AF323314

World Scientific Proceedings Series on
Computer Engineering and Information Science 3

Computational Intelligence in Business and Economics

Proceedings of the
MS'10 International
Conference

World Scientific Proceedings Series on Computer Engineering and Information Science

Series Editor: Da Ruan, *Belgian Nuclear Research Centre (SCK•CEN)*
& Ghent University, Belgium

World Scientific Proceedings Series on
Computer Engineering and Information Science 3

Computational Intelligence in Business and Economics

Proceedings of the MS'10 International Conference

Barcelona, Spain   15–17 July 2010

editors

Anna M. Gil-Lafuente
University of Barcelona, Spain

José M. Merigó
University of Barcelona, Spain

NEW JERSEY · LONDON · SINGAPORE · BEIJING · SHANGHAI · HONG KONG · TAIPEI · CHENNAI

Published by

World Scientific Publishing Co. Pte. Ltd.

5 Toh Tuck Link, Singapore 596224

USA office: 27 Warren Street, Suite 401-402, Hackensack, NJ 07601

UK office: 57 Shelton Street, Covent Garden, London WC2H 9HE

British Library Cataloguing-in-Publication Data
A catalogue record for this book is available from the British Library.

**World Scientific Proceedings Series on Computer Engineering and
Information Science — Vol. 3**
COMPUTATIONAL INTELLIGENCE IN BUSINESS AND ECONOMICS
Proceedings of the MS'10 International Conference

ISBN-13 978-981-4324-43-4
ISBN-10 981-4324-43-4

Printed in Singapore by B & Jo Enterprise Pte Ltd

The MS'10 Barcelona International Conference is supported by

PREFACE

The Association for the Advancement of Modelling & Simulation Techniques in Enterprises (AMSE) and the University of Barcelona are pleased to present the main results of the International Conference of Modelling and Simulation in Engineering, Economics and Management, held in Barcelona, 15 – 17 July, 2010, through this Book of Proceedings published in the Book Series *"World Scientific Proceedings Series in Computer Engineering and Information Science"*.

MS'10 Barcelona is co-organized by the AMSE Association and the University of Barcelona, Spain. It is co-supported by the Spanish Royal Academy of Financial and Economic Sciences and the Spanish Ministry of Science and Innovation. It offers a unique opportunity for researchers, professionals and students to present and exchange ideas concerning modelling and simulation and related topics and see how they can be implemented in the real world.

In this edition of the MS International Conference, we want to give special attention to the emerging area of Computational Intelligence. In particular, we want to focus on the implementation of these techniques in the Economic Sciences. Thus, the title of this book is *"Computational Intelligence in Business and Economics"*. Computational Intelligence is a very broad research area that includes fuzzy set theory, neural networks, evolutionary computation, probabilistic reasoning and chaotic comuting as particular research topics of this discipline. The growing importance of Computational Intelligence in the Economic Sciences is obvious when looking to the complex world we are living in. Every year new ideas and products are appearing in the markets making them very flexible and with strong unpredicted fluctuations. Therefore, in order to deal with our world in a proper way, we need to use models that are able to assess the imprecision and the uncertainty.

MS'10 Proceedings is constituted by 88 papers selected from 141 submissions from 36 countries, making an acceptance rate of 62%. We have also included a summary of the presentation given by the plenary speakers: Jaime Gil Aluja, Janusz Kacprzyk and Korkmaz Imanov. The book is divided in 7 parts: (1) Theoretical Foundations, (2) Accounting and Finance, (3) Management, (4)

Marketing, Sports and Tourism, (5) Economics and Politics, (6) Applications in Engineering, and (7) Applications in Other Fields.

We would like to thank all the contributors, referees and the scientific and honorary committees for their kind co-operation with MS'10 Barcelona; to Jaime Gil Aluja for his role as the President of AMSE and the President of the honorary committee; to the whole team of the organizing committee, including Lluis Amiguet, Luciano Barcellos, Carolina Luis Bassa, Josefa Boria, Jaime Gil Lafuente, Mª Carmen Gracia, Aras Keropyan, Pilar López-Jurado, Onofre Martorell, Carles Mulet, Camilo Prado, Mª Luisa Solé and Emilio Vizuete; and to Chelsea Chin (Editor, World Scientific) for her kind advise and help to publish this volume. Finally, we would like to express our gratitude to World Scientific and in particular to Da Ruan (editor-in-chief of the book series "*WS Proceedings Series in Computer Engineering and Information Science*") for his support in the preparation of this book.

Anna M. Gil Lafuente, MS'10 Barcelona Chair.
José M. Merigó, MS'10 Barcelona Co-chair.
Barcelona, March 2010.

HONORARY COMMITTEE

Special thanks to all the members of the Honorary Committee for their support in the organization of the MS'10 Barcelona International Conference.

President of the Honorary Committeee

Jaime Gil-Aluja — President of *AMSE* and President of the *Spanish Royal Academy of Financial and Economic Sciences*

Honorary Committee

André Azoulay — Le Conselleir de *Sa Majesté le Roi du Royaume du Maroc*

Ernest Benach — President of the *Parlament de Catalunya*

Alessandro Bianchi — Ex Rector of the *University of the Mediterranean Studies of Reggio di Calabria*

José Casajuana — President of the *Royal Academy of Doctors*

Jacques Delruelle — President of the *Censor School of Accounting of Belgium's National Bank*

Ricardo Díez Hotchleitner — Honorary President of the *Club de Roma*

Isidre Fainé Casas — President of *La Caixa*

Lorenzo Gascón — Vicepresident of the *Spanish Royal Academy of Financial and Economic Sciences*

Mohamed Laichubi — Former Minister and *Algerian Ambassador*

Juan José Pinto — Former President of *Caixa Barcelona*

Dídac Ramírez — Rector of the *University of Barcelona*

Eugen Simon — President of *the National Foundation for the Science and the Art of Romania*

Lotfi A. Zadeh — *University of California at Berkeley*

SCIENTIFIC COMMITTEE

Special thanks to all the members of the Scientific Committee for their kind support in the organization of the MS'10 Barcelona International Conference.

Christian Berger-Vachon
(Co-President)

Anna M. Gil-Lafuente
(Co-President)

Jihad M. Alja'am, Qatar
Said Allaki, Morocco
Mª Teresa Anguera Argilaga, Spain
Noura Al-Khaabi, UAE
Jacques Marie Aurifeille, France
José Daniel Barquero, Spain
Pietro Burrascano, Italy
Fernando Casado, Spain
Houcine Chafouk, France
Nashaat El-Khameesy, Egypt
Kurt Engemann, USA
Farahat Farahat, Egypt
Joan Carles Ferrer, Spain
Fares Fraij, Jordan
Jaime Gil Lafuente, Spain
Federico González Santoyo, Mexico
Rainer Hampel, Germany
Francisco Herrera, Spain
Kedi Huang, P.R. China
Korkmaz Imanov, Azerbaijan
Janusz Kacprzyk, Poland
Yuriy Kondratenko, Uckraine
Viktor Krasnoproshin, Belarus
Prabhat Kumar Mahanti, India
Leonid A. Kuztnesov, Russia
Vicente Liern Carrión, Spain

Enrique López González, Spain
Jesús Marín Solano, Spain
Luis Martínez López, Spain
José M. Merigó Lindahl, Spain
Ramir Mirsalinov, Azerbaijan
Francesco C. Morabito, Italy
Vladimir S. Neronov, Kazakhstan
Ahmad Nuseirat, Jordan
Ahmed Oulad Said, Morocco
Witold Pedrycz, Canada
Emmanuel Perrin, France
Ramón Poch Torres, Spain
Joan Francesc Pont Clemente, Spain
José Antonio Redondo, Spain
Alfredo Rocafort, Spain
Alfonso Rodríguez, Spain
José Jaime Ronzón Contreras, Mexico
Da Ruan, Belgium
Mohamed Saighi, Algeria
Petr Sternbeck, Czech Rep.
Antonio Terceño, Spain
Jaime Tinto Arandes, Venezuela
Emili Vizuete, Spain
Iskander Yaacob, Malaysia
Ronald R. Yager, USA
Aladin Zayegh, Australia

ORGANIZING COMMITTEE

Special thanks to all the members of the Organizing Committee for their support during the preparation of the MS'10 Barcelona International Conference.

Chair of the Organizing Committee

Anna M. Gil Lafuente, Chair MS'10 Barcelona

Co-Chair of the Organizing Committee

José M. Merigó Lindahl, Co-Chair MS'10 Barcelona

Organizing Committee

Lluís Amiguet Molina, Spain

Luciano Barcellos de Paula, Brazil

Josefa Boria Reverter, Spain

Jaime Gil Lafuente, Spain

Mª Carmen Gracia Ramos, Spain

Aras Keropyan, Turkey

Pilar López-Jurado, Spain

Carolina Luis Bassa, Spain

Onofre Martorell Cunill, Spain

Carles Mulet Forteza, Spain

Camilo Prado Román, Spain

Mª Luisa Solé Moro, Spain

Emili Vizuete Luciano, Spain

ACKNOWLEDGEMENT TO REVIEWERS

Special thanks to all the referees for their advice in the revision process of the papers submitted to the MS'10 Barcelona International Conference:

Latif Adnane

Gerardo G. Alfaro Calderón

Jorge de Andrés

Luciano Barcellos

Ahmed Benzaoui

Josefa Boria

José M. Brotons

Matteo Cacciola

Alain Calzadilla

Agusti Casas

Mª Elvira Cassú

Omar Danilo Castrillón

David Ceballos

Edwin Dado

Rekioua Djamila

José Antonio Díaz

Djordje N. Dihovicni

Kurt J. Engemann

Elena Escrig

Aurelio Fernández

María José Fernández

Joan Carles Ferrer

Pedro Flores

Ever Angel Fuentes

Javier Garcia Fronti

Pablo García

Rosario Garza Ríos

Vasile Georgescu

Anna M. Gil Lafuente

Jaime Gil Lafuente

Egils Ginters

Jaime A. Giraldo

Mª Carmen Gracia

Calin Gurau

Escid Hammoud

Rubén Huertas

Nazhad A. Hussein

Rozita B. Jailani

Shawnim R. Jalal

Mariano Jiménez

Jelena Jovanovic

Aras Keropyan

Magda Komornikova

Yuriy Kondratenko

Victor Krasnoproshin

Hocine Labar

Luisa Lucila Lazzari

Monica Leba

Salvador Linares

Bárbara Llacay

Carolina Luis Bassa

Aiyed Maree

Jesús Marín

Luis Martínez

Giuseppe Megali

Samir Mehrez

José M. Merigó

Sjoerd Mevissen

Francesco Carlo Morabito

Kelaiaia Mounia

Anna Petrickova

Ileana Pérez

Giselle Pino

Emil Pop

Camilo Prado

Toufik Rekioua

Alfredo Rocafort

S. Rominus Valsalam

Mohamed Saighi

Emilio Vizuete

Changfan Xin

CONTENTS

PART 2: ACCOUNTING AND FINANCE   99

PLENARY SPEAKERS

THE SCIENTIFIC RESEARCH OF A FUTURE SUSTAINABLE ECONOMIC DEVELOPMENT

JAIME GIL ALUJA

Emeritus Professor, Department of Business Administration, Rovira i Virgili University,
Reus, Spain
Spanish Royal Academy of Financial and Economic Sciences,
Barcelona, Spain

Abstract

The important advancement which has taken place during the last decade in the process of the creation of a society with progress without precedent throughout history, has led to a quasi generalized economic and financial crisis that has ended by stirring up the very foundations of our life in society.

These achievements that have been attained are the result of a whole conglomerate of effort carried out by the most diverse classes, with the common denominator of freedom in stability. The development of research in the different spheres of knowledge, in our opinion constitutes one of the fundamental axes around which the progress attained has revolved. This progress can be seen today as menaced by the ghost of the crisis, which is hitting, particularly all the under privileged, so hard.

Nevertheless, we feel that the problem which has caused so much concern to so many families cannot be reduced solely to the economic-financial sphere but it must also be considered as a consequence of another far deeper and extensive problem: this is a crisis of values. In fact, historical evolution has accumulated a considerable residue of knowledge supported on certain principles that were believed unchangeable. The explosion of the economic-financial crisis has brought to light the fragility of our social systems, in such a way that we are becoming aware of the disappearance of these principles and, what is far most serious is the lack of any that substitute them. The result is disorientation in all walks of life in society: politics, economics, teaching, research, morals, etc., this can even be found in our very model of coexistence.

The reality is that now we find ourselves with the fact that the ghost of the crisis is to be found in every corner of our planet, presenting itself disguised in the most varied clothes. But also from ghostly apparitions the light of an opportunity can arise, the opportunity of change that must be a systemic change.

Thus, what has occurred, in a slow but inexorable manner, is a rupture between the theoretical of society model and the real society. As a consequence of this the inevitable result has been the loss of confidence of citizens of all countries. To regain this confidence it will require an important teaching effort and an effort in dialogue. But this alone will not be sufficient. And this is so since what it is in play is the design of a new cultural model. The drawing up of this cultural model must also respond effectively not only to the economic and financial consequences of globalisation but also take into account the process of shifting towards a society that it is all the time becoming more complex and full of uncertainties.

A good number of scientists have placed, stone by stone, the foundations of what can be a new building of knowledge. But still required is a large close of imagination in order to break the links that ties us with the past, placing in their place "non linear" differential equations.

Three fundamental axes make up the search for a new way of thought in economic science: uncertainty, irregularity and complexity. They would then appear to be the principal challenges that the changeable realities of our days are placing before social and economic research. It is necessary to delve into the depth of each one of the levels of knowledge in order to attempt to find, in each one of them the keys that allow us to open the doors to an efficient treatment of present realities.

The reflexions that we suggest in this work are oriented to put attention that the science must play an important role in the rules that in the future govern the international relations. We are very confidence in the future contributions made within the heart of the new fields that have opened in research activities. These contributions must be the ones to expand the light of science, and at the same time, strengthen solidarity and well being of all citizens. Only this way will lead us to the desired sustainable social progress.

DECISION MAKING, DECISION PROCESSES AND DECISION SUPPORT SYSTEMS

JANUSZ KACPRZYK

Systems Research Institute, Polish Academy of Sciences,
ul. Newelska 6, 01-447 Warszawa, Poland

Abstract

We start with a brief introduction to modern approaches to decision making. We concentrate mainly on a formal, mathematical approach and analyze various models. We discuss the main elements of those models, notably issues related to preferences, utilities and rationality. We consider specifics of the basic setting with one quality criterion, one decision maker and a static setting. Then, we proceed to the analysis of multiple criteria, multiple decision makers, and dynamics. Some other approaches, notably in the behavioral and cognitive direction will also be briefly mentioned, and some inspirations from neuroeconomics will be mentioned.

Then, we proceed to the analysis of modern approaches to the analysis and solution of complex real world decision making problems which are heavily human centered in the sense of both a crucial importance of human related aspects, judgments, assessment, and of a key role played by a human decision maker(s). We advocate the use of modern tools and techniques emphasizing the need for involving more factors and aspects like: the use of explicit and tacit knowledge, intuition, analysis of emotions, individual habitual domains, non-trivial rationality, different paradigms, etc. We also mention some relations to behavioral and cognitive approaches, and some new ideas in this respect coming from neuroeconomics and related areas. We stress the need for intelligent computer based decision support systems that should exhibit some intelligence and human consistency.

We survey various views on how intelligence may be meant, both from a human and machine perspective. In addition to more traditional views from an individual perspective, we mention new concepts related to collective intelligence which are more and more important for the present increasingly complicated decision situations, involvement of multiple actors/agents, and also some personal computational devices, exemplified by smart phones, attained better courses of actions using some "intelligent" tools. We give an overview of main types of modern decision support systems.

We present some new so-called computing paradigms that try to attain a synergy, and bridge the gap between the human user and computer systems that is mainly caused by the fact that natural language is the only fully natural means of communication and articulation for a human being but it is "strange" to the computer. We mainly present: human centric computing, human centered computing, human computing, collaborative intelligence, etc. that can help bridge this gap.

We mention a need for appropriate tools to implement these concepts of new human centric/centered computing paradigms, and human consistency, and suggest that Zadeh's paradigm of computing with words (and perceptions) may be such a tool that may help bring computing closer to the human being by an explicit use of (quasi)natural language in many phases of computing, problem solving, etc.

We show some implementations of the line of though proposed by using linguistic data summaries and some tools of natural language generation (NLG) and Systemic Functional Linguistics (SFL) in a business context for supporting decisions in a computer retailer.

IMPRECISE PROBABILITY FOR ESTIMATED FORECASTING VARIANTS OF THE ECONOMICAL DEVELOPMENT

G.C. IMANOV

Fuzzy Economics Department, Cybernetic Institute of NAS, Baku, Azerbaijan

Abstract

The problem of uncertainty of the socioeconomic systems is the subject of the fuzzy economics. Problems in economical uncertainty and their solution by methods of fuzzy logic are widely described in the investigations by professor J.Gil-Aluja. Between problems of economical uncertainty, very important meaning has been found not only in economical information uncertainty but also in forecasting problems of economical event and process.

Economical systems are being grounded in the human intuition. Intuitive opinions are fundamental for the hypothesis, which is being used in the forecasting of economical events and processes.

Nowadays, methods of mathematical statistics, probability theory and fuzzy logic are widely used for forecasting. All these methods are only applicable when we have preliminary hypotheses. Recently, a wide range of methods based on the use of imprecise probability have been developed for forecasting and for the prediction of different events and processes.

Framework of imprecise probability includes measures of fuzziness, possibility and upper and lower probabilities.

In a recent report by L.Zadeh, R.Aliev *et al*, for the solution of the problem of the decision-maker in uncertain situation, some models of the imprecise probability were proposed. These models were applied for different economical processes.

In this presentation we do certain attempts to apply some methods of imprecise probability (conditional fuzzy granulation, Sugeno metrics, Choquet integral) for evaluation of forecasted variants of the economical development of the country.

PART 1:
THEORETICAL FOUNDATIONS

THE INDUCED GENERALIZED OWAWA DISTANCE OPERATOR

JOSÉ M. MERIGÓ, ANNA M. GIL-LAFUENTE

Department of Business Administration, University of Barcelona,
Av. Diagonal 690, 08034 Barcelona, Spain

We present the induced generalized ordered weighted averaging – weighted average distance (IGOWAWAD) operator. It is a new distance aggregation operator that uses order-inducing variables to represent complex reordering processes in the aggregation of the information. It provides a unified framework between the weighted average and the OWA operator considering the degree of importance that each concept has in the aggregation. It also uses generalized aggregation operators providing a more robust formulation that includes a wide range of particular cases including the induced OWA distance, the Hamming distance, the induced Minkowski OWA distance, the induced OWAWA distance and the induced Euclidean OWAWA distance. We further generalize this approach by using quasi-arithmetic means obtaining the induced quasi-arithmetic OWAWA distance (Quasi-IOWAWAD) operator.

1. Introduction

The distance measure [2-5] is a very useful tool for comparing different elements. For example, we can compare the elements of two sets or two fuzzy sets. In the literature, we find a wide range of distance measures. For example, we can use a general representation that includes many particular cases such as the Minkowski distance. Usually, when calculating the distance between two elements, sets or fuzzy sets, we need two develop a normalization process in order to obtain an average of all the individual distances considered in the problem. For doing so, we need to use an aggregation operator [1,5]. The most common ones are the arithmetic mean and the weighted average that combined with the Minkowski distance forms the normalized Minkowski distance (NMD) and the weighted Minkowski distance (WMD), respectively.

Another aggregation operator that can be used is the ordered weighted averaging (OWA) operator [9,10,12]. By using the OWA, we are able to provide a parameterized family of distance aggregation operators between the minimum distance and the maximum distance. More complex formulation of the OWA that could be used are the induced OWA (IOWA) operator [11], the generalized

OWA (GOWA) operator [4-5] and the induced generalized OWA (IGOWA) operator [7]. Moreover, it is also possible to use a more complete formulation that unifies the weighted average and the OWA operator in the same formulation considering the degree of importance that each concept has in the aggregation. That is, the ordered weighted averaging – weighted average (OWAWA) operator [5-6].

The aim of this paper is to present a new approach that uses a more general formulation with distance measures. We call it the induced generalized OWAWA distance (IGOWAWAD) operator. It is a new distance aggregation operator that uses order-inducing variables to deal with complex reordering processes and generalized means in a unified framework between the weighted average and the OWA operator. Its main advantage is that it includes a wide range of particular cases including the induced OWA distance (IOWAD), the Minkowski OWA distance (MOWAD), the OWA distance (OWAD), the OWAWA distance (OWAWAD), the induced quadratic OWAWA distance (IOWQAWAD) and the induced geometric OWAWA distance (IOWGAWAD).

We further extend this approach by using quasi-arithmetic means obtaining the induced Quasi-OWAWA distance (Quasi-IOWAWAD) operator. The main advantage of this approach is that it includes the IGOWAWAD operator as a particular case.

In order to do so, this paper is organized as follows. In Section 2, we briefly review some basic concepts. Section 3 presents the new approach. Section 4 introduces the Quasi-IOWAWAD operator and Section 5 summarizes the main conclusions.

2. Preliminaries

In this section we briefly review the Minkowski distance, the induced generalized OWA (IGOWA) operator and the OWA distance (OWAD) operator.

2.1. *The Minkowski Distance*

The Minkowski distance is a very useful technique for calculating the differences between two elements, two sets, etc. In fuzzy set theory, it can be useful, for example, for the calculation of distances between fuzzy sets, interval-valued fuzzy sets and intuitionistic fuzzy sets. For two sets A and B, it can be defined as follows.

Definition 1. A weighted Minkowski distance of dimension n is a mapping WMD: $[0, 1]^n \times [0, 1]^n \rightarrow [0, 1]$ that has an associated weighting vector W of dimension n such that the sum of the weights is 1 and $w_j \in [0, 1]$. Then:

$$WMD\,(A, B) = \left(\sum_{i=1}^{n} w_i \mid a_i - b_i \mid^{\lambda} \right)^{1/\lambda} \tag{1}$$

where a_i and b_i are the ith arguments of the sets A and B respectively.

Note that it is possible to generalize this definition to all the real numbers by using $R^n \times R^n \rightarrow R$. For the formulation used in fuzzy set theory, see for example [4]. Note also that if $w_i = 1/n$, then, the WMD becomes the normalized Minkowski distance (NMD).

2.2. *The Induced Generalized OWA Operator*

The IGOWA operator [7] is a generalization of the IOWA operator by using generalized means. It is defined as follows.

Definition 2. An IGOWA operator of dimension n is a mapping IGOWA: $R^n \rightarrow R$, which has an associated weighting vector W with $w_j \in [0, 1]$ and $\sum_{j=1}^{n} w_j = 1$, such that:

$$IGOWA\,(\langle u_1, a_1 \rangle, \langle u_2, a_2 \rangle, \ldots, \langle u_n, a_n \rangle) = \left(\sum_{j=1}^{n} w_j b_j^{\lambda} \right)^{1/\lambda} \tag{2}$$

where b_j is the a_i value of the IGOWA pair $\langle u_i, a_i \rangle$ having the jth largest u_i, u_i is the order inducing variable, a_i is the argument variable and λ is a parameter such that $\lambda \in (-\infty, \infty)$.

2.3. *The OWA Distance Operator*

The OWAD (or Hamming OWAD) operator [5] is an extension of the traditional normalized Hamming distance by using OWA operators. The main difference is the reordering of the arguments of the individual distances according to their values. Then, it is possible to calculate the distance between two elements, two

14

sets, two fuzzy sets, etc., modifying the results according to the interests of the decision maker. It can be defined as follows.

Definition 3. An OWAD operator of dimension n is a mapping OWAD: $[0, 1]^n \times [0, 1]^n \rightarrow [0, 1]$ that has an associated weighting vector W, with $\sum_{j=1}^{n} w_j = 1$ and $w_j \in [0, 1]$ such that:

$$OWAD\left(\langle \mu_1, \mu_1^{(k)} \rangle, \ldots, \langle \mu_n, \mu_n^{(k)} \rangle\right) = \sum_{j=1}^{n} w_j D_j \tag{3}$$

where D_j represents the jth largest of the $|\mu_i - \mu_i^{(k)}|$, $\mu_i \in [0, 1]$ for the ith characteristic of the ideal P, $\mu_i^{(k)} \in [0, 1]$ for the ith characteristic of the kth alternative P_k, and $k = 1, 2, \ldots, m$.

Note that this definition can be generalized to all the real numbers R by using OWAD: $R^n \times R^n \rightarrow R$. Note also that it is possible to distinguish between ascending and descending orders.

3. The Induced Generalized OWAWA Distance Operator

The IGOWAWA operator is an aggregation operator that provides a generalized model between the OWA operator and the weighted average by using generalized means. It also uses distance measures in the analysis providing a more complete representation of the aggregation process. Furthermore, it also uses order inducing variables in order to deal with complex reordering processes. The main advantage of this approach is that it unifies the weighted Minkowski distance with the induced Minkowski OWA distance in the same formulation considering the degree of importance that each concept has in the aggregation process. It can be defined as follows.

Definition 4. An IGOWAWAD operator of dimension n is a mapping $IGOWAWAD$: $R^n \times R^n \times R^n \rightarrow R$ that has an associated weighting vector W of dimension n such that $w_j \in [0, 1]$ and $\sum_{j=1}^{n} w_j = 1$, according to the following formula:

$$IGOWAWAD\ (\langle u_1, x_1, y_1\rangle, \ldots, \langle u_n, x_n, y_n\rangle) = \left(\sum_{j=1}^{n} \hat{v}_j D_j^{\lambda}\right)^{1/\lambda} \tag{4}$$

where D_j is the $|x_i - y_i|$ value of the IGOWAWAD triplet $\langle u_i, x_i, y_i\rangle$ having the jth largest u_i, u_i is the order inducing variable, each argument $|x_i - y_i|$ has an associated weight (WA) v_i with $\sum_{i=1}^{n} v_i = 1$ and $v_i \in [0, 1]$, $\hat{v}_j = \beta w_j + (1-\beta)v_j$ with $\beta \in [0, 1]$ and v_j is the weight (WA) v_i ordered according to D_j, that is, according to the jth largest of the u_i, and λ is a parameter such that $\lambda \in (-\infty, \infty)$.

Note that we can also formulate the IGOWAWAD operator in the following way separating the part that affects the OWA and the part that affects the WA.

Definition 5. An IGOWAWAD operator is a mapping $IGOWAWAD: R^n \times R^n \times R^n \to R$ dimension n, if it has an associated weighting vector W, with $\sum_{j=1}^{n} w_j = 1$ and $w_j \in [0, 1]$ and a weighting vector V that affects the WA, with $\sum_{i=1}^{n} v_i = 1$ and $v_i \in [0, 1]$, such that:

$$IGOWAWAD\ (\langle u_1, x_1, y_1\rangle, \ldots, \langle u_n, x_n, y_n\rangle) =$$

$$= \beta\left(\sum_{j=1}^{n} w_j D_j^{\lambda}\right)^{1/\lambda} + (1-\beta)\left(\sum_{i=1}^{n} v_i |x_i - y_i|^{\lambda}\right)^{1/\lambda} \tag{5}$$

where D_j is the $|x_i - y_i|$ value of the IOWAD triplet $\langle u_i, x_i, y_i\rangle$ having the jth largest u_i, u_i is the order inducing variable, and λ is a parameter such that $\lambda \in (-\infty, \infty)$.

Note that if the weighting vector is not normalized, i.e., $\hat{V} = \sum_{j=1}^{n} \hat{v}_j \neq 1$, then, the IGOWAWAD operator can be expressed as:

$$IGOWAWAD\ (\langle u_1, x_1, y_1\rangle, \ldots, \langle u_n, x_n, y_n\rangle) = \left(\frac{1}{\hat{V}}\sum_{j=1}^{n} \hat{v}_j b_j^{\lambda}\right)^{1/\lambda} \tag{6}$$

Note also that it is possible to distinguish between descending and ascending orders. The IGOWAWAD operator is monotonic, bounded and idempotent. Several measures can be studied for characterizing the weighting vector such as the orness measure, the entropy of dispersion and the balance operator.

Another interesting issue that we could consider is the use of infinitary aggregation operators [8]. Thus, we can represent the IGOWAWAD operator in a situation where there is an unlimited number of arguments to be considered. Note that $\sum_{j=1}^{\infty} \hat{v}_j = 1$. By using, the IGOWAWAD operator we get the infinitary IGOWAWAD (∞-IGOWAWAD) operator as follows.

$$\infty-IGOWAWAD\ (\langle u_1, x_1, y_1 \rangle,\ \ldots,\ \langle u_n, x_n, y_n \rangle) = \sum_{j=1}^{\infty} \hat{v}_j b_j \tag{7}$$

Note that the reordering process is very complex because we have an unlimited number of arguments. Thus, the process cannot be directly assessed considering all the arguments. For further reading in the usual OWA, see Mesiar and Pap [8].

The IGOWAWAD operator includes a wide range of aggregation operators. If we analyze the parameter β, we get the following:

- The weighted Minkowski distance: When $\beta = 0$.
- The induced Minkowski OWA distance: When $\beta = 1$.

And if we analyze the parameter λ, we can obtain the following special cases of the IGOWAWAD operator:

- The induced OWAWAD (IOWAWAD) operator: When $\lambda = 1$.
- The induced ordered weighted quadratic averaging weighted quadratic averaging distance (IOWQAWQAD) operator (the Euclidean case): When $\lambda = 2$.
- The induced ordered weighted geometric averaging weighted geometric averaging distance (IOWGAWGAD) operator: $\lambda \to 0$.
- The induced ordered weighted harmonic averaging weighted harmonic averaging distance (IOWQAWQAD) operator: $\lambda = -1$.
- The induced ordered weighted cubic averaging weighted cubic averaging distance (IOWCAWCAD) operator: When $\lambda = 3$.

Note that a lot of other families of IGOWAWAD operators could be obtained following [5,7,10].

4. The Quasi-IOWAWAD Operator

The IGOWAWAD operator can be further generalized by using quasi-arithmetic means in a similar way as it was done in [1,5,7]. We will call it the quasi-arithmetic IOWAWAD (Quasi-IOWAWAD) operator. It is defined as follows.

Definition 6. A Quasi-IOWAWAD operator of dimension n is a mapping $QIOWAWAD: R^n \times R^n \times R^n \rightarrow R$ that has an associated weighting vector W of dimension n such that the sum of the weights is 1 and $w_j \in [0, 1]$. Then, the distance between two sets is:

$$QIOWAWAD \left(\langle u_1, x_1, y_1\rangle, \langle u_2, x_2, y_2\rangle, \ldots, \langle u_n, x_n, y_n\rangle\right) = g^{-1}\left(\sum_{j=1}^{n} \hat{v}_j\, g\left(D_{(j)}\right)\right) \quad (8)$$

where D_j is the $|x_i - y_i|$ value of the QIOWAWAD triplet $\langle u_i, x_i, y_i\rangle$ having the jth largest u_i, u_i is the order inducing variable, each argument $|x_i - y_i|$ has an associated weight (WA) v_i with $\sum_{i=1}^{n} v_i = 1$ and $v_i \in [0, 1]$, $\hat{v}_j = \beta w_j + (1-\beta)v_j$ with $\beta \in [0, 1]$ and v_j is the weight (WA) v_i ordered according to D_j, that is, according to the jth largest of the u_i, and g is a strictly continuous monotonic function.

As we can see, when $g(b) = b^\lambda$, then, the Quasi-IOWAWAD becomes the IGOWAWAD operator. Note that it is also possible to distinguish between descending (Quasi-DIOWAWAD) and ascending (Quasi-AIOWAWAD) orders.

Note that all the properties and particular cases commented in the IGOWAWAD operator are also applicable in the Quasi-IOWAWAD operator.

5. Conclusions

We have presented a new distance aggregation operator that uses induced and generalized aggregation operators in a unified model between the weighted average and the OWA operator that considers the degree of importance that each concept may have in the aggregation. We have called it the IGOWAWAD operator. Its main advantage is that it includes a wide range of aggregation operators such as the IMOWAD operator, the Minkowski distance, the arithmetic weighted generalized distance and the arithmetic IOWAD operator. We have also presented the Quasi-IOWAWAD operator. It is a further generalization that includes the IGOWAWAD operator as a particular case.

We see that the applicability of the IGOWAWAD operator is very broad because we can apply it in a wide range of studies that use the weighted average or the IOWA operator. In future research we will further extend this approach by using more complex formulations such as the use of unified aggregation operators and uncertain information. We will also study the applicability of the IGOWAWAD in different fields such as statistics, economics and engineering.

Acknowledgements

Support from the Spanish Ministry of Science and Innovation under project "JC2009-00189" is gratefully acknowledged.

References

1. G. Beliakov, A. Pradera, T. Calvo, *Aggregation functions: A guide for practitioners* (Springer-Verlag, Berlin-Heidelberg, 2007).
2. R.W. Hamming, Error-detecting and error-correcting codes, *Bell Systems Technical J.* **29**, 147 (1950).
3. N. Karayiannis, Soft learning vector quantization and clustering algorithms based on ordered weighted aggregation operators, *IEEE Trans. Neural Networks* **11**, 1093 (2000).
4. A. Kaufmann, *Introduction to the theory of fuzzy subsets*, (Academic Press, New York, 1975).
5. J.M. Merigó, *New extensions to the OWA operators and their application in decision making* (PhD thesis (in Spanish), Department of Business Administration, University of Barcelona, 2008).
6. J.M. Merigó, On the use of the OWA operator in the weighted average and its application in decision making. In: *Proceedings of the WCE 2009 Conference*, London, United Kingdom, pp. 82-87, 2009.
7. J.M. Merigó and A.M. Gil-Lafuente, The induced generalized OWA operator, *Inform. Sci.* **179**, 729 (2009).
8. R. Mesiar and E. Pap, Aggregation of infinite sequences, *Inform. Sci.* **178**, 3557 (2008).
9. R.R. Yager, On ordered weighted averaging aggregation operators in multi-criteria decision making, *IEEE Trans. Syst. Man Cybern. B* **18**, 183 (1988).
10. R.R. Yager, Families of OWA operators, *Fuzzy Sets Syst.* **59**, 125 (1993).
11. R.R. Yager and D.P. Filev, Induced ordered weighted averaging operators, *IEEE Trans. Syst. Man Cybern. B* **29**, 141 (1999).
12. R.R. Yager and J. Kacprzyk, *The ordered weighted averaging operators: Theory and applications.* Norwell: Kluwer Academic Publishers, 1997.

PROBABILISTIC MODELING USING COPULA FUNCTIONS BASED BAYESIAN APPROACH

PRANESH KUMAR[*]

Department of Mathematics and Statistics, University of Northern British Columbia, Prince George, BC, V2N 4Z9, Canada

Pearson's correlation coefficient is a measure of linear dependence only and has played a pivotal role in stochastic modeling. However the correlation coefficient is appropriate under some regularity conditions. It may affect the validity of correlation based models especially in the situations where there is evidence of non-linear dependence among model variables. Alternatively stochastic dependence, linear or non-linear, can be modeled by a copula function that overcomes most limitations of the linear correlation. Copulas are functions that join multivariate distribution functions to their one-dimensional marginal distribution functions. The Bayesian approach analyses the relationship between the conditional and unconditional probabilities. In this paper we discuss copula based Bayesian approach in modeling dependence. We model the nonlinear dependence using the concept of conditional copulas and illustrate with an application to adopt a sequential real options strategy.

1. Introduction

In project risk management, capital budgeting stresses the value of an asset as the present value of future cash flows or benefits. When cash flows are certain, future cash flows can be discounted at the risk-free rate. Uncertainty in cash flows either have to be discounted at a rate that includes a market risk-premium or expected cash flows can be replaced with their certainty equivalents and discounted using the risk free rate. The discounted cash flow based shareholder value approach has also been criticized. The NPV criterion is insufficient in capturing the managerial flexibility to delay, grow, scale down or abandon projects. A real option that combines strategy with valuation is increasingly attracting attention. The insight that underlies this approach is that an investment opportunity can be conceptually compared to a financial option. Many researchers both in corporate finance and management accounting have emphasized the importance of real option analysis for corporate investments

---

[*] Work partially supported by discovery grant of the Natural Sciences and Engineering Research Council of Canada.

decisions. Some researchers have used real option analysis to value natural resource development projects, patents, and licenses with limiting quotas, software development and insurance policy decisions, among many other applications. Application of real option pricing has also been proposed for valuing R&D projects in the capital budgeting literature [14]. There has been extensive growth in research both in the standard and game theoretic (competitive and cooperative) framework, with applications in forestry, oil and gas, information technology. One area, however, that has received relatively less attention in real option literature is the integration of Bayesian analysis that allows for modeling learning options. Bayesian modeling allows updating beliefs about past shocks which gives rise to trade-off between investing now and waiting to learn. In this paper we discuss application of copula based Bayesian approach for modeling dependent risk as a tool in the Bayesian real option models. We first describe copula functions and why copulas are appropriate to model dependent risk. Then we present a copula based Bayesian approach. We conclude with an illustration and discussion of potential real option applications.

2. Copula Functions

Copulas are a relatively new concept in modeling dependence. Sklar [16] first used copula to describe the joining (or coupling) of a collection of one-dimensional marginal distributions to form a multivariate distribution. The basic idea is that the bivariate joint distribution of the random variables X and Y, denoted by $H(x, y)$ and marginal distribution function $F(x)$ and $G(y)$, can be expressed as a copula function $C(u,v)$ defined by $H(x, y) = C(F(x), G(y)) = C(u,v)$ where $u, v \in$ [0, 1]. Copulas allow one to study scale-free measures of dependence and to construct families of multivariate distributions for simulation. Copula is unique if the marginal distributions are continuous. A large and growing literature on copulas has been developed in the recent years [1,6-8,12,15]. Copulas are found useful in several situations like in modeling nonlinear dependence and extreme events. Copulas can be constructed with any choice of marginal distribution functions. There has been a growing interest in copula applications in insurance and finance [2-5,9,14]. Armstrong et al. [2] developed a novel form of Bayesian updating based on Archimedean copulas and applied the methodology to value an oil project. In finance and risk management reference to [1,10,11]. Using the normal copula, Clemen and Reilly [5] demonstrate the benefit of using correlations and copulas to construct probabilistic models for risk analysis. In a recent article [9], Herath and Kumar apply copula to capital budgeting problems and suggest using copulas to model nonlinear dependence in Bayesian setting. There are several methods of constructing copulas or specifying families of copulas [13]. We consider a widely studied family of copulas known as the bivariate Archimedean copulas. A number of known copula families belong to this class.

2.1. *Family of Bivariate Archimedean Copulas*

Let $\varphi(.)$ be a convex decreasing function defined on $(0, 1]$ such that $\varphi(1) = 0$ and let $\varphi^{[-1]}(.)$ be its pseudo-inverse exits. Then the function $C(u,v) = \varphi^{-1}[\varphi(u) + \varphi(v)]$, is a copula. The function $\varphi(.)$ is called a generator of the copula and different choices of generator function gives different families of copulas. Scale invariant dependent measures can be expressed as copula functions of random variables. The two standard non-parametric dependence measures Kendall's Tau and Spearman's Rho expressed in copula form are

$$\tau = 4 \iint_{I^2} C(u,v) \, dC(u,v) - 1 , \tag{1}$$

$$\rho = 12 \iint_{I^2} C(u,v) \, du \, dv - 3 . \tag{2}$$

Kendall's Tau is estimated from the data set $(x_i, y_i), i = 1, \ldots, n$ by

$$\tau = 2 \sum_{i<j} \text{Sign}\left[(x_i - x_j)(y_i - y_j)\right] / n(n-1) . \tag{3}$$

It may be noted that the linear correlation coefficient is not expressible in a copula form. The parameter θ is estimated from τ. The parameter θ in each case measures the degree of dependence and controls the association between two variables. When $\theta \to 0$ there is no dependence and if $\theta \to \infty$ there is perfect dependence. Schweizer and Wolff [15] show that the dependence parameter θ which characterizes a family of Archimedean copulas can be related to Kendall's τ.

The general dependence structure, especially the dependence structure of the extreme events, strongly influences the analysis and should be considered in analysis. Tail dependence refers to the amount of dependence in the tails of a bivariate distribution or alternatively the dependence in the corner of the lower-left quadrant or upper-right quadrant of a bivariate distribution. Tail dependence in terms of a bivariate copula function C(u,v) is measured by

$$\lambda_{upper} = \lim_{u \to 1}[1 - 2u + C(u,u)]/(1 - u) \quad \text{and} \quad \lambda_{lower} = \lim_{u \to 0} C(u,u)/u.$$

The distribution is upper (lower) tail dependent if λ_{upper} (λ_{lower}) > 0 and upper (lower) tail independent if λ_{upper} (λ_{lower}) $= 0$.

2.2. *Algorithm to Generate Archimedean Copulas*

The following algorithm generates random variables (U, V) whose joint distribution is an Archimedean copula $C(u, v)$ with generator function $\varphi(t)$.

1. Generate two independent uniform random variables p and q on $[0,1]$.
2. Set $t = K_C^{-1}(q)$, where $K_C = K_C(t) = t - \varphi(t)/\varphi'(t)$ is a copula $C(u,v)$.
3. Set $u = \varphi^{-1}[p \cdot \varphi(t)]$ and $v = \varphi^{-1}[(1 - p) \cdot \varphi(t)]$.
4. Calculate $x = F^{-1}(u)$ and $y = F^{-1}(v)$.
5. Repeat n times steps 1 through 4 to generate data $(x_i, y_i), i = 1,...,n$.

3. Bayesian Updating Using Copulas

In Bayesian approach the joint distribution need to be specified for arriving at the posterior distribution. Since the joint distribution is defined by the copula, Bayesian updating can be done using copula functions. The joint distribution function from a copula $C(u,v)$ is $c(u,v) = \partial^2 C(u,v)/\partial u \partial v$. In the proposed copula approach, from a Bayesian view, the conditional distribution of $v \mid u$ is

$$c_u(v) = P[V \leq v \mid U \leq u] = \frac{\partial}{\partial u} C(u,v).$$ The above conditional distribution $c_u(v)$ is the posterior distribution of v. Now we simulate the pairs (u,v) using copula based Bayesian updating as follows:

1. Simulate two *independent* random numbers u, t between 0 and 1.
2. Let $v = c_u^{-1}(t)$, where c_u^{-1} denotes the quasi inverse of c_u.
3. The desired pair of values is (u,v).

The conditional distributions for some Archimedean copulas are presented in Table 1. Using Maple® software, we have for Ali-Mikhail-Haq copula

$$c_u^{-1}(t) = [1 - \theta - 2t\theta(1-u)(1-\theta+u\theta)$$

$$- \sqrt{(1-\theta)^2 + 4tu\theta(1-\theta+u\theta)}] / 2\theta[t\theta(1-u)^2 - 1], \tag{4}$$

for Clayton copula

$$c^{-1}{}_u(t) = \exp[-\frac{1}{\theta}\ln\{\exp(-\theta\frac{\ln(tu)+\theta\ln u}{1+\theta}) - u^{-\theta} + 1\}], \tag{5}$$

and for Frank copula

$$c^{-1}{}_u(t) = 1 - \frac{1}{\theta}\ln\frac{(t-1)e^{-(u-1)\theta}-t}{(t-1)e^{-u\theta}-t}. \tag{6}$$

Table 1: Archimedean Copulas and Conditional Distributions.

Copula	$C(u,v)$	$c_u(v)$
AMH	$\dfrac{uv}{1-\theta(1-u)(1-v)}; \theta \in [-1,1]$	$\dfrac{v[1-\theta(1-v)]}{[1-\theta(1-u)(1-v)]^2}$
Clayton	$(u^{-\theta}+v^{-\theta}-1)^{-1/\theta}; \; \theta \in [-1,\infty)\setminus\{0\}$	$(u^{-\theta}+v^{-\theta}-1)^{-(1+\theta)/\theta}u^{-(1+\theta)}$
Gumbel	$\exp[-\{(-\ln u)^\theta + (-\ln v)^\theta\}^{1/\theta}]; \; \theta \in [1,\infty)$	$\dfrac{C(u,v)}{u}\left[1+\left(\dfrac{\ln v}{\ln u}\right)^\theta\right]^{(1-\theta)/\theta}$

4. An Application

A new production process is being contemplated for manufacturing stainless steel bearings. A company is planning to invest in the adoption of this new process to improve its current manufacturing process. It is planning to adopt a sequential real options strategy approach by first trying out new process in one location and then based on the new information to go ahead and expand new process to other locations. The parameter of interest is the diameter of stainless

24

steel bearings. Measurements of the diameters of random samples of bearings from the old (say, variable Y) and the new (say, variable X) processes are recorded. The prior here is the distribution of the diameter measurements of bearings (Y) from the old process. The sample data refers to the diameter measurements of bearings (X) after implementing the new process. In the real options approach, the corporate managers would revise the prior with new information and obtain the posterior distribution. Posterior distribution then will be used to decide whether or not to invest in new technology at other locations. This type of decision making is akin to real options since the company delays the immediate full investment in all locations to capture the upside potential. The option involved is a learning real option. For suggested copula based Bayesian approach, we first estimate the marginal distributions from prior Y and the data X. The prior probability distribution of $Y \sim \mathrm{Gamma}(5781.9, 0.002759)$ and the estimated distribution of $X \sim \mathrm{Gamma}(7111.1, 0.00225)$. We use the Ali-Mikhail-Haq copula to generate the posterior distribution from Eq. (10). Estimated posterior distribution $Y \sim \mathrm{Gamma}(4541.8, 0.003514)$. The distributions are shown in Figure 1. The managers of the company use the posterior distribution to make inference about the population parameter and to decide on whether or not to invest in the new technology.

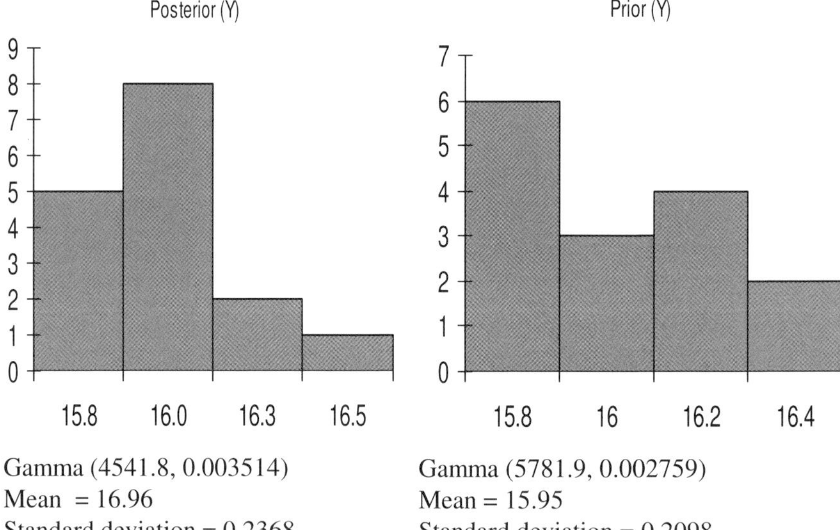

Gamma (4541.8, 0.003514)
Mean = 16.96
Standard deviation = 0.2368

Gamma (5781.9, 0.002759)
Mean = 15.95
Standard deviation = 0.2098

Figure 1. Prior and Posteriors Distributions.

5. Conclusion

There has been lot of emphasis on the importance of real option analysis to make corporate investments decisions, value natural resource development projects, patents, and licenses with limiting quotas, software development and insurance policy decisions, value IT security investments, valuing R&D projects in the capital budgeting etc. Understanding and quantifying dependence among contributing factors is often required in real options. Recently, however, the problems associated with correlation have attracted attention of researchers. An alternate measure of dependence known as a copula has been suggested to overcome many of limitations of linear correlation. There are several advantages in using copulas to model dependence. For example, copulas allow modeling non-linear dependence, any choice of marginal distributions can be used, and extreme events can be modeled.

Copulas also have been considered in Bayesian analysis with focus on real options. Although, the frequentist approach for defining the probability of an uncertain event is all well and good provided that we have been able to record accurate information about many past instances of the event. However, if no such historical database exists, then we have to consider a different approach. More formally, since there are no previous instances of such occurrence we cannot use the frequentist approach to define our degree of belief of this uncertain event. Bayesian probability is a formalism that allows us to reason about our beliefs under conditions of uncertainty and include them in the analysis. The basic expressions about uncertainty in the Bayesian approach are statements about conditional probabilities. The joint distribution has to be specified for determining posterior distribution. Since the joint distribution is defined by the copula, Bayesian updating can be done using copula functions as illustrated in this article.

References

1. L. Andersen and J. Sidenius, "Extensions to the Gaussian Copula: Random Recovery and Random Factor Loadings," *Journal of Credit Risk,* Vol. 1, pp. 29-70, 2004.
2. M. Armstrong , A. Galli, W. Bailey and B. Couet, "Incorporating Technical Uncertainty in Real Option Valuation of Oil Projects," *Journal of Petroleum Science and Engineering,* Vol. 44, pp. 67-82, 2004.
3. M. N. Bennett, and J. E. Kennedy, "Quanto Pricing with Copulas," *Journal of Derivatives,* Vol. 12, no. 1, pp. 26-45, 2004.
4. U. Cherubini and E. Luciano, "Bivariate Option Pricing with Copulas", *Applied Mathematical Finance*, Vol. 8, pp. 69-85, 2002.

5. R. T. Clemen, and T. Reilly, "Correlations and Copulas for Decision and Risk Analysis," *Management Science,* Vol. 45, no. 2, pp. 208-224, 1999.
6. E. W. Frees, and E. Valdez, "Understanding Relationships Using Copulas," *North American Actuarial Journal,* Vol. 2, no. 1, pp. 1-25, 1998.
7. C., Genest, "Frank's Family of Bivariate Distributions", *Biometrika*, Vol. 79, pp. 549-555, 1987.
8. C. Genest, and L. Rivest, "Statistical Inference Procedures for Bivariate Archimedean Copulas,"*Journal of the American Statistical Association,* Vol. 88, pp. 1034-1043, 1993.
9. H. S. B. Herath and P. Kumar "RESEARCH Directions in Engineering Economics-Modeling Dependencies with Copulas", *Engineering Economist,* Vol. 45, No. 1, 2007, pp. 1-36.
10. J., Hull and A. White., "Valuation of a CDO and n^{th} to Default CDS without Monte Carlo Simulation," *Journal of Derivatives*, Volume 12, No. 2, pp. 117-131, 2004.
11. S. A., Klugman and R. Parsa, "Fitting Bivariate Loss Distributions with Copulas," *Mathematics and Economics,* Vol. 24, pp. 139-148, 1999.
12. A. W., Marshall, and I. Olkin, "Families of Multivariate Distributions," *Journal of the American Statistical Association,* Vol. 83, pp. 834-841, 1988.
13. R. B., Nelsen, *An Introduction to Copulas*, Springer-Verlag New York, Inc., 2006.
14. C. S. Park and H. S. B. Herath, "Exploiting Uncertainty - Investment Opportunities as Real Options: A New Way of Thinking in Engineering Economics", *Engineering Economist*, Vol. 45, No. 1, 2000, pp. 1-36.
15. B. Schweizer and E. F. Wolff, "On Nonparametric Measures of Dependence for Random Variables," *The Annals of Statistics*, Vol. 9, no. 4 (July), pp.879-885, 1981.
16. A. Sklar, "functions de repartition a n dimensions et leurs merges," *Publ. Inst. Statist. Univ. Paris*, Vol. 8, pp.229-231, 1959.

ON HYBRIDIZATION OF PROBABILISTIC AND FUZZY APPROACHES TO PROPAGATE RANDOMNESS AND EPISTEMIC UNCERTAINTY IN RISK ASSESSMENT MODELS

VASILE GEORGESCU

Department of Mathematical economics, University of Craiova, 13 A.I.Cuza Craiova, 200585, Romania

This paper discuses hybrid probabilistic and fuzzy approaches to propagating randomness and uncertainty in risk assessment models. Analytic and stochastic methods such as Probability bounds analysis, Fuzzy α-levels analysis, and the theory of Fuzzy random vectors can be combined in different ways or can be integrated in a Fuzzy Monte Carlo simulation framework in order to find the output of a model that has both random variables (given by probability distributions) and fuzzy variables for the inputs.

1. Probabilistic risk assessment

According to EPA's guidance (EPA, 2001), *probabilistic risk assessment* (PRA) is a general term for risk assessments that use probability models to represent the likelihood of different risk levels in a population (i.e., randomness) or to characterize uncertainty in risk estimates. In the probabilistic approach, inputs to the risk equation are described as *random variables* that can be defined mathematically by a probability distribution. The CDF for risk can be especially informative for illustrating the percentile corresponding to a particular risk level of concern.

1.1. *Ontological versus epistemic uncertainty*

An essential concept in probabilistic risk assessment is the distinction between ontological and epistemic uncertainty.

Ontological uncertainty (also called randomness, variability, or aleatory/ objective/irreducible uncertainty) arises from natural stochasticity, environmental variation across space or through time, genetic heterogeneity among individuals, and other sources of randomness. Although variability can often be better characterized by further specific study, it is not generally reducible by empirical effort. Variability can be translated into risk (i.e., probability of some adverse consequence) by the application of an appropriate probabilistic model.

Epistemic uncertainty (also called subjective/reducible uncertainty) arises from incomplete knowledge about the world. Sources of uncertainty include measurement uncertainty, small sample sizes, detection limits and data censoring, ignorance about the details of the mechanisms and processes involved and other imperfections in scientific understanding. Uncertainty can in principle be reduced by focused empirical effort. It cannot be translated into probability, but it can be used to generate bounds on the risk assessments (the range within which the risk distribution might vary given the uncertainty present in the risk model).

1.2. *Propagating randomness in risk models with no parameter uncertainty: one-dimensional Monte Carlo Analysis (1D MCA)*

A Monte Carlo analysis that characterizes either uncertainty or variability in each input variable can be described as a one-dimensional Monte Carlo analysis (1D MCA). In its general form, the risk equation can be expressed as a function of multiple risk exposure variables (V_i) : Risk $= f(V_1, \ldots, V_n)$.

Often the input distributions are assumed to be independent. The value of one variable has no relationship to the value of any other variable. In this case, a value for each variable (V_i) is selected at random from a specified PDF and the corresponding risk is calculated. This process is repeated many times (e.g., 10,000). Each iteration of a Monte Carlo simulation should represent a plausible combination of input values. A unique risk estimate is calculated for each set of random values. Repeatedly sampling (V_i) results in a frequency distribution of risk, which can be described by a PDF or a CDF. A sufficient number of iterations should be run to obtain numerical stability in percentiles of the output (e.g., risk distribution). The risk distributions derived from a PRA allow for inferences to be made about the likelihood or probability of risks occurring within a specified range of the input variables.

More complex Monte Carlo simulations can be developed that quantify a dependence between one or more input distributions by using conditional distributions or correlation coefficients.

1.3. *Propagating randomness and epistemic uncertainty simultaneously: two-dimensional Monte Carlo Analysis (2D MCA)*

A 2D MCA is a term used to describe a model that simulates both uncertainty and randomness in one or more input variables. Uncertainty in the parameter estimates can be represented in a PRA model as follows. Consider a random input variable whose parameter estimates are affected by uncertainty. Assume normal PDFs can be specified for both uncertain parameters: the mean and the standard deviation. Uncertainty in the mean is described by the normal PDF with parameters ($\mu_{mean}=5$, $\sigma_{mean}=0.5$); similarly, uncertainty in the standard deviation is described by the normal PDF with parameters ($\mu_{SD}=1$, $\sigma_{SD}=0.5$). A variable described in this way is called a second order random variable.

A two-dimensional Monte Carlo simulation is a nesting of two ordinary Monte Carlo simulations. Typically, the inner simulation represents natural variability of the underlying processes, while the outer simulation represents the analyst's uncertainty about the particular parameters that should be used to specify inputs to the inner simulation. This structure means that each iterate in the outer simulation entails an entire Monte Carlo simulation, which can lead to a very large computational burden.

2. Probability bound analysis in risk assessment

2.1. *Computing with probability bounds*

Probability bounds analysis combines probability theory and interval arithmetic to produce probability boxes (p-boxes), structures that allow the comprehensive propagation of both randomness and uncertainty through calculations in a rigorous way.

If we have only a partial information about the probability distribution, then we cannot compute the exact values $F(x)$ of the CDF. Instead, we can circumscribe $F(x)$ by a pair of functions $\underline{F}(x)$ and $\overline{F}(x)$, each one representing a CDF, which bounds the (unknown) actual CDF. Such a pair of CDFs is called a *probability bound*, or a *p-bound*, for short. For every x, the possible values of the probability $F(x)$ belongs to the interval $[\underline{F}(x), \overline{F}(x)]$.

In computations, it is often convenient to express a p-box in terms of its inverse functions ℓ and u defined on the interval of probability levels $[0,1]$. The function u is the inverse function of the upper bound on the distribution function and ℓ is the inverse function of the lower bound. These monotonic functions are bounds on the inverse of the unknown distribution function F

$$\ell(p) \ge F^{-1}(p) \ge u(p) \tag{1}$$

where p is probability level. Note that ℓ corresponds to $\overline{F}$ and u to $\underline{F}$.

It is simple to compute probability bounds for many cases in which the distribution family is specified, but only interval estimates can be given for the parameters. For instance, suppose that, from previous knowledge, it is assumed that a distribution is normal, but the precise values of the parameters that would define this distribution are uncertain. If there exist bounds on μ and σ (mean and standard deviation), bounds on the distribution can be obtained by computing the envelope of all normal distributions that have parameters within the specified intervals. These bounds are

$$\ell(p) = \max_{\theta} F_{\theta}^{-1}(p); \quad u(p) = \min_{\theta} F_{\theta}^{-1}(p); \tag{2}$$

where

$$\theta \in \{(\mu, \sigma) \mid \mu \in [\mu_{\ell}, \mu_{u}], \sigma \in [\sigma_{\ell}, \sigma_{u}]\} \tag{3}$$

and F is the CDF of a normal distribution with such parameters. In principle, making these calculations might be a difficult task since θ indexes an infinite set of distributions. However, in practice, finding the bounds requires computing the envelope over only four distributions: those corresponding to the parameter sets $(\mu_{\ell}, \sigma_{\ell})$, (μ_{ℓ}, σ_{u}), (μ_{u}, σ_{ℓ}), and (μ_{u}, σ_{u}). This simplicity is the result of how the family of distributions happens to be parameterized by μ and σ.

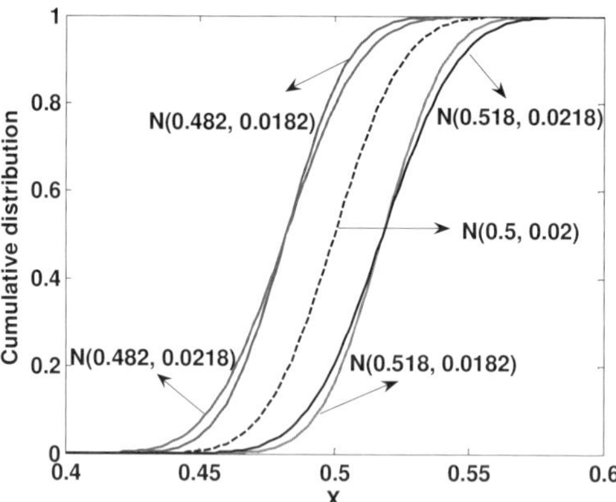

Figure 1. Bounds on the CDF of a normal distribution with $\mu = [0.482, 0.518]$ and $\sigma = [0.0182, 0.0218]$. The dotted line is the CDF for the normal distribution with $\mu = 0.5$ and $\sigma = 0.02$.

Nevertheless, it is just as easy to find probability bounds for cases with other commonly used distribution families such as lognormal, uniform, exponential, Cauchy, and many others.

2.2. *Probability bounds analysis compared to Monte Carlo simulation*

When one or more point estimates defined in the risk model are uncertainty, a Monte Carlo analyst might employ a two-dimensional Monte Carlo simulation that includes an uncertainty (inner) loop for each uncertain point estimate.

In a probability bounds analysis, the same interval of possible values used in the Monte Carlo analyst's uncertainty loop replaces the point estimate; however the semi-analytic nature of the probability bounds analysis results in an exact representation of the stated uncertainty. As the number of times the inner loop is called in the Monte Carlo simulation approaches infinity, the result of the Monte Carlo analysis converges on the probability bounds result.

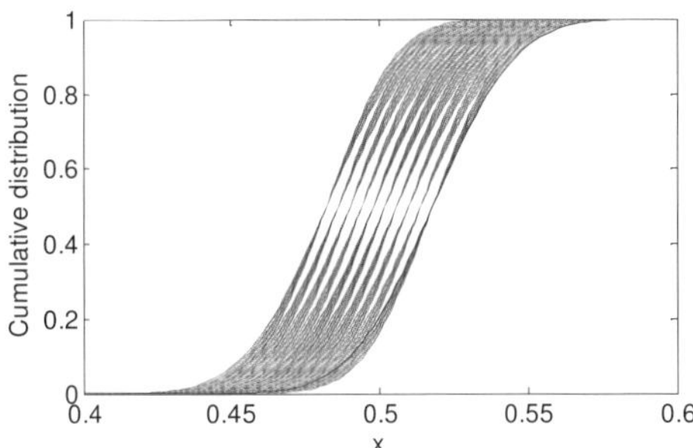

Figure 2. Monte Carlo vs. Probability Bounds: uncertainty regarding the exact value of the parameters of a probability distribution, where $\mu = [0.482, 0.518]$ and $\sigma = [0.0182, 0.0218]$.

3. Fuzzy randomness approaches to risk assessment

3.1. *Fuzzy random variables*

We consider an extension of the probability space $[\Omega; \mathcal{A}; P]$ by the dimension of fuzziness, i.e., by introducing a membership scale. This enables the consideration of imprecise observations as fuzzy realizations $\tilde{x}(\omega) = (\tilde{x}_1, \ldots, \tilde{x}_n) \subseteq X$ of each elementary event $\omega \in \Omega$.

For constructing probability measures on fuzzy sets, an appropriate metric is needed. We consider the well-known Hausdorff metric d_H, on the class $K_c(\Re)$ of nonempty compact intervals

$$d_H(K, K') = \max\left\{\sup_{k\in K}\inf_{k'\in K'} |k - k'|,\ \sup_{k'\in K'}\inf_{k\in K} |k - k'|\right\} \tag{4}$$

$$= \max\left\{\left|\inf K - \inf K'\right|, \left|\sup K - \sup K'\right|\right\}$$

A *fuzzy random variable* $\tilde{X}$ is the fuzzy result of the uncertain mapping

$$\tilde{X} : \Omega \to \mathbf{F}_c(\mathfrak{R}) \tag{5}$$

such that for each $\alpha \in [0, 1]$ the α-level mapping

$$X_\alpha : \Omega \to \mathbf{K}_c(\mathfrak{R}), \text{ with } X_\alpha(\omega) = \left[\inf(X(\omega))_\alpha, \sup(X(\omega))_\alpha\right], \forall \omega \in \Omega \tag{6}$$

is a (compact convex) random set, (i.e., it is Borel-measurable w.r.t. the Borel σ-field generated by the topology associated with d_H).

The fuzzy probability distribution function $\tilde{F}(x)$ of $\tilde{X}$ is the set of probability distribution functions of all originals X_j of $\tilde{X}$ with the membership values $\mu(F(x))$. The cuantification of fuzziness by fuzzy parameters leads to the description of the fuzzy probability distribution function $\tilde{F}(x)$ of $\tilde{X}$ as a function of the fuzzy bunch parameter $\tilde{s}$.

$$\tilde{F}(x) = F(\tilde{s}, x) \tag{7}$$

For the purposes of numerical evaluation, α-discretization is advantageously applied.

$$F(\tilde{s},x) = \left\{F_\alpha(x);\ \mu(F_\alpha(x)) \mid F_\alpha(x) = [\underline{F}_\alpha(x), \overline{F}_\alpha(x)],\right.$$
$$\left.\mu(F_\alpha(x)) = \alpha,\ \forall \alpha \in [0,1]\right\} \tag{8}$$

with $\underline{F}_\alpha(x) = \inf\{F(s,x) \mid s \in s_\alpha\}$, $\overline{F}_\alpha(x) = \sup\{F(s,x) \mid s \in s_\alpha\}$.

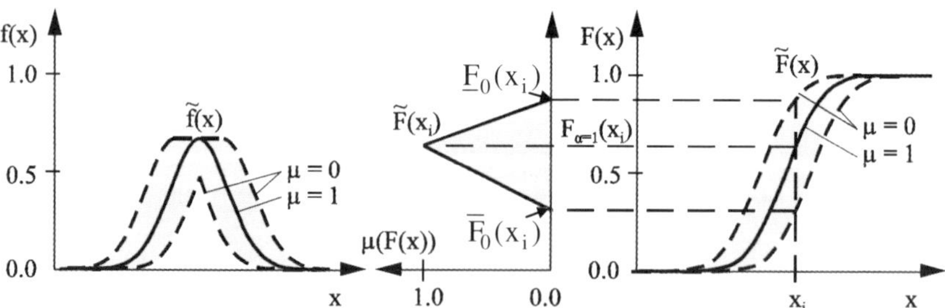

Figure 3. Fuzzy probability density function and fuzzy cumulative distribution function.

With the aid of α-discretization a fuzzy random function may be formulated as a set of α-level sets of ordinary random functions

$$\tilde{X}(t) = \left\{ X_\alpha(t); \mu(X_\alpha(t)) \mid X_\alpha(t) = \left[\underline{X}_\alpha(t), \overline{X}_\alpha(t) \right], \right.$$
$$\left. \mu(X_\alpha(t)) = \alpha, \forall \alpha \in [0, 1] \right\} \tag{9}$$

3.2. *Hybrid approaches to propagating randomness and fuzziness in risk assessment*

The idea is to find the output of a model $g(X_1, ..., X_n, \tilde{X}_1, ..., \tilde{X}_m)$ that has both random variables $X_1, ..., X_n$, given by probabilistic distributions, and fuzzy variables $\tilde{X}_1, ..., \tilde{X}_m$, for the inputs. To estimate the output of this generalized model, most researchers attempt to eliminate or transform one type of uncertainty to another before performing a simulation (e.g. possibility to probability transformation). Guyonnet et al. (2003) first proposed a "hybrid approach" with both fuzzy and random types of uncertainty without transforming one type to another. They calculated the Inf and Sup values of the model g considering all the values that are located within the $\alpha -$ cuts of the input fuzzy sets and suggested that minimization and maximization algorithm can be used for finding Inf and Sup values of a general model. However, in their application, the model was a simple monotonic function, and the Inf and Sup values were identified directly without using minimization or maximization algorithms.

A more tractable way to propagating both randomness and fuzziness is based of a fuzzy generalization of the Monte Carlo (FMC) simulation framework, which integrates fuzzy arithmetic method with Monte Carlo simulation to find the output of a model with both fuzzy and probabilistic inputs.

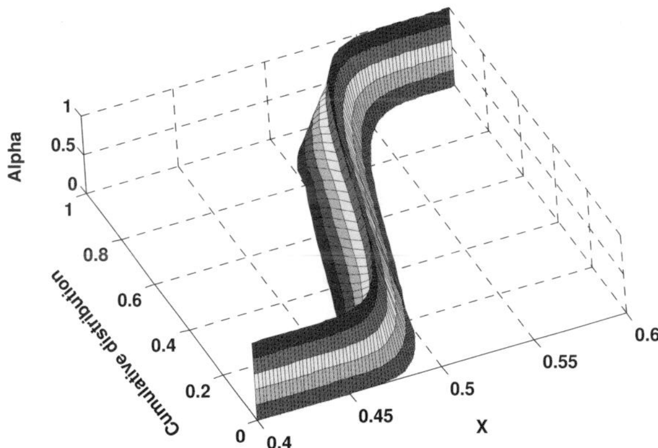

Figure 4. 3D view of fuzzy CDF resulting from the output of FMC by aggregating α-CDF bounds.

34

Since in FMC, fuzzy arithmetic (in α-cut form) is performing for each sample set, the output of FMC is represented as a number of fuzzy sets with random variation. This randomness results from random sampling of random input parameters. The fuzzy CDF is used for finding the *fuzzy probability* of not exceeding a given threshold and a *fuzzy quantile* corresponding to a given probability.

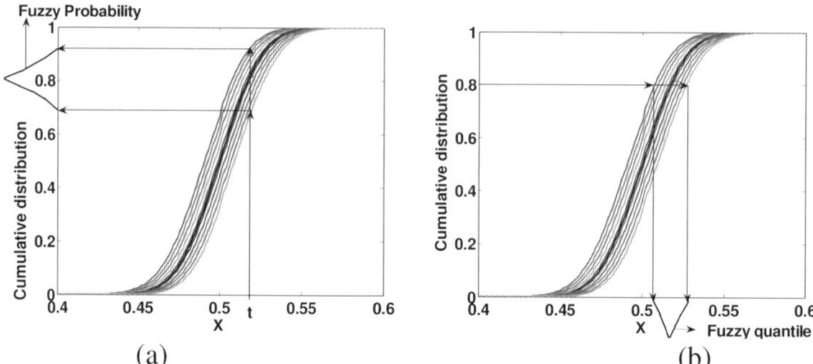

Figure 5. (a) The fuzzy probability of not exceeding a specific threshold $t \in X$
(b) A fuzzy quantile corresponding to a given probability.

References

1. C. Baudrit, D. Guyonnet and D. Dubois, "Postprocessing the Hybrid Method for Addressing Uncertainty in Risk Assessments." *Journal of Environmental Engineering* 131(12), 1750-1754, (2005).
2. EPA's guidance: "Risk Assessment Guidance for Superfund (RAGS) Volume III – Part A: Process for Conducting Probabilistic Risk Assessment", 2001, www.epa.gov/oswer/riskassessment/rags3adt/index.htm
3. S. Ferson and W.T. Tucker, "Probability Bounds Analysis in Environmental Risk Assessments" (Technical report), *Applied Biomathematics*, Setauket, New York (2003). Available at www.ramas.com/pbawhite.pdf.
4. S. Ferson, L, Ginzburg, V. Kreinovich, H.T.Nguyen and S.A. Starks, "Uncertainty in risk analysis: towards a general second-order approach combining interval, probabilistic, and fuzzy techniques", *Proceedings of the 2002 IEEE Int. Conference on Fuzzy Systems*, pp. 1342-1347. (2002)
5. D. Guyonnet, B. Bourgigne, D. Dubois, H. Fargier, B. Côme and J. Chilès, "Hybrid approach for addressing uncertainty in risk assessments." *Journal of environmental engineering* 129(1), 68-78 (2003).
6. B. Möller and M. Beer, *Fuzzy Randomness – Uncertainty Computational Mechanics*, Springer, Berlin and New York, (2004).
7. P. Terán, "Probabilistic foundations for measurement modeling with fuzzy random variables", *Fuzzy Sets and Systems* 158(9), 973-986, (2007).

STRUCTURAL OPTIMIZATION OF LINGUISTIC KNOWLEDGE BASE OF FUZZY CONTROLLERS

YURIY P. KONDRATENKO

Intelligent Information Systems Department, Petro Mohyla Black Sea State University
10, 68th Desantnykiv Str., Nikolaev, 54003, Ukraine, y_kondrat2002@yahoo.com

LEONID P. KLYMENKO

Ecology Department, Petro Mohyla Black Sea State University
10, 68th Desantnykiv Str., Nikolaev, 54003, Ukraine, rector@kma.mk.ua

EYAD YASIN MUSTAFA AL ZU'BI

College of Science and Arts, King Saud University, p/o Box 30
Shagra,11961, Kingdom of Saudi Arabia, eyad19762000@yahoo.com

The paper considers the problem of developing effective methods and algorithms for optimization of fuzzy rules bases of Sugeno-type fuzzy controllers that can be applied to control of dynamic objects, including objects with non-stationary parameters. Proposed approach based on calculating the coefficient of influence of each of the rules on the formation of control signals for different types of input signals provides optimization of a linguistic rules database by using exclusion mechanism for rules with negligible influence.

1. Introduction

Fuzzy sets theory and fuzzy logic have been widely introduced into research and design practice recently. From the first study of fuzzy sets [16] researches received the theoretical foundation introducing fuzzy sets for successful solving of various problems in uncertainty [2,3,4]. Especially it is important and effective for control of such objects with non-stationary functioning conditions as ships, underwater robots, manipulated systems with moving base and others. Special attention should be paid to structural-parameter optimization of fuzzy systems for their applications in engineering where fuzzy controllers are components of embedded computer systems [7,8]. A number of methods of fuzzy controllers synthesis [1,6,9] have been developed to date. They provide the desired quality control in fuzzy systems by optimizing parameters of membership functions of linguistic terms. As an objective function in the implementation of these methods an integral quadratic criterion or standard deviation of the real transition from desirable are usually used. At the same time rules, that determine the control strategy, are based on expert assessments for all possible combinations of linguistic terms. The described above approach does not take into account the redundancy of complete database rules, which makes the structure of fuzzy controllers too complicated and does not use the ability of fuzzy logic systems for extrapolation. Thus, the development of algorithms to optimize the structure of fuzzy controllers is quite necessary [5,10,12,13,15], as it will simultaneously improve the performance of fuzzy control devices by decreasing the number of computer operations and reduce the complexity of the synthesis process of fuzzy controllers by decreasing the number of optimization parameters in the tasks of nonlinear programming.

2. Problem Statement and Description of Tested Fuzzy Controller

This paper offers the introduction stage of structural optimization to the procedures of forming the base of linguistic rules of fuzzy controllers. This stage is based on the identification of the impact level of linguistic rules on the defuzzyfied output control signal and building the appropriate ranked series of rules according to this specified parameter. The obtained ranked series will allow to delete the rules, whose impact on the formation of controller output signal is negligible, from the linguistic base. The correctness of excluding certain rules must be confirmed by comparing the quality of fuzzy control systems for two options: the complete and optimized knowledge bases of rules.

To test the proposed approach, the solution to the structural optimization problem of fuzzy PID controller [9] for non-stationary control objects will be analyzed. This fuzzy controller is based on the fuzzy inference engine of Sugeno-type [14] with linear functions of input signals in the consequents of linguistic rules. The output component of each rule is a PID-law control variable which was formed by parametric optimization within the gradient method according to the input signal vector of fuzzy controller, which looks like

$$X=\left\{x_1(t),x_2(t),x_3(t)\right\}=\left\{\varepsilon(t),\int\varepsilon(t)dt,\frac{d\varepsilon}{dt}\right\},$$

where ε is the error of fuzzy control system. The integral quadratic criterion of the control quality plays the role of the objective function during parametric optimization. For fuzzyfication of each input signal we will use three linguistic terms with Gaussian form of membership function [11,12], which uniformly cover the range of possible values of corresponding input signals. Thus, the full linguistic knowledge base of the considered fuzzy controller consists of 27 linguistic rules such as:

$$i: \quad \text{IF} \ \ x_1(t) \in \mu_{1,(i \, \text{div} \, 9)+1} \quad \text{AND} \ \ x_2(t) \in \mu_{2,\left[(i \, \text{div} \, 9) \, \text{mod} \, 3\right]+1} \quad \text{AND} \ \ x_3(t) \in \mu_{3,(i \, \text{mod} \, 3)+1}$$

$$\text{THEN} \ \ u = k_{i,1}x_1 + k_{i,2}x_2 + k_{i,3}x_3,$$

where i is number of rules; div and mod are operations integer division and taking remainder of the division, respectively; $x_j(t)$ is component of input signal vector of fuzzy controller, $j = 1, 2, 3$ ..

3. Analysis of the Linguistic Rules Impact on the Formation of Control Signals in Fuzzy Control Systems

The information in a fuzzy controller during the process of forming the output signal is undergoing a number of successive stages of transformation, such as fuzzyfication, aggregation, activation, accumulation, and defuzzyfication [5,6,11,12]. In fuzzy Sugeno-type controllers the output control signal is calculated as the position of the centre of material points masses located on the abscissa axis. The coordinates of these material points describe the output signal values formed at the output of each rule according to PID-law control, and points mass describes the degree of truth of the corresponding rule, calculated at the stage of aggregation. It is obvious that the smaller the weight of a point, the smaller its impact on the overall centre of mass and, consequently, on the value of the control signal. Thus, assessing (on the stage of designing fuzzy controllers) the change of the rules' truth degree in the control process enables to rank the rules according to their influence on the value of output control signal and henceforth to optimize the fuzzy linguistic database by deleting those rules, whose influence is too low. Changing the degree of truth of i-th rule in the control process with corresponding reference signal is expressed by the following function of model time, t :

$$\mu_i^R(t) = \overset{m}{\underset{j=1}{U}}\mu_j^i\big(x_j(t)\big) = \underset{j=1}{\overset{m}{\inf}}\,\mu_j^i\big(x_j(t)\big), \tag{1}$$

where $\mu_i^R(t)$ is the degree of truth of i-th rule in time moment t ; $x_j(t)$ is j-th input fuzzy controller signal, $j = 1 \ldots m$, $m = 3$; μ_j^i is the result of fuzzyfication of j-th input signal $x_j(t)$ by the corresponding linguistic term of i-th rule.

The nature of transients in fuzzy control systems greatly depends on the type of reference signal and disturbing influence. Therefore to ensure comparability of simulation conditions and real conditions of control system functioning it is advisable to conduct model experiments, in which the most common types of reference and disturbing inputs are combined (control input: step, harmonic, linear-rising; disturbing input: step, linear-rising, harmonic, pulse, stochastic).

Fig. 1 shows the calculated by expression (1) dynamic dependences of the rules validity degrees in the control process at the output of a single step reference signal with permanent disturbance. As shown in Fig. 1, the truth value of the rules set $\mathbf{R}_1 = \{4, 23, 10, 11, 5, 16, 20, 17, 1, 7, 2, 8, 6, 21, 25, 26, 9, 15, 18\}$ does not exceed $\mu=0,1$, and for the rules set $\mathbf{R}_2 = \{3, 12, 23, 27\}$ the truth throughout the transient process is zero. Thus, the impact of rules that are members of sets $\mathbf{R}_1$ та $\mathbf{R}_2$ is lower than that of other rules.

The next step is forming a ranked series of rules. It is necessary to choose such evaluative function $G\left[\mu_i^R(t)\right]$, the input for which is dependence $\mu_i^R(t)$ of i-th rule influence in time moment t on the control signal and the output is scalar value G_i, which represents a generalized characteristic of the rule impact on the control signal formation during the entire transient process.

One of the possible ways of building an assessment functional $G\left[\mu_i^R(t)\right]$ is the integration of expression (1) with subsequent averaging of functional values obtained in different conditions of the transient flow. The analytical representation of the proposed estimated functional is:

$$G_i\left[\mu_i^R(t)\right] = \frac{1}{T_{max}}\int_0^{T_{max}}\mu_i^R(t)dt = \frac{1}{T_{max}}\int_0^{T_{max}}\inf_{j=1}^m \mu_j^i\left(x_i(t)\right)dt, \tag{2}$$

where G_i is the evaluation function value for i-th rule; T_{max} is the duration of the transient process.

It is suggested that prior to ranking rules the values of the assessment functional, obtained in different simulation conditions, and should be averaged according to the algorithm:

$$G_i^{av}\left[\mu_{i,1}^R(t), \mu_{i,2}^R(t), \ldots \mu_{i,s}^R(t)\right] = \frac{1}{s}\sum_{k=1}^s G_{i,k}\left[\mu_{i,k}^R(t)\right], \tag{3}$$

The average values of functional (3) for all 27-linguistic rules of the investigated fuzzy PID-controller are presented in the diagram (Fig. 2).

The series formed by the ranking rules in descending order of their degree of influence on the control signal, is the following

$$R = \{13, 22, 14, 19, 4, 23, 10, 11, 5, 16, 20, 17, 1, 7, 2, 8, 6, 21, 25, 26, 9, 15, 18, 3, 27, 24, 12\}. \tag{4}$$

Later, it is possible to determine the critical (minimum) number of rules from (4), for which the index value of control quality will remain within acceptable limits. The task can be solved by simulation and analysis of transients in the fuzzy control system, starting with minimal linguistic database – a single rule with the highest rank, in particular rule 13. In this case, the fuzzy Sugeno-type controller functionally transforms into the traditional PID-regulator. Modelling process is repeated, the gradually adding rules to the linguistic knowledge base

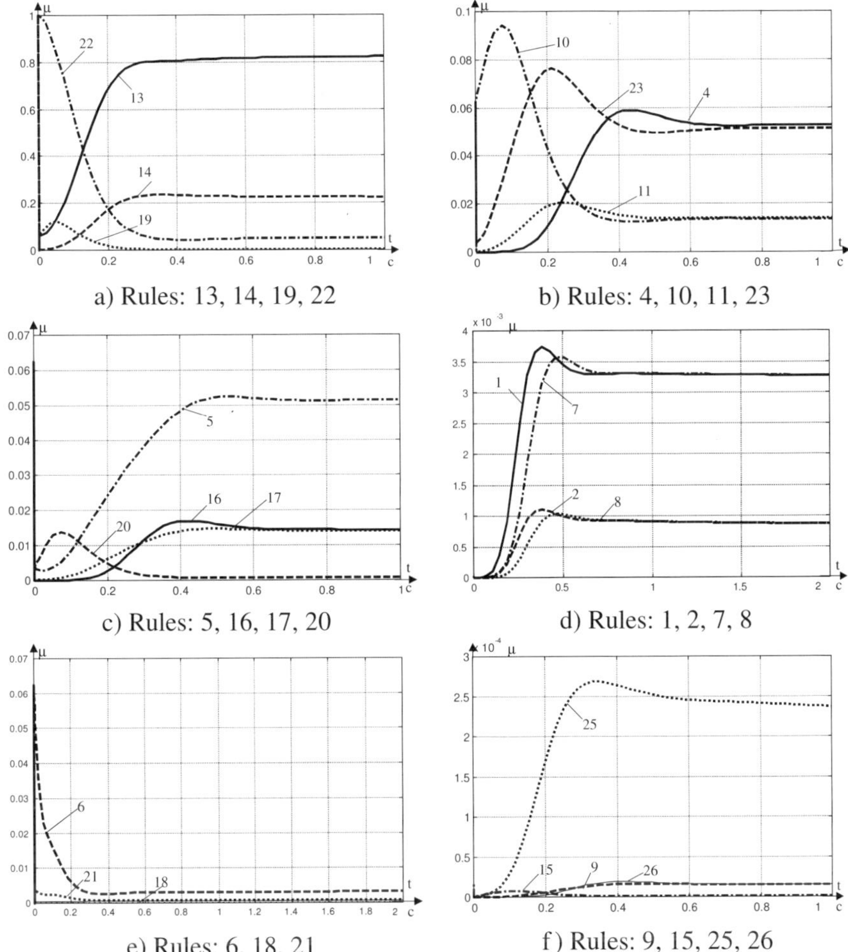

a) Rules: 13, 14, 19, 22

b) Rules: 4, 10, 11, 23

c) Rules: 5, 16, 17, 20

d) Rules: 1, 2, 7, 8

e) Rules: 6, 18, 21

f) Rules: 9, 15, 25, 26

Fig. 1. Dependences of the rules impact on the control signal value

of fuzzy Sugeno-type controller in the order determined by the ranked series (4) until the control quality indices are within the limits determined by technical requirements.

The described procedure was used for all abovementioned combinations of reference inputs and disturbing influences. The simulation enabled to determine

40

the nature of the transient characteristics changes of fuzzy control systems with increasing number of rules (Fig. 3, 4).

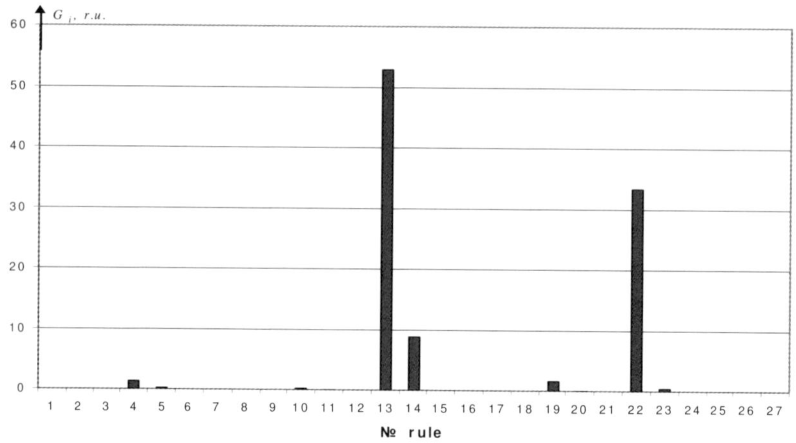

Fig. 2. Averaged values of evaluation functional $G_i\left[\mu_i^R(t)\right]$ for the Sugeno-controller base of rules

Thus, analyzing Fig. 3 and Fig. 4, one can conclude that after the inclusion of the first seven rules of ranked series (4) to an optimized knowledge database, its

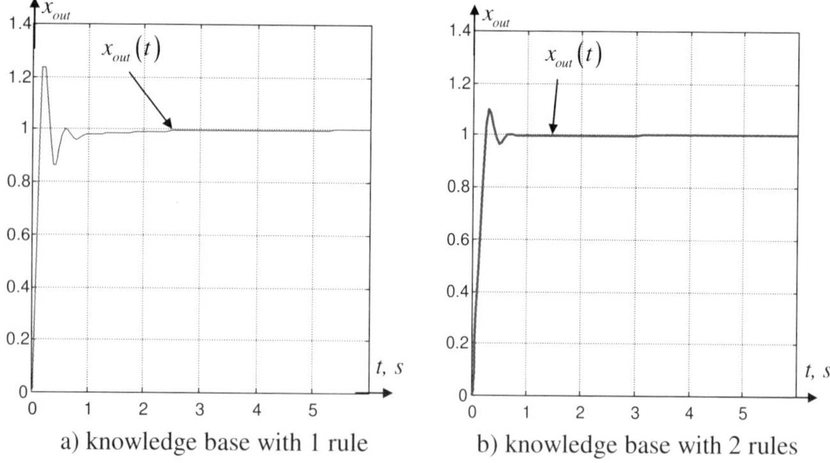

a) knowledge base with 1 rule   b) knowledge base with 2 rules

Fig. 3. Transient processes in fuzzy control system with 1 and 2 rules

further expansion does not significantly affect the improvement of control quality. Based on the proposed conception of fuzzy controllers structural optimization it is possible to formalize the following algorithm to reduce the amount of linguistic rules in knowledge database:

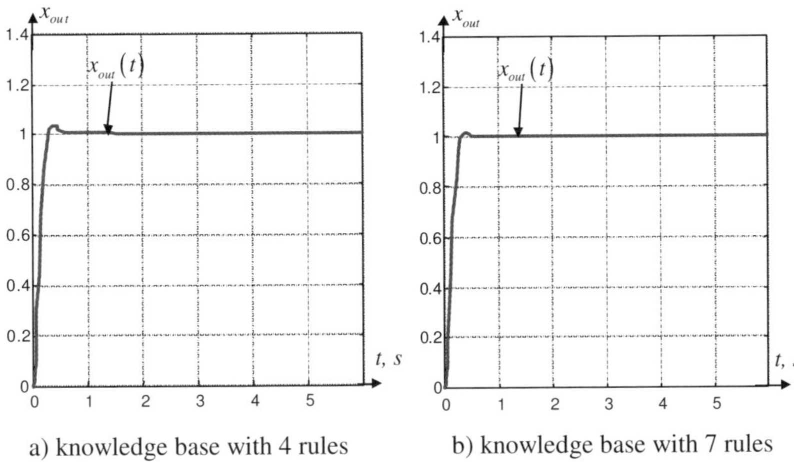

a) knowledge base with 4 rules   b) knowledge base with 7 rules

Fig. 4. Transient processes in fuzzy control system with 4 and 7 rules

Step 1. Calculating according to the expression (1) the functions of truth changes $\mu_i^R(t)$ for all the rules during control process.

Step 2. Calculating evaluation $G_i\left[\mu_i^R(t)\right]$ with expression (2) and their averaging according to (3) for different modes of simulation.

Step 3. Ranking the base of linguistic rules of fuzzy controller based on their impact on the control signal according to the value of evaluation functional $G_i\left[\mu_i^R(t)\right]$.

Step 4. The formation of an optimized rules database by gradually adding rules to it (as defined in ranked series) with permanent monitoring of quality control indices.

4. Conclusions

The concept and algorithm for optimization of fuzzy linguistic rules database of fuzzy controllers was tested on a fuzzy PID controller for control of a non-stationary object of second order. As a result of the optimization the total number of rules in the linguistic base was successfully reduced from 27 to 7 without compromising the quality of the fuzzy control system, which confirms the effectiveness of the proposed approach. It is possible to expand such research onto the development of optimized linguistic rules database for different types of fuzzy information processing algorithms.

References

1. V.I. Arkhangelsky, I.N. Bohaenko, G.G. Grabowski and N.A. Ryumshyn, Fuzzy-control systems. Technica, Kiev (1997).
2. J. Gil-Aluja, Investment in uncertainty. Kluwer Academic Publishers, Dordrecht (1999).
3. A.M. Gil Lafuente, El analissis de las inmovilizaciones en la incertidumbre. Ariel Economia, Barcelona (2004).
4. R. Hampel, M. Wagenknecht and N. Chaker (Eds.), Fuzzy Control:Theory and Practice. Physika-Verlag, Heidelberg, New York (2000).
5. J. Jantsen, A robustness study of fuzzy control rules. Proc. Int. Conf. EUFIT'97, vol.2, Aachen, Germany, pp. 1223-1227 (1997).
6. Y. Kondratenko and E.Y.M. Al Zubi The optimisation approach for increasing efficiency of digital fuzzy controllers. Annals of DAAAM for 2009 & Proceeding of the 20th Int. DAAAM Symp., Publ. by DAAAM International Vienna, pp. 1589-1591 (2009).
7. Z. Kovacic and S. Bogdan, Fuzzy Controller Design: Theory and Applications. Taylor & Francis Group: CRC Press, Boca Raton (2006).
8. K. Michels, F. Klawonn, R. Kruse and A. Nurnberger, Fuzzy Control: Fundamentals, Stability and Design of Fuzzy Controllers. Springer-Verlag, Berlin Heidelberg (2006).
9. M. Mizumoto, Realisation of PID controls by fuzzy control methods. Fuzzy Sets and Systems, № 70, pp. 171-182 (1995).
10. A.A. Oleynik and S.A. Subbotin, The fuzzy rule base reduction based on multiagent approach. Herald of the National Technical University "KhPI", Kharkov, № 43, pp. 126–137 (2009).
11. W. Pedrycz, Fuzzy control and fuzzy systems. John Willey and Sons, New York (1993).
12. A. Piegat, Fuzzy Modelling and Control. Physika-Verlag, Heidelberg (2001).
13. V. L. Sanchez and J. Otero, Boosting fuzzy rules in classification problems under single-winner inference. Int. Journal of Intelligent Systems, № 9 (22), pp. 1021-1035 (2007).
14. T. Takagi and M. Sugeno, Fuzzy identification of systems and its applications to modeling and control. IEEE Trans. Systems, Man & Cybernetics, vol. 15, №1, pp. 116-132 (1985).
15. R. Yager and D. Filev, Essentials of fuzzy modeling and control. John Willey and Sons, New York (1994).
16. L.A. Zadeh, Fuzzy sets. Information and Control, no.8, pp. 338-353 (1965).

2G: A CLASSIFICATION ALGORITHM BASED ON PATTERN RECOGNITION AND DECISION TREES

COTA O. MARIA DE GUADALUPE AND FLORES P. PEDRO

Departamento de Matemáticas, Universidad de Sonora, Boulevard. Luis Encinas y Avenida Rosales S/N.
Hermosillo, Sonora CP 83000. México

This paper presents the details of the design of the algorithm 2G, which is based on techniques of pattern recognition and decision trees, and describes original contributions that consist in: the use a method different from the existing ones in the stage of values discretización, eliminating redundancies and taking into account values for which there are overlapping classes, considering them, at this stage, as values grouped into 'virtual classes' that allows them to have representation on the set of values involved in the selection of attributes; the application of the criterion for minimizing the amount of attributes to construct the corresponding decision tree, which results in the decreasing number of conditions required to evaluate the instances for which there is not known the class to which they belong; and to allow the classification of new examples with no explicit rules derived from the rules generated, with the only restriction that these rules must belong to the same class. In addition, it also includes classification results obtained with the 2G algorithm using cross-validation, which almost always improves the results reported in the literature

1. Introduction

In this work is shown an algorithm based in decision tress [1], that we named 2G, which according to the test realized is very efficient in the treatment of problems with real attributes, especially in those that have attributes with continuous values. Moreover, in the procedure to generate the rules obtained with the 2G algorithm, in the stage of discretization of values, are grouped values with overlapping classes in what we call "virtual classes" which allows them to have representation in the set of values that will formed later, based in what we call "breaking of the class" that is used to select the attributes with major gain of information to build the corresponding decision tree for.

In order to evaluate the performance of 2G algorithm we chose several classic problems in the area and used open source of algorithms like C4.5 [2], See5 [3] and J48 [4] to compare the results reported in the literature [1], [5], [6],

[7], [8], [9], [10] with those obtained with 2G algorithm. It is important to notice that in almost all cases the algorithm 2G produced better results than those presented in literature.

2. 2G algorithm description

2G algorithm is an alternative method for constructing decision trees on a secific problem and orders the attributes of the training set by applying the concept of entropy as a measure of data variability and information gain.

2.1. *Entropy and information gain*

The specification of 2G algorithm is described below:

S original set of training examples Sr reduced set of training examples
p total number of S or Sr examples e instance of p
c class to which belongs e k number of classes
z index of the class value c n number of examples of a class e_i
    related to e and $z = \{1, ..., c\}$
l number of attributes of the A set of attributes
    set S or Sr
Ar selected set of attributes t number of examples of A or Ar
    from $G(Ar)$
v set of values of the set A or Ar m number of examples of v
T number of values of v in A or Ar $prob_i$ probability that an example
    (e_i) of Ar belongs to a class c
    with $i = \{1, ..., t\}$

The previous variables together with the entropy set H(Sr), the entropy of attributes H(Ar), the entropy of values H(v) and the attributes gain of the reduced set G(Ar) are applied through the following expressions:

$$\text{H}(Sr) = \sum_{i=1}^{p} - prob_i * log_2 (prob_i)$$

$$\text{H}(Ar) = \sum_{r=1}^{T} \text{H}(Sr) - prob_i * \text{H}(v) \tag{1}$$

$$\text{H}(v) = \sum_{j=1}^{l} - prob_j * log_2 (prob_j)$$

$$\text{G}(Ar) = \sum_{x=1}^{l} \text{H}(S) - \text{H}(Ar)$$

2.2. *Value discretization*

To discretize the values of attributes, we are based on methods used in algorithms like C4.5 [2], See5 [3] and J48 [4], but for best results we use distinct operations, wich are described below:

One of the traditional methods of selection of representative values of an attribute is to select a set of values that are at the point where a change is detected in the vector class, then choose the average values of the adjacent values that meet these criteria, ignoring repeated values and implement a process to reduce the resulting list, to which is applied a heuristic selection or statistical estimate as the mean, median, etc. An example of this is shown in Table I, which describes the values for the attribute 'A'. The values involved in sampling and averaging the values found in items where a class change is detected are marked with an 'x', obtaining the following vector: (67.5, 80.0, 95.0).

TABLE I.-EXAMPLE OF DISCRETIZATION OF VALUES. TRADITIONAL METHOD.

Value	65	70	70	80	80	85	86	86	90	99	100
Class	-1	1	-1	1	-1	1	1	1	-1	-1	1
	x								X		x

In our case, for greater accuracy in the generation of rules, about us select for each attribute the values that are the point where it changes of class vector to what we call "breaking of the class" an then eliminate redundances (Table II). Later, it is selected the maximum value for each group of values continuous of the same class to form a set of representative values per attribute. As an exception, and unlike traditional methods, we include the maximum value of the groups of values that present "overlapping classes", identifying them as groups of values that belong to "virtual classes" allowing them to participate in the selection of values and being part of the set of values that will eventually be used in the attributes selection stage. To make the final selection of representative values it was constructed a matrix where the values of the resultant vector of representative values selected by every attribute are set as column headings. For each class is added a row, and in the internal cells of the matrix where the column value matches with the class value it is used the variable "ninst" that can take the value of 1 if there exists at least one example that meets the properties of the row and column, and the value 0 if otherwise.

An example of this is shown in the section highlighted in gray in Table II. So that the resultant vector for us is: (65, 80, 86, 99, 100), which has a positive impact when applying the algorithm 2G because important values rejected by other methods are now included.

TABLE II.- EXAMPLE OF DISCRETIZATION OF VALUES. ALGORITHM 2G.

Value	65	70	80	85	86	90	99	100
Class -1	1	1	1	0	0	1	1	0
Class 1	0	1	1	1	1	0	0	1
	X		X		X		X	X

2.3. 2G algorithm procedure

a) Information recorded:

- Classes (c)
- Attribute values (v)
- Attributes (Ar)
- Training examples (e)

b) Calculation of values using (1):

- $p, k, n, l, t, m, T.$
- Combined entropy H(Sr).
- H(Ar) it is applied for each attribute
- G(Ar) it is applied just one time and the four attributes that present the biggest degree of information gain are selected

c) Building of the decision tree (Ar):

- The biggest values representatives of the attributes are taken for each combination of class. The level of the tree is limited to four and the permutation between the first and second selected node is realized.

d) Rules generation

- The rules are generated only with two conditions and for each rule are fixed the minimum and maximum values.

e) Evaluation of the test set.

- To evaluate new examples it is taken as reference the tree structure.
- During the process of assignment of class there are examples for which do not exist rules that can classify them. To treat this type of instances, these are allowed to be classified with more than one rule, only if they belong to the same class. If even so, some examples can not conclude this procedure it is possible to classify these examples using the attribute that provides greater information gain and assign to them the class of the rule that matches a very close value to the maximum value of the minimum recorded for the rule.

Below is a brief description on the application of the procedure called "no explicit virtual patterns" (figure 1):

1. We selected the first class of the attribute that has a higher gain

2. An instance can be classified assigning different rules to its attributes, but must be of the same class. An example of this is shown in Figure 1, where C+ and C- are the classes and sections in gray are the different rules. The arrows indicate the route of evaluation of new instances that are classified with this technique. Sample 1 is classified by a rule of class C+ and Sample 2 is classified

with two rules of class C+. Moreover, Rn represents the number of rule with n = 1, 2..., N. When we can not classify the values of an instance in one class, we choose the attribute that has more gain of information and analyze three options:

a. Select the class that has the first rule.
b. Choose the rule that has the maximum value of the minimum value.
c. Select the majority class of the ruleset candidates.

The second option of abovepresented the best performance

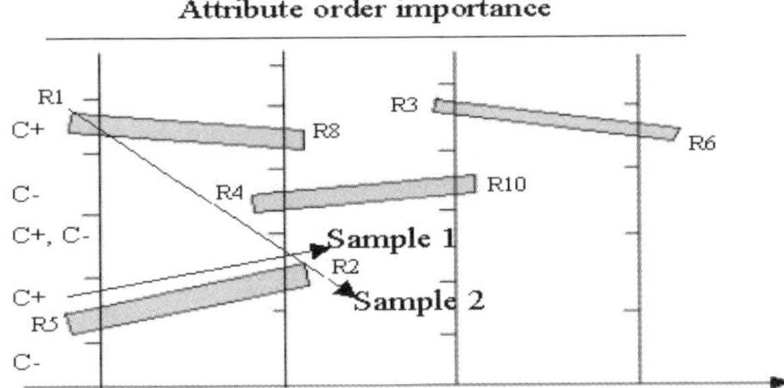

Figure 1. Representation of "no explicit virtual patterns".

3. Classification results with 2G algorithm

Contrary to algorithms such as C4.5 [2], See5 [3] and J48 [4], in our case we obtain the biggest degree of information from the attributes in one chance. With regard to the order obtained, it is swapped the first attribute with the second one and the corresponding process of the decision tree building continues. This decision tree is built to provoke bigger data variability. The results obtained from the selection of attributes are similar to those reported in algorithms in [11]. K-fold Cross Validation [12] is used with K = 10. The best results are shown in the gray section of Table III.

TABLE III.-RESULTS COMPARISON.

Dataset name	Instances	Attrib	Class	Balanced Error Rate (%)				
				AdaBoost	See5	C4.5	J48	2G
Breast	699	10	2	2.96	3.01	4.87	5.44	1.0
Pima	768	8	2	24.75	26.03	29.29	26.17	2.47
Sonar	208	60	2	21.35	14.53	28.97	28.84	4.66
Wine	168	13	3	3.14	2.25	8.83	6.18	2.64
Ionospher	351	34	2	6.61	6.23	7.96	8.55	3.5

4. Conclusions

Among the existing classification techniques, decision trees have proved to be very efficient and accurate enough to generate new knowledge. The 2G algorithm designed with this approach offers original contributions that are not covered by the revised algorithms.

The main contributions of the 2G algorithm are: that instead of trying to reduce the number of values in the process of discretization process, we apply a selection method that includes values than by other methods are ignored, as are the values of overlapping classes, that in this case, we include in the groups that we called "virtual class", so, we manage to give them representation in the final set of values that are used to select the attributes with the greatest information gain. This has allowed us to maintain better accuracy in the generation of rules, which together with the application of 'no explicit virtual patterns' and additional criteria has led us to have better results in most cases reported in Table III, which includes results for comparison with the algorithms mentioned in the literature.

References

1. Quinlan J., "Induction of Decision Trees", *Kluwer Academic Publishers, Machine Learning*. (1986).
2. http://www2.cs.uregina.ca/~dbd/cs831/notes/ml/dtrees/c4.5/tutorial.html.
3. http://www.rulequest.com/see5-info.html.
4. http://www.cs.waikato.ac.nz/ml/weka/.
5. Bartlett L. & Traskin M., "ADABOOST is Consistent", *Neural Information Processing Systems Conference*. (2006).
6. Díaz M., Fernández M.z & Martínez A., "See5 Algorithm versus Discriminant Analysis. An Application to the Prediction of Insolvency in Spanish Non-life Insurance Companies", Universidad Complutense de Madrid (2004).
7. Kohavi, R., Li, C.-H., "Oblivious decision trees, graphs, and top-down pruning", *Fourteenth International Joint Conference on Articial Intelligence*. (2005).
8. http://kdd.ics.uci.edu/databases/kddcup99/kddcup99.html.
9. http://www.ailab.si/orange/doc/datasets/breast-cancer-wisconsin.htm.
10. http://archive.ics.uci.edu/ml/datasets.html.
11. http://www.grappa.univ-ille3.fr/~torre/guide.php?id=accueil.
12. Kohavi Ron, *A Study of Cross-Validation and BootStrap for Accuracy Estimation and Model Selection*. International Joint Conference on Artificial Intelligence. (1995). http://robotics.stanford.edu/users/ronnyk/.

A TOOL FOR OBJECTIVES DEFINITION IN THE MKDD METHODOLOGY FOR DATA MINING STUDIES

ANNA MARIA GIL-LAFUENTE[*], EMILI VIZUETE LUCIANO,
SEFA BORIA REVERTER

*Department of Economics and Business Administration, University of Barcelona, Avda.
Diagonal 690, 08034 Barcelona, Spain*

Lately it has been possible to witness the fast evolution of computational resources. This evolution was naturally followed by an increasing facility in the data obtaining. Thus the use of huge databases and data warehouses went on to be used in ample scale, what made the mining of useful information for business transactions an important research area. The process known by KDD (Knowledge Discovery in Databases) is pointed out by the existing bibliography on the subject as a solution for the need to transform data into applicable information to help in problem solving and it is formed by a sequence of procedures that include the popular data mining.

1. Introduction

Lately it has been possible to witness the fast evolution of computational resources. This evolution was naturally followed by an increasing facility in the data obtaining. Thus the use of huge databases and data warehouses went on to be used in ample scale, what made the mining of useful information for business transactions an important research area [17, 18]. The process known by KDD (Knowledge Discovery in Databases) is pointed out by the existing bibliography on the subject [9, 16] as a solution for the need to transform data into applicable information to help in problem solving and it is formed by a sequence of procedures that include the popular data mining.

The procedures that compose the KDD are better executed when it is added some steps at the beginning, in order to identify and to delimit the objective of

---

[*] Corresponding author: Tel: +34 93 402 19 62; Fax: +34 93 402 45 80.
E-mail addresses: amgil@ub.edu (A.M. Gil), evizuetel@ub.edu (E. Vizuete), jboriar@ub.edu (S. Boria).

the problem to be worked; and in the end, where one applies the information acquired to business actions and conclude the study with a reflection about the acquired knowledge [1, 10]. With the aim of structuring in an efficiently way the traditional steps of the KDD process and these new ones above cited, a methodology known by MKDD (Managerial Knowledge Discovery in Databases) was created: it is an integration between the already famous KDD with the established management method PDCA.

Meanwhile the definition of the objective in data mining studies is not trivial: the business men generally have a very vague idea about the type of information that they need to obtain from the databases.

The interest of this article is to present a tool to make easier the translation of the managerial objectives proposed by the business men into analytical objectives, oriented to give a course to the data mining studies.

The proposed tool is quite simple: it consists of a matrix that connects the managerial objectives to representations of the analytical objectives, and this relation is measured by fuzzy logic functions.

In Section 2, we present a general vision of MKDD methodology, and in Section 3 includes a brief discussion on the importance and difficulties about the definition of analytical objectives, and the proposed tool is presented. Conclusion are pointed in Section 4.

2. A structured methodology for data mining studies

An effective data mining study includes a series of stages for data preparation and organization: selection, pre-processing, transformation, data mining and analysis. These steps make up the KDD process, which is widely explored in the bibliography. This process management takes to results more consistent than data mining studies that are executed separately, but there still existing the problem of integrating the conclusions to the executive scene.

On the other hand, there are an ample range of structures known like problem solving methodologies, which were developed to lead studies from the objectives exposition to the conclusions interpretation and application. These methodologies have an ample application in managerial circles, leading to success lots of process and product improvement/ innovation projects.

The precursor of the problem solving methodologies is the Deming Cycle (PDCA or PDSA), that is a continuous quality improvement model made up of a logical sequence of four steps represented in Figure 1: Plan, Do, Check or Study and Act [6, 8]. Nowadays many other improvement methodologies exist based on the PDCA - like the also famous DMAIC - but all has in common the stages structure going from the planning step to the conclusion and results implementation stage, always watching the problem from the general to the specific and so focusing the actions in a more effective way. It is this structure the responsible by the success of studies that make use of the problem solving methodology, in several knowledge fields.

With the objective to bring similar abilities in terms of arrangement and integration to data mining procedure [5], it has been developed the MKDD process that organizes stages of the traditional KDD within the robust structure of PDCA methodology [15]. This way it is possible to take the study from the translation of managerial objectives into analytical data mining objectives, until the integration of analytical conclusions to the business language, going through the commonly used data bases analysis. Figure 2 presents the MKDD structure and following the process steps will be described briefly.

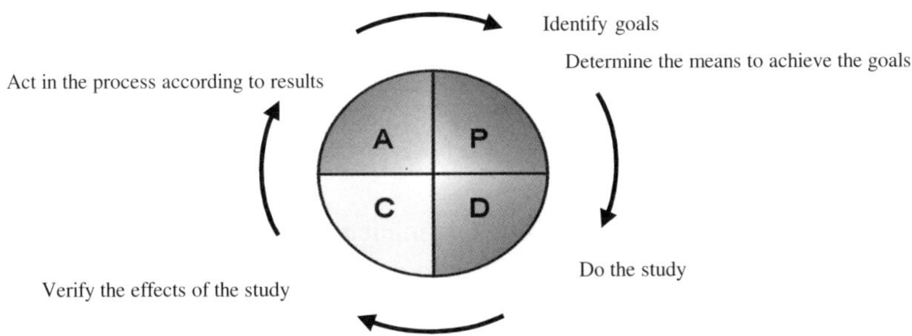

Figure 1. Representation of Deming Cycle steps.

3. Making it easy the objectives definition

After the MKDD steps were presented and it was possible to observe that it is a really simple and well structured methodology to being employed by the data mining analysts, the proposed tool will be presented to help in the job of translating the decision-makers desires into concrete objectives under the analysts' views [2, 3, 6]. This transition from the executive-managerial world into technical-analytical words is not always something simple to do, since the people involved in this process have different views and perceptions respect to the subject "objective of the study".

Figure 2. The MKDD process.

For a correct conduction of the data mining studies, it is necessary to focus well on the type of information that is desired to obtain from the data bases, since there are a host of data mining techniques congregated in several different models. Starting a study without defined objectives is a loss of time, while it will never be possible to evaluate if the decision-makers desires are being satisfied or not.

Another difficulty found by the analysts is as to define what data mining models and tools are better to employ to solve the problems, and the definition of analytical objectives facilitates the election of these models since there are a narrow association between analytical objective and models of analysis.

In order to facilitate this task of defining analytical objectives based on the managerial objectives, we present a tool based on the fuzzy logic [14], in which the business men and analysts can collectively define the relationship degrees between each managerial objective and the possible analytical objectives through fuzzy subgroups. These relationship degrees finally are compared to predefined ideally required cut points, obtaining the high-priority order to lead the studies focusing at each analytical objective.

The managerial objectives are designated by C_i, i= 1, 2, …, n, and the analytical objectives are named as P_j, $j = 1,2,...,m$. The relationship degree cut points ideally required are called $c_i \in [0.1]$, $i = 1,2,...,n$ (although at this application it is suggested $c_i = 1$ $\forall$ i), and could come expressed by the following way:

$$C = \begin{array}{ccccccc} C_1 & C_2 & C_3 & C_4 & & \cdots & C_n \\ \hline c_1 & c_2 & c_3 & c_4 & & \cdots & c_n \\ \hline \end{array}$$

This level is the relationship degree expression, in the sense of which a managerial objective c_i can be translated or worked in a data mining study like the analytical objective P_j, and will be measured in the [0,1] interval in a way that the more it approaches to 0 smaller is the relationship; and the more it approaches to 1 higher is this relationship. Traditionally and to facilitate the expression given by the experts, usually the hendecandarian scale is used (11 values between 0 and 1), since it represents the numerical scale fraction that is easier to understand and to use considering that it agrees with our traditional numerical system. With the object of allowing the experts to express their opinions in a semantic way and to come later to a numerical transformation usually it is employed semantic scales [11]. A semantic scale suggestion is the following one:

$c = 0$: No relationship.

$c = 0,1$: Practically no relationship.

$c = 0,2$: Hardly any relationship.

$c = 0,3$: Very weak relationship.

$c = 0,4$: Weak relationship.

$c = 0,5$: Average relationship.

$c = 0,6$: Notable relationship.

$c = 0,7$: Quite heavy relationship.

$c = 0,8$: Heavy relationship.

$c = 0,9$: Very heavy relationship.

$c = 1$: Total relationship.

If we have m analytical objectives P_m, and after the discussion between managers and analysts it has been obtained for each one of them the pertinent fuzzy subgroups, where $Pi_{(j)}$ are the relationship attributions between managerial and analytical objectives, it will be represented by:

	C_1	C_2	C_3	C_4	$\cdots$	C_n
$P_{\sim 1} =$	$P^{(1)}{}_1$	$P^{(1)}{}_2$	$P^{(1)}{}_3$	$P^{(1)}{}_4$	$\cdots$	$P^{(1)}{}_n$
$P_{\sim 2} =$	$P^{(2)}{}_1$	$P^{(2)}{}_2$	$P^{(2)}{}_3$	$P^{(2)}{}_4$	$\cdots$	$P^{(2)}{}_n$
$P_{\sim m} =$	$P^{(m)}{}_1$	$P^{(m)}{}_2$	$P^{(m)}{}_3$	$P^{(m)}{}_4$	$\cdots$	$P^{(m)}{}_n$

The suggested arrangement criterion for the analytical objectives is based on the distance concept [11, 12]. Among the different distances possible to consider, it is common to choose the Hamming relative distance by its simplicity and operability. This distance is obtained by the simple weigh up of the calculated differences, for each element, of the ownership characteristic functions taken with the defined objectives. In this sense, the relative distance is obtained from the corresponding absolute distances, like it is indicated as follow. This measurement between $C_{\sim}$ and $P_{\sim j}$ can be described as:

$$d(C_{\sim}, P_{\sim j}) = \sum_{i=1}^{n} |C_i - P_i^{(j)}| \tag{1}$$

But, in general, what is employed is the relative distance, which consists in divide the absolute distance $d(C_{\sim}, P_{\sim j})$ by the number of referential elements that is n. It comes:

$$\delta(C_{\sim}, P_{\sim j}) = \frac{d(C_{\sim}, P_{\sim j})}{n} = \frac{\sum_{i=1}^{n} |C_i - P_i^{(j)}|}{n} \tag{2}$$

The priority order to utilize the analytical objectives sighting to reach the raised managerial objectives will be, then, from the minor to the greater obtained distance.

4. Conclusions

The application of the analytical objectives definition tool was considered simple and effective by both the technical body (data mining analysts) and the company's director. He added that the tool clarified him about the type of study that was being applied on his website data. Thus, the purpose of developing a useful and of easy application tool to help in the hard task of translating the managerial objectives into analytical objectives was successfully reached. The incorporation of qualified techniques for the uncertainty treating on this investigation area favors, mainly, the possibility of incorporating more trustworthy information and with greater flexibility level to the existing models. Try to provide more reliability to the models given by the scientists and professionals has been the basic proposed objective in this work. In this sense, the different fuzzy subgroups instruments contributions have been decisive for reaching our objectives.

As future works, we see the developing of new tools able to help in key points of the MKDD method. These points are generally those in which it is necessary to connect managerial and analytical worlds on a more structured way through a quantifiable model based on an information several times objective other than subjective, but carried of a high load of uncertainty.

References

1. Araya, S., Silva, M., Weber, R., "A methodology for web usage mining and its application to target group identification", Fuzzy and Sets Systems (148), 139-152, (2004).
2. Au, W.H., Chan, K.C.C., "Mining changes in association rules: a fuzzy approach", Fuzzy Sets and Systems (149), 87-104, (2005).
3. Berzal, F., Blanco, I., Sanchez, D., Serrano, J.M., Vila, M.A., "A definition for fuzzy approximate dependences", Fuzzy Sets and Systems (149), 105-129, (2005).
4. Bosc P., Kraft D., Petry F., "Fuzzy sets in database and information systems: Status and opportunities", Fuzzy and Sets Systems (156), 418-426, (2005).

5. Box, G.E.P,, Cox, D.R., "An analysis of transformations (with discusision)", J. R. Statistic (vol. 26), 211-252, (1964).
6. Crespo, F., Weber, R., "A methodology for dynamic data mining based on fuzzy clustering", Fuzzy Sets and Systems (150), 267-284, (2005).
7. Diniz, C.A.R. e Louzada-Neto, F., "Data Mining: uma introdução", XIV SINAPE – Associação Brasileira de Estatística (ABE), Brasil, (2000).
8. Fernandez, D.X., Riboldi, J., "MKDD: data mining no contexto de estatística e gerenciamento", Anais do IX SEAGRO – ESALQ/USP, Brasil, 593-597, (2001).
9. Gil Aluja, J., "Fuzzy sets in the management of uncertainty", Ed. Springer-Verlag, Berlin Heidelberg, (2004).
10. Gil Lafuente, A.M., "Fuzzy Logic in financial analysis", Ed. Springer-Verlag, Berlin Heidelberg, (2005).
11. Gil Lafuente, A.M., "Nuevas estrategias para el análisis financiero en la empresa", Ed. Ariel, Barcelona, (2001).
12. Gil Lafuente, J., "Marketing para el nuevo milenio", Ediciones Pirámide, Madrid, 258-266, 447-448, (1997).
13. Hair, D.F., Anderson, R.E., Tatham, R.L., Black, W.C., "Multivariate Data Analysis", Practice Hall, New Jersey (1998).
14. Han, J., Kamber, M., "Data Mining – Concepts and Techniques", Morgan Kauffmann Publishers, San Francisco, (2001).
15. Hong, T.P., Lin, K.Y., Wang, S.L., "Fuzzy data mining for interesting generalized association rules", Fuzzy Sets and Systems (138), 255-269, (2003).
16. Petry F.E., Zhao L., "Data mining by attribute generalization with fuzzy hierarchies in fuzzy databases", Fuzzy Sets and Systems (160), 2206-2223, (2009).
17. Srivastava, R., Cooley, M., Deshpande, P., "Web usage mining: discovery and applications of usage patterns from web data", SIGKDD Explorations (2), 12-23, (2000).

SOLUTION OF APPLIED PROBLEMS: FORMALIZATION, METHODOLOGY AND JUSTIFICATION

VICTOR KRASNOPROSHIN, VLADIMIR OBRAZTSOV

*Belarus State University, 4 Nezavisimosti Avenue, Minsk, 220050 Belarus,
e-mail: krasnoproshin@ bsu.by, obraztsov@bsu.by*

HERMAN VISSIA

*Byelex Multimedia Products BV Argon 1 – 4751 XC Oud Gastel, the Netherlands,
e-mail: h.vissia@byelex.com*

The paper deals with questions of management of the applied problem solution. Three groups of problems have been considered. The problems concern the formalization, selection and construction of the model, method and algorithm of the solution as well as the justification of the obtained results.

1. Introduction

With the development of the society, the role of theoretical knowledge and computer technology in solving applied problems is constantly rising. However, the theory and practice are developing in some sense independently of each other. Each of them has its own specific features and priorities. Using the theory for practice usually occurs on formal grounds, without posing questions of the justification, solvability, the intended aim, etc. All this has a negative impact on the final result when solving applied problems.

Why is it important to know how to solve applied problems? Because such problems form the majority, and the accumulation and standardization of the solution means result in a possibility to automate the solution in general. Besides, a correct understanding of the problem is a substantial and important part of the solution [1, 8].

The paper deals with questions of management of the applied problem solution.

2. Definition of an applied problem

We define first the notion of an "arbitrary problem". For this we consider the basic components that are commonly used in its formulation and do not depend on the subject area, informal meaning of information, etc. (See Fig. 1).

The first element is the Cartesian product $I^{input} \times I^{output}$. The second element is the computational process $\mathrm{Pr} : I^{input} \to I^{output}$.

Thus, by a "problem" we mean a certain relation $T \subseteq I^{input} \times I^{output}$ for which at least two elements are defined $i_i^{in} \in I^{input}, i_k^{out} \in I^{output}$ ($i, k \in N$).

For stating an arbitrary problem T, it is necessary to explicitly specify elements $(i_i^{in}, i_k^{out}) \in T$, which define restrictions to the process Pr.

Thus, by a "problem" we mean a certain relation $T \subseteq I^{input} \times I^{output}$ for which at least two elements are defined $i_i^{in} \in I^{input}, i_k^{out} \in I^{output}$ ($i, k \in N$).

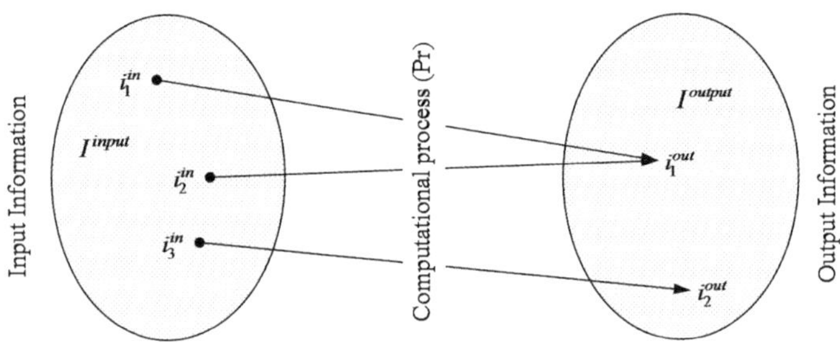

Fig. 1. The main components of a problem

Let T_0 denote a set of explicitly defined elements $(i_i^{in}, i_k^{out}) \in T$. It is easy to see that $T_0 \subseteq T$. In this case a "problem" can be defined through the relation $T \subseteq I^{input} \times I^{output}$ for which there is the implication: $T \Rightarrow T_0$.

Depending on the method of forming the Cartesian product $I^{input} \times I^{output}$, the class of problems T can be divided into two non-overlapping subsets [2, 4]. If the components I^{input}, I^{output} are associated with any real objects, then the corresponding problem will be called an "applied" one (T^{ap}). Otherwise, it is a theoretical problem (T^{th}).

We can certainly say that $T = T^{ap} \cup T^{th}$, but semantic relationship between these classes, apparently, does not exist.

As noted by several authors [1, 3, 4], applied problems are primary in relation to the theory, and therefore they are of particular interest. To establish a relationship between classes T^{ap} and T^{th}, it is necessary to determine the characteristic properties of each of them.

3. Formalization

In general, the computational process for the problem $T \in T^{ap}$ is unknown. Therefore, a model of the process is used for its solution.

It is reasonable to provide two levels [4] i.e. an informal level, at which the problem is formed, and a formal one, intended for building the model. Relationship between the levels and their specific content are universal. In the general scheme of problem solution the relationship is shown in Fig. 2.

At the formal level, problems are formed from the set T^{th}. Here, $T^{th} \subseteq X \times Y$, and $p_2 : X \to Y$. In this case the condition $T^{th} \neq \varnothing$ is ensured by the presence of the problem on the informal level with some additional conditions of consistency on coding (p_1) and interpretation (p_3) mapping.

Really, this means that a formal level for a new problem can be regarded as an informal one. Thus, the general scheme of problem solution is not limited to the single (primary) scheme shown in Fig.1. In fact, it can be considered as a superposition of the primary schemes. In this case the recursion [7] can be used for constructing a formal model:

$$
\begin{aligned}
h((x, y), 0) &\cong f(i^{in}, i^{out}), \\
h((x, y), i+1) &\cong g((x, y), i, h((x, y), i)),
\end{aligned}
\tag{1}
$$

where the two-place function $f(i^{in}, i^{out})$ is the process $\Pr(i^{in}) = i^{out}$, and $i \in N$. In regard to the three-place function g, its arguments are defined by the following relations

$$
h((x, y), i) \cong h_{\tilde{k}_i}((x, y), i), \quad (x, y) \in X_{\tilde{k}_i} \times Y_{\tilde{k}_i},
$$

$$
\tilde{k}_i \cong \tilde{k}_{i-1} \times \tilde{N}, \tilde{k}_0 = \{(0)\}, \tilde{N} \subset N, |\tilde{N}| < \infty.
$$

Besides,

$$
\forall i > 0 \exists p_1, p_2, p_3 \ p_1 : X_{\tilde{k}_{i-1}} \to X_{\tilde{k}_i}, p_2 : X_{\tilde{k}_i} \to Y_{\tilde{k}_i}, p_3 : Y_{\tilde{k}_i} \to Y_{\tilde{k}_{i-1}},
$$

$$
h_{\tilde{k}_i}((x, y), i) \cong p_3 \circ p_2 \circ p_1(x).
$$

In this scheme there is only a unique informal level, at which the set T^{ap} is formed, and the final (in the limit - countable) set of formal levels, at which the corresponding sets T^{th} are formed.

Construction of a formal model with the use of the recursion (1), can be considered as a complete scheme of formalization necessary for solving any problem within T. It is necessary either to find a suitable scheme with the existing theoretical work, or somehow to build it.

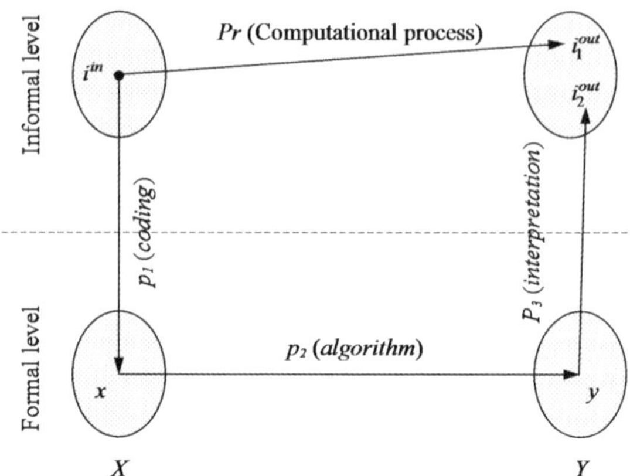

Fig. 2. Problem solution scheme

For any scheme there is a problem, which is thematically close to the problem of the algorithm statement [7]: how many levels is it necessary to build, and in what sense can we speak of the original problem solution? In terms of mathematical formalization, the latter question is directly related to the problem of justification [1, 5, 6].

4. Justification

Let's consider the problem solution scheme from T^{ap} in Fig. 2. We can write

$$\Pr(i^{in}) = i_1^{out} \in I^{output},$$
$$p_3 \circ p_2 \circ p_1(i^{in}) = i_2^{out} \in I^{output}. \tag{2}$$

Realization of the condition (2) is associated with the computability [7] of the function (1). We call such a problem the algorithmically solvable one.

That is, we can state that for the problem there exists an algorithm that realizes the function (1) under all conditions associated with the implementation (1) and the fulfillment of the condition (2). But this is not enough, it is also necessary to establish a relationship between i_1^{out} and i_2^{out}. Ideally, it could take the form

$$\forall i^{in} \in I^{input} \, ((\Pr(i^{in}) = p_3 \circ p_2 \circ p_1(i^{in})) \Leftrightarrow (i_1^{out} = i_2^{out})). \tag{3}$$

Condition (3) makes sense on the entire set of the set T.

If we assume that we can formally prove the fulfillment of condition (3) on the set T, then the resulting solution we'll call the "justified" one. For example, justified are solutions of propositional calculus problems, but the propositional calculus this property no longer has [1, 5, 6]. These are the problems that arise in the process of problem construction of mathematical formalisms [1].

The condition (3) is stringent enough and for applied problems it is not appropriate [1, 4]. To be able to describe the nature of the solvability of problems with unjustified solutions we'll modify the condition.

Initially, we note that condition (3) is a consequence of one of the types of relationships, which can be introduced on the Cartesian product $I^{output} \times I^{output}$. The equivalence relation generated by the function of equality in this product. In general, any relationship $I^{out} \subseteq I^{output} \times I^{output}$ can be described by the function

$$\psi : I^{output} \times I^{output} \to R^{+},$$

where R^{+} is a subset of non-negative real numbers. In this case ψ realizes a variant of "similarity" of elements in I^{output}. This, for example, may be proximity ($\psi(i^{out}, i^{out}) = 0$), similarity ($\psi(i^{out}, i^{out}) = 1$) or some other variant.

Let's introduce a function of the type

$$\varphi : R^{+} \to [0,1],$$

and require that it be monotonic and satisfy the condition ($r, r_1, r_2 \in R^{+}$)

$$\varphi(r) = \begin{cases} 1, r = r_1, \\ 0, r = r_2. \end{cases} \tag{4}$$

The selection of the function φ, corresponding to the condition (4), is determined by the nature of ψ mapping. In case of proximity $r_1 = 0, r_2 = +\infty$, and for similarity $r_1 = 1, r_2 = 0 \vee +\infty$. Obviously with such a choice, the superposition $\varphi \circ \psi$ makes sense. The superposition is the basis for introducing the function

$$\Phi(I^{input}) = \sum_{i^{in} \in I^{input}} \varphi(\psi(\Pr(i^{in}), p_3 \circ p_2 \circ p_1(i^{in}))) \cdot |I^{input}|^{-1}. \tag{5}$$

It is easy to see that (3) is a special case of (5). With a suitable choice of φ and ψ mapping, the condition (3) can be written as: $\Phi(I^{input}) = 1$.

When calculating $\Phi(I^{input})$ there are only two possibilities

$$\begin{cases} \exists i^{in} \in I^{input} \ \forall \alpha \in [0,1] \ \Phi(i^{in}) \neq \alpha, & (6) \\ \forall i^{in} \in I^{input} \ \exists \alpha \in [0,1] \ \Phi(i^{in}) = \alpha. & (7) \end{cases}$$

Upon fulfillment of (6) Φ is noncomputable [7]. The reasons of noncomputability may be different. In the above formalization no restrictions are placed on the structure of sets I^{input}, I^{output}. And since they can be infinite, this can lead to a situation when resources are not sufficient to calculate Φ. The case (7) deals with the computability of Φ on the whole set I^{input}. And, specifically obtained number $\alpha \in [0,1]$ is in principle irrelevant.

We introduce two classes of problems. As stated above, upon $\Phi(I^{input}) = 1$ the solution of problem T is justified. It is known [1, 5], that the logical basis for this conclusion is the principle of deduction. And because the condition $\Phi(I^{input}) = 1$ is logically connected with computability at the whole interval $[0,1]$, then the principle of deduction can be extended to the whole class of problems for which there is the condition (7). Therefore, the relevant class of problems T can be called "deductively solvable" (or "algorithmically deductively solvable").

For the class of problems T with a noncomputable function Φ, in accordance with the problem definition, it is still possible to specify a subset T_0: $\Phi(I_0^{input}) = 1$ (where I_0^{input} is the projection of the set I^{input} onto the subset T_0). Otherwise, the problem does not exist.

Between conditions $\Phi(I^{input}) = 1$ and $\Phi(I_0^{input}) = 1$ there is an obvious link

$$\Phi(I^{input}) = 1 \Rightarrow \Phi(I_0^{input}) = 1.$$

However, the converse implication is interesting. Therefore, when trying to build something opposite to deductive solvability, it is appropriate to call this class of problems T "inductively solvable". Although, unlike the first case, no single principle of induction exists.

Is it possible to build a reverse implication? For example, in [9], such an implication is built for the so-called representative problem T_0. However, this is done only for the problems of pattern recognition. But this result is easily generalized to the case of the problem of recognizing the truth. Other generalizations or similar results are unknown.

We now turn to the characterization of the set of problems T^{ap}. It contains problems of two classes: inductively solvable and insolvable ones (for which there is (6)). For the latter class there is always a possibility of transition to the inductively solvable class. This possibility appears as a result of cognition. And problems in the class of inductively solvable can never pass to the class of deductively solvable.

In turn, a set of problems T^{th}, can include problems of all three classes: deductively solvable, inductively solvable and insolvable. Moreover, the fundamental difference between T^{th} and T^{ap} is that for T^{th} and only for it, any problem can pass to a class of deductively solvable ones.

5. Methodological aspects

It was found that the characteristic features of a class of applied problems are:

- position in the solution scheme (only for such problems the informal level is directly connected with the reality);
- algorithmic inductive solvability/insolvability.

It is clear that the above features should influence the methods and way of organizing such a solution. These issues relate to the field of methodology [4], we consider them in more detail.

Let's make the corresponding particularization and specific filling of the solution shown in Fig. 2. At the informal level, there are several components that make up the solution process. Any problem is described by information, and obtaining a solution is associated with its processing. Therefore, the problem and the corresponding process have informational and computational components. Transformation of information is implemented in a certain environment, which naturally affects the informational and computational components. Therefore, we can single out another one, the so-called "technological" component.

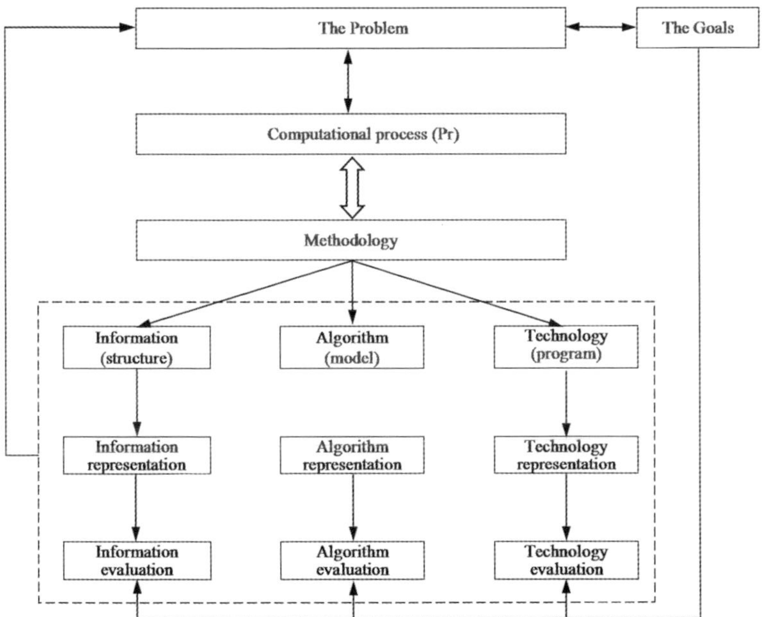

Fig. 3. Scheme of the general step of recursion

These components are naturally carried over to the level of formal constructions. The essence of management in this case is the solution of problems of representation and evaluation [6]. The problem of representation is typical for mathematical formalization. The concept of goal is associated with the two sides of the solution process: it is necessary to ensure the availability of a solution and to assess its quality from the standpoint of validity. These goals are also associated with the result and are characteristic of the process.

The implementation of any process is concerned with the recursion (1). At each step, a standard universal procedure is performed, the scheme of which is shown in Fig. 3. According to the results of evaluation, the problem can be corrected through its components. Among all the problems the one is chosen for which the best results are obtained. Further development of the theory occurs in the direction of such a problem as long as possible, or simply feasible.

The most general description of the methodology for problem solution is given above. It also applies to the inductively solvable problems from T^{th}.

The described approach to a practical problem does not pretend to any finality or completeness. Our aim is to show that investigating such a complex issue, it is possible to set some base points, but in the ideal case - the border.

References

1. M.Kline. *MATHEMATICS. The Loss of Certainty*. Oxford University Press, New York: 447 p. (1980)
2. V.Turchin. *The Phenomenon of Science*. Columbia University Press, New York: 368 p. (1977)
3. A.Foss. *The Essence of Mathematics*. Knizny Dom "Librokom", Moscow: 120 p. (2009)
4. Blekhman I.I., Myshkis A.D., Panovko Ya.G. *Mechanics and Applied Mathematics. Logics and Peculiarities of Mathematics Application*. Nauka, Moscow: 328 p. (1983)
5. V.Ya. Perminov. *Philosophy and Mathematics Justification*. Progress-Tradition, Moscow: 320 p. (2001)
6. Yu.A.Gastev. *Homomorphisms and Models. Logico-algebraic Aspects of Modeling*. Nauka, Moscow: 152 p. (1975)
7. N.Cutland. *Computability. An introduction to recursive function theory*. Cambridge University Press, London: 256 p. (1980)
8. G.Polya *How to Solve It: A New Aspect of Mathematical Method*. (2nd ed.), Princeton University Press, Princeton, New York: (1957)
9. V.V.Krasnoproshin, V.A. Obraztsov *Problem of Solvability and Choice of Algorithms for Decision Making by Precedence. Pattern Recognition and Image Analysis*, 16 (2): 155-169 (2006)

OPTIMAL PLANIFICATION OF BIDIMENTIONAL TABLES WITH FUZZY NUMBERS AND SUMMATORY RESTRICTIONS

XAVIER BERTRAN I ROURE, JOAN BONET I AMAT,
GUILLEM BONET I CARBÓ, SALVADOR LINARES I MUSTARÓS

Department of Business Administration
University of Girona. Spain

In the present communication we present a solution of the bidimentional tables planning problem which elements belong to the support of some triangular fuzzy numbers that fulfil the summatory restrictions of the problem. In order to solve that, we present a computer program developed for the research group GRHCS16 (Mathematics for the analysis of the uncertainty in Economics) of the University of Girona. This program runs the following three optimization functions of the solutions: the sum of the quadratic distance between the solution points and the kernel, the sum of the characteristic function of the solution points and the minimum of the characteristic functions to the solution points.

1. Introduction

We start from a bidimentional table which elements are relied between them through summatory restrictions on each row and column, as it is showed below:

$$\begin{pmatrix} x_1 & x_2 \\ x_3 & x_4 \end{pmatrix} \qquad \begin{array}{l} x_1 + x_2 = S_{F1} \\ x_3 + x_4 = S_{F2} \end{array} \quad [1]$$

$$x_1 + x_3 = S_{C1} \qquad x_2 + x_4 = S_{C2}$$

From the following equality,

$$S_{F1} + S_{F2} = x_1 + x_2 + x_3 + x_4 = S_{C1} + S_{C2},$$

We can deduce that the equation $x_1 + x_2 = S_{F1}$ depends on the others. Then, the general problem gets reduced to the search of the values x, y, z, t that solve the following lineal equations:

$$\begin{cases} x_1 + x_3 = S_{C1} \\ x_2 + x_4 = S_{C2} \\ x_3 + x_4 = S_{F2} \end{cases} \quad [2]$$

Because the main matrix determinant of [2] is different from zero, we deduce that the rank of the main matrix is three, and consequently we can classify the system as an indeterminate compatible system with one degree of freedom.

It is important to take into account that when we choose a possible value for one of the unknowns, all the solutions has fewer decimals than the number of decimals of the value chosen or the number of decimals of the restriction values.

For instance, let's imagine that we want to find the value of the unknowns x, y, z, t that solve the following equation system:

$$\begin{cases} x + z = 3,1 \\ y + t = 2,33 \\ z + t = 1,23 \end{cases} \quad [3]$$

Let's consider that the value of x equals to 2'1, then we obtain that z=1, t=0'23 and y=2'1. In none of the cases the number of decimals of the solutions is bigger than:

Maximum(decimals x, decimals S_{C1}, decimals S_{C1}, decimals S_{C1})
$$= Maximum(1,1,2,2) = 2$$

Let's imagine that the unknown values x_1, x_2, x_3, x_4 belong to the compact supports of some triangular fuzzy numbers $\tilde{X}_1 = [a_1,b_1,c_1]$, $\tilde{X}_2 = [a_2,b_2,c_2]$, $\tilde{X}_3 = [a_3,b_3,c_3]$, $\tilde{X}_4 = [a_4,b_4,c_4]$.

Our final goal is to choose the optimal values of the unknowns x_1, x_2, x_3, x_4, among the infinite solutions that solve the system.

A first choice could be, for instance, a solution that minimizes the sum of the quadratic distances between the solution values and the kernel of the fuzzy numbers.

Formally, let's suppose that $[a_i , c_i]$ is the support of the fuzzy numbers $\tilde{X}_i$ and b_i the value of its kernel. We are looking for such values $x_i \in [a_i , b_i]$ i=1,2,3,4 that solve the summatory restrictions and make minimum the following function:

$$D = \sum_{i=1}^{4} (y_i - b_i)^2$$

A second option would be choosing some solution values that maximize the function sum of the characteristic functions of the solution values.

Formally, let's say that $[a_i , c_i]$ is the support of the fuzzy numbers $\widetilde{X}_i$ and b_i the value of its kernel. We are looking for such values $x_i \in [a_i , c_i]$ $i=1,2,3,4$ that solve the summatory restrictions and make maximum the following function:

$$S = \sum_{i=1}^{4} \mu(y_i)$$

A third option would be choosing the solution values that make maximum the function minimum of the characteristic functions of the solution values.

Formally, let's suppose that $[a_i , c_i]$ is the support of the fuzzy numbers $\widetilde{X}_i$ and let b_i be the value of its kernel. We are looking for such values $x_i \in [a_i , c_i]$ $i=1,2,3,4$ that solve the summatory restrictions and the following function:

$$M = \min_{i=1,2,3,4} (\mu(y_i))$$

reaches a maximum on them.

In the real life the solutions with infinite decimals don't exist. Actually, because of the errors committed by the measuring devices or the physic limitations, we got used to work with a limited numbers of decimals (let's say two approximation decimals for instance). Because of the last observation, with the number of decimals to work with fixed, we can run a computer program that calculates every possible solution, finding the ones that optimize every one of the three functions. As an example, if we consider that x belongs to the support of the triangular fuzzy number (2,5,6) and we found every possible solution with a precision of two decimals, we obtain that we only have to check (6-2).100 possible solutions.

The research group of the University of Girona GRHCS16, has created a computer tool that offers the possible points solution of every one of the three mentioned functions using for that an initial form in which the user must introduce the extreme values of the supports and the kernel of the four triangular fuzzy numbers, the independent terms of the restrictions and, of course, the maximum number of decimals that the solutions has to have.

2. The program step by step

In the following picture we can appreciate the initial form of the tool created:

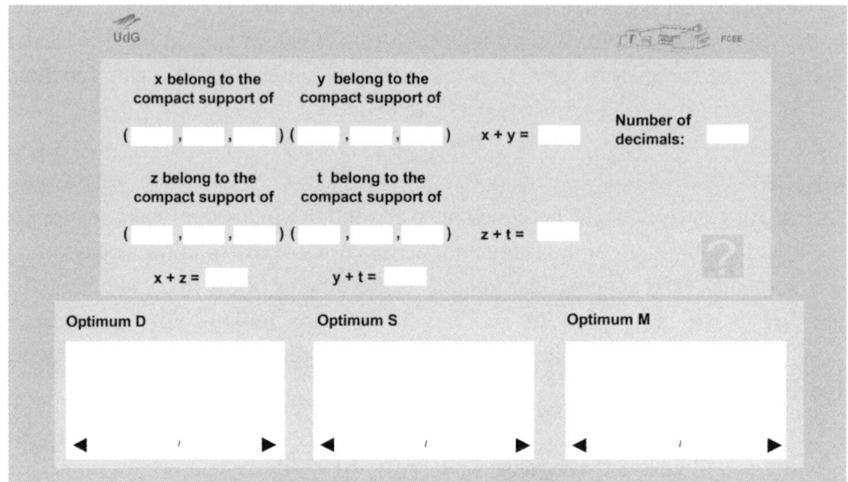

Figure 1

With the purpose of making clear the theoretical foundations of the program we propose a numerical example based on a decision business problem:

Let's imagine a water park with 400 employees. Between them there are only 120 qualified lifeguards. The premises are divided into two separate zones: 1 with 240 employees, and the second one with 160.

It is thought to reduce the staff according to a plan previously designed the optimal condition of which are specified by the following conditions:

1. The number of lifeguards working in Zone 1 has to be between 84 and 100, with an optimal value of 92.
2. The lifeguards' number working in Zone 2 should be between 26 and 64, reaching its optimal value at 44.
3. The number of employees that are not lifeguard in Zone 1 must belong to the interval [120,152], finding its optimal value at 136.
4. Finally, according to the needs of the water park, the number of common employees in Zone 2 must be between 120 and 144, considering its optimal value is 132.

If we consider the problem and synthesized in a table, we obtain:

Table 1

	Zone 1	Zone 2
Qualified lifeguards	$x \in \text{Support}(84,92,100)$	$y \in \text{Support}(24,44,64)$
Non lifeguards employees	$z \in \text{Support}(120,136,152)$	$t \in \text{Support}(120,132,144)$

being x, y, z, t the solutions of the following lineal equations:

$$\begin{cases} x + y = 120 \\ z + t = 280 \\ x + z = 240 \\ y + t = 160 \end{cases} \quad [4]$$

Once the different data are introduced, we can run the program to find the solution.

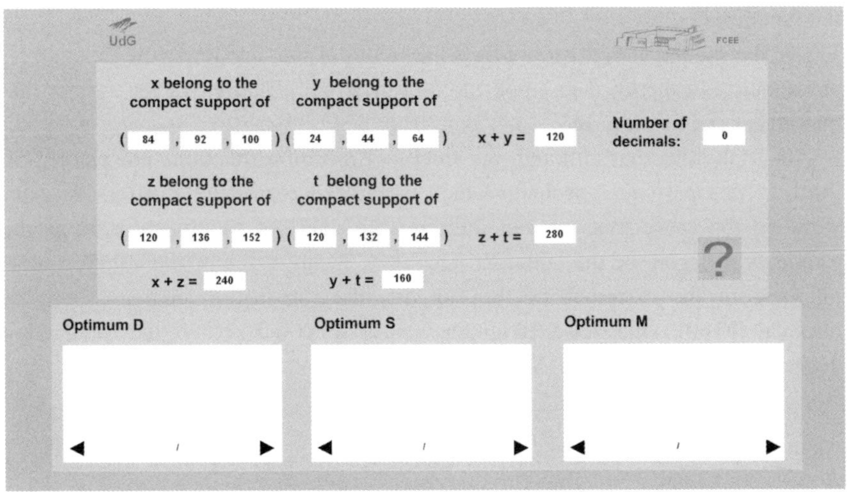

Figure 2

In the following picture it is shown how it appears three different boxes of text with all the possible different values, and the value of the three different functions, showing them for if the user wants the solution that mix two or three of the functions.

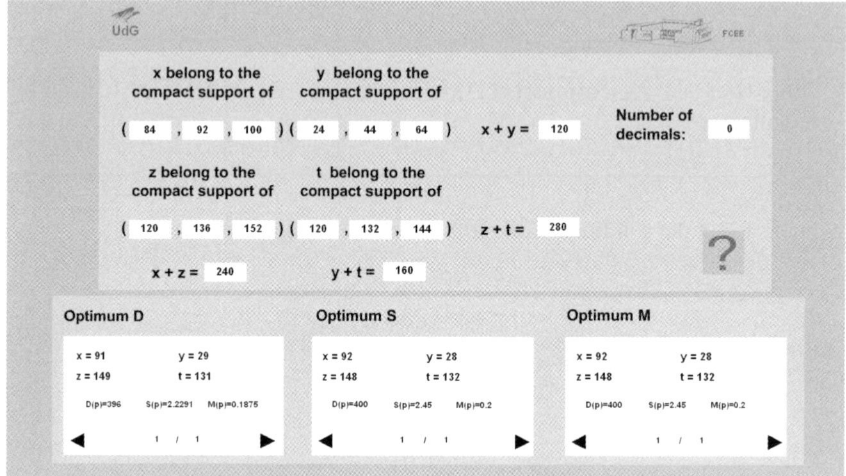

Figure 3

In the first of the three text boxes the tool shows the solutions that minimize the function D

In the second one, the tool offers the solutions that maximize the function S

Finally, in the third text box the tool gives the solutions of the system that maximizes the function M

It is obvious that although the three optimization functions are viable, the third, in this particular problem which we are concerned with, offers an extra value in the sense that we can interpret the value of the function M as the satisfaction degree of the solution. This way, if any value of the solution were obtained in the extremes of the support, the satisfaction degree would be minimal (M=0). Otherwise, if all the values were the kernels the satisfaction degree would be maximum (M=1).

3. Conclusions

The problem of optimization of functions D, S or M in bidimentional tables, which terms belong to the support of some triangular fuzzy numbers which fulfil some summatory restrictions and which have a limited number of decimals, have a solution even though it may not be unique. The computer tool created by the research group GRHCS16 of the University of Girona finds these solutions. The program available for business practice at the website http://web2.udg.edu/grmfcee/optimum.swf is a useful tool for finding the possible solutions for this type of problems.

References

1. Aubanell, A.; Bernseny, A.; Delshams, A.: *Útiles básicos de Cálculo numérico.* Ed. Labor. (1993)
2. Bonet, J.; Bertran, X.; Cassú, C. i Ferrer J.C. Algebra moderna: conjunts, relacions i aplicacions. Girona, Universitat de Girona. (1994)
3. Castellet, M.; Llerena, I.: *Àlgebra lineal i geometria.* Publicacions de la Universitat Autònoma de Barcelona. (1990)
4. Chiang, Alpha C.: Métodos fundamentals de Economía Matemática. Ed. McGrawHill. (1987)
5. De la Cruz, D.; Zumbado, C.: Flash, Php y Mysql. Ediciones Anaya Multimedia. (2006)
6. Gil Aluja, J.: *Fuzzy sets in the management of uncertainty.* Ed. Springer-Verlag. (2004)
7. Kaufmann, A.; Gil Aluja, J.: *Introducción de la teoría de los subconjuntos borrosos a la gestión de las empresas.* Ed. Milladoiro. (1986)
8. Kaufmann, A.; Gil Aluja, J.; Terceño, A.: *Matemática para la economía y la gestión de empresas. Vol I: artimética de la incertidumbre.* Ed. Foro Científico. (1994)

INDUCED GENERALIZED PROBABILISTIC OWAWA OPERATOR

JOSÉ M. MERIGÓ

Department of Business Administration, University of Barcelona,
Av. Diagonal 690, 08034 Barcelona, Spain

We introduce the induced generalized probabilistic ordered weighted averaging –
weighted average (IGPOWAWA) operator. It is a new aggregation operator that provides
a unified framework between the probability, the weighted average and the ordered
weighted averaging (OWA) operator considering the degree of importance that each
concept has in the aggregation. Moreover, the IGPOWAWA operator also uses
generalized means providing a more general formulation that includes the arithmetic, the
geometric and the quadratic version. Furthermore, this approach is able to deal with
complex reordering process by using order-inducing variables. We study some of its
main properties and particular cases obtaining the induced POWAWA, the induced
geometric POWAWA and the induced quadratic POWAWA operator.

1. Introduction

In the literature, we find a wide range of methods for aggregating the information
[1-13]. The weighted average (WA) is one of the most common aggregation
operators found in the literature. It can be used in a wide range of different
problems including statistics, economics and engineering. Another interesting
aggregation operator that has not been used so much in the literature is the
ordered weighted averaging (OWA) operator [9].

A very practical extension of the OWA is the induced OWA (IOWA)
operator [12]. It is an extension of the OWA operator that uses order-inducing
variables in the reordering of the arguments. Its main advantage is that it can
represent more complex situations because it can include a wide range of factors
in the reordering process rather than simply consider the values of the
arguments. Recently, several authors have developed different extensions and
applications of the IOWA operator [4,6].

A more general formulation of these aggregation operators is by using
generalized means such as the generalized weighted average (GWA) and the
generalized OWA (GOWA) operator [11]. Moreover, it is possible to further

generalize this approach by using quasi-arithmetic means obtaining the Quasi-WA and the Quasi-OWA operator [3].

Several studies have tried to use the WA and the probability in the OWA operator. In [7], Torra developed a model for using OWAs and WAs in the same formulation called the weighted OWA (WOWA) operator. Later [8], Xu and Da developed another approach called the hybrid averaging (HA) operator. The use of the OWA operator in the probability has been analyzed in several papers [2,4]. More recent approaches for unifying the OWA with the probability and the WA are the probabilistic OWA (POWA) operator and the OWA weighted average (OWAWA) operator introduced in [4]. Another interesting approach is the one that unifies the probability with the weighted average, known as the probabilistic weighted averaging (PWA) operator [4]. A more general approach to the previous ones is the one suggested by Merigó in [5]. He suggested a unified model between the probability, the weighted average and the OWA operator. This new model is the probabilistic ordered weighted averaging – weighted average (POWAWA) operator.

The aim of this paper is to present a more general formulation that it is able to deal with probabilities, WAs and OWAs in the same formulation and considering the degree of importance that each concept has in the aggregation. We call it the induced generalized probabilistic ordered weighted averaging – weighted average (IGPOWAWA) operator. The main advantage is that it uses order-inducing variables in order to deal with complex reordering processes and generalized means providing a more general formulation of the model that includes a wide range of particular cases such as the induced POWAWA (IPOWAWA), the geometric IPOWAWA (IPOWGAWA), the quadratic IPOWAWA (IPOWQAWA), the harmonic IPOWAWA (IPOWHAWA), the induced OWAWA (IOWAWA) and many other types.

This paper is structured as follows. In Section 2, we briefly review some basic concepts about the IOWA, the GOWA and the POWAWA operator. In Section 3 we present the IGPOWAWA operator and in Section 4 we study several families of the IGPOWAWA. Section 6 summarizes the main results of the paper.

2. Preliminaries

In this section we briefly describe some basic concepts about the IOWA, the GOWA and the POWAWA operator.

2.1. *The IOWA Operator*

The IOWA operator was introduced by [12] and it represents an extension of the OWA operator. Its main difference is that the reordering step is not developed with the values of the arguments a_i. In this case, the reordering step is developed with order-inducing variables. The IOWA operator also includes as particular cases the maximum, the minimum and the average criteria. It can be defined as follows.

Definition 1. An IOWA operator of dimension n is a mapping $IOWA: R^n \times R^n \to R$ that has an associated weighting vector W of dimension n with $\sum_{j=1}^{n} w_j = 1$ and $w_j \in [0, 1]$, such that:

$$IOWA\left(\langle u_1, a_1 \rangle, \langle u_2, a_2 \rangle, \dots, \langle u_n, a_n \rangle\right) = \sum_{j=1}^{n} w_j b_j \tag{1}$$

where b_j is the a_i value of the IOWA pair $\langle u_i, a_i \rangle$ having the jth largest u_i, u_i is the order-inducing variable and a_i is the argument variable.

2.2. *The GOWA Operator*

The generalized OWA (GOWA) operator was introduced by Yager [11]. It generalizes a wide range of aggregation operators that includes the OWA operator with its particular cases, the ordered weighted geometric (OWG) operator, the ordered weighted harmonic averaging (OWHA) operator and the ordered weighted quadratic averaging (OWQA) operator. It can be defined as follows.

Definition 2. A GOWA operator of dimension n is a mapping $GOWA: R^n \to R$ that has an associated weighting vector W of dimension n with $\sum_{j=1}^{n} w_j = 1$ and $w_j \in [0, 1]$, such that:

$$GOWA\left(a_1, a_2, \dots, a_n\right) = \left(\sum_{j=1}^{n} w_j b_j^{\lambda} \right)^{1/\lambda} \tag{2}$$

where b_j is the jth largest of the a_i, and λ is a parameter such that $\lambda \in (-\infty, \infty)$.

2.3. *The POWAWA Operator*

The probabilistic OWA weighted average (POWAWA) operator [4-5] is an aggregation operator that uses probabilities, weighted averages and OWAs in the same formulation. It unifies these three concepts considering the degree of importance we want to give to each case depending on the situation considered. It can be defined as follows.

Definition 3. A POWAWA operator of dimension n is a mapping *POWAWA*: $R^n \rightarrow R$ that has an associated weighting vector W of dimension n with $w_j \in [0, 1]$ and $\sum_{j=1}^{n} w_j = 1$, such that:

$$POWAWA\,(a_1, \ldots, a_n) = \sum_{i=1}^{n} w_j b_j \tag{3}$$

where b_j is the jth largest of the a_i, each argument a_i has an associated weight v_i with $\sum_{i=1}^{n} v_i = 1$ and $v_i \in [0, 1]$, a probability p_i with $\sum_{i=1}^{n} p_i = 1$ and $p_i \in [0, 1]$, $\hat{v}_j = C_1 w_j + C_2 v_j + C_3 p_j$, with C_1, C_2 and $C_3 \in [0, 1]$, $C_1 + C_2 + C_3 = 1$, and v_j and p_j are the weights v_i and p_i ordered according to b_j, that is to say, according to the jth largest of the a_i.

3. The Induced Generalized Probabilistic OWAWA Operator

The induced generalized POWAWA (IGPOWAWA) operator is a generalization of the POWAWA operator that uses generalized means and order-inducing variables. Thus, it is an aggregation operator that uses generalized means in a unified framework between the probability, the weighted average and the OWA operator. Moreover, it is able to assess complex reordering processes by using order-inducing variables. Its main advantage is that it provides a more robust formulation than the POWAWA operator because it includes a wide range of particular cases including the induced POWAWA (IPOWAWA), the geometric IPOWAWA (IPOWGAWA), the quadratic IPOWAWA (IPOWQAWA) and the harmonic IPOWAWA (IPOWHAWA) operator. It can be defined as follows.

Definition 4. An IGPOWAWA operator of dimension n is a mapping $IGPOWAWA: R^n \times R^n \rightarrow R$ that has an associated weighting vector W of dimension n with $w_j \in [0, 1]$ and $\Sigma_{j=1}^n w_j = 1$, such that:

$$IGPOWAWA\ (\langle u_1, a_1 \rangle, \langle u_2, a_2 \rangle, \ldots, \langle u_n, a_n \rangle) = \left(\sum_{j=1}^n \hat{v}_j b_j^\lambda \right)^{1/\lambda} \tag{4}$$

where b_j is the a_i value of the IGPOWAWA pair $\langle u_i, a_i \rangle$ having the jth largest u_i, u_i is the order-inducing variable, each argument a_i has an associated weight v_i with $\Sigma_{i=1}^n v_i = 1$ and $v_i \in [0, 1]$, a probability p_i with $\Sigma_{i=1}^n p_i = 1$ and $p_i \in [0, 1]$, $\hat{v}_j = C_1 w_j + C_2 v_j + C_3 p_j$, with C_1, C_2 and $C_3 \in [0, 1]$, $C_1 + C_2 + C_3 = 1$, v_j and p_j are the weights v_i and p_i ordered according to b_j, that is to say, according to the jth largest of the a_i, and λ is a parameter such that $\lambda \in (-\infty, \infty)$.

Note that this definition could also be presented using the following equivalent definition.

Definition 5. An IGPOWAWA operator of dimension n is a mapping $f: R^n \times R^n \rightarrow R$, that has an associated weighting vector W, with $\Sigma_{j=1}^n w_j = 1$ and $w_j \in [0, 1]$, a weighting vector V, with $\Sigma_{i=1}^n v_i = 1$ and $v_i \in [0, 1]$, and a probabilistic vector P, with $\Sigma_{i=1}^n p_i = 1$ and $p_i \in [0, 1]$, such that:

$$f(\langle u_1, a_1 \rangle, \ldots, \langle u_n, a_n \rangle) =$$

$$= C_1 \left(\sum_{j=1}^n w_j b_j^\lambda \right)^{1/\lambda} + C_2 \left(\sum_{i=1}^n v_i a_i^\lambda \right)^{1/\lambda} + C_3 \left(\sum_{i=1}^n p_i a_i^\lambda \right)^{1/\lambda} \tag{5}$$

where b_j is the a_i value of the IGPOWAWA pair $\langle u_i, a_i \rangle$ having the jth largest u_i, u_i is the order-inducing variable, C_1, C_2 and $C_3 \in [0, 1]$ with $C_1 + C_2 + C_3 = 1$, and λ is a parameter such that $\lambda \in (-\infty, \infty)$.

Example 1. Assume the following arguments in an aggregation process: (60, 20, 40, 80) and $\lambda = 1$. Assume the following weighting vector $W = (0.2, 0.2, 0.3,$

0.3), $V = (0.3, 0.3, 0.2, 0.2)$, and the following probabilistic weighting vector $P = (0.3, 0.3, 0.3, 0.1)$. Note that the probabilistic information has a degree of importance of 40%, the weighted average a degree of 40% and the OWA a degree of 20%. We assume that $\lambda = 1$ and the following order-inducing variables $U = (12, 16, 30, 24)$. If we want to aggregate this information by using the IGPOWAWA operator, we will get the following. The aggregation can be solved either with Eq. (4), (5) or (6). With Eq. (4) we get the following.

$$\hat{v}_1 = 0.4 \times 0.3 + 0.4 \times 0.2 + 0.2 \times 0.2 = 0.24 \,,$$

$$\hat{v}_2 = 0.4 \times 0.1 + 0.4 \times 0.2 + 0.2 \times 0.2 = 0.16 \,,$$

$$\hat{v}_3 = 0.4 \times 0.3 + 0.4 \times 0.3 + 0.2 \times 0.3 = 0.3 \,,$$

$$\hat{v}_4 = 0.4 \times 0.3 + 0.4 \times 0.3 + 0.2 \times 0.3 = 0.3 \,.$$

As we can see, the sum of the new weights is still one. Now, we calculate the aggregation process as follows:

IGPOWAWA = $0.24 \times 40 + 0.16 \times 80 + 0.3 \times 20 + 0.3 \times 60 = 46.4$.

As we can see, the induced GOWA (IGOWA) [6], the generalized WA (GWA) and the generalized probability are included in this formulation as special cases.

- If $C_1 = 1$, we get the IGOWA operator.
- If $C_2 = 1$, we get the GWA.
- If $C_3 = 1$, we get the generalized probabilistic aggregation.
- If $C_1 = 0$, we form the generalized probabilistic weighted average (GPWA).
- If $C_2 = 0$, we form the induced generalized probabilistic OWA (IGPOWA) operator.
- If $C_3 = 0$, we form the induced generalized OWAWA (IGOWAWA) operator.

Note that it is possible to distinguish between the descending IGPOWAWA (DIGPOWAWA) and the ascending IGPOWAWA (AIGPOWAWA) operator by using $w_j = w^*_{n-j+1}$, where w_j is the jth weight of the DIGPOWAWA and w^*_{n-j+1} the jth weight of the AIGPOWAWA operator.

Note that if the weighting vectors of the three concepts are not normalized, i.e., $W = \sum_{j=1}^{n} w_j \neq 1$, $V = \sum_{i=1}^{n} v_i \neq 1$, $P = \sum_{i=1}^{n} p_i \neq 1$, then, the IGPOWAWA operator can be expressed as:

$$f(\langle u_1, a_1 \rangle, \ldots, \langle u_n, a_n \rangle) =$$

$$= \frac{C_1}{W} C_1 \left(\sum_{j=1}^{n} w_j b_j^{\lambda} \right)^{1/\lambda} + \frac{C_2}{V} \left(\sum_{i=1}^{n} v_i a_i^{\lambda} \right)^{1/\lambda} + \frac{C_3}{P} \left(\sum_{i=1}^{n} p_i a_i^{\lambda} \right)^{1/\lambda} \tag{6}$$

The IGPOWAWA is monotonic, bounded and idempotent. Note that it is interesting to mention that with the IGPOWAWA operator, we get new boundary conditions based on the minimum and the maximum probabilistic weighted aggregation. Other properties and particular cases will be considered in future research.

4. Families of IGPOWAWA Operators

A further interesting issue of the IGPOWAWA operator is to analyze different particular cases such as the following ones obtained by using different representations in the weighting vectors.

- The GPOWAWA and all its particular cases (when the ordered position of u_i is the same than the ordered position of b_j such that b_j is the jth largest of a_i).
- The arithmetic GPWA aggregation (if $w_j = 1/n$, for all j).
- The arithmetic IGPOWA operator (if $v_i = 1/n$, for all i).
- The arithmetic IGOWAWA operator (if $p_i = 1/n$, for all i).
- The double arithmetic IGOWA operator (if $p_i = 1/n$, for all i, and $v_i = 1/n$, for all i).
- The double arithmetic GWA operator (if $p_i = 1/n$, for all i, and $w_j = 1/n$, for all j).
- The double arithmetic generalized probabilistic aggregation (if $v_i = 1/n$, for all i, and $w_j = 1/n$, for all j).
- The generalized average (if $v_i = 1/n$, for all i, $p_i = 1/n$, for all i, and $w_j = 1/n$, for all j).
- The maximum GPWA ($w_p = 1$ and $w_j = 0$, for all $j \neq p$, and $u_p = \text{Max}\{a_i\}$).

- The minimum GPWA ($w_p = 1$ and $w_j = 0$, for all $j \neq p$, and $u_p = \text{Min}\{a_i\}$).
- The maximum arithmetic probabilistic aggregation ($w_1 = 1$ and $w_j = 0$, for all $j \neq 1$, and $v_i = 1/n$, for all i).
- The maximum arithmetic WA aggregation ($w_1 = 1$ and $w_j = 0$, for all $j \neq 1$, and $p_i = 1/n$, for all i).
- The minimum arithmetic probabilistic aggregation ($w_n = 1$ and $w_j = 0$, for all $j \neq n$, and $v_i = 1/n$, for all i).
- The minimum arithmetic WA aggregation ($w_n = 1$ and $w_j = 0$, for all $j \neq n$, and $p_i = 1/n$, for all i).
- The IGPOWAWA Hurwicz criteria ($w_1 = \alpha$, $w_n = 1 - \alpha$ and $w_j = 0$, for all $j \neq 1, n$).
- The step-IGPOWAWA operator ($w_k = 1$ and $w_j = 0$, for all $j \neq k$).
- The olympic-IGPOWAWA operator ($w_1 = w_n = 0$, and $w_j = 1/(n - 2)$ for all others).
- Etc.

Note that other families of IGPOWAWA operators could be studied following Merigó [4] and Yager [10,13].

Moreover, if we analyze different values of the parameter λ, we obtain another group of particular cases such as:

- The usual IPOWAWA operator: When $\lambda = 1$.
- The geometric IPOWAWA (IPOWGAWA) operator: When $\lambda \to 0$.
- The harmonic IPOWAWA (IPOWHAWA) operator: When $\lambda = -1$.
- The quadratic IPOWAWA (IPOWQAWA) operator: When $\lambda = 2$.
- The maximum: When $\lambda \to \infty$.
- The minimum: When $\lambda \to -\infty$.

Note that many other families could be studied by using other values in the parameter λ and mixing different values of λ in the same aggregation.

Moreover, it is possible to further generalize the IGPOWAWA operator by replacing the parameter λ by a strictly continuous monotonic function $g(b)$ as follows. We call it the quasi-arithmetic IPOWAWA (Quasi-IPOWAWA) operator:

$$QIPOWAWA\ (\langle u_1, a_1 \rangle, \langle u_2, a_2 \rangle, \ldots, \langle u_n, a_n \rangle) = g^{-1}\left(\sum_{j=1}^{n} \hat{v}_j\, g\big(b_{(j)}\big) \right) \tag{7}$$

Note that we will study in more detail the Quasi-IPOWAWA operator in future research [4].

5. Conclusions

We have presented the IGPOWAWA operator. The main advantage of this approach is that it unifies the probability, the WA and the OWA in the same formulation and considering the degree of importance that each concept has in the aggregation. Another key aspect of this model is that it uses order-inducing variables in order to assess complex reordering processes. Furthermore, this approach includes a wide range of aggregation operators such as the IPOWAWA, the maximum-PWA, the minimum-PWA, the double arithmetic OWA, the double arithmetic WA, the double arithmetic probability, the arithmetic OWAWA, the IPOWGAWA, the IPOWQAWA and the IPOWHAWA operator. Moreover, we have also obtained many other new aggregation operators included in the IGPOWAWA such as the arithmetic PWA, the probabilistic double WA, the arithmetic IPOWA and the arithmetic IOWAWA.

In future research, we expect to develop further extensions of this approach by considering more complex formulations by using unified aggregation operators and uncertain information represented in the form of interval numbers, fuzzy numbers, linguistic variables, expertons and more complex structures.

Acknowledgements

Support from the Spanish Ministry of Science and Innovation under project "JC2009-00189" is gratefully acknowledged.

References

1. G. Beliakov, A. Pradera, T. Calvo, *Aggregation functions: A guide for practitioners* (Springer-Verlag, Berlin-Heidelberg, 2007).
2. K.J. Engemann, R.R. Yager, D.P. Filev, Modelling decision making using immediate probabilities, *Int. J. General Syst.* **24**, 281 (1996).
3. J. Fodor, J.L. Marichal, M. Roubens, Characterization of the ordered weighted averaging operators, *IEEE Trans. Fuzzy Syst.* **3**, 236 (1995).
4. J.M. Merigó, *New extensions to the OWA operators and their application in decision making* (PhD thesis (in Spanish), Department of Business Administration, University of Barcelona, 2008).
5. J.M. Merigó, On the unification between the probability, the weighted average and the OWA operator. In: *Intelligent Decision Making Systems* (World Scientific, Singapore, pp. 375-381, 2009).

6. J.M. Merigó and A.M. Gil-Lafuente, The induced generalized OWA operator, *Inform. Sci.* **179**, 729 (2009).
7. V. Torra, The weighted OWA operator, *Int. J. Intelligent Syst.* **12**, 153 (1997).
8. Z.S. Xu and Q.L. Da, An overview of operators for aggregating information, *Int. J. Intelligent Syst.* **18**, 953 (2003).
9. R.R. Yager, On ordered weighted averaging aggregation operators in multi-criteria decision making, *IEEE Trans. Syst. Man Cybern. B* **18**, 183 (1988).
10. R.R. Yager, Families of OWA operators, *Fuzzy Sets Syst.* **59**, 125 (1993).
11. R.R Yager, Generalized OWA aggregation operators, *Fuzzy Optim. Decision Making* **3**, 93 (2004).
12. R.R. Yager and D.P. Filev, Induced ordered weighted averaging operators, *IEEE Trans. Syst. Man Cybern. B* **29**, 141 (1999).
13. R.R. Yager and J. Kacprzyk, *The ordered weighted averaging operators: Theory and applications*. Norwell: Kluwer Academic Publishers, 1997.

FUNCTIONAL COORDINATES

SAMIR ZAKI MOHAMED MEHREZ
19 Omar Ibnel Khattab St., Ismaillyia Squ., Heliopolis,
Cairo, Egypt

There is no limit to the number of functional scales that can be constructed, and many functions other than logarithmic ones are commonly used in applications of scales. The paper will focus on two functional scales; adjacent and nonajacent, in addition to their relative characteristics through illustrative numerical examples, and graphs.

1. Functional Scales

In order to construct a functional scale, certain characteristics of the scale must be known. These include the kind of function involved, the approximate length of the scale desired, and the range or domain of the variable. In laying out distances on the scale, inches are normally used. However, the number of inches in the length of the scale seldom will agree with the total range of numerical values of the function, and it is usually necessary to proportion the numerical values involved to correspond to the desired scale length. This proportioning is best accomplished through the use of the scale equation, containing a modulus or "stretch factor". The form of such an equation is as follows:

$$\delta_X = m(X - K) \tag{1}$$

where δ_X = distance along the scale, m = modulus, X = function of the variable x, K = a constant.

The first requirement is to determine the value of K. This must equal to the value of the function X corresponding to the value of the variable x for which δ_X is zero. Then, the computed value of δ_X for the value of x will be zero, and this value of x should be placed at one end of the scale. The next step is to determine the value of the modulus m. The maximum value of δ_X will have been established, and this value must apply to the point at the other end of the scale. When the maximum value of δ_X and the value of X corresponding to the maximum value of x are substituted in the scale equation, m becomes the only unknown quantity in that equation. Thus if δ_{xmax} and X_{max} denote these values of the distance and the function,

$$m = \frac{\delta x\,\text{max}}{X_{\text{max}} - K} \tag{2}$$

After the value of m has been computed, Eq. (1) can be used to plot on the scale as many intermediate points as desired. The proper value of x should be placed at each point thus located. The scale may be plotted on either a curved axis or a straight axis, but the latter is more common in ordinary applications.

To show an example of a functional scale, let it be required to plot a scale for x^2 that will meet the following requirements: The scale is to be approximately 8 inches in length, and the range of the variable is to be from 2 to 5. since δ_X will be zero when x = 2, the value of K will be 2^2, or 4, and the modulus will be

$$m = \frac{8}{5^2 - 4} = \frac{8}{21}$$

Ordinarily, a functional scale need not have the exact length specified. So the fraction 8/21 will be reduced to 0.38, which will require only a slight change in the length of the scale. The scale equation that will be used to located points on the scale is thus

$$\delta_X = 0.38(x^2 - 4) \tag{3}$$

A scale should be easily readable. Therefore, enough graduation marks should be used to permit easy interpolation. Also, it is desirable to make the major graduation marks longer than the less important ones, and to calibrate at least the major graduations. The space along the scale between two major graduations may be called a major division. Sometimes the length of a major division is such that only one group of subdivisions is needed. Where the length of such a subdivision would be fairly large, it may be desirable to further subdivide each subdivision. Then a larger subdivision would be called a major subdivision, and a smaller one would be a minor subdivision. Usually, it is advisable to start drawing a scale by locating the points at its ends. The major intermediate graduations should be plotted next, and finally the graduations for the major and minor subdivisions should be located. For the scale in the assumed example, the major graduations would be at the whole numbers, which are 2, 3, 4 and 5. As each of these values is substituted for x in Eq. (3), the corresponding distance δ_X can be plotted along the scale from the zero (or end) position. The value of 2.0 is placed at the minimal end of the scale, as shown in Figure 1. observe that graduations on the scale are located according to the function and are numbered according to the variable. The value shown at the opposite end of the scale in figure 1 is of course the specified maximum value of the variable, or 5.0. The distance from the initial point (origin) of the scale to the graduation marked 5.0 is found by substituting the value 5.0 for x in Eq. (3). This distance is

7.98 inches, which showed that the actual scale length is only 0.25% different from the desired length (an unimportant difference). The distances from the origin of the scale to the other whole-number points are determined in like fashion by substitution of values in Eq. (3).

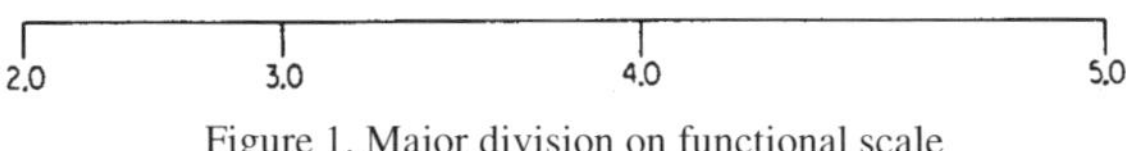

Figure 1. Major division on functional scale

The next practical step is to observe the distances between successive major graduations and to decide upon the most practical number of subdivisions in each instance. If the space between 2.0 and 3.0 is 1.90 inches long, ten subdivisions would seem quite desirable, since the average length of these subdivisions would be 0.19 inch and interpolation would be reasonable. It is customary to elongate the fifth mark in such a group of ten, but still to have this mark shorter than the marks used for the whole numbers. Therefore, in this portion of the scale there are three lengths of graduation marks. The whole number marks are the longest; the mark representing 2.5 is of intermediate length; and the remaining marks are the shortest. Since the distance between graduations is only 1.90 inches, it would be impractical to calibrate the scale at any of the intermediate graduations; in fact, to do so might actually make reading of the scale quite difficult. Thus, it would probably be impractical to include more than ten subdivisions in the portion of the scale between 2.0 and 3.0. The graduation for each subdivision is located by substituting the appropriate value for x in Eq. (3) and laying off the corresponding distance δ_x from the origin of the scale. If the space between 3.0 and 4.0 is 2.68 inches long, then again ten major subdivisions are indicated. However the average length of the subdivision would then be 0.268 inch, which is probably too great to permit easy interpolation. If each of these major subdivisions is further divided into two minor subdivisions, so that the total number of subdivisions between 3.0 and 4.0 is 20, the average length of the minor subdivisions becomes 0.134 inch, which is a much more suitable distance for interpolation. These minor subdivisions will of course require shorter graduation marks on the scale than those used for the major subdivisions. As a result four different lengths of marks will be necessary between 3.0 and 4.0. Let the distance from 4.0 to 5.0 be 3.42 inches. When this space is divided into ten major subdivisions, the average length of these subdivisions is 0.342 inch. Further division of each major subdivision into two minor subdivisions will reduce the average length of the minor subdivisions to 0.171 inch and will permit easy interpolation. Therefore, as in the case of the space from 3.0 to 4.0, a total of 20 subdivisions is indicated. The complete scale is shown in Figure (2).

Figure 2. Completed scale

When scale-equation values are computed by hand, it is sometimes possible to reduce the work involved by manipulating the equation in some way. For example, let us suppose that the function is $3x^2$, that the length of the scale is to be 8 inches, and that the range is to be from 2 to 5. The minimum value of X would be 12, the maximum value would be 75, and the modulus would be

$$m = \frac{8}{75-12} = \frac{8}{63} = 0.127 \tag{4}$$

the scale equation will be

$$\delta_X = 0.127 \, (3x^2 - 12) \tag{5}$$

If 3 is factored out of the expression in the parentheses, and the scale equation is written in the form

$$\delta_X = 0.381 \, (x^2 - 4) \tag{6}$$

Although the modulus is changed, the scale will not be affected in any way by this change, since Eq. (6) is the equivalent of Eq. (5). The modulus shown in Eq. (5) is the actual or true modulus, while the modulus indicated in Eq. (6) can be called the effective or applied modulus.

A functional scale by itself has no value. Such a scale becomes useful only when it is combined with uniform scales or with other functional scales in particular ways.

1.1 *Adjacent Scales*

Many equations involving two variables are used for conversion purposes. For instance, the relationship between the volume and the radius of a sphere is expressed by the equation

$$3V = 4\pi R^3 \tag{7}$$

where V is the volume in cubic units and R is the radius in linear units.

Let it be desired to obtain one of these quantities, when the other is known, by locating the given value on one scale and then reading the corresponding value on a second scale. A range of diameters from 1 to 6 inches will be considered sufficient. Obviously, each scale must have enough subdivisions to permit easy interpolation. It will be necessary to lay out the two scales independently, but they should be placed on the same axis so that easy transfer from one to the other will be possible. Eq. (7) shows that the V scale will be uniform, since 3V is a linear or uniform function, while the R scale will be cubic in nature. A scale equation can be written for each of these variables, but it is more practical simply to divide the V scale geometrically into the proper number of uniform divisions, and to use a scale equation only for the R scale. However, it should be noted that each scale will actually have a modulus, and that both scales must have the same modulus. The modulus is an expansion or stretch factor, and two scales placed along the same axis obviously must be expanded or contracted by the same amount. In order that the V and R scales may be laid out, the scale length must be known. Let this be 6 inches. Because the graduations on the R scale are dependent on a scale equation, it will be necessary to determine the modulus for that equation, in case the scale length must be adjusted slightly, by substituting appropriate values in Eq. (2), the modulus is found to be

$$m = \frac{6}{4\pi(3.0)^3 - 4\pi(0.5)^3} = \frac{6}{(12.56)(26.875)} \tag{8}$$

For practical purposes, m can be taken as 0.0177. The scale equation then becomes

$$\delta_R = 0.0177\,(4\pi r^3 - 1.5708) \tag{9}$$

The R scale can now be plotted as a functional scale. The conversion chart, with the complete scales, is shown in Figure (3). A simplification can be made in Eq. (7), because there are constants on each side. If both sides are divided by 4π, it will not be necessary to make an extra computation in the scale equation for R or to use an effective modulus. Thus, the scale equation for the R scale would be

$$\delta_R = m(R^3 - 0.125) \tag{10}$$

And the modulus would be

$$m = \frac{6}{26.875} = 0.223 \text{ approximately} \tag{11}$$

The R scale could then be plotted by use of the scale equation

$$\delta_R = 0.223\,(R^3 - 0.125) \tag{12}$$

Naturally, the modulus in Eq. (12) will not be the same as that in Eq. (9) because the constants in the original equation have been changed. However, the new modulus will not change the positions of the graduations on the R scale or of those on the V scale. The truth of this statement can be shown by computing

88

the effective modulus for Eq. (9). That modulus would be 4π times 0.0177, or 0.2223, which is in good agreement with the modulus in Eq. (12). Therefore, the effective modulus for the original arrangement of Eq. (7) becomes the true modulus for the altered arrangement. The conversion chart, with the complete scales is shown in Figure (3).

Figure 3. Adjacent scales for sphere dimensions

When the rearrangement of an equation is contemplated, the effect on the functional scales should be considered. The transposing of a constant from one side of a given equation to the other side will, in general, have no effect on the positions of the graduations on a functional scale. Thus, dividing both sides of Eq. (7) by 4π had no effect on the graduations on the R scale in Figure (3). However, if the form of a variable is changed, then the positions of the graduations on the scale will probably be changed. Such a change can be a serious matter in the interpretation of the relationship between the variables. For instance, let us consider the relationship between the surface area of a sphere and its volume. The conversion chart would represent a single equation in which there are two variables. This equation is obtained by expressing the surface area and the volume in terms of the radius and then eliminating the radius from those two equations. Thus, the surface area A is $4\pi R^2$, and the volume V is $(4/3)\pi R^3$. Hence

$$V = \frac{A^{3/2}}{6\sqrt{\pi}}$$

(13)

This equation could also be written in the form

$$A = \sqrt[3]{36\pi}\, V^{2/3} \tag{14}$$

Also, the constants could be transposed so as to given other relationships. Transposing a constant would not affect the locations of the graduations on the A and V scales, but changing the powers of the variables as in the conversion from Eq. (13) to Eq. (14) would change the positions of the graduations on the scales.

1.2 *Nonadjacent Scales*

Conversion scales need not be placed along the same axis in every instance. If they are separated, they would be called nonadjacent scales.

Such scales would probably be placed on parallel axes, and there would be a turning position through which a straightedge could be placed to line up corresponding values on the two scales. The only practical reason for using nonadjacent scales would be the necessity of using scales of different lengths. Obviously the moduli would have to be different and would have to be computed separately. Of course, the distance between two values on either scale of a pair of nonadjacent scales might also be different from the corresponding distance on one of two adjacent scales. Another important difference would be that the direction in which values increase on one of the two nonadjacent scales would have to be reversed from the direction which would have been proper for adjacent scales. The reason should be evident from Figure (4), where a pair of scales for conversion of temperatures have been drawn in this fashion.

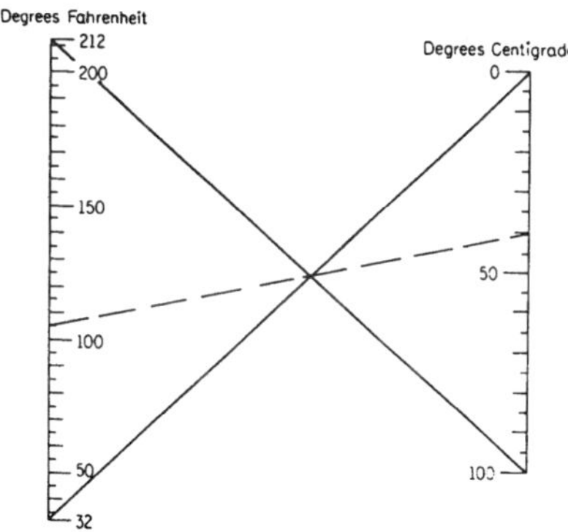

Figure 4. Nonadjacent scales

Obviously, when the straightedge passes through the turning point and when one point of the straightedge is raised to give a certain reading on one scale, the other part of it must be lowered to get the corresponding reading on the other scale.

The turning point is readily located by drawing lines connecting two pairs of corresponding values and finding the intersection of these two lines. In Figure (4) the extreme values, or the corresponding ends of the scales, were used.

2. Conclusion

From the above presented matter, we can deduce that when the rearrangement of an equation is contemplated, the effect on the functional scales should be considered. The transposing of a constant from one side of a given equation to the other side will, in general, have no effect on the positions of the graduations on a functional scale. Where as, if the form of a variable is changed, then the positions of the graduations on the scale will probably be changed. Such a change can be a serious matter in the interpretation of the relationship between the variables.

References

1. W.H. Burrows, Graphical Techniques for Engineering computation (1965).

2. Forrest Wood Worth, Graphical Simulation (1981).

3. J. Molnar, Ann Arbar, Nomographs: What They Are and How to Use Them (1981).

4. Jhon H. Fasal, Nomography (1968).

EASY COMMUNICATION ENVIRONMENT FOR DISTRIBUTED SIMULATION

ARTIS SILINS, EGILS GINTERS, DACE AIZSTRAUTA

Sociotechnical Systems Engineering Institute, Vidzeme University of Applied Sciences, Cesu Street 4, Valmiera LV-4200, Latvia

The development of simulation enables the researchers to explore more sophisticated problems at a more detailed level. This implies a necessity to use several models, or even different simulation tools. There are several solutions, but they are complicated, expensive and not suitable for people without specific knowledge. This paper describes a solution that would give the opportunity to ensure the communication between different parts of the joint model written by different simulation tools within HLA communication architecture at the same time being unsophisticated and appropriate for users without extensive technical skills. The easy communications system consists of three main elements simulation tool, communication adapter and HLA.

1. Introduction

The development of simulation enables the researchers to explore more sophisticated problems at a more detailed level. At the same time this implies a necessity to use several models, or even different modelling tools. The real systems often deal with complicated socio-technical systems that can not be explored at the sufficient level of quality with one modelling tool. Different simulation approaches (multi agent systems, discrete events simulation, system dynamics, etc.) usually envisage the use of different simulation tools (software). This makes the issue of their mutual communication. There are several solutions, but they are complicated, expensive and not suitable for people without specific knowledge. This is an important constraint that impedes the development of distributed simulation especially within social and behavioural sciences.

Hence this paper describes a solution that would give the opportunity to ensure the communication between simulation tools within HLA communication architecture at the same time being unsophisticated and appropriate for users without extensive technical skills.

2. Former Research in Field of Distributed Simulation – Lessons Learned

This paper is based on previous research made by authors. First of them examined multi level modelling of environmental systems in the Ligatne Natural Trails. Different routes ensure movement of visitors either by foot or by car. The total amount of visitors and cars is permanently growing and that leads to plans for expanding of parking and traffic dispatching. But at the same time permanently growing amount of visitors makes pressure on functioning of ecosystem and regeneration possibilities of lawns in sightseeing places. Therefore, potential workload forecasting of the tourism object, which depending of tourists flows intensity, becomes important. In 2006 two separate simulation models were elaborated [3].

First - for throughput analysis of the trails and scenic routes, and planning the parking places. Functional model in this case was described as discrete event system and was simulated in EXTEND [1]. The second model was provided for estimation of other critical resource as capacity and quality of the sight place. Under the quality we understood the capabilities of regenerating of the nature resources (lawn, for instance) in given area influenced by the flow of the tourists with predefined intensity. In this case agent based approach was used and NetLogo [10] environment was selected. Only one problem still remained related with communication and synchronizing the separate models located on different places and operated in the real time.

EXTEND [1] is modelling environment supporting modelling, analysis and optimisation of the discrete-event and continuing processes. The environment is relatively open and well-linked with MS Office. It is possible to create user's component's using embedded ModL language, which is similar to C language. EXTEND allows the communications with ODBC, ActiveX and C classes.

NetLogo [10] is multi-platform multi-agent programming and modelling environment designed mostly for analysis of environmental systems and social phenomena. NetLogo is created in Java ensuring the platform independent environment, possibilities of object-oriented structuring and good programming options. NetLogo allows designing different extensions for communication with outer environment.

To ensure interoperability and information exchange among the models the convenient communication environment was necessary.

In further research it was concluded that although serious amount of simulation tools and simulators are created for modelling technical (EXTEND, ARENA, Witness, AutoMod, Simul8, STELLA etc.) as well as social systems (NetLogo,

AgentSheets, SWARM, RePast, MIMOSA etc.), nevertheless designing of heterogeneous simulation models is still difficult. One of the reasons is lack of suitable techniques for communications and synchronization of the various models inside the joint systems model. [2]

Thereafter test models were made to examine the possibilities to connect two different simulation tools using communication architecture. Two communication architecture environments were compared – CORBA and HLA – by experimenting with them and their capacity to work with certain load [2, 4]. Besides the technical comparison, it was concluded that one needs to have a good knowledge of programming otherwise it is impossible to organize and manage communication between simulation tools [2]. Therefore the aim of this paper is to analyze a new comprehensible or Easy Communication Concept and describe the mechanism for ensuring the communication of simulation tools for users without programming skills.

3. Communication Environment for Distributed Simulations

This section first describes the existent communication mechanisms and observed disadvantages. Afterwards the authors propose their communication system and describe its requirements in detail.

3.1. *Communication Mechanisms in Distributed Models*

One of them is HLA Blockset™ - a commercial product created by ForwardSim Inc. The HLA Blockset™ provides a library of Simulink® blocks specifically designed for the integration of HLA services into Simulink®. Using the HLA Blockset, you can connect your Simulink models to a distributed simulation using the High Level Architecture standard HLA 1.3 or IEEE 1516 [6]. But the product is supposed for the Simulink® modelling tool only.

Similarly in their research on distributed simulation systems Hibino *et.al* [5] uses similar approach. They propose a manufacturing adapter to connect manufacturing system simulators with HLA using a plug-in style and evaluate it using a hypothetical manufacturing system. To be more precise three major commercial based manufacturing system simulators as QUEST, SIMPLE++, and GAROPS are connected using the developed manufacturing adapter.

Both above mentioned examples share the central solution that permits to implement HLA functionality in the simulation tool. However to be able to use any of these communication systems, modelling expert needs to immerse oneself in HLA structure and principles of operation.

Therefore it is necessary to develop a communication adapter that would enable the co-operation between simulation tools without making the modelling expert to master the infrastructure of HLA in detail. The communication adapter should instead facilitate the work of modelling software user, so there is no need to think at the level of communication abstraction, but it is enough to define the name of communication channel and its properties (function and parameters).

3.2. *Requirements to Alternative Communication Mechanism*

The proposed communications system consists of three main elements: simulation tool, communication adapter and HLA. The main goal of this communication system is to provide a mechanism that does not demand from the user any special knowledge of HLA infrastructure nor the principles of its action nor programming skills. Further each of the elements and its role in the communication system is described.

3.2.1. *Simulation tool*

In order to be able to function in a communicative system, simulation tools have to be able to communicate in HLA and/or with different software. In this article strictly focus only one of these versions, namely, where simulation tools are not able to communicate in HLA, but can perform communication with other software (adapters) instead. In most cases this function is performed with some additional plug-ins, extensions or libraries. For example, NetLogo, that is a multi agent-modelling tool, uses different extensions [10], as well as discrete event modelling tool Extend that also allows using extensions [1].

But it is important that independent developers are allowed to create these extensions, thus promoting HLA communication. One should take into account that it is common for modelling tools to use extensions as functional libraries – i.e. they do not keep any live extension instances. That means there is no possibility to realise HLA communication in a direct way therefore an adapter is used. The adapter is carrying out the HLA communication and passing on the information to the extension of the simulation tool.

3.2.2. *HLA*

High Level Architecture (HLA) [8] is a concept of the architecture for distributed simulation systems. HLA ensures interoperability and reuses among simulations. It consists of rules that separate parts of distributed simulation model (federates) must follow to achieve proper interaction during a federation execution; Object Model Template that defines the format for specifying the set of common objects used by a federation (federation object model), their attributes, and relationships among them; Interface Specification, which provides interface to the Run-Time Infrastructure, which can be distributed and ties together federates during model execution. The distributed time management can be done, because all federates' nodes directly undertake synchronization roles. Therefore, the total simulation takes less time and the system is safer, unfortunately, implementation is more complex and laborious.

For this reason adapter that will ease the communication of simulation tools using HLA needs to be developed.

3.2.3. *Communication adapter*

Adapter is the central element from the perspective of this paper. It embraces communication from both sides – communication with simulation tool and communication with HLA. Adapter is like an interpreter that interprets HLA data to the format that is comprehensible for the simulation tool.

The communication among different simulation tools will be accomplished using HLA communication architecture. For the model to be able to perform its tasks in HLA environment, one needs an adapter. The communication adapter would provide the data exchange between the modelling tool and communication architecture. At the same time also the adapter needs to be easily manageable, so that the adjustment of simulation model would be possible for users without programming skills. The user has to be able to define understandable model communication parameters with the help of GUI, and another model has to be able to receive information according to pre-defined parameters.

3.2.4. *Description of communication systems operation using adapter*

The adapter is software module that is executed on the same machine as the simulation tool. The adapter will ensure the functions of a model within HLA architecture. HLA itself is used to make the functionality of these models and the results universal, so that they can be used by anyone that is able to connect to this federation.

The adapter (*Communication adapter* in Figure 1) may receive the data at any moment. This article does not refer to situations, where HLA Time Management ensures federation time advancing, as described by Ke Pan *et al.* [7], including the time advancing of the modelling tools.

The adapter should be able to store data and be ready to pass those to the simulation tool, whenever it requests for them. For this reason the data storage is used (*Data storage* in Figure 1). This data storage will ensure that the model receives all data in a time, even if it falls behind from other models. Additional reason for this solution would be the inability to inject data into running model. Therefore the receipt of data is organised by requests. See Figure 1 for a description of one model communication using adapter. The *Model* in Figure 1 represents the model that is created with a certain simulation tool or environment.

The communication between the model's library and the adapter is carried out using XML that ensures extensive and universal opportunities for data and communication description.

To ensure the communication with the model in this manner, the adapter has to look for communication requests at certain port at local host. Simulation tool will connect to the adapter with a request once in a certain period of time. This request is specified as XML-based document and hidden for end-user.

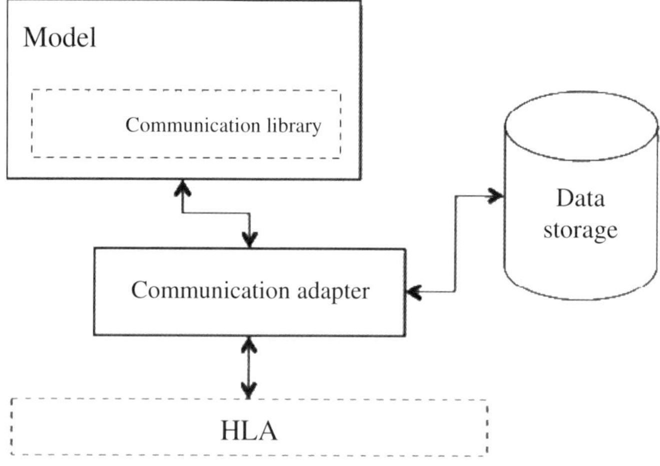

Figure 1. Model communication with adapter and data storage.

After the adapter returns data from data storage, which corresponds to the interaction for which the adapter has subscribed to in the HLA federation.

With the help of the adapter, the user can define information that he wants to interchange. The HLA sign-up configuration is accomplished with the help of adapter and has to be user-friendly. The adapter has to let the user to view all interactions of federation and all their properties, as well as the user needs to be enabled to subscribe to the interactions he is interested in with GUI.

When the user has signed up to an interaction, it has access to modelling tool. Further the user calls out the interaction in the modelling environment and receives data (the reception of data depends on the realization of extension). At the same time the user can define his interactions itself. It should be taken into account that the user has to be able to do this only with the input of the interactions name and parameters. In this case we assume that all parameters are defined with string data type, as this is very important when generating Federation Object Model (FOM). When the user has defined all parameters, then the adapter generates FOM and signs up to the federation (*adapter federer*). Every user-defined interaction is transmitted to a custom made federer – the configuration federer. This federer is located in another federation and it is responsible for FOM file. That means that configuration federer maintains the FOM file, according to which the modelling adapters create their federation.

Based on FOM the adapter connects to the federation (if there is no federation, then one is created), that functions according to the "rules" described in FOM. All interactions and their parameters are described in FOM. And also in conformity with FOM the adapters offer user functionality (published by adapters of other models) that can be used in simulation tools.

Configuration federer operates on the same machine where HLA. This federer operates independently from modelling federers, that means, modelling users are not responsible for its operations and do not have any direct impact on it.

4. Conclusions

Finally some important conclusions can be drawn regarding the distributed simulations and communication between models. First, it can be observed that the developers of simulation tools do not pay attention to the opportunities of models to communicate with other models, even of the same modelling environment. The paper outlines the structure of a comprehensible communication system and points out to its advantages.

Second, the existent mechanisms do not offer time synchronization option; therefore there is a need to invent data storage. Further research should be aimed at searching for such time synchronising options.

Third, future research should also seek for possibilities to ensure the transmission of more complicated data types.

At the same time it should be noted that not all simulation tools offer the creation of extensions, therefore the comprehensible communication system described in this paper would not be applicable for such tools.

Therefore if it is observed that computational modelling is revolutionizing the social and organizational sciences [9], then there are new challenges for engineering scientists in terms of enabling this process and empowering the researchers from other disciplines.

References

1. D. Krahl, The EXTEND Simulation Environment, in Proceedings of the 2002 Winter Simulation Conference/E. Yücesan, C.-H. Chen, J. L. Snowdon, and J. M. Charnes, eds., (2002).
2. E. Ginters, A. Silins, J. Andrusaitis, Communication in distributed simulation environment, In Proceedings of 6th WSEAS International Conference on Systems Science and Simulation in Engineering, Venice, Italy, (2007), 217-221.
3. E. Ginters, A. Silins, Multi-level Approach for Environmental Systems Modelling in the Ligatne Natural Trails. WSEAS Transactions on Systems, Issue 4, Volume 6, (2007), 795-801.
4. E. Ginters, A. Silins, Simulation Data Exchange in Distributed E-learning Environment, Proceedings of the 4th WSEAS/IASME International Conference on EDUCATIONAL TECHNOLOGIES (EDUTE'08), Corfu, Greece, (2008),138-143.
5. H. Hibino, Y. Fukuda, Y. Yura, K. Mitsuyuki, K. Kaneda, Manufacturing adapter of distributed simulation systems using HLA, Simulation Conference, Proceedings of the Winter conf., vol 2, (2002) 099-1107.
6. HLA Blockset™, ForwardSim Inc, High Tech Park of Québec, http://www.forwardsim.com/en/prod_hlab.php, (2009).
7. K. Pan, S.J. Turner, W. Cai, Z. Li, A Hybrid HLA Time Management Algorithm Based on Both Conditional and Unconditional Information, Parallel & Distrib. Comput. Center, Nanyang Technol. Univ., Singapore, (2008), 203-211.
8. K. Perumalla, Tutorial. Handling Time Management under the High Level Architecture, http://www.ornl.gov/~2ip/doc/perumalla-tutorialslides-iitsec06.pdf, (2009).
9. K.M. Carley, Computational organizational science and organizational engineering, Simulation Modelling Practice and Theory 10 (2002) 253–269.
10. U. Wilensky, NetLogo, Center for Connected Learning and Computer-Based Modeling, Northwestern University, Evanston, IL, http://ccl.northwestern.edu/netlogo/, (2009).

PART 2:
ACCOUNTING AND FINANCE

FUZZY ANALYSIS FOR ASSETS REPLACEMENT

GONZÁLEZ SANTOYO F., FLORES ROMERO B., FLORES JUAN J.
*Universidad Michoacana de San Nicolas de Hidalgo, Ciudad Universitaria,
Morelia, Michoacán, 58030, Mexico*

GIL-LAFUENTE A.M.
*Universidad de Barcelona
Barcelona, Spain*

CHÁVEZ R.
*Centro de Investigacion del Estado de Michoacan
Morelia, Michoacán, 58030, Mexico*

This paper presents a methodology to study the problem of fixed assets. The methodology is explained through the analysis of a company to solve the fixed assets problem. Fixed assets are of great value since they represent an important issue in a system's operation; their contribution to the efficient operation of the system is a key concept in the generation of the economic surplus of every company.

1. Introduction

The formulation of an equipment replacement plan plays an important role in determining the basic technology and the economical progress of every company. Changing machinery and equipment in a rush or inadequately, generates a decrease in the organization's equities, and therefore a decrease in cash availability to start new profitable projects. On the other hand, a late replacement originates (excessively) high operation and maintenance costs. Those are the reasons why a company must plan effectively and efficiently the replacement of all its assets, or else it will be in disadvantage with respect to other companies in the market, who do perform opportune replacements.

This is a common situation for business and government companies, as well as for individuals. They have to face the decision whether or not to stop using a given asset and replace it for a new one, or else, to continue using it. This kind of decision is found more and more often; as the competitive pressures increase in the business world, more high-quality goods and services are required in shorter and shorter response times.

Mass production seems to be the cheapest method to satisfy the market's needs. Thuesen H.G. et al. [5], establish that mass production demands a large amount of equity assets to be consumed in the process. Assets quickly become obsolete and inadequate for the job; they become replacement candidates. Not upgrading these assets continually may take the company to the point of generating important losses in its operation.

Replacement decisions face two basic options: the first one is to keep the asset for an additional period of time, the second one requires to immediately remove the current asset and replace it by a new one that guarantees the company a contribution to efficiency, effectiveness, and profitability.

The problem under study is to determine the optimal time and conditions when a given asset must be replaced, given that it is no longer contributing from the technical and financial points of view. Furthermore, this asset is no longer providing the quality expected and required by the global market.

2. Factors Causing Replacement

According to Coss Bu R. [1], the causes leading to replace a given asset are insufficiency and ineptitude, excessive maintenance, decreasing efficiency, and aging. Sullivan W.G. et al. [4] state that the replacement analysis and evaluation comes from changes in the economical conditions of its usage in the operation environment. The most important reasons to perform such an analysis are: wear off, requirements changes, technology, financial, economical, physical, and useful life of the asset.

Thuesen H.G. et al [5] present two basic reasons to consider asset replacement: physical deterioration and obsolescence.

In conclusion, the basic factors leading to replacement analysis are:
Insufficiency and ineptitude
Excessive maintenance
Decreasing efficiency
Aging
Physical Inadequacy (wear off)
Requirements modifications
Technology
Financing
Economic life
Possession life

Physical life

Useful life

Physical deterioration

The above factors need to be defined for an appropriate interpretation and use.

Insufficiency: The installed capacity is not enough to satisfy the demand level in the slot of time required for the machinery and equipment under study.

Excessive maintenance: The cost level associated to maintenance of the asset becomes excessive, so much that an economical-technical analysis is needed to determine if the required service could be provided at lower costs using other alternatives, and still providing efficiency, effectiveness, and quality.

Decreasing efficiency: When the costs caused by operation inefficiency of the asset are excessive, decreasing the quality of the product/service.

Aging: The result of research and development, causing better assets, making them more suitable, and with better technological features, cost, and quality than those of the previous generation, currently used in the company. Obsolescence is characterized by changes external to the asset, reason that fully justifies the replacement.

Physical inadequacy (wear off): Changes in the physical condition of the asset. It is common that by continuous use (aging) the asset operation becomes less efficient. The asset's routine maintenance costs increase notably. Equipment breaks more often and energy consumption increases. Unexpected events (accidents) affect the physical condition of drivers, possession economy, and machinery usage.

Requirements modification: Modified assets are used to produce goods/services that satisfy human needs. When demand increases or decreases, or its design changes, the economy of the involved assets may be modified.

Technology: The impact of technological changes varies for different kinds of assets. For instance, heavy machinery used in construction is less affected by technological changes than automatic manufacturing equipment. In general, unitary production costs and quality are influenced favorably by technological changes; as a result, newer and better ones replace current assets more frequently.

Financing: Financing factors imply opportunistic economical changes external to physical operation or usage of assets, producing important considerations. For instance, a company must take a decision to rent or buy a certain kind of asset. Replacement studies consider time, so it is necessary to determine the lifetime of the different types of assets. These types are:

104

Economic life: There exist several points of view. One is the lapse of time (years) that originates the minimum uniform annual cost for the possession and operation of an asset. This state is reached at the point where the decision agent is not willing to accept the marginal utility level. The criterion is:

$$CMa = \text{Marginal Cost} \tag{1}$$

$$UMa = \text{Marginal Utility} \tag{2}$$

Table 1. Decision rules

STATE	DECISION
CMa = UMa	Replacement (1st priority)
CMa < UMa	Keep asset
CMa > UMa	(late) replacement

Possession life: Elapsed time between date of purchase and the date when the asset is dismissed from the inventory.

Physical life: Elapsed time between date of purchase and its final dismissal, along a succession of owners.

Useful life: Elapsed time (years) during which an asset remains in productive service (main or backup). Estimated time where the asset is expected to be active in a company to generate an economic income.

3. Economic Life of a New Asset (Challenger)

In practice the useful life of an asset is unknown (defender or challenger). You cannot estimate it in a reasonable and adequate form, either.

The time an asset remains in productive service could extend indefinitely with the proper maintenance. In such a situation, it is convenient to know the economic life, the minimum equivalent uniform annual cost, annual total cost - EUAC (marginal), so that we can compare challenger and defender based on the evaluation of their economic lives and most favorable costs for each of them.

One of the classical definitions of an asset's economic life is the time that minimizes the EUAC. Economic life also refers to minimal cost life, or optimal replacement interval.

To compute the EUAC for a new asset one needs to have precise estimations of the Equity Investment, annual expenses, and market values for each year.

According to Sullivan W.G. et al. [4], estimations of the initial Equity Investment, annual expenses, and market value are useful to determine the present value (PV) during period k, before taxes. The equation used to compute PV is:

$$VP_k = I - VM_k\left(\frac{P}{F}, i\%, k\right) + \sum_{j=1}^{k} E_j\left(\frac{P}{F}, i\%, k\right)$$

$$VP_k = I - VM_k\left(\frac{P}{F}, i\%, k\right) + \sum_{j=1}^{k} E_j\left(\frac{P}{F}, i\%, k\right) \tag{3}$$

where I is the equity investment, VM_k the market value at period (k), E_j the annual expenses at period (j), and $(P/F, i\%, k)$ the future value factor brought to present from period (k)

$$\left(\frac{P}{F}, i\%, k\right) = \frac{1}{(1+i)^k} \tag{4}$$

$$\left(\frac{P}{F}, i\%, j\right) = \frac{1}{(1+i)^j} \tag{5}$$

To estimate the total marginal cost for every year (k), (CT_k), we use the following equation:

$$CT_k = VM_{k-1} - VM_k + iVM_{k-1} + E_k \tag{6}$$

We use the marginal total costs (or yearly), to determine the EUAC on every year before and including year (k), based on the equation for (CT_k). The minimum $EUAC_k$ during the asset's useful life identifies its economic life (Nc^*). Where $Nc^* = Min_k\{EUAC_k\}; k = 0,1,L\ ,n$

A new bulldozer (a powerful tractor with a broad upright blade at the front for clearing ground) will require an investment of $20,000.00, and is expected to have the market values and annual expenses indicated in columns 2 and 5, respectively in Table 2. If the TREMA before taxes is 10% annual, ¿How long should it be in service?

Table 2. Determination of the economic life of an asset

1	2	3	4	5	6	7
End of year (k)	VM End of year (k) ($)	Market value loss (VM) during year (k)	Equity Cost. 10% of VM starting year (k)	Annual Expenses (Ek)($)	CTk Margina l Total Cost	EUAC To Year (k)
0	20,000	---	---	---	---	---
1	15,000	5,000	2,000	2,000	9,000	9,000
2	11,250	3,750	1,500	3,000	8,250	8,643
3	8,500	2,750	1,125	4,620	8,495	8,598
4	6,500	2,000	850	8,000	10,850	9,084
5	4,750	1,750	650	12,000	14,400	9,084

4. Computing the Total Marginal Cost (CT_k)

The following equation is used to compute the Total Marginal Cost.

$$CT_k = VM_{k-1} - VM_k + iVM_{k-1} + E_k \tag{7}$$

Therefore:

$$CT_1 = VM_0 - VM_1 + i\,VM_0 + E_1 = 9,000$$

$$CT_2 = VM_1 - VM_2 + i\,VM_1 + E_2 = 8,250$$

$$CT_3 = VM_2 - VM_3 + i\,VM_2 + E_3 = 8,495$$

$$CT_4 = VM_3 - VM_4 + i\,VM_3 + E_4 = 10,850$$

$$CT_5 = VM_4 - VM_5 + i\,VM_4 + E_5 = 14,400$$

To compute the EUACk we use the following equation

$$EUAC_k = \left[\frac{\sum_{j=1}^{k} CT_j}{(1+i)^j} \right] (A/P, i\%, k) \tag{8}$$

$$= \left[\frac{\displaystyle\sum_{j=1}^{k} CT_j}{(1+i)^j} \right] \left[\frac{i(1+i)^k}{(1+i)^k - 1} \right]$$

For k = 1

$$\left[\frac{CT_1}{(1+i)^1} \right] \left[\frac{i(1+i)^1}{(1+i)^1 - 1} \right]$$

For k = 2

$$\left[\frac{CT_1}{(1+i)^1} + \frac{CT_2}{(1+i)^2} \right] \left[\frac{i(1+i)^2}{(1+i)^2 - 1} \right]$$

Generalizing up to (k) you obtain:

$$\left[\frac{CT_1}{(1+i)^1} + \frac{CT_2}{(1+i)^2} + \mathsf{L} + \frac{CT_k}{(1+i)^k} \right] \left[\frac{i(1+i)^k}{(1+i)^k - 1} \right]$$

Table 2 shows the values obtained in the computation. To determine the economic life Nc^*, we have:

$$Nc^* = Min_k \{ EUAC_k \}; k = 0,1,\mathsf{L}, n \tag{9}$$

Therefore:

$$Nc^* = Min_k \{ 9000, 8643, 8598, 9084, 9954 \} = 8598$$

Which corresponds to $N_t = 3$; i.e., replace machine at the end of year 3. The asset's EUAC at different times in its life are depicted in Figure 1.

In a replacement analysis, it is very important to determine the most adequate economic life of the defender (Nd^*). The decision rule is given in Table 3.

108

Table 3. Replacement decision rules

State	Decision
EUAC for Nd^* = EUAC for Nc*	Replacement
EUAC for Nd^* < EUAC for Nc*	Keep the asset
EUAC for Nd^* > EUAC for Nc*	Replacement

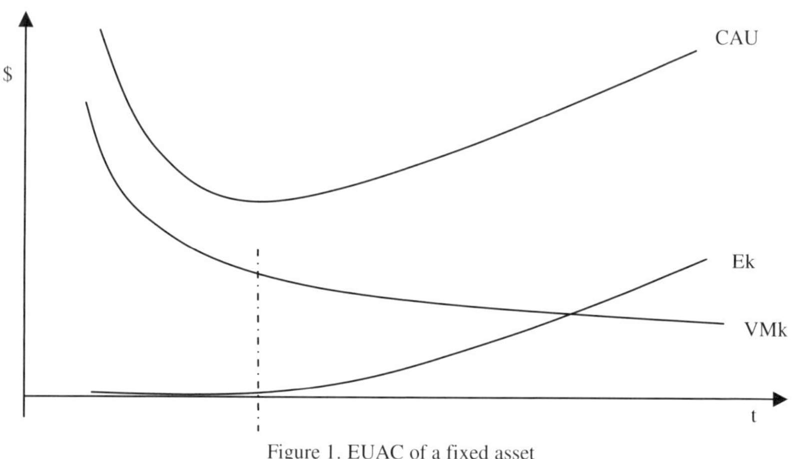

Figure 1. EUAC of a fixed asset

It is important to note that it does not matter how the remaining economic life of a defender (Nd^*) is determined, the decision to keep it does not mean that this must be done only for this period; on the contrary, the defender must be kept longer than its apparent economic life, while its marginal cost (total cost for an additional year of service) be less than the minimum EUAC of the best challenger. The replacement analysis may also determine the best economic life (Nd^*) for the defender.

This gives the opportunity to keep the defender as long as its EUAC on (Nd^*) be less than the minimum EUAC of the challenger, as shown in Table 3.

5. Fuzzy Analysis

Let us consider the preceding problem under uncertain or fuzzy criteria. With that in mind, we will consider VM to take on three values, supplied by field experts, considering possible market variations. After a considerable time, its market value will be much lower, due to depreciation. Assume the market value does not vary and after five years of life it is \$4,750.00. Let us consider an exponential depreciation behavior (negative k), so the derivative of VM with respect to time is:

$$\frac{d(VM)}{dt} = kVM \tag{10}$$

Estimated values for the equipment are VM_r, VM_m, and VM_s, with values of 19700, 20000, and 20150, respectively.   Given those values, formulating the differential equation, and integrating, we obtain:

$$\frac{d(VM)}{VM} = kdt, \qquad \int\frac{d(VM)}{VM} = k\int dt, \qquad VM = VM_0 e^{-kt}$$

Computing for each estimate on increasing order of value: For each estimate at t=0 and VM_0=values for each estimate at the beginning, the depreciated final value of the equipment at t=5 and VM_5 for all estimate is p=\$4,750.00, we obtain:

$$VM_r = 19700_0 e^{-0.284t}, \qquad VM_m = 20000_0 e^{-0.289t},$$
$$VM_s = 20150_0 e^{-0.29t}$$

From the above equations, we obtain Table 4, computing VM for each differential equation. VM_r is considered from its lowest value to average value, VM_m the average, and VM_s above average superior. VM_m is the same as in the previous case, taking also 10% of the cost of equities at the beginning of the year. Using the same annual expenses, Table 5 shows the results for CT_k, in terms of NBT:

Table 4. Fuzzy estimation of Vm

k	VMr	VMm	VMs
0	19700	20000	20150
1	14822	14980	15092
2	11152	11220	11304
3	8391	8403.9	8467
4	6313	6294.6	6342
5	4750	4714.6	4750

Table 5.

k	TREMA (10%)r	TREMA (10%)m	TREMA (10%)s	Ek	CTkr	CTk m	CTks	(EUAC) kr	(EUAC) km	(EUAC) Ks
0										
1	1970.0	2000.0	2015.0	2000	8848	9020	9072.6	8847.8	9019.9	9073
2	1482.2	1498.0	1509.2	3000	8152	8258	8297.4	8516.6	8657.1	8703
3	1115.2	1122.0	1130.4	4620	8497	8558	8587.8	8510.5	8627.2	8668
4	839.0	840.3	846.6	8000	10917	10950	10972	9029	9127.7	9165
5	631.3	629.4	634.1	12000	14194	14209	14226	9875.1	9960	9994

From Table 5, you can see that the economic life (ND) lies at year 3, for all estimates, since EUAC values are the minimum from the 5 years.

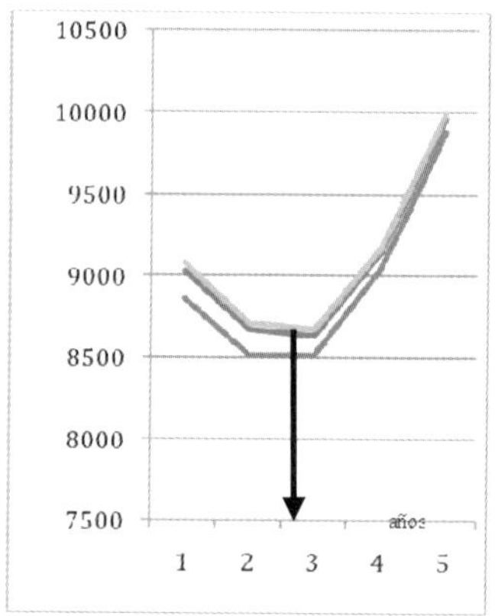

Figure 2. EUAC for each estimate

Nevertheless, when the estimate VM_r decreases below 19,604, the economic life of the equipment is 2 years (see Tables 6 and 7). Those results were not unexpected, since on Table 5, we observe that values at years 2 and 3 are close together. We have the same effect in this exercise, where values for years 2 and 3 are very close together, so taking a decision on any of these would be correct.

111

Table 6. Decreasing VMr

K	VMr	VMm	VMs
0	19604	20000	20150
1	14764	14980	15092
2	11119	11220	11304
3	8374	8403.9	8467
4	6307	6294.6	6342
5	4750	4714.6	4750

Table 7. Equipment replacement at constant interest rate

k	TREMA (10%)r	TREMA (10%)m	TREMA (10%)s	Ek	CTkr	CTkm	CTks	(EUAC) kr	(EUAC) km	(EUAC) Ks
1	1960.4	2000.0	2015.0	2000	8800	9020	9072.6	8800.0	9019.9	9073
2	1476.4	1498.0	1509.2	3000	8121	8258	8297.4	8476.8	8657.1	8703
3	1111.9	1122.0	1130.4	4620	8477	8558	8587.8	8476.8	8627.2	8668
4	837.4	840.3	846.6	8000	10905	10950	10972.0	9000.0	9127.7	9165
5	630.7	629.4	634.1	12000	14188	14209	14226.0	9849.7	9960.0	9994

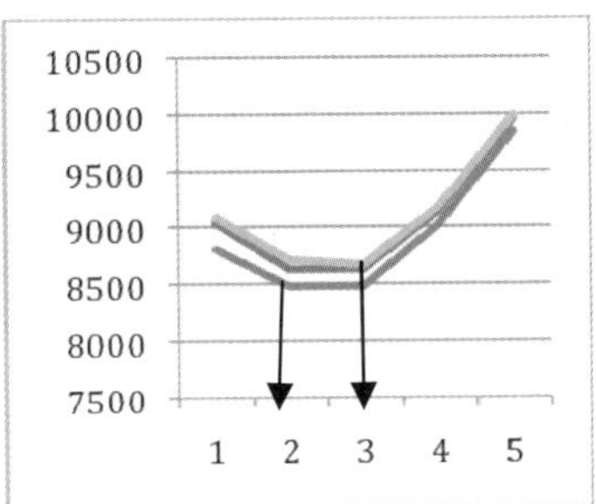

Figure 3.

Now let us consider the variations on interest rates, on the triplet (r, m, s), where the value of VM remains constant during the equipment's initial life. According to the group of experts, the results of forecasting interest rates for each year are shown in Table 8. Table 9 shows how variations on the interest rate affect directly the CT and EUAC.

According to the values of interest rates in their respective years, computed values for EUAC for triplet (r, m, s), (EUAC)kr indicates replacement must be done at the end of year 2, while (EUAC)km and (EUAC)ks indicate replacement is due at the end of year 3 (see Figure 4).

Table 8. Interest rate assignment for each year, given by experts

K (year)	Ir (%)	Im (%)	is (%)
1	9	10	13
2	8	10	14
3	9	10	12
4	7	10	12
5	9	10	11

Table 9. Results considering interest rate variations

k	TREMAr	TREMAm	TREMAs	Ek	CTkr	CTkm	CTks	(EUAC) kr	(EUAC) km	(EUAC) Ks
1	1800.0	2000.0	2600.0	2000	8797.5	8997.5	9597.5	8797.5	8997.5	9597.5
2	1200.2	1500.2	2100.3	3000	7948.9	8249.0	8849.1	**8393.4**	8641.0	9241.1
3	1012.8	1125.3	1350.4	4620	8444.8	8557.4	8782.4	8408.9	**8615.8**	**9102.5**
4	590.9	844.1	1013.0	8000	10700.3	10953.5	11122.4	8902.7	9119.5	9537.7
5	569.9	633.2	696.5	12000	14152.2	14215.5	14278.8	9762.5	9954.2	10314.

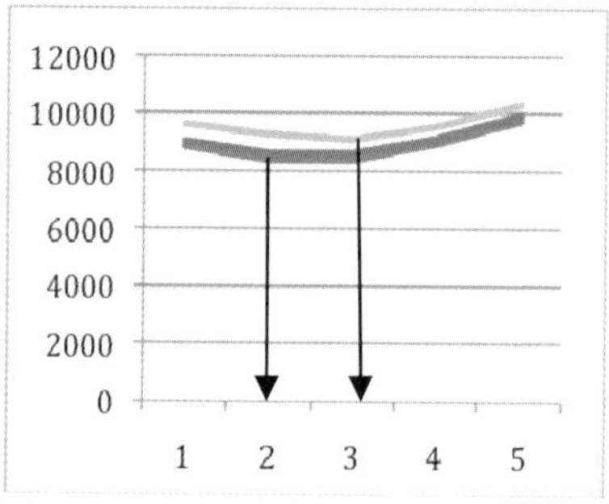

Figure 4.

According to the obtained results on the worst case (r), replacement is due at the end of year 2, while on the middle (m) and optimistic (s) cases, it is due at the end of year 3. This fact indicates that the equipment replacement can take place anywhere between those two periods. As mentioned before, if VM_r is less than 19604, replacement is also due in year 2.

The following example illustrates this case. An investor "W" needs to determine how long a bulldozer must be kept in service before replacing it by a new one (challenger). The defender is 2 years old, obtained with an original cost of $13,000.00, with a current VM of $5,000.00. If we keep it in service, its market values and annual costs are expected to be as indicated in Table 4.

It is important to determine the optimal time to keep the defender before replacing it by the challenger. For the previous case, the equities cost is represented by the TREMA corresponding to each interest rate on Table 8. Using the same methodology as in the previous case, we have:

Table 10. Market values and annual expenses

End of year (k)	(VM) End of year (k) ($)	Annual expenses (Ek) ($)
1	4,000	5,500
2	3,000	6,600
3	2,000	7,800
4	1,000	8,800

For this case, $Nd^{*}_{r,m,s} = Min_k \{ EUAC_k \} = 1$

The minimal values of $EUAC_{r,m,s}$ are \$6950, \$7,000, and \$7150, corresponding to keep the defender one more year.

Table 11. Computation of economic life

End of year (k)	(VM) eoy (k)	Loss (VM) dy (k)	Equity cost (VMr) boy	Equity cost (VMm) boy	Equity cost (VMs) boy	Annual Expenses (E_k)	(CT_{kr})	(CT_{km})	(CT_{ks})	(EUACkr)	EUACkm	EUACks
0	5,000	---		---			---	---	---	---	---	---
1	4,000	1,000	450	500	650	5,500	6950	7,000	7150	6950	7,000	7150
2	3,000	1,000	320	400	560	6,600	7920	8,000	8160	7417	7,476	7622
3	2,000	1,000	270	300	360	7,800	9070	9,100	9160	7919	7,966	8081
4	1,000	1,000	140	200	240	8,800	9940	10,000	10040	8385	8,405	8490

The marginal costs (CTk) of keeping the defender one more year are \$7920, \$8,000, and \$8160. Those values are less than the minimum EUAC of the challenger, which is \$8,598.

CT3 of the defender is greater than the minimal $EUAC_{r,m,s}$ (\$8444.87, \$8,598, \$8582.48) of the challenger. Therefore, the recommendation based on the obtained information from the analysis, we have:

"It is cheaper to keep the defender two more years and then replace it by the challenger"

The equipment replacement is required in situations where its efficiency tends to deteriorate with time - Sasieni M. et al. [3]. The efficiency level can be restored to a previous level using some corrective action. The problem to solve is to determine the times when such a corrective action must be performed, to optimize the equipment effectiveness

6. Conclusions

Given the above results, we conclude that to reach a better tecno-financal operation point in a company, we need to know accurately the different processes that form part of the company, given that those processes are responsible for the generation of the added value; similarly the fixed assets composing those processes. The determination of the operative evolution, computed from the economic perspective, and the flexibility of the decision making process using fuzzy techniques, allow us to know until what point in their lives machinery and equipment efficiently and effectively contribute to the economic goals of the company.

References

1. Coss Bu, Raúl. *Análisis y Evaluación de Proyectos de Inversión*. Limusa, México, 4ta. reimpresión, 1992.
2. González Santoyo, F. *Estrategias para la toma de decisiones empresariales en un entorno de incertidumbre*. Tesis de Doctor en Ciencias. Centro de Investigación y Desarrollo del Estado de Michoacán (CIDEM). Morelia México. 2008.
3. Sasieni, M. et al. *Investigación de Operaciones*. Limusa, México. 1980.
4. Sullivan, W. G. et al. *Ingeniería Económica de Degarmo*. Pearson Prentice Hall. México. 2004.
5. Thuesen, H. G. et al. *Ingeniería Económica*. Prentice Hall Internacional. México. 1981.

INVESTIGATION AND SCIENTIFIC EVOLUTION OF COST ACCOUNTING PROGRAMMES[*]

ALFREDO ROCAFORT NICOLAU, FRANCISCO MARTÍN PEÑA
*Accounting Department, Area of Financial Economics
and Accounting, University of Barcelona,
Diagonal 690-696, 08034-Barcelona, Spain*

JOSÉ DANIEL BARQUERO CABRERO
*Economy and Business Department,
ESERP Business School,
Girona, 24, 08010-Barcelona, Spain*

The scientific contents of cost accounting are the object of diverse subjective interpretations. This debate will begin with a terminology discussion (cost accounting, management accounting) and will become more acute when referring to the widely understood description of its evolution. This study approaches the debate by proposing the analysis of five investigation programmes which the authors consider both necessary and sufficient in order to explain the current reality of cost accounting.

1. Accounting as a scientific building in process

1.1. The logical-deductive model

In the attempt of formalizing proposed by R. Mattessich (1964), accounting as measurement tool remains configured as a model supported in axioms and basic definitions; deductivism accounting eases the establishment of inter-relationships between the original terms and the axioms and the reach of general application norms or set of statements similar to mathematical theorems.

Another method of scientific construction was the way of the postulates and principles, within whose proposals that of M. Moonitz (1961)[†] stands out, which classifies the postulates in three categories: environment, accounting and

---

[*] This investigation work is supported by the Accounting Department from the University of Barcelona.

[†] Cf. C. Mallo (1982); J. Túa Pereda (1982), L Cañibano Calvo (1979).

imperatives; with quantification, exchange of goods, entities, time periods and units of measurement being the environment postulates referred to.

1.2. Scientific progress and paradigm - programme dilema

The cited formulae allow the drawing of the scientific building of accounting such as it is found here and now. It fits to adopt an evolutionary method: starting from the present reality and taking into account the distinct lines of investigation open, outline how it has reached here with the aim of not only understanding more coherently what has been achieved concretely up to the present but also to anticipate the future of accounting science, evading past errors.

To approach this way, a large group of authors today still consider the paradigm concept defined by T. Kuhn (1962) as a useful tool not only to describe the evolution of the empirical sciences, but also to explain, within social sciences, the polyhedral history of accounting in its most recent stage.

But there are those who, in the same way as the authors of this work, rule out the sociological approach based on conflict implicit in the kuhnian paradigm concept, and prefer to use the alternative investigation programme concept, outlined by I. Lakatos (1965) at the time of examining the historical development of accounting science[*].

The defenders of the paradigmatic evolution show as a main argument the fact that the paradigm, reduced to a programme, is removed from the inherent conflictive passion and only investigative passion remains, which is not sufficient enough to explain the existence of periods of extreme scientific creativity, such as that experienced by cost accounting in the decade 1985-1995, and periods of creative lethargy such as the previous years[†].

Deep down, the dispute between defenders of Kuhn and defenders of Lakatos exposes two beliefs found around the true cause of scientific progress: the mere emotion of discovery or the *Sturm und Drang* unleashed from generational collisions. Our contribution tries to corroborate the lakatosian conception applied to cost accounting.

---

[*] *"According to my methodology the great scientific achievements are research programmes which can be evaluated in terms of progressive and degenerating problem shifts; and scientific revolutions consist of one research programme superseding (overtaking in progress) another"*: Imre Lakatos (ed. by John Worrall, Gregory Currie), The methodology of scientific research programmes, Press Syndicate of the University of Cambridge, UK, (1980), p.110.

[†] M. Kelly– M.Pratt (1992), *Purposes and paradigms in management accounting: beyond economic reductionism*, Accounting Education, 1 (3), 225 – 246.

2. Evolutive theory of cost accounting

2.1. Postulations and principles in cost accounting

Moving the postulations and principals generally accepted of the theory of cost accounting is arduous and often fruitless work which opens the necessary formulation of the basic presumptions and from those the opportune precision in internal information of decisional type which represent cost accounting.

In this way accounting, configured as a science, has to recompose its versatility when applied to cost accounting. As Bueno Campos warned: *"For accounting to become an operative instrument there is a need to restructure its methodology, economic and logical criteria must be used, more than simple mechanics or of judicial- patrimonial characteristics, as conventional accounting has come managed."*[*]

2.2. Crisis and change of paradigm in the 1990's

Was there a change of paradigm in the 1990's? The answer of J. Lee is negative: in the decade of the 90's there was no change of paradigm, but a decade which began "in the atmosphere that a new paradigm was needed in cost accounting".[†] At the same time the cited author pleaded for "a new paradigm within which to map the proper courses of action in cost accounting research".[‡]

But in spite of some authors identifying the vast diffusion of ABC (*Activity Based Costing*) as a change of paradigm, given that its defenders usually confronted *traditional* cost accounting with accounting of the company of the future, what is certain is that the best revolutionaries which were invoked and the accounting answers to improve the management control and competitiveness of occidental companies against Japanese ones, it did not take off, given that deep down the ABC did not represent a new model either (J. Lee, 2003).

---

[*] Bueno Campos, Eduardo; *Direct costing*, Hervi, Madrid, (1972) p.

[†] John Y. Lee, *Cost System Research Perspectives*, M.J.Epstein – J.Y.Lee, Advances in Management Accountig, vol 11, Kidlingtong, Oxford, Elsevier Science Ltd., (2003) p. 41.

[‡] John Y. Lee, *Managerial accounting changes for the 1990's*, Reading MA, Addison-Wesley (1987).

3. The evolution of investigation programmes

3.1. Programmes valid for cost accounting

Our presentation aims to explain the recent evolution of cost accounting through the identification of its investigation programmes. The origin and description of the five following programmes will be converted into necessary and sufficient indicators of the progress reached to this date by the discipline, especially during the last three decades.

- Programme focused on calculation of costs and valuation problems.
- Programme based on concepts and processes of planning and control.
- Programme on information of relevant costs for decision making.
- Programme on binomial technological cost-value.
- Programme on cost information in public and environmental entities.

The simultaneous relevance of these cost accounting programmes in the last decades, far from representing a doctrinal contradiction, has an internal cohesion meaning with the same essence as cost accounting (A. Rocafort and F. Martín. 1991).

3.2. Cost and valuation

In the origins of the Industrial Revolution of the 19th Century the initial posing of cost accounting to resolve problems as simple as the cost of industrial products arose and, as a consequence, to designate the necessary sale prices. In this pre-scientific period, the essential objective was the operating calculation of product costs. With posterity, now entering the 20th Century, the development of this focus puts emphasis on the valuation of factors and products, in the procedures and implementation of the cost system, in the distribution tables between direct and indirect costs, etc.

One of the most representative works of this focus was constituted by Th. Lang (1944), in which four essential characteristics are combined: a) the preponderance of the informative character, analytical and of control, b) the analysis of the projected system to the cost of products through the aggregation of the distinct factors of cost, inventory control and types of production, c) the generalized use of inorganic or product costs, margining the meaning of cost localization, d) the beginning of formulae and variations of standard costs. In the same way as considered by Th. Lang, among the authors most representative of the American school, in the European school, with certain clarifications, the Danish professor P. Hansen (1962) stands out.

This first programme, of the five listed also spans the focuses of direct costing (1940-1950) and ABC (1990's): The ABC focus contains the precise elements which structure the calculation of costs referred to as the activities which occur in the sphere of the company, in whichever area of work and not only in production.

3.3. Planning and control

The formulation of this programme is owed in the majority to Continental-European authors. The assumption from the beginning is none other than the global modeling of business planning, projecting as a manifesto objective the determination of the internal result of the company.

The origin of this programme may be found in the School of Cologne, represented by Eugen Schmalenbach (1873 - 1955). A programme which crystallized in the proposal of Account Planning of Business Accounting. The Decree of 11th November 1937, in the period of Nazi Germany, collected the proposal. E. Schmalenbach formulated an account system incardinated to radical monism and, although it observes the limitations it may entail, proposes a decimal classification of the accounts. The French Accounting Plan of 1947, adapted in 1957 and revised in 1982, as much as the approval in Spain in 1978 of the Ministerial Order over Exploitation Analytical Accounting or Group 9 of the General Accounting Plan, design a countable planning attempt for internal accounting, in the way that this is the second investigation programme.

Plans facilitate computerization and, because of this, can provide an unquestionable usefulness. Once World War II had passed, the phenomenon of countable planning and standardization extended universally, backed by professional associations, the state and transnational organizations. The Accounting Plan for North American corporations came driven in the U.S.A. by the American Accounting Association and other organizations such as the AIA (*American Institute of Accountants*) and the AICPA (*American Institute of Certified Public Accountants*); in the scope of cost accounting, in 1971 and with the backing of the AICPA, the Congress of the United States created the Cost Accounting Standard Board destined to the emission of internal accounting norms and the calculation of costs, to initially establish this in companies the Defense Department was contracted, projecting a notable influence throughout the accounting profession.

In spite of the fact that the cited CASB (*Cost Accounting Standard Board*) disappeared in 1980, the significance of the norms which were emanated (CAS norms) is unquestionable: the 19 norms in force in its day have had a lasting impact on the accounting profession. The CASB which emerged through federal law in 1988 deal with the controlling of these norms, which performed an important part for the contractors of the time who operated with the state.

3.4. Decision making

This programme experienced a strong expansion in the 1960's and 1970's between cost accounting investigators, and this situation has repeated in present times. The intention to contribute is understood as a programme based on decision making, from the countable scope to the rational formation of prices and to conclude, the economical analysis of distinct business options from short to long term. Following this programme, the costs, as well as offering a base to determine profits, for the planning of results and for control, contribute valid information for decision making. Its decisional projection converts cost accounting into the information system positioned to provide, valid information for planning, the control and making of decisions.

C.T. Horngren (2008) affirms that *"the essence of the administrative process is decision making"*, and for this identifies management accounting with cost accounting. However, many mentors of the management accounting concept observe the insufficiency of traditional cost accounting to the effects of decision making, marking an evolution up to the amplitude of the field of investigation of the discipline. Management accounting would overflow, for its extension, into classical cost accounting, which remains implicitly integrated in the previous.

M.I. Blanco Dopico and S. Gago Rodríguez (1993) openly point that the lines of investigation of management accounting in the 1970's and beginning of the 1980's, went bound to management accounting as a decision system, management accounting as an information system and management accounting as a system of control.

3.5. The binomial technological cost-value

In the decade of the eighties, as a consequence of relevant technological development produced in the international economic sphere, criticisms of management accounting were formed which justified, maybe excessively, what came to be called the management accounting crisis. In essence, this programme assumes to move the focus of interest towards the synchronization of the client's expectations (value) and the production of the product or service of the firm (cost).

A. Rocafort and F. Martin (1991) signalled three reasons which justified the criticisms mentioned: a) the evident fact that very few businesses use a very academically defined counting system and almost perceive it as superfluous, b) the appearance of new focuses and production management models (JIT, Lean Production), c) the existence of more and more refined information and telecommunication technology.

In this time P. Mevellec (1988) promoted *"a revolution in the field of technical data collecting and in the form of understanding the processes of analytical accounting"*. That time is now a reality, and as a more immediate consequence it is observed how the necessary time for the elaboration of the internal reports relative to cost control has inverted its structure, drastically reducing the time that the former inverted in the sampling and treatment of the production data phase.

The traditional focus of cost accounting had economic control of production as an objective. To the extent that the productive systems advanced in complexity, analytical accounting complicated in itself the methods of calculation and cost control. Specifically in that gradual complication of the accounting system is where some authors began to see one of the main weaknesses of analytical accounting against the current methods of production simplification.

In line with this programme, R.S. Kaplan (1988) cited the case of a transport company which considered itself satisfied with the operation control system in its more than five thousand centres. Difficulties arose when tariff restrictions were relaxed on the services offered. From then on the company considered it necessary – and managed to stabilize – a cost calculation and analysis system which allowed it to face the challenges of the competition.

For R.S. Kaplan a single system capable of satisfying the demands which the diverse functions of any cost system raises does not exist. Although companies can use a single method to obtain all the corresponding data for the transactions they perform, the treatment of that information demands independent and specific development depending on the recipients and the objectives.

In the same way the protracted and debatable classical analysis of the deviations is substituted by a simpler system of variations of the real costs faced with the estimated costs as competitive for a determined market. Beginning from the previous statement of inferior costs-objective to the actual costs of the company, the evolution of the last with respect to those, still always registering unfavourable deviations, signals the level of compromise of the company with the purpose of continuous improvement and following reduction of costs. More than alarm signals for a given period, the new deviations are converted into an interesting chronological register of the progress (or deterioration) operated by the adopted production system.

3.6. Efficiency and control of public and environmental spending

It is generally accepted that a rising field of financial law is composed of the sector of legal order whose object is the control of execution of deposits and public spending. The sociological and political tendency which characterizes the last decades is projected in the economical field with requirements of financial transparency and of holding different types of control over financial activity.

Following J.M. Buchanan (2003) the political programme should contain a fiscal offer (of income and costs) which the citizen, by voting for one option or another, will assume, demanding one alternative or another. The tendency of control of public spending is directed towards two specific objectives: 1) eficiency control in the application of alternative resources to satisfy public needs; 2) Control of effectiveness of public spending.

The fiscal "revolution" at the end of the 1970's in some states of North America came to capture the growing concern of citizens of information and control of state activity. Setting a precedent, the trial of budgets for programmes or the technique of a budget base zero are clearly accounting applied to the management of the public.

It fits to establish a costs information system based specifically not on management techniques and rendering of accounts to budgetary style, but, considering that it is necessary but insufficient, instigate the conscience of costs through the specific development of analytical accounting for the public sector. An extension of this programme is the incorporation of a new sensibility which has overflowed into the doctrine of CSR (*Corporate Social Responsibility*) and also into rendering of accounts (*accounting*).* In spite of the fact that in this sector a great profusion of legal rules, efficient management of the limited resources is called to be a central element of accounting investigation for decision making in public entities, which exceed the budgetary focus and confer in administrative organizations the necessary decisive elements for an

---

* M. Kelly and M. Alam, *Management Accounting and the Stock Value Model*, JAMAR, vol. 6, nº 1 (2008), p. 76.

indispensable innovation facing international competitiveness of the economic group. The aforementioned programmes do not consider the environmental problem as a field of analysis of cost accounting.[*]

4. Conclusions

The investigation into and through the five programmes which remain open to investigators of cost accounting not only allows the demarcation of a wide field over which the scientific building of cost accounting has at present been constructed, but also the drawing of the evolution of the discipline, pointing to its immediate future.

However, and apart from the time of emergency of the Japanese challenge in the commercial field (1980's), it is not possible to recognize the generational tensions foreseen by Kuhn for the moment of birth of new paradigms. This shows that accounting evolution can be explained through analysis and enumeration of investigation programmes, without need to fall back on paradigmatic changes.

References

1. M. I. Blanco Dopico, and S. Gago Rodríguez; *Las líneas de investigación en la Contabilidad de gestión*: Sáez Torrecilla, Ángel (coord.); *Cuestiones actuales de contabilidad de costes*, McGraw Hill - ACDDI, Madrid, (1993), pp. 67 a 110.
2. M. Bromwich and A. Bhimani, *Management accounting: evolution not revolution*, CIMA, Londres (1989).
3. J. M. Buchanan, *The origins and development of a research program*, Center for Study of Public Choice, George Mason University, Fairfax, Virginia, (2003).
4. L.Cañibano Calvo; *Teoría actual de la contabilidad*, ICE, Madrid (1979).
5. S.Carmona Moreno, *Cambio tecnológico y contabilidad de Gestión*, Instituto de Contabilidad y Auditoría de Cuentas, Madrid (1993).
6. P.Hansen, *The accounting concept of profit: an analysis and evaluation in the light of the economic theory of income and capital*, København, Einar Harcks Forlag (1962).

---

[*] D.R.Hansen and M.M. Mowen, *Environmental Cost Management*, Management Accounting, Thomson-South-Western, (2005), pp. 490-526.

7. Ch.T.Horngren, G.Foster, S.M.Datar, and M.Rajan, *Cost accounting: a managerial emphasis*, Prentice Hall; 13th edition (2008)

8. H.T.Johnson and R.S.Kaplan, *Relevance lost. The rise and fall of management accounting,* Harvard Business School Press, Boston Mss., (1987).

9. R.S.Kaplan. *One cost system isn't enough*, Harvard Business Review, Jan-Febr (1988).

10. T.Kuhn, *The structure of scientific revolutions*, International Encyclopedia of Unified Science, ed. O. Neurath and R. Carnap (1962).

11. Th.Lang, *Cost accountants' handbook.* The Ronald Press Company, New York (1944).

12. I.Lakatos and A. Musgrave (eds.), *Criticism and the Growth of Knowledge:* Proceedings of the International Colloquium in the Philosophy of Science, London 1965, Cambridge, UK: Cambridge University Press Vol. 4 (1970).

13. J.L.Luft, *Long-term change in management accounting: Perspectives from historical research*, Journal of Management Accounting Research, (1997).

14. C.Mallo Rodríguez; *Contabilidad analítica. Costes, rendimientos, precios y resultados,* Instituto de Planificación Contable, Ministerio de Hacienda, Madrid, 2ª ed. (1982).

15. R.Mattessich, *Accounting and analytical methods*, RD. Irwin, Homewood, Illinois (1964).

16. P.Mévéllec, La comptabilité analytique face à l'évolution technologique, Revue Française de Gestion, Jan-Febr (1988).

17. M.Moonitz, The basic postulates of accounting, Accounting Research Study, n° 1, AICPA (1961).

18. A.Rocafort Nicolau and F.Martín Peña; Just in time para empresas españolas, Ed. Miquel, Barcelona (1991).

19. J.Túa Pereda; Principios y normas de contabilidad. Historia, metodología, y entorno de la regulación contable, Instituto de Planificación Contable, Ministerio de Economía y Hacienda, Madrid, (1983).

CLAIM RESERVING WITH FUZZY REGRESSION AND THE TWO WAYS OF ANOVA

JORGE DE ANDRES-SÁNCHEZ

University Rovira i Virgili Department of Business Administration
Facultat de Ciencies Econòmiques, Reus, Spain

The mutant and uncertain behaviour of insurance environments does not make advisable to use a wide data-base when calculating claim reserves and so, quantifying provisions with Fuzzy Numbers becomes suitable. This paper develops a claim reserving method that combines Ishibuchi and Nii's extension (2001) to the fuzzy regression method with the scheme for claim reserving proposed by Kremer (1982).

1. Introduction

Fuzzy Sets Theory (FST) has been applied successfully in several areas of Business Management as capital budgeting, accounting, marketing or human resources. Several outstanding examples are [9, 10, 11, 12]. Regarding actuarial analysis, one of the most interesting areas of FST is Fuzzy Data Analysis (FDA). As Statistics, FST provides many techniques for searching and ordering the information contained in empirical data. Within an actuarial context, FDA has been used in several areas. So [7] and [17] use FDA for underwriting and reinsurance decisions, whereas [21] proposes using FDA for ratemaking and risk clustering. Likewise [1,14,15,21] adjust functions of actuarial interest with FST techniques.

Within claim reserving field, [1] adapts the schema developed in [3] to the use of Fuzzy Regression (FR) and [2] has extended Taylor's geometric separation model also to the use of FR. In this way, the present paper proposes a claim reserving method that mixes FR with the methodology by Kremer in [16], which has been used intensively in actuarial literature.

The structure of the paper is as follows. In the next section we shall describe the aspects of fuzzy arithmetic and the FR method in [13] that generalises well-known Tanaka's regression method [19]. Section 3 develops our claim reserving method. We then show a numerical application based on real data. Finally, we state the most important conclusions of the paper.

126

2. Fuzzy arithmetic and fuzzy regression

2.1. *Some aspects of fuzzy numbers*

For practical purposes, Triangular Fuzzy Numbers (TFNs) are widely used Fuzzy Numbers (FNs) since they are easy to handle arithmetically and they can be interpreted intuitively. We shall symbolise a TFN $\tilde{a}$ as $\tilde{a} = (a, l_a, r_a)$ where a is the centre and l_a and r_a are the left and right spreads, respectively. A TFN is characterised by its membership function $\mu_{\tilde{a}}(x)$ or by its α-cuts, a_α, as:

$$\mu_{\tilde{a}}(x) = \begin{cases} \dfrac{x - a + l_a}{l_a} & a - l_a < x \le a \\[2ex] \dfrac{a + r_a - x}{r_a} & a < x \le a + r_a \\[2ex] 0 & \text{otherwise} \end{cases} \tag{1a}$$

$$a_\alpha = \left[\underline{a}(\alpha), \overline{a}(\alpha)\right] = \left[a - l_a(1 - \alpha), a + r_a(1 - \alpha)\right] \tag{1b}$$

Let be a real valued function $y = f(x_1, x_2, \ldots, x_n)$. Then, if $x_1, x_2, \ldots, x_n$ are the FNs $\tilde{a}_1, \tilde{a}_2, \ldots, \tilde{a}_n$, $f(\cdot)$ induces the FN $\tilde{b} = f(\tilde{a}_1, \tilde{a}_2, \ldots, \tilde{a}_n)$ whose α-cuts, b_α, can be obtained from $a_{1_\alpha}, a_{2_\alpha}, \ldots, a_{n_\alpha}$, by doing:

$$a_\alpha = f(\tilde{a}_1, \tilde{a}_2, \ldots, \tilde{a}_n)_\alpha = f(a_{1_\alpha}, a_{2_\alpha}, \ldots, a_{n_\alpha}) \tag{2}$$

Likewise [4] shows that if the function $f(\cdot)$ is increasing with respect to the first m variables, $m \le n$, and decreasing with respect to the last $n-m$, then:

$$b_\alpha = \left[\underline{b}(\alpha), \overline{b}(\alpha)\right] = \left[f\left(\underline{a_1}(\alpha), \ldots \underline{a_m}(\alpha), \overline{a_{m+1}}(\alpha), \ldots \overline{a_n}(\alpha)\right), f\left(\overline{a_1}(\alpha), \ldots \overline{a_m}(\alpha), \underline{a_{m+1}}(\alpha), \ldots \underline{a_n}(\alpha)\right)\right] \tag{3}$$

If a FN $\tilde{b}$ is obtained from a linear combination of the TFNs $\tilde{a}_i = (a_i, l_{a_i}, r_{a_i})$, $i = 1, \ldots, n$, i.e. $\tilde{b} = \sum_{i=1}^{n} k_i \tilde{a}_i$, $k_i \in \Re$, $\tilde{b}$ will be the TFN, $\tilde{b} = (b, l_b, r_b)$, where:

$$b = \sum_{i=1}^{n} a_i k_i \,, \quad l_b = \sum_{\substack{i=1 \\ k_i \ge 0}}^{n} l_{a_i} |k_i| + \sum_{\substack{i=1 \\ k_i < 0}}^{n} r_{a_i} |k_i| \,, \quad r_b = \sum_{\substack{i=1 \\ k_i \ge 0}}^{n} r_{a_i} |k_i| + \sum_{\substack{i=1 \\ k_i < 0}}^{n} l_{a_i} |k_i| \tag{4}$$

To defuzzify FNs we propose using the expected value of a FN developed in [5], which for $\tilde{a}$, we symbolise as $EV[\tilde{a}, \beta]$. This value can be obtained by introducing the decision-maker risk aversion with the parameter β, $0 \le \beta \le 1$:

$$EV[\tilde{a}, \beta] = (1 - \beta) \int_0^1 \underline{a}(\alpha) \, d\alpha + \beta \int_0^1 \overline{a}(\alpha) \, d\alpha \tag{5a}$$

Notice that the expected value of a FN is an additive measure, and so:

$$EV\left[\sum_{i=1}^{n}\tilde{a}_i,\beta\right]=\sum_{i=1}^{n}EV[\tilde{a}_i,\beta] \qquad (5b)$$

2.2. *Fuzzy regression model with asymmetric coefficients*

We use the fuzzy regression (FR) method developed in [13], which is an extension of [19]. The explained variable is a linear combination of the explanatory variables and this relationship should be obtained from a sample of n observations $\{(y_1,x_1),\ (y_2,\ x_2),\ldots,(y_j,x_j),\ldots,(y_n,x_n)\}$ where x_j is the jth observation of the explanatory variable, which is m-dimensional: $x_j = (x_{1j},x_{2j},\ldots,x_{ij},\ldots,x_{mj})$. Moreover x_{ij} is the observed value for the ith variable in the jth observation which is crisp. So, y_j is the jth observation of the explained variable, $j=1,2,\ldots,n$ and may either be a crisp value or a confidence interval. It can be represented as $y_j = \left[\underline{y_j},\overline{y_j}\right]$, where $\underline{y_j}$ ($\overline{y_j}$) is the lower (upper) extreme of the interval y_j. We must estimate the following fuzzy linear function:

$$\tilde{Y}_j = \tilde{a}_0 + \tilde{a}_1 x_{1j} + \ldots + \tilde{a}_m x_{mj} \qquad (6)$$

where $\tilde{Y}_j$ is the estimation of y_j after adjusting $\tilde{a}_0,\tilde{a}_1,\tilde{a}_2,\ldots,\tilde{a}_m$

As it is usually assumed we model the parameters $\tilde{a}_i$ as TFN, and so: $\tilde{a}_i = (a_i, l_{a_i}, r_{a_i})$, $i=0,1,\ldots,m$. Thus, the estimate of y_j, $\tilde{Y}_j$, in (6) is a TFN that we will name $\tilde{Y}_j = (Y_j, l_{Y_j}, r_{Y_j})$. It is calculated from (4):

$$Y_j = a_0 + \sum_{i=1}^{m} a_i x_{ij}\ ,\ \ l_{Y_j} = l_{a_0} + \sum_{\substack{i=1\\x_{ij}\geq 0}}^{m} l_{a_i}\left|x_{ij}\right| + \sum_{\substack{i=1\\x_{ij}<0}}^{m} r_{a_i}\left|x_{ij}\right|\ ,\ \ r_{Y_j} = r_{a_0} + \sum_{\substack{i=1\\x_{ij}\geq 0}}^{m} r_{a_i}\left|x_{ij}\right| + \sum_{\substack{i=1\\x_{ij}<0}}^{m} l_{a_i}\left|x_{ij}\right| \qquad (7)$$

To fit $\tilde{a}_0,\tilde{a}_1,\tilde{a}_2,\ldots,\tilde{a}_m$ we first have to determine the cores $a_0, a_1,\ldots,a_m$ with OLS. These estimates are named as $a_0{}',\ a_1{}',\ldots,a_m{}'$. To do this, we reduce $y_j=1,2,\ldots,n$ to crisp representative values (e.g. the centres of the confidence intervals). Subsequently, we have to determine the parameters l_{a_i} and r_{a_i}, that must minimise the spreads of $\tilde{Y}_j$ and simultaneously maximise the level at which y_j $j=1,2,\ldots,n$ are contained within $\tilde{Y}_j$. If we require a minimum accomplishment level α^* for the second objective, to fit the spreads we have to solve the following linear programming problem:

$$\text{Minimise } z = \sum_{j=1}^{n}\sum_{i=0}^{m} l_{a_i}\left|x_{ij}\right| + \sum_{j=1}^{n}\sum_{i=0}^{m} r_{a_i}\left|x_{ij}\right| \qquad (8a)$$

subject to:

$$a_0'+\sum_{i=1}^{m}a_i'\,x_{ij} - \left(l_{a_0} + \sum_{\substack{i=1\\x_{ij}\geq0}}^{m}l_{a_0}\left|x_{ij}\right| + \sum_{\substack{i=1\\x_{ij}<0}}^{m}r_{a_i}\left|x_{ij}\right|\right)\left(1-\alpha^*\right) \leq \underline{y_j}\ ,\, j=1,2,...,n \quad (8b)$$

$$a_0'+\sum_{i=1}^{m}a_i'\,x_{ij} + \left(r_{a_0} + \sum_{\substack{i=1\\x_{ij}\geq0}}^{m}r_{a_i}\left|x_{ij}\right| + \sum_{\substack{i=1\\x_{ij}<0}}^{m}l_{a_i}\left|x_{ij}\right|\right)\left(1-\alpha^*\right) \geq \overline{y_j}\ ,\, j=1,2,...,n \quad (8c)$$

3. A fuzzy regression method for claim reserving

3.1. *Fitting the evolution of claiming with fuzzy regression*

The historical data on the evolution of the claims is usually presented in a *run-off* triangle similar to that of Table 1, where $s_{i,j}$ is the claim cost of the insurance contracts originated in the ith period ($i=0,1,...,n$) within the jth claiming period ($j=0,1,...,n$). Given that the past claiming costs of the ith occurrence period are $s_{i,j}$, $j=0,1,...,n-i$, calculating claim reserves implies forecasting and adding the claim costs of future development periods: $s_{i,j}$, $i=1,2,...,n$; $j=n-i+1$, $n-i+2,...,n$.

Table 1. Run-off triangle

		Development period						
		0	**1**	**...**	**j**	**...**	**n-1**	**n**
	0	$s_{0,0}$	$s_{0,1}$	...	$s_{0,j}$	...	$s_{0,n-1}$	$s_{0,n}$
	1	$s_{1,0}$	$s_{1,1}$	...	$s_{1,j}$	...	$s_{1,n-1}$	
Occurrence/ origin period	$\vdots$	$\vdots$	$\vdots$	$\vdots$	$\vdots$	$\vdots$	$\vdots$	
	i	$s_{i,0}$	$s_{i,1}$	...	$s_{i,j}$	...		
	$\vdots$	$\vdots$	$\vdots$	$\vdots$	$\vdots$			
	n-1	$s_{n-1,0}$	$s_{n-1,1}$	...				
	n	$s_{n,0}$		...				

Kremer in [16] , as classical chain ladder, supposes that $s_{i,j}$ can be represented by the product $C_i{\cdot}p_j$ where C_i is the total claiming cost in the ith origin period, whereas p_j is the proportion of this cost paid in the jth development period. Therefore, [16] proposes adjusting C_i, $i=0,1,...,n$ and p_j, $j=0,1,...,n$ by using linear regression since $\ln s_{i,j} = \ln C_i + \ln p_j$. In that paper it is supposed that the uncertainty about claiming is probabilistic. On the other hand, we consider that the uncertainty comes from fuzziness. So, we will obtain an estimate of the incremental claim cost $s_{i,j}$ by means of the fuzzy number $\tilde{s}_{i,j}$:

$$\tilde{s}_{i,j} = \tilde{C}_i \tilde{p}_j \tag{9}$$

then, the linear regression model to fit is:

$$\ln \tilde{s}_{i,j} = \tilde{a} + \tilde{b}_i + \tilde{c}_j \tag{10}$$

We suppose that $\tilde{a}, \tilde{b}_i, \tilde{c}_j$ are TFNs and therefore $\ln \tilde{s}_{i,j}$ is also a TFN. If we symbolise $\tilde{a} = (a, l_a, r_a)$, $\tilde{b}_i = (b_i, l_{b_i}, r_{b_i})$, $i=1,2,...,n$ and $\tilde{c}_j = (c_j, l_{c_j}, r_{c_j})$, $j=1,2,...,n$, we obtain from (4) and (10):

$$\ln \tilde{s}_{i,j} = \left(\ln s_{i,j}, l_{\ln s_{i,j}}, r_{\ln s_{i,j}} \right) = \left(a + b_i + c_j, l_a + l_{b_i} + l_{c_j}, r_a + r_{b_i} + r_{c_j} \right) \tag{11}$$

Notice that in the fuzzy regression model (10) $\tilde{a}$ is the independent term whereas $\tilde{b}_i, \tilde{c}_j$ are the coefficients of dichotomous explanatory variables in such a way that their observations are equal to one when the period in which they are located is equal to the parameter period, and zero in the other case.

To adjust (11), we must first obtain the estimates for the centres of $\tilde{a}, \tilde{b}_i$, $i=1,2,...,n$ and $\tilde{c}_j$, $j=1,2,...,n$ by means of least squares or, alternatively, with the algorithm described in [16]. Subsequently, we must solve:

$$\underset{l_a, l_{b_i}, l_{c_j}, r_a, r_{b_i}, r_{c_j}}{\text{Minimise}} z = \frac{(n+1)^2 + (n+1)}{2}(l_a + r_a) + \sum_{i=1}^{n}(n+1-i)(l_{b_i} + r_{b_i}) + \sum_{j=1}^{n}(n+1-j)(l_{c_j} + r_{c_j}) \tag{12a}$$

subject to:

$$a' + b_i' + c_j' - (l_a + l_{b_i} + l_{c_j})(1-\alpha^*) \leq \ln s_{i,j}, \ i=1,2,...,n; \ j=1,2,...,n-i \tag{12b}$$

$$a' + b_i' + c_j' + (r_a + r_{b_i} + r_{c_j})(1-\alpha^*) \geq \ln s_{i,j}, \ i=1,2,...,n; \ j=1,2,...,n-i \tag{12c}$$

$$a' + b_i' + c_j' - (l_a + l_{b_i} + l_{c_j}) \geq 0 \ \ i=1,2,...,n; \ j=1,2,...,n-i \tag{12d}$$

$$l_a, l_{b_i}, l_{c_j}, r_a, r_{b_i}, r_{c_j} \geq 0, \ i=1,2,...,n; \ j=1,2,...,n \tag{12e}$$

Notice that (12b), (12c) and (12e) are the constraints (8b), (8c) and (8d) whereas (12d) ensures non-negativity in fitted log-incremental claiming costs.

3.2. Determining the cost of future claims and calculating claim reserves

We can now predict the claiming cost of all origin periods in the development periods in which they are unknown. Given that the logarithm of incremental claim costs $\ln \tilde{s}_{i,j}$, $i=1,2,...,n$; $j \geq n-i+1$ are the TFNs in (11) and that the incremental claim cost $\tilde{s}_{i,j}$ is:

$$\tilde{s}_{i,j} = e^{\ln \tilde{s}_{i,j}} = e^{\tilde{a}+\tilde{b}_i+\tilde{c}_j} \tag{13a}$$

Here, $e^{\tilde{a}}$ is the incremental claim cost in the initial origin and development periods ($i=0$, $j=0$). Thus, $\tilde{b}_i$ is the logarithmical growth rate of total claiming during the origin period i, with respect to the initial origin period. Analogously, for a given origin period, $\tilde{c}_j$ is the logarithmical growth rate of the incremental cost of claims during the development period j with respect to the cost of claims declared during the development period $j=0$. Then, the α-cuts of $\tilde{s}_{i,j}$, s_{i,j_α} are obtained from (1b) and (3):

$$s_{i,j_\alpha} = \left[\underline{s_{i,j}}(\alpha), \overline{s_{i,j}}(\alpha)\right] = \left[e^{a+b_i+c_j - \left(l_a+l_{b_i}+l_{c_j}\right)(1-\alpha)}, e^{a+b_i+c_j + \left(r_a+r_{b_i}+r_{c_j}\right)(1-\alpha)}\right] \tag{13b}$$

The expected $EV\left[\tilde{s}_{i,j};\beta\right]$ is obtained by applying (5a) to (13b):

$$EV\left[\tilde{s}_{i,j};\beta\right] = (1-\beta)\int_0^1 e^{a+b_i+c_j-\left(l_a+l_{b_i}+l_{c_j}\right)(1-\alpha)}\,d\alpha + \beta\int_0^1 e^{a+b_i+c_j+\left(r_a+r_{b_i}+r_{c_j}\right)(1-\alpha)}\,d\alpha$$

$$= (1-\beta)\frac{e^{a+b_i+c_j-\left(l_a+l_{b_i}+l_{c_j}\right)}}{l_a+l_{b_i}+l_{c_j}}\left[e^{l_a+l_{b_i}+l_{c_j}} -1\right] + \beta\frac{e^{a+b_i+c_j+\left(r_a+r_{b_i}+r_{c_j}\right)}}{r_a+r_{b_i}+r_{c_j}}\left[1-e^{-\left(r_a+r_{b_i}+r_{c_j}\right)}\right]$$

$$\tag{13c}$$

Of course, if $l_a = l_{b_i} = l_{c_j} = 0$, the first summand of (13c) is $(1-\beta)e^{a+b_i+c_j}$ and when $r_a = r_{b_i} = r_{c_j} = 0$, the second summand of (13c) is $\beta e^{a+b_i+c_j}$.

The provision corresponding to the ith origin period is then:

$$P\tilde{R}O_i = \sum_{j=n-i+1}^{n} \tilde{s}_{i,j} \tag{14}$$

So the provision for all the occurrence periods is:

$$P\tilde{R}O = \sum_{i=1}^{n} P\tilde{R}O_i = \sum_{i=1}^{n}\sum_{j=n-i+1}^{n} \tilde{s}_{i,j} \tag{15}$$

Of course, from the α-cuts of $\tilde{s}_{i,j}$ in (13b) we can derive the exact value for the α-cuts of $P\tilde{R}O_i$ and $P\tilde{R}O$ by applying (3). To account for the claim provision in the financial statements, we must transform $P\tilde{R}O_i$ and $P\tilde{R}O$ into the crisp numbers PRO_i^* and PRO^* respectively. To do so, we propose using the expected value of a FN, which we have described in (5a) and (5b). To fix β we must bear in mind that actuarial decisions must be prudent, that is, $\beta>0.5$. Given that the expected value of FN is an additive measure, we can obtain PRO_i^* and PRO^* in such way:

$$PRO_i^* = EV\left[P\tilde{R}O_i; \beta\right] = \sum_{j=n-i+1}^{n} EV\left[\tilde{s}_{i,j}; \beta\right] \qquad (16a)$$

$$PRO^* = EV\left[P\tilde{R}O; \beta\right] = \sum_{i=1}^{n} \sum_{j=n-i+1}^{n} EV\left[\tilde{s}_{i,j}; \beta\right] \qquad (16b)$$

4. Numerical application

Our numerical example is developed over the run-off triangle at Table 2 used in [6, p. D5.4], which is based on real data from an automobile insurance company. From Table 2, we can immediately obtain the log-incremental payments in Table 3.

Table 2. Run off triangle. The amounts are the cost of the claims from the ith origin year paid at the jth development year ($s_{i,j}$, i=0,1,2,3, j=0,1,...,3-i)

		Development year			
	$i\backslash j$	0	1	2	3
	0	11073	6427	1839	766
Origin year	1	14799	9357	2344	
	2	15636	10523		
	3	16913			

Table 3. Run off triangle in which the quantities are ln$s_{i,j}$, i=0,1,2,3, j=0,1,...,3-i

		Development year			
	$i\backslash j$	0	1	2	3
	0	9.312	8.768	7.517	6.641
Origin year	1	9.602	9.144	7.760	
	2	9.657	9.261		
	3	9.736			

First we need to fit the parameters $\tilde{a} = (a, l_a, r_a)$, $\tilde{b}_i = (b_i, l_{b_i}, r_{b_i})$, i=1,2,3 and $\tilde{c}_j = (c_j, l_{c_j}, r_{c_j})$, j=1,2,3. The results are:

$\tilde{a}$ =(9.288, 0.024, 0.000); $\tilde{b}_1$ =(0.303, 0.000, 0.000); $\tilde{b}_2$ =(0.404, 0.011, 0.016); $\tilde{b}_3$ =(0.447, 0.000, 0.000); $\tilde{c}_1$ =(-0.466, 0.030, 0.019); $\tilde{c}_2$ =(-1.801, 0.006, 0.030); $\tilde{c}_3$ =(-2.647, 0.000, 0.000)

Now, we must evaluate (13a) and (13b) to calculate the future cost of claims $\tilde{s}_{i,j}$, i=1,2,3; j=3-i+1,...,3. Table 6 indicates the values of α-cuts s_{i,j_α} for α=0,0.5,1. The value s_{i,j_1} gives us a prediction of the most feasible point estimate of the future incremental claim whereas the 0-cut quantifies its estimated range. Subsequently, we calculate the α-cuts of provisions (Table 6).

132

Table 4. Values of s_{i,j_α} $i=1,2,3$, $j=3-i+1,...,3$ for the α-levels $\alpha=0, 0.5, 1$.

	$s_{1,3_\alpha}$	$s_{2,2_\alpha}$	$s_{2,3_\alpha}$
$\alpha=1$	[1036.86, 1036.86]	[2672.95, 2672.95]	[1147.35, 1147.35]
$\alpha=0.5$	[1012.38, 1036.86]	[2564.96, 2799.47]	[1107.81, 1166.06]
$\alpha=0$	[988.48, 1036.86]	[2461.33, 2931.96]	[1069.64, 1185.08]
	$s_{3,1_\alpha}$	$s_{3,2_\alpha}$	$s_{3,3_\alpha}$
$\alpha=1$	[10611.44, 10611.44]	[2791.62, 2791.62]	[1198.29, 1198.29]
$\alpha=0.5$	[10054.03, 10813.80]	[2708.94, 2876.83]	[1170.00, 1198.29]
$\alpha=0$	[9525.91, 11020.01]	[2628.71, 2964.63]	[1142.37, 1198.29]

Table 5. Values of the reserves for the α-levels $\alpha=0, 0.5, 1$.

	$PROV_{1\alpha}$	$PROV_{2\alpha}$	$PROV_{3\alpha}$	$PROV_\alpha$
$\alpha=1$	[1036.86, 1036.86]	[3820.30, 3820.30]	[14601.35, 14601.35]	[19458.51, 19458.51]
$\alpha=0.5$	[1012.38, 1036.86]	[3672.77, 3965.53]	[13932.97, 14888.91]	[18618.12, 19891.30]
$\alpha=0$	[988.48, 1036.86]	[3530.97, 4117.05]	[13296.99, 15182.94]	[17816.43, 20336.84]

To account provisions in financial statements it is necessary to defuzzify the fuzzy provisions. By using the expected value of (13c) and taking a risk aversion coefficient $\beta=1$, we obtain:

$$PRO_1^* = EV\left[P\tilde{R}O_1;1\right] = 1036.86;\ PRO_2^* = EV\left[P\tilde{R}O_2;1\right] = 3966.58;$$

$$PRO_3^* = EV\left[P\tilde{R}O_3;1\right] = 14889.99;\ PRO^* = EV\left[P\tilde{R}O_i;1\right] = 19893.42$$

5. Conclusions

Few data must be used to adjust an insurer's claim reserves. In this context we think that Fuzzy Set Theory is a suitable alternative to the usual statistical methods. Specifically, we have combined Fuzzy Numbers (FNs) and Fuzzy Regression (FR) with claim reserving scheme in [16]. Our claim-reserving method makes predictions as complete as "stochastic" methods since it allows us to estimate both a fair value for claim reserves as well as their variability. On the other hand, "classical methods", such as the grossing up technique, focus the problem deterministically and therefore produce poorer predictions because they only fit an expected value of the future claims. Obtaining a reference quantity not only for the fair value of claim provisions but also for their "variability" is interesting for actuaries because it enables them to determine well-founded safety margins.

In our opinion, the fuzzy claim reserving method we propose in this paper has other interesting characteristics: the estimates obtained after adjusting FR models are FNs, which are easy to handle arithmetically without losing much of the information from the available data. Fuzzy Numbers provide both a prediction of the fair value of reserves (the 1-cut of FNs and their expected value) and an estimate of their variability, since the provisions are quantified as confidence intervals. In both cases, we obtain closed formulas that are easy to compute. Moreover, using non-symmetrical TFNs allows us to capture the asymmetric distribution of the data with respect to their central values (e.g. the skewness of the OLS regression errors).

The fuzzy estimation of claim reserves normally needs to be transformed into a crisp equivalent in order, for example, to compute them in financial statements. In this paper, we propose the concept of the expected value of a FN because this defuzzification method makes it possible to introduce the actuarial risk aversion easily and intuitively.

References

1. Andrés, J. de, Terceño, A., 2003. Applications of Fuzzy Regression in Actuarial Analysis. Journal of Risk and Insurance 70, 4, 665-699.
2. Andrés-Sánchez, J. de, 2007. Claim reserving with fuzzy regression and Taylor's geometric separation method. Insurance: Mathematics and Economics 40, 145-163.
3. Benjamin, S., Eagles, L.M., 1986. Reserves in Lloyd's and the London market. Journal of the Institute of Actuaries 113, 2, 197-257.
4. Buckley, J.J., Qu, Y., 1990. On using α-cuts to evaluate fuzzy equations, Fuzzy Sets and Systems 38, 309-312.
5. Campos, L.M., González, A., 1989. A subjective approach for ranking fuzzy numbers. Fuzzy Sets and Systems 29, 145-153.
6. Christofides, S., 1989. Regression models based on log-incremental payments. In: Institute Of Actuaries, 1990. Claims reserving manual, Volume 2. London, Institute of Actuaries.
7. Derrig, R.A., Ostaszewski, K., 1995. Fuzzy techniques of pattern recognition in risk and claim classification. Journal of Risk and Insurance 62, 447-482.
8. Dubois, D., Prade, H., 1992. Foreword. In: Fuzzy Regression Analysis. Physica-Verlag, Heildelberg.
9. Gil-Aluja, J. Investment on uncertainty. Dordretch. Kluwer Academic Publishers, (1998).
10. Gil-Aluja, J. Elementos para una teoría de la decisión en la incertidumbre. Ed. Milladoiro. Vigo, (1999).
11. Gil-Lafuente, A.M. Fuzzy logic in financial analysis. Springer-Verlag Berlin Heidelberg (2005).
12. Gil-Lafuente, J. Marketing para el nuevo milenio. Ed. Pirámide. Madrid, (1997).

13. Ishibuchi, H., Nii, M., 2001. Fuzzy regression using asymmetric fuzzy coefficients and fuzzified neural networks, Fuzzy Sets and Systems 119, 273-290.

14. Koissi, M.C. Shapiro, A.F., 2006. Fuzzy formulation of the Lee–Carter model for mortality forecasting. Insurance: Mathematics and Economics 39, 289-307.

15. Koissi, M.C. Shapiro, A.F., 2008. Fuzzy regression and the term structure of interest rates- A least squares approach. Actuarial research clearing house newsletters vol. 2009.1.

16. Kremer, E., 1982. IBNR claims and the two way model of ANOVA. Scandinavian Actuarial Journal, 1, 47-55.

17. Lai, L.-H., 2006. Underwriting profit margin of P/L insurance in the fuzzy-ICAPM. The Geneva risk and insurance review 31, 23-34.

18. Straub, E., 1997. Non-life insurance mathematics. Springer, Berlin.

19. Tanaka, H., 1987. Fuzzy data analysis by possibilistic linear models, Fuzzy Sets and Systems 24, 363-375.

20. Tank, F., Gebizlioglu, O.L.; Apaydin, A., 2006. Determination of dependency parameter in joint distribution of dependent risks by fuzzy approach. Insurance: Mathematics and Economics 39, 189-194.

21. Verrall, R.J., Yakoubov, Y.H., 1999. A fuzzy approach to grouping by policyholder age in general insurance. Journal of Actuarial Practice 7, 181-203.

22. Yakoubov, Y.H., Haberman, S., 1998. Review of actuarial applications of fuzzy set theory. Actuarial Research Paper n. 105. Department of Actuarial Science and Statistics of the City University, London.

INTEGRATING SUSTAINABILITY THROUGH FUZZY LOGIC: FORTUNE GLOBAL 100 SUSTAINABILITY RATING[*]

ELENA ESCRIG-OLMEDO[†]
JUANA MARÍA RIVERA-LIRIO
MARÍA JESÚS MUÑOZ-TORRES
MARÍA ÁNGELES FERNÁNDEZ-IZQUIERDO

*Department of Finance and Accounting, Universiat Jaume I,
Campus del Riu Sec, 12071 Castellón, Spain*

Many organizations currently publish ratings that quantify the sustainability of firms by aggregating scores. However, some of these scores are associated with problems of how positive and negative assessments are offset. This work proposes a methodology for using fuzzy logic in the design of a comprehensive sustainability rating for firms. The approach is applied to information taken from the 2008 Accountability Rating and aims to correct one of the weaknesses revealed by methodologies based on the aggregation of scores –the offset effect. The proposal in this paper enables a decision-maker to manage this offset effect.

1. Introduction

The ranking of firms according to their sustainable performance has become relevant, and as a result the number of agencies or associations that provide ratings of corporate social responsibility (CSR) has increased rapidly [1]. Despite the growth of environmental, social, and governance (ESG) rating agencies, there is no standard methodology for the evaluation of firms. A major reason is the complexity of developing synthetic sustainability indices. There are calls in the academic world for the establishment of a standard assessment methodology for use by ESG rating agencies [2, 3, 4].

Given the complexity of CSR and its assessment, there are several issues that must be tackled during the development of a synthetic sustainability index: (1) selection of the domains and variables; (2) construction of the scoring system; (3) choice of statistical techniques for aggregation and weighting; and (4) the possible offsetting effect of scores. Some of these problems have been

---

[*] This work is supported by grant FPU-AP2008-01043 and project SEJ2006-08317/ECON, as well as the Universitat Jaume I via the P1•1A2006-16 research project.
[†] Corresponding author: eescrig@cofin.uji.es, fax number 00 34 964728565

solved within the stock markets, because of the activities of sustainability rating agencies and sustainability stock indices.

But the problems of weighting and possible offsetting in the scorings remain unresolved. Work included under the term 'triple bottom line' involves keeping balanced scorecards in the areas analysed under the focus of sustainability, so that good results in some of the pillars cannot hide the absence or inadequacy of policies or processes in other areas. In these sense, the offsetting effect is unwanted when high scores in one domain may have on very low scores in another domain because under our assumptions a firm is socially responsible when there is a balance between the analysed domains.

In this context, the objective of this paper is to propose a methodology for designing a comprehensive index for assessing organisational sustainability. Specifically, fuzzy logic is applied to the CSR information supplied by Accountability Rating for 2008 (AR2008), and this information is used as a proxy for sustainability practices. This technique is suitable for measuring sustainability addresses the complexity of the concept and enables the incorporation of expert knowledge into the system of assessment. There are other ways to weight the importance of the three sustainability pillars, like the Analytic Hierarchy Process (AHP), widely used as a way for generating aggregate sustainability measures [5, 6]. Nevertheless, the flexibility of our system allows for different weightings to be yielded or various scenarios to be generated by the decision makers, not only with a technical approach but also under other considerations according to the profile of the stakeholder. However, it is possible to combine both methodologies [6] when the introduction of independent assessments into indicators weights is relevant for the decision maker.

2. The Accountability Rating

Accountability Rating was jointly developed by a leading British CSR consultancy (**CSR**network) and an international group of experts known as 'AccountAbility'. Authors such as Schäfer et al., [7] highlight the relevance of this rating and have studied its methodology for analysing sustainability in organisations. Moreover, Eccles et al. [8] consider this rating as a reference in their studies. Accordingly, we focused on Accountability Rating because it provides a publicly available and well-known annual rating system. The Accountability Rating (AR) is applied to firms in the Fortune Global 100. The AR evaluates these firms in terms of CSR in four key domains: *strategic intent, governance and management, engagement, and operational performance*. These four domains are widely used in the literature for operationally implementing the CSR concept. Firstly, in relation to *strategic intent*, the AR assesses whether an organisation seeks to address social, environmental, and economic issues in its core business strategy. CSR is considered the commonly accepted sustainability triple bottom line approach applied at corporate level. As Kleine and von Hauff [9] remarked, modern corporations are complex institutions that must take into account not only economic, but also social and ecological aspects. Recent studies have emphasised the importance for firms of integrating the concepts of CSR and corporate strategy in terms of financial performance and competitive advantage [10, 11]. The second most highly valued aspect in the AR is *governance and management*. Corporate governance is a concept with implications for an organization's approach to CSR [12] and involves questions such as transparency and accountability [13]. The implementation of CSR strategies requires the formalization of management systems that define policies, procedures, or mechanisms for the measurement of economic, social, and environmental performances – among others [14]. As Kleine and von Hauff [9] stressed: *"Corporate Social Responsibility as an 'organizational innovation' must be integrated (...) at all management levels in the corporate development processes"*. An important issue when considering the integration of CSR into an organization is the management of stakeholder relations [15]. The AR has primarily placed this issue under the domain of *engagement*. This domain takes into consideration aspects such as dialogue with stakeholders, the preparation and publication of information on sustainability, and the quality of the information in terms of whether it is subject to credible independent monitoring. Finally, AR assesses a firm's effectiveness in implementing its social and environmental strategies, management systems, and engagement mechanisms through the *operational performance* domain. The translation of the concept of 'social responsibility' into operational terms and the development of the appropriate and implied measurement mechanisms are key issues for analyzing the positioning of an organization in the context of sustainability and CSR [16].

For the task of generating various assessments, each criterion is currently evaluated by giving firms a score in each of the four AR domains. The maximum score for each domain is 25 and the maximum score for a firm is 100. In this way, the final overall rating is the result of adding the scores in each of the key domains. However, this overall rating has a number of limitations: (1) higher scores for one domain may hide very low scores in another domain; (2) the balance is not reflected between the various aspects of management necessary for a firm to be listed as socially responsible; and (3) the varying assessments that different stakeholders may give to each criterion are not included.

Bearing in mind the potential of fuzzy logic for generating synthetic measurements of sustainability [17, 18], we propose addressing these limitations by developing a comprehensive sustainability rating based on applying fuzzy logic to the AR2008.

3. Design of Study

Authors such as Phillis and Andriantiatsaholiniaina [19], Muñoz et al. [16], and Rivera and Munoz [18] state that there are several reasons why fuzzy logic [20] is an appropriate methodology for assessing the concepts of sustainability: (1) fuzzy logic uses linguistic variables and these enable the treatment of complex concepts and polymorphs that are difficult to quantify; and (2) fuzzy logic is a mathematical tool that enables the simulation of system dynamics without a detailed mathematical description. Fuzzy logic can be combined with other methodologies, such as the Analytic Hierarchy Process (AHP), in cases when the introduction of independent assessments into score weightings is relevant for the decision-maker.

On this basis, we propose using fuzzy logic methodologies for making models to generate a synthetic index for comprehensively measuring CSR.

3.1. *Generating a synthetic sustainability index using fuzzy logic*

The fuzzy inference system (FIS) is a methodology for implementing fuzzy logic [21]. Jang [22] states that there are five functional blocks that form FIS (A.1). Numeric variables are the system inputs. These crisp variables are transformed through a fuzzification process into grades of membership for linguistic terms of fuzzy sets, with the help of previously defined membership functions. There are various types of membership functions – such as triangular, trapezoidal, or Gaussian [23]; while the triangular membership function is commonly used [24] because it is intuitively easy for decision-makers to use and calculate [25]. The resulting linguistic variables become the fuzzy inputs for the inference engine. Following the application of IF-THEN rules, a fuzzy output is obtained and expressed in linguistic terms. The IF-THEN rules represent knowledge and describe a logical evolution of the system according to linguistic values [19].

It is possible to distinguish between different types of fuzzy inference systems [23]. The Mamdani fuzzy model (A.1) has been commonly mentioned in the application of fuzzy theory to sustainability [19] because it is widely accepted, intuitive, and well-suited to human input. A fuzzy output is changed into numeric values using a defuzzification process. There are several defuzzification methods in the literature [26], and the centroid method is the most frequently used [24].

Using the previously mentioned methodology, the following section describes the system defined to assess the ranking of the Fortune Global 100 firms by generating a sustainability rating from the scores given in the AR2008 for the four domains (system inputs): strategic intent (SI), governance and management (GM), engagement (E), and operational performance (OP). The fuzzy computations will be performed using MATLAB's The MathWorks.

The defined membership functions for the input and output variables are triangular membership functions because of their simplicity [25], and because they can approximate most non-triangular functions [27]. The linguistic values assigned for the inputs are low (L)- parameters: (-12.5 0 12.5)-, medium (M) -parameters: (0 12.5 25)-, and high (H) -parameters: (12.5 25 37.5). Finally, the values of the Fuzzy Sustainability Rating (FSR) output have been expressed as poor sustainability (PS), low sustainability (LS), medium sustainability (MS), high sustainability (HS), and top sustainability (TS).

Table 1. Rule design for both scenarios

ANTECEDENT			CONSEQUENT
Number of LOW inputs	Number of MEDIUM inputs	Number of HIGH inputs	
4 or 3	0	0	PS
2	2 or 1	0	LS
2	0	2	MS
1	1 or 2 or 3 or 0	2 or 1 or 0 or 3	MS
0	4 or 3 or 2	0 or 1 or 2	HS
0	1 or 0	3 or 4	TS
0	0	4	TS
1 (OP input)	3 or 2 or 1	3 or 2 or 1	Not TS[a]

Note: [a] Rule 82 added in the second scenario.

The linguistic rule generation process has been guided by expert knowledge (Table 1). Two scenarios have been created. In the first scenario, the sum total of the generated rules equals 81.In the second scenario, another rule has been added: "IF operational performance is LOW, THEN Fuzzy Sustainability Rating IS NOT top sustainability" (assuming that the remaining inputs do not have a 'LOW' rating). This introduces a new constraint on the system that penalizes firms with low OP – even higher scores are obtained for the other domains. In this way, the importance of this domain in the comprehensive sustainability index is internalised.

4. Results

We have performed an exploratory factor analysis of the sample using the Principal Components Method, in order to have previous knowledge about the variables (domains) that make up the Accountability Rating and to detect the suitability to design a synthetic index that allow us to resume all the available information. The result shows a single factor, so confirming the work in finding a synthetic index.[b]

The system based on a fuzzy logic design methodology is applicable to any sample of firms that form part of the AR, and is therefore not context-dependent.

---

[b] The results of these analyses are available upon request to the authors.

Moreover, this methodology decreases the offsetting effect that very high scores in one domain may have on very low scores in another domain. Table 2 shows the differences between the AR2008 and the Fuzzy Sustainability Rating (FSR) developed under the first scenario for the first ten firms. The results reveal that 60% of the firms in the top ten of the AR2008 are also in the top ten in the FSR. In addition, it is worth noting that the first and last firms ranked by both systems coincide. However, 48% of the firms have lost positions in the ranking, while 43% have gained positions. There are changes in the ranking of ten positions or more, with 9% of all the firms losing rank, while 12% of firms gain at least ten positions. Moreover, there is a 90% agreement regarding the firms rated among the top 50. The AR2008 and FSR almost entirely coincide in ranking the top 50 firms, but show significant divergence regarding the exact position each firm holds. Indeed, it is worth emphasizing that all of the firms that lost at least ten positions in the ranking are in the top 50. Therefore, it appears that firms in the top 50 of the AR2008 were the most penalized in the FSR, caused primarily by a reduced offset effect for poor results in a previously discussed domain.

Table 2: Scenario 1. Classification according to FSR without OP restriction

AR	Firms	SI	GM	E	OP	AR Overall Score (0-100)	FSR Overall Score (0-1)	FSR	FSR - AR
1	Vodafone	21.30	19.50	22.10	14.80	77.70	0.7906	1	0
2	General Elec.	20.60	19.60	17.60	12.30	70.10	0.7654	3	-1
3	HSBC	20.60	18.30	17.30	11.60	67.80	0.7412	9	-6
4	France Tel.	19.00	16.90	17.30	14.10	67.30	0.7685	2	2
5	HBOS	18.50	17.80	15.80	14.10	66.20	0.7615	4	1
6	Nokia	20.10	17.80	14.00	11.90	63.80	0.7325	12	-6
7	EDF	18.80	16.40	15.40	11.60	62.20	0.7279	14	-7
8	GDF Suez	14.70	16.20	13.20	17.70	61.80	0.7554	5	3
9	**BP**	**18.00**	**18.30**	**16.20**	**9.10**	**61.60**	**0.6765**	**30**	**-21**
10	Royal D./Shell	18.00	17.10	14.70	11.30	61.10	0.7172	17	-7

Table 3 shows the results obtained by the system described in the second scenario (FSR-restricted), that is, the scenario that establishes a restriction penalizing poor OP scores. The results reveal that 50% of the firms in the top ten of the AR2008 are also in the top ten of the FSR with the OP restriction. In addition, it is worth noting that the first and last firms ranked by AR2008 and the FSR coincide. The main difference in comparison with the previous scenario is related with the percentage of firms showing a major change in their position. The position changes are greater because 20% of the firms fell ten positions or more, and 23% rose by more than ten positions. In overall terms, the AR2008 and FSR-restricted rankings show a 78% agreement for their top 50 firms, but also show major differences regarding the exact position given to each firm. Some 95% of the top 50 firms dropped ten positions or more.

Table 3: Scenario 2. Classification according to FSR with OP restriction

AR	Firms	AR Overall score	FSR restricted Overall Score (0-1)	FSR restricted	FSR AR
1	Vodafone	77.70	0.7906	1	0
2	General Elec.	70.10	0.7540	5	-3
3	**HSBC**	**67.80**	**0.6951**	**15**	**-12**
4	France Tel.	67.30	0.7685	2	2
5	HBOS	66.20	0.7615	3	2
6	Nokia	63.80	0.6997	14	-8
7	**EDF**	**62.20**	**0.6789**	**19**	**-12**
8	GDF Suez	61.80	0.7554	4	4
9	**BP**	**61.60**	**0.5578**	**64**	**-55**
10	**Royal D./Shell**	**61.10**	**0.6582**	**25**	**-15**

It is worth noting that there is 84% agreement regarding the top 50 firms in scenarios 1 and 2; however, considerable differences exist regarding the exact position. Moreover, there is a 90% match for the top ten firms. The introduction of a rule that controls low scores for OP has highlighted imbalances in the AR 2008 and first-scenario rankings. The restricted result provides a rating that agrees with the hypothesis of a decision-maker managing the offsets. Firms with a low OP score have been penalized – even if they do not have poor scores in the other domains.

5. Conclusions

The development of a synthetic sustainability index faces difficulties related with the complexity of the term CSR (considered as the organisational integration of sustainability) and its measurement using scores; as well as difficulties in the application of appropriate statistical techniques for managing the problem of possible score offsets. In this context, the objective of this work has been the development of a comprehensive sustainability rating using methodologies based on fuzzy logic. The sample of firms and inputs for the fuzzy system are taken from information made publicly available in the 2008 Accountability Rating. Given the importance of organizational outcomes related to sustainability, we have considered two possible scenarios. The second scenario differs from the first scenario by including a restriction penalising firms that, despite not having low scores in strategic engagement, corporate governance, or the management of stakeholder relations, do have low scores for these issues in terms of performance. The most remarkable aspect of the results obtained using the defined fuzzy system, relates to the greater balance shown between the four domains in the FSR when compared to the AR2008 – with the balance being even greater in the restricted FSR. This approach corrects one of the main weaknesses of methodologies based on the aggregation of scores, i.e. the possible offsetting of negative scores with good scores and introduces the role of the decision-maker in the assessment.

The main limitation is the fact that the developed sustainability rating uses inputs previously defined by the AR. Therefore, it has been impossible to correct, where appropriate, any limitations that the assessment of these inputs may contain.

Appendix

A Fuzzy Inference System (22)   ### Mamdani FIS (21)

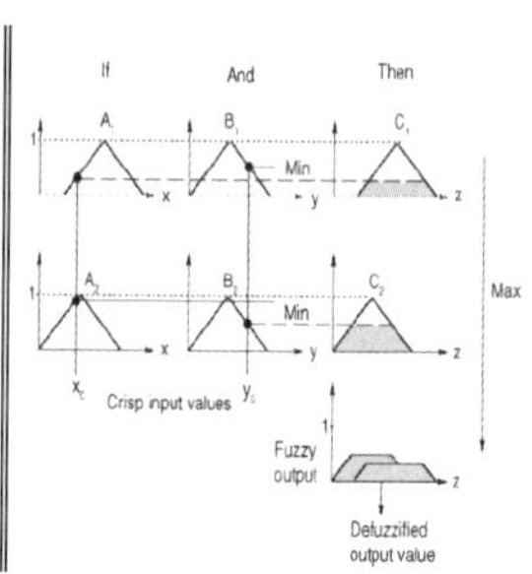

(A.1)

References

1. M.J. Epstein and J-F. Manzoni, Performance Measurement and Management Control: Improving Organizations and Society. *Emerald Group Publishing*, (2006).
2. E. Escrig, M.J. Muñoz and A. Fernández, *International Journal of Sustainable Economy*, ISSN Online: 1756-5812 (Forthcoming) (2009).
3. D. Krajnc and P. Glavič, *Ecol. Econ.* **55**, 551 (2005).
4. S. Waddock, *Acad. Manag. Perspect.* **22**, 87 (2008).
5. B.M. Ruf, K. Muralidhar and K. Paul, *J. Manag.* **24**, 119 (1998).
6. K.F.R Liu, *Environmental Management* **39**, 721 (2007).
7. H. Schäfer, J. Beer, J. Zenker and P. Fernandes, 'Who is who in Corporate Social Responsibility Rating?' Bertelsman Foundation. University Stuttgart. Institute of Business Administration (2006).
8. N.S. Eccles, V. Pillay and D. De Jongh, *African Business Review* **13**, 21 (2009).
9. A. Kleine and M. Von Hauff, *J. Bus. Ethics*, DOI 10.1007/s10551-009-0212-z (2009).
10. Z. Sharp and N. Zaidman, *J. Bus. Ethics,* DOI 10.1007/s10551-009-0181-2 (2009).
11. J.M. Moneva, J.M. Rivera-Lirio and M.J. Muñoz-Torres, *Ind. Manage. Data Syst.* **107**, 84 (2007).
12. I. Bonn and J. Fisher, *Corporate Governance* **13**, 730 (2005).

13. I. Ferrero, M.A. Fernández and M.J. Muñoz, A proposal for corporate governance rating in Spanish Saving Banks. In Angela, C. et al, *New Frontiers in Insurance and Bank Risk Management*, McGraw-Hill, Milano (2009).

14. M.J. Munoz-Torres, M.A. Fernandez-Izquierdo, L. Nieto-Soria, J.M. Rivera-Lirio, E. Escrig-Olmedo and R. Leon-Soriano, *International Journal of Sustainable Economy* **1**, 270 (2009).

15. Y. Fassin, *J. Bus. Ethics* **84**, 113 (2008).

16. M.J. Muñoz, J.M. Rivera and J.M. Moneva, *Ind. Manage. Data Syst.* **108**, 829 (2008).

17. Y.A. Phillis and B.J. Davis, *J. Intell. Robot. Syst.* **55,** 3 (2009).

18. J.M. Rivera and M.J. Muñoz, *J. Bus. Ethics*, DOI 10.1007/s10551-009-0278-7 (2009).

19. Y.A. Phillis and L.A. Andriantiatsaholiniaina, *Ecol. Econ.* **37**, 435 (2001).

20. L.A. Zadeh, *Information and Control* **8**, 338 (1965).

21. A.F. Shapiro, *Insur. Math. Econ.* **35**, 399 (2004).

22. J-S. R. Jang, *IEEE Trans. Syst. Man Cybern.* **23**, 665 (1993).

23. J-S. R. Jang and C-T. Sun, *Proc. IEEE* **83**, 378 (1995).

24. W-W. Wu and Y-T. Lee, *Expert Syst. Appl.* **32**, 499 (2007).

25. H-Y. Lin, P-Y. Hsu and G-J. Sheen, *Expert Syst. Appl.* **32**, 939 (2007).

26. C.C. Lee, *IEEE Trans. Syst. Man Cybern.* **20**, 419 (1990).

27. W. Pedrycz, *Fuzzy Sets Syst.* **64**, 21 (1994).

QUALITY EVALUATION OF THE HUMAN ACTION PERFORMING IN A WORKING SYSTEM USING FUZZY LOGIC

ANDREEA IONICA

*Management Department, University of Petrosani, University Street,
No 20 Petrosani, Romania*

MONICA LEBA

*System Control, Applied Informatics and Computer Engineering Department,
University of Petrosani, University Street,
No 20 Petrosani, Romania*

EDUARD EDELHAUSER

*Management Department, University of Petrosani, University Street,
No 20 Petrosani, Romania*

A review of the working systems' elements shouldn't omit the influence of the human factor, even if the latter is difficult to quantify and predict. The inquiry is supported by the ever more serious impact on all the elements of the working systems. The paper attempts to point out the importance of the impact of the human factor influence on all the elements of the working systems and propose a fuzzy model for quality evaluation of performing a human action.

1. Introduction

Independent of its nature, in every productive activity it is necessary that the following four elements exist and interact: operators/executants, working task, production means, working environment.

The most difficult is to express the action of human factor to the executants' level and to the decisional factor level by imposing a quantification and unitary treatment of the subjectivism [1].

Due to the complexity of the role played by the human factor, all action categories should be taken into account, and a risk evaluation pattern for a given action should include the interconnection between all the actions regarding the elements of the working system.

If the risk represents the possibility to put oneself into a possible danger, it can express a criterion for quality evaluation of performing a human action. Thus the extent to which it can produce unwanted effects is shown, including malfunctions of the working system upon the person, technical equipment or working environment.

The degree of risk associated to a human action is connected to a group of internal factors of risk which shall act through the human error and external risk factors related to technical equipment, protection systems and organizational framework where the humans carry out their activities.

The proposed model is based on the evaluation of the terms of the scope-means relationship. It is not a mathematical relationship, but a symbolic one. The evaluation of the terms allows us to identify the correspondence between the working system elements and the groups of risk factors above mentioned.

We propose a fuzzy model, because in general the fuzzy logic is related to the science that treats the interface man and working system. Also, fuzzy logic offers "the tool" that makes possible the quantification of the subjective incertitude, and operates with the imprecise notions as nuances that describe the state of a system.

2. The research methodology

The research methodology is based on the evaluation of the terms of the scope-means relationship. First are determined the membership values for each of the inputs and then is designed the fuzzy model of the evaluation system.

2.1. *The scope-means relationship*

$$s+e=m+t \ [3] \quad (1)$$

where:

s – *Scope value* – the optimum level of safety of the working system (the functioning probability of the system for diminishing the risk of appearing the defect state)

m – *Means value* – the quantity of materials means and also of measures of working safe necessary for diminishing the risk of appearing the defect state;

t – *Cognitive means* – quantity and quality of the knowledge and habits used for diminishing the risk of appearing the defect state;

e – *Collateral effects value* – the value of the prejudices followed the risk manifestation

The terms of the relationship are in the equilibrium value; "the weight" of the left terms tips the balance for increasing the risk, while "the weight" of the right terms leads to the diminution of the risk.

s>0 if and only if m+t>e. So, the scope is rewarding only if the means are valuable, and better the means are, more valuable the scopes are.

After analyzing a human action as a scope-means relationship it must be appreciated or estimated the "value" of each term.

The estimation depends on the nature of each term, so the scope is subjective (fuzzy assessed), the means are quantitative (value and/or fuzzy assessed), the cognitive means are quantitative related to the human factor (fuzzy assessed) and effects are quantitative and qualitative (value and/or fuzzy assessed). So, the scope is represented by the levels of the functioning probabilities, the means are represented by the classes delimited on the basis of the conformity level of the equipments resulting after auditing, the cognitive means are represented by the marks obtained after being evaluated periodically and the effects are represented by the levels of defects importance.

After having applied the specific steps of the fuzzy logic, by obtaining the defuzzyfication result, it should be appreciated the action of the human factor by framing into an action typology.

Table 1. Action typologies

FULL EFFCIENT	VERY GOOD EFFICIENT	GOOD EFFICIENT	MIN EFFICIENT	NON EFFICIENT
SUCCES	SUCCES	SUCCES/RISC	RISC	RISC
100%-80%	80%-50%	50%-20%	20%-10%	10%-0%

The framing into an action typology will allow determining the help of the human factor to appearance of the deficiencies/malfunctions, even if it is about the decisional errors or the execution errors [1].

2.2. *Fuzzy system modeling and simulation*

In order to model the fuzzy evaluation system described above there was used the Fuzzy toolbox from the MatLab simulation environment.

First, there were implemented the membership functions for all the inputs and for the output of the system (figure 1), based on the evaluation of each linguistic variable. There were used only triangular and trapezoidal functions.

148

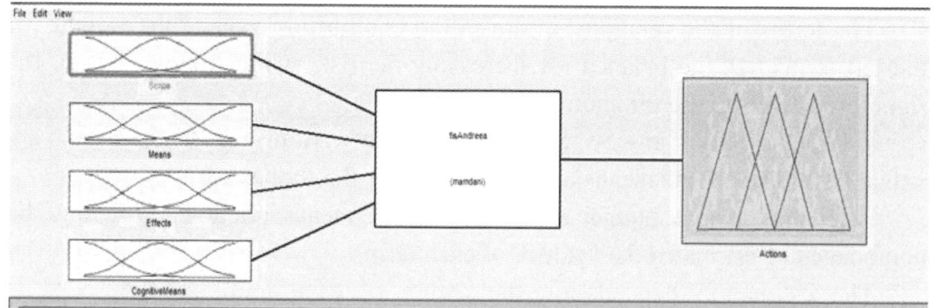

Figure 1. The fuzzy system

In figures 2 to 6 there are presented the membership functions.

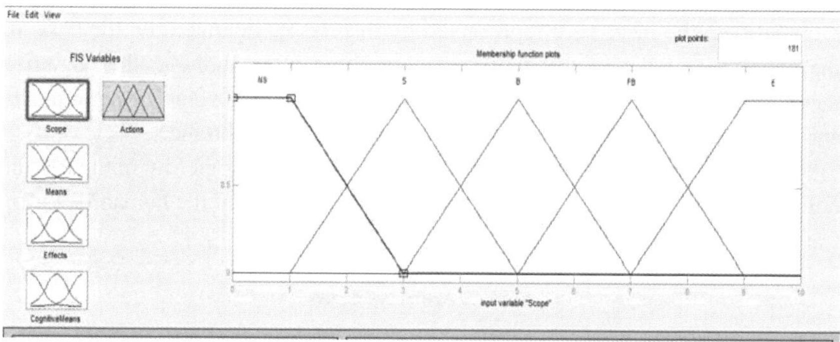

Figure 2. The description of the linguistic variable *Scope*

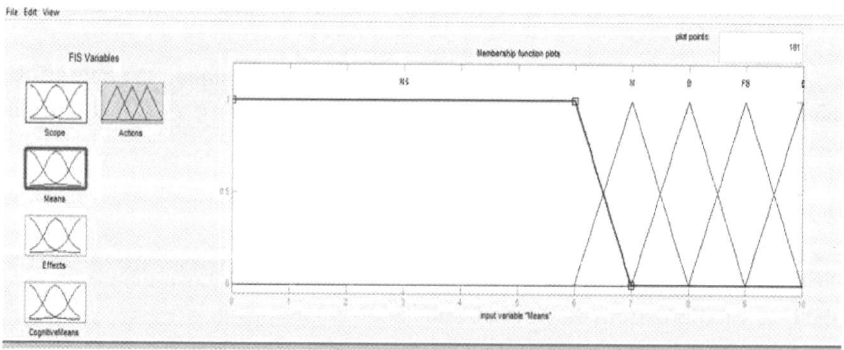

Figure 3. The description of the linguistic variable *Means*

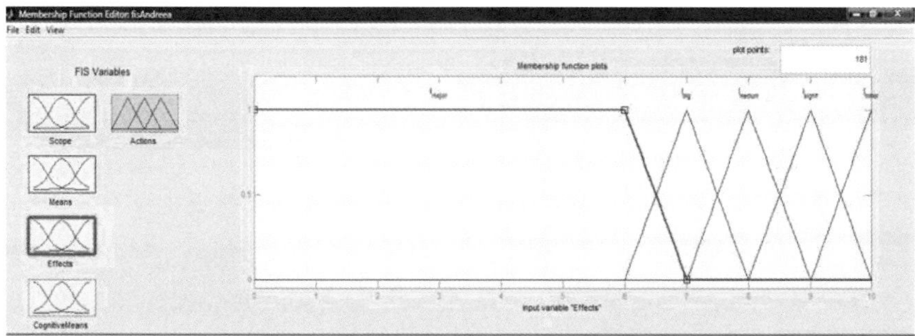

Figure 4. The description of the linguistic variable *Effects*

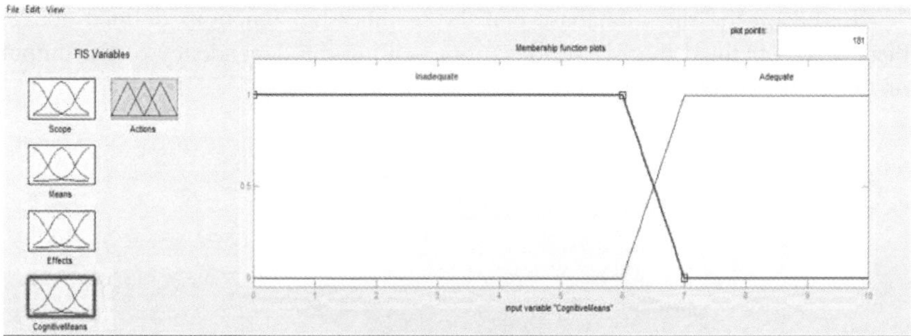

Figure 5. The description of the linguistic variable *Cognitive means*

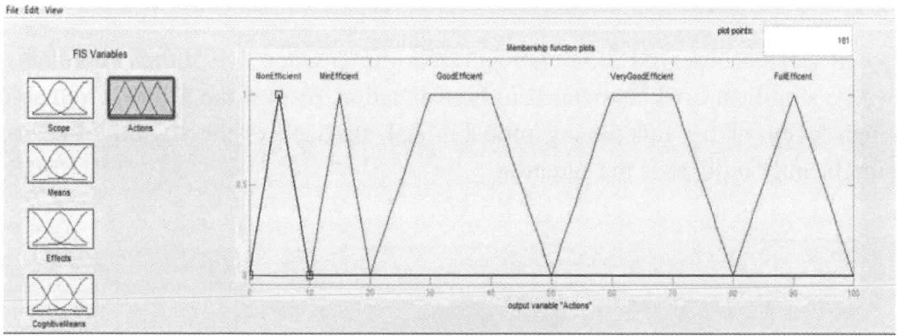

Figure 6. The description of the linguistic variable *Actions*

3. Quality evaluation of a human action: a fuzzy model, discussions and concluding remarks

In order to use the fuzzy model there was built the rules database, as in figure 7.

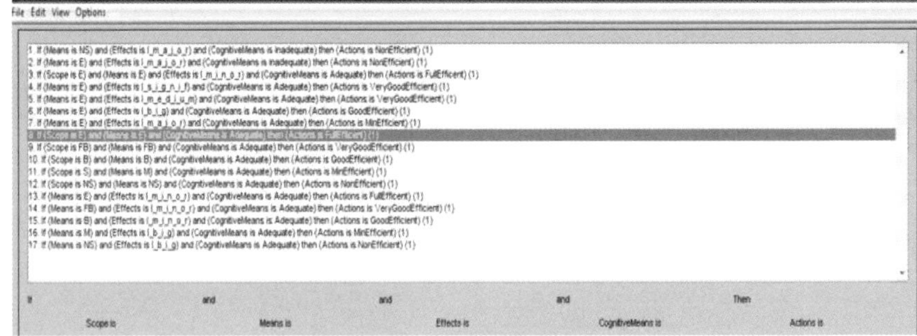

Figure 7. The data base of rules

Based on the rules database and the membership functions defined above, there were obtained the 3D surfaces representing the dependency of the output on two of the inputs.

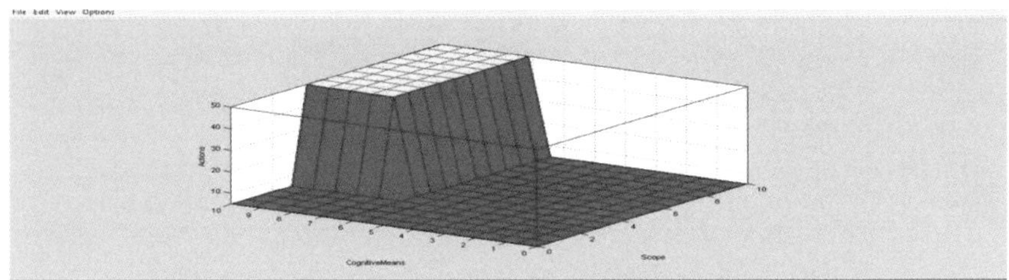

Figure 8. Scope-Cognitive Means-Actions relationship surface

It can be observed *Minimum Effective Actions* and *Non Efficient Actions,* with a significant risk associated to human action, even if the scope is valuable (high levels of the functioning probabilities), the lack of the cognitive means, significantly influences the situation.

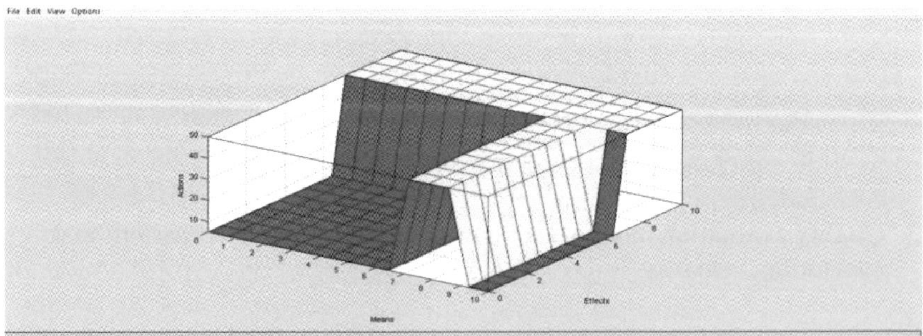

Figure 9. Effects-Means-Actions relationship surface

It can be analyzed the efficiency of the actions that tend to *Very Good Efficient Actions*, when we have *Excellent* means, *Minor Importance* effects that do not cause long term interruptions of productive activities with impact on the all elements of the working system.

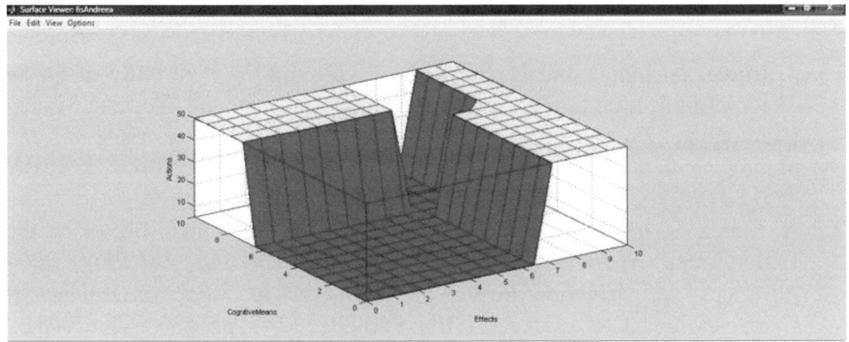

Figure 10. Effects-Cognitive Means-Actions relationship surface

It can be observed the high level of the risk associated to *Non Efficient Actions* when the cognitive means are *Inadequate,* and the effects generate malfunctions in the entire working system.

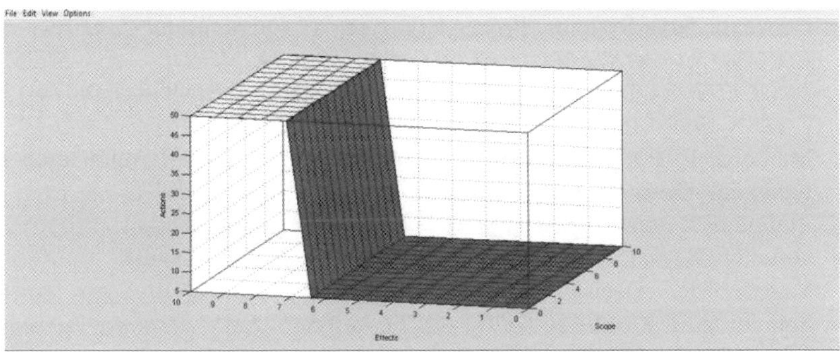

Figure 11. Scope-Effects- Actions relationship surface

Also, it can be emphasized the importance of the appropriate identification and evaluation of the effects and framing them in a class of importance depending on the peculiarities of the working system.

The evaluation of the human action performing in a working system, using fuzzy logic, generates interpretations concerning the quality improvement of the working process. The actions will concentrate, for examples, on the organization at the working place (working groups dimensioned correctly, special intercession team), purchase of appropriate equipment, spare parts materials, necessity of collaboration regarding the improvement of the quality at the suppliers, staff-forming-training program.

References

1. S. Irimie, A. Ionica and D. Surulescu, Exploring the Possibility of Fuzzy Theory Application to the Case of the Man - Underground Working System Interactions, *Proceedings of the 4th International Conference on the Management of Technological Changes,* Chaina, Greece, Book 2, ISBN 960-8475-05-8, pp. 41-46, **BGR15**, (2005).
2. A. Ionica, S. Irimie, C. Jujan, The Influence of the Human Factor on the Underground Working System, *Proceedings of the AMIREG 2004 Advances in Mineral Resources Management and Environmental Geotechnology*, Creta, Grecia, ISBN: 960-88153-0-4, pp. 635-640, (2004).
3. I. Sava, Contributions to the elaboration of some unconventional methods in order to prevent and eliminate the causes that may generate technical damages and accidents, *PhD. Thesis*, University of Petrosani, Romania (1999).
4. E. Sofron, Fuzzy Control Systems. Modelling and Computer Added Design, *ALL Press*, Bucharest, Romania (1998).
5. E. Pop, C. Covaciu, A. Avram, F. Neghina. Adaptive Control Strategy for Conveyor Drve Systems, *Proceeding of the 8th International Conference on CIRCUITS, SYSTEMS, ELECTRONICS, CONTROL & SIGNAL PROCESSING*, Puerto de la Cruz, Tenerife, Spain, ISBN 978-960-474-139-7, ISSN 1790-5117, pp.156-161, (2009).
6. M. Leba, E. Pop, A. Badea, Adaptive Software Oriented Automation for Industrial Elevator, *Proceedings of the 11th International Conference on Automatic Control, Modelling & Simulation*, Istanbul, Turkey, ISBN 978-960-474-082-6, ISSN 1790-5117, pp.128-133, **BLX36**, (2009).
7. Yager, RR, <u>Decision making with fuzzy probability assessments</u> Source: *IEEE TRANSACTIONS ON FUZZY SYSTEMS   Volume: 7 Issue: 4* pp. 462-467 (1999)
8. Yager, RR, <u>Human behavioral modeling using fuzzy and Dempster-Shafer theory</u>, *the 1st International Workshop on Social Computing, Behavioral Modeling   and   Prediction,   Phoenix   AZ Source: SOCIAL COMPUTING, BEHAVIORAL MODELING AND PREDICTION pp. 89-99 (2008)*

MAIN FACTORS TO MAINSTREAM DEBT FOR SHAPING CAPITAL STRUCTURE IN SERVICE, TRADE, TRANSFORMATION, CONSTRUCTION SECTORS, MINING INDUSTRY AND TELECOMUNICATION IN MEXICO

JUAN GAYTÁN CORTES[*], JOSÉ SÁNCHEZ GUTIÉRREZ

*University Center of Economic-Administrative Sciences
Universidad de Guadalajara,
Guadalajara, Jalisco, México*

JOEL BONALES VALENCIA

*Institute of Economic and Enterprise Investigations
Universidad Michoacana de San Nicolás de Hidalgo
Morelia, Michoacán, México*

ABSTRACT

The purpose of this study was to construct a mathematical model to identify key institutional factors of the country and the company, its mathematical relationship and their discrepancies, by incorporating debt, forming the capital structure of the service, trade, processing, construction and extractive industries as well as telecommunications. The context that enabled the analysis of this phenomenon was shaped by companies in each sector that were quoted within the Mexican Stock Exchange (MSE) in the period 2000-2007.

The financial data was sorted, graphed and analyzed. Afterwards, it was used to power the E-Views version 4.1. The long-term debt was the dependent variable. The independent variables were the main factors of the country and company. The positive or negative mathematical relationship was calculated, using the statistical technique which is known as *panel data*. Finally, discrepancies between the sectors were shown.

Keywords: capital structure, institutional factors of the company, the country's institutional factors, sectorial differences.

---

[*] This work was to construct a mathematical model to identify key institutional factors of the country and the company, its mathematical relationship and discrepancies, by including debt, forming the capital structure of the service, trade, processing, construction, mining and telecommunications industries in Mexico.

1. Introduction

The theoretical models which were developed in the last half century have sought to validate and generalize, sometimes, the irrelevance thesis by Modigliani and Miller [20], They have tried to adapt some others as well, the maximum indebtedness by Modigliani and Miller [18] to the empirical evidence that the market limits the indebtedness capacity of the company. From the convergence of two research lines, in the 60's came a renewed theory of capital structure, which postulates the existence of an optimal capital structure as the suitable solution to the problem.

Decisions of the capital structure are even more complicated when examined in an international context, particularly in developing countries where markets are characterized by the limitations of government institutions, Boateng [4].

We reviewed the theories that have been addressed on the factors and the relationship and influence they exert by determining the capital structure, mentioning the following ones among the others: theory of optimal capital structure, tax base theory, theory of asymmetric information, hierarchical selection theory and *pecking order theory* (POT). Moreira and Mesquita [21] found evidence in favor of this theory. Fama and French [9] found a positive relationship between debt and profitability supporting the theory (POT). Brown and Lima [3], found that small firms borrow more short-term and verified a positive relationship between total debt and long term confirming the theory (POT). In the theory of agency costs and the theory of free cash flow, Faulkender and Petersen [11] developed a model to analyze the funding's source effect for firms in determining their capital structure.

We also reviewed empirical studies that support these theories, highlighting among others the study by Rajan and Zingales [23], and the Wald's study [31]. These studies provided empirical evidence for G7 countries, Bradley, Harrell and Kim [2] Kester [18], Van der Wijst the [30], Chung [8], Filbeck and Gorman [13]. Just as Booth, Aivazian, Demirguc-Kunt, and Maksimovic [6], who examined the determinants of capital structure in ten developing countries during 1980-1990 and providing the evidence that the determinants are similar in developed countries. Chang and Maquieira [6] replicated the study by Rajan and Zingales [24], for Latin American companies issuing American Depositary Receipt, ADR, checking the sign and significance of three out of four determinants studied: growth opportunities (-), size (+) and profitability (-).

Famá and Perobelli [10], using the study of Titman and Wessels [29], found a negative relationship between resource growth, size and profitability with the degree of short-term debt. Gomes [15], Fried and Lang [14], considering the size, growth, risk and industry, found a negative relationship between debt and profitability factors, growth and size.

In relation to the sector, empirical evidence has been presented by Gupta [16], Scott and Martin [28], Schwartz and Aronson [27] and Archer and Faerber [1], among others, showing that the kind of industry influences financial structure.

Authors Ferri and Jones [12], using data on U.S. companies re-examined this relationship and concluded that there is a definite relationship between capital structure and the sector or industry classification. Moreover, the evidence presented dissenting studies by Remmers, Stonehill, Wright and Beekhuis [23], who argue that the kind of industry is not a determinant element of capital structure.

2. Objective

The *Financial Theory* considers the optimization of capital structure is part of the problem of financial goal, which is identified with the normative principle of maximization of shareholder wealth regarded as a rational guide for the efficient placement cash surpluses in the capital market or investment of tangible and intangible.

Given this assumption it is necessary to identify the factors and relationship to determine the design of the new rules of behavior that will replace the company's structure prescriptive models that are supported by "should be" and replaced by a satisfactory explanation of the capital structures used by companies.

Most of the literature that looks at an association between capital structure and the specific characteristics of the firm or the country has been conducted in developed economies. However, in emerging markets, conversely that in developed countries, there are many institutional differences between some researches in these scenarios may be mentioned Schulman et al. [26] for New Zealand, Wiwattanakantang [32] for Taiwan, Chen [7] for China, Boateng [4] to Ghana, Sayılgan Güven, Hakan Karabacak, Güray Küçükkocaoglu [17] to Turkey.

Considering the theories and empirical studies that have been already analyzed, this research was guided by the following general objectives:

1. Identifying key institutional factors of the country and the company as well as its mathematical relationship with the addition of debt to make capital structure used by firms in service sectors, trade, processing, construction and telecommunications in Mexico.

2. Identifying discrepancies between the main institutional factors of the company and the country, incorporating debt in the formation of the capital structure used by firms in service, trade, processing, construction and mining sectors as well as telecommunications in Mexico.

3. Methodology of Research and Development

The statistical technique used to estimate the multivariate mathematical relationship is known as the "panel data", and the information is processed using the electronic "E-Views" version 4.1. The general specification of the regression model with panel data is as follows, Pindik and Rubinfeld [22]:

$$Y_{it} = \alpha_{it} + X_{it} \qquad \beta + u_{it}$$

Con i = 1,......N;   t = 1,...T.

Where:
I = refers to the individual or study unit (cross section)
t = refers to a time dimension
α =refers to a vector of intercepts of n parameters
β = refers to a vector of K parameters
X it = refers to the "ith" observation at the t time for the K explanatory variables
The total sample of observations within the model would be given by: N x T.

4. Verification

The results obtained after applying the statistical tests using the technique of panel data show that the main country´s institutional factors and companies are related to the debt addition by forming capital structure which is used by service, trade, transformation, construction mining and telecommunication companies in Mexico, are not the same and they do not have the same mathematical relation to each of the sectors. See summary tables shown in No.1 and No.2.

Table No. 1 Summarizes the main factors of the country and the company that is related to the addition of debt in the considered sectors:

TABLE 1: KEY FACTORS BY SECTOR

TRADE

Interest Rate
Income Tax
Inflation
Sales
Utility
Parity

SERVICES

Interest Rate
Income Tax
Inflation
Sales
Utility

TELECOMMUNICATIONS

Interest Rate
Inflation
Sales
Utility

TRANSFORMATION

Income Tax
Sales
Parity
Capital

CONSTRUCTION

Interest Rate
Inflation
Sales
Parity

EXTRACTIVES INDUSTRIES

Interest Rate
Inflation
Income Tax
Sales
Active

Source: Prepared by the leaving results of E-views software

TABLE 2: DISCREPANCIES IN MAJOR SECTORAL FACTORS INCORPORATE IN THEIR DEBT TO CAPITAL STRUCTURE

Concept	Saes	Int_Rate	Inflation	Utility	Active	Inc. Tax	Parity	Capital
Trade	*	*	*	*		*	*	
Services	*	*	*	*		*		
Telecommunications	*	*	*	*				
Extractives	*	*	*		*	*		
Construction	*	*	*				*	
Transformation	*					*	*	*
	5	4	4	3	1	4	3	1

Source: Prepared by the leaving results of E-views software

5. Conclusions

The research achieved its object of study which was to identify some key quantitative factors of the country and the company that are associated with the addition of debt to make capital structure, and the discrepancies among the major factors of business service, trade, processing, construction, mining and telecommunications industries in Mexico. We acknowledge factors arising from the qualitative characteristics such as culture, power, country risk, and personal values are factors that can influence and change the results, which turn out to be considerable reasons why we suggest to be included in further investigations.

References

1. S.H. Archer, and L. G. Faerber, "Firm Size and Cost of Equity" *Journal of Finance*, p. 69-84, (1996).
2. M. Bradley, G. A. Harrel, and E. H. Kim E. H., "On the Existence of and Optimal Capital Structure: Theory and Evidence", *The Journal of Finance*, Vol. XXXIX, No. 3, pp. 857-880, (1984).
3. R. D. Brito, and M. R. Lima, "Que Determina la Estrutura de Capital en Brasil?", Análisis del 3o. Encuentro Brasil-Financia, realizado de 21 a 22 de julho de 2003, em São Paulo, SP, (2003).
4. Boateng, "Determinants of capital structure: evidence from international joint ventures in Ghana". *International Journal of Social Economics*, Vol. 31, No. 1/2, 56-66, (2004).
5. L. Booth, V. Aivazian, A. Demirguc-Kunt, and V. Maksimovic, "Capital Structures in Developing Countries," *Journal of Finance* 56 (1), 87-130, (2001).
6. J. Chang, and C. Maquieira, "Determinantes de la estructura de endeudamiento de empresas latinoamericanas emisoras de ADRs", *Estudios de Administración*, vol. 8, núm. 1, pp. 55-86, (2001).
7. J. J. Chen, "Determinants of capital structure of Chinese-listed companies". *Journal of Business Research*, Vol. 57, 1341-1351, (2003).
8. C. B. Chung, "Industrial Management & data Systems", *MCB University PressLimited*, Vol. 93, No. 9, pp. 19-29, (1993).
9. E. F. Famá, and K. R. French, "Testing tradeoff and Pecking Order Predictions about Dividend and Debt," *Review of Financial Studies* 15(1), 1-37, (2002)
10. R. Famá, F. Perobelli, and C. Finotti, "Factores Determinantes de la Estrutura de Capital: Aplicado a Empresas de Capital Abierto en Brasil",

Análisis del Primer Encuentro Brasil-Financia, realizado los días 23 y 24 de julho de 2001 en São Paulo, SP, (2001).

11. M. W. Faulkender, and A. M. Petersen, "Does the Source of Capital Affect Capital Structure?". AFA 2004 San Diego Meetings, (2003).

12. M. G. Ferri, and W. H. Jones, "Determinants of Financial Structure: A New Methodological Approach," *Journal of Finance*, 631-644, (1979).

13. G. Filbek, and R. F. Gorman, "Capital Structure and Asset Utilization: The Case of Resource Intensive Industries", *The Cuarterly Review of Economics and Finance,*Vol. 26, No. 4, pp. 211-228, (2000)

14. Fried, and L. H. P. I. Lang, "An Empirical Test of the Impact of Managerial Self-Interest on Corporate Capital Structure", *The Journal of Finance*, Vol. 43, No. 2, pp. 271-81, (1998).

15. G. L. Gomes, and R. P. Câmara, "Determinantes de la Estrutura de Capital de Empresas Brasileñas con Acciones Negociadas en Bolsas de Valores. In *Finanças Corporativas*. São Paulo, 2001).

16. M. C. Gupta, "The Effect of size, Growth, and Industry on the Financial Structure of Manufacturing Companies", *Jounal of Finance,* Vol. 24, No. 3, pp. 517-529, (1969).

17. S. Güven, H. Karabacak and G. Küçükkocaoglu, "The firm-specific determinants of corporate capital structure: evidence from turkish panel data" Investment Management and Financial Innovations, Volume 3, Issue 3, (2006).

18. W. C. Kester, "Capital and Ownership Structure: A Comparison of United States and Japanese Manufacturing Corporations", *Financial Management in Japan*, pp. 5-16, (1986).

19. F. Modigliani and M. Miller, "Corporate Income, Tax and the Cost of Capital: A Correction". *The American Economic Review*, Vol. 53, pp. 433-443, (1963).

20. F. Modigliani and M. Miller, "The Cost of Capital, Corporation Finance and The Theory of Investment", *American Economic Review*, Vol. 48, pp. 261-297, (1958).

21. M. Moreira and F. P. Mesquita, "Como una Indústria Financia su Crescimento: un Análisis de Brasil Pós-Plano Real, *Revista Econômica Contemporânea*, v. 5, pp. 35-67, (2001).

22. R. S. Pindyck and D. L. Rubinfeld, *Econometría: Modelos y Pronósticos*, McGraw Hill/Interamericana Editores, México, (2001).

23. R. G. Rajan and L. Zingales, "What do we know about capital structure? Some evidence from international data", *The Journal of Finance*, Vol. 50, No. 5, pp. 1421-1460, (1995).

24. R. G. Rajan and L. Zingales, "Financial dependence and growth", *The American Economic Review*, Nashville, Vol. 88, pp. 559-586, (1998).

25. L. Remmers, A. Stonehill, R. Wright and T., "Industry and Size as Debt Ratio Determinants in Manufacturing Internationally", *Financial Management*, pp. 24-32, (1974).

26. T. Schulman, W. T. Deborah, K. F. Sellers and D. B. Kennedy, "Effects of tax integration and capital gains tax on corporate leverage". *National Tax Journal*, Vol. 49, No. 1, 31-54, (1996).

27. E. Schwartz and J. R. Aronson, "Some Surrogate Evidence in Support of the Concept of Optimal Financial Structure," *Journal of Finance*: 10-18, (1967).

28. D. F. Scott and J. D. Martin, "Industry Influence on Financial Structure," *Financial Management*, (1976).

29. S. Titman, and R. Wessels, "The Determinants of Capital Structure Choice", *Jounal of Finance*, Vol. 43, No. 1, pp. 1-19, (1988).

30. D. Van el Der Wijst, "Financial Structure in Small Business: Theory, test and application", *Lecture Notes in Economics and Mathematical Systems series*, No. 320, Nueva York, Londres y Tokyo, (1989).

31.J. K. Wald, "How firm characteristics affect capital structure: and international comparison", *The Journal of Financial Research*, Vol. XXII, No. 2, pp. 161-187, (1999).

32. Y. Wiwattanakantang, "An empirical study on the determinants of the capital structure of Thai firms". *Pacific-Basin Finance Journal*, Vol. 7, 371-403, (1999)

A NANOTECHNOLOGY JOINT INVESTMENT FRAMEWORK[*]

MARIA TERESA CASPARRI

CMA, Facultad Ciencias Económicas, Universidad de Buenos Aires

JAVIER GARCIA FRONTI

CMA, Facultad Ciencias Económicas, Universidad de Buenos Aires

This paper captures three main characteristics of the nanotechnology market in a valuation framework: (a) uncertainty due to technological and political (regulation) factors; (b) cooperation between companies (One specialized in R&D and a manufacturer) and (c) government's incentives. The valuation model proposed here includes these characteristics in a joint investment valuation framework. This construction could be used by policymakers to analysed incentives in the R&D market.

Keywords: nanotechnology, real options, cooperative game, investment valuation.

1. Introduction

The term nanotechnology has been formed both from scientific community as from the public imagination. Among scientists, who first used the term was Norio Taniguchi [1]. For the general public, was K. Eric Drexler [2] who popularized the term and using a visionary speech about the possibility of building robots to scale "nano" (nanobots). Along with him, visionaries promise nanotechnology solutions to major problems of mankind, but we still have to wait for these active devices being available for the general public. However, there is a current reality of nanomaterials in many consumer products unthinkable a few years ago.

Wood, Jones and Geldart [3] present the identification of three perspectives on nanotechnologies: a) incremental Nanotechnology, where work is essentially a continuation of the research over the past 50 years in science materials, b) evolutionary Nanotechnology, which addresses the reduction of existing

---

[*] The authors thank valuable comments from two anonymous referees and gratefully acknowledge the financial support of the UBACyT E008, PICT 00770 (Agencia) y UBACyT E012. Corresponding author: Javier García Fronti (fronti@econ.uba.ar)

technologies to the nanoscale. It focuses on rare materials that allow an evolution of information technology, and c) radical Nanotechnology, which includes active devices. Currently Nano products in the market are primarily from the incremental category. Towards the end of 2007, the inventory of consumer products that include nanotechnology, by Project on Emerging Nanotechnologies [4], had 580. This presence in the market and the future explosion of the offering, immediately requires thinking about how to assess private investments in nanotechnology together with its risks: level of toxicity to humans [5, 6] or to environment [7].

Like other technologies, nanotechnology refers not only to a size problem, but also the economic and social interaction between the actors involved that gives meaning. Its market is a concept in process of formation, which is constructed by the constant interaction of the actors involved. The scientific practice is co-constituted with a corresponding market. Understanding the latter as a coordination mechanism in which agents maximize their interests through economic calculations and where conflicts are resolved by setting prices [8]. These agents are part of a network of relationships and social connection[†].

This paper captures three main characteristics of this market into a valuation framework. Firstly, this market is uncertain due to technological and political (regulation) factors. Secondly, to reach the retail market with a product including nanotechnology, it is necessary cooperation between companies: One specialized in R&D and a manufacturer capable of reaching retail market. This work relies in real option theory to calculate the present value and flexibility of the investment. Moreover, and to account for interaction between companies, game theory concepts are also included. Finally, this market usually needs government's intervention, supporting companies doing R&D.

Therefore, and based in the methodology proposed by Savva and Scholtes [10], this paper proposes a basic framework to understand the interaction between a nanotechnology company and a manufacturer when they start a joint investment aiming to sell one consumer product that includes nanomaterials. Moreover, the role of the government is analysed. To do so, the paper is organised into three sections. The following one is an overview of the model. The next section specifies the participation constrains for the Nanotechnology

---

[†] However, the dynamics of this practice and its market, poses new risks. The latest reports from the UK government and business organizations are some examples of this [9]. They stressed that nanotechnology may be the main engine of economic growth, replacing the information technology. In this view, opposing pressure groups (many of whom were and are in the GM debate) that postulate that nanotechnology is likely to have adverse effects to be studied and regulated.

Company and for the producer. The last section is an extension that includes government incentive to the project in the form of a option. Finally some conclusions are stated and some further research is proposed.

2. A joint investment model

This section presents a model for investment valuation in the Nano market. In the economy proposed there are two companies. One is a Nanotech company that has specialisation in R&D (with no access to the consumer market). The second one is a national manufacturer with huge experience selling consumer products. They need each other to deliver a product with nanotechnology to the market.

Before the project started, the agents know how much money want to invest (K_N, K_A), the expected income at the end of the project (Y), the probability of good state (p), the volatility (σ) and the discount factor (β). The timeline is as follow: At time "0", Nanotech (N) invests in R&D a quantity KN. By time "1", the manufacturer invests KA to start the production. With these two investments in place, at the end of the project they receive a total output of "Y". However, due to uncertainty, the project could be above mean (uY) or below (dY). In any case, the final output is shared among companies, Nanotech receives αY and the manufacturer $(1 - \alpha$Y).

The intuition behind this uncertainty could be a competitor targeting the same market with a similar product. If the competitor has succeeded, the final output is lower than expected (and higher if the competitor failed). To take this into account, the model assumes that final outcome of the project follows a geometric Brownian motion with no drift; agents have zero risk aversion and the project has a failure probability of "p" [11, 12]. To ensure that the initial valuation of "Y" is consistent with the assumptions of the scenario, these expressions are the first order approximation for the upwards and downwards:

$$u = 1 + \sigma\sqrt{\frac{1-p}{p}}; \quad d = 1 - \sigma\sqrt{\frac{p}{1-p}}$$

Summing up the basic structure of the game is as follow (see figure 1). At time zero Nanotech calculates the parameters of the project and calculates its present value (with discount factor β) and he decides to invest or not. If he enters into the game, the technology is ready for production at time 1. At this point, the national producer values the project and decides if she wants to invest KA (agreeing to pay Nanotech a fraction α of the final income at time 2). The project is subject to uncertainty with probability "p" and volatility "σ". At the end of the project the value of "Y" is realised and each company receives the fraction promised at the beginning.

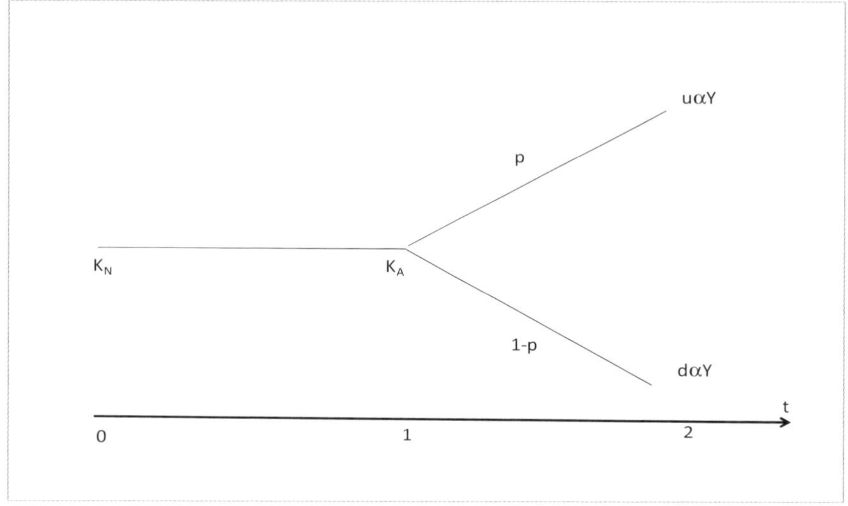

Figure 1: Timeline

3. Participation constraints

As it mentioned above, each agent values the project from their point of view. Nanotech will receive a fraction α of the final outcome; so he discounts it two periods to compare it with the initial investment in R&D. The national producer values the project knowing that she will receive the rest of the outcome and discounting it back one period. Therefore the following participation constraints have to be satisfied:

$$\text{Nanotech } \beta^2[puY\alpha + (1-p)dY\alpha] \geq K_N \tag{1}$$

$$\text{Producer } \beta[puY(1-\alpha) + (1-p)dY(1-\alpha)] \geq K_A \tag{2}$$

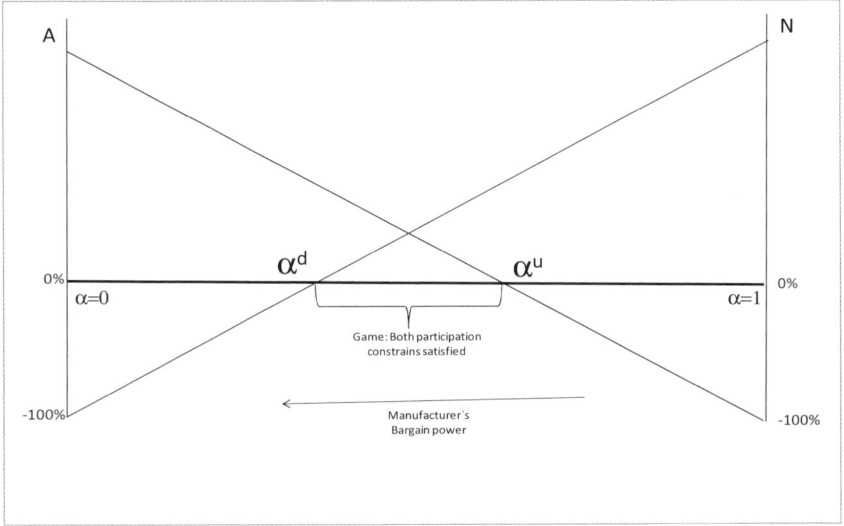

Figure 2: Present value of revenues depending on α

Clearly, the present value of each revenue depends on α. If all the income is for the manufacturer (α = 0), her revenue is maximum. On the contrary, if α = 1, Nanotech receives maximum revenue (see Figure 2). In the two boundaries, there is no game due to a violation of the participation constrains. As far as the joint project is profitable, Nanotech will participate if receives an expected share (present value) bigger than the initial investment (α ≥ α^d) and the producer will join if α ≤ α^u. Therefore, the joint investment will take place if α ∈ [α^d, α^u]. From (1) and (2) we obtain:

$$\alpha \geq \frac{K_N}{Y\beta^2} = \alpha^d$$

$$1 - \alpha \geq \frac{K_A}{Y\beta} = 1 - \alpha^u$$

Assuming that the national producer has bigger bargain power than Nanotech, she could impose α^d (maximising her revenue into the game). Moreover, she also could enforce a smaller value using her bargaining power, forcing nanotech out of the game and destroying the possibility of the joint project. Next section analyses how government intervention could help to keep both on board assuming that the project has positive externalities for society.

4. Participation constraints with governmental incentive

This section analyses the situation where the manufacturer have enough bargain power to enforce $\alpha < \alpha^d$, so Nanotech opts out due to a violation of his participation constrain. Let introduce a new player in the game: the government. Clearly, an investment in R&D will produce a multiplicative effect in the economy increasing the tax income in the long run. Therefore the government has an evident incentive to bring Nanotech back into the game.

Let assume the government guarantee a minimum repayment of $xY < uY$ at time "2" to Nanotech. Therefore, his participation constraints changes accordingly; while the producer´s one remain unchanged (See Figure 3):

$$\text{Nanotech} \quad \beta^2[puY + (1-p)\max(dY\alpha xY)] \geq K_N \tag{3}$$

$$\text{Producer} \quad \beta[puY(1-\alpha) + (1-p)dY(1-\alpha)] \geq K_A \tag{4}$$

from (3) and (4):

$$(pu + (1-p)\max(d\alpha, x)) = \overline{\alpha}^d \leq \alpha^d$$

$$1 - \alpha \geq \frac{K_A}{Y\beta} = 1 - \alpha^u.$$

Therefore, the joint investment will take place if $\alpha \in [\overline{\alpha}^d, \alpha^u]$, extending the interval where the game will take place.

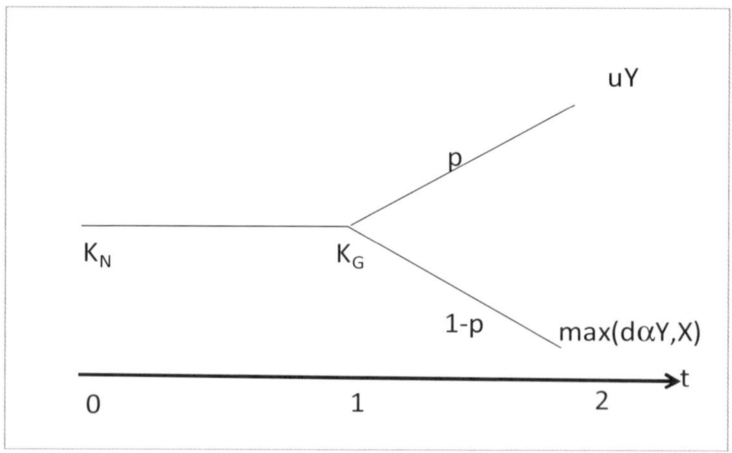

Figure 3: Time line with one-sided option

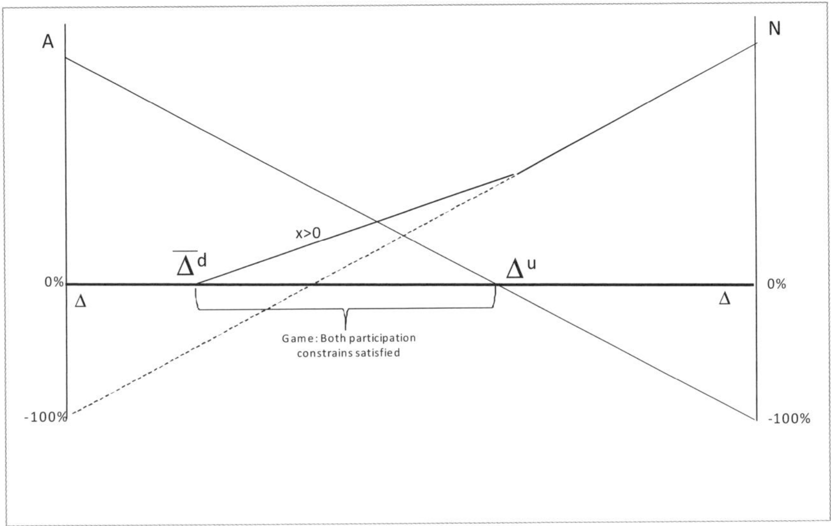

Figure 4: Revenues under government intervention depending on α

The revenues depending on α, changes accordingly for Nanotech. Meanwhile $\alpha \geq \dfrac{x}{d}$, there is no government intervention so the figure is exactly like the previous case. However if $\alpha < \dfrac{x}{d}$, Nanotech will receive an incentive to participate. This is reflected in figure 4.

Finally some policy remarks are presented. The government´s incentive is paid at time 2. Clearly this is a counter cycle strategy. The government could contribute to increase employment in recession, with no payment at time "0". Moreover, if the government is credible, it is also possible to sell this option into the market.

5. Conclusion

This work proposed a model for joint-investments valuation. Firstly a cooperative project is analysed. If it is no possible for both players to participate, an extension is presented where a government incentive is included.

This framework could be used by policymakers to analysed incentives in the R&D market. One important feature of the present proposal is that do not require cash payment from the government at the moment the project start.

References

1. N. Taniguchi, *On the basic concept of nanotechnology*, Proc. Int. Conf. Prod. Eng (1974), 18-23.
2. K. E. Drexler, *Engines of creation: [the coming era of nanotechnology]*, Doubleday/Anchor Press, 1986.
3. S. Wood, R. Jones and A. Geldart, *Nanotechnology: From the science to the social. The social, ethical and economic aspects of the debate.*, ESRC, London, 2007.
4. Project on Emerging Nanotechnologies, "An inventory of nanotechnology-based consumer products currently on the market," Woodrow Wilson International Center for Scholars and the Pew Charitable Trusts. http://www.nanotechproject.org/inventories/consumer/, 2008.
5. D. Cui, F. Tian, C. S. Ozkan, M. Wang and H. Gao, *Effect of single wall carbon nanotubes on human hek293 cells*, Toxicol.Lett. **155** (2005), 73-85.
6. C. W. Lam, J. T. James, R. McCluskey and R. L. Hunter, *Pulmonary toxicity of single-wall carbon nanotubes in mice 7 and 90 days after intratracheal instillation*, Toxicol Sci **77** (2004), 126-134.
7. V. L. Colvin, *The potential environmental impact of engineered nanomaterials*, Nature Biotechnology **21** (2003), no. 10, 1166-1170.
8. M. Callon, "Actor-network theory: The market test," *Actor network theory and after*, J. Law and J. Hassard (Editors), 1999, pp. 181-195.
9. The Royal Society & The Royal Academy of Engineering, *Nanoscience and nanotechnologies: Opportunities and uncertainties*, The Royal Society & The Royal Academy of Engineering, Plymouth, UK, 2004.
10. N. D Savva and S. Scholtes, "Real options in partnership deals: The perspective of cooperative game theory," Discussion paper. Cambridge: Judge Business School, University of Cambridge, 2005.
11. J. Hull, *Options, futures. And other derivative securities (6e)*, New York: Prentice-Hall. Englewood Clis, 2006.
12. D. G. Luenberger, *Investment science*, Oxford University Press New York, 1998.

ORIGIN AND DIFFUSION OF DIRECT COSTING: EVOLUTION OR SCIENTIFIC REVOLUTION?

ALFREDO ROCAFORT NICOLAU

*Accounting Department, Area of Financial Economics and Accounting,
University of Barcelona, Diagonal 690-696, 08034-Barcelona*

The origin and evolution of *direct costing* (DC) approaches is a field rarely covered by cost accounting historians. This study does not only aim to systematize the historical evolution account which explains the appearance of DC, but also to show how this proposal, based on distinct accounting treatment of fixed costs and variable costs, adjusts more to the scheme of birth and development of a research programme as foreseen by I. Lakatos, than that outlined on the origin of a scientific revolution implicit in the kuhnian theory of the paradigm.

1. Introduction

To face the problem of the origin and evolution of direct costing (DC), the scholars of this approach tend to adopt one of the following two perspectives:

a) The perspectives which concentrate on the internal reality of the proposal, that is to say the technical and doctrinal framework, for which the study of the gradual theoretical- practical birth and development of the DC approaches are asked of the historian.

b) The perspective which enlightens the external reality, apparently more epidermal and anecdotal but equally clarifying, which consists of describing the impact of the reactions that this approach produces between academics and professionals.

This investigation adopts an eclectic attitude, voluntarily moving between both points of view, with the intention of stressing in the first place the continuist and non ground-breaking character of the DC proposal. This first objective will lead to an attempt to place the family of DC sub-approaches within a united interpretation of the historical trajectory marked by Cost Accounting.

170

1.1. *The NACA statements*

In its bulletin of April, 1953, the NACA - *National Association of Cost Accountants* (at the present time, IMA - *Institute of Management Accounting)* stated a series of considerations on the long and large investigation carried out on DC by the scientific and professional community within the association. These conclusions, found in the 23 *Research Report,* outlined the first version of the direct costing approach.

Following the cited report, the proposal to record in the books products on the unique base of variable costs was considered to be of special usefulness for managers and investors of a company. As far as fixed costs are concerned, a rigorous examination of their nature seemed to justify that they were deemed period charges and were not assigned to the products: a fixed cost is a cost which serves the company to be able to *be* in business, no to *do* business, following the conclusion of the controller J. Freeman (1961) at an association meeting.

Starting from the year 1953 a period of diffusion and analysis of the new accounting doctrine began in all kinds of forums and publications. A task of diffusion in which the same NACA bulletins played a key role, welcoming both defenders and detractors of the proposal.

The publication of two institutional reports which appeared in the same year (1961) should be mentioned in particular: one again coming from the NACA and the other from the ICMA *(Institute of Cost and Management Accountants)* emphasising the practical interest of the DC model.[*] One year later W. Wright (1962) signalled that the key to *direct costing* was in the separation of the variable costs linked to the production volume of the fixed costs, linked to the period. The first two alone form the value of the inventories, allowing the need to reclassify fixed costs according to the maintaining or not of a tight relationship with a determined product (direct fixed costs). These precisions outlined the second of the two versions of DC: the simple and the developed.

---

[*] The 37 NACA Research Report bore the significant title *Current application of direct costing* and contained well thought out affirmations on the model, given that the previous year two congresses had been celebrated on the subject. Compare the following reflection with previous others: *"Manufacturing costs of the period arise from supplying capacity to production and by maintaining this capacity at a certain point, independent to the level of intensity used. And given that the opportunity to use the capacity expires over time, the costs which support said capacity should also be considered to expire over time"*.

1.2. *DC approaches before 1953*

The original proposal ratified by the NACA in 1953 originated several years earlier, with it being possible to be confirm that its formal gestation comes from the years before and after 1929. Nowadays the paternity of the global proposal tends to not be attributed to only one author, but two. In effect, in 1937 G. Charter Harrison finally achieved the publication of a polemic article, which he had written years before and which the secretary of NACA, R. Marple, did not dare to include in the bulletin because of its bold radicalism, beginning with the biblical echoing title: *New wine in old bottles: Why most profit and loss statements are wrong*. For G. Charter Harrison the new ideas on the accounting treatment of fixed and variable costs (*the new wine*) clearly clashed with the traditional conceptual brand (*the old bottles*).

The other author was J. N. Harris, to whom should be attributed not only the fact that he proposed an identical DC approach which Harrison had proposed in parallel, but the exclusive paternity of the term *Direct Costing*, a term which would be converted into a source of continuous mistake making. After having implanted the DC accounting calculation system in the chemical company where he worked as a controller (with lukewarm results) in 1934, J. Harris achieved the approval of the cited secretary of the NACA, R. Marple, who, after serious doubts, allowed the publication of his article which, together with that of G. Harrison, would fuel the controversy of fixed and variable costs, ignited in the previous decade. In January 1936, the regular readers of the monthly NACA bulletin could read (volume 17), many with great surprise and some with indignation, the 25 page document entitled *How much did we earn last month?*, written by J. Harris.

For historiographical purposes, the DC polemic can be enclosed in the two decades from 1935 to 1955, and its appearance date can be stated as 1936. Even though it is possible to contribute indications that the proposal as such was already taking shape at the beginning of the 20th century and even before. In this way O. Nielsen (1966) contributed an early sample of a document from 1919 belonging to the Midland Club, an association of Midwestern candy manufacturers, dated in Sioux Falls, South Dakota. An Association which proposed an accounting solution close to DC methodology.[*]

---

[*] O. Nielsen (1966), A predecessor of Direct Costing, Journal of Accounting Research, spring. In this document he pleaded for a uniform system of accounting and a definition of the gross margin close to DC: *The practical man wants (...) direct methods, devoid of complicated procedure, so that every step to the final result may be clearly traced (...) It means practically nothing to one manufacturer for another to tell him that his Gross Profits do average or should average a certain percent of his sales, because the second manufacturer does not know what that means*

2. The DC proposal, a supposed paradigmatic change

2.1. *The polemical diffusion of the DC approach in the U.S.A.*

Following S. Specthrie (1963), the first significant implementation of the model was in 1947 by the company Pittsburgh Plate Glass Co. Shortly after the case of Staley Manufacturing, a corn factory, was discussed. This was seasonally strong and presented results which were not convincing with the traditional complete costs model.

The same author signalled that in 1953 the NAA *(National Association of Accountants,* earlier NACA*)* only counted among its thousands of members some 17 companies which used DC. A decade later, in 1962, The magazine *Business Week* (24-03-62) counted the number of large companies which had adopted the model at 250.

In 1962 the same S. Specthrie predicted a notable increase in the number of companies adopting DC, if it could be achieved, as was the interest of its defenders, that United States fiscal institutions (specifically the IRS) approved DC as a base for the valuation of inventory.

But judging by the reactions found by accounting professionals and theorists, it can be said that none of the DC family approaches had an easy path to acceptance. In fact, in the year 1936, the cited article by J. Harris *(How much did we earn last month?)* raised a storm of criticism and defenders without precedent.

What must be stressed here, in the same way, is that this kind of polemic took place between the members themselves and in the heart of one institution, such as the NACA. (And, in passing, it must also be stated the importance that at the head of these institutions personalities such as R. Marple, who occupied the post of secretary of the NACA for 30 years , were to be found).

2.2. *The European debate: from the British cost war to the Schneider-Schmalembach dispute*

In my opinion, one of the most severe criticisms received by DC, although not the most rigorous, is owed to O. Gelinier (1966). This French engineer, General Director of C.E.G.O.S., did not mind affirming, in spite of worldwide

---

unless he knows how the first manufacturer arrives at his Cost and Gross Profits. Manufacturers might as well talk in all languages of the earth as talk in terms of Gross Profit and Cost, unless they know that they are considering elements of cost in a like manner.

commotion, that the named direct cost system was a crude and primitive method, was at the core a return to the system used in the previous century and could only give results in some simple cases.[*]

Still in the 1960's, the Belgian professor G. de Bodt (1964) echoed the effervescence produced by the new proposal between heads of the company, economists and financiers in charge, heads of industrial accounting and costs specialists. Practically every professional, technician or theoretician felt questioned by the atmosphere to opt for their own theoretical positions and their habitual accounting practises. A description of the *battles* between 'fullcosters' and 'directcosters' in UK can be read in the article by D; T. Dugdale and J. Colwyn.[†]

Following G. Dorn (1961)[‡] the first classification of cost accounting in fixed and variables is owed to E. Schmalembach (1873-1955), author of the article "Accounting and calculations in the factory" which appeared in 1899 in the metallurgical sector magazine *Renscheid.* Without doubt the 'theory of fixed costs' was one of the doctrinal field of attention for the German author. In 1919 he returned to the subject in a series of articles in the magazine *Commercial Scientific Investigation* and in 1937 he published *Der Kontenrahmen*, where he offered a practical vision of the problem. For E. Schmalembach it is essential that all companies separate, as far as possible, fixed costs of proportionals and permanently control of their evolution.[§]

But this interest contrasts with the lack of enthusiasm with which another of the more distinguished German authors of the age, E. Schneider covered the subject. This question is significantly dealt with in the last chapter of his book most recognised by cost accountants,[**] it did not bring anything to the progress of cost accounting. The proof is that the author has been able to elaborate a full costs methodology (the method by sections) without seeing the necessity of using the fixed costs doctrine approach at any time.

---

[*] O. Gelinier (1967), *Le secret des structures competitives*, Paris, Éditions Hommes Et Techniques, 1967.

[†] G. de Bodt, (1968), *Direct costing et programmation économique de l'entreprise à produits multiples*, Dunod, París, 1968: D; T. Dugdale and J. Colwyn (2003) Battles in the costing war: UK debates, 1950-75, *Accounting, Business & Financial History,* volume 13, issue 3, november

[‡] G. Dorn, The development of industrial cost calculation in Germany, Duncker & Humboldt, Berlín, 1961.

[§] E. Schmalembach, Der Kontenrahmen, Leipzig, 1937, 5th ed.

[**] E. Schneider (1969), *Industrielles Rechnungswesen. Grundlagen und Grundfragen*, J.C.B. Mohr, Tübingen, 5th ed. (first edition in the year 1939).

2.3. *Paradigm or research programme*

Before and after the description of the most prominent facts of the birth and development of DC, it fits to ask oneself if we find ourselves before a phenomenon which, with the due distances, has affiliated to the group of changes which Kuhn described as paradigm changes or if on the other hand it deals with the contrary, of a simple, but valuable, contribution destined to compliment the doctrinal body of cost accounting, configured up to the present time.

Formulating the question in a direct way: Can DC be considered as a new Kuhn paradigm, orientated to displace other out of date paradigms?, and in this case; Can the age from the years 1935 to 1955 be qualified as an age of scientific change and revolution?

The answer that we give to the question is negative. DC, as has been seen, provoked intense literary activity, followed by practical attempts, with the purpose of bringing points for and against it. But, examined from its posterior evolution, the typical dialectic forcefulness of the paradigmatic changes described by Kuhn does not appear.

Without doubt it was a notable effort of the defenders of DC for confronting accounting of traditional costs, bound to an out of date accounting theory, with some modern approaches, also linked to the practices of economists. But, in spite of this effort, what is certain is that from the 1960's, the disputes ceased and a period of peaceful coexistence of the two previously conflictive approaches existed. This shows that during twenty years an equivocal debate had taken place, beginning with the same name DC. The return of AC, as pronounced by R. Anthony (1975) had brought about this pacification.

3. Working hypothesis for a conciliating vision of accounting history

The evolutionary and non revolutionary interpretation of the history of DC demands a logical component which shows the trajectory followed by the proposal, not only an objective component (the documentary "tests"). This component is that which is considered a priority contribution in this study, leaving for another work the documented conclusions. In the following a personal interpretation of this history in the form of "working hypothesis" is proposed.

3.1. *Why did DC arise?*

The birth of DC can be explained for various reasons, between which two stand out: a) approximation accountants – economists that had a place after the second world war; and b) the ever growing necessity of agile and reliable information for decision making.

Thanks to the new margin concept of contribution it was possible, as its defenders state, to satisfy the demands of studies on policies of price fixing such as that of R. Hall and C. Hitch.[*] It was also possible to apply cost-volume-profit analysis techniques which the incipient economists of the company were designing. But, it was also possible to move away from the real complexity of the companies, and here is where Johnson and Kaplan (1987) saw the beginning of the loss of relevance of cost accounting.

It is important to take into account the polemic on which Direct Cost turned during the years of its first gestation and development, around the adequacy between valuation of inventories and users of accounting information. Following the specific interpretation of what happened offered by H. Johnson and R. Kaplan (1988) if this polemic today seems to be overcome it is because the different duties of financial accounting and management accounting are understood more each day. What happened between 1930 and 1960 is the appearance in history of accounting practice of a figure that disorientated cost accountants: the figure of the external auditor, with the consequent proliferation of generally accepted accounting valuation norms which eased their work as an arbitrator.

But another reason exists which is worthy to take into account today. The passing of time has shattered the same substance of this debate, by which certain fiscal advantages attributable to DC are referred. The current problem is not so much the use of inventories as a fiscal management mechanism, such as its minimization. From 1973, first in Japan and later in all the Occident, a slogan of "frugality" has spread in the production and storage of goods. It is obvious that, faced with the generalization of zero-stock objectives, the demand of storable assets of certain companies has converted the polemic of how to value inventories as irrelevant. As a matter of fact, at the present time the best valuation is that which results as unnecessary.

---

[*] R. Hall and C. Hitch (1939), *Price theory and business behaviour*, Oxford Economics Papers, May.

176

3.2. *The multiple DC sub-proposals*

Another working hypothesis is the permanent "ambiguity" attributable to the concept of Direct Cost. When we speak of inventory valuation it seems a proposal in favour of the objectivity of the direct costs which reject the arbitrariness of the traditional allocations of the indirect, simply not assigned. But, when we speak of its usefulness for analysis and decision making the approach is openly based on the concept of variable costs, taken from the investigations of the business economics theorists.

Actually, and even though each updated exhibition of DC tries to place it in one of these two positions (direct costs- variable costs), the deposit of more than half a century passed since the official existence of the approach would justify a classification of the sub-approaches as in the following:

DC SUB-APPROACHES		
• Direct Cost (literal sense) • Hierarchical Costs • Costs for responsibilities	• Direct Cost vs Variable Cost • Variable costs (Anglo-Saxon approach) • Variable costs (European approach)	• Mixed direct cost (evolved) • Anglo-Saxon approach. • German approach

As far as the two remaining DC methods are concerned, many authors prefer to use the term *Variable Cost* in place of *Direct Cost* to make the orientation of the sub-approach which is being treated understood. (The expression Marginal Costs seems to be permanently relegated to the specific investigation of economists, despite the exceptional fact that some modern author prefers this term). The distinction between the Anglo-Saxon approach and the European approach is really a question of accents not only exclusive between the authors of one or other geographical environment. However, it is true that in the European models (particularly French and German) the localization of variable costs and fixed costs in homogeneous sections or centres of activity is stressed.

The "mixed" DC is almost exclusively fruit of an evolution in the study of decision making, particularly intense in the decade of the 1970's, and of a dispassionate assimilation of the most reasoned criticisms of the opponents of DC. With this model interest started to section the global "pool" of fixed costs in order to classify them in more detail. It was not only observed that certain fixed costs were related directly with determined product lines, but also that deepening in this line, some European authors – especially the Germans K. Agthe and P. Riebel – proposed a generalization of the concepts of contribution margin and direct fixed costs to whatever management object a cost calculation demanded. To this last model the denomination *Direct Costing for multiple calculation objects* is extremely suitable.[*]

3.3. *The logical component of the historical trajectory*

The story after the 1960's (that is to say, practically the last fifty years) of *Direct Cost* is a story of *fair neighbourhood* with *full costing*. All authors are of the opinion that both models are necessary, taking in the axiom already established at the beginning of the 20th century and remembered by R. Kaplan, that one cost system is not enough. Nevertheless, E. Schneider and other more modern European and Anglo-Saxon authors aim their suspicions against the place in which fixed costs are relegated (in Germany, in the time of Schneider and Schmalembach, the disputed question was denominated of the *fixed costs*, and not the variable and direct costs). It has been seen how the defenders of DC had to fall back when faced with the radical approaches of the first version of DC. First was the indiscriminate exclusion of fixed costs. Then a theory adjustment of direct fixed costs was formed. Finally the Germans proposed a generalized application model of this theory to the distinct objects of cost.

Following this, it is possible to confirm that the key which allows unity to the historical trajectory of cost accounting in the 20th century is that of fixed costs (the denominated *overhead*) and the way in which they are treated in internal accounting information. It must not be forgotten that in 19th century times before the explicitness of the *full costing* model, the overhead received little or no attention in the accounting reports especially created to take note of material consumption cost and man hours.

Gradually analytical thinking was taking a greater awareness of the importance it took for all the investigation system of the possible identification or traceability of fixed costs and, in general, of the indirects of other times. Only that this time the interest can be well explained by the necessity arising with the new configuration of companies in the 1960's and 1970's (multinationals, holdings, associations...) where the imposing volume of costs due to the complex structures of the same forced the accountants to look back on them.

This current of "rediscovery" of the indirects has overflowed at present times into ABC (*Activity Based Costing*). ABC, which aroused a similar debate to DC, today presents a known advantage: its approach allows the identification

---

[*] Cfr.: J. Weber - B. Weissenberger (1997), *Relative Einzelkosten- und Dechungsbeitragsrechnung: a critical evaluation of Riebel's approach, Management Accounting Research*, vol 11.

178

(trace) of costs, until now classified as indirect or fixed. Actually, with respect to the evolved DC models of the Germans, ABC only performs a slight displacement of the interest for determined "objects of cost" previously forgotten, which obliges the rethinking of the classic distinction between fixed and variable costs. Here we also find ourselves, according to J. Bromwich, before an *evolution* more than a *revolution*. A change of emphasis and approach.

In accordance with this work hypothesis, the evolutionary trajectory of the approaches in cost accounting would be that described in the following table:

FULL COST	SIMPLE DIRECT COST	EVOLVED DIRECT COST	GERMAN DIRECT COST	ABC
Inclusion of indirect costs in the calculation method, neglecting as much their behaviour standards as their traceability with respect to the product.	Exclusion of indirect costs of the calculation method, considering irrelevant as much their behaviour standards as their traceability.	Partial inclusion of indirect costs in calculation method, together with some limited attempts to examine as much their behaviour standards as their traceability.	Inclusion of indirect costs in calculation method, together with a generalized attempt to examine as much their behaviour standards as their traceability.	Overcoming of the direct-indirect and fixed-variable distinction, with the explicit objective of examining as much the behaviour standards as traceability of all costs.
Key concepts: Product costs and business results.	**Key concepts:** Product costs, gross contribution margin and business result.	**Key concepts:** Product costs, gross and net contribution margin and business result.	**Key concepts:** Product costs, net contribution margin by activity of business and business result.	**Key concepts:** Product costs, complete cost of activities, non financial means for continuous improvement and business result.

In the opinion of the writer, the evolution of cost accounting in the 20th century is a story of apparently opposed, but deep down complementary, contributions. From there the coexistence of all arising and identified models. Once again, the conception of the lakatosian scientific change seems to adjust better than that proposed by Khun, to the historical reality in which cost accounting has developed.

References

1. R. N. Anthony (1975), The rebirth of cost accounting, *Management Accounting* (October).
2. G. de Bodt (1968), *Direct Costing*, Dunod, París, 1968.
3. J. Brown (1991), Marginal Costing, *Handbook of Management Accounting*, coord. R. Cowe, Gower Publishing Co., Aldershot (Hms.), England 2nd ed.

4. O. Gelinier (1967), *El secreto de las estructuras competitivas*, TEA, Madrid.
5. J. Harris (1936), *How much did we earn last month*, en N.A.C.A. Bulletin, January.
6. H. T. Johnson, R. S. Kaplan (1987), *Relevance Lost: The Rise and Fall of Management Accounting*. Boston: Harvard Business School Press.
7. V. Serra Salvador, J. Vilar Sanchís (1993), *Contabilidad de costes parciales (modelos Direct Cost), Cuestiones actuales de contabilidad de costes*, coord. A. Sáez Torrecilla, ACODI-McGrawHill, Madrid
8. E. Schmalembach (1937), *Der Kontenrahmen*, Leipzig, 5th ed. The quote is taken from the book by E. Schneider (1969).
9. E. Schneider (1969), *Industrielles Rechnungswesen. Grundlagen und Grundfragen*, J.C.B. Mohr, Tübingen, 5th ed.
10. S. W. Specthrie (1963), *Basic Cost Accounting*, Prentice Hall, Englewood Cliffs, N. J.

DECISION MAKING TECHNIQUES IN A UNIFIED MODEL BETWEEN THE WEIGHTED AVERAGE AND THE OWA OPERATOR

JOSÉ M. MERIGÓ, ANNA M. GIL-LAFUENTE

Department of Business Administration, University of Barcelona,
Av. Diagonal 690, 08034 Barcelona, Spain

We develop a new decision making model that uses a unified framework between the weighted average and the ordered weighted averaging (OWA) operator. This model is based on the use of similarity measures such as the adequacy coefficient and the index of maximum and minimum level. Moreover, it also uses the ordered weighted averaging – weighted average (OWAWA) operator. Thus, we get some new aggregation operators such as the OWAWA adequacy coefficient (OWAWAAC) and the OWAWA index of maximum and minimum level (OWAWAIMAM) operator. We develop an application of the new approach in a decision making problem concerning the selection of strategies. We see that each method may lead to different results.

1. Introduction

Decision making problems are very common in the literature. One methodology for carrying out the decision process is by using ideals that are compared with the available alternatives. This can be done with a wide range of similarity measures. One of the most common one is by using distance measures [1-3,5-6]. Another way for doing so is by using t-norms and related techniques. A very popular technique is the adequacy coefficient [2]. It uses a Luckasiewicz t-norm in the comparison process in such a way that if the result of the available alternative is higher than the ideal, the result is neutralized and if it is equal or lower it is calculated as in the Hamming distance. In [1], J. Gil-Lafuente suggested an index that used the Hamming distance and the adequacy coefficient in the same formulation depending on the specific characteristic considered. Recently, some new generalizations have been suggested by using the ordered weighted averaging (OWA) operator and related techniques [3,6].

The OWA operator [7] is an aggregation operator that provides a parameterized family of aggregation operators between the minimum and the maximum. Since its introduction, it has been studied and applied by a lot of authors [3-4,8]. Recently, Merigó [3-4] has suggested a new aggregation operator that unifies the OWA operator with the weighted average considering the degree of importance that each concept has in the aggregation. He called it the ordered weighted averaging – weighted average (OWAWA) operator.

When dealing with similarity measures, Merigó and A.M. Gil-Lafuente [3,6] have suggested the use of the OWA operator and its extensions in the adequacy coefficient and in the index of maximum and minimum level. They called it the OWA adequacy coefficient (OWAAC) and the OWA index of maximum and minimum level (OWAIMAM) operators.

In this paper, we suggest a new methodology by using the OWAWA operator. Thus, we get a more complete representation of the aggregation process because we consider the weighted average and the OWA operator in the same formulation. We call these techniques the OWAWA adequacy coefficient (OWAWAAC) and the OWAWA index of maximum and minimum level (OWAWAIMAM) operator. The main advantage of these approaches is that they are able to deal with the weighted average and the OWA operator in the same formulation considering the degree of importance that each concept has in the aggregation. Thus, the weighted adequacy coefficient, the OWAAC, the weighted index of maximum and minimum level and the OWAIMAM operator, are included as special cases of this general framework. We study some of their main properties and particular cases.

We also develop an application in a decision making problem concerning strategic selection where we can see the applicability of the OWAWAAC and the OWAWAIMAM operators.

In order to do so, this paper is organized as follows. In Section 2, we briefly describe some basic concepts. Section 3 presents the OWAWAAC and the OWAWAIMAM operators. Section 5 presents a decision making application in strategic selection and Section 6 summarizes the main conclusions.

2. Preliminaries

In this section we briefly review the adequacy coefficient, the index of maximum and minimum level and the OWAWA operator.

2.1. *The Adequacy Coefficient*

The adequacy coefficient [2] is an index used for calculating the differences between two elements, two sets, etc. It is very similar to the Hamming distance with the difference that it neutralizes the result when the comparison shows that the real element is higher than the ideal one. For two sets $A = \{a_1, \ldots, a_n\}$ and $B = \{b_1, \ldots, b_n\}$, it can be defined as follows.

Definition 1. A weighted adequacy coefficient (WAC) of dimension n is a mapping WAC: $[0, 1]^n \times [0, 1]^n \rightarrow [0, 1]$ that has an associated weighting vector W of dimension n such that the sum of the weights is 1 and $w_j \in [0, 1]$. Then:

$$WAC\,(A\,,B) = \sum_{i=1}^{n} w_i [1 \wedge (1 - \mu_i + \mu_i^{(k)}] \tag{1}$$

where a_i and b_i are the ith arguments of the sets A and B respectively.

2.2. *The Index of Maximum and Minimum Level*

The index of maximum and minimum level (IMAM) [1] is an index that provides similar results than the Hamming distance but with some differences that makes it more complete. Basically, we could define it as a measure that includes the Hamming distance and the adequacy coefficient [2-3,6] in the same formulation. It can be defined as follows.

Definition 2. A weighted IMAM (WIMAM) of dimension n is a mapping $IMAM$: $[0, 1]^n \times [0, 1]^n \rightarrow [0, 1]$ that has an associated weighting vector W of dimension n with $\sum_{j=1}^{n} w_j = 1$ and $w_i \in [0, 1]$, such that:

$$WIMAM\,(\langle \mu_1, \mu_1^{(k)} \rangle, \ldots, \langle \mu_n, \mu_n^{(k)} \rangle) =$$

$$= \sum_u w_i(u) \times \left| \mu_i(u) - \mu_i^{(k)}(u) \right| + \sum_v w_i(v) \times \left[0 \vee (\mu_i(v) - \mu_i^{(k)}(v)) \right] \tag{2}$$

where μ_i and $\mu_i^{(k)}$ are the ith arguments and $u + v = n$.

2.3. *The OWAWA Operator*

The ordered weighted averaging – weighted averaging (OWAWA) operator is an aggregation operator that unifies the WA and the OWA operator in the same formulation considering the degree of importance that each concept has in the analysis [3-4]. It can be defined as follows.

Definition 3. An OWAWA operator of dimension n is a mapping OWAWA: $R^n \to R$ that has an associated weighting vector W of dimension n such that $w_j \in [0, 1]$ and $\sum_{j=1}^{n} w_j = 1$, according to the following formula:

$$OWAWA\,(a_1, \ldots, a_n) = \sum_{j=1}^{n} \hat{v}_j b_j \tag{3}$$

where b_j is the jth largest of the a_i, each argument a_i has an associated weight (WA) v_i with $\sum_{i=1}^{n} v_i = 1$ and $v_i \in [0, 1]$, $\hat{v}_j = \beta w_j + (1 - \beta) v_j$ with $\beta \in [0, 1]$ and v_j is the weight (WA) v_i ordered according to b_j, that is, according to the jth largest of the a_i.

3. New Aggregation Techniques with the OWAWA Operator

In this Section we briefly introduce the OWAWAAC and the OWAWAIMAM operator and study some of its main properties.

3.1. *The OWAWA Adequacy Coefficient*

The OWAWAAC operator is an aggregation operator that normalizes the adequacy coefficient by using the OWAWA operator. Thus, it is able to represent the adequacy coefficient with a unified model between the weighted average and the OWA operator that considers the degree of importance that each concept has in the aggregation. It can be defined as follows.

Definition 4. An OWAWAAC operator of dimension n is a mapping $OWAWAAC: [0, 1]^n \times [0, 1]^n \to [0, 1]$ that has an associated weighting vector W, with $w_j \in [0, 1]$ and $\sum_{j=1}^{n} w_j = 1$, such that:

$$OWAWAAC\,(\langle \mu_1, \mu_1^{(k)} \rangle, \ldots, \langle \mu_n, \mu_n^{(k)} \rangle) = \sum_{j=1}^{n} \hat{v}_j K_j \tag{4}$$

where K_j represents the jth largest of $[1 \wedge (1 - \mu_i + \mu_i^{(k)})]$, each argument $[1 \wedge (1 - \mu_i + \mu_i^{(k)})]$ has an associated weight (WA) v_i with $\sum_{i=1}^{n} v_i = 1$ and $v_i \in [0, 1]$, $\hat{v}_j = \beta w_j + (1 - \beta) v_j$ with $\beta \in [0, 1]$ and v_j is the weight (WA) v_i ordered according to K_j, that is, according to the jth largest of the $[1 \wedge (1 - \mu_i + \mu_i^{(k)})]$.

Note that the WAC and the OWAAC operators are included as special cases of the OWAWAAC operator:

- WAC: When $\beta = 0$.
- OWAAC: When $\beta = 1$.

Note that if the weighting vector is not normalized, i.e., $\hat{V} = \sum_{j=1}^{n} \hat{v}_j \neq 1$, then, the OWAWAAC operator can be expressed as:

$$OWAWAAC\ (\langle \mu_1, \mu_1^{(k)} \rangle, \ldots, \langle \mu_n, \mu_n^{(k)} \rangle) = \left(\frac{1}{\hat{V}} \sum_{j=1}^{n} \hat{v}_j K_j^{\lambda} \right)^{1/\lambda} \tag{5}$$

The OWAWAAC operator is monotonic, bounded and idempotent. Note that if $\mu_i \geq \mu_i^{(k)}$, for all i, then, the OWAWAAC operator becomes the OWAWA distance (OWAWAD) operator [5].

3.2. *The OWAWA Index of Maximum and Minimum Level*

The OWAWAIMAM operator is an aggregation operator that normalizes the IMAM with the OWAWA operator. Therefore, we are able to provide an aggregation of the IMAM that considers both the weighted average and the OWA operator in the same formulation and considering the degree of importance that each concept has in the formulation. It can be defined as follows.

Definition 5. An OWAWAIMAM operator of dimension n, is a mapping $OWAWAIMAM: [0, 1]^n \times [0, 1]^n \to [0, 1]$ that has an associated weighting vector W, with $w_j \in [0, 1]$ and $\sum_{j=1}^{n} w_j = 1$, such that:

$$OWAWAIMAM\ (\langle \mu_1, \mu_1^{(k)} \rangle, \ldots, \langle \mu_n, \mu_n^{(k)} \rangle) = \sum_{j=1}^{n} \hat{v}_j K_j \tag{6}$$

where K_j represents the jth largest of all the $|\mu_i - \mu_i^{(k)}|$ and the $[0 \vee (\mu_i - \mu_i^{(k)})]$ arguments; each argument has an associated weight (WA) v_i with $\sum_{i=1}^{n} v_i = 1$ and $v_i \in [0, 1]$, $\hat{v}_j = \beta w_j + (1 - \beta) v_j$ with $\beta \in [0, 1]$ and v_j is the weight (WA)

v_i ordered according to K_j, that is, according to the jth largest of the $|\mu_i - \mu_i^{(k)}|$ and the $[0 \vee (\mu_i - \mu_i^{(k)})]$.

Note that the WIMAM and the OWAIMAM operators are included in this formulation as special cases:

- WIMAM: When $\beta = 0$.
- OWAIMAM: When $\beta = 1$.

If the weighting vector is not normalized, i.e., $\hat{V} = \sum_{j=1}^{n} \hat{v}_j \neq 1$, then, the OWAWAIMAM operator can be expressed as:

$$OWAWAIMAM\ (\langle \mu_1, \mu_1^{(k)} \rangle, \ldots, \langle \mu_n, \mu_n^{(k)} \rangle) = \left(\frac{1}{\hat{V}} \sum_{j=1}^{n} \hat{v}_j K_j^{\lambda} \right)^{1/\lambda} \tag{7}$$

The OWAWAIMAM operator is also monotonic, bounded and idempotent. Note that if $\mu_i \geq \mu_i^{(k)}$, for all i, then, the OWAWAIMAM operator becomes the OWAWA distance (OWAWAD) operator [5] and if we use $[0 \vee (\mu_i - \mu_i^{(k)})]$ for all i, then, it becomes the OWAWAAC operator. Note also that the OWAWAD operator can also be formed when we only use $|\mu_i - \mu_i^{(k)}|$ in the aggregation.

Following the OWA and the OWAWA literature [3-8] we can analyze a lot of families of OWAWAIMAM and OWAWAAC operators.

4. Decision Making Application

In the following, we are going to present a numerical example of the new approach concerning political decision making problems.

Assume a group of investors is planning its investment strategy for the next year and they consider three possible alternatives.

1) A_1: Invest in Europe.
2) A_2: Invest in North America.
3) A_3: Invest in Asia.

After careful review of the information, the investors establish the following general information about the alternatives. Note that the results are evaluations between [0, 1] being 1 the best result. The results are shown in Table 1.

Table 1. Characteristics of the investments.

	C_1	C_2	C_3	C_4	C_5
A_1	0.4	0.8	0.9	0.6	0.9
A_2	0.5	0.7	0.9	0.7	0.7
A_3	0.9	0.7	0.7	0.5	0.7

Note that C_1 = Benefits in the short term, C_2 = Benefits in the mid term, C_3 = Benefits in the long term, C_4 = Risk of the investment, C_5 = Other variables. According to their objectives, they establish the following ideal investment. The results are presented in Table 2.

Table 2. Ideal investment.

	C_1	C_2	C_3	C_4	C_5
I	0.8	0.9	1	0.9	0.8

With this information, it is possible to develop different methods for selecting a fiscal policy. In this example, we consider the WAC, the OWAAC, the OWAWAAC, the WIMAM, the OWAIMAM and the OWAWAIMAM operators. Note that for the IMAM, we assume that C_1, C_2 and C_3 has to be treated with the adequacy coefficient and C_4 and C_5 with the Hamming distance. We assume that the weights are: W = (0.3, 0.2, 0.2, 0.2, 0.1) and V = (0.1, 0.2, 0.4, 0.2, 0.1). Note that the weighted average V has a degree of importance of 80%. The results are shown in Table 3.

Table 3. Aggregated results.

	WAC	OWAAC	OWAWAAC	WIMAM	OWAIMAM	OWAWAIMAM
A_1	0.84	0.86	0.844	0.17	0.23	0.182
A_2	0.83	0.82	0.828	0.16	0.20	0.168
A_3	0.74	0.82	0.756	0.25	0.24	0.248

As we can see, with the adequacy coefficient (AC), the optimal choice is A_1 and with the IMAM, A_2 is optimal. Note that in the AC we look for the highest result while in the IMAM we look for the lowest one.

5. Conclusions

We have introduced a new decision-making model based on the use of similarity measures and OWAWA operators. The main advantage of this approach is that we are able to compare ideals with the available alternatives in a unified framework between the weighted average and the OWA operator by using the OWAWA operator. Thus, we can consider the degree of importance that the WA and the OWA has in the specific problem considered. Furthermore, by using the OWAWAAC we are able to use a norm similar to the Hamming distance but with some differences that makes it more complete. By using the OWAWAIMAM we are able to include the adequacy coefficient and the Hamming distance in the same formulation.

We have illustrated this approach with an application in strategic decision making where we have seen the usefulness of the new methods suggested.

In future research we expect to develop further developments such as the use of induced and generalized aggregation operators.

Acknowledgements

Support from the Spanish Ministry of Science and Innovation under project "JC2009-00189" is gratefully acknowledged.

References

1. J. Gil-Lafuente, El "índice del máximo y mínimo nivel" en la optimización del fichaje de un deportista. In: *X Congreso Internacional de la Asociación Europea de Dirección y Economía de la Empresa* (AEDEM), Reggio Calabria, Italia, pp. 439-443, 2001.
2. A. Kaufmann and J. Gil-Aluja, *Introduction to the theory of fuzzy subsets in business management* (Milladoiro, Santiago de Compostela, Spain, 1986).
3. J.M. Merigó, *New Extensions to the OWA operators and their application in decision making* (PhD thesis (in Spanish), Department of Business Administration, University of Barcelona, 2008).
4. J.M. Merigó, On the use of the OWA operator in the weighted average and its application in decision making. In: *Proceedings of the WCE 2009 Conference*, London, United Kingdom, pp. 82-87, 2009.
5. J.M. Merigó, Decision making with distance measures, weighted averages and OWA operators. In: *Proceedings of the SIGEF 2009 Conference*, Lugo, Spain, pp. 482-495, 2009.
6. J.M. Merigó and A.M. Gil-Lafuente, New decision-making techniques and their application in the selection of financial products, *Inform Sci.* **180** (2010) in press, doi: 10.1016/j.ins.2010.01.028.
7. R.R. Yager, On ordered weighted averaging aggregation operators in multi-criteria decision making, *IEEE Trans. Syst. Man Cybern. B* **18** (1988) 183-190.
8. R.R. Yager, Families of OWA operators, *Fuzzy Sets Syst.* **59** (1993) 125-148.

REALISTIC AGENT-BASED SIMULATION OF FINANCIAL CRISES: THE 1998 TURMOIL

BÀRBARA LLACAY and GILBERT PEFFER

Dept. for Economic, Financial, and Actuarial Mathematics, University of Barcelona
Av. Diagonal, 690, 08034 Barcelona, Spain

International Centre for Numerical Methods in Engineering, Ed. C1, Campus Nord UPC
c/Gran Capità, s/n, 08034 Barcelona, Spain

Agent-based models have a great potential for the simulation of historical episodes that has to date barely been explored. We focus in particular on the simulation of historical episodes in financial markets, and present here an empirically grounded model of the 1998 turmoil that caused the collapse of the LTCM hedge fund. This model allows us to explore the effects of VaR risk management techniques on market prices, a problem that some market participants and regulators believe lies at the heart of the instabilities experienced in summer 1998.

1. Introduction

The analysis of historical episodes involves a number of challenges: as a historical event is unique, it is difficult to find comparable episodes and this increases the possibility of making incorrect inferences; as historical research naturally focuses on past events, counterfactuals can only be analysed theoretically since it is not possible to run a confirming experiment in practice. Social simulation opens up a possibility of counterfactual experiment in the historical social sciences. More specifically, agent-based models show a great potential to study the evolution of social systems. Our objective in this article is to use this potential of agent-based models for the simulation of large-scale phenomena in financial markets, which up to now has been a much neglected area of agent-based modelling. In particular, we focus on studying financial crises, a topic that has gotten renewed attention as a result of the 2007/08 credit crunch. We moreover stress the importance of building on a range of empirical data and studies to design a *realistic* model which allows us to explore in more detail the intrinsic dynamics of a historical episode.

2. The LTCM Crisis

To illustrate the potential of multi-agent systems for historical research in financial crisis, we have chosen the LTCM collapse that took place in summer 1998. LTCM (Long-Term Capital Management) was a highly successful hedge fund. Its main strategy was relative-value arbitrage, that is, the exploitation of temporal price divergences between related assets – for example, due to a difference in their liquidity – by simultaneously buying the cheaper asset and selling the expensive one. Due to the sustained, impressive profits the firm achieved over the years, LTCM was much admired by its competitors, who also sought to imitate its strategies and exploit similar arbitrage opportunities [15]. However, this situation changed radically within a matter of weeks: in September 1998 LTCM found itself on the brink of collapse and only a rescue concerted by the Fed saved it from bankruptcy.

The origins of this crisis can be traced back to the moratorium on ruble-denominated debt announced by the Russian government on the 17th of August 1998. Although LTCM had only minor exposure to the Russian market, many institutional investors and also arbitrage traders that were active in the Russian debt market had to unwind their loss-making trades, thereby setting off a marked decline in investor confidence in emerging markets across the board. This trend triggered a flight to liquidity: investors sold off their riskiest and most illiquid assets in order to buy safer government securities. The resulting price adjustments were especially damaging for LTCM, who was a large liquidity provider and thus heavily invested in illiquid assets.

The LTCM crisis has been analysed by a number of scholars, who have put forward different explanations for the dry-up of market liquidity and LTCM's collapse in 1998. Paradoxically, the value-at-risk management systems used by market participants have been blamed for being partially responsible for the turmoil. In the next section we briefly introduce the value at risk methods and the controversy about the role they played in the 1998 crisis.

3. Risk Management Systems: Value-at-Risk

VaR is one of the most widely used measures of market risk in banks and financial institutions all over the world [13]. The value-at-risk of a portfolio is defined as "the maximum loss, from an adverse market move, within a given level of confidence, for a given holding period" [13: 112]. In general terms, the maximum loss is calculated as a function of the portfolio historical volatility: when volatility rises or drops, so does value-at-risk [5].

The VaR method was initially born as a methodology to measure risk and report on it in easy terms. In the second half of the 90s, it was widely adopted by financial institutions and its use was stimulated by the BIS when the Capital Accord allowed banks to use their internal risk VaR models to calculate the regulatory capital for market risk [13].

Apart from using VaR models for regulatory purposes, banks also employ these models to allocate capital among different business units and set internal risk limits to trading desks and individual investors [10]. When VaR exceeds the limits defined for a desk or investor, positions are partly liquidated to reduce the exposure [13].

Well-documented analysis of LTCM crisis such as those provided by MacKenzie [15] and Holzer and Millo [8] have pointed to the danger created by VaR systems in a herding context where agents have overlapping positions. Holzer and Millo, together with other authors (e.g. [6], [16]) hold that as value-at-risk (VaR) of trading increases when volatility rises, some institutions breached their limits after the initial instability due to the Russian moratorium, which forced them to cut positions and in turn increased the volatility, leading to a vicious circle of market instabilisation. However, there is controversy on this theory. For example, Jorion [11] rejects this thesis outright, while pointing to other mechanisms which might have transmitted the instability (e.g. margin calls or stop-loss rules).

4. Research Questions

Agent-based models allow us to replicate real markets realistically enough as to test the different theoretical arguments put forward by the commentators. Specifically, we explore the conditions under which the use of VaR techniques could have caused the market collapse observed in Summer 1998 and will compare their effects to the results of implementing alternative mechanisms such as stop-loss rules and margin calls which have also been blamed for playing a role in 1998 turmoil. Moreover, Jorion [11] argues that regulatory capital requirements stipulated in the BIS Capital Accord and the 1996 Amendment [3] do not have a destabilising effect because of different 'smoothing' mechanisms. Hence, in a second series of simulations we will explore this thesis and study the effect of VaR systems when implemented exactly as put forth by BIS.

5. Description of the Agent-Based Model

To use simulations in order to draw reliable conclusions on the effects of VaR systems, we have built a model that realistically replicates the market situation

192

where the crisis took place. Crisis accounts such as [15] and [8] present an overview of the episode and some information on the market structure and the agents involved. However, as we need more detail on the market and the participants to build a realistic model, we have to turn to a range of complementary, technical sources and market data that provide us with deep additional knowledge.

5.1. *Market Structure*

Our artificial model simulates the fixed-income market, since it is the market where LTCM mainly operated. More specifically, we focus on one of LTCM's (and most bond arbitrageurs') paradigmatic trades [14]: the arbitrage opportunity offered by the spread between the newly issued Government bonds ('on-the-run') and older bonds ('off-the-run') of similar maturity. On-the-run bonds are more liquid because they are benchmark issues and for this reason they usually trade at a premium (their yield is lower or, equivalently, their price is higher than for older issues) [17]. However, their prices forcibly converge when the Government issues new debt, since the former on-the-run bonds become now off-the-run. So arbitrageurs take long positions in cheaper OFF bonds and short-sell the more liquid, expensive ON bonds, profiting from the price difference when prices converge. So there are two risky assets in our artificial market – ON bonds (generally more liquid and expensive) and OFF bonds – apart from cash.

Apart from the sale and purchase of bonds, our model further implements a key mechanism in the fixed-income market: the repurchase agreement ('repos'). A government bond repo is an agreement in which one party sells the bond to the buyer and commits to repurchase the bond on the following day or at some other specified date. In effect this transaction is a collateralised loan, where on maturity the borrower, that is, the short-seller of the bond pays back the cash plus an interest rate ('repo rate') in return for the bond [4]. Repos are fundamental for bond arbitrageurs: on the one hand, repos provide them with a source of financing, allowing them to leverage their operations and multiply their profits. On the other hand, repos are a means of borrowing securities, what allows investors to short-sell expensive bonds [12]. Our model reproduces these mechanics, together with the margining practices used in real repo operations: the borrower pays an initial margin, or 'haircut', to provide some protection to the lender in case the other party fails [12], and both parties must mark the bonds used as collateral to market daily and pay a margin to the other if the price has fallen or risen [5].

A range of market participants make use of repos, for leveraging or for financing their inventories: hedge funds, proprietary desks at investment banks, market makers and so on [5]. As in real markets, repo loans in our model are offered by banks through their repo desk.

5.2. *Market Making in Bonds*

Government bonds are traded in over-the-counter markets, that is, trades are not made through a central exchange institution, but directly between parties. A group of entities – banks and securities houses – are registered as dealers and are in charge of making markets. They must maintain liquidity by being ready to buy at the bid price and sell at the ask price, profiting by the average difference (the so-called bid-ask spread) as the return for their services [5].

The marking making desks of bank agents in our artificial market play the role of bond dealers. They post prices for ON and OFF bonds which are driven by two main factors: the order imbalance [2] and the volume of trading [12]: when the demand for a given bond increases, its price rises, and spreads are larger in thin markets.

5.3. *Other Market Participants*

A range of agents take part in the global secondary bond markets: central banks, investment and commercial banks, hedge funds, mutual funds, pension funds or insurance companies [17]. Some of these participants (especially pension funds and insurance companies) use passive strategies, buying for instance government bonds and holding them for long period, making only slight adjustments to their portfolios [5]. As we focus on a historical episode that is relatively brief – the market turmoil took only a few weeks – and operations by passive traders are infrequent and small, we can neglect their effect on market dynamics. We will thus concentrate on those agents who use active trading, and distinguish three types of participants: hedge funds, mutual funds, and banks. These market participants use the most frequent strategies in bond trading, both based on taking advantage of price changes in individual bonds [5]: the *switch* strategy consists in selling those bonds in portfolio which are overpriced with respect to their historical quotes and buying those which are underpriced; the *relative-value* strategy follows the same principle, but short-selling the overpriced bonds and purchasing the underpriced ones at the same time.

Although the agents in the model use similar trading strategies[a], they differ in their characteristics:

Hedge funds are extremely active agents who make extensive use of short positions and leverage to enhance their profits [18]. They engage in relative-value arbitrage – resembling LTCM and its imitators – exploiting the ON-OFF spread, and although they use VaR models to manage their risk [9] they have more flexible limits than other agents (because real hedge funds usually have credit lines or ask their investors to lock in the capital for long periods [7]).

Laws typically prevent *mutual funds* from short-selling securities, engaging in leveraging practices or investing in illiquid assets ([1], [18]). For this reason, the mutual funds in the model do not use the arbitrage strategy, which involves short-selling, but only the switch strategy, and restrict themselves to investing in the liquid bond. Mutual fund agents moreover can only face limited losses to avoid investor withdrawals, so they are forced to liquidate positions when prices fall [7].

Banks are more complex than the other agents, because actual banks have different business lines [18]. As we have mentioned above, banks have market making and repo desks. Moreover, they also have proprietary trading desks where they trade both on switch and arbitrage trades. Like hedge funds, they use leverage aggressively but – somewhat like mutual funds – they cannot afford huge losses [15].

5.4. *Risk Management*

Agents in our model manage their daily risk using a VaR model. Taking the data on previous bond prices, they calculate their volatilities and correlations and, assuming that returns follow a normal distribution, they estimate the maximum expected loss [5].

Agents apply the VaR model for the double usage observed in real markets: they use VaR to compute the capital that must be set aside to meet regulatory requirements, and to internally allocate capital among the different desks and control market risk.

Apart from VaR, our artificial agents also implement stop-loss rules to manage their risk (when losses surpass a specific limit, positions are reduced), as

---

[a] Note that agents have overlapping positions and use similar strategies as put forward by MacKenzie [15] and Holzer and Millo [8] in their 'superportfolio' argument. This reproduces the herding context where the crisis broke out.

this widespread method has also been suspected for contributing to heightened instability in falling markets [11].

VaR and stop-loss limits can be seen as a proxy of the agents' risk tolerance. As mutual fund and bank agents can only afford more limited losses than hedge funds, this will be reflected in a higher sensibility to losses and lower limits.

6. Simulation Results

We have implemented three different scenarios which differ in the methods used by agents to manage risk. We next briefly describe the three scenarios and the results obtained in each case:

Scenario 1: All agents in the model use VaR as the only method to manage their market risk (i.e. they do not implement stop-loss rules). An initial volatility and price shock represents the market instability following the Russian moratorium in August 1998. The simulations show that after this initial shock, the use of VaR limits has indeed the potential of instabilising markets: a rise of volatility leads to an increase in VaR, and if those agents with lowest risk limits breach these, they are forced to cut positions and sell part of their assets, which in turn lowers prices and increases volatility further, forcing other agents to also reduce their exposure and leading to a vicious circle as described by [8].

Scenario 2: In this case, all agents use a stop-loss rule instead of VaR to bound their losses. The stop-loss limits are heterogeneous among agents, although they remain constant along time. Also an initial volatility and price shock is implemented, after which simulations reveal that stop-loss rules have an instabilising effect similar to that caused by VaR methods: the initial price shock causes losses to agents, and if those agents with lower stop-loss limits breach these, they are coerced to cut positions and sell part of their assets, which in turn lowers prices further and heightens losses for the rest of agents, resulting in a downward spiral.

Scenario 3: In this third scenario we explore the thesis by [11] which argues that risk management measures implemented exactly as advocated in the BIS Capital Accord do not have a destabilising effect because of different 'smoothing' mechanisms. In this case, only banks implement VaR measures, and regulatory capital is calculated using the smoothing mechanisms described by Jorion: at least one year of historical data must be used, and VaR must be averaged over 60 days. Under these conditions, the sensibility of agents to a volatility shock gets notably reduced, and simulation results support Jorion's argument that 'market risk charges move very slowly in response to changing market conditions' [11: 125-126].

7. Conclusions

We have advocated the potential of agent-based models for the simulation of large-scale phenomena in financial markets, in particular financial crises. We would like to stress the usefulness of building on empirical sources and take advantage of the clear correspondence between real and artificial agents to build realistic models that can provide reliable insights on empirical markets dynamics. To illustrate our approach, we have presented a model of the LTCM crisis that has allowed us to throw light on the discussions about the role that VaR methodologies played in 1998 turmoil. As Jorion [11] claims, it is true that the regulatory capital requirements put forth by BIS cannot be blamed for those instabilities. However, the actual use of VaR by market participants for setting risk limits can indeed transmit instability in contexts of heightened volatility.

References

1. Axis financial source [online], http://forex-managedaccount.com/hedge-funds/mutual-funds.html, consulted on 7 Jan 2010
2. M. Brandt and K. Kavajecz, *J. Financ.* **59**, 2623 (2004).
3. BSBC, Basle Committee on Banking Supervision, Jan 1996.
4. M. Choudhryy, *An introduction to repo markets* (1999).
5. M. Choudhry, *The bond and money markets* (2001).
6. N. Dunbar, *Investing Money* (2000)
7. B. Eichengreen and D. Mathieson, *Econ. Issues*, **19** (1999)
8. B. Holzer and Y. Millo, ESRC Centre for Analysis of Risk and Regulation, LSE, Discussion Paper No. 29 (2004).
9. IMF, *Global Financial Stability Report*, Oct 07 (2007).
10. P. Jorion, *Value at Risk* (2001)
11. P. Jorion, *Financial Stability Review*: Dec 2002.
12. M. Livingston, *Bonds and Bond Derivatives* (1999).
13. M. Lore and L. Borodovsky, *The professional's handbook of financial risk management* (2000).
14. R. Lowenstein, *When Genius Failed* (2000)
15. D. MacKenzie, *Econ. Soc.* **32**, 349 (2003).
16. A. Persaud, *Erisk*, Dec 2000.
17. J. Saxton, (2001). *Federal Debt: Market Structure and Economic Uses for U.S. Treasury Debt Securities* (2001).
18. USA, *Hedge Funds, Leverage, and the Lessons of Long-Term Capital Management* (1999).

FINANCIAL RELATIONS OF NATIONAL PARK AGENCIES IN LATVIA: OPPORTUNITIES FOR ICT AND DYNAMIC MODELING

ILUTA BERZINA, AGITA LIVINA

*Sociotechnical Systems Engineering Institute, Vidzeme University of Applied Sciences,
Cesu Street 4, Valmiera LV-4201, Latvia*

Protected areas in the world are very popular tourism destinations. Using ICT in the management of the protected area should be one of the tools for managers to make effective and qualitative decision making process, save time and expenses etc., as well as forecast the operation of a system by modeling. In this article a three level conceptual infological model has been created: (1) financial relations process what characterizes the simplified structure of the system and the links between objects: stakeholder's interests, achievements and financial capacity of national park (NP) agencies of Latvia – a basic operation field for (2) evaluating NPs and stakeholders' financial relations and (3) applying dynamic modeling and forecasting possibilities.

1. Introduction

Protected areas in the world are very popular tourism destinations. There are more than 120000 several nature protected areas in the world, int.al. 3900 national parks (NP). Four of them are established in Latvia [1]. NP is a natural area of land and/or sea, designated to protect the ecological integrity of ecosystems for present and future generations. NPs are managed mainly for ecosystem protection and recreation [2]. World praxis shows that NPs are able to provide important economical benefit through nature tourism [3]. Using ICT in the management of NPs should be one of the tools for managers not to make mistakes in decision making process, save time and expenses etc., as well as forecast by modeling the operation of a financial system.

2. Problem formulation

By this time modern technologies (ICT) (also GIS, digital and mobile information systems) in the world are more widely used by the agencies of protected areas in marketing and communication with visitors [4]. From the point of view by the management of NPs, in the USA ICT are used, for instance, for calculations of economical impact with products like Money Generation Model 2 (MGM2) which is a multi-page Excel 7.0 workbook that estimates the direct and total economic impacts of visitor spending [5]. For calculations of regional economical impact calculations of national parks IMpact analysis for PLANning Professional (IMPLAN Pro) is used, which is Microsoft Excell and Access files [6]. Despite this, it must be agreed with the view of Korea Tourism Organization (KTO) – technologies in tourism are occasionally used in the current travel industry (as an exception are on-line booking systems) [7]. Presently technologies in nature protection and tourism managerial level in Latvia are only known as scientific achievements or some engineering-related images they are used or adapted very rarely and are not created. Mainly, lack of financial capacity is suggested as the reason of obstructing development.

3. Problem solutions

We believe the reasons must be searched in: (1) the form of maintaining and managing NPs; (2) finance attraction as money generation. To create a general platform, we set a target – to show a conceptual finance flow of NPs as a process and the fields of using ICT in it. To achieve this, such objectives are set: (1) to study the organization of finance flow in NPs in the best praxis of the world and scientific cognitions and on its basis (2) to create a conceptual infological model of finance flow that is in conformance with the situation of NPs in Latvia and shows potential financial feedback and ICT use fields in it; (3) to create a dynamic model of finance flow as an example by using the software STELLA.

4. Organization of finance flow of NPs in the best praxis of the world and scientific cognitions

4.1. *NP's governance and management*

Traditionally, NPs have been managed by government agencies. [8].

In the 20th century in the agencies of NPs two management models operate: (1) "exclusive" and (2) "inclusive". In the first – largely adopted in the USA – management plans were developed with the intention of de-coupling the interests of local people from protected areas, with options ranging from an open anti-participatory attitude to the outright resettlement of the resident communities. In the second model – more frequently adopted in Western Europe – the interests of local societies were central, private ownership of land within protected areas was common and local administrators were largely involved in management planning. While "exclusive" management approach is generally successful, the "inclusive" approach, which widely expanded in Europe, including Latvia, still affects local life quality and development [9]. According to the latest scientific literature, there is a new trend in the world – new management approaches in nature protection and development, for instance, in effective stakeholders' collaboration [10]. Therefore, problems and new objective setting become similar in the NPs territories where both management models are represented.

P.F.J. Eagles in a World Parks Congress (2003) outlined some trends what affecting park management, int.al., park management shifts to financially flexible and entrepreneurial forms [11].

Partnerships are increasingly important in the management of public agencies, specifically parks and recreation service providers. Through collaboration managers of park agencies provide goods for supporting their agencies [12].The main stakeholders in the operation of NPs are: local society, local councils, NGOs at various levels, local governance, agencies with legal jurisdiction over NP at stake, political party structures, religious bodies, volunteers, commercial enterprises, foundations, universities and research organizations, national governments, foreign aid institutions, international organizations, staff, visitors, etc. [9]. They all are persons whose interests are conformed and balanced.

In Latvia in the middle of the year 2009 reforms in all state governing and administrative structures were started, including the sector of nature protection and administrative sectors. Currently the Agency of Nature Protection (ANP) almost singly provides the operation of NPs. NP agencies are structural units of ANP. By the change of the management approaches of NPs there must be integrated "collaborative management" elements because stakeholders are usually aware of their interests in the management of the NP and they are usually willing to invest (e.g., time, political authority, money) [9].

4.2. *NPs financing*

Not long before existing tendency to perceive every protected area as a separate entity is to be broken and good practice now recommends that they be planned, managed and financed as a system [13]. Protected areas in developing countries receive an average of less than 30 % of the funding that is necessary. All the various ways of financing protected areas fall under three basic categories:

(1) Annual budget allocations from a government's general revenues; (2) Grants and donations from individuals, corporations, foundations, and international donor agency; (3) User fees, conservation taxes, fines, and other revenues. Most protected areas in developing countries will need to rely on a combination of all these sources [14]. Income of NPs in Latvia is basically formed by state budget allocations what does not provide full accomplishment of all NP functions. The other and most important source of income in NPs of Latvia is forest cutting or selling in low protection status areas. New models are emerging, by changing of the governance forms of the protected area putting more stress on collaboration. Such new approaches may provide flexibility and be innovative in securing financial resources from public and private sources [15].

5. A conceptual infological model of finance flow organization in NPs, fields for ICT application and dynamic modeling

Fig.1. is a conceptual infological model – NPs and different level (international, national, local) stakeholders' financial relations as a closed, cyclic process that characterizes the simplified structure of a system and the links between objects: stakeholders' interests (sponsors), their achievements and NPs financial capacity. Financial inputs in NPs management, as well as outputs and outcomes are the systems attributes that depend on object decision or operation interaction and also its effectiveness [16], [17], [18].

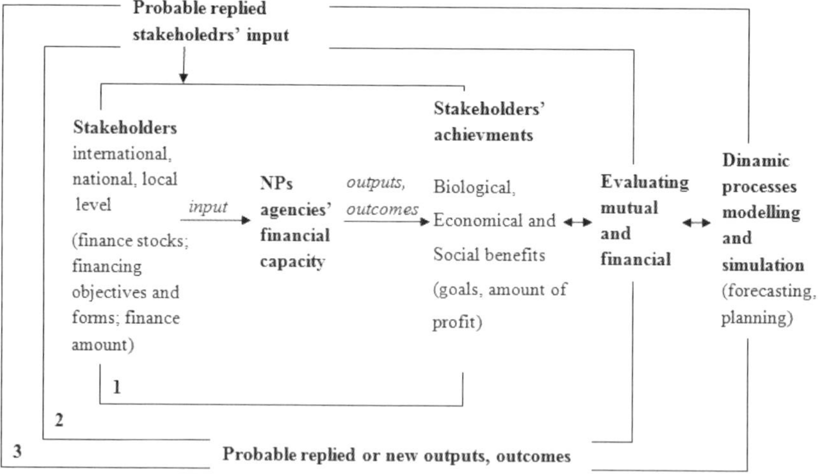

Figure 1. Financial relations as a process in the NPs agencies and fields for ICT application (created by authors)

Fig. 1. includes three the most important blocks of information flow which hierarchy of mutual relation dependence is subordinated and perceived in the order from 1. – 3. Basic cycle of finance flow in NPs operates in the 1st block during the 1st year which is like a reference. In this block all accountancy software are used and they are the only obligatory and used condition in the finance management in Latvia.

The second information block is connected with the business management praxis and theory of NPs that includes assessment of finance flow as well as stakeholders' financial relations towards NPs and each stakeholder's aims where decisions to the next period(s) follow (further motivation of financing). Management of information flow in this block by using ICT currently is a free choice of NPs administration and it depends of its innovations. According to Leverington et al. (2008), the latest praxis shows that main dimensions of NPs assessment management are: Conserving natural integrity; conserving cultural/spiritual and aesthetic; socio-economic, community engagement and recreation; capacity to manage/governance. In turn, the criteria are: context, planning, input, process, outputs, outcomes. For evaluating NPs management effectiveness the most widely used methodologies across the world are: Rapid Assessment and Prioritization of Protected Areas Management (RAPPAM), Parks in Peril Site Consolidation Scorecard, PROARCA, ParksWatch Parks Profiles, etc. [19], [20]. Several methods are used MS Excell combinations with derivative software, for instance, such as Scorecards (quantification possibilities). Especially created ICT products as an independent assessment tool for NPs are not.

NPs agencies revenue generation evaluation results would be a valid base for modelling system operation. The advantage of process modeling becomes apparent in forecasting the results that is useful for planning further actions for replied inputs and new outcomes, and facilitating outputs For instance, relations of some components of conceptual model objects by using stochastic data and software STELLA 9.0 (Fig. 2), (Fig. 3).

202

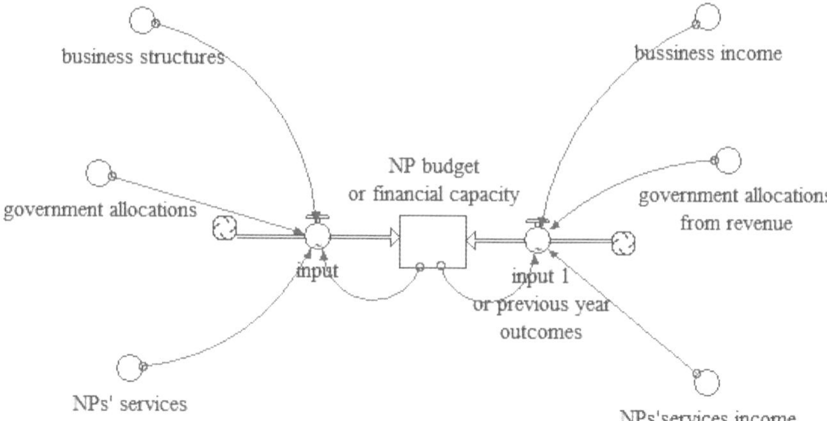

Figure 2. Dynamic model of NPs finance flow from local stocks (created by authors)

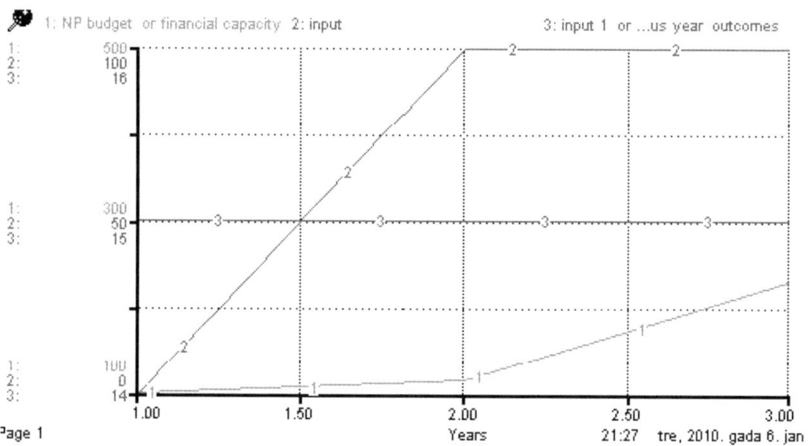

Figure 3. Dynamic of NPs finance flow from local stocks in three years (created by authors)

Fig. 3. shows that financial capacity of NPs in three years would be rapidly growing if the proportion of total investment increases but still slowly growing in relation to constant outcomes (15%) and changes of finance proportion are necessary, increase of the role of money generation for the balance of financial relation or decrease the load for some of financial sources, for instance, state budget.

In the verification of dynamic model operation such world wide methods as input-output (I/O), cost-benefits (B/C), travel-cost (T/C) mathematic calculation models can be used. In turn, for the validation of dynamic model Chi – square test can be used, because the system is a real and existing research objects [21]. If it was not like this, compliance of the modeled process to reality could be validated statistically by using Kolmogorov – Smirnov (K – S test) or Anderson – Darling (goodness-of fit test) tests, as well as by doing *face validation* (experts' audit approach) [21].

6. Conclusions

The idea of the article is directed to implementing business principles in the management of NPs because the role of tourism as well as the role of using ICT increases. Using ICT in NPs has possibilities to be one of the tools with which to evaluate the management of NPs as well as to forecast by modeling the operation effectiveness. In the article there is created a 3 level conceptual infological model for NPs financial relations that is a basic operation field for using modeling and forecasting approaches. Therefore, with a condition that the feedback is provided between stakeholders' financial interests, there are found two new fields of ICT use in the management of financial flow of NPs: in (1) assessment; (2) modeling, forecasting and planning of financial relations.

References

1. EUROPARC Federation (ed.) Living Parks : 100 Years of National Parks in Europe, Kessler Druck + Medien, Germany, Bobingen, (2009)
2. IUCN. Defining Protected Area. Available at:
   http://www.unep-wcmc.org/protected_areas/categories/index.html
3. Department of Environment and Conservation NSW. Impacts of Protected Areas on the Regional Economy of North-East NSW, (2006) Available at:
   http://www.environment.nsw.gov.au/projects/NortheastEconomicStudy.htm
4. Dias, E. Beinat, C. Rhin, H. Scholten. Location Aware ICT in Addressing Protected Areas' Goals. Available at:
   http://www.webparkservices.info/Assets/LOCATION%20AWARE%20ICT%20IN%20ADDRESSING%20PROTECTED%20AREAS%20GOALS%20v2.pdf
5. MSU, Money Generation Model Version 2. Available at:
   http://web4.canr.msu.edu/mgm2/MGM2web.htm
6. MSU, Running Tourism Impact Analysis in IMPLAN Pro. Available at:
   https://www.msu.edu/~changwe4/ipro/index.htm
7. KTO. Tourism Technologies: KTO's New Tourism Strategy, (2006) Available at:
   http://english.visitkorea.or.kr/enu/FU/FU_EN_15.jsp?cid=289722
8. GoBi Research Group. Protected Area Governance, (2009) Available at:
   http://www.biodiversitygovernance.de/project_details.php?p=gir

9. Borrini-Feyerabend G. Collaborative management of Protected Areas: Tailoring the Approach to the Context, 1996. IUNC. Available at: http://data.iucn.org/dbtw-wpd/commande/&MR=20&RL=0&DL=0

10. Buckley R., Weaver D.B., Pickering C., Nature-based Tourism, Environment and Land management, (2003) Biddles Ltd, Kinsg's Lynn, UK

11. Eagles, P. International Trends in Park Tourism: a Macro View of Park Tourism Finance. World Parks Congress, South Africa, Durban, (2003) Available at:
http://www.conservationfinance.org/Workshops_Conferences/WPC/WPC_d ocuments/Apps_12_Eagles_v1.pdf

12. Borrini-Feyerabend G. Governance of Protected Areas – Innovation in the Air, (2003) Available at:
http://www.earthlore.ca/clients/WPC/English/grfx/sessions/PDFs/session_1/ Borrini_Feyerabend.pdf

13. Weddell M.S., Fedorchak R., Wright B.A. The partnership phenomenon, Journal Park Science, Fall, No. 2, Vol. 26 (2009). Available at:
http://www.nature.nps.gov/ParkScience/print.cfm?PrintFormat=pdf

14. Spergel B., Raising Revenues for Protected Areas: a Menu of Options, WWF, (2001) Available at:
http://www.worldwildlife.org/what/howwedoit/conservationfinance/WWFBi naryitem7128.pdf

15. Eagles P., Hillel O. Improving protected area finance through tourism, 2008. Available at:
http://www.ahs.uwaterloo.ca/~eagles/documents/EaglesandHillelArticleonE conomicsandFinanceofTourisminProtectedAreas.pdf

16. Gilbert N., Troitzsch K.G., Simulation for the Social Scientist, Bell&Bain, Glasgow, (2005)

17. Merkurjevs J., Merkurjeva G., Pečerska J., Tolujevs J., Sistēmu imitācijas modelēšanas tehnoloģija, Rīga, (2008)

18. Nilsson A., Nellborn C., Tolis C. Perspectives on business modelling: understanding and changing organizations, Springer, Berlin (1999)

19. Leverington F., Hockings M., Costa K.,L., Management effectiveness eveluation in protected areas – a global study, (2008) IUNC WCPA. Available at:
http://cmsdata.iucn.org/downloads/maangementeffectiveness2008.pdf

20. Hockings M., Evaluating Management of Protected Areas: Integrating Planning and Evaluation, (1998) Available at:
http://www.springerlink.com/content/3q6g3tulq8fc8np9/

21. Engineering Statistics Handbook, Available at:
http://www.itl.nist.gov/div898/handbook/eda/section3/eda35.htm

DURATION AND UNCERTAINTY: A COMPARATIVE ANALYSIS FOR INDEXED BONDS

AURELIO FERNÁNDEZ

Universitat Rovira i Virgili, Department de Gestió d'Empreses
Avinguda de la Universitat 1, CP 43204, Spain
CECyT, FACPCE, Argentina

MARÍA-JOSÉ GARBAJOSA-CABELLO, MARIA-BELÉN GUERCIO

Universitat Rovira i Virgili, Department de Gestió d'Empreses
Avinguda de la Universitat 1, CP 43204, Spain

The duration of a bond is a weighted average of the cash flows generated by the bond, where the weights are the proportion that each flow represents within the total value of the bond. Classical duration is computed considering crisp variables such as bond's price, coupon and maturity. However, there are bonds, issued with distinctive characteristics, whose magnitudes are not crisp. The aim of this paper is to determine the duration of this kind of bonds. In order to do so, we will perform a numerical example for selected bonds of the fixed income financial market for two countries.

1. Purpose and Introduction

Inflation indexed bonds are fixed income securities whose nominal cash flows are adjusted to an inflation index. The increasing use of the inflation indexed bonds has stimulated the interest of many authors to analyze its structure, understand its functioning, pricing, risk management, etc. For this reason, the aim of this work is twofold. On the one hand to propose a measure to the duration of an inflation indexed bond from a fuzzy methodology. On the other hand to determinate the suitability of this kind of bonds for an immunization strategy. As a side effect we also are testing the Efficient Market Hypothesis. In an efficient market, inflation expectations are fully anticipated in prices. Therefore duration should not be affected by this effect.

The specific properties of fuzzy methodology allow us to assess the duration when one of variable is uncertain. Index linked bonds have got one uncertain variable, the future inflation rate. Fuzzy duration had been developed by Terceño et al. (2007) when the bond is issued with variable coupon, specifically, linked to interest rate. In order to analyze the behavior of this new measure, we apply the methodology to index linked bonds in the British and the American markets.

The structure of the present work is as follows. The next section briefly summarizes aspects related to inflation indexed bonds. In Section 3 we present the methodology that we will use in order to compute the duration. Section 4 is dedicated to describe data. Section 5 makes an empirical application for UK and US inflation indexed bond market. Finally, Section 6 draws the main conclusions.

2. Background Information

After the pioneering decision by the United Kingdom; several countries began to issue securities whose principal is linked to a specific index. According to Price (1997), one of the reasons that induced the UK and New Zealand to issue indexed bonds was that inflation expectations seemed too exaggerated for the monetary authorities. The rationale for such high inflation projections was the mistrust in the anti-inflationary policies pursued by public authorities. If inflation expectations overestimate actual inflation, it favors the alternative of issuing indexed bonds.

Among the arguments to issue indexed bonds are the savings in financing costs (which benefits the issuer), the completion of the market (benefiting the borrowers, allowing to generate an optimal portfolio), and the reinforcement of the credibility of the anti-inflationary policies (which benefits the central bank).

An additional argument that applies especially to countries with a tradition of inflation is that it favors saving. This is so because economic agents, in order to hedge against inflation, put their savings in real goods or in foreign currency causing monetary problems in the domestic economy. In this sense, Tobin (1963) argues that indexed bonds are a close substitute for physical goods. The existence of these bonds would benefit savings in domestic currency, avoiding government's currency mismatching.

Rational investors demand an interest rate to compensate them for inflation. Within the classic Fisherian framework, the interest rate has a real interest component and a component of inflation expectations. Changes in inflation expectations make interest rate to fluctuate in the short-term (ceteris paribus the real interest). Given this scenario, treasury bills are not safe assets for long-term investors inflation indexed bonds fill this gap by offering a truly riskless long-term investment (Fischer, 1982; Campbell and Shiller, 1996; Brennan and Xia, 2002; Campbell, Shiller and Viceira, 2009).

3. Duration of a Bond in a Fuzzy Environment

Macaulay (1938) defined duration as the weighted average duration of maturities of the bond's cash flow. The weighting is made by the present value of cash flow associated with each maturity.

In the initial stage of analysis, future cash flows generated by the bond may be uncertain. In the case of an inflation indexed bond, we know de principal value but not the amount indexed for inflation, since we don't know the future inflation. To deal with future inflation, stochastic models are usually used. Unfortunately, these adaptations mask some econometric problems, principally in the form of systematic biases which are difficult to evaluate. Normally these models make cash flows to follow a certain stochastic process. In uncertain environments, classical statistics become insufficient to deal with vague data. Therefore, to calculate the duration there is a need for another methodology. Under these circumstances, fuzzy techniques emerge as an alternative to model the uncertainty inherent in expected inflation. Fuzzy numbers allow an intuitive interpretation and their manipulation is rather simple.

Thus, inflation can be expressed by a fuzzy number $\tilde{\pi}$ as: $\tilde{\pi} = (\pi_c, l_\pi, r_\pi)_{LR}$, where $(\pi_c, l_\pi, r_\pi)_{LR}$ is a symmetrical L-R Dubois and Prade, π_c is the nucleus of the mentioned number and l_π and r_π are the left and right radii. Therefore, the value of the bond, V_n, can also be expressed by a fuzzy number as: $\tilde{V}_{..} = V_{..}\tilde{\pi} = V_{..}(\pi_{..}, l_{..}, r_{..})_{...}$. Therefore, in a fuzzy environment, the cash flows of the bond, Q_j, are calculated as: $\tilde{Q}_j = i \cdot \tilde{V}_n \ \forall \ j=1,\ldots,(n-1)$ and $\tilde{Q}_j = i \cdot \tilde{V}_n + \tilde{V}_n$ if $j=n$, where i is the coupon's interest rate.

Finally, we express $\tilde{Q}$ cash flows by means of a symmetric triangular fuzzy number $\tilde{Q} = (Q_C, l_Q, r_Q)$.

Thus, the fuzzy duration of the bond, $\tilde{D}_0$, is defined as:

$$\tilde{D}_0(\tilde{Q}_j) = \frac{\sum_{j=1}^{n} j \, \tilde{Q}_j (1+k)^{-t_j}}{\sum_{j=1}^{n} \tilde{Q}_j (1+k)^{-t_j}}$$

where k is the discount rate and t_j is are coupon's maturities.

Since cash flows $\tilde{Q}_j$ are expressed by fuzzy numbers, duration becomes also a triangular fuzzy number and will be defined by a center (D_c) and its right (r_D) and left (l_D) radii.

4. Data

4.1. *US market*

The US Treasury has been issuing Treasury inflation-protected securities (TIPS) since 1997. TIPS pay interest biannually at a fixed rate. The rate is applied to the adjusted principal. Consequently interest payments, as well as the principal, rise with inflation and fall with deflation.

The U.S. Treasury publishes daily index ratios that are used to adjust the principal of TIPS. The index ratios are based on the latest changes to the Bureau of Labor Statistics Consumer Price Index for All Urban Consumers U(CPI-U): US City Average, by expenditure category and commodity and service group. The expected inflation is based on the opinion of different forecasters.

In order to compute the fuzzy duration measure, we select a TIPS, issued in April 15, 2009, with 5 years maturity, and with a 1 1/4 % coupon. We take as initial date for our estimation April 15, 2009 (issue date). In this date the implicit discount rate (6 months) for a zero-coupon bond issued by the US Treasury was 1.71%.

4.2. *UK market*

United Kingdom was among the first countries to issue inflation index linked securities, called index-linked gilts, on a regular issues since 1981. These bonds pay biannual cash flows indexed to the Retail Prices Index (RPI). In practical terms this means that both the coupons and the principal are adjusted to take into account the accrued inflation since the gilt's first issue date. Depending on the date of first issue, index-linked gilts have different indexation lags, and hence different methodologies for calculating cash flows. Index-linked gilts issued prior to 2005 have an eight-month indexation lag, while those issued from 2005 onwards use a three-month indexation lag methodology.

In order to do the fuzzy duration measure, we select an index-linked gilt, issued in 1985, with 28 years maturity, and with a 2 ½ % coupon. The present value has been computed following the rules of the United Kingdom Debt Management Office (DMO). For doing this, we consider the RPI published by HM Treasury, in the Forecasts for the UK Economy. This office surveys the most important financial firms, asking them on inflation forecasts and other macroeconomic variables. Although it is very extensive in the number of firms surveyed, we will consider only City forecasters, which are firms located in the London financial district and whose activity is closely related with bond trading.

We select as initial date for our estimation March 2, 2009. There is no special reason for selecting this date, except that it is close to a coupon payment, and this avoids the presence of accrued interest in the market price. In this date the LIBOR rate (6 months) used to calculate the theoretical price was 2.04%.

5. Application and Results

5.1. *US market*

For the US market we consider forecasts on inflation, for the years 2009-2014 from the following sources: Congressional Budget Office, Federal Reserve Governors, Scotiabank Group, Maine Consensus Economics and Conway Pedersen Economics Inc. Taking into account these forecasts, we compute the center π_C, right radius r_π and left radius l_π for fuzzy inflation $\tilde{\pi} = (\pi_C, l_\pi, r_\pi)$. We set the center π_C as the mean value revealed by forecasters and as the radius $r_\pi = l_\pi$ we set the standard deviation of the forecasts.

In Table 1 we present the following information: coupon date, coupon interest rate i, fuzzy inflation $\tilde{\pi} = (\pi_C, l_\pi, r_\pi)$ and fuzzy cash flows $\tilde{Q} = (Q_C, l_Q, r_Q)$.

Table 1. Data

Coupon date	i coupon interest rate	Fuzzy inflation $\tilde{\pi} = (\pi_C, l_\pi, r_\pi)$			Fuzzy cash-flow $\tilde{Q} = (Q_C, l_Q, r_Q)$		
		π_C	$\pi_C - l_\pi$	$\pi_C + r_\pi$	Q_C	$Q_C - l_Q$	$Q_C + r_Q$
15/10/2009	0.00625	-0.0002	-0.0037	0.0032	-0.0002	-0.0037	0.0032
15/04/2010	0.00625	0.0036	-0.0030	0.0102	0.0036	-0.0030	0.0102
15/10/2010	0.00625	0.0115	0.0027	0.0204	0.0115	0.0027	0.0204
15/04/2011	0.00625	0.0196	0.0077	0.0316	0.0196	0.0077	0.0316
15/10/2011	0.00625	0.0279	0.0120	0.0440	0.0279	0.0120	0.0440
15/04/2012	0.00625	0.0358	0.0157	0.0563	0.0358	0.0157	0.0563
15/10/2012	0.00625	0.0435	0.0189	0.0687	0.0435	0.0189	0.0687
15/04/2013	0.00625	0.0512	0.0220	0.0812	0.0512	0.0220	0.0812
15/10/2013	0.00625	0.0591	0.0253	0.0939	0.0591	0.0253	0.0939
15/04/2014	0.00625	0.0663	0.0275	0.1066	0.0663	0.0275	0.1066

From the above data and taking into account the fuzzy duration, then we calculate center and upper and lower bounds of $\tilde{D}_0$ (duration of a TIPS bond, in a fuzzy environment).

$$\tilde{D}_0 = \left(\frac{506.96}{104.11}, \frac{488.71}{100.43}, \frac{525.89}{107.93} \right) = (4.869, 4.866, 4.873)$$

From the result obtained, the duration of the bond analyzed can be expressed by a triangular fuzzy number (TFN), whose center is 4.869, 4.8666 left radius and right radius 4.873. Thus, the TFN has a very small radius and therefore a very short interval oscillation. Thus, we can say that the duration is not sensitive to changes in inflation expectations.

5.2. UK market

For the UK market we consider the following inflation forecasters: Bank of America, Citigroup, Commerzbank, Daiwa Institute of Research, Goldman Sachs, Hermes, Lloyds and RBS Global Banking & Markets. With these data, we operate in the same way as described in the previous paragraph.

In Table 2 we present the following information: coupon date, interest rate i, fuzzy inflation $\tilde{\pi} = (\pi_C, l_\pi, r_\pi)$ and fuzzy cash flows $\tilde{Q} = (Q_C, l_Q, r_Q)$.

Table 2. Data

Coupon date	i coupon interest rate	Inflation $\tilde{\pi} = (\pi_C, l_\pi, r_\pi)$			Cash-flow $\tilde{Q} = (Q_C, l_Q, r_Q)$		
		π_C	$\pi_C - l_\pi$	$\pi_C + r_\pi$	Q_C	$Q_C - l_Q$	$Q_C + r_Q$
16/08/2009	0.0125	0.0318	0.0187	0.0450	1.29	1.27	1.31
16/02/2010	0.0125	0.0423	0.0240	0.0609	1.30	1.28	1.33
16/08/2010	0.0125	0.0529	0.0293	0.0770	1.32	1.29	1.35
16/02/2011	0.0125	0.0666	0.0393	0.0946	1.33	1.30	1.37
16/08/2011	0.0125	0.0805	0.0494	0.1125	1.35	1.31	1.39
16/02/2012	0.0125	0.0955	0.0614	0.1308	1.37	1.33	1.41
16/08/2012	0.0125	0.1108	0.0735	0.1493	1.39	1.34	1,44
16/02/2013	0.0125	0.1267	0.0861	0.1688	1.41	1.36	1.46
16/08/2013	0.0125	0.1428	0.0987	0.1887	115.71	111.24	120.35

From the above data and taking into account fuzzy duration, then we calculate center and upper and lower bounds of $\tilde{D}_0$ (duration of an index-linked gilt, in a fuzzy environment).

$$\tilde{D}_0 = \left(\frac{494.454232}{116.03}, \frac{475.564169}{111.680023}, \frac{514.0808243}{120.5479932} \right) = \left(4.261, 4.258, 4.265 \right)$$

From the result obtained, the duration of the bond analyzed can be expressed by a triangular fuzzy number (TFN), whose center is 4.261, 4.258 left radius and right radius 4.265. Thus, the TFN has a very small radius and therefore a very short interval oscillation. Thus, we can say that the duration is not sensitive to changes in inflation expectations.

6. Conclusions

In this paper we studied the duration of inflation indexed bonds in the British and the American markets. In a previous paper, Fernández et al. (2009) simulated the duration of British indexed bonds in a scenario with strong uncertainty, concluding that even in the situation of divergence of opinions regarding inflation forecasts, the duration measure remains almost unaltered. In this paper, we compare the duration of two bonds, both in developed capital markets. In both cases, the sensitivity of duration to changes in expected inflation is very low. However, the characteristics of the bonds are different. According to conditions of issuance of the British bonds under analysis, they exhibit a lag of 8 months, whereas the American bond has no lag. These results implied that the existence of a lag does not influence significantly the duration's interval. The consequence of such behavior is that inflation indexed bonds become a suitable instrument for portfolio immunization in the long run, minimizing the periodical portfolio rebalancing. From the other point of view, we can conclude that the market incorporates correctly the inflation projections, reinforcing the idea of a well-functioning market as predicted by the Efficient Market Hypothesis. In order to generalize our results, we would like to study in future works the behavior of duration of an indexed bond in developing markets, which can include a larger component of uncertainty.

References

1 M.J. Brennan and Y.D. Xia, Dynamic Asset Allocation Under Inflation, *Journal of Finance*, **57**, 1201 (2002).
2. J.Y. Campbell and R.J. Shiller, A Scorecard for Indexed Government Debt, *Cowles Foundation Discussion Papers* **1125**, Cowles Foundation, Yale University. (1996).

3. J.Y. Campbell, R.J. Shiller and L.M. Viceira, Understanding Inflation indexed bond markets. *NBER working paper series*, **15014**. Available at: http://www.nber.org/papers/w15014. (2009).
4. DMO. Gilt Market Estimated Redemption Payments for Index-linked Gilts. Available at:
www.dmo.gov.uk/rpt_parameters.aspx?rptCode=D9C&pag=D9C. (2009).
5. D. Dubois, and H. Prade, Ranking fuzzy numbers in the setting of possibility theory, *Information Sciences*, **30** 184 (1983).
6 A. Fernández, M.J. Garbajosa, and M.B. Guercio, Duration and convexity of a fixed income bond in an fuzzy environment, *Proceedings of the XV SIGEF Congress*. October, 29-30, 2009. Lugo (Spain) (2009).
7. S. Fischer, Welfare aspects of government issue of indexed bonds, *NBER Working paper series*, **874**, (1982).
8. HM Treasury, Forecasts for the UK economy. A comparison of independent forecasts, available: hm-treasury.gov.uk/forecasts. (2008).
9. F. Macaulay, The Movements of Interest Rates. Bond Yields and Stock Prices in the United States since 1856, New York: *National Bureau of Economic Research*. (1938).
10. R. Price, The Rationale and Design of Inflation indexed Bonds, *IMF Working Paper* **97/12**, (1997).
11. A. Terceño, J.M. Brotons, and A. Fernández, Immunization strategy in a fuzzy environment, *Fuzzy Economic Review*, **XII**, 2, 95. (2007).
12. J. Tobin, An essay on the Principles of Debt Management. *Fiscal and Debt Management Policies*. Englewood Cliffs: Prentice Hall. (1963).
13. Treasury of USA available at:
http://www.treasurydirect.gov/instit/annceresult consulted on 12/18/2009.

INTRODUCING FUZZY NUMBERS IN THE STUDY OF THE VIABILITY OF A TREASURY FORECAST

SALVADOR LINARES MUSTARÓS, JOAN CARLES FERRER COMALAT, ELVIRA CASSÚ SERRA, DOLORS COROMINAS COLL

Department of Business Administration
University of Girona. Spain.

One of the most difficult problems for an entrepreneur consists in determine whether he will have enough cash to cope with all future payments during a certain period. This work shows a technique for predicting viability of treasury using fuzzy numbers, including an example with a forecast model used in the practice to create a new business.

1. Introduction

One of the most important prognosis tools used to estimate whether an entrepreneur may be required to provide more money than the normal operations of the company to prevent a lack of funds, is the study of the operation called "Treasury Forecast" (TF).

The variables that are important to know or to estimate in order to make the TF are on the one hand the cashing and, on the other hand the payments.

A simple graphic presentation of the TF used in the most centers that give advice to new entrepreneurs in Catalonia (Spain) and used in this work as a model example is the following:

Table 1

CONCEPT	period 1	period 2	...
CASHING AND INPUTS			
Sales			
Other cashing			
PAYMENTS AND OUTPUTS			
Shopping (Suppliers)			
Staff			
Salaries nets of workers			
Social Security			
Salaries nets of entrepreneurs			
Self insurance			
Other structural costs			
Rentals			
Maintenance and repairs			
Transport			
Insurances			
Utilities (electricity, water, phone,...)			
Advertising and promotion			
External services			
Bank charges			
Taxes			
Other expenses			
Public Taxes payments			
VAT payment			
IRPF payment			
ST (society tax) payment			
Payment investments			
Credit dues			
CASHING – PAYMENTS			
DISPONIBILITY			
SURPLUS/DEFICIT			

In general, the future values of these variables are uncertain. With the establishment of the theory of fuzzy sets introduced by Zadeh, we have a new framework that allows us to formalize the viability of treasury in a natural way, according to human reasoning and providing quantitative techniques to make this forecast process.

In this sense we think that if we can do some quantification, the entrepreneur could obtain a more precise idea that the mere risk of his intuitive forecast.

Consequently, the main goal of this work is to create a mathematical model for quantitative prognosis of lack of funds for an enterprise project using fuzzy numbers.

2. Theoretical calculation of the Treasury Forecast using fuzzy numbers

Using the representation of a triangular fuzzy number for each item of the Treasury Forecast, formed by the sum of the values until the period n from the pessimistic viewpoint, the highest level of confidence and finally from the optimistic viewpoint respectively , we have a natural way to introduce the fuzzy numbers in the compute of the Treasury Forecast.

We propose that any item of accumulate cashing where the value a represents the pessimistic value, b is the value that represents the highest level of confidence, and c is the optimistic value, could be represented by a positive triangular fuzzy number (a, b, c). In this way, if we think, for instance, that we will cash at least 100 m.u., at most 200 m.u. and we believe that our highest confidence value is 170 m.u., then we obtain the triangular fuzzy number (100,170,200).

In a similar way, we propose that any item of accumulate payment where c represents the pessimistic value, b the value that represents the highest level of confidence, and a the optimistic value for the accumulated payments, could be represented through a negative fuzzy number $(-c,-b,-a)$. In this situation, if you believe that we will pay at least 10, at most 15 and our highest confidence value is 12, then we will use the triangular fuzzy number (-15, -12, -10).

Through this modeling process, using the fuzzy arithmetic we can obtain the triangular fuzzy number CASHING − PAYMENT. After that, if we add the triangular fuzzy number that represents the disponibility, we obtain a new triangular fuzzy number called SURPLUS/DEFICIT. This number will give us an idea of the possibilities associated with excess or lack of funds for each period.

3. Study for the viability of a Treasury Forecast modelled using fuzzy numbers

Using the former triangular fuzzy number SURPLUS/DEFICIT ($\tilde{S}$), we dispose a new technique to study the feasibility of a treasury forecast through a new parameter called "possibility degree policy" (that represents a certain degree of confidence to measure the future necessity to order a new credit policy). This parameter will give us a measure of the risk for the entrepreneur to have lack of funds in a next period in the future.

So, in this way, we define this parameter called "possibility degree policy" as follows:

Possibility degree policy = value of negative area $\tilde{S}$ /value of total area $\tilde{S}$

Note that always:

$$0 \leq \text{Possibility degree policy} \leq 1$$

In order to make understandable the different possible situations, in the figure 1 we illustrate through visual examples of various situations that might occur in a particular period when we determine the final result of the TF using triangular fuzzy numbers (a, b, c). Besides, each situation is accompanied by the simplified expression of their corresponding number of possibility degree policy.

Finally, if N_i denotes the number that represents the possibility degree policy in the period p_i (i = 1,2,...,n), then we define the level of viability of the treasury for a determinate enterprise project as the value:

$$\text{Level of the viability of the treasury} = 1 - \text{maximum } (N_1, N_2, \ldots, N_n)$$

For the entrepreneurs, we propose the criterion based on the fact that the Treasury Forecast is considered feasible when the level of viability is above the value 0.5, because it is a situation where it is more possible to avoid having to ask for a credit policy.

c ≤ 0

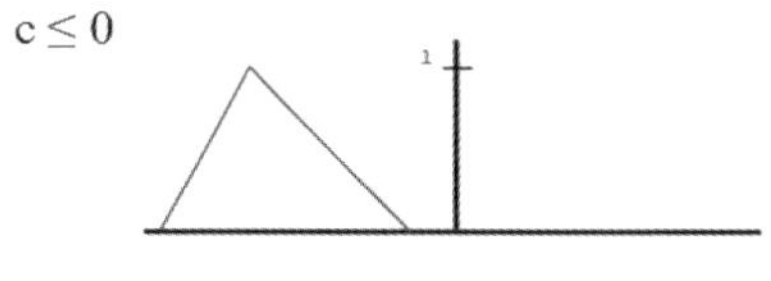

Possibility degree policy = 1

Note that in this case, it is clear that we must search for a credit policy because we will have with security a lack of founds

b < 0

c > 0

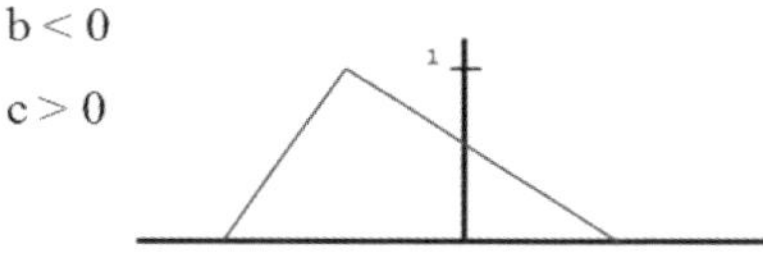

Possibility degree policy $= 1 - \dfrac{c^2}{(c-b)(c-a)}$

In this case, it seems quite possible that we will request a credit policy

b = 0

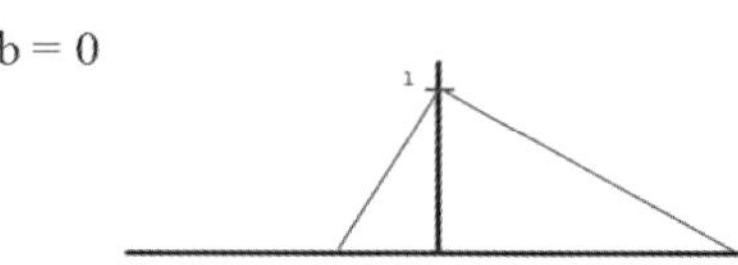

Possibility degree policy $= \dfrac{a}{a-c}$

In this situation, it seems that the possibility of having to apply a policy will not reach 0.5

b < 0

c > 0

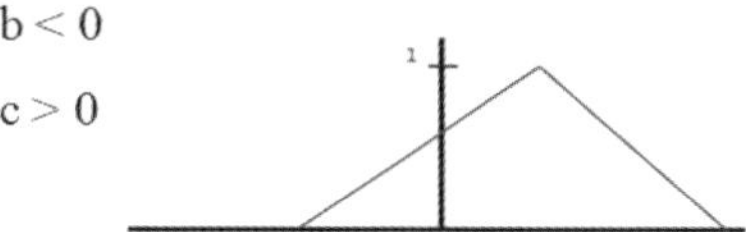

Possibility degree policy $= \dfrac{a^2}{(c-a)(b-a)}$

In this graphical example, there will be a low possibility of having to apply a credit policy.

a ≥ 0

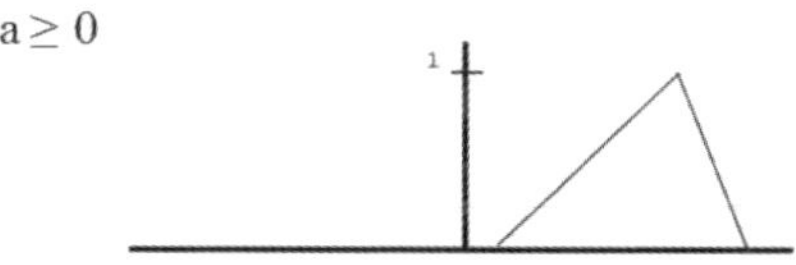

Possibility degree policy = 0

Finally, note that in this case we will not need to ask for a credit policy

Figure 1

4. A numerical example for calculate the Treasury Forecast using fuzzy numbers.

We suppose that we want to begin a new business. We know that the price of the premises for the business is 2,000 m. u. a month including cleaning, water, electricity, telephone and Internet. Also, we know with certainty that we will have an initial cost of 26,000 m. u. in computer equipment and 5,500 m.u. in furniture. We estimate that probably we will need to buy three types of raw materials in a month. For a first month we think that we will need a minimum of 300 m. u. and a maximum of 600 m. u. For a second month we know that we will need 100 m. u. Finally, we think that in the third month we will need a minimum of the 100 m. u. and a maximum of 150 m. u. We consider that in this estimations the indirect taxes (VAT) are included.

In order to advertise our new business, we will spend 2,000 m. u. for advertising during the first month.

The initial capital destined for beginning the new business is 20,000 m. u. Moreover, we have been conceded an initial loan of 10,000 m. u. free of interest tax, that we have to return during the next 5 months with a quote of 2,000 m. u. per month.

We assign 8,000 m. u. for salaries, including taxes. The workers are self-employers, and, for this reason, there are no spends in Social Security and other recruitment expenses.

The estimated sales for the first two months under the different points of view are:

	First month	Second month
Pessimistic	14.400	15.000
Maximum level of confidence	17.600	19.400
Optimistic	20.800	20.600

Using the information included in the table 1, we can build the treasury forecast fuzzy:

Table 2

CONCEPT	First month	Second month
CASHING	**(14.400,17.600,20.800)**	**(29.400,37.000,41.400)**
Sales	**(-32350,-32300,-32000)**	**(29.400,37.000,41.400)**
Other cashing	**(0,0,0)**	**(0,0,0)**
PAYMENTS	**(-46.350,-46.300,-46.000)**	**(-592.00,-59.100,-58.500)**
Shopping (Suppliers)	**(-32350,-32300,-32000)**	**(-33.200,-33.100,-32.500)**
Staff	**(-8.000,-8.000,-8.000)**	**(-16.000,-16.000,-16.000)**
Salaries	(-8.000,-8.000,-8.000)	(-16.000,-16.000,-16.000)
...	(0,0,0)	(0,0,0)
Other structural costs	**(-4.000,-4.000,-4.000)**	**(-6.000,-6.000,-6.000)**
Rentals	(-2.000,-2.000,-2.000)	(-4.000,-4.000,-4.000)
...	(0,0,0)	(0,0,0)
Advertising and promotion	(-2.000,-2.000,-2.000)	(-2.000,-2.000,-2.000)
...	(0,0,0)	(0,0,0)
Payment investments	**(-2.000,-2.000,-2.000)**	**(-4.000,-4.000,-4.000)**
CASHING − PAYEMENTS	**(-31.950,-28.700,-25.200)**	**(-29.800,-22.100,-17.100)**
DISPONIBILITY	**(30.000,30.000,30.000)**	**(30.000,30.000,30.000)**
SURPLUS/DEFICIT	**(-1.950, 1.300, 4.800)**	**(200, 7.900, 12.900)**

The graphical representation of the fuzzy numbers SURPLUS/DEFICIT during the first and the second period are:

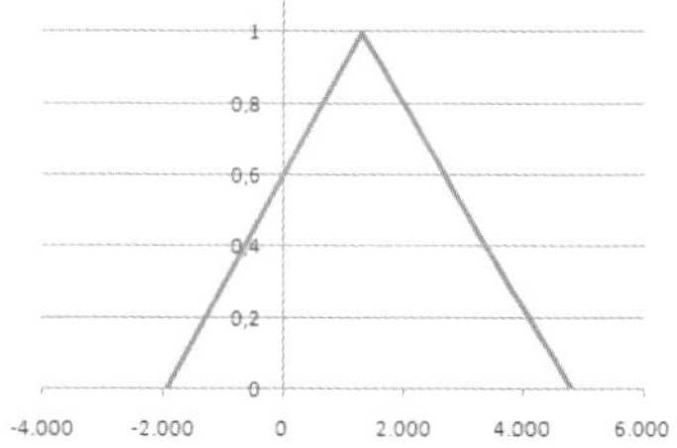
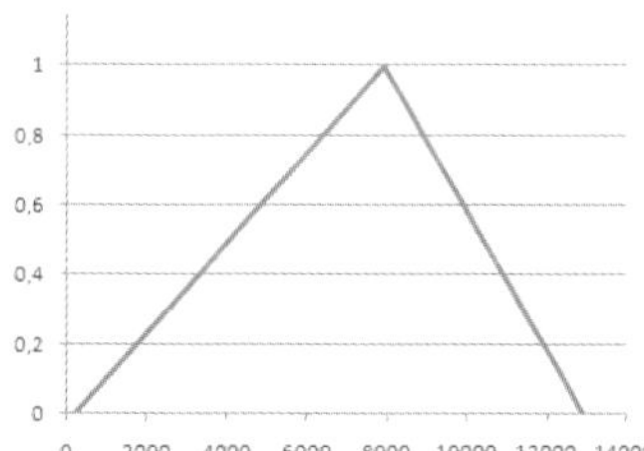

Figure 2

In this situation, we have:

Possibility degree policy for (**-1.950, 1.300, 4.800**) = 0.17

Possibility degree policy for (**200, 7.900, 12.900**) = 0

Level of the viability of the treasury $= 1 -$ maximum $(0.17, 0) = 0.83$
and so, we accept the viability of fuzzy treasury forecast

5. Conclusions

1. In this work, we have seen a practical methodology under uncertainty to estimate the viability for a treasury forecast modeled through fuzzy numbers.
2. This new methodology is directly applicable in real situations and could be a useful tool for the entrepreneurs and organisms that give advice to the new entrepreneurs.
3. We have programmed also practical software for this process with the goal to solve this problem and to do simulations in different real situations. The program available for business practice at the website http://web2.udg.edu/grmfcee/treasuryfuzzy.xls is a useful tool for finding the possible solutions for this type of problems.
4. The fuzzy arithmetic is an interesting tool to compute the treasury forecast for a new business project, using triangular fuzzy numbers for modelling uncertainty data, but it is also possible to use trapezoidal fuzzy numbers if we have an interval of the maximum confidence.

References

1. Bojadziev, G.; Bojadziev, M. (1998): *Fuzzy sets, fuzzy logic, applications.* Advances in Fuzzy Systems-Applications and Theory vol. 5. World Scientific.
2. Gil Aluja, J. (2004): *Fuzzy sets in the management of uncertainty.* Ed. Springer-Verlag.
3. Gil Lafuente, A. M. (2005): *Fuzzy logic in financial analysis.* Ed. Springer-Verlag.
4. Kaufmann, A.; Gil Aluja, J.: (1986) *Introducción de la teoría de los subconjuntos borrosos a la gestión de las empresas.* Ed. Milladoiro.
5. Kaufmann, A.; Gupta, M. M. (1991): *Introduction to fuzzy arithmetic. Theory and applications.* International Thomson Computer Press.
6. Ludevic, M.; Ollé, M. (1991) *Como crear su propia empresa.* Ed. Marcombo. Barcelona.
7. Pindado, J. (2001): *Gestión de tesorería en la empresa: teoría y aplicaciones prácticas.* Universidad de Salamanca.

VALIDATING THE PECKING ORDER THEORY IN THE SPANISH CHEMICAL INDUSTRY

XAVIER CÀMARA-TURULL, XAVIER BORRÀS BALSELLS, MARIA TERESA SORROSAL FORRADELLAS

Departament de Gestió d'Empreses, Universitat Rovira i Virgili
Avda. Universitat, 1, E-43204 Reus, Spain

FERNÁNDEZ IZQUIERDO, M.A.

Departamento de Finanzas y Contabilidad, Universitat Jaume I
Avda. Sos Baynat s/n, E-12071 Castellón de la Plana, Spain

The financial crisis that began in 2008 has revived interest in the significance of the capital structure of corporations. This paper analyses the Pecking Order Theory using a sample of Spanish chemical companies. We pose the same hypotheses first presented by Fama and French in 2002, but employ a different methodology: self-organizing maps, specifically Kohonen maps. Our research reaches similar conclusions to those of Fama and French (2002): More profitable companies present lower leverage and companies with higher growth rates also have higher leverage.

1. Introduction

There has been ongoing theoretical and empirical research into the capital structure of corporations since Modigliani and Miller presented their seminal article in 1958 about the irrelevance of capital structure in terms of a firm's value in perfect markets.

Since then, many theories have been developed that, building upon this research, have tried to adapt it to market imperfections. The first of these was the Trade-Off Theory which incorporates the tax benefits of debt (Modigliani and Miller, 1963) and the bankruptcy costs that it might generate (Kraus and Litzemberger, 1973). Another line of research is derived from the Agency Theory (Jensen and Meckling, 1976), which deals with the conflict between shareholders and debt-holders. Finally, a third approach is based on the costs that asymmetric information generates, which leads to another two theories: signalling theory (Ross, 1977; Leland and Pyle, 1977) and the Pecking Order Theory (Myer and Majluf, 1984). Despite numerous empirical studies, there is still no general consensus among researchers on the decisive factors in determining a company's optimal capital structure. As Myers (1984) says, the theories are not designed to be general, but to explain the behaviour of a subsample of firms. So, if the sample is big enough, more than one theory can be validated.

The global financial crisis of the 21st century has revived this topic by pointing to the alteration of the capital structure of the economy brought about by the low interest rate policy between 2002 and 2006 as the leading cause of widespread economic troubles.

Therefore, the main purpose of our research is to examine financing capital decision-making in the Spanish chemical sector through the Pecking Order Theory, using the method proposed by Kohonen based on an unsupervised neuronal net (self-organizing maps, SOMs).

Neuronal nets have frequently been applied in the field of finance because they present clear advantages over other methods. They allow non-linear processes to be used which involve the net's increasing capacity to approximate functions, classify patterns, increase its immunity to noise, and improve interconnectivity.

The main advantage of an unsupervised training rules net is that the net learns to adapt through experiences collected during previous training patterns without being influenced by the subjective decisions of experts.

In the following section we describe the main contributions of the Pecking Order Theory and define the working hypotheses used by Fama and French (2002). Next, we present the sample of companies and the variables used in the study and the methodology applied. We then present our results and finish with the primary conclusions that can be drawn from this work.

2. The Pecking Order Theory

The Pecking Order Theory proposed by Myers and Majluf in 1984 is widely accepted in the world of finance. The theory is based on the costs of the asymmetric distribution of information that exists between companies and capital markets. Company managers have access to and use internal information about the expected returns of future investments. This asymmetrical information leads investors to think that company managers will only issue new shares to finance investments when these are overvalued. Investors react to this extension with a down-correction of the share price. To prevent this from happening, managers will first use financial sources not affected by the costs of the asymmetric information, such as internal funds, and only if these are not sufficient will they resort to other capital sources less affected by those costs: first debt, then hybrid securities like convertible bonds, and finally equity issues.

Several empirical studies that have attempted to validate the Pecking Order Theory have reached differing conclusions. Fama and Fench confirmed the Pecking Order Theory in their research of 2002 only to then reject it in their research of 2005.

This research aims to provide a new empirical contribution to the existing literature by attempting to validate the Pecking Order Theory in the chemical industry sector. In keeping with Fama and French (2002), we present four hypotheses about the relation between debt and different financial-economic variables: return, growth, volatility and non-debt tax shelter:

1. According to the Pecking Order Theory, the relationship between a firm's leverage and its return should be negative, because the higher the return a company has, the greater the volume of internally generated funds it should have, and therefore the lower its debt.
2. The relationship between a firm's leverage and its potential growth is positive. The more the company grows, the bigger its need for debt should be. It can also be interpreted as the greater future potential a firm has, the smaller its leverage should be in order to maintain a low level of risk and undertake future investments without needing to issue risky assets (Myers and Majluf, 1984)
3. The greater the volatility of a company, the smaller its leverage should be because the reliability of future cash flows should be smaller as well.
4. Finally, a bigger tax shelter increases internally generated company funds (unless the EBITDA is not enough to cover amortizations).

3. Methodology

3.1. *Sample design*

The information used in this research comes from the SABI database. We considered the companies with the code CNAE 24, Chemical Industry, during the period between the 1999 and 2006 financial years, both of them included.

From the original sample all the firms that did not have all the information needed or whose information was illogical were removed. In the end, the sample consisted of 158 companies for the 1999-2006 period, equalling a total of 1,264 observations per variable.

3.2. *Variables*

The proxy variable for company leverage is the debt to equity ratio. The proxy variables for company returns are return on assets (ROA) and return on equity (ROE). Growth opportunities were measured by means of increases in sales and assets from one period to next. The proxy variable for volatility is the real assets log (Fama and French, 2002) and the proxy variable for tax shelter (not generated from debt) is the amortization ratio measured as amortization over total assets.

3.3. *Self-organizing maps (SOM)*

Self-Organizing Maps (SOMs) are a specific type of artificial neural network developed by T. Kohonen. These networks distribute the input information (data or patterns in n-vectors components) in a bi-dimensional space, according to the similarity among patterns.

SOMs are hetero-associated networks (input patterns are associated with different nature outputs), with off-line learning (training and function phases are clearly differentiated), unsupervised (there is no prior information about the groups that the network may create so self-organized) and competitive (when a new pattern is presented there is only one active unit on the map).

The network structure features an input and an output layer. The input layer has n neurons that collect one pattern component. The output layer is made up of m x p neurons of the map of characteristics.

There are three connections between the neurons: i) Feed-forward connections between every neuron of the input layer and output layer. ii) Lateral connections between the neurons of the input layer and those of the output layer defined in their neighbouring area. iii) Recurrent connections in which every unit connects to itself in the output layer.

The SOM function is carried out in four stages: first, the data is entered and it flows throughout the connections between the input and output layers. In the second stage, the m x p output layer units collect the information received and create lateral connections (increasing the influence to those nearby) and recurrent connections that emit an exit signal modified by a continuous transfer function.

In the third stage, a competition is set up in the output layer in order to achieve a winner neuron that minimizes the distance between the weights associated with its connections and the components of the input patterns. In the last step, the weights of the winner neuron and its neighbours are modified according to the distance by a learning coefficient that decreases as the network learns to ensure the convergence to equilibrium. The process is repeated with the rest of input patterns and new iterations are conducted until the final map of characteristics is defined.

The SOM can be applied to solve multiple problems in many different fields, including those that require pattern recognition, data codification, optimization or data grouping. In our research we have applied the SOM to analyze the relationship between some relevant indicators of the performance of chemical companies and their capital structure. The SOM allows companies to be grouped according to their relevant performance indicators and the relationship between the firms and their leverage to be evaluated.

4. Results

This construction work was performed using a toolbox for Matlab designed by professor Kohonen's research group at Helsinki University. After the training process we achieved the map shown in Figure 1.

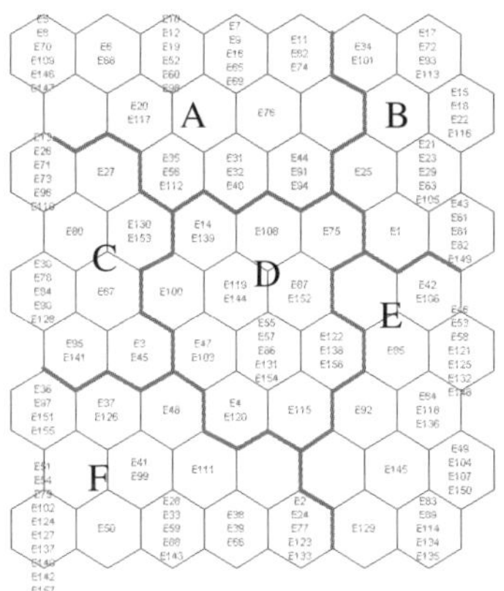

Figure 1: Map of Spanish chemical firms

We identified the clusters from the U-matrix for the variables described above and for the eight-year period ending in 2006. The resulting map was built by a double optimisation: i) maximum homogeneity within each group and ii) a minimum number of groups.

Our interpretation of the defined groups based on the weight maps is as follows:

- Group A: This group consists mainly of mid-low profitability, mid-low growth, low volatility and high non-debt fiscal shelter companies. These are also the oldest and largest companies in the sample.
- Group B: These are the companies with lower profitability and growth, high volatility and mid-low non-debt fiscal shelter. They are small but old companies.
- Group C: This group consists mainly of companies with mid-high profitability and low volatility. Growth and non-debt fiscal shelter are average. This group is comprised of the largest companies.
- Group D: The companies in this group have slightly lower profitability than those in group A but their growth and non-debt fiscal shelter are above average. This group has very low volatility. It is comprised of mid-small companies that are younger than average.
- Group E: These are the youngest and smallest companies of the sample and present very high volatility, low profitability and average growth.
- Group F: This group has the highest profitability and growth. Both volatility and non-debt fiscal shelter are below average. The companies in this group are small and mid-aged.

According to the resulting maps:

Hypothesis 1. There is a relationship between profitability and leverage. The best companies in terms of profitability are those that use less debt to finance their assets. For those with lower profitability we have to distinguish between old and young companies as the former present a lower level of leverage while the latter have greater leverage.

Hypothesis 2. The companies with lower growth have lower leverage, but higher growth only corresponds to higher leverage in the case of mid-low profitability.

Hypothesis 3. There is no relationship between volatility and leverage. However, there is a relationship between volatility and company age: the younger the company the more volatile it is.

Hypothesis 4. Companies with a high non-debt fiscal shelter mainly present low leverage and vice versa, but there are two groups (group F and group D) that do not follow this behaviour.

5. Conclusions

This research aims to validate the Pecking Order Theory for the Spanish chemical industry using Kohonen's self-organizing maps. We used a sample of 158 companies for the period 1999-2006.

After analysing the results of our study, we can conclude that there is a relationship between profitability and leverage and between growth and leverage, which validate the first and second hypotheses described in section 2. Only Group A does not verify these hypotheses. The companies within this group present low leverage despite their low profitability, which may be explained by the fact that they have low growth rates and that they have acquired high levels of funds through amortizations.

This cannot be extended to volatility and non-debt fiscal shelter, which do not have this relationship with leverage. Therefore the third and fourth hypotheses cannot be validated.

On the other hand, we found that the company size and age are relevant factors in that: i) the largest and oldest companies mainly have higher non-debt fiscal shelters, lower growth rates and consequently lower leverage; ii) the older companies mainly present low volatility rates, while younger firms display higher volatility.

Although we used a different methodology, some of our results are similar to those obtained by Fama and French (2002). However, because we were not able to validate some of the hypotheses posed, we will complement this research by repeating the analysis using other methodologies such as factor analysis, analysis of panel data and neural backpropagation. We will also extend this research to include other Spanish industry sectors.

References

1. B. Back, K. Sere and H. Vanharanta, Managing complexity in large data bases using self-organizing maps. *Accounting management and information technologies*. 8 (1998).
2. E.F. Fama and K. French, Testing trade off and pecking order predictions about dividends and debt. *Review of financial studies*. 15 (2002).
3. E.F. Fama and K. French, Financial decisions: who issues stock?. *Journal of financial studies*. 76, (2005).
4. M. Jensen and W. Meckling, Theory of the firm: managerial behaviour, agency costs and ownership structure. *Journal of financial economic*. 5 (1976).
5. T. Kohonen, Self-Organization and Associative Memory. Berlin: Springer-Verlag (1989).
6. T. Kohonen, Self-Organizing Maps. Berlin: Springer-Verlag (1997).
7. A. Kraus and R. Litzenberger, A state-preference model of optimal financial leverage. *The journal of finance*. 28 (1973).

8. H.Y. Leland and D. Pyle, Information asymmetric financial structure, and financial intermediation. *The journal of finance.* 32 (1977).
9. F. Modigliani and M.H. Miller, The cost of capital, corporation finance and the theory of investment. *American economic review.* 48 (1958).
10. F. Modigliani and M.H. Miller, Corporate income, taxes and the cost of capital: a correction. *American economic review*, 53 (1963).
11. S.C. Myers, The capital structure puzzle. *Journal of finance.* 39 (1984).
12. S.C. Myers and N. Majluf, Corporate investment decisions when firms have information that investors don't have. *Journal of financial economics.* 13 (1984).
13. S. Ross, The determination of financial structure: the incentive-signalling approach. *The Bell journal of economic.* 8 (1977).

APPLICATION OF THE AFFINITIES THEORY IN A PROBLEM OF THE LATIN AMERICAN BUSINESS COMPETITIVENESS

ERIKA ANSELIN-AVILA, ANNA M. GIL-LAFUENTE

Faculty of Economical Sciences and Business Studies,
Department of Economic and Business Organization,
Barcelona University,
Av. Diagonal 690, 08034 Barcelona, Spain
E-mails: eanselav8@docd2.ub.edu, eanselin@gmail.com, amgil@ub.edu

The Affinities Theory has been an investigation subject approached from subjective perspectives. The article aims to showing a new technical procedure to integrate similar but not identical problems in the countries in Latin American. These items are fundamental in the decision making for the international agencies about of de Business Competitiveness. In order to consolidate this theory a small and medium business simulation whit results of an investigation in eight countries in South America, describing all outcomes and conclusions generated by the analysis, is shown.

Keywords: affinities theory; business competitiveness; problems Latin American; economical problems.

1. Introduction

Over time the research needs in all circumstances as economic, political and social, correspond to human development itself. Talk about globalization these days is to refer to systems where countries, companies and societies are interrelated, there is no place where the restriction for the purchase of services or products, be they national and international levels, the large or small firms today does not require such complex systems to international supply.

The macroeconomic effect has a sensitive impact principality in the small and medium enterprises (SMEs), by its special and limited characteristics, e.g. they do not have protection about currency change, do not have reserves economics in case of economical crisis, their patrimony is banker credit guaranty; but is important to considerate than the effect is different in each business sector or size.

The moments of major impact owe to the economic crises that have affected to a great extent to the least protected sectors (SMEs), which are more sensitive to the consequences derived from a country's macroeconomics situation. Izquierdo, Romero and Talvi [5] suggest that: the Tequila crisis in 1995 (the most importantly for Latin America), the Russian crisis of 1998 and the resulting collapse in capital inflows to the region with direct economic consequences – in accord by Calvo, Izquierdo and Talvi [2] – support the premonitory concerns raised by Calvo, Leiderman and Reinhart [3]. The drought in capital inflows to the region following the Russian crisis lasted until the end of 2002. Since then, external capital has returned to the region whit a vengeance due to abundant international liquidity and a dramatic rise in commodity prices. Zhang and Si [9] define that in recent years, many studies have documented the important role of various factors on the Chinese growth entrepreneurial enterprises, e.g. innovation capability, location factors, being located in a regional industry cluster, guanxi and networking opportunities, entrepreneurial skills including international business experience, access to more financial sources and capital for developing the business [1, 4 and 7]. Not surprisingly, Latin América economics have since then been experiencing a new phase of booming asset prices, appreciating real exchange rates, booming investment and strong growth performance.

In order to provide support to this analysis, this document shows a tool that will evaluate the variables of an economic zone with similar characteristics and obtain results that allow us to identify affinity between countries in the same region, so that with this International Institutions in conjunction with national measures can multiply acquired in one country with similar characteristics to make it to the other and offer support for this statement in its competitive environment business.

2. Application of the Affinities Theories

The creation and sustainability of SMEs have been part of the agenda of development agencies and government over the past thirty years. Several routes have been tried, but recently there has been increasing international attention on how to reform the business environment.

This environment covers all factors which are outside the company and have an impact on business competitiveness and growth prospects. Such factors include government policies, laws and regulations, infrastructure, the state of macroeconomics, taxes, exchange rates, the quality of skilled workers available, the culture of doing business, access to markets, etc..

The moot point is how the business environment can be more or less conducive to facilitating and promoting business development? "There is a view among experts in business development a more conducive environment could be a key element in improving competitiveness and survival of private enterprises, especially SMEs" [8].

In order to provide an analysis of this problem, then presents a process described by teachers Kaufmann and Gil Aluja, called Affinities Theory [6], whose foundations are based on the grouping of concepts that will deliver results-focused institutions development of this sector in Latin America in order to identify the factors affecting this area and seek to multiply the measures that are workable solution for their compatibility with the problem.

For the development of this study are considered assessments by Zeballos, Emilio and FUNDES International [9], which identifies the environmental barriers identified by managers in 8 countries evaluated by a taste of 4,200 small and medium entrepreneurs companies, in depth interviews with over 200 people (public officials, representatives of private and intermediate sector - experts in the field, representatives of guilds, employers, private operators, etc.-) in Argentina, Bolivia, Chile, Colombia, Costa Rica, El Salvador, Panama and Venezuela, as well as information contained in reports from focus groups and depth interviews.

3. Description and Development of the Process

The grouping of products, with more or less common features may be of obvious importance for executives who are forced to make decisions in the complex world of international economics and economic analysis of enterprises.

In order to facilitate the solution of this problem, we describe a scheme whose bases are: In an economic environment there are m countries P_j, j = 1,2,3 ... .. m, certain characteristics C_i, i = 1,2,3, ..., n. These characteristics for a company a degree of acceptance that will be valued by $\alpha = [0,1]$ so that the higher the estimate are given values closer to unity and as the estimate be reduced figures are assigned close to zero. Each variable P_j may well be described through the fuzzy subset whose reference is given by C_i characteristics:

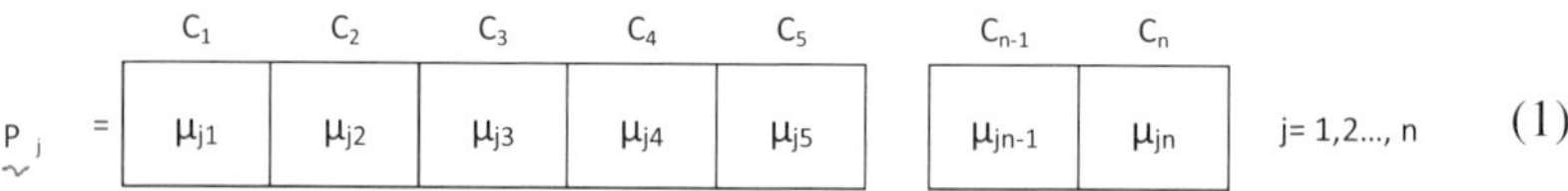

$$P_{\underset{\sim}{j}} = \begin{array}{|c|c|c|c|c|} \hline C_1 & C_2 & C_3 & C_4 & C_5 \\ \hline \mu_{j1} & \mu_{j2} & \mu_{j3} & \mu_{j4} & \mu_{j5} \\ \hline \end{array} \quad \begin{array}{|c|c|} \hline C_{n-1} & C_n \\ \hline \mu_{jn-1} & \mu_{jn} \\ \hline \end{array} \quad j = 1,2..., n \qquad (1)$$

Applying this theory to the case, we should define the characteristics that present problems of nations of the 8 countries in this study (P_1 = Argentina, P_2 = Bolivia, P_3 = Chile, P_4 = Colombia, P_5 = Costa Rica, P_6 = El Salvador, P_7 = Panamá, P_8 = Venezuela) and described below in the figure No. 1:

C_1	Access to bank credit	C_{21}	Legal uncertainty
C_2	Access to external markets	C_{22}	Labor law / obligations associated with recruitment
C_3	Access to technology	C_{23}	Internal market and competition conditions inside
C_4	Support and social recognition to the employer	C_{24}	New forms of financing
C_5	Support / functioning of the state	C_{25}	Get skilled labor
C_6	Environmental Aspects	C_{26}	Public Order
C_7	Barriers to market entry	C_{27}	Commercial Banking Platform inappropriate
C_8	Offer export quality	C_{28}	Little public support instruments use
C_9	Workloads	C_{29}	Private Policy support
C_{10}	Unfair Competition	C_{30}	Politicization and representation of Guilds
C_{11}	Concentration of supply / demand	C_{31}	Issues in Infrastructure and SS
C_{12}	Cost / quality of public services	C_{32}	Relationship between large firms is not conducive to SME
C_{13}	Difficult to sell to public sector	C_{33}	Relationship with suppliers
C_{14}	High social security charges	C_{34}	Relationship with distributors
C_{15}	Entrepreneurship	C_{35}	Consultancy services / training inadequate
C_{16}	Missing import regulation	C_{36}	Macroeconomic situation
C_{17}	Taxes and patents	C_{37}	Trading in influence / corruption
C_{18}	Inadequacy of business organizations	C_{38}	Complicated procedures in foreign trade
C_{19}	Informality of business	C_{39}	Publics Procedures and Services
C_{20}	RRHH qualified	C_{40}	Linking sectoral

Figure No. 1 Problems identified for the American Latin Business.

The values were obtained by the investigation of Zeballos, as noted in previous lines, are showing in the figure No. 2:

	P_1	P_2	P_3	P_4	P_5	P_6	P_7	P_8
C_1	76.0	28.0	26.8	20.0	10.7	17.0	15.2	43.0
C_2		1.8	8.2	3.0	2.7	3.0		
C_3		0.5	10.9			5.0	0.3	
C_4		1.8						
C_5			26.4	7.0	10.4	14.0		23.0
C_6								10.0
C_7							1.3	
C_8	8.0		8.8					
C_9		1.3						9.0
C_{10}		28.8	41.6					
C_{11}	30.0							
C_{12}							12.3	34.0
C_{13}						5.0		
C_{14}					28.8			
C_{15}								6.0
C_{16}	46.0							
C_{17}		2.8	19.5	13.0	5.0	8.0	10.2	16.0
C_{18}	7.0							
C_{19}							4.7	
C_{20}								20.0

	P_1	P_2	P_3	P_4	P_5	P_6	P_7	P_8
C_{21}	47.0	4.0		1.0			2.9	
C_{22}		1.3	30.1	3.0		1.0	20.6	
C_{23}		10.0		11.0	3.8	30.0		
C_{24}					2.1			
C_{25}		1.8						6.0
C_{26}			3.0					
C_{27}	39.0							
C_{28}	23.0	1.0	11.9					
C_{29}					0.9			
C_{30}		1.3	14.5	1.0			0.8	11.0
C_{31}	54.0		9.0	2.0	11.2	12.0	3.3	
C_{32}	6.0				2.8			
C_{33}			7.4					
C_{34}			5.5					
C_{35}	13.0				0.6			
C_{36}		11.8	39.1	28.0				44.0
C_{37}	18.0				12.1		6.3	12.0
C_{38}	33.0							
C_{39}		5.3			2.3		12.1	6.0
C_{40}					0.9			

Figure No. 2 Valuation of Problems identified for the American Latin Business.

According to the estimation of the experts interviewed, has made a valuation on [0,1] expressed in percentage, according to the importance given by the respondents in each country, this estimate gave the following data matrix (figure No. 3):

	P_1	P_2	P_3	P_4	P_5	P_6	P_7	P_8
C_1	1.0	1.0	0.7	0.9	0.7	0.7	0.9	0.9
C_2		0.1	0.2	0.2	0.3	0.3		
C_3		0.1	0.4			0.4	0.1	
C_4		0.1						
C_5			0.6	0.5	0.7	0.7		0.7
C_6								0.2
C_7							0.2	
C_8	0.1		0.3					
C_9		0.1						0.2
C_{10}		1.0	1.0					
C_{11}	0.4							
C_{12}							0.8	0.8
C_{13}						0.4		
C_{14}					1.0			
C_{15}								0.1
C_{16}	0.7							
C_{17}		0.2	0.5	0.7	0.5	0.5	0.6	0.5
C_{18}	0.1							
C_{19}							0.4	
C_{20}								0.6

	P_1	P_2	P_3	P_4	P_5	P_6	P_7	P_8
C_{21}	0.8	0.3		0.1			0.3	
C_{22}		0.1	0.8	0.2		0.2	1.0	
C_{23}		0.8		0.6	0.4	1.0		
C_{24}					0.3			
C_{25}		0.1						0.1
C_{26}				0.2				
C_{27}	0.6							
C_{28}	0.3	0.1	0.4					
C_{29}					0.2			
C_{30}		0.1	0.4	0.1			0.1	0.3
C_{31}	0.9		0.3	0.1	0.8	0.6	0.3	
C_{32}	0.1				0.4			
C_{33}			0.2					
C_{34}			0.1					
C_{35}	0.2				0.1			
C_{36}		0.8	0.9	1.0				1.0
C_{37}	0.2				0.8		0.5	0.4
C_{38}	0.5							
C_{39}		0.4			0.3		0.7	0.1
C_{40}					0.2			

Figure No. 3 Valuation of Experts about of the Problems identified for the American Latin Business.

Through this table we can see the relationships for each level, through the α-cuts. As has been identified with different color, you can display the different brands of values:

$$\alpha = 1, \alpha \geq 0.9, \alpha \geq 0.8, \alpha \geq 0.7, \alpha \geq 0.6, \alpha \geq 0.5, \alpha \geq 0.4, \alpha \geq 0.3, \alpha \geq 0.2, \alpha \geq 0.1$$

To establish relations of affinity, we use the method called MOORE families. We call $E^{(1)}$ to set P_j and $E^{(2)}$ to set C_i. Thus we have:

$$E^{(1)} = P_1, P_2, P_3, P_4, P_5, P_6, P_7, P_8 = A,B,C,D,E,F,G,H \qquad (2)$$

$$E^{(2)} = C_1, C_2, C_3, C_4, C_5, C_6, C_7, C_8, C_9, C_{10}, C_{11}, C_{12}, C_{13}, C_{14}, C_{15}, C_{16}, C_{17}, C_{18}, C_{19},$$
$C_{20}, C_{21}, C_{22}, C_{23}, C_{24}, C_{25}, C_{26}, C_{27}, C_{28}, C_{29}, C_{30}, C_{31}, C_{32}, C_{33}, C_{34}, C_{35}, C_{36}, C_{37}, C_{38},$
C_{39}, C_{40} = 1, 2, 3, 4, 5, 6, 7, 8, 9, 10, 11, 12, 13, 14, 15, 16, 17, 18, 19, 20, 21, $\qquad (3)$
22, 23, 24, 25, 26, 27, 28, 29, 30, 31, 32, 33, 34, 35, 36, 37, 38, 39, 40.

Make up, then, the greatest set possible with the elements of $E^{(2)}$ called "Power Set $E^{(2)}$"" which will:

$P(E^{(2)}) = \tilde{(}$, 1, 2, 3, 4, 5, 6, 7, 8, 9, 10, 11, 12, 13, 14, 15, 16, 17, 18, 19, 20, 21, 22, 23, 24, 25, 26, 27, 28, 29, 30, 31, 32, 33, 34, 35, 36, 37, 38, 39, 40, 1-2, 1-3,1-4, 1-5, 1-6, 1-7, 1-8, 1-9, 1-10, 1-11, 1-12, 1-13, 1-14, 1-15, 1-16, 1-17, 1-18, 1-19, 1-20, 1-21, 1-22, 1-23, 1-24, 1-25, 1-26, 1-27, 1-28, 1-29, 1-30, 1-31, 1-32, 1-33, 1-34, 1-35, 1-36, 1-37, 1-38, 1-39, 1-40, 2-3,2-4, 2-5, 2-6, 2-7, 2-8, $\qquad (4)$

2-9, 2-10, 2-11, 2-12, 2-13, 2-14, 2-15, 2-16, 2-17, 2-18, 2-19, 2-20, 2-21, 2-22, 2-23, 2-24, 2-25, 2-26, 2-27, 2-28, 2-29, 2-30, 2-31, 2-32, 2-33, 2-34, 2-35, 2-36, 2-37, 2-38, 2-39, 2-40, $E^{(2)}$)

For each element of $P(E^{(2)})$ will correspond to the elements or $P(E^{(1)})$ for different levels of α taking into account the above table, determining in each case the correspondence of the values obtained in each assigned between α level (0.7-1).

This considering that executives considered sufficient level $\alpha \geq 0.7$ for finding the relations of affinity, therefore, be taken at this level, the empty elements of $P(E^{(1)})$ and the subsets of $E^{(2)}$ that are not covered by other, this way, the result would be:

$$
\begin{array}{ll}
\text{A --- C16, C21, C31} & \text{AB --- C1} \\
\text{B --- C23, C36} & \text{BC --- C10} \\
\text{C --- C36} & \text{CEF ---C1} \qquad (5) \\
\text{D ----C17, C36} & \text{GH ----C12} \\
\text{E ----C14, C37} & \text{DGH --C1} \\
\text{F ---- C23} & \text{EFH ---C5} \\
\text{G ---- C22, C39} &
\end{array}
$$

Whit this information is possible to analyze:

a) Of the 40 problems identified in the economic zone, 14 of which are the most representative.

b) In different levels but, all countries agree that the Access to de bank credit is the most important factor for to development in its country.

c) Bolivia and Chile are saying that their main problems are in the Unfair Competition; Chile, Costa Rica, El Salvador and Venezuela are affinities in considerate than have great problems whit Support / functioning of the state; Panamá and Venezuela said than the Cost / quality of public services are constraints to growth.

d) That there are problems that countries are given the same importance and value of this highlights the affinity between them, but if we consider that the indicator considered by experts as evaluation range [1-0.7], there are more matches and shorten the to assess problems in an industry. This is the case: C23= Internal market and competition conditions inside, C31= Issues in Infrastructure and SS and C36= Macroeconomic situation.

4. Conclusions

As we can see, it highlights the similarities existing between the different countries in relation to the characteristics that problems identified during the investigation.

This analysis allows international institutions to focus attention on issues of greater importance in the economic zone, leaving each country to address specific problems.

Allows repetition of models on display in a country, thereby assessing viability in a second or third country.

The schedule features 14 general problems, but the affinities are given only 4 points: Access to bank credit, Support / functioning of the state, Unfair Competition and Cost / quality of public services. In this case the government in each country has many problems for to found the answers about its SMEs necessities, or in other order change the mindset of their businessmen, making them independent of government efforts.

References

1. Ahlstrom, D. and Bruton, G. An institutional perspective on the role of culture in shaping strategic actions by technology focused entrepreneurial firms in China, Entrepreneurship Theory and Practice, Vol. 26, pp.53–70. (2002).
2. Calvo, G., Izquierdo, A. and Talvi, E. Phoenix miracles in emerging markets: recovering without credit from systemic financial crisis, NBER Working Paper 12101. (2006).
3. Calvo, G., Leiderman, L. and Reinhart C. Capital inflows and real exchange rate appreciation in Latin America: the role of external factors, IMF Staff Papers, Vol. 40, pp.108–151. (1993).
4. Gibb, A. and Li, J. Organising for enterprise in China: what can we learn from the Chinese micro, small, and medium enterprise development experience, Futures, Vol. 35, pp.403–421. (2003).
5. Izquierdo, A., Romero, R. and Talvi, E., Business Cycles in Latin America: the role of external factors, CERES, Working Paper. (2007).
6. Kaufmann, A. and Gil Aluja, J. Técnicas Especiales para la gestión de expertos, Santiago de Compostela: Ed. Milladoiro. (1993).
7. Watkins Mathys, L. and Foster, M.J. Entrepreneurship: the missing ingredient in China's STIP?. Entrepreneurship and Regional Development, No. 18, pp.249–274. (2006).
8. Zevallos V. Emilio - Restricciones del entorno a la competitividad empresarial en América Latina. FUNDES Internacional, Bolivia. (2007).
9. Zevallos V. Emilio.- Micro, Pequeñas y medianas empresas en América Latina. Revista CEPAL Volumen 79. (Abril 2003).
10. Zhang, Y. and Si, C. The Impacts of external factors on the growth of Chinese entrepreneurial enterprises. An empirical study, (Emerald Group Publishing Limited) Journal of Small Business and Enterprise Development, Vol. 15, pp.689–703. (2008).

MODELLING OF THE ECONOMIC EFFECT OF ROTATION AND FINANCIAL LEVERING IN THE FIELD OF PROFITABILITY

ALFREDO ROCAFORT NICOLAU

*Accounting Department, Area of Financial Economics
and Accounting, University of Barcelona,
Diagonal 690-696, 08034-Barcelona, Spain*

MANUEL FLORES CABALLERO

*Financial Economy and Accountancy Department,
University Rey Juan Carlos, Campus de Vicálvaro,
Paseo de los Artilleros, s/nº, 28032-Madrid, Spain*

In the study of the rates of return of coefficients two large magnitudes exist which explain the different effects which are produced from the margin of business to financial profitability. The repercussion of rotation from an economic point of view on the economical profitability and financial levering on the ROI and the financial profitability we define as rotation effect and levering effect. The joint study of both effects allows us to represent the so-called "global effect" which is produced from the margin of business to financial profitability.

1. Analysis of the Effects Produced on Profitability

The field study of profitability allows us to establish some fixed relationships between the profit of the financial year with respect to three large types of variables, two of equity and one economical, specifically these are:

- The business Net;
- The level of investment made by the company in their assets, and finally;
- Revenues or volume of net sales reached in the financial year.

These relationships and those which determine the two large fields which we express through the following figure: those of financial levering and rotations over assets.

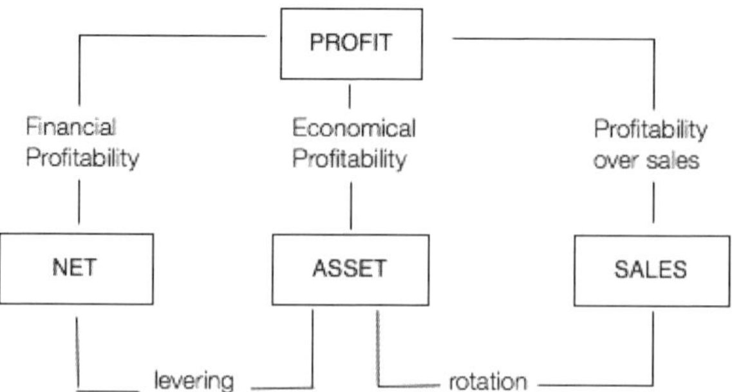

The study of the relationships between these three large magnitudes is decisive in the world of company profitability as much for the relationships which are produced between the same as for their relationships with the different profit levels of the company.

The relationships between the variables Assets and Business Net allow us to know the financial levering which is produced in the company and which will affect the profitability field, for which we will designate "financing effect" and "structural charge effect".

$$\text{Rate of levering} \quad = \quad \frac{\text{Total Assets}}{\text{Business Net}}$$

While the relationships between the variables of revenues with respect to assets allows us to know the rotation field and which will affect the profitability field, which we will designate "investor effect".

$$\text{Rate of rotation} \quad = \quad \frac{\text{Business Revenue}}{\text{Total Assets}}$$

In the graph below we can observe that the points at which the lines cross which express profit, specifically that of profit before interest and taxes (PBIT) and the Net Benefit (NB) on the three magnitudes: Net, Total Assets and the volume of Business Revenue are precisely the profitability coefficients which we have studied: the general margin on sales, economical profitability, the Net ROI and financial profitability.

Graph showing the impact of rotation and levering on profitability

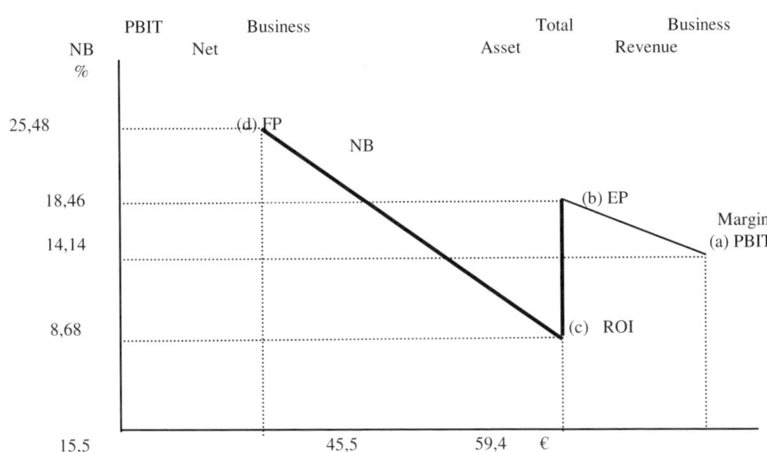

The point (a) expresses the general margin on sales, point (d) expresses financial profitability. Between these the study of the three financial relationships which are decisive on the results of the company is contained.

As we can observe in the previous graph, the four ratios on profitability will allow us to study these effects as we can see in the following:

Points	Magnitude Relationships	Effects
(a)-(b)	Business Revenue – Total Assets	Investment
(b)-(c)	PBIT – Net Profit	Structural Costs
(c)-(d)	Total Assets- NET	Financing

In the same way we can see how the business which can be found in the Annex is affected by the two large relationships

- Those of levering which are expressed by the relationship between the columns of Total Asset and Net and which are quantified in the field of profitability by two large effects: those of structural costs and financial costs.
- Those of rotation which are expressed by the relationship between the two magnitudes of volume of net sales and Total Asset of the company and which are quantified in the field of profitability by the investing effect.

In continuation we will proceed to study the financial relationships mentioned and their effects.

2.   Study of Investment Effect

In the business world we know that the co-efficient of economic profitability is formed by two catalyst coefficients; those of the general margin on sales and rotation.

For this reason, we can observe in the graph that the difference between the coefficients over the general margin on sales and the ratio of Economic Profitability shows us the effect which rotation of sales on Total Assets in the company will produce exactly.   We will call the effect produced by the difference between these ratios "investment effect".

Graph showing Investment Effect

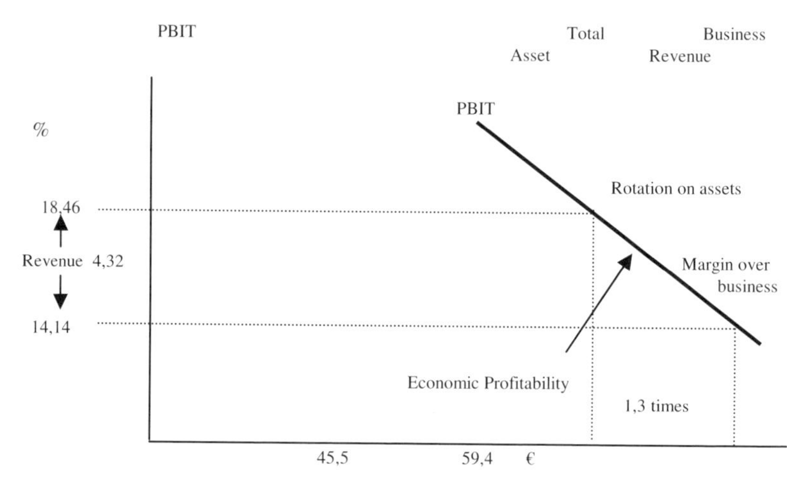

$$\text{Margin over Business Revenue} = \frac{\text{PBIT}}{\text{Business Revenue}} \times 100 = \frac{8'40}{59'4} = 14.14\,\%$$

$$\text{Rotation of Total Assets} = \frac{\text{Business Revenue}}{\text{TA}} = \frac{59'4}{45'5} = 1.30837 \text{ times}$$

$$\text{Economic Profitability } \frac{\text{PBIT}}{\text{TA}} = \frac{8'4}{45'5} = 18.46\,\%$$

The greater the difference between the Economic Profitability coefficient with the ratio of General Margin on Business Revenue, the higher the rotation of business revenue over the Total Assets of he company.

It is clear that even though the coefficients of the general margin on business revenue and economic profitability use the same numerator, the PBIT, the difference between them is produced by having distinct denominators. While one compares the PBIT over Total Assets, or investment made by the company, the other does this over business revenues achieved.

Within a determined sector we will say that an establishment, area or point of sale of the scale where the relationship between volume of sales with total asset is most viable. This relationship will be optimized to the scale when less assets are necessary to reach a determined volume of sales, or merely that to reach a set volume of sales we require lower investments in assets.

With respect to the relationship Assets – Business Revenue, the company will select their investments based on the following criteria: on the scale when the difference between Business Revenue and the total of the most favourable assets is the greatest, given that less investment in assets is required to reach a determined volume of sales.

3.   Structural Cost Effect Analysis

The designated structural costs effect is a purely financial nuance effect, essentially formed by two magnitudes:

- The cost of loans which finance the assets of the company, also designated as the structural charge costs or uncontrolled financing with costs.
- Tax on the financial year results of the company, such as income tax on the company.

We can determine the effect of structural costs on the fields of profitability by means of the known coefficients of Economic Profitability or Gross ROI and Net ROI. The difference between these ratios is the percentage incidence of the structural costs.

Graph showing "structural costs" effect

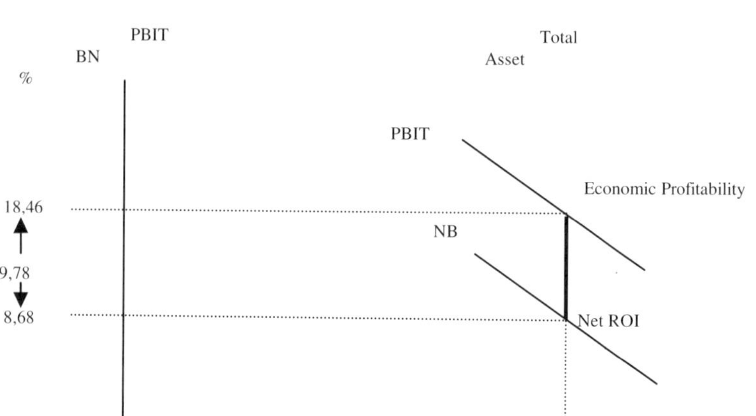

The difference of the calculation between Economic Profitability and Net ROI comes given because both coefficients have the same denominator, and on the other hand they have different numerators.

$$\text{Economic Profitability} \quad \frac{\text{PBIT}}{\text{TA}} = \frac{8'40}{45'5} = 18.46\ \%$$

$$\text{ROI} \quad \frac{\text{NB}}{\text{TA}} = \frac{3'95}{45'5} = 8.68\ \%$$

In equivalent conditions of PBIT, we can observe that companies with a higher level of self-financing undergo very reduced financing costs and very high costs for taxes on profits, and also the opposite; when the company has a higher debt level a lower level of taxes on profits and higher structural financing interests will be registered.

On the scale that companies reach a greater level of financing beyond their control, they will have more structural financing costs and profits will be reduced and, for this reason, the taxes on the same.

4. Financing or Capitalizing Effect Study

The financing effect comes determined by the level of levering of the company, a relationship which is established between the magnitudes of investment in assets and self financing of the company.

In the field of profitability this effect comes expressed by the existing difference between the ratios; Net ROI and Financial Profitability.

In the graph we can observe the effect produced by the difference between the two ratios and which we will call "the financing effect or capitalizing effect".

Graph showing "financing" effect

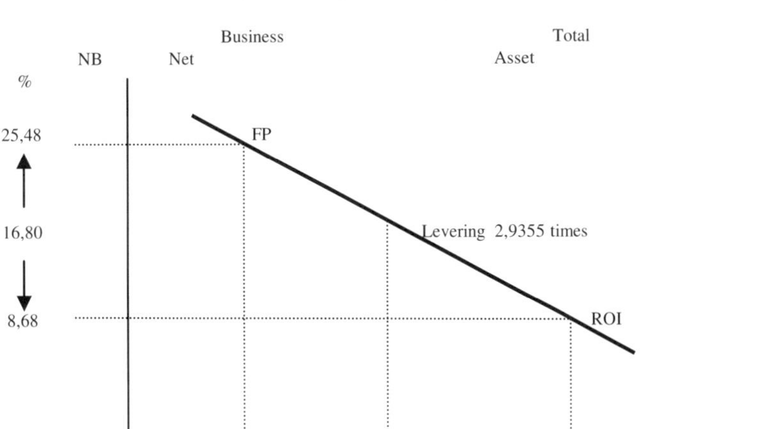

When the co-efficient of levering is higher this indicates that the company has contributed less self means with respect to its investment in assets and vice versa, when the greater level rate of self financing is lower than the assets which the company has.

They are ratios which have the same numerator, NB, and with different denominators, TA and Net, respectively.

$$\text{ROI} \quad \frac{\text{NB}}{\text{TA}} = \frac{3'95}{45'5} = 8.68\ \%$$

$$\text{Levering of Total Assets over Business Net} \quad \frac{\text{TA}}{\text{NET}} = \frac{45'5}{15'5} = 2.9355\ \text{Times}$$

$$\text{Financial Profitability} \quad \frac{\text{NB}}{\text{NET}} \;=\; \frac{3'95}{15'5} \;=\; 25.48\,\%$$

When the difference between both ratios is higher this means that a greater level of levering will be produced in the company over its own means of financing and vice versa, when the difference between Net ROI on Financial Profitability is lower then the existence of Total Assets being financed by own means will be brought closer.

In the field of profitability the differences between the ratios Net ROI and Financial Profitability are specifically those which determine the percentage quantification of this capitalizing effect.

5. Global View of the Effects Produced Between Financial Profitability and the General Margin on Company Revenue

As we have been able to confirm, the difference between rates of Financial Profitability and General Margin on sales comes determined by the sum of three large effects: the investment effect, the structural charge effect and the financing effect.

Using the data collected from the company in the Annex of a company 50% self financed and 50% non-affiliated financed, the analysis of profitability and its effects, expressed in millions of u.m. is the following:

The determination of the ratios is the following:

Calculation of the ratios over profitability

		%
General Margin over sales	(Mr)	14.14
Economic Profitability	(EP)	18.46
Net ROI	(RN)	8.69
Financial Profitability	(FP)	25.48

The company reaches a margin over sales of 14.14% and financial profitability of 25.48%, producing a difference between the ratios of 11.34 points, produced by various effects; two positive character effects and one negative as can be seen in the following table:

Effects between the ratios of financial profitability and the margin over Business Revenue

%
a) Financing effect: FP - Net ROI   = 25'48 - 8'68   =   16'80
b) Structural costs effect: NET ROI – EP   = 8'68 - 18'46   = - 9' 78
c) Investing effect: RE - Margin over sales = 18'46 - 14'14   =   4 '32

Total difference (Financial Profitability – Margin over sales) =   11.34

Graphically we express the effects in the following way:

Graph showing effect of rotation and levering on profitability

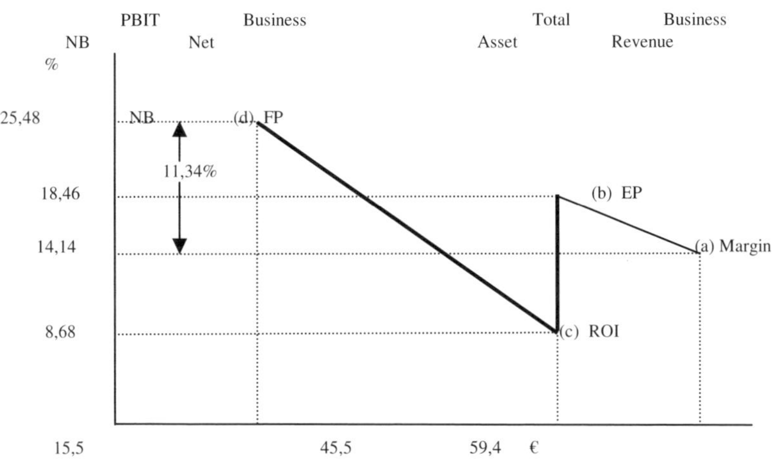

As can be understood from the graph, the detail of the effects is the following:

a) The effects produced by the amount of levering of the company is 7.02 %, produced by the decomposition of two effects:
·   The financing effect with a favourable balance of 16.80%
·   The effect of the structural charge which produces a negative effect quantified at -9.78 points
b) The effect produced by the level of rotation over the assets of the company and which produce an investing effect which is also favourable of 4.32 points.

References

1. A.P. Arenal Vera, E. Bolado Echevarria, *Análisis de Correlación entre la rentabilidad de la empresa y la cotización bursátil de sus títulos. Aplicaciones a la Cía. Telefónica Nacional de España, decenio 1975-1984, Técnica Contable*, Madrid 1988, págs 223-235.
2. L.A. Bernstein, *Análisis de los Estados Financieros*, Editorial Deusto, Bilbao 1984, 299 pp.
3. L. Cañibano Calvo, E. Bueno Campos, *Autofinanciación y tesorería en la empresa*, Madrid 1983, 413 pp.
4. A. Cuervo Garcia, P. Rivero Torres, *El análisis económico-financiero de la empresa*, Revista Española de Financiación y Contabilidad. nº 49, Madrid 1986, págs 15-33.
5. M. Flores Caballero, *Análisis de la rentabilidad,* Técnica Contable, Madrid 1991, págs 487-504.
6. M. Flores Caballero, *Análisis de los efectos: inversión, costes estructurales y capitalización en el estudio de la rentabilidad*, Comunicación IV Encuentro Profesores Universitarios de Contabilidad, Santander 1991, 1207 pp.
7. M. Flores Caballero, *Aspectos económicos del análisis de los estados financieros*, Universidad de Huelva, Huelva 1993, 336 pp.
8. M. Flores Caballero, *Análisis de la relación del Neto empresarial, Activo Total y Volumen de ventas en el análisis de la rentabilidad*, Comunicación a la 1ª Jornada de Trabajo sobre análisis contable, Granada 1994, págs 7-96.
9. J. Gonzalez Pascual, *Rentabilidad, endeudamiento e inflación, XXV años de Contabilidad universitaria en España*, IPC, Madrid 1988, págs. 391-410.
10. B. Lev, *Análisis de Estados Financieros, Un nuevo enfoque*, Esic.
11. A. Novales, *Evolución del saneamiento financiero de las empresas industriales en España: 1984-1986*, Papeles de Economía, nº 38, Madrid 1989, págs 159-178.
12. J. Rivero Romero, Mª.J. Rivero Menéndez, *Análisis de Estados financieros*, Madrid 1998, 686 pp.
13. P. Rivero Torre, *Análisis de Balances y Estados Complementarios*, Madrid 1991, 469 pp.
14. A. Rocafort Nicolau, *Análisis e integración de Balances*, Barcelona 1983, 492 pp.
15. Ph D. J.K. Shim, J.G. Siegel, *Administración Financiera*, McGraw - Hill, Madrid 1989.

A BUSINESS INTELLIGENCE SOFTWARE MADE IN ROMANIA, A SOLUTION FOR ROMANIAN COMPANIES DURING THE ECONOMIC CRISIS

EDUARD EDELHAUSER, ANDREEA IONICA

Management Department, University of Petroşani, Petroşani, Romania

LUCIAN LUPU – DIMA

Info 98 Computing Centre Company, Siveco Implementer, Petroşani, Romania

The paper focuses on a modern prospective IT&C sector, which embeds simulation and assistance tools for managerial decisions. The team of authors studies aspects of this field by using the IT&C methods as management tools, and here we refer to Decision Support Systems (DSS), Business Intelligence (BI) and Enterprise Resource Planning (ERP). In addition, they have been implementing integrated information systems in Romanian organisations for more than 10 years and they are now studying the effects that these implementations have induced regarding the management of Romanian organisations. The effects are studied through the efficiency of hard and software platforms usage, as well as by the improvement of operational and strategic managers' training in using tools such as DSS or BI, and the training of the human resources of Romanian organisations in the IT&C field.

1. Introduction

In the present context of economic crisis, considering our opinion and the managerial one in Eastern Europe regarding the particular case of Romania, one of the solutions for economic revival is constituted by the usage of some advanced management methods, based on IT&C tools and modelling and simulation of the economic and management processes methods that can offer the foundation of high-performance management.

The evaluations of the local BI market, carried out by means of the main local implementers indicate an unusual tendency, namely, in the context of a severe reduction of the volume of global sales regarding company informational applications, in 2009 the BI market registered an increase almost 8 times higher than in 2008, and this trend seems to be maintained in 2010 as well.

The paper is organised in four chapters and deals with the essential characteristics of the BI concept regarding two aspects, namely the spatial aspect by analyzing the worldwide and national BI market and the temporary aspect regarding design, implementation and maintenance, corroborated with the continuous update to the customer's needs by the analyzed feedback of the support decision systems.

The first chapter highlights the status of the main competitors on the BI market as it is presented in the studies of the prestigious companies IDC and Gartner regarding the years 2008 and 2009. There are presented both the software tools used and the fields of implementation of the informational systems in the BI category. The second chapter expounds the degree of involvement of the four main worldwide players on the BI market, respectively SAP, Oracle, IBM and Microsoft, on the Romanian market these great actors owning 60% of the entire BI market worldwide. Moreover there is punctuated a problem specific to Romanian economy, valid for all the small and incompletely globalized markets, namely the importance of SMEs. Taking into account the fact that the large Romanian companies represent companies with public capital and subsidiaries of large multinational companies, and the large actors have already managed to implement the assisted managerial decision software within these companies, a market that is very attractive for the companies that create BI and DSS software in the management field is still that of SMEs. This market is the target of both large actors mentioned before as well as the local developers such as Siveco by Siveco Business Analyzer, S&T by MicroStrategy, Spectrum Solutions by Oracle BI and Wizrom by Panorama, out of which Siveco represents by far an autochthonous leader of the ERP and BI market. The third chapter is dedicated to the BI application of Siveco, application fully designed in Romania, and describes the main modules and types of analysis proposed by the SBA component such as what if and top bottom analysis and various types of simulations, as well as some design characteristics of the application. The last chapter is intended to be a result of the first three chapters and represents the essence of the effects induced by the implementation of the BI applications in the Romanian organisations. When quantifying these effects we relied on a questionnaire directed to a population made up of representative companies in the public and private field where Siveco carried out implementations of company applications.

Thus, modelling and simulation prove to be useful, reaching a maximum level of efficiency, consistency and importance by means of the BI tools. The applications in the category of informational systems for the support of managerial decision that the team of authors studied, promoted and implemented are especially BI solutions made in Romania. In this way, more and more Romanian organisations benefit from the advantages of special Romanian decision-making oriented software, and here we refer to the applications of Siveco software house. The implementation of the BI applications is studied worldwide as well as at a national level, and the efficiency of local BI software usage is assessed and quantified especially by means of managerial research carried out on the Siveco customers.

2. The performance of leading worldwide BI tools vendors in 2008

The main objective of any company is to earn profit. In order to achieve it, the company has to be efficient, to bring financial benefit. To that effect, there are necessary models of decision making in order to measure, manage and optimize the performance of different activities in the company. These decisions are made because of information, and Business Intelligence is exactly the concept that, if implemented correctly, leads to capitalization of the information necessary to measure, manage, make decisions and optimize performances. The essence of Business Intelligence (BI) is to gain information and knowledge from data in order to enable people to make better decisions. Especially in times of economic turmoil, the quality and efficiency of this process can be a crucial advantage for any company. BI is a highly dynamical field and builds an interface of growing importance between IT and management.

In presenting the worldwide BI market, we relied on two authorized sources of IT&C market study, namely Gartner and IDC. To start with, we emphasized the fact that in 2008, a year when the crisis made its presence felt all over the world, worldwide BI revenue reached $8.8 Billion and the growth in business intelligence software continues despite economic pressures, with a 22 percent.

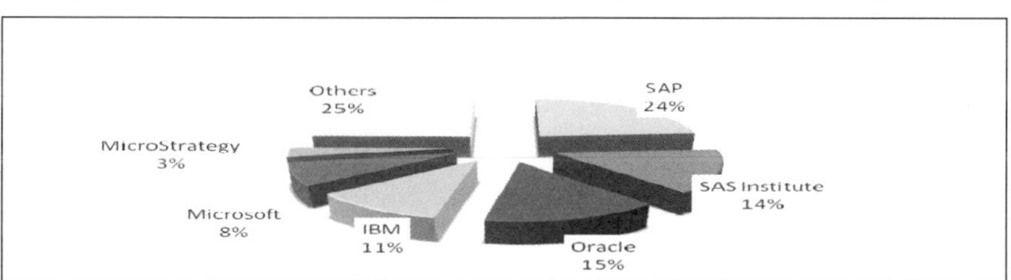

Figure 1. Worldwide BI, Analytics and Performance Management Revenue Estimates for 2008 (Source: Gartner, June 2009)

Gartner reports very significant revenue growth in both BI platforms (24.3 percent) and analytics and performance management applications (20.4 percent), summing up approximately $3.1 billion and $5.7 billion.

3. BI market, the only IT&C market in Romania that registered a significant increase in 2009

We tried to identify the main obstacles hindering the penetration of BI solutions on the Romanian market. Therefore, we reached the conclusion that poor technical abilities, poor education in the IT&C field regarding the top management in Romanian companies and the limited budgetary resources are impediments that we are frequently confronted with, when we are talking to a potential customer. This is not, however, a particular situation – it does not happen only in Romania, it is a situation that all the other markets are confronted with. We consider these impediments as opportunities for the solutions we promote. Nevertheless, this does not mean that there are no real obstacles, and the most frequent problem consists of the fact that the direction towards a BI solution is not seen as a business decision, but as one prevailingly technical. Or a successful deployment of a BI solution is always realized when it benefits from the support of those decision persons that are the main beneficiaries and direct users of these types of solutions, that understand the business vision, business strategy and motivation of that precise company.

There are two distinct situations on the Romanian market: the case of local companies that enter the category "large enterprise" that are aware of the necessity for BI tools, and the sector represented by Small & Medium Enterprise, a case in which is difficult to assert that a Business Intelligence solution becomes a "must have". As for the segment of large and very large companies and multinational corporations, we can say that they have reached an awareness threshold. There are some market verticals that reached maturation very rapidly and that progressed up to the international standards such as banking, mobile telephony, big retail chains, oil industry, services etc. These verticals (as well as others), where competition is very strong, generate especially the demand for BI.

4. SIVECO Business Analyzer a high performance Information Management System

Business Intelligence Solutions of SIVECO Romania monitors and correlates all the levels of company's activities, positively influencing its performances. SIVECO Business Analyzer (SBA) is a high performance Information Management System, capable to be adapted and customized according to the business particularities of any company. SBA supports the decision making process during the activities of planning monitoring, controlling, forecast and prognosis, provides information support for the adoption of strategies for cost control and the identification of sources to increase profit. It also provides synthesis, coherent, consistent and real-time information, and represents the requested analyses under the form of graphs and tables in an appealing manner, easy to manage and customize.

The second application in the field of BI is SIVECO Balanced ScoreCard (SBSC) is a software solution for strategic management and a latest generation information product launched on the Romanian market, able to monitor, analyze and compare the organization's performance in order to improve it. Placing the strategy at the centre, the proposed solution provides the beneficiary with relevant information regarding the manner in which the organization is heading towards reaching its strategic objectives.

We exemplified four simulation analysis and models of SBA and SBSC that are useful in the management activity and in the researches and which are highly used by the managers of Romanian enterprises that purchased this type of product. The analysis of the evolution of an indicator allows the representation of the values in the database under the form of diagrams or charts.

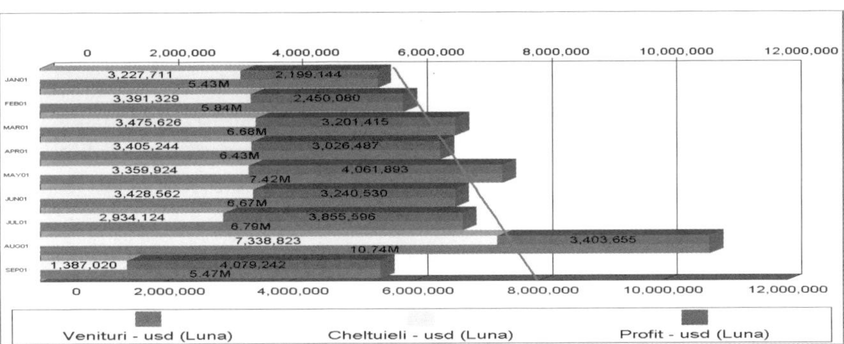

Figure 2. The status of revenues, costs and profit regarding the entire enterprise, in which the user may change the selection of the displayed values while the program is running

"What if?" Analysis consists of the possibility to modify the entrance parameters of an indicator and to see how this indicator varies after this modification. One can easily imagine potential situations when this type of analysis would be useful. For example, what happens with costs and profit if there is a certain percentage increase of the salary or power costs? What happens if the number of employees decreases or increases? On the other hand, if the value of certain taxes is modified (VAT, income taxes).

Top/Bottom Analysis. This analysis enables the selection of one of the most important types of incomes or the most important customers. The existence of this possibility is necessary especially in case the dimensions have many values (Customers in example below) that cannot be monitored each at large, but you want to monitor the extreme values: the highest ones and the lowest ones.

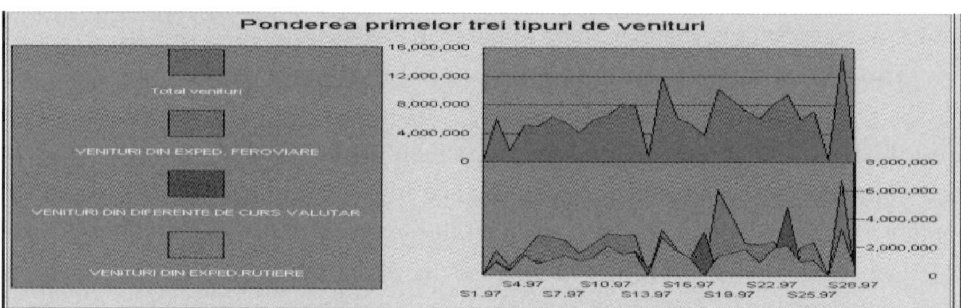

Figure 3. Exemplification of Top/Bottom Analysis by the first three types of incomes in comparison to total incomes

Forecasting is a simulation process in which the forecast values are based on the existing data history and the richer this history is the higher the accuracy of the forecast.

5. Effects induced by implementing BI applications in Romanian organisations

We asked the respondent companies a series of questions regarding the main obstacles in the penetration of BI solutions on the local market. Taking into account the "scores" they provided, the results are the following (ranking according to the degree of importance):
- Defective knowledge of the "concept" and of the advantages offered by the BI solutions;
- Romanian companies' prevailingly focusing on the operational aspect (to the detriment of the strategic one);
- Low technical "appetite" of decision factors;
- BI solution vendors' difficulty to demonstrate the possibility to obtain a real RoI and a TCO according expectances;
- Low financial power of potential customers;
- Low technical abilities of potential customers;
- Inadequate IT&C infrastructure.

Still in the virtue of the questionnaire, we achieved the results and we were able to formulate and validate research assumptions. Thus, we formulated an assumption presuming that in the private domain there is a more efficient usage of money than in the public domain. This hypothesis would be explained by the following specifications:

- In private companies hardware facility is correlated with the number of employees
- In private companies hardware facility is correlated with software facility

We used statistical techniques in order to define the differences between the groups, using T test. For this purpose, we tested the average equality of two paired samples (Paired Samples T Test) for six variables grouped in four pairs each. Out of the six variables three pertain to the companies with public capital (pers_public, calc_public and BI_public), respectively three to companies with private capital (pers_privat, calc_privat and BI_privat).

Table 1. The result of the T test for six variables grouped in four pairs each

	N	Correlation	Sig.
Pair 1 pers_public & calc_public	4	0.997	0.003
Pair 2 pers_privat & calc_privat	4	0.632	0.368
Pair 3 calc_public & BI_public	4	0.613	0.387
Pair 4 calc_privat & BI_privat	4	0.979	0.021

We noticed that if in the public domain exists a better correlation between the number of employees and the number of computer-related equipment (0.997 in comparison with 0.632), the situation is different regarding the correlation hardware – software which we defined as using computers for BI applications. (In this case, the figures in the private domain are 0.979 in comparison with 0.613 in the public domain). We reach the conclusion that providing with excessive hardware is not necessarily a useful thing to do, if that hardware is not then correlated with the software devices. There was also validated the hypothesis referring to the better efficiency of investing money in the private domain, and also a better correlation between the efficiency of the hardware and employee resources and the implementation of a BI in the private domain in comparison to the public one.

6. Conclusions

We are trapped in the middle of an economic-financial crisis, and Romania, we dare to assert, is affected more by the faulty management of some of its leaders than by the crisis itself. Thus in a country where we ask ourselves if there are more retiring persons than employees or if the salaries of the public employees are higher than those of the employees in the private sector or the production and services sector, we definitely have to change fundamental things. One of the ways that I consider possible would be the use of some advanced management methods in the Romanian organisations.

The conclusion of the authors is that in the 2010 Romania, a country that has lately managed to make itself known worldwide, most often by means of local achievements in the field of software industry, and less in other fields of industry, should take advantage of this appetite of the Romanians for the computer-science field and try to improve the management of the organisations. This could be made by prevailingly using the management methods from the category of DSS and BI that are based on informational tools; and if possible the product has to originate in the Romanian market and at the same time, we should always monitor especially the efficiency of the implementation and the efficiency of the investment in informational software.

References

1. E. Edelhauser, Study Regarding the Implementation of Enterprise Resource Planning in the Romanian Companies, *The 9th International Conference on Informatics in Economy, Education, Research & Business Technologies,* Bucharest, pp. 157-162, (2009).
2. E. Edelhauser, A. Ionica, Enterprise Resource Planning through Structural Founds in the Romanian Economy, *The 6th International Conference Management of Technological Changes,* Alexandroupolis, Greece, pp. 485-488, **BMO93,** (2009).
3. M. Leba, E. Pop, A. Badea, Adaptive Software Oriented Automation for Industrial Elevator, *Proceedings of the 11th International Conference on Automatic Control, Modeling & Simulation,* Istanbul, Turkey, pp.128-133, **BLX36,** (2009).
4. E. Pop, E. Padurariu, M. Leba, D. Ciodaru, Software Engineering Approach on Administration Management, *Proceeding of the 8th International Conference on Circuits, Systems, Electronics, Control & Signal Processing,* Puerto de la Cruz, Tenerife, Spain, pp.186-191 (2009).
5. D. Vesset, B. McDonough, Worldwide Business Intelligence Tools 2008 Vendor Shares, *IDC Competitive Analysis, Report, Volume: 1, Business Intelligence and Data Warehousing Strategies,* (2009).
6. ***, Market Share: Business Intelligence, Analytics and Performance Management Software, *Worldwide 2008, Gartner report,* (2008).

PART 3:
MANAGEMENT

ALGORITHM APPLIED IN THE IDENTIFICATION OF STAKEHOLDERS

ANNA MARÍA GIL-LAFUENTE, LUCIANO BARCELLOS PAULA[†]

*Faculty of Economics and Business, University of Barcelona, Av. Diagonal 690
Barcelona, Catalonia 08034, Spain*

To do sustainable business, companies must have good knowledge of all actors with influence in its sphere of activity. This identification of stakeholders is the first step. Based on stakeholder theory we discuss the importance of management with stakeholders in the pursuit of sustainability in business. In this paper we will focus our research on identifying the stakeholders through an analysis of an empirical study by a consulting firm in Brazil. In this case, the company needs to identify the stakeholders that can exert some influence in its sphere of activity. To achieve this objective, the consultant hired has used fuzzy logic algorithm, applying the theory of Clans. To complete the study, we present the contributions, the empirical results and conclusions of our investigation.

1. Introduction

The stakeholders of a company are individuals or groups who affect, or are affected by an organisation and its activities [12]. There is no generic list of stakeholders for all companies, or even for a single company, because these will change over time – those who affect and are affected depends on the industry, company, geography and the issue in question. New business strategies and changes in the business environment will often mean a new set of stakeholders [13]. As Post *et al.* [6], the stakeholders of a firm are individuals and groups who contribute voluntarily or involuntarily, to its capacity and wealth creation activities and, therefore, are potential beneficiaries and/or risk bearers. The stakeholders cover a wide variety of actors, including shareholders, employees, customers, local communities, government, NGOs, suppliers. The Stakeholder Theory [11] predicts that sustainability should have a positive impact on financial results because companies benefit from "addressing and balancing the claims" of the many key stakeholders.

[†] Scholar of the MAEC-AECI.

In this paper we will focus our research on identifying the stakeholders through an analysis of an empirical study by a consulting firm in Brazil. In this case, the contracting company needs to identify the stakeholders that can exert some influence in its sphere of activity. Because of the importance and complexity that is the identification of stakeholders for companies is essential to address the analysis with an approach based on complex systems and models that help entrepreneurs in making decisions. For these reasons, it is justified to analyze the stakeholder identification algorithms using fuzzy logic, in this specific case; the consultancy contract has applied the "Theory of Clans" [10]. We believe that our contribution will serve to support future research on the application of algorithms to business sustainability, a field that has been only scarcely investigated.

2. Methodology - The Theory of Clans [5]

K defines a clan from a finite referential E which satisfies the following conditions:

$$E \in K \tag{1}$$

$$\text{If } C \subset E : (C \in K) \Rightarrow \left(\overline{C} \in K\right) \tag{2}$$

where C is any of the subsets that compose K.

$$\left(C_1, C_2, ..., C_m \in K\right) \Rightarrow (C_1 \cup C_2 \cup ... \cup C_m \in K) \tag{3}$$

It is also verified:

$$\phi \in K \text{ , as } E \in K \text{ and then } \overline{E} = \phi \in K \tag{4}$$

$$\left(C_1, C_2, ..., C_m \in K\right) \Rightarrow (C_1 \cap C_2 \cap ... \cap C_m \in K) \tag{5}$$

following DE MORGAN´S Theorem.

According to Gil-Aluja [5], from the concept of clan relations affinities found. The road taken to obtain affinities can describe the following algorithm:

1) It begins in a Boolean matrix [B] from a fuzzy relation of the sets E_1 and E_2 levels cut about relevant.

2) We get the "family" of subsets of objects, each of which brings together those who possess the same characteristics.

3) From the "minterms" or "atoms" is not empty the corresponding "clan".

4) For each of the elements of the clan are calculated intersections of subsets of characteristics possessed by members of the respective elements of the clan.

5) When more than one subset of features that is repeated as a result of the intersection, we choose the corresponding element of the clan that owns the largest number of components.

6) The gathering of the clan elements of the subsets of features is repeated maximal affinities.

3. Application of Fuzzy Logic in the Identification of Stakeholders

To do sustainable business, companies must have good knowledge of all actors with influence in its sphere of activity. This identification of stakeholders is the first step. Once organizations have become aware of the various publics that interact with them, it is important to categorize in terms of expectations, problems, geographic areas, their impact on the company's business and vice versa. The result of the identification and segmentation is called a map of the stakeholders. Subsequently, companies must establish a hierarchy among them, in order to determine the relevance of their modes of interaction. In reviewing the literature, we found different methods used in identifying stakeholders. Mitchell *et al.* [13] have proposed a framework of three core criteria to inform the management process of identifying stakeholders. They are based on the relationship attributes of power, legitimacy and urgency. For Olcese *et al.* [2] can be identified interest groups through the analysis of the origin of the various financial transactions or business processes. Another way would be identified according to the type of relationship [4]. In this case, there are a number of different dimensions that you can consider when identifying stakeholders:

1. By responsibility: people to whom you have, or in the future may have, legal, financial and operational responsibilities enshrined in regulations, contracts, policies or codes of practice.

2. By influence: people who are, or in future may be, able to influence the ability of your organisation to meet its goals – whether their actions are likely to drive or impede your performance. These can include those with informal influence and those with formal decision making power.

3. By proximity: the people that your organisation interacts with most, including internal stakeholders, those with longstanding relationships, those you depend on in your day-to-day operations, and those living next to your production sites.

4. By dependency: the people that are most dependent on your organisation, for example employees and their families, customers who are dependent on your products for their safety, livelihood, health or welfare or suppliers for whom you are a dominant customer.

5. By representation: the people that are through regulatory structures or culture/tradition entrusted to represent other individuals; e.g. heads of a local community, trade union representatives, councillors, representatives of membership based organisations, etc.

In reviewing the literature, we find fuzzy logic applied to sustainability in many ways. For example, the analysis of organic purchase decisions by consumers [3], the decision analysis and evaluation of "green" suppliers [9], the selection process elements that contribute to the sustainable growth of the company [7], and the algorithms applied in the sustainable management of human resources [8]. However, the application of fuzzy logic to business sustainability, dealing mainly with identification of stakeholders, has been investigated only minimally to date. In this context, the consultant hired to identify chosen based stakeholders to identify the type of relationship [4].

4. Results

The empirical study was conducted in August 2009 by *Ideas and Solutions Consulting* in Brazil. At the request of the contractor, the study data were treated with strict confidentiality. The company studied belongs to food industry and the main objective is to identify your key stakeholders using fuzzy logic from the Theory of Clans. It considers two sets of reference $E_1=\{a,b,c,d\}$ and $E_2=\{A,B,C,D,E\}$. The set E_1, represents people or groups who may have some relationship with the company. The set E_2, represents the types of relationships in various dimensions *(A)* by responsibility; *(B)* by influence; *(C)* by proximity; *(D)* by dependency; *(E)* by representation. The consulting firm has convened a workshop that was attended by five heads of departments who know about the subject in analysis. Once submitted to the directors of the company the subject, they specify their views through the scale [0,1], whereby, as the estimate is closer 1, the greater the importance of the relationship of the person or group with the company. The elements of these two sets are related through a fuzzy relationship matrix (table 1), which allows it to be studied using α-cuts.

Table 1. Fuzzy relationship matrix

	A	B	C	D	E
a	1	0.8	0.6	0.4	0.3
b	0.5	0.9	0.7	0.5	0.8
c	0.8	0.6	0.8	0.9	0.7
d	0.9	0.8	0.9	0.7	0.6

$[\tilde{R}] =$

Certain levels are chosen for each element of E_2, $\alpha_A = 0.9, \alpha_B = 0.8, \alpha_C = 0.8, \alpha_D = 0.7, \alpha_E = 0.7$ and we find a Boolean matrix [B] as shown in table 2.

Table 2. Boolean Matrix

$$[B] = \begin{array}{c|ccccc} \text{☞} & A & B & C & D & E \\ \hline a & 1 & 1 & & & \\ b & & 1 & & & 1 \\ c & & & 1 & 1 & 1 \\ d & 1 & 1 & 1 & 1 & \\ \end{array}$$

It is observed in this matrix (table 2), which objects have their respective qualities, through the following subsets:

$$A_A = \{a,d\}, A_B = \{a,b,d\}, A_C = \{c,d\}, A_D = \{c,d\}, A_E = \{b,c\} \tag{6}$$

Taken together, these subsets form which in theory is known clan the family name. In this case the family F is:

$$F = \{\{a,d\},\{a,b,d\},\{c,d\},\{c,d\},\{b,c\}\} \tag{7}$$

Since the family is the "clan". They A_i^* are:

$$A_A = \{a,d\}, A_B = \{a,b,d\}, A_C = \{c,d\}, A_D = \{c,d\}, A_E = \{b,c\} \tag{8}$$

$$\overline{A_A} = \{b,c\}, \overline{A_B} = \{c\}, \overline{A_C} = \{a,b\}, \overline{A_D} = \{a,b\}, \overline{A_E} = \{a,d\} \tag{9}$$

Then calculate the minterms or atoms. To obtain the "clan" engendered by the family F, the atoms do not take all possible gaps and joints, adding ϕ:

$$K = \{\phi,\{a\},\{b\},\{c\},\{d\},\{a,d\},\{a,b,d\},\{c,d\},\{b,c\},E_1\} \tag{10}$$

We find the intersection of characteristics for each element of the clan. Since there exists a subset with the same characteristics, affinity relationships are thus:

$$
\begin{array}{lcl}
\phi & \rightarrow & \{A,B,C,D,E\} \\
\{b\} & \rightarrow & \{B,E\} \\
\{c\} & \rightarrow & \{C,D,E\} \\
\{d\} & \rightarrow & \{A,B,C,D\} \\
\{a,d\} & \rightarrow & \{A,B\} \\
\{b,c\} & \rightarrow & \{E\} \\
\{c,d\} & \rightarrow & \{C,D\} \\
\{a,b,d\} & \rightarrow & \{B\}
\end{array}
\tag{11}
$$

If added, formal purposes, also the relationship E_1, ϕ. This allows you to submit the following Galois Lattice [1], shown in Figure 1.

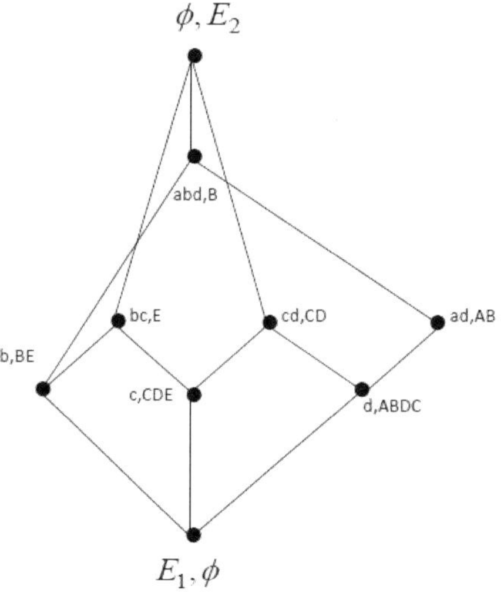

Figure 1. Galois Lattice

This lattice shows visually the affinities between the various stakeholders, considering the type of relationship they have on the company. We emphasize the relationship of affinity between the stakeholders *{a,b,d}*. This result shows that they have an important role in influencing *(B)* the activities of the company. Having done the identification, the next steps the company would obtain the segmentation and prioritization of the stakeholders.

5. Conclusions

The stakeholder study shows that compared with the changes we are living is essential to find models that will help employers in making decisions, especially in an uncertain environment. Because of the importance and complexity that is the identification of stakeholders for companies in our research we try to analyze these complex systems using fuzzy logic. In applying the model through empirical study has been possible to provide a tool based on the use of clustering algorithm that can facilitate decision making by obtaining qualitative data from a dialogue with managers or specialists on a particular topic. This is an innovation and a useful tool to be used in the process of identifying stakeholders. The model also serves to establish the level of relationship between different stakeholders and obtain affinities. The Galois lattice shows a structured way the affinities between the various actors in relation to degrees of compliance with them. Also it allows making decisions based on the features that are considered a priority in every situation and moment. The result has shown that people o groups {a,b,c,d} were identified as stakeholders, while we know the type of relationship that each company has on the affinities and relationships between them.

The paper's main contribution is the application of algorithms in the identification of stakeholders considering sustainability criteria in enterprises, and providing a useful model in making decisions. We believe that our contribution will serve to support future research in the field of application of algorithms to business sustainability in general and particular aspects of it such as environmental management, economic and social, among many other approaches.

References

1. A. Kaufmann and J. Gil-Aluja. *Técnicas especiales para la gestión de expertos*. Milladoiro, Santiago de Compostela, 151-175 (1993).
2. A. Olcese, M. Rodríguez Ángel and J. Alfaro. *Manual de la empresa Responsable y Sostenible*. Madrid: McGraw-Hill. (2008).
3. A.M. Gil Lafuente and L. Salgado Beltrán. "Models for analysing purchase decision in consumers of ecologic products". *Fuzzy Economic Review*, **X**, 47-62. (2005).
4. Accountability, UNEP and Stakeholder Research Associates Canada Inc. *From words to action. The Stakeholder engagement Manual. The practitioner's handbook on stakeholder engagement*. Vol. **2**, 39. (2005).
5. J. Gil-Aluja. *Elementos para una Teoría de la Decisión en la incertidumbre*. Editorial Milladoiro, 247-256 (1999).

6. J.E. Post, L.E. Preston and S. Sachs. "Managing the Extended Enterprise: The New Stakeholder View". *California Management Review*. **45(1)**, 5-28. (2002).

7. L. Barcellos Paula and A.M. Gil Lafuente. "Proceso de selección de elementos que contribuyen al crecimiento sostenible de la empresa". *Proceeding of International Conference and Doctoral Consortium for ISEOR and Academy of Management, held at Lyon, France*, **(1)**, 773-788. (2009a).

8. L. Barcellos Paula and A.M. Gil Lafuente. "Algoritmos aplicados en la gestión sostenible de los recursos humanos". Economic and Financial Crisis:"New challenges and Perspectives". *Proceeding of XV Congress of International Association for Fuzzy-Set Management and Economy (SIGEF), Lugo, Spain.* (2009b).

9. Lu Lyy, Wu Ch and Kuo Tc. "Environmental principles applicable to green supplier evaluation by using multi-objective decision analysis". *International Journal of Production Research*. **45(18-19)**, 4317-4331. (2007).

10. M. Courtillot. "Structure cononique des fichiers". *A.I.E.R.-A.F.G.E.T.* Vol. **7**. Enero, 2-15. (1973).

11. R.E. Freeman and W. Evan. "Corporate Governance: A Stakeholder Interpretation". *Journal of Behavioral Economics*. **19(4)**, 337–359. (1990).

12. R.E. Freeman. *Strategic Management: A Stakeholder Approach*. Pitman Series in Business and Public Policy. (1984).

13. R.K. Mitchell, B.R. Agle and D.J. Wood. "Toward a Theory of Stakeholder Identification and Salience: Defining the Principle of who and what really Counts". *The Academy of Management Review*. **22(4)**, 853-886. (1997).

JOB SHOP PROBLEM ANALYSIS THROUGH AN EVOLUTIONARY ALGORITHM

OMAR DANILO CASTRILLÓN GOMEZ, WILLIAM ARIEL SARACHE, JAIME ALBERTO GIRALDO

Industrial engineering department Universidad Nacional de Colombia
Manizales, Caldas, 17001, Colombia

The aim of this paper[*], is to design a new methodology based on an evolutionary algorithm that allows a reduction in the makespan time and increases the machine utilization time, reducing the idle time ,in job shop environments (Open Shop). In these environments there are m machines and each job needs to be processed once in each of the machines. The processing order is not important.
This paper has two parts: The first part is the identification and definition of the methodology. The second part is the demonstration of its effectiveness. The production planning optimization is achieved through an evolutionary algorithm, that improves the total make span time and the total idle time. This research was carried out in an enterprise of the metal-mechanic sector.

1. Introduction

Due to new trends in world markets (new dynamic processes such as globalization and huge developments in information technologies and communications), different enterprises have needed to acquire more flexible and versatile manufacturing systems [1]. These systems are defined by different effectiveness criteria that provide a considerable and widely varying degree of control in the manufacturing processes.

Because of the short available time to plan tasks [2], it is necessary to develop operations planning with less time under multi-criteria objectives and variables that make the decisions more difficult. This aspect has been studied by different authors, especially in the Operations Research Area [3].

It is important to note that the majority of the sequencing and scheduling problems are Np-hard class. These problems present a functional dependence

---

[*] This paper derives from the participation of the authors in a research Project financed by the Research Vice-presidency of the Universidad Nacional de Colombia, entitled **"production sequencing using evolutionary algorithms. Application to Job Shop environments"**.

that is not possible to delimit by a polynomial [4]. The number of machines and the number of orders define the size of the problem to be solved with restrictions that must be considered.

According to the objectives of the enterprise, these problems are guided by an objective function [5] aimed at finding the best solution for the enterprise that can be established by the minimizing of the next parameters [6]: a) Makespan (C_M), the time necessary to finish all the orders. b) Maximal machine workload (W_M), the maximum required work time on a machine; its purpose is to keep the balance of the work distribution on all machines and to avoid excess of work on anyone machine. c) Total workload (W_T), represents all the machine's work time; the objective is to achieve a feasible solution for the distribution of work to all the machines [7]. d) Total Idle Time represents the non-utilization total time of the machines.

Different techniques have been used to optimize the variables above such as linear programming, branch and bound algorithms and some other techniques based on artificial intelligence. (For example heuristics techniques, taboo search [8], and evolutionary algorithms [9] that include stochastic search techniques).

The evolutionary algorithms are usually composed by: initial problem encoding, choice of the initial population, the fitness function evaluation, the selection of the best individuals, generation of new population [10], and stopping criterion [6].

Different studies have shown the efficiency and effectiveness of the genetic algorithms over other methods and its usefulness to define new genetic hybrid algorithms [12, 13] that apply to all types of problems. The fundamental objective of this paper is to design a new methodology to optimize the two major objectives in a job shop problem, (Open Shop): the total make span time and the total idle time. In these environments there are **m** machines and each job needs to be processed once in each of the machines. The processing order is not important. This methodology is based on an evolutionary algorithm.

According to the literary reviews there are a few studies on this topic. This area has not been studied and/or documented with enough effort, especially when it comes to a third world country, where the production systems are handmade with low competitive levels [14]. The interest of the authors in this topic is to achieve a higher understanding and explore possibilities when it comes to the applications of this technique in the central region of Colombia. The reasons above make this topic interesting for the industry, professionals in engineering, trades, enterprise directors and all the community.

2. Methodology

A new methodology based on evolutionary algorithms is proposed to improve the solution of these types of problems. This methodology begins by considering the assumptions proposed in [14].

Step 1. Representation: The JSSP problem is represented by a two dimensional matrix, the number of the rows represents the workplaces and the number of the columns represents the orders. Each value (row, col), is the process time of machine j of order i . [15]

Table 1. Representation of the $JSSP_{NXM}$ problem.

	Ord$_1$	**Ord$_2$**	**...**	**Ord$_n$**
C$_1$		**Pt**		
..				
C$_m$				

Step 2. Initial solution: The initial solutions of the problem under study are coded using the structure shown in Figure 1. In each coded solution of chromosome shape, the genes represent the position in which an order is served by each of the different machines. The genes alleles represent the order number. Based on these initial solutions, an evolutionary algorithm begins to build new solutions. In the construction of these solutions, genetic crossover operators are used with a probability of 97% and mutations with a probability of 3%.

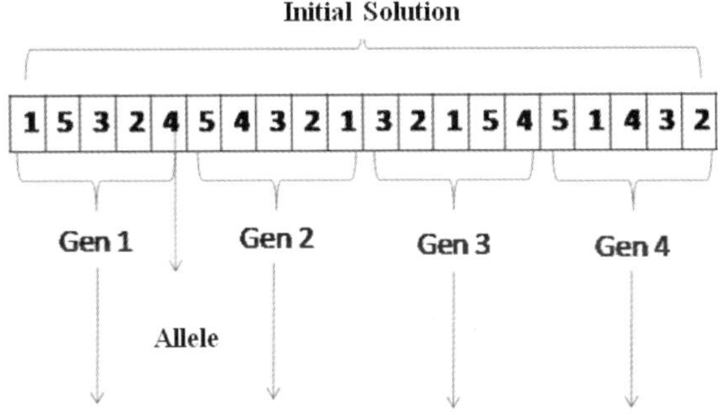

Figure 1. Initial solution codification

Step 3. Sequencing: For each of the solutions established in the previous step, a Gant chart is defined, which sets the order of processes in time in each of

268

the different workplaces. Once the previous diagram assesses each of the different solutions, a total make span time and total idle time calculation using the following functions is performed (Fitness):

$$Fitness_{makespan} = \min\left(\max_{1<=i<=N} \left(\max_{1<=j<=M} (P_{ij}) \right) \right) \quad \text{eq. (1)}$$

$$Fitness_{idle} = \min \sum_{j=1}^{m} f_j \quad \text{eq (2)}$$

The fundamental objective is to maximize the two fitness functions. **N** is the number of orders, **M** is the number of machines, P_{ij} is the process time of order i of machine j and f_j is the total idle time of machine **j.**

Step 4. Optimal estimation: In order to calculate the approximation of the solutions found, regarding the best solution, it is necessary to estimate the optimal solution. It is not always possible to calculate an optimal solution for a problem, due to its size. Therefore, it is necessary to make an optimal estimate, which is accomplished when a solution is found in which there is a workplace with zero idle time.

The effectiveness and the approximation percentage of each possible solution found may be calculated by the optimal value.

Experimentation: This methodology was carried out on a metal-mechanic enterprise, specifically in its key product called "Bar". Although in the original problem the product must pass through five workplaces regardless of the order, the experimentation was conducted based on a problem with general characteristics: 5 workplaces and 30 orders; restrictions were made only for computational reasons. (See Table 2).

Table 2. Makespan times. $2.37376*10^{62}$ possible solutions.

	P1	P2	P3	P4	P5	P6	P7	P8	P9	P10	P11	P12	P13	P14	P15	P16	P17	P18	P19	P20	P21	P22	P23	P24	P25	P26	P27	P28	P29	P30
C1	4	7	6	5	7	9	11	12	10	8	7	10	10	8	9	11	10	7	4	6	8	8	1	19	6	7	1	17	6	1
C2	7	4	5	13	11	14	8	6	4	13	5	6	13	9	4	12	6	0	10	11	17	0	16	5	12	9	8	6	4	1
C3	9	4	8	7	10	5	11	9	11	9	6	15	7	6	17	13	5	6	11	4	5	4	13	16	14	5	7	4	11	15
C4	12	6	4	8	4	0	12	14	8	7	1	4	8	12	4	11	8	9	6	5	4	6	10	8	6	8	11	9	4	1
C5	6	7	8	12	12	8	7	5	7	12	10	9	9	11	13	7	7	6	7	6	5	5	8	17	11	0	9	10	12	1

3. Results and discussions

Step 1. Representation: According to the methodology described, the problem under analysis is represented by the structure proposed in the table 2. This table shows the make span time of the 30 orders in the workplaces or machines.

Step 2-4: The greatest solutions found using the techniques described in steps 2, 3 and 4 of the proposed methodology are illustrated in table 3. Likewise, figure 2 shows the Gant chart of the best solution represented in table 3, which is the optimal solution in this case.

Table 3. Make span time. Found solutions.

Solution	Total makespan time	Idle time.	Approximation. Optimal estimation. (make span time = 269)	Approximation. Optimal Estimation (idle time = 137)
1	270	142	99.62%	96.47%
2	271	147	99.26%	99.26%
3	272	152	98.89%	93.19%
4	272	152	98.53%	93.19%
5	270	142	99.62%	96.47%
6	269	137	100%	100%
7	272	152	98.89%	93.19%
8	270	142	99.62%	96.47%
9	269	137	100%	100%
10	271	147	99.26%	99.26%
Average	**270.6**	**145**	**99.36%**	**96.75%**

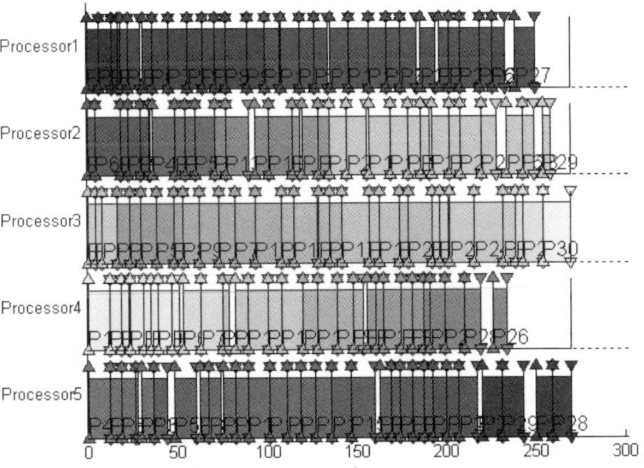

Figure 2. Optimal solution found. Make span time = 269. Idle time = 137.

An analysis of Figure 2 establishes that in the workplace 3 (processor 3), there is no idletime, and consequently the solution illustrated in Figure 2, is one of the optimal solutions.

4. Discusions

Of the various literary reviews [16], we can conclude that the use of AI techniques in solving sequencing problems in Job Shop environments has not been widespread. While there are some authors [17] that use different AI techniques to sequence a series of orders, none of them achieve results as close to the optimal results as those illustrated in this article. However, it is important to note that these processes must be involved in sequencing cost functions, which allow determining the efficiency of the solutions found in economic terms, thus requiring a multi-objective analysis of the problem which will be subject of future lines research.

5. Conclusions

Evolutionary algorithms are an excellent technique for solving sequencing processes in JSSP environments. They make possible to find values proximate to the optimal.

Taking as reference the different results obtained, it is possible to conclude that this new methodology obtains solutions with an approximation to the optimal solution of the 99.36% and 96.75% measured by the variables of total make span time and total idle time respectively.

Acknowledgments

Acknowledgments to all GTA members (Category A) in Innovation and Technological Development of the Universidad Nacional de Colombia, Manizales. A special thanks to Natalia Ruiz Mazuera, Industrial Engineering Student for her collaboration.

References

1. L. De Giovanni and F. Pezzella, An Improved Genetic Algorithm for the Distributed and Flexible Job-shop Scheduling problem. European Journal of Operational Research. Vol. 200, No. 2, 2010, pp 395-408.
2. A. Correa and E. Rodríguez, Secuenciación de operaciones para configuraciones de planta tipo flexible Job Shop: Estado del arte. Avances en Sistemas e Informática. Vol. 5, No. 3, 2008, pp 151-161.

3. Q.K. Pan, L. Wang and B. Qianb, A novel differential evolution algorithm for bi-criteria no-wait flow shop scheduling problems. Computers & Operations Research. Vol. 36, No. 8, 2009, pp 2498-2511.

4. H. Zhou, C. Waiman and L. Lawrence, Minimizing weighted tardiness of job-shop scheduling using a hybrid genetic algorithm. European Journal of Operational Research. Vol. 194, No. 3, 2009, pp 637-649

5. A. Manikas, and Y. L. Chang, Multi-criteria sequence-dependent job shop scheduling using genetic algorithms. Computers & Industrial Engineering. Vol. 56, No. 1, 2009, pp 179-185.

6. F. Pezzella, G. Morganti and G. Ciaschetti, A genetic algorithm for the Flexible Job-shop Scheduling Problem. Computers & Operations Research. Vol. 35, No. 10, 2008, pp 3202-3212.

7. C. Low and Y. Yeh, Genetic algorithm-based heuristics for an open shop scheduling problem with setup, processing, and removal times separated. Robotics and Computer-Integrated Manufacturing. Vol. 25, No. 2, 2009, pp 314-322.

8. M. Andresen, H. Brasel, M. Morig, et al, Simulated annealing and genetic algorithms for minimizing mean flow time in an open shop. Mathematical and Computer Modelling. Vol. 48, No. 7-8, 2008, pp 1279-1293

9. I. Essafi, Y. Mati and S. Dauzère-Pérès S, A genetic local search algorithm for minimizing total weighted tardiness in the job-shop scheduling problem. Computers & Operations Research. Vol. 35, No. 8, 2008, pp 2599-2616.

10. S. Marimuthu, S.G. Ponnambalam and N. Jawahar, Evolutionary algorithms for scheduling m-machine flow shop with lot streaming. Robotics and Computer-Integrated Manufacturing. Vol. 24, No. 1, 2008, pp 125-139.

11. G. I. Zobolas, C.D. Tarantilis and G. Loannou, Minimizing makespan in permutation flow shop scheduling problems using a hybrid metaheuristic algorithm. Computers & Operations Research. Vol. 36, No. 4, 2009, pp 1249-1267.

12. C.H. Pan and H.C. Huang, A hybrid genetic algorithm for no-wait job shop scheduling problems. Expert Systems with Applications. Vol. 36, No. 3, 2009, pp 5800-5806.

13. C.H. Martin, A hybrid genetic algorithm/mathematical programming approach to the multi-family flowshop scheduling problem with lot streaming. Omega. Vol. 37, No. 1, 2009, pp 126-137.

14. M. W. Rohrer, Simulating of Manufacturing and Material Handling Systems. Procedente de Handbook of Simulation, John Wiley. 2000.

15. D.A. Koonce, Using data mining to find patterns in genetic algorithm solutions to a job Shob schedule. Computer & Industrial Engineering. Vol. 38, No. 1, 2000, 361-374.

16. F. Nilgün, O. Celal, E. Orhan, et al, Investigation of Ant System parameter interactions by using design of experiments for job-shop scheduling

problems. Computers & Industrial Engineering. Vol. 56, No. 1, 2009, 538-559.

17. O. López, I. Ortega and V. Medina, A multi-agent system to construct production orders by employing an expert system and a neural network. Expert Systems with Applications. Vol. 36, No. 1, 2009, 2937-2946.

SEARCHING FOR ENTREPENEURIAL EXCELLENCE: AN APPROACH TO ELECTRE II PHILOSOPHY

GISELLE PINO LEÓN

Port Manning Enterprise AGEMPORT, Industrial Engineer, Number 73 apartment 8 Alberro, Cotorro, Havana City, Zone:14000, Cuba. E-mail: ctssuzgis@ceniai.inf.cu

ROSARIO GARZA RÍOS, ILEANA PÉREZ VERGARA

Quality Branch, Faculty of Industrial Engineering, ISPJAE, Industrial Engineer, 114 street , Marianao, Havana City, Zone: 10400, Cuba. E-mail: rosariog@ind.cujae.edu.cu, ileper@ind.cuja.edu.cu

Models of Excellence do not define that an enterprise should perform its self-evaluation before applying for an award; neither have they defined a methodology to help in the decision-making process of the organization to submit for a quality award related to entrepreneurial management. To answer this question, the authors propose the use of an approach based on ELECTRE perspective, specifically the Test of Veto suggested in ELECTRE II, a recommended procedure which allows ascertaining whether the enterprise has the conditions to apply for an award.

1. ELECTRE and Excellence Enterprises

1.1. *ELECTRE approach in the search of excellence*

Quality Awards have become an international practice aiming to benefit and show excellence in organizational management. They are based upon upgrading, collective learning and sustained improvement, in order to reach with efficiency and efficacy a level of proficiency and constant management results.

Quality Awards identify and recognize leading enterprises due to their success in quality and entrepreneurial management, in the long road to excellence. At present, the number of organizations which make use of models related to entrepreneurial management is growing.

The use of numerous math tools to reach multiple criteria, consensus and quality tools has become crucial in order to adjust excellence models in the organizations.

None model of excellence consulted states that an enterprise should perform a self-evaluation before submitting for an award, neither there is a methodology to help the enterprise to adopt such a decision.

Once the organization obtains a self-evaluation after the use of those models, then the following question arises:

How do we know if the enterprise is in conditions to submit an application for a quality award related to entrepreneurial management?

To answer this question, the authors recommend to use an approach the utilization of a focus based on the philosophy of the ELECTRE specifically the Test of Veto included in the ELECTRE II, proposing a procedure that leads to determine if the enterprise is in condition to apply for an award.

This procedure allowed determining gaps corresponding to each stated criteria in the Self-evaluation Guidelines. It was implemented at a Maritime Containers Terminal in Cuba.

1.2. *Selecting critical criteria*

Once the Guidelines for Self-evaluation are applied, it is possible to determine the present state of the enterprise or level of excellence according to the rating scale shown in Table 1.

Table 1. Rating used to determine the enterprise level of excellence.

Scale	Level of Excellence
0-200	Poor
201-500	Low
501-700	Medium
701-850	High
851-1000	First-class

If the enterprise achieves a First-Class level of excellence, then there is no doubt: it may submit an application for an enterprise management quality award. But, if the level reached is High or Medium, then uncertainty may arise regarding such a decision; thus, it becomes a major issue to determine the critical criteria and their influence in the enterprise level of excellence.

A criterion is considered critical when: It exercises a negative influence upon the level of excellence, it is away from the ideal situation, it is the major gap between the present situation and the optimum one the organization wants to reach.

How many criteria can be found in an unfavourable situation and even though, the enterprise may submit for an award?

To answer this question, the authors propose the use of two approaches:

A. ELECTRE Approach

A criterion is considered unfavourable when its weight or importance is beyond the medium weight of criteria. They are main criteria for the organization.

The ELECTRE II, specifically the Test of Veto, explains:

The affirmation a S b
If:
$J- \neq \varnothing$
$j \in (J- \wedge J_{CRIT})$
Where:
$J_{CRIT} = \{ j \varepsilon \ F / w_j > w_{med} \}$

The application of the Test of Veto, in this case results:

$$C_{crit} = \{ j \in J: W_j > W_{med} \} \qquad [1]$$

$$W_{med} = \frac{\sum_{j=1}^{m} Wj}{m} \qquad [2]$$

Where:

C_{crit}: Group of criteria considered critical.

W_j: Weight or importance of the j criterion.

W_{med}: Average weight or importance.

m: Total of criteria included in the Self-evaluation Guidelines.

B. SCC Approach (Selection of Critical Criteria)

The authors propose to make use of the procedure shown in Fig. 1 and Table 2, indicating the path to be followed in order to find critical criteria.

Table 2. Number of Critical Criteria.

Number of Critical Criteria										
1	2	3	4	5	6	7	8	9	10	11
Critical	> 50 1	> 60 1	> 60 1	> 60 1	> 60 1	> 60 1	> 60 1	> 60 1	> 60 1	> 60 1
	≥ 40 2	≥ 40 2	≥ 40 2	≥ 40 2	≥ 40 2	≥ 40 2	≥ 40 2	≥ 40 2	≥ 40 2	≥ 40 2
		≥ 30 3	≥ 30 3	≥ 30 3	≥ 30 3	≥ 30 3	≥ 30 3	≥ 30 3	≥ 30 3	≥ 30 3
			≥ 20 4	≥ 20 5	≥ 20 4	≥ 20 4	≥ 20 4	≥ 20 4	≥ 20 4	≥ 20 4
			≥ 10 1	≥ 10 1	≥ 10 6	≥ 10 7	≥ 10 8	≥ 10 9	≥ 10 10	≥ 10 9
					*	*	X	X	X	X

Rank in %

Top number of possible critical criteria in this rank

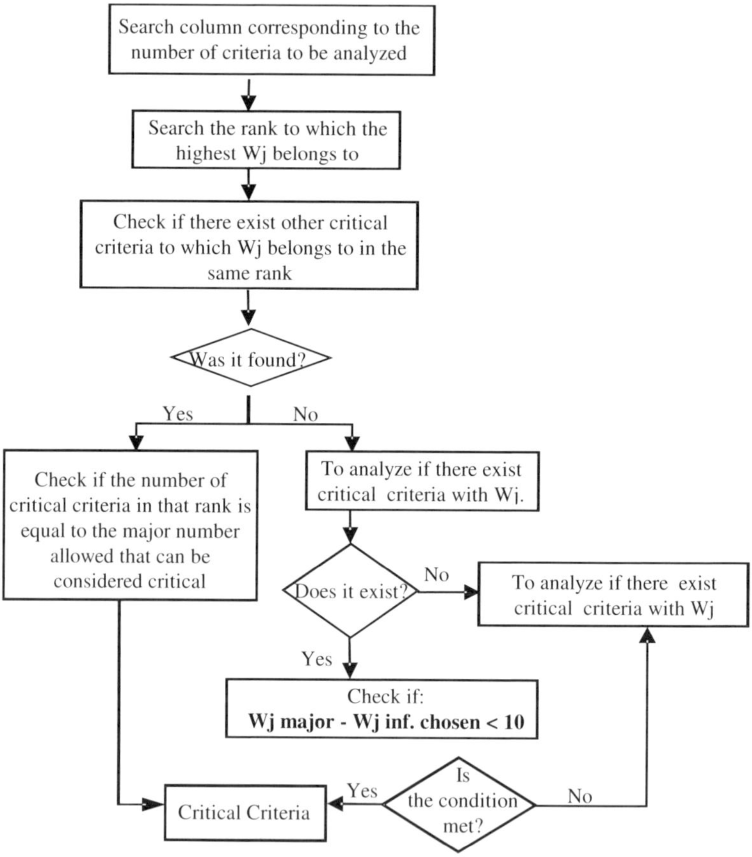

Search column corresponding to the number of criteria to be analyzed

↓

Search the rank to which the highest Wj belongs to

↓

Check if there exist other critical criteria to which Wj belongs to in the same rank

↓

Was it found?

Yes → Check if the number of critical criteria in that rank is equal to the major number allowed that can be considered critical

No → To analyze if there exist critical criteria with Wj.

Does it exist?

No → To analyze if there exist critical criteria with Wj

Yes → Check if:
Wj major - Wj inf. chosen < 10

Is the condition met?

Yes → Critical Criteria

No →

Fig 1. Procedure to determine the number of critical criteria.

1.3. *Determination of gaps*

Once the number of critical criteria is determined, we are able to know the enterprise level of excellence but we still do not know the existing gaps; accordingly, it is interesting to determine them.

Gaps are the existing distance between the actual and the ideal state of the criteria, and at the same time, of the enterprise in general.

The authors recommend the use of a tool called "Graph Radar", which shows in a graphic way what is stated above. It is possible to observe in Table 3 the Level of Excellence (LE) corresponding to each criterion according to the score obtained.

Table 3. Score to be established.

Level	Scale	Level of Excellence
0	0	Poor
1	0-20	Poor
2	21-30	Low
3	31-40	Low
4	41-50	Low
5	51-60	Medium-Low
6	61-70	Medium-High
7	71-84	High
8	85-100	First-class

The authors recommend using this rating (Table 3) whenever the enterprise has a number of 8 criteria, in other cases the rating should be adjusted again.

The percentage accomplished for each criterion should be the information to present in the "Graph Radar", since each criterion has a different maximum ranking depending on: total of sub-criterion included in the questionnaire, number of questions developed for each sub-criterion in the same questionnaire, and the probability that each question answered obtains the same rating.

1.4. *Use of the ELECTRE approach in order to determine whether the enterprise may apply for an award*

Whenever an enterprise performs its self-evaluation, it knows its level of excellence, and then it may determine its critical criteria and also to identify the gaps but, how is it possible to know whether the enterprise may apply for an award?

Taking as a reference the philosophy of the ELECTRE II, the authors propose the following condition to be fulfilled:

Condition:

$$L = \{\, j \in C_{crit} : LE \leq Medium \,\}$$

If *Card L* $\leq c$ Then, you may apply for an award.

Where:

L: group of critical criteria, which level of excellence (LE) may be Medium, Low or Poor.

LE: Level of Excellence (may be: First-class, High, Medium, Low or Poor)

c: concord rate, could be consider as ¾ or 2/3 (Ostanello, 1984), the authors propose to use the value of ¾ , which means that up 75% of the critical criteria belonging to L may obtain a medium level of excellence or below it, to apply for an award.

If the condition is not fulfilled, then the enterprise no matter whether it obtains a high level of excellence should not apply for an award until its action plan of improvement is completed. After, it should perform its self-evaluation once again and only then, it shall determine the evolution obtained.

1.5. *Application at a Maritime Terminal of Containers in Cuba*

The results of the application are shown in Fig. 2. The level of excellence obtained was HIGH. The number of critical criteria determined were a total of 4, they were: Development and Management of Human Capital, Client's Satisfaction, Leadership, Quality Process.

Of these 4 critical criteria only two of them are related to a medium level of excellence, they represent 50% of the total critical criteria; therefore this enterprise may apply for the "Giraldilla" Award. After these results were reached, the organization prepared the report to be forwarded to the ONN (Normalization/Standardization National Office), with the request to apply for the "Giraldilla" Award (Award to Entrepreneurial Quality Management granted by the ONN, Havana City, Cuba). The file was approved and an official group of experts audited the enterprise, since positive results were obtained the "Giraldilla" Award was granted to the enterprise, in his 2009 edition.

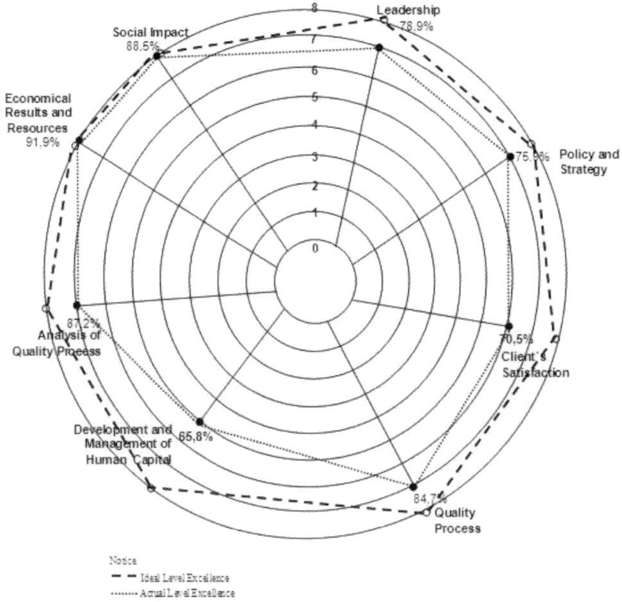

Fig 2. Results of the application of "Graph Radar".

References

1. Barba Romero S, Pomerol J.C (1997): Decisiones multicriterio Fundamentos teóricos y utilización práctica, Universidad de Alcalá, España.
2. Begoña, B, Diez, J. (2000): Evaluación multicriterio de la calidad de vida urbana: El caso de la ciudad de Lugo. España: 51st meeting of the European working group "Multicriteria aid for decision".
3. Benítez Benigni, Yanela y Vizcaíno Rodríguez, Dayamis: *Utilización de herramientas matemáticas en la adaptación de Modelos de Excelencia*. Trabajo de Diploma. Ciudad de la Habana, Cuba, 2007.
4. Brans J, P, Vincke Ph (1985): A preference ranking Organization method: The Promethee methods for multicriteria decision making. Revista Management Science.
5. Casadeus Fa, Martí, Heras S., Iñaki, Merino D. Javier (2005): Calidad Práctica: una guía para no perderse en el mundo de la calidad. Ed. Prentice hall, Madrid, España
6. Fernández E., Torrens R, (1997): El método EDIPO para la ayuda a la decisión. Revista Ingeniería Industrial, Cuba.

7. Fodor J., Roubens M. (1994): Fuzzy Preference Modeling and Multicriteria Decision Support, Dordrech.
8. French S. (1986): Decision Theory: An introduction to the mathematics of rationality. Halsted Press New York – Brisbane – Toronto.
9. Ostanello, A. (1984): Outranking Methods. Proceding of the first summer school on MCDM. Sicilia.
10. Romero C. (1993): Teoría de la decisión multicriterio: Conceptos, técnicas y aplicaciones. Alianza Editorial S. A. Madrid.
11. Romero, C. (1997): Análisis de las decisiones multicriterio. Madrid.
12. Roy B. (1984): The outranking approach and the foundation of Electre methods. En Reading in Multiple Criteria Decision Aid. Editores Bana e Costa.
13. Roy B. (1990): The outranking approach and the Foundations of Electre methods. Berlin.
14. Roy, B. (1996): Multicriteria methodology for Decision Aiding, Kluwer Academic Publisher, Dordrecht- Boston- London
15. Tabucanon M. (1988): Multiple Criteria Decision Making in Industry, Studies in Production and Economic Engineering, Elserver, Amsterdam - Oxford - New York, Tokyo.

DECISION SUPPORT MODEL FOR INFORMATION SYSTEMS INTEGRATION IN SUPPLY CHAINS: A FUZZY APPROACH

DANIA PÉREZ ARMAYOR[†], JOSÉ A. DÍAZ BATISTA

Facultad de Ingeniería Industrial, Instituto Superior Politécnico J. A. Echeverría, CUJAE, Ave. 114 # 11901, Marianao, La Habana, Cuba

The need to satisfy a more demanding customer in a scenery where deadlines and costs must be ever smaller to maintain competitiveness, together with increased uncertainty about demand, has been leading organizations to collaborate to such a level that now the competition is not between isolated enterprises, but between supply chains. The integration of information systems in the chain is a recognized problem that is still far from solved because the selection complexity of a combination of technologies to support, to the greatest possible extent, the supply chain performance. This paper proposes an approach for a decision support model based on compensatory fuzzy logic, to facilitate the selection of technologies to be used for integrating the information systems in a supply chain.

1. Introduction

The need to satisfy an increasingly more exigent customer, reduce delivery times and decrease overall costs in order to keep competitive, plus the increasing uncertainty in the demand, has paved the way for inter-organizational collaboration leading businesses to group themselves into supply chains creating an environment where the competition is no longer among enterprises but among supply chains [1-3]. Supply chain management (SCM) is a coordination and collaboration challenge that require a decision making process based on the latest and best information from every component of the chain in order to archive a better total system performance rather than optimization of single members [1, 4].

The existence of such inter-organizational collaboration is possible due the intensive use of information systems (IS) supported by information and communication technologies (ICT), nevertheless, the evolution of the IS has resulted in a surplus of applications that are not designed for working in a

---

[†] Work partially supported by the "Very Large Business Applications" department, university "Carl von Ossietzky" from Oldenburg, Germany.

interoperable way [3, 5, 6], considering interoperability as "the ability of two or more systems or components to exchange information and to use the information that has been exchanged" [7], letting a long way between the high-level vision of the integrated supply network and the basic reality in the development and implementation of these needed supporting technologies [2, 5].

An increasingly more exploited path to overcome integration problems is the enterprise application integration (EAI), which reuse the existing technologies in the inter-organizational environment, incorporating functionalities from disparate applications and leading to cheaper, more functional and manageable ICT infrastructures, and making easier the investment returns, the cost reductions and the collaboration among the involved entities [3, 5, 6, 8, 9].

However, the complexity regarding the permutations of integration technologies that can be used to piece together information systems remains as an important barrier to achieve the benefits expected from SCM, due to the inexistence of a unique solution able to solve all the integration problems [3, 8].

This paper proposes an approach for a decision support model based on compensatory fuzzy logic (CFL), to facilitate the selection of technologies to use for integrating the information systems in a supply chain.

2. The Integration Problem

Traditionally the information systems have been deployed to support specific departmental needs, each application specializing on some specific activity type, in order to reduce time and increase effectiveness in each specific area of work. These autonomous and dissimilar systems were not made to collaborate among them, holding related data without the proper global administration [6], generating as well that several applications present similar functionalities in such way that exist more than one software available for do a task with different quality and efficiency according to the application that has been used. This isolated information systems have a very negative impact on business efficiency and their effectiveness [10]. The need to overcome these deficiencies and give a coordinate answer to the clients, regardless of how many internal systems were necessary to consult, highlight the integration of information systems as a solution to guarantee continuous and harmonic information flow in the enterprise frame [5, 6].

Among the developed solutions for intra-organization integration, the most involving, and therefore the most popular, have been the enterprise resource planning (ERP) systems [2, 3, 5, 6, 11]. The ERP systems provide an integration framework by re-implementing disparate enterprise application systems on the basis of an integrated and consistent database and accommodate many features of an organization's business processes. But they are highly complex, integrated systems that require careful consideration before selection, implementation, and use [6, 11] given the tremendous implementation cost and the difficulties to adapt the enterprise to the system [11] specially in small and medium-sized enterprises (SME) [12].

Supply chains need to work as a synchronized entity in order to reduce buffered inventory, lead times and, therefore, be able to reduce total cost across the entire system and increase responsiveness in order to match supply and demand in the market in ever-shorter time-frames. That is a complex task involving a great challenge of coordination and information integration in order to allow visibility and reduce uncertainty in the demand through the complete network [1, 13]. In order to accomplish this every member of the network must be connected to each other by means of shared information [1]. This situation makes the integration of information systems across the whole network a necessary element in order to provide a shared foundation of information. The information systems are responsible for the visibility and for accomplishing that they must be design in relation to common predetermined objectives for all members involved. "The use of these systems has the potential to convert supply chains into demand chains in the sense that the system can now respond to known demand rather than having to anticipate that demand through a forecast" [1].

Nevertheless, to enable these benefits represents a tremendous task that requires a high level of process alignment [1]. The problems that make this task so difficult find their source in technological, strategic and organizational reasons. On one hand, there are findings arguing that companies share information selectively. Organizations are often willing to share information to ensure the flow of materials through the network. But very few seem to be willing to provide online access to their ERP systems or access to sensitive areas such as design or strategic decisions, due to potential loss of proprietary information and loss of control [2].

Also the interoperability problems (e.g. the lack of ability to collaborate and the danger of data inconsistencies) among the coexisting systems in the enterprise frame are aggravated in the supply chains context [3, 6, 10]. A mayor challenge in order to rise above these difficulties is related to the uncertainty in the selection of the technologies that can better support the performance of the supply chain. There are many technologies to connect information systems, but none of them have claimed to beat all the integration problems and, therefore, is necessary the use of combinations of technologies[3] that must be different according to the integration requirements of the supply networks [1, 14]. So, the problem is which combination fits better a given integration necessity, but the lack of tools that support these process [8] affects the supply chain managers as much as the technology developers.

The variety of integration technologies, the various functionalities that are partially or completely repeated in many technologies or the quality with which these technologies perform their functions are a known barrier in the selecting process of the combination in which supply chain members should invest to obtain certain benefits [3, 5, 8].

3. Decision Support Model

The fundamental question of the given problem is in determining how good a combination of technologies for the integration of certain supply chain is. The hypothesis is that a combination of technologies is good for a supply chain if it satisfies the requirements of integration in this type of chain, applying the rule that the characteristics of an integration requirement determine which technologies, or combination of technologies, can be "suitable" for the chain. This last issue introduces vagueness in the analysis because it depends on the criterion of more or less experienced people.

In this scenario several aspects should be considered: first, the procedure for validation of the hypothesis involves the participation of those interested in the decision (decision makers), whether supply networks managers interested in acquiring the technologies or providers of integration solutions.

Secondly, the way in which technologies meet integration requirements is a fuzzy variable, given the terms "good" and "important" that can be used to quantify the veracity of the hypothesis. These terms allow a scale in natural language that captures the decision makers' perceptions regarding the veracity of the hypothesis. This scale of subjective values (such as very good, good, fair or bad) can be turned into numerical values between 0 and 1, seeking to reach an objective sort of the priority with which technologies should be considered for application in certain types of chain, despite the subjectivity of the scale used to obtain the criteria for decision-makers.

Thirdly, the supply chain types (i=1,...,M), the integration requirements (j=1,...,N) and technologies or technology combinations (k=1,...,L) used in the model must be previously defined. These three aspects constitute theoretical basis of the model, therefore, the more objective and explicit definition made of them the better the outcome. At present the number and diversity of technologies, the highly specific and vaguely spelled out integration requirements, and the many dimensions that can be applied to classify supply chains are significant barriers to integration technology choice.

The proposed model to validate the hypothesis, in its initial approach, is planned in three main steps, which must result in the matrices represented in Figure 1.

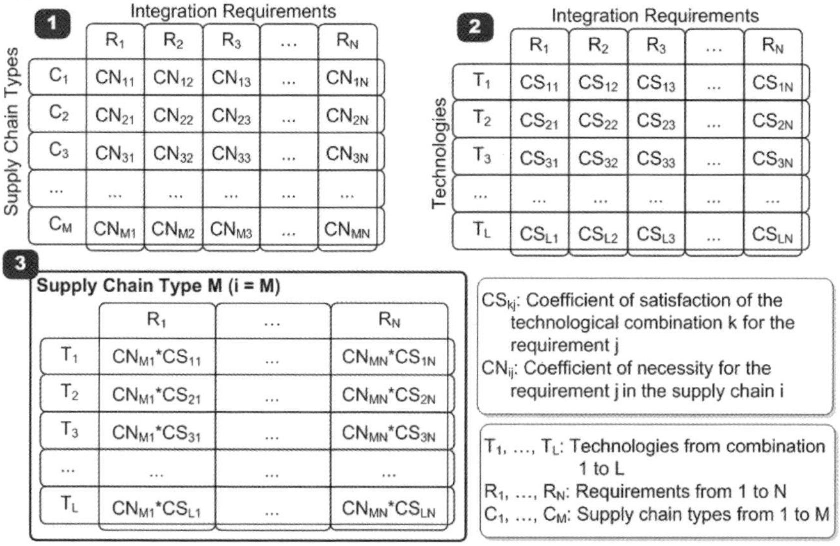

1 — Integration Requirements (Supply Chain Types)

	R_1	R_2	R_3	...	R_N
C_1	CN_{11}	CN_{12}	CN_{13}	...	CN_{1N}
C_2	CN_{21}	CN_{22}	CN_{23}	...	CN_{2N}
C_3	CN_{31}	CN_{32}	CN_{33}	...	CN_{3N}
...	...	...	...	...	...
C_M	CN_{M1}	CN_{M2}	CN_{M3}	...	CN_{MN}

2 — Integration Requirements (Technologies)

	R_1	R_2	R_3	...	R_N
T_1	CS_{11}	CS_{12}	CS_{13}	...	CS_{1N}
T_2	CS_{21}	CS_{22}	CS_{23}	...	CS_{2N}
T_3	CS_{31}	CS_{32}	CS_{33}	...	CS_{3N}
...	...	...	...	...	...
T_L	CS_{L1}	CS_{L2}	CS_{L3}	...	CS_{LN}

3 — Supply Chain Type M (i = M)

	R_1	...	R_N
T_1	$CN_{M1}*CS_{11}$	...	$CN_{MN}*CS_{1N}$
T_2	$CN_{M1}*CS_{21}$	...	$CN_{MN}*CS_{2N}$
T_3	$CN_{M1}*CS_{31}$	...	$CN_{MN}*CS_{3N}$
...	...	...	...
T_L	$CN_{M1}*CS_{L1}$	...	$CN_{MN}*CS_{LN}$

CS_{kj}: Coefficient of satisfaction of the technological combination k for the requirement j
CN_{ij}: Coefficient of necessity for the requirement j in the supply chain i

$T_1, ..., T_L$: Technologies from combination 1 to L
$R_1, ..., R_N$: Requirements from 1 to N
$C_1, ..., C_M$: Supply chain types from 1 to M

Figure 1. Relation matrices

The first step focuses on determining the extent in which the integration requirement (j) is necessary for the performance of the given supply chain type (i), expressing such a result in the so-called coefficient of necessity (CN_{ij}).
The second step is based on obtaining the coefficient of satisfaction (CS_{kj}) expressing the extent in which the technology (k) satisfies the requirement (j).

The third step is to obtain a sub-matrix from the matrix built in step 2, which would achieve an ordering of the technologies considered for a specific supply chain type.

The sub-matrix of step 3 takes into account only the significant requirements (columns of matrix in step 2) for the i-th desired supply chain, considered as significant those requirements in the matrix in step 1 with, for example, $CN_{ij} \geq$ 0.6, as shown in Figure 2. Then the ordering of the technologies is obtained by summing of the coefficients of satisfaction (CS_{kj}) weighed up by the coefficients of necessity (CN_{ij}).

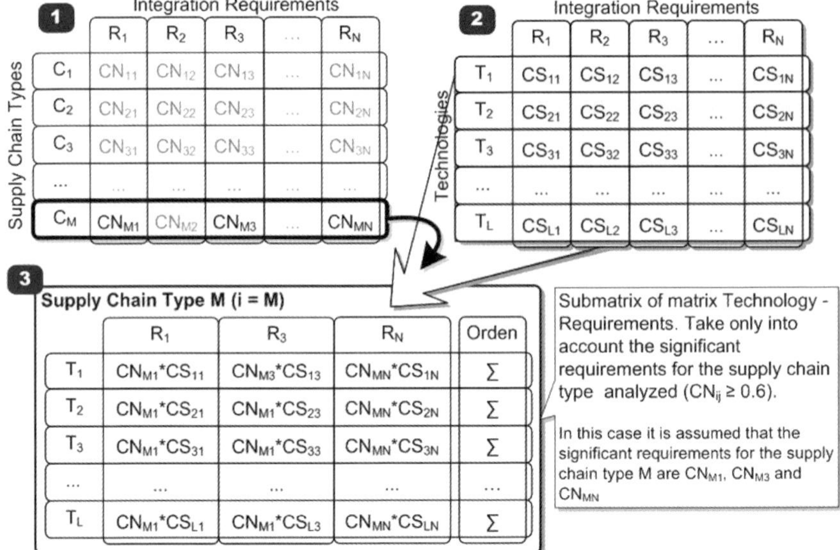

Figure 2. Building matrix for step 3

In the case of several decision makers (p) there would be as many matrices 1 and 2 as people involved in the decision process. All these matrices 1 and 2 are combined to obtain unique matrices for steps 1 and 2 using the "geometric mean" expressions (1) and (2).

$$CN_{ij} = \sqrt[p]{CN_{ij1}\ CN_{ij2}\ ...\ CN_{ijp}} \tag{1}$$

$$CS_{kj} = \sqrt[p]{CS_{kj1}\ CS_{kj2}\ ...\ CS_{kjp}} \tag{2}$$

Where:

CN_{ij} is the coefficient of necessity of the requirement j for chain type i.

CN_{ijp} is the coefficient of necessity of the requirement j for chain type i given by the person p (p=1,…,P).

CS_{kj} is the coefficient of satisfaction of the requirement j for the technological combination k.

CS_{kjp} is the coefficient of satisfaction of the requirement j for the technological combination k given by the person p.

CN_{ijp} and CS_{kjp} are subjective values that quantify each decision maker perception, while CN_{ij} and CS_{kj} represent a sort of consensus for a group of decision makers, that's why step 3 will result in a unique ordering of importance for a given set of technological combinations, considering a specific type of supply chain previously defined.

The compensatory fuzzy logic (CFL) is a multivalent system that incorporates the benefits of fuzzy logic. Given its ability to formalize the reasoning is suitable for building semantic models from natural language. It facilitates the evaluation and multi-criteria decision making from verbal descriptions that commonly appear ambiguously defined, including the structuring of problems that require ranking or selection of alternatives [15].

Once the array of technologies is obtained it provides a basis for finding which technological variant may be "more satisfactory", taking into account other factors such as the cost of using the technology in question.

4. Conclusions

The decision support model takes into account the subjectivity and vagueness present in a decision that involves several people, even from different organizations in the supply chain, for the selection of technologies for integration.

The model considers the potential compensations that may occur due to different measures in which combinations of technologies are able to meet certain supply chain requirements for non-dominant cases.

The fact that decision makers select the coefficients of the matrices in steps 1 and 2 from scales formed in a natural language makes easier the process.

Critical to have a good model is to properly define the supply chain types and the integration requirements.

References

1. M. Christopher, *Logistics & Supply Chain Management: creating value-adding networks*. 3 ed. Financial Times Series, Harlow, England: Prentice Hall. 320 (2005).
2. P. K. Bagchi, B. C. Ha, T. Skjoett-Larsen and L. B. Soerensen, *Supply chain integration: a European survey*. The International Journal of Logistics Management. **16**(2): p. 275-294 (2005).
3. M. Themistocleous, Z. Irani and P. E. D. Love, *Evaluating the integration of supply chain information systems: a case study*. European Journal of Operational Research. **159**(2): p. 393-405 (2004).
4. H. Günter, G. Grote and O. Thees, *Information technology in supply networks. Does it lead to better collaborative planning?* Journal of Enterprise Information Management. **19**(5): p. 540-550 (2006).

5. G. Hohpe and B. Woolf, *Enterprise Integration Patterns : Designing, Building, and Deploying Messaging Solutions*: Addison-Wesley (2004).

6. M. Weske, *Business Process Management. Concepts, Languages, Architectures*: Springer (2007).

7. IEEE Standards, *IEEE Standard Computer Dictionary* in *A Compilation of IEEE Standard Computer Glossaries* Institute of Electrical and Electronics Engineers (IEEE), (1990).

8. K. Khoumbati and M. Themistocleous, *Application of fuzzy simulation for the evaluation of enterprise application integration in healthcare organisations.* Transforming Government: People, Process and Policy. **1**(3): p. 230-241 (2007).

9. N. Erasala, D. C. Yen and T. M. Rajkumar, *Enterprise Application Integration in the electronic commerce world.* Computer Standards & Interfaces. **25**(2): p. 69-82 (2003).

10. J. Woznica and K. Healy, *The level of information systems integration in SMEs in Irish manufacturing sector.* Journal of Small Business and Enterprise Development. **16**(1): p. 115-130 (2009).

11. F. Adam and D. Sammon, eds. *The Enterprise Resource Planning Decade: Lessons Learned and Issues for the Future.* Idea Group Publishing (2004).

12. N. Brehm, *Föderierte ERP-Systeme auf Basis von Web Services. Dissertation*, Aachen: Shaker Verlag(2009).

13. A. Rushton, P. Croucher and P. Baker, *The Handbook of Logistics and Distribution Management* 3ed: Kogan Page. 612 (2006).

14. P. Helo, Y. Xiao and J. R. Jiao, *A web-based logistics management system for agile supply demand network design.* Journal of Manufacturing Technology Management. **17**(8): p. 1058-1077 (2006).

15. A. Racet Valdés, R. A. Espín Andrade and J. C. Marx Gómez, *Compensatory Fuzzy Ontology*, in *ICT Innovations 2009*, D. Davcev and J.C. Marx Gómez, Editors, Springer: Berlin, Germany. p. 35-44 (2010).

ANALYSIS OF CONTRACTFLEXIBILITY BY USING MODELLING AND SIMULATION

WENDY HADDAD CARRARO

Federal University of Rio Grande do Sul, Avenida Guido Mondin, 830. São Geraldo. ZIP: 90230-260. Porto Alegre/RS, Brazil

JOÃO LUIZ BECKER

GESID, Federal University of Rio Grande do Sul - Management School, Rua Washington Luiz, 855. Centro. ZIP: 90010-460. Porto Alegre/ RS , Brazil

The current paper aims at modeling a tool in order to help business people in charge of decision making regarding service or production contracts. It intends to offer a correct analysis and evaluation of the elaboration of contract clauses which behold flexibility for the contractual relationship in terms of the variables price and quantity. The use of such tool will allow business people from different segments to analyze the sensitivity of some variables as well as risk and uncertainties of the business.

1. Introduction

Flexibility, as the capacity of a company to permanently co-align its own environment with the environment in which the business is established [1]. In a world where uncertainties are inexistent and all future changes in the environment could be perfectly predicted, the company could make decisions in the present about all future actions, without any considerations about other contingencies. Therefore, actions aiming at increasing flexibility are justified whenever uncertainties regarding environmental changes are present [5]. Contracts are effective tools to deal with the information asymmetry. A great deal of literature has explored how to make a supply chain work with different types of contract, such as: return policies, quantity discounts, quantity flexibility, technical assistance agreements, revenue-sharing contracts, sales-rebate contracts, preferences. The cost structure of companies offering a contract is supposed to be known before signing the contract [3].

2. Flexibility Concept

In operational research, flexibility is usually seen as a system's ability to respond to environmental uncertainties [4]. They may be internal to the company (e.g. machine breakdown, inappropriate plans and stock) or external to the company (e.g. uncertainties based on the behavior of customers and competitors, need for higher speed and supplier failures).

Flexibility could guarantee possible adaptations under conditions of economic changes or when unpredicted disturbances emerge due to errors and omissions [6]. According to this definition, uncertainties related to environmental changes provide a higher value to flexibility.

3. Applied Method

The methodology used in this paper for the elaboration of a decision-support tool has comprised the following stages, as suggested by Freitas [7]: planning, modeling, experimenting and project conclusion. The software *Microsoft Excel*® was the computational resource used, including the use of electronic plans for the compilation of data, collection of statistical indicators, simulation modeling using macros, obtainment of comparative results using graphs resources included in the software.

The company which provided the database is a laboratory of clinical analysis whose contracts with health insurance companies are rigid. The context of the demand flow and financial situation existent in the health segment is determinant for a possible applicability or non-applicability of flexible contracts, considering there are four different types of participants in the contracts: the contracted company, the contracting company.

The information and data about the examined system were collected both *in situ* and from historical records of the company, serving as object for the development of the research. The research was carried out on an exploratory basis, with both qualitative and quantitative analysis of data [8].

Face and content validations have been performed in order to verify whether the curves and equations generated were appropriate or not and, thus, guarantee that the results obtained from the modeling produces reliable and representative results, according to the initial premises.

4. Flexibility Modeling in Contracts – Price (P) and Quantity (Q)

Aiming at the validation of the fundamental hypothesis of this article the objective is to identify the best conditions in terms of price, quantity, flexibility policies and structure of fixed costs, in which both contracted and contracting companies have advantage, considering the existence of risk and uncertainties sharing. As a base for the definition of the equilibrium curve and function, data from typical contracts between the company and mid-range health insurance companies has been used. This kind of contract represents approximately one third of the total volume of services rendered by the laboratory.

4.1 Definition of Simulation Types

In order to model different scenarios, some classifications have been defined, known as types of contract: rigid, flexible-symmetric and flexible-asymmetric. In Figure 1, a scheme with the definition of contract types used as criteria for the simulation tool is presented.

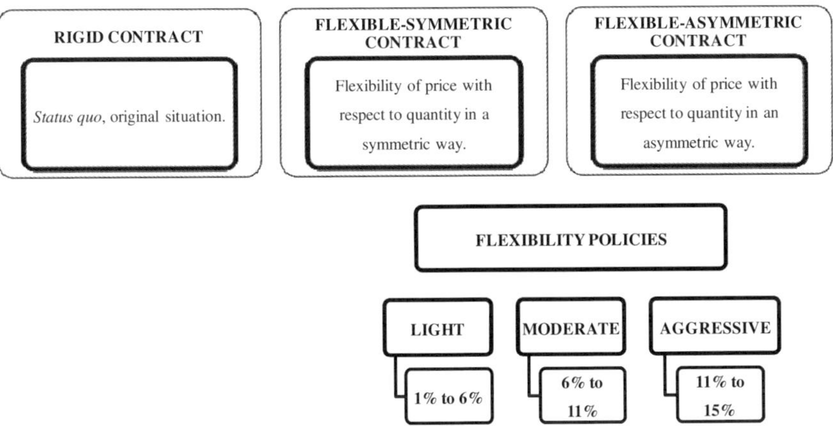

Figure 1 – Definition of simulations and policies types.
Source: Elaborated by the authors.

A rigid contract is a contract containing fixed prices, regardless of the demanded quantity, not subject to negotiation. The contracting company will not obtain any gains per volume, since the price is the same, regardless of the demand. A flexible contract is a contract in which price may vary according to the quantity effectively demanded. The contracting company may benefit depending on the volume effectively demanded.

Flexible-symmetric contracts are depicted in the current paper as those in which prices vary up or down symmetrically with respect to the reference price according to relative variations in the quantity effectively demanded in relation to the agreed reference quantity. Flexible-asymmetric contracts, in turn, are those in which prices vary up or down asymmetrically with respect to the reference price according to relative variations in the quantity effectively demanded in relation to the agreed reference quantity.

4.1.1 Definition of the Equilibrium Function Q = F(P) and Construction of the Demand Curve

Table 1 presents the amount of examinations carried out and their respective billings under the auspices of the considered contracts during a specific period.

Table 1 – Average price/quantity of examinations ratio for different contracting companies

CONTRACTING COMPANY	Quantity of Examinations	Total Billing	Average Price R$*	% Q Variation	% AP Variation
Contract A	459	55.424,25	120,75		
Contract B	332	58.123,24	175,07	-28	45
Contract C	279	38.061,18	136,42	-39	13
Contract D	203	35.594,02	175,34	-56	45
Contract E	162	30.851,28	190,44	-65	58
Contract F	113	22.772,89	201,53	-75	67
Contract G	95	20.414,55	214,89	-79	78
Contract H	59	13.450,82	227,98	-87	89
TOTAL	1702	362.100,50	212,75		

The percent variation in quantity and average price presented in Table 1 corresponds to the comparison between the values in each contract as compared to those in contract A. The variations in price and quantity are not regular or proportional when considering quantity *versus* price. Based on the definition of price *versus* demanded quantities data it is possible to elaborate a demand curve, relating quantity Q and the corresponding average prices P. By that means, quantity with respect to price is obtained:

$$Q = f(P).$$

The adjusted equation is:

$$Q = 3.951,44 \cdot e^{-0,018 \cdot P} \quad (1)$$

Assuming R-square = 0,856. Graph 1 presents the demand curve, obtained from the collected data.

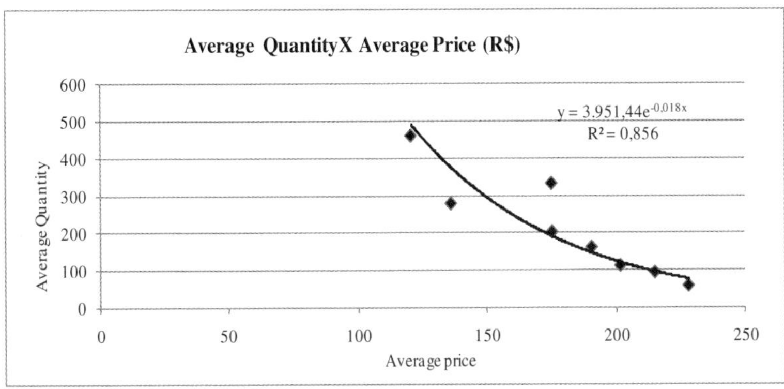

Graph 1 – Average Quantity x Average Price (R$)

A more detailed statistical analysis is presented in Table 2.

Table 2 – Statistical Analysis of Average Q x P Curve for the main agreements – Mid-Range

Regression Statistics		ANOVA				
		df	*SS*	*MS*	*F*	*Significance F*
Multiple R	0,925					
R-Square	0,856	**Regression**	1	2,852	2,852	35,667	0,001
Adjusted R-Square	0,832	**Residual**	6	0,480	0,080		
Standard Error	0,283	**Total**	7	3,332			
			Coefficients	*Standard Error*	*t Stat*	*P-Value*
Observations	8					
		Intersept	8,282	0,531	15,588	0,000
		Variable X1	-0,017	0,003	-5,972	0,001

Based on this curve, it is possible to experimentally simulate situations considering different prices. Given a price, the expected demanded quantity by lab services can be determined.

4.1.2 *Randomization of the Q = f(P) Curve*

Equation (1) is equivalent to:

$$\ln Q = \ln(3.951,44) - 0,018 \cdot P$$

It is proposed to model the variable $\ln Q$ as a normal distribution, with mean μ_Q and standard deviation σ_Q. That is:

$$\ln Q \sim N(\mu_Q; \sigma_Q^2)$$

294

The $\ln Q$, μ_Q mean will be modeled by the deterministic equation (1), which is,

$$\mu_Q = 3.951,44 \cdot e^{-0,018 \cdot P}$$

The random perturbation will be modeled by its standard-deviation value σ_Q estimated from empirical data on the analyzed company, assuming:

$$\sigma_Q = 0,557$$

4.2 Developed Experiment

The inverse transformation method was used in order to generate a random simulation of Q [2], using the functional facilities of *Microsoft Excel*®. That is:

$$Q = \mu_Q \cdot e^{INVNORM(RANDOM(); \; 0; \sigma_Q)} \quad (2)$$

For each price, eight different percentage combinations have been used. Based on the three different types of contract, the three flexibility policies, the sixteen selected prices and the eight percentage combinations for each price, considering each combination of contract and policy, it was possible to compose a database with a total of 1.152 simulated scenarios. For each price P, 300 random independent values were generated for Q, using equation (2).

4.2.1 Input Data and Output Data

Variables considered as input data for the tool: initial prices of contract; Percentage for each flexibility policy; Fixed Costs for the quantities considered; Expected Net Margin; Maximum Production Capacity; Added Value of Fixed Costs, in case demanded quantities exceed the Maximum Production Capacity; and Value of Variable Costs. The output data of the simulation tool are: average demand; standard deviation; Total billing; Total variable cost; Gross Margin; Fixed cost; Need to increase the production capacity in order to meet the demand; Net Profit; Performance Indicators; Net Margin; Probability of Profit below the expected Average Net Margin.

4.2.2 Result Analysis and Ideal Scenarios

Based on the simulation data, it is observed that almost all options of symmetric and asymmetric flexibility result in price reduction in relation to the rigid contract. In 67.2% of the observed situations, prices in contracts considered flexible, are better than in those considered rigid. It is also observed that 29.6%

of contracts present higher demanded quantities, 26% present a lower Probability of Profit below the expected Average Net Margin, 14.1% result in better billings and 7.5% present a better net margin, comparatively to rigid contracts.

Contracts with improvements in their expected average net margin for the contractor were filtered (86 situations). Out of these 86 situations, it was identified those which presented a better average final price, those which presented a lower probability of profit below the expected average net margin for the contracted, those which presented a higher demanded quantity and those which presented a higher total billing. Results prove the theory that there will be flexible contracts with benefits for both parties. In 95.3% of the situations, flexible contracts improved their margin and also met a higher demanded quantity, which is advantageous not only for the contracted but also for the contracting company, since a higher demand reduces the security liabilities with patients.

5. Conclusions

The current paper aimed at proving the hypothesis that it is possible to identify levels of price and quantity to be demanded, assuring the viability of contract formulation with flexibility clauses. During the modeling elaboration, it was also possible to identify the best conditions in terms of price, quantity, flexibility policies and structure of fixed costs, in which there is gain for both the contracted and the contracting companies, considering the existence of risk.

It is suggested that this subject should be further explored and developed in future research papers. Likewise, organizations and researchers should search for alternatives with the use of flexibility, in order to share risks and its respective reduction by using and choosing uncertainty variables that result in gains for all the parties involved in contractual relations.

References

1. A. J. Verdu-Jover, J. M. Gomez-Gras, F. J. Llorens-Montes, Managerial flexibility: determinants and performance implications. *Industrial Management & Data Systems*, 108(1-2), p. 70-86 (2008).
2. A. M. Law, W. D. Kelton, *Simulation modeling and analysis.* (3a. ed.) Boston: McGraw-Hill (2000).
3. D. Ding, J. Chen Coordinating a three level supply chain with flexible return policies. *Omega-International Journal of Management Science*, 36(5), p. 865-876 (2008).

4. D. Gerwin, Manufacturing flexibility: a strategic perspective. *Management science*, 39(4), p. 395-410 (1993).
5. J. E. Fensterseifer, Incerteza, Aprendizagem, Eficiência e o Valor da Flexibilidade de Produção. *Encontro Nacional de Engenharia da Produção - ENEGEP*, Belo Horizonte, MG, Brasil, 10 (1990).
6. O. Williamson, *The theory of the firm as governance structure*: from choice to contract. (2002).
7. P. J. de Freitas, *Introdução à modelagem e simulação de sistemas com aplicações em arena*. Florianópolis: Visual Books (2001).
8. S. Roesch, *Projetos de estágio e de pesquisa em administração*: guia para estágios, trabalhos de conclusão, dissertações e estudos de caso. São Paulo: Atlas (1999).

DECISION MAKING IN STRATEGIC BUSINESS MANAGEMENT

ARAS KEROPYAN, ANNA MARIA GIL-LAFUENTE

Department of Economics and Business Organization, University of Barcelona
Avinguda Diagonal, 690
08034 Barcelona, Spain

In this paper, we investigate different decision style models for decision making and decision support system cases within the strategic management processes. We build our model on a system which is based on fuzzy logic methodology. This methodology will allow us to examine the relations between decision making styles and strategic management processes. The result will enable us to make the most proper decision making style in a strategic management process. We are leaving more research topics for further studies that may be applied to different styles of decision making within the strategic management process.

1. Introduction

Decision making is one of the most important activities for managers. Over the years, researchers have discussed the influence of the ability of managers on organizational outcomes. Some authors have argued that managers have a remarkable impact on organizational performance. S. Robins (1999) describes in his book the manager's impact as the essence of the manager's job and a critical element of organizational life. Meanwhile Rowe (1994) suggests that decision making is synonymous with managing. Different kinds of computer-based information systems have been developed to support decision making and decision support systems, group support systems and executive information systems. In order to be more competitive organizations in though market conditions, it is widely agreed that managers must make good decisions which affect their organizations significantly.

We believe that by using fuzzy logic methodology, we can propose good examples of decision making in strategic management and present a useful application. In this study we are going to discuss different styles of decision making in strategic management process and try to propose the most adequate decision making style using the fuzzy logic method. We are going to leave topics for further research so that our model can be approved afterwards by applying data to different techniques of fuzzy logic.

2. Fuzzy Logic

Zadeh (1965) has published first fuzzy set theory. Zimmermann (1991) explained fuzzy set theory as a strict mathematical framework in which vague conceptual phenomena was precisely and rigorously studied. The theory can also be thought as a modeling language which suited well for situations that were containing fuzzy relations, criteria and phenomena. Afterwards, Rowe (1994) have proved the portfolio matrix and 3Cs model which were enabling companies to analyze their strategic business units and projects, and providing strategic directions in an efficient way. This hasn't worked very well. Certain values in the decisions making aren't always correct. Because there are always vague processes and it is difficult to estimate decision making processes with an exact numerical value. Pap and Bosnjak (2000) defined the main problem of using the classical portfolio matrix as the precise determination of the numerical value for the criteria. As a result, it would be useful to use the linguistic assessments which have been introduced by Zadeh (1965) and Bellman (1970) instead of numerical indicators.

2.1. *Fuzzy number and linguistic variable*

Dubois and Prade (1970) have defined the fuzzy numbers. They have described its meaning and features. A fuzzy number $\tilde{N}$ is a fuzzy set which membership function is $\mu_{\tilde{N}}(y): R \to [0,1]$. A triangular fuzzy number $\tilde{N} = (a,b,c)$ can conform to different set of a, b, c characteristics. If we explain those characteristics in management terms, a value is the optimistic estimate, when everything goes great. The value b is the most likely estimate, which implies to the situation not very good either very bad. The c value is a pessimistic estimate, when everything goes badly.

Zadeh and Bellmann (1970) defines a linguistic variable as a variable whose values are not numbers but words or phrases in a natural or synthetic language. In a problem when we are working on linguistic variables we can present their means. At that moment, we can rate and weight the various conditions by using the fuzzy numbers and linguistic variables. Linguistic variables represent the relative importance and appropriateness of each ranking method that simultaneously considers the metric distance and fuzzy mean value is proposed. The distance from the ideal solution and the fuzzy mean value are usual criteria for ranking fuzzy numbers.

Moon, Lee and Lim defines fuzzy numbers as if Y is a collection of objects represented of generated of y's, then a fuzzy set $\tilde{N}$ in Y is a set of ordered pairs:

$$\tilde{N} = \{(x, \mu_{\tilde{N}}(y)) \mid y \in Y\}$$

$\mu_{\tilde{N}}(y)$ is the membership function or grade of membership of y in $\tilde{N}$ that maps Y to the membership space N (when N contains only the two points 0 and 1, $\tilde{N}$ is no fuzzy and $\mu_{\tilde{N}}(y)$ is identical to the characteristic function of a no fuzzy set). The range of the membership function is a subset of the nonnegative real numbers whose supreme is finite. Elements with a membership of zero degrees are normally not listed. The authors characterize a linguistic variable by a quintuple $(y, F(y), A, B, \tilde{N})$ in which y is the name of the variable; $F(y)$ denotes the term of y set; for example the set of names of linguistic values of y, with each value being a fuzzy variable denoted generically by Y and ranging over a universe of discourse A that is associated with the base variable a; B is a syntactic rule for generation of the name, Y, of values of y; and $\tilde{N}$ is a semantic rule for associating with each Y its meaning $\tilde{N}(y)$ which is a fuzzy subset of A.

In this study we propose following semantics for the set of five terms to point different styles of decisions on the strategic management process:

A) VG = Very Good = (8, 9, 10)
B) G = Good = (6, 7, 8)
C) M = Medium = (4, 5, 6)
D) B = Bad = (2, 3, 4)
E) VB = Very Bad = (0, 1, 2)

We use triangular fuzzy numbers and therefore we present the following semantics in Figure 1:

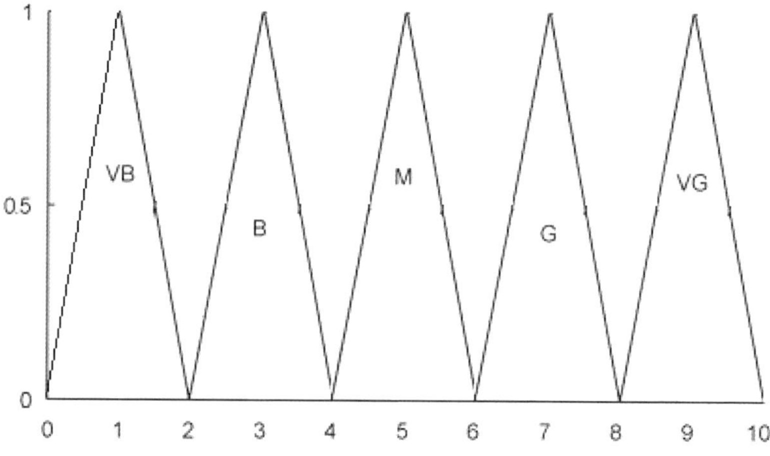

Figure 1. The membership functions for fuzzy numbers

3. Strategic Decision Making and Decision Making Styles

Ultimately, in management research topics strategic decision making has become to be one of the most appealing areas. Behavioral decision theory and transaction cost economics have fed the area and the studies about strategic decision making have increased during 1990's (Schwenk, 1995). Although there are many studies about this area, the knowledge of strategic decision making is inadequate. Eisenhardt and Zbaracki (1992) implied in their study that strategic decisions have vital roles for companies but strategy process subject has not been researched considerably from a stage of being based on mature paradigms and incomplete assumptions.

Strategic decision making and different styles of decision making are strongly connected. For this reason when we are talking about strategic decision process we should also investigate decision making styles. In the literature there are many types of decision makers and decision making styles. For example, in 1980's there were studies that investigated personality types and therefore different decision making styles. More recently, Rowe and Boulgarides (1994) proposed a model of decision styles that recognizes the influence of values and perceptions. In Figure 2, their model is shown. Rowe and Boulgarides in their model suggest that decision makers are driven by four forces.

<table>
<tr><td></td><td colspan="2">Left brain hemisphere</td><td colspan="2">Right brain hemisphere</td></tr>
<tr><td rowspan="2">High</td><td colspan="2">Analytic

Enjoys solving problems/puzzles
Uses considerable data
Undertakes careful analysis

Strong need for achievement
(in the form of challenges)</td><td colspan="2">Conceptual

Creative and humanistic
Broad and long-term focus
Seeks independence

Strong need for achievement
(in the form of recognition)</td></tr>
<tr></tr>
<tr><td rowspan="2">Low</td><td colspan="2">Directive

Aggressive and autocratic
Acts rapidly
Uses rules and intuition

Strong need for power</td><td colspan="2">Behavioral

Supportive and empathetic
Prefers communication/discussion
Uses intuition rather than data

Strong need for affiliation</td></tr>
<tr></tr>
</table>

Cognitive Complexity

Task Oriented   People Oriented

Values

Figure 2. Decision style model (Rowe and Boulgarides, 1994)

The four forces – directive, analytic, conceptual, and behavioral – can be related to the typology of needs developed by McClelland (1962) who had proposed that behavior is motivated by the needs for achievement, power and affiliation. Subsequently, he recognized that the need for achievement may be satisfied in two different ways, either intrinsically by taking on new challenges or extrinsically by receiving praise and recognition. According to Rowe and Boulgarides, the primary need of directive decision makers is power. They are results oriented, but also want to dominate others. They have a low tolerance for ambiguity and prefer low levels of cognitive complexity. This preference limits the amount of information that they gather and the number of alternatives that they consider. Analytic decision makers have a strong need for achievement in the form of new challenges. They have greater tolerance for ambiguity than their directive counterparts. Their comfort with cognitive complexity strongly encourages data collection and processing. They make decisions slowly because they want to examine the situation thoroughly and consider many alternatives systematically. Conceptual decision makers are achievement oriented like their analytic counterparts, but crave extrinsic rewards, such as praise, recognition, and independence. They are comfortable with a high degree of cognitive complexity and also have a strong people orientation. Conceptual decision makers typically gather information from multiple sources and consider many alternatives. They tend to take a long-term perspective, exhibiting considerable

302

creativity and idealism. Behavioral decision makers are driven primarily by a need for affiliation. This type has a low cognitive complexity, but a strong people orientation. Behavioral style managers tend to communicate easily and be very concerned with the well-being of their peers and subordinates. They are typically receptive to suggestions, willing to compromise, and prefer loose controls. It is interesting to analyze different styles of decision making. In their study, Rowe and Boulgarides (1994) present a Decision Style Inventory (DSI) to measure the relative propensity to make use of the four decision styles. This instrument does not measure absolute values on each style. Instead, scenario-based items are used to determine the relative scores of either an individual or a sample drawn from one population compared to samples drawn from other populations or the population as a whole. In the end, DSI is a useful utility to compare the decision-making styles of specific individuals or groups. Likewise in the other studies the inventory's reliability and validity have been confirmed. It has "a very high face validity and reliability".

4. Application

In this study, our objective is to find out the best decision making styles that we have presented before for the different strategic management processes. In order to do that, in Table 1 we present a matrix that refers to the correlations between different kind of management strategies and different strategic decisions. The decisions that we are presenting below can pertain different styles of management.

Table 1. Semantic representations of the relations between decision making and management styles

Decision Making Style/Strategic Decisions	New Business Investment	New Product Introduction	Pressure	Decision Uncertainty	Threat/Crisis
Analytic	(VB, B, M, G, VG)	(VB, B, M, G, VG)	(VB, B, M, G, VG)	(VB, B, M, G, VG)	(VB, B, M, G, VG)
Conceptual	(VB, B, M, G, VG)	(VB, B, M, G, VG)	(VB, B, M, G, VG)	(VB, B, M, G, VG)	(VB, B, M, G, VG)
Directive	(VB, B, M, G, VG)	(VB, B, M, G, VG)	(VB, B, M, G, VG)	(VB, B, M, G, VG)	(VB, B, M, G, VG)
Behavioral	(VB, B, M, G, VG)	(VB, B, M, G, VG)	(VB, B, M, G, VG)	(VB, B, M, G, VG)	(VB, B, M, G, VG)

a) New Business Investments: Consist the decisions of acquisitions, mergers, joint ventures, new company establishment, and investments in capital equipment and also consists of internal reorganization investments such as information systems, internal reorganization.

b) New Product Introduction: It concerns expansion of production equipment, storing facilities, modernization of production equipment, and investment in the marketing domain. (V. M. Papadakis, S. Lioukas and D. Chambers, 1998)

c) Pressure: It is the extent of pressure exerted either on the organization or the time pressure felt by the participants in the strategic decision process. (Beach and Mitchell, 1978)

d) Decision Uncertainty: As Beach and Mitchell implies (1978) it is the composite variable which consists of three 7-point Likert-type scales measuring the uncertainty about actions to be taken, general uncertainty surrounding the decision, and uncertainty concerning the information to be collected.

e) Threat/crisis: Is a variable that consists of two scales measuring the extent to which the SD is perceived as a crisis situation and the second the threat of financial loss. (Billings et. al, 1980)

5. Conclusion and Further Research

In this study, we are proposing a fuzzy based model which can be applied in strategic decision making process. We present 4 kind of decision making styles (analytic, conceptual, directive and behavioral) and 5 kind of strategic decisions (new business investment, new product introduction, decisions under pressure, decisions with uncertainty and decisions among threat/crisis). In further studies, the correlations between those decision making styles and strategic decisions can be identified and pointed by fuzzy numbers according to their correlations {VG = Very Good = (8, 9, 10); G = Good = (6, 7, 8); M = Medium = (4, 5, 6); B = Bad = (2, 3, 4); VB = Very Bad = (0, 1, 2)}. From here, a fuzzy model can be presented and the results can be discussed. We think that a fuzzy-based AHP model can be applied which can be built on the model that we present in this study. Once the correlations between decision making styles and strategic decisions are recognized the practical business and managerial results can be shown in further research.

References

1. J. G. Aluja, The Interactive Management of Human Resources In Uncertainty, (1996).
2. J. G. Lafuente, Algoritmos Para La Excelencia. Claves para el éxito en la gestión deportiva. Editorial Milladoiro, Vigo, Spain. (2002).
3. J. G. Aluja, A. M. Gil-Lafuente and A. Klimova, Elementos técnicos para la obtención de las afinidades. Reticulos de Galois, (2007).

4. G. Birkoff, Lattice Theory, American Mathematical Society Colloquim Publications, **25**, (1991).

5. A. J. Rowe and J. D. Boulgarides, Managerial Decision Making, Prentice-Hall, Englewood Cliffs, NJ, (1994).

6. C. Moon, J. Lee and S. Lim, *Applied Soft Computing*, 10, 512 (2009).

7. M. G. Martinsons and R. Davison, *Decision Support Systems*, 43, 284 (2007).

8. S. P. Robbins, *Management, 6*, Prentice Hall, Englewood Cliffs, NJ, (1999).

9. H. J. Zimmermann, Fuzzy Set Theory and Its Application, *Kluwer Academic Publishing*, Boston (1991).

10. L. A. Zadeh, *Fuzzy set, Information and Control.* **8,** 338 (1965).

11. E. Pap, Z. Bosnjak and S. Bosnjak, Application of fuzzy sets with different t-norms in the interpretation of portfolio matrices in strategic management, *Fuzzy Sets and Systems.* **114,** (2000).

12. R. E. Bellman and L. A. Zadeh, Decision-making in a fuzzy environment, *Management Science* **17,** (1970).

13. D. Dubois and H. Prade, Operation on fuzzy numbers, *International Journal of Systems Service* **9,** 613, (1978).

14. C. R. Schwenk, Strategic decision making, *Journal of Management*, **21 (3),** (1995).

15. K. M. Eisenhardt and M. J. Zbaracki, Strategic decision-making, *Strategic Management Journal*, Winter Special Issue, **13,** (1992).

16. D. C. McClelland, Business drive and national achievement, *Harvard Business Review* **40,** (1962).

17. N. H. Leonard, R. W. Scholl and K. B. Kowalski, Information processing style and decision making, *Journal of Organizational Behavior,* **20,** (1999).

18. V. M. Papadakis, S. Lioukas and D. Chambers, Strategic Decision-Making Processes: The Role of Management and Context, *Strategic Management Journal* **19,** 115, (1998).

19. R. S. Billings, T. W. Milburn and M. L. Schaalman, A model of crisis perception: A theoretical and empirical analysis, *Administrative Science Quarterly*, **25,** 300, (1980).

20. L. R. Beach and T. R. Mitchell, A contingency model for the selection of decision strategies, *Academy of Management Review*, **3,** 439, (1978).

THE IMPROVEMENT OF THE KEY PROCESSES IN A TERMINAL OF CONTAINERS: AN APPLICATION OF THE DISCRETE SIMULATION

ILEANA PÉREZ VERGARA, ROSARIO GARZA RÍOS

Instituto Superior Politécnico "José Antonio Echeverría"
Ciudad de La Habana, Cuba

A better knowledge and interpretation about how systems works can be obtained by using simulation, improving its control and getting sensitive benefits on their operation. The objective of the construction of models of simulation permits , not only evaluating the present-day performance of the production facilities and services, but also the alternatives of improvement proposals for these facilities, as much in economic terms as in measures of performance of production and the services, such as time of cycle of the products or clients, size of queues, workers' appropriate number in the work positions, or servers's number at centers of attention to the clients, etc. Presently work show an application of the discreet simulation to the operation of the reception/delivery process in a terminal of containers, that allowed after carrying out a study of the same one, to propose solutions to the detected problems related with to the rational use of the resources to offer an appropriate level of service, those that were studied starting from the designed simulation models. It is proposed as a result of the study, the redesign of the door system with impacts expected in the level of customer service.

1. Introduction

A maritime terminal of containers is a complex system in which processes of modal transporting interchange or of logistic steps (marine and terrestrial traffic) of containers are   developed. A basis to undertake the improvement of the performance of a maritime terminal of containers (TMC) it is to identify the processes that are developed and the interrelations among these. Although they can be said that in general two key processes exist: The load and unloading of ships and the reception and terrestrial delivery, other processes like the storage and the internal transport of containers, considered as of support they also take place, that is shown in the figure 1.

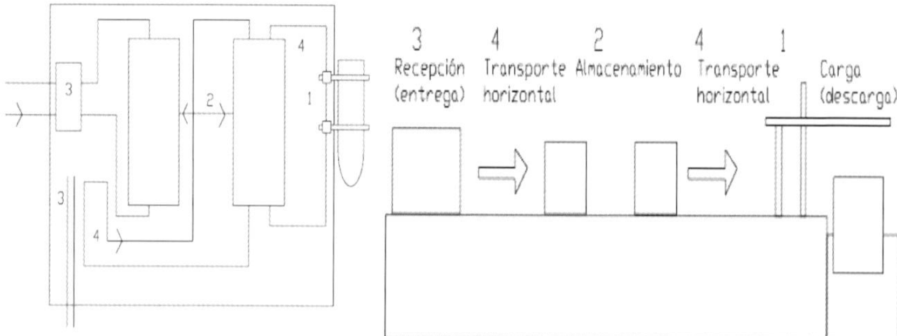

Figure 1. Outline of the processes of a terminal of containers. Sight in plant (left) and sight in upright projection (right).

The elevated number of external factors that can get to intervene in maritime and terrestrial traffic, as well as the great volume and volatility of the data that these negotiate conform an environment of relationships of the specially complex terminal; scenario that gets complicated for the wide typology of containers, ships and vehicles of terrestrial transport that they relate to each other in the system.

The changes that are generated in kind of system make that the behavior of the same one classifies as dynamic discreet that permits its modelation starting from the use of the discreet simulation Like tool for the analysis of the same.

The use of the simulation like work methodology is a very old activity, and It could be told than inherent to the human being's learning process.

The objective of the construction of models of simulation permits, not only evaluating the present-day performance, but also the alternatives of improvement proposals for these facilities, as much in economic terms measures of performance of production and the services, such as time of cycle of the products or clients, size of queues, workers' appropriate number in the work positions, or servers's number at centers of attention to the clients, etc

Although it is certain that these techniques present certain complexity, The fact to take decisions on a model of reality of simulated form, permits the construction of scenarios in those that it is possible the adoption of decisions where the time, the costs and risks of the decisions that are adopted are minimum and the immediate feedback of the effects of this decisions cannot only contribute to the improvement of them but also to the process of formation of a culture of the taking of decisions.

2. The discreet simulation and the focus of processes

The simulation is one of the most powerful analysis tool available for the design and operation of processes or complex systems. It is defined as "the process of to design a model of a real system and to drive experiments with that pattern, with the purpose of understanding the behavior of the system and/or to evaluate several strategies for the operation of the same one" [2], [3].

This definition adapts to situations in the managerial and/or organizational environment, since in many occasions different alternatives exist among those that should decide which it is the one that adds bigger values to the processes or which ones are the ones that satisfy determined restrictions or objectives.

The focus of processes has become for the engineering in organization in a key element in the process of taking of decisions. This focus that is sustained in the focus of systems, present that a process is a set of activities mutually related or that they interact, which turn entries into results With the aim of satisfying the needs that they go for directed those exits, and to add value. [1].

It comes into question that two basic forms to obtain information on the factors that affect a process exist: to observe the process without modifying it, or experimenting in the process, making changes and studying their consequences [6].

The utility of the simulation still evidenced in anyone of two basic previous forms. However is more appreciated its utility in the second, when permitting the experimentation in a model simulated of the real system, what supports that presented in the own ISO 9000:2000 that establish like one of their principles that the taking of decisions should be based on data and in the analysis of the processes.

To make decisions can be interpreted as the change in the levels of the factors on which the man can act directly and to analyze how these changes modify the behavior of the process, in this case they can be varied the operation rules for example, the form in that are carried out the same ones, The availability of resources, etc.

The principle of the continuous improvement of quality is present as another of the principles of the same ISO 9000:2000. In order to guarantee an improvement they require changes in processes that imply a bigger quality, and the elevation of the productivity, and, the discreet simulation turns out to be an useful technique for it.

At the same time, in oneself process could be of interest to measure several characteristics to the exit, what is correspond in studying several variables at the same time.

2.1 The problem to study

The terminal of containers study object presents problems in the reception process and terrestrial delivery whose main objective is to facilitate the reception/delivery of goods in a quick, but compatible with safenesses for the obtaining of the information that is necessary in its.

In this process they have gathered complaints of clients due to the lofty time of sojourn of trucks, for the administration considered necessary to find a solution to this problem.

A diagnosis came true and they determined the principal problems that affect the process:

1. Excessive documentation to present in the different control points along the reception process and delivery of containers
2. The capacity of parking of the Terminal, in the revision interior's area, is insufficient.
3. The Door System that allows the terrestrial access to the And the one in which the trucks are received, it is inspected the documentation of the full or empty containers that entered, an it is considered "bottle neck" since it doesn't allow to guarantee the continuous flow of the trucks that request the service.

2.2 The simulation models

Taking into account that the civil and technological infrastructure of the Terminal was conceived for a regimen of inferior operation to the current one that imposes restrictions for its Enlargement in the interior area, were decided to study the system and to analyze possible solutions to the 2nd and 3rd problems, through a simulation study that took into account the logical interactions between activities and operative decisions of the process, among those that highlight:

1. Access Vial (point of control of documents and expedition)
2. Inspection
3. Entrance order to the Terminal
4. Control of the documentation in the front door
5. Scale
6. Process of load/unload of full containers
7. Process of load/unload of empty containers
8. Control in the exit door
9. Confection of the remission of exit

The above-mentioned was captured in the simulation pattern developed in Sand version 7.01 [4] that is shown in the figure 2.

They were defined as entities the vehicles, according to the activities that carry out, differentiated by the attribute t:

1. t1: trucks that only operate with full containers.
2. t2: trucks that only operate with empty containers.
    t3: trucks that carry out double operation.

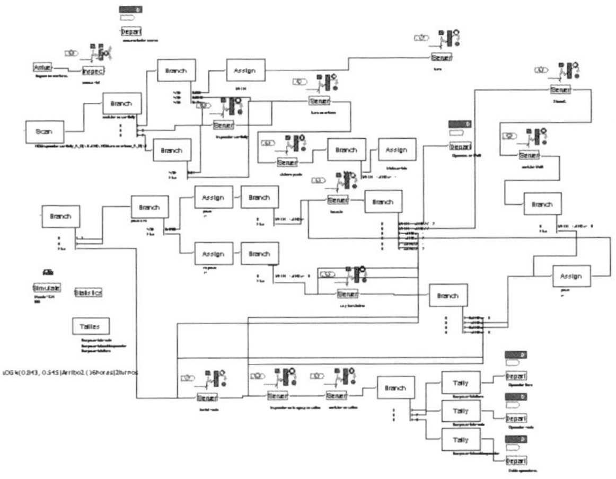

Figure 2. I Model of simulation of the Process reception/delivery in the Terminal.

For the obtaining of the times of duration of the activities were carried out samplings of times and analysis of data, those that were processed by the option Input Analizer

The study variables, related with the characteristics of quality, were:

- Total of operations: total of vehicles with received service for operations
- Average of the waiting time in door: it constitutes the time that should wait the trucks in the door to be able to carry out their operations in the Terminal.
- Average of time in system: the one understood from the arrival of the vehicles to the access vial until it leaves the Terminal.
- Percent of use of the door.

The Outputs of the option of the Statistics was used for the obtaining of blended values of the same, being carried out the corresponding experimental design of the simulation that threw the number of necessary races to be able to infer about the behavior of this system [4], [7].

The results yielded than the half number of trucks expecting in road access era of 24.38 with a peak of 25 trucks and a level of occupation of the door of entrance of 100%, what corroborates the opinion of the clients.

This motivated a proposal of redesign of the process that included Doing simultaneously the activities of the 1 to the 4 described previously, but in an external area to the Terminal, since like it had been said, it is not possible to enlarge the current capacity of parking in the Revision Interior's area, for reasons of the civil infrastructure. The redesign it required to modify the distribution in plant of the Terminal and it involve the realization of a new model that allowed to simulate the behavior of the system under the new conditions to determine the quantity of necessary doors that guaranteed an appropriate flow of trucks in the Terminal. The new model is shown in the figure 3.

The obtained results of the simulation pattern developed for the proposal allowed to determine that the quantity of necessary doors to guarantee a better level of service and the fluency of the system is of 2 doors.

A comparative analysis of the results was made obtained in the current conditions and the proposal, what is shown in the Table No. 1.

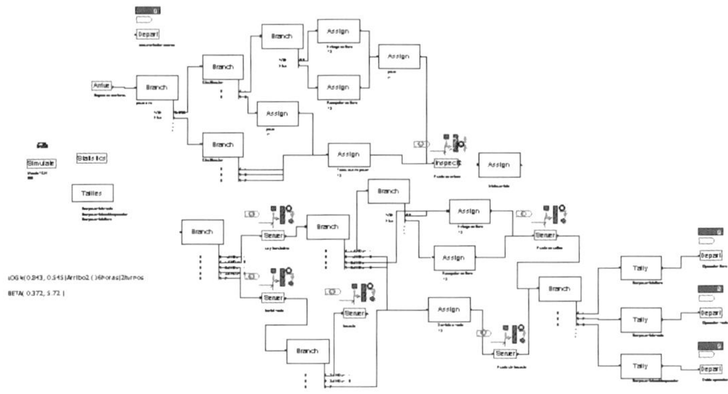

Figure 3. I Model of simulation for the proposed solution.

Table No. 1 Outputs obtained for the current variant and the proposed.

Variables		Blended value		Impact
		Before	**Proposed**	
Average number of	Quantity of loaded trucks	63	145	+82
trucks that carry out	Quantity of Unloaded trucks	174	128	-46
operations in the				
Terminal. (Trucks)	Quantity of loaded/unloaded trucks	59	76	+17
	Total of Operations	296	349	+ 53
Average waiting time of trucks in the door. (min)	Time of wait in the entrance door	59,15	2.15	- 57
Average time in the system. (min)	Time of trucks that load	97	45	-52
	Time of trucks that unload	79	42	-37
	Time of trucks that carry out double operation	102	68	-34
% of use of the doors.	Use of the doors	100	92	-8

The results obtained by means of the races of the simulation models allow to evidence that with the solution proposal substantial increments can be achieved in the level of borrowed service in the Terminal seen through the increase of the average number of trucks that carry out operations in 50, the decrease of an average of 57 minutes of average time of wait of the trucks in the door and the remarkable decrease of the average time, in the system, of the trucks according to the activity to develop.

References

1. ISO 9000:2000. *Sistemas de Gestión de la Calidad. Requisitos.*
2. Kelton W.D. y Law A.M. *Simulation Modeling & Analysis.* Second Edition. McGraw Hill, New York, 1991.
3. Kelton W.D. y Law A. M. *Simulation Modeling & Analysis.* Third Edition. Mc Graw Hill, New York, 2000.
4. Kelton W.D. y Sadowski R.P. *Simulation with Arena.* Mc Graw Hill. New York, 2004.
5. Peña, D. *Estadísticas Modelos y Métodos.* Segunda Edición. Madrid, 1994.
6. Pérez V. Ileana. *Procedimiento para la optimización de experimentos simulados,* Tesis para optar por el grado de Doctor en Ciencias Técnicas, La Habana, Cuba. 2001.
7. Walpole R. E., Myers R. M., Myers S. L *Probabilidades y Estadística para Ingenieros.* Prentice Hall, México, 1999.

NETWORKING AND LOGISTIC STRATEGIES ENACTING ASSEMBLING SYNERGISM[*]

RAUL O. DICHIARA

Depto. de Economía, UNS-CONICET, 12 de Octubre 1198, Piso 7º
Bahía Blanca, B-8000 CTX, Buenos Aires, Argentina

BLANCA I. NIEL

Depto. de Matemática, Universidad Nacional del Sur, Av. L. N. Alem 1253
Bahía Blanca, B-8000, Buenos Aires, Argentina

This paper shows selected strategies to propel synergism into distinct sets of entities. These have been identified amongst enterprises, factories, service facilities, economic agents, etc. After bringing together the specified items we assume a proposed target to this constituted group in order to drive efficiently toward the specific group's aim that contributes with a singled out effect in relation to the whole. Any posed objective should be produced with a minimum cost in terms of resources input. Hence, we introduce the associative rules for each assembling: cooperative network architecture and weighted linkages. Then, we display alternative logistic decision strategies: greedy, farthest neighbor, exhaustive, optimum search, heuristic strategies, etc. Finally, we exhibit for the case studies the better feasible response or almost optimum admissible response prompted from our systematic reasoning based on a series of concatenated papers that we have written in topics of associative networking, network architectures, transportation planning and decision making strategies.

---

[*] This work was partially supported by General Science and Technology Secretary, UNS. Grants 24-24-E/073 ("Desarrollo de redes y sistemas logísticos en el transporte de cargas como componente de la competitividad sistémica de la agroindustria y ramas industriales específicas en Argentina") and 24-E/074 ("Estrategias de organización y trayectorias productivas de Pymes Regionales. Desempeño en los mercados internos y de exportación").

1. Introduction

The positive externalities in the industry today are related to the *network* concept, contrary to the tradition in the industrial economics, based on the economies of scale. The proposition of the information economics *"it's better, ceteris paribus, to be connected to one bigger network than to a smaller one"* take the shape of *network externalities*, which have been described in three laws of the information economics, i.e. Sarnoff's, Metcalfe's and Reed's laws.

The aim of this research is to explain the role of the descentralized organization and the new information technology in order to obtain competitive strategic advantages related to the interdependent firms, manufacturing and/or service facilities, economic agents, etc. all of them as part of one network, growing so the added value of their production and/or logistic services.

The cooperation strategies herein networking markets make necessary to identify allies between customers, suppliers, competitors and innovators, with which one positive flow of feedbacks effects are set up. This new organizational paradigm introduces the concept of *virtual organization,* as one possibility to expand the production potential and improve the competitiveness of the Small and Medium Sized Enterprises.

2. Economies of Network

Decisions making of economic agents are pending on available information, which generally is not complete. More and better information brings about more accurate but expensive decisions.

The economic meaning in order to obtain, process and transfer information is then right away known. The information, defined as *"all of that which can be codified as a flow of bits"* (Carl Shapiro and Hal Varian, 1999)[1], is characterized as a good to which customers give different values according to different applications (e.g. entertainment or business). The customer's utility coming from the information is basic in order to price building in this market, since the production of this kind of goods has high fix costs but low marginal costs: when the first copy is produced, most of the costs are sunk costs and then will be no frontiers to obtain additional quantities (e.g. copies).

Other as common industrial markets, characterized as oligopoly, the new information economics is well know as one temporary monopoly. The reason is that the new economics is based on the network economy and the basic concept is the positive feedback.

The meaning of the positive externalities in the industry today is coming from the concept of network. There are *real* and *virtual* networks, depending on whether the links between nodes are physical or invisible connections. The basic economic characteristic of networks is that the connections value depends on the team member number before connected. The results to be integrated into a network are beneficial for all team members and there are explained by three basic laws:

1. David Sarnoff [a]: The spreading network's value growths proportional to n, the number of members in the audience, because the communications are only one way: one issuer and n receivers.
2. Robert M. Metcalfe[b] [2]: If there are n members within one network, and the network's value for each one is proportional to the number of others users, then the total value of the network for all members is proportional to $n(n-1)$. In fact, the n network's members want to be connected with all others, except with themselves (because it has no sense), as much time as members are into the networks. If this number is n, then the all possible contacts are $(n.n - n) = n^2 - n$. In other words, when the network's scale growths in the magnitude of one dozen, its value growths nearly in the magnitude of hundreds.
3. David P. Reed [3]: The Metcalfe's law undermines[c] the value of all connections because the utility of big networks, particularly social networks, grows exponentially with the network's scale. The reason for that is that the number of all possible members subgroups within the network is $2^n - n - 1$ where n is the number of members. Then, the linking possibilities between the n members are stated by 2^n parts of the body, minus the empty group (which is only one) and minus n, the number of network's members. Then, the number of subgroups grows faster than the number members (Sarnoff's law) other the number of possible links pairs (Metcalfe's law).

---

[a] Sarnoff, David (1891-1971) was bonn in Uzlian near Minsk in Bielorussia. He was radio and TV pioneer and entrepreneur in USA. He founded the NBC (National Broadcasting Company) and was Director of RCA (Radio Corporation of America) during different times from 1919 until his retirement in 1970.

[b] Metcalfe, Robert Melancton. During the '70 R.M. Metcalfe and D. R. Boggs did invent Ethernet, technology of local area which is used to connect thousands of computers all over the world. One thousand people connected to a network can take place at nearly one million different calls.

[c] Reed, David Patrick. "In 1995, the on-line business estimated for 1998 was U$S 2 until 3 billions, meanwhile the real value was nearly U$S 13 billlions".

If the set of entities is X, $P(X)$ symbolizes all the subsets *built from X*, e.g. $X(a,b,c)$, $P(X) = \{\phi\}, \{a\}, \{b\}, \{c\}, \{a,b\}, \{a,c\}, \{b,c\}, \{a,b,c\}$, i.e. $P(X)$ has $2^3 = 8$ subgroups. Each subgroup cardinality is computed according to the Tartaglia triangle procedure. In this case 1, 3, 3, 1. In general by the combinatorial numbers $\binom{n}{p} = \dfrac{n(n-1)...(n-p+1)}{p!}$. Consequently, if all subgroups are included in the network, its value grows exponentially compared with the case when only the original assembled nodes are considered.

3. Networking Enterprises

Each enterprise is one node in the network, whose aim is to add so much value as possible in the production and supplying process as member of that organization. The organizational scheme of enterprises has been changed from one hierarchical system (with economies of scale) to other one of networking enterprises, where economies of scope and flexible production systems, including the so called *virtual enterprise*, are the main distinctive features.

3.1. Cooperation in horizontal subnets

Each enterprise within the network has the same decision making capacity and the same possibility to set up a question interesting for all network's members. The firms have full capacity to link pairwise together. The links between Small and Medium Sized enterprises within the network and/or subnet are building following some rules in order to improve the better resource allocation [4]:

- To select step by step among those enterprises which bear more resemblance in this horizontal outlying structure;
- To select step by step its opposite among those enterprises which bear no resemblance in this horizontal outlying structure;
- To select the strategy (ies) leading to the most efficient outcome minimizing the total weights;
- To select the strategy (ies) leading to the most efficient outcome maximizing the total weights.

The aim of different linking strategies between enterprises is to improve the efficiency of groups (or subgroups) in order to optimize some magnitudes such as benefits, distance, cost, time, etc. improving the synergism into the network. The members of network are identified and they have $n(n-1)$ pairwise linkages. This network works subject to the restriction that all and each one enterprises must be connected into the final decision making circle and it can make it only one time, e.g. there are $(n-1)!$ linking cycles. For example, if $n = 7$ firms, then $(7-1)! = 6! = 720$ is the number of ways (both, coming and going) or communication possibilities between the seven enterprises.

Each network is built according to the principle that *"Each member enterprise within its own subnet develops one economic activity which defines the subnet of the firm"*. Each enterprise has a specific location and the linkages between them can be settled according to the following rules:

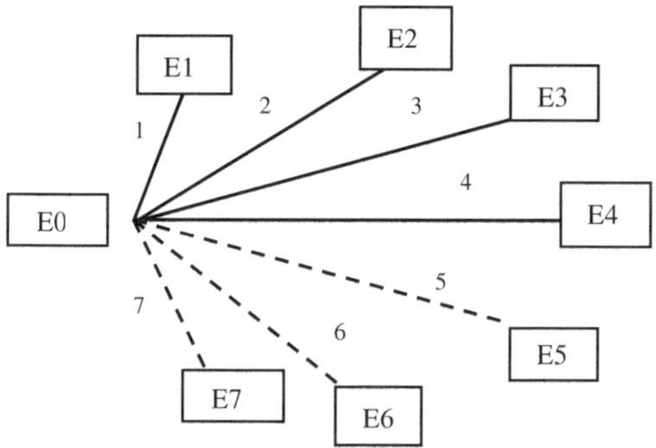

Figure 1. Integer weights of the links

- Rule 1: It goes from one enterprise E_0 to another one nearest E_1 according to clock wise. The rule 7: (n - 1) goes from one enterprise E_7 to another one nearest E_0 according to the counterclock wise. In both cases, the value of the link or *weight* is minimal $(w_1 = w_7 = 1)$.

- Rule 2: It goes from one enterprise E_0 over the next immediately arriving to the subsequent firm E_2 according to the clock wise. The rule 6: (n-2) means coming from one firm E_6 going over the next and arriving to the subsequent enterprise E_0 according to the counterclock wise. In both cases, the value of the link or *weight* is quasi minimal $(w_2 = w_6 = 2)$.

- Rule 3: It goes from one enterprise E_0 over the two next immediately arriving to the following firm E_3 according to the clock wise. The rule 5: (n-2) means coming from one firm E_5 going over the two next and arriving to the following enterprise E_0 according to the anti clock wise. In both cases, the value of the link or *weight* is quasi maximal $(w_3 = w_5 = 3)$.

318

In general, the rule k means coming from one firm E and going over (k -1) enterprises according to the clock wise. The rule (n - k) means going out from one enterprise and going over (k - 1) firms according to the counterclock wise.

- Rule 4: To select the opposite enterprise E_4. This is one particularly case and it is possible only if n is one even number. In fact, if n is one odd number, then the diameter (i.e. the opposite) does not exist. In first case (n is even), the value of link or *weight* positive is maximal $(w_4 = 4)$.

3.2. Cooperation in hub-subnets

One among other enterprises acts as manager decisions making (or *broker*) in relation to the other firms within the subnet. Each cyclical possible connection starts and finishes by this firm. This organizational structure can be used in case of any relation between SME purveyors and one big enterprise [5; 6].The interconnection strategy setting off from the hub enterprise and then to travel along all peripheral one according to some approximation strategy (e.g. greedy, anti-greedy, nearest neighbour, farthest neighbour, heuristic algorithm, etc.) to reach the optimum (or quasi-optimum) solutions for a specific aim. After the firms' aggregation, the methodology renders the existence or absence of full connectivity and all feasible connections. From the beginning of the disclosure we merge the words *connectivity* and *cooperation* as synonyms in any net, sub-net or hub sub-net architecture. The possible strategies are following [7]:

- Minimal Hub Net: One big enterprise is located at the hub of the horizontal architecture and all open cyclical results are used. In case of those strategies, whose aim is to connect with the nearest enterprises, it will be used the minimal journey with link 1; or with link 2; or with link 3 or with link 4 open. If $n = 8$, the cases finish there.
- Maximal Hub Net: In case of those strategies, whose aim is to connect with farthest enterprises, it will be used the maximal journey achieved with link 1; or with link 2 ; or with link 3 or with link 4 open. If $n = 8$, the cases finish there.

If n is even, then will be opened the link 1 (other case is to open the link 2, other is to open link 3). In general, it will be opened link $\frac{n}{2}$. There are $\frac{n}{2}$ different cases for the different connection strategies.

If n is odd, then can be opened the link 1. Other hub net will be achieved if it is opened the links 2, 3, etc. The open link (it can be link 1, or 2, or 3,...) is where the hub must in going and out going to the enterprises (or nodes) located in the peripheria.

4. Case Studies

4.1. Horizontal network of n local SMEs

Table 1. Socio economic attributes of SMEs in one horizontal network [d]

	Attribute	C	$-C$
1	Foundation's year of the firm	Before or during 1970 $\rightarrow c_1 = 1$	After 1970 $\rightarrow c_1 = -1$
2	¿Is the firm foundation related to the growth of big enterprises?	Yes $\rightarrow c_2 = 1$	No $\rightarrow c_2 = -1$
3	The enterprise is belonging to:	Only owner $\rightarrow c_3 = 1$	Society $\rightarrow c_3 = -1$
4	¿Which were the sale revenues during 2001 (incl. AVT)?	i) (\$0 a \$50.000]; ii) (\$50.000 a \$100.000]; iii) (\$100.000 a \$160.000]; iv) (\$160.000 a \$300.000]; v) (\$300.000 a \$1.000.000]; vi) (\$1.000.000 a \$1.500.000]; vii) (\$1.500.000 a \$3.000.000]; viii) (>\$3.000.000]	
5	¿The SME trades with big enterprises?	Yes $\rightarrow c_5 = 1$	No $\rightarrow c_5 = -1$
6	Number of employees of the firm. The scale is made with one threshold of 5 between 0 and 40		
7	¿Did the enterprise participate in training courses joining the personnel of big enterprises ?	Yes $\rightarrow c_7 = 1$	No $\rightarrow c_7 = -1$
8	¿Did the enterprise join universities, institutes and training centers?	Yes $\rightarrow c_8 = 1$	No $\rightarrow c_8 = -1$

Source: R.O. Dichiara et al., op.cit

The subnet architecture weighted the slight, mild and strong differences between members of each economic activity when they are located in the vertices of a

---

[d] Information obtained from the data basis of the project "Estudio de impacto económico. Empresas de la Cámara de Concesionarios y Permisionarios del Puerto de Bahía Blanca". R. O. Dichiara et al., Departamento de Economía, UNS. August, 2002.

regular $n-$gon. N_6^E subnet is built with suppliers related to the "road construction machinery" needs in the economic area. Moreover, the enterprises provide maintenances and services for the machinery, however they do not have the machineries for sale.

Each N_6^E enterprise member specific location abides with the rule of clockwise decreasing of the average turnover as well as of the amount of steady employees, from the starter node, that is to say from the best positioned firm, herein, the enterprise E_{140}. Hence, the strategy of connecting step by step between less differentiated firms is $E_{140} \rightarrow E_{145} \rightarrow E_{139} \rightarrow E_{67} \rightarrow E_{97} \rightarrow E_{104} \rightarrow E_{140}$ (Figure 2).

On the contrary, the strategy of connecting step by step between quasi-opposite or opposite firms is $E_{140} \rightarrow E_{139} \rightarrow E_{97} \rightarrow E_{145} \rightarrow E_{104} \rightarrow E_{67} \rightarrow E_{140}$ (Figure 2). The application of this methodology releases the existence of at least one cyclic connectivity ($E_{140} \rightarrow E_{139} \rightarrow E_{97} \rightarrow E_{145} \rightarrow E_{104} \rightarrow E_{67} \rightarrow E_{140}$) given a supposed strategy composed by four links between quasi-opposite firms and two linkages between opposite ranked firms.

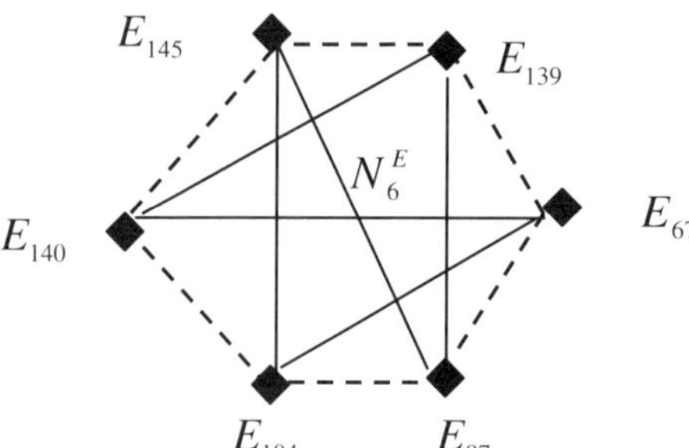

Figure 2. Nearest (dashed line) and Farthest (full line) strategies in N_6^E net

On the other hand, if the constraints were two links of each one of the available weighted connections, the method renders the absence of any cyclic strategy of linkage for the six firms integrated in N_6^E subnet. The linkage $E_{140} \rightarrow E_{139} \rightarrow E_{67} \rightarrow E_{140} \rightarrow E_{139} \rightarrow E_{67} \rightarrow E_{140}$ foresees the redundancy of the case (B.I. Niel, 2007) [8].

4.2. Hub subnet

The ensuing paragraph deploys a *hub subnet scheme* built by a horizontal peripheral architecture of SME's and a hub firm that eventually has whichever size and is engaged in another economic activity. The hub enterprise starts and ends up the cyclic information flux.

Let N_{H7}^{E} be the hub subnet of *"providers of electrical, electronic and/or computerized system service"* constructed with the small firms { E_8, E_{45}, E_{71}, E_{73}, E_{89}, E_{128}, E_{135} } and the role of the concentrator played by H_7^{E}. The paradigm of farthest neighbour renders the longest connectivity, e.g. $H_7^{E} \rightarrow E_{135} \rightarrow E_{89} \rightarrow E_{71} \rightarrow E_{73} \rightarrow E_{45} \rightarrow E_8 \rightarrow E_{128} \rightarrow H_7^{E}$ (Figure 3). The nearest neighbour step by step linkage renders the shortest feasible connectivity, e.g. $H_7^{E} \rightarrow E_{135} \rightarrow E_8 \rightarrow E_{73} \rightarrow E_{89} \rightarrow E_{128} \rightarrow E_{45} \rightarrow E_{71} \rightarrow H_7^{E}$ (Figure 3).

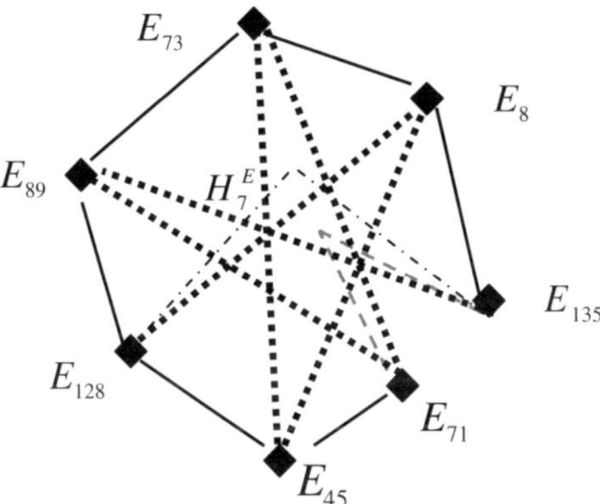

Figure 3. Nearest minimal bridge (full line) and farthest maximal bridge (dot line) Neighbour paradigms in N_{H7}^{E} hub subset

5. Conclusions

The SMEs surveyed firms constituted the entities of two case studies of networks built by cooperative principles. In detail, a horizontal architecture of SMEs and its hub-net variation. Each network's dynamics renders the pathways of feasible and optimum strategies and the shortest viable tours. These gathering of entities under an implemented organization and dynamics unveil knowledge about of several social, cultural, and economic aspects. In conclusion, business has the advantage of a logistics and distribution solution available in its surroundings. Furthermore, cost savings and faster turn-around decrease the rate of death of SMEs and will realize regional synergism.

References

1. C. Shapiro & H. Varian, Information Rules. A Strategic Guide to the Network Economy. Harvard Business Press (1999).
2. R. M. Metcalfe, Internet Collapses and Other InfoWorld Punditry (2000).
3. D. P. Reed, Weapon of Math Destruction. Context Magazine (1999).
4. R. O. Dichiara & B. I. Niel, Fostering connectivity in specific subnets of small and medium-sized enterprises. AMSE MS'08, Universitat de les Illes Balears, Spain (2008).
5. H. H. Erbe, Creation and management of networks of Small and Medium-Sized Enterprises in: R. O. Dichiara (Editor*) University Research and Education Requirements for Small and Medium Sized Enterprises.* Programme ALFA (2000-2005). ISBN 987-9871171-99-6. EdiUNS, Bahía Blanca (2008).
6. R. O. Dichiara, Relationships between Small and Big Enterprises in Suppliers Networks. The Case of Mass Production Industry. ICSB 48th World Conference. Belfast, Vol. 1, pp. 211 (2003).
7. R. O. Dichiara; B. I. Niel & Claverie, A., Networking and transportation planning for regional synergism. EMNet 2009, University of Sarajevo, Bosnia-Herzegovina (2009).
8. B. I. Niel, On a General Method for Finding the Longest Traveling Salesman Paths in Specific Networks. Proceedings of the XIV Congress of SIGEF. Poaina Brasov, Romania (2007).

FUZZY DECISION MAKING WITH PROBABILITIES AND INDUCED AGGREGATION OPERATORS[*]

JOSÉ M. MERIGÓ[1,2], KURT J. ENGEMANN[2]

[1]*Department of Business Administration, University of Barcelona,*
Av. Diagonal 690, 08034 Barcelona, Spain
[2]*Department of Information Systems, Hagan School of Business,*
IONA College, 10801 New Rochelle, NY, USA

We present a new approach for decision making under risk and uncertainty environments by using imprecise information that can be assessed with fuzzy numbers (FNs). We introduce the fuzzy induced probabilistic ordered weighted averaging (FIPOWA) operator. It is an aggregation operator that uses probabilities and OWAs in a unified framework that considers the degree of importance that each concept has in the analysis. Moreover, it also uses induced aggregation operators that represent a complex attitudinal character and FNs that considers the minimum and the maximum results and the possibility that the internal values may occur. We study some of its main properties and particular cases. We develop an application in a decision making problem about selection of strategies.

1. Introduction

The probability is a very useful tool for aggregating the information in risk environments. Another interesting aggregation operator is the ordered weighted averaging (OWA) operator [7]. It provides a parameterized family of aggregation operators that range from the minimum to the maximum. For further reading on the OWA operator and some of its applications, see [4,8,11].

We study different properties of the FIPOWA operator and different particular cases such as the fuzzy arithmetic Recently, some authors have tried to unify the probability and the OWA in the same formulation. It is worth noting the work developed by [2,9] about the concept of immediate probabilities. However, this model is not able to consider the degree of importance that each concept may have in the aggregation. This problem can be solved with the probabilistic OWA (POWA) operator [4,5] because it gives different degrees of

---

[*] This work is supported by the Spanish Ministry of Science and Innovation under project JC2009-00189.

importance to each concept so we are able to include them taking into account how relevant they are in the specific problem considered.

A more complete way for representing the OWA operator can be carried out by using induced aggregation operators [4,6,10] that use order inducing variables in the reordering step of the aggregation process. The main advantage is that it permits to consider more complex attitudinal characters of the decision maker that consider other aspects rather than the degree of optimism/pessimism such as psychological factors, time pressure and personal issues. Applying this concept to the POWA operator, we get the induced POWA (IPOWA) operator [4].

Usually, when using these approaches it is considered that the available information are simple exact numbers. However, this may not be the real situation found in the specific problem considered. Sometimes, the available information is vague or imprecise and it is not possible to analyze it with exact numbers. Then, it is necessary to use another approach that is able to assess the uncertainty such as the use of fuzzy numbers (FNs) [1,12]. By using FNs, we can consider a wide range of possible results included between the maximum and the minimum according to a membership function. Note that in the literature, there are a lot of studies dealing with uncertain information represented in the form of FNs such as [3-4].

In this paper, we present a new approach that unifies the IOWA operator with the probability when the available information is uncertain and can be assessed with FNs. We call it the fuzzy induced probabilistic ordered weighted averaging (FIPOWA) operator. The main advantage of this approach is that it unifies the IOWA and the probability taking into account the degree of importance that each concept has in the formulation and considering that the information is given with FNs. Thus, we are able to consider situations where we give more or less importance to the OWA and the probability depending on our interests and the problem analysed. Furthermore, by using the FIPOWA, we are able to use a complex reordering process in the OWA operator in order to represent complex attitudinal characters.

We also analyze the applicability of the new approach and we see that it is possible to develop an astonishingly wide range of applications. For example, we can apply it in a lot of problems about statistics, economics, engineering, decision theory and soft computing. In this paper, we focus on a decision making application in strategic management. We develop a decision making problem where a decision maker want to select an optimal strategy. The main advantage of the FIPOWA in these problems is that it is possible to consider the objective probability and the attitudinal character of the decision maker at the same time.

This paper is organized as follows. In Section 2 we revise some basic concepts. In Section 3 we present the new approach. Section 4 analyzes different families of FIPOWA operators. In Section 5 we develop an application of the new model and in Section 6 we summarize the main results of the paper.

2. Preliminaries

In this section we briefly review the FNs, the OWA, the IOWA and the POWA operator.

2.1. *Fuzzy Numbers*

The FN was first introduced by [1,12]. Since its introduction, it has been studied and applied by a lot of authors.

A FN is a fuzzy subset of a universe of discourse that is both convex and normal. Note that the FN may be considered as a generalization of the interval number although it is not strictly the same because the interval numbers may have different meanings.

In the literature, we find a wide range of FNs [3-4]. For example, a trapezoidal FN (TpFN) A of a universe of discourse R can be characterized by a trapezoidal membership function $A = (\underline{a}, \overline{a})$ such that

$$\begin{aligned}
\underline{a}(\alpha) &= a_1 + \alpha(a_2 - a_1), \\
\overline{a}(\alpha) &= a_4 - \alpha(a_4 - a_3).
\end{aligned} \tag{1}$$

where $\alpha \in [0, 1]$ and parameterized by (a_1, a_2, a_3, a_4) where $a_1 \le a_2 \le a_3 \le a_4$, are real values. Note that if $a_1 = a_2 = a_3 = a_4$, then, the FN is a crisp value and if $a_2 = a_3$, the FN is represented by a triangular FN (TFN). Note that the TFN can be parameterized by (a_1, a_2, a_4).

In the following, we are going to review the FN arithmetic operations as follows. Let A and B be two TFN, where $A = (a_1, a_2, a_3)$ and $B = (b_1, b_2, b_3)$:

1. $A + B = (a_1 + b_1, a_2 + b_2, a_3 + b_3)$
2. $A - B = (a_1 - b_3, a_2 - b_2, a_3 - b_1)$
3. $A \times k = (k \times a_1, k \times a_2, k \times a_3)$; for $k > 0$.

Sometimes, it is not clear how to reorder the arguments. Then, it is necessary to establish a criterion for comparing FNs. For simplicity, we recommend the following method. Select the FN with the highest value in its highest membership level, usually, when $\alpha = 1$. Note that if the membership level $\alpha = 1$ is an interval, then, we will calculate the average of the interval. If there is still a tie, we recommend the use of an average or a weighted average of the FN according to the interests of the decision maker.

Note that other operations and ranking methods could be studied [3-4] but in this paper we focus on these ones.

2.2. *The OWA Operator*

The OWA operator was introduced by Yager [7] and it provides a parameterized family of aggregation operators that include the arithmetic mean, the maximum and the minimum. It can be defined as follows.

Definition 1. An OWA operator of dimension n is a mapping OWA: $R^n \to R$ that has an associated weighting vector W of dimension n such that the sum of the weights is 1 and $w_j \in [0, 1]$, then:

$$OWA\ (a_1, a_2, \ldots, a_n) = \sum_{j=1}^{n} w_j b_j \tag{2}$$

where b_j is the jth largest of the a_i.

2.3. *The Induced OWA Operator*

The IOWA operator [10] is an extension of the OWA operator that uses order inducing variables in the reordering step. It can be defined as follows:

Definition 2. An IOWA operator is a mapping IOWA: $R^n \times R^n \to R$ that has an associated weighting vector W with $w_j \in [0, 1]$ and $\sum_{j=1}^{n} w_j = 1$, such that:

$$IOWA\ (\langle u_1, a_1 \rangle, \langle u_2, a_2 \rangle, \ldots, \langle u_n, a_n \rangle) = \sum_{j=1}^{n} w_j b_j \tag{3}$$

where b_j is the a_i value of the IOWA pair $\langle u_i, a_i \rangle$ having the jth largest u_i, u_i is the order inducing variable and a_i is the argument variable.

2.4. *The Probabilistic OWA Operator*

The probabilistic ordered weighted averaging (POWA) operator is an aggregation operator that unifies the probability and the OWA operator in the same formulation considering the degree of importance that each concept has in the problem [4-5]. It can be defined as follows.

Definition 3. A POWA operator of dimension n is a mapping POWA: $R^n \rightarrow R$ that has an associated weighting vector W of dimension n such that $w_j \in [0, 1]$ and $\sum_{j=1}^{n} w_j = 1$, according to the following formula:

$$POWA\ (a_1, \ldots, a_n) = \sum_{j=1}^{n} \hat{p}_j b_j \tag{4}$$

where b_j is the jth largest of the a_i, each argument a_i has an associated probability p_i with $\sum_{i=1}^{n} p_i = 1$ and $p_i \in [0, 1]$, $\hat{p}_j = \beta w_j + (1-\beta)p_j$, being β a parameter such that $\beta \in [0, 1]$ and p_j is the probability p_i ordered according to b_j, that is, according to the jth largest of the a_i.

3. The Fuzzy Induced Probabilistic OWA Operator

The fuzzy induced POWA (FIPOWA) operator is an aggregation operator that uses the probability and the OWA in the same formulation. It also uses order inducing variables in order to represent the reordering process, from a more general point of view. Moreover, the FIPOWA also deals with an uncertain environment that cannot be assessed with exact numbers but it is possible to use FNs. It can be defined as follows.

Definition 4. Let Ψ be the set of FNs. A FIPOWA operator of dimension n is a mapping FIPOWA: $\Psi^n \times \Psi^n \rightarrow \Psi$ that has an associated weighting vector W of dimension n such that $w_j \in [0, 1]$ and $\sum_{j=1}^{n} w_j = 1$, according to the following formula:

$$FIPOWA\ (\langle u_1, \tilde{a}_1 \rangle, \ldots, \langle u_n, \tilde{a}_n \rangle) = \sum_{j=1}^{n} \hat{p}_j b_j \tag{5}$$

where b_j is the $\tilde{a}_i$ value of the FIPOWA pair $\langle u_i, \tilde{a}_i \rangle$ having the jth largest u_i, u_i is the order inducing variable, each argument $\tilde{a}_i$ is a FN and it has an associated weight p_i with $\sum_{i=1}^{n} p_i = 1$ and $p_i \in [0, 1]$, $\hat{p}_j = \beta w_j + (1-\beta) p_j$ with $\beta \in [0, 1]$ and p_j is the weight p_i ordered according to b_j, that is, according to the jth largest of the $\tilde{a}_i$.

Note that it is also possible to formulate the FIPOWA operator separating the part that strictly affects the OWA operator and the probability.

Definition 5. Let Ψ be the set of interval numbers. A FIPOWA operator is a mapping FIPOWA: $\Psi^n \times \Psi^n \to \Psi$ of dimension n, if it has an associated weighting vector W, with $\sum_{j=1}^{n} w_j = 1$ and $w_j \in [0, 1]$ and a weighting vector P, with $\sum_{i=1}^{n} p_i = 1$ and $p_i \in [0, 1]$, such that:

$$FIPOWA\ (\langle u_1, \tilde{a}_1 \rangle, \ldots, \langle u_n, \tilde{a}_n \rangle) = \beta \sum_{j=1}^{n} w_j b_j + (1-\beta) \sum_{i=1}^{n} p_i \tilde{a}_i \tag{6}$$

where b_j is the $\tilde{a}_i$ value of the FIPOWA pair $\langle u_i, \tilde{a}_i \rangle$ having the jth largest u_i, u_i is the inducing variable, each argument $\tilde{a}_i$ is a FN and $\beta \in [0, 1]$.

Note that different types of FNs could be used in the aggregation such as TFNs, TpFNs, L-R FNs, interval-valued FNs, intuitionistic FNs and more complex structures.

When using FNs in the OWA operator, we have the additional problem of how to reorder the arguments. In the FIPOWA operator, this is not a problem because the reordering process is developed with order inducing variables and it is independent of the values of the arguments. However, in a decision making problem, we need to carry out a ranking process between the final results of each alternative considered. For these cases, we recommend to use, for example, the method commented in the section of FNs.

Note that it is possible to distinguish between the descending FIPOWA (DFIPOWA) and the ascending FIPOWA (AFIPOWA) operator.

If the weighting vector is not normalized, i.e., $W = \sum_{j=1}^{n} w_j \neq 1$, or $P = \sum_{j=1}^{n} p_i \neq 1$, then, the FIPOWA operator can be expressed as:

$$FIPOWA\ (\langle u_1, \tilde{a}_1 \rangle,\ \ldots,\ \langle u_n, \tilde{a}_n \rangle) = \frac{\beta}{W} \sum_{j=1}^{n} w_j b_j + \frac{(1-\beta)}{P} \sum_{i=1}^{n} p_i \tilde{a}_i \qquad (7)$$

Note that it is possible to consider that the weights of the FIPOWA operator are also FNs or other uncertain techniques such as interval numbers.

The FIPOWA operator is monotonic, bounded and idempotent. Another interesting issue when analysing the FIPOWA operator is the problem of ties in the order inducing variables. In order to solve this problem, we recommend to follow the policy explained by Yager and Filev [10]. Basically, the idea is to replace each argument of the tied inducing variables by its fuzzy average.

A further interesting issue to consider is the different families of FIPOWA operators that are found by analyzing the weighting vector W and the coefficient β. If we look to the coefficient β, we get the following particular cases.

- If $\beta = 1$, we get the FIOWA operator.
- If $\beta = 0$, we get the fuzzy probabilistic approach.

Note that other families of FIPOWA operators could be studied following Merigó [4] and Yager [8].

4. Application in Strategic Decision Making

In the following, we are going to develop a brief example where we will see the applicability of the new approach. We will focus in a decision making problem about selection of strategies. Note that other business decision making applications could be developed such as financial decision making or human resource selection. Note that the FIPOWA operator may be applied in similar problems than the IOWA and the probabilistic approach such as in statistics, engineering, economics and soft computing.

Assume a company that operates in North America and Europe is analyzing the general policy for the next year and they consider 5 possible strategies.

- A_1 = Expand to the Asian market.
- A_2 = Expand to the South American market.
- A_3 = Expand to the African market.
- A_4 = Expand to the 3 continents.
- A_5 = Do not develop any expansion.

In order to evaluate these strategies, the group of experts considers that the key factor is the economic situation of the next year. Thus, depending on the situation, the expected benefits will be different. The experts have considered 5 possible situations: S_1 = Very bad, S_2 = Bad, S_3 = Regular, S_4 = Good, S_5 = Very good. The expected results depending on the situation S_i and the alternative A_i are shown in Table 1. Note that the results are TFNs.

Table 1. Available strategies.

	S_1	S_2	S_3	S_4	S_5
A_1	(30,40,50)	(50,60,70)	(70,80,90)	(90,100,110)	(70,80,90)
A_2	(60,70,80)	(60,70,80)	(50,60,70)	(80,90,100)	(50,60,70)
A_3	(70,80,90)	(70,80,90)	(70,80,90)	(50,60,70)	(40,50,60)
A_4	(50,60,70)	(40,50,60)	(70,80,90)	(80,90,100)	(70,80,90)
A_5	(20,30,40)	(50,60,70)	(60,70,80)	(90,100,110)	(70,80,90)

In this problem, the experts consider the weighting vector W = (0.3, 0.3, 0.2, 0.1, 0.1) and the probabilistic vector P = (0.3, 0.3, 0.2, 0.1, 0.1). Note that the probabilities have a degree of importance of 60% and the OWAs, 40%. Due to the fact that the attitudinal character is very complex the experts use order inducing variables to express it.

Table 2. Order inducing variables.

	S_1	S_2	S_3	S_4	S_5
A_1	20	13	14	45	12
A_2	30	26	7	12	32
A_3	12	21	43	16	30
A_4	12	15	17	30	47
A_5	23	28	31	12	10

With this information, we can aggregate it in order to take a decision. In Table 3, we show different results obtained by using different types of FIPOWA operators.

Table 3. Aggregated results.

	FIOWA	FPOWA	FIPOWA
A_1	(62,72,82)	(60.4,70.4,80.4)	(57.2,67.2,77.2)
A_2	(58,68,78)	(61,71,81)	(58.6,68.6,78.6)
A_3	(59,69,79)	(65,75,85)	(62.6,72.6,82.6)
A_4	(68,78,89)	(60.8,70.8,80.8)	(60.8,70.8,80.8)
A_5	(53,63,73)	(56.2,66.2,76.2)	(50.6,60.6,70.6)

If we establish an ordering of the alternatives, we get the following results shown in Table 4. Note that in this example it is not necessary to establish a criterion for ranking FNs because it is clear which alternative goes first, second and so on, in the ordering process. Note also that "$\succ$" means "preferred to" and "=" means "equal to".

Table 4. Ordering of the strategies.

	Ordering
FIOWA	$A_4 \succ A_1 \succ A_3 \succ A_2 \succ A_5$
FPOWA	$A_3 \succ A_2 \succ A_4 \succ A_1 \succ A_5$
FIPOWA	$A_3 \succ A_4 \succ A_2 \succ A_1 \succ A_5$

As we can see, depending on the aggregation operator used, the ordering of the strategies may be different. Therefore, the decision about which strategy select may be also different. For example, A_3 is the optimal choice with the FPOWA and the FIPOWA. With the FIOWA we select A_4.

5. Conclusions

We have presented the FIPOWA operator. It is a new aggregation operator that unifies the IOWA operator with the probability when the available information is uncertain and can be assessed with FNs. The main advantage of this operator is that it provides more complete information because it represents the information in a more complete way considering the maximum and the minimum results and the possibility that the internal values will occur. We have studied some of its main properties and particular cases.

We have analysed the applicability of the new approach and we have seen that it is very broad because it can be applied in a lot of problems that were previously studied with the probability or the OWA. In this paper, we have focussed on an application in strategic management. We have seen that depending on the particular type of FIPOWA operator used the results may lead to different decisions.

In future research, we expect to develop further developments by using other types of information such as linguistic variables. We will also add other characteristics in order to obtain a more complete formulation such as generalized and quasi-arithmetic means, distance measures and t-norms. Finally, we will also develop different types of applications especially in decision theory but also in other fields such as statistics, engineering and economics.

Acknowledgements

Support from the Spanish Ministry of Science and Innovation under project "JC2009-00189" is gratefully acknowledged.

References

1. S.S.L. Chang and L.A. Zadeh, On fuzzy mapping and control, *IEEE Trans. Syst. Man Cybern. B* **2**, 30, (1972).
2. K.J. Engemann, D.P. Filev and R.R. Yager, Modelling decision making using immediate probabilities, *Int. J. General Syst.* **24**, 281 (1996).
3. A. Kaufmann and M.M. Gupta, Introduction to fuzzy arithmetic (Publications Van Nostrand, Rheinhold, 1985).
4. J.M. Merigó, *New extensions to the OWA operators and their application in decision making* (PhD thesis (in Spanish), Department of Business Administration, University of Barcelona, 2008).
5. J.M. Merigó, Probabilistic decision making with the OWA operator and its application in investment management, *Proc. IFSA-EUSFLAT 2009*, Lisbon, Portugal, 2009, pp. 1364-1369.
6. J.M. Merigó and A.M. Gil-Lafuente, The induced generalized OWA operator, *Inform. Sci.* **179**, 729 (2009).
7. R.R. Yager, On ordered weighted averaging aggregation operators in multi-criteria decision making, *IEEE Trans. Syst. Man Cybern. B* **18**, 183 (1988).
8. R.R. Yager, Families of OWA operators, *Fuzzy Sets Syst.* **59**, 125 (1993).
9. R.R. Yager, K.J. Engemann and D.P. Filev, On the concept of immediate probabilities, *Int. J. Intelligent Syst.* **10**, 373 (1995).
10. R.R. Yager and D.P. Filev, Induced ordered weighted averaging operators, *IEEE Trans. Syst. Man Cybern. B* **29**, 141 (1999).
11. R.R. Yager and J. Kacprzyk, *The ordered weighted averaging operators: Theory and applications*. Norwell: Kluwer Academic Publishers, 1997.
12. L.A. Zadeh, The Concept of a Linguistic Variable and its application to Approximate Reasoning. Part 1, *Inform. Sci.* **8** (1975) 199-249, Part 2, *Inform. Sci.* **8** (1975) 301-357, Part 3, *Inform. Sci.* **9** (1975) 43-80.

ARTIFICIAL INTELLINGENCE ON THE ROUTING PROCESS OPTIMIZATION

OMAR DANILO CASTRILLÓN, DIANA MARIA CARDENAS, JAIME ALBERTO GIRALDO, LINA ELIANA AVILA

Industrial engineering department Universidad Nacional de Colombia
Manizales, Caldas, 17001, Colombia

The aim of this paper[*] is to optimize the routing process in companies of distribution in parcel delivery sector, thus increasing using times of vehicle, reducing idle time, through the study of major techniques among artificial intelligence. This paper has two parts: The first part is the identification and definition of a methodology for the sequencing of orders in the delivery process. The second part is the demonstration of effectiveness of this computer system in comparison with the optimal solution. This research was carried out in a parcel delivery company in the sector, where scheduling orders are improved through a evolutionary algorithm, diminishing the total processing time and hence total idle time. Likewise, in this document people can analyze the behavior of other variables, taking into account different sequencing techniques.

1. Introduction

Traditionally, companies have focused on production process (To Produce) and marketing (To sell), but organizations or enterprises are more complex. Areas such as: Marketing, purchasing, customer service, accounting, among others, depend on a good logistic, which allows an adequate customer chain integration Provider [1, 2]. One aspect in which, the quality is highly related to the satisfaction of service [3].

This article, study problems of logistics in a courier company, where the requirement for a fast and efficient transportation has great importance [4]; especially when analyzing the current speed of delivery to markets, aspects that together with another factors, point out a great demand and efficiency in transport [5].

---

* This paper derives from the participation of the authors in a research Project financed by the Research Vice-presidency of the Universidad Nacional de Colombia, entitled "production sequencing using evolutionary algorithms. Application to Job Shop environments".

In these companies, the transportation problem is integrated with the inventory behavior, where the main difficulty is minimize transportation costs and inventory at each site of the company, while the delivery time must be defined, for the different orders, increased its efficiency [6, 7]. Sometimes it is necessary to include transportation costs, deliveries cost, like the car rental cost, a cost proportional to the number of vehicles used [8].

Some authors [9] have attempted to provide more complex solutions to this problem, where the variables considered above, and the deviations of workloads are described.

Similarly the Artificial intelligence techniques, as expert systems, ant colony, fuzzy logic, particle swarm optimization, binary particle swarms optimization, neural networks, clone selection, etc, these techniques are capable to imitate the complex processes of a human mind. They found solutions very quickly.

Based on above techniques, intelligent transportation systems have been designed [10], algorithms of efficient search, in order to optimize or sub optimize the main variables of the previous problem [11]. In general, artificial intelligence techniques have been applied to solve all sorts of problems related to transport systems [12, 13, 14, 15].

The objective of this work is to find, the best possible way to collect all the orders in a courier company. When these orders are sending to their final destination, the most appropriate way for distribution must be found. A problem that due to its large number of possibilities N! (Number of orders) may be considered as a NP-Hard problem. This problem will be resolved by the following techniques: genetic algorithms, randomized algorithms and genetic-random algorithms, etc.

2. Methodology

Step 1: Representation. This route scheduling problem can be represented by a vector U. The value of each position will represent the order number and position of the vector will determine the position in which the order J is treated. $U = [U_1, U_2, U_3, ..., U_J, ..., U_n]$. For example, in the figure 1, the vector $V = [1, 2, 4, 6, 5, 3, 7, 8]$ will represent the sequence that must be routed in each of the different orders. Several initial solutions are randomly constructed, which represent a valid solution to the problem.

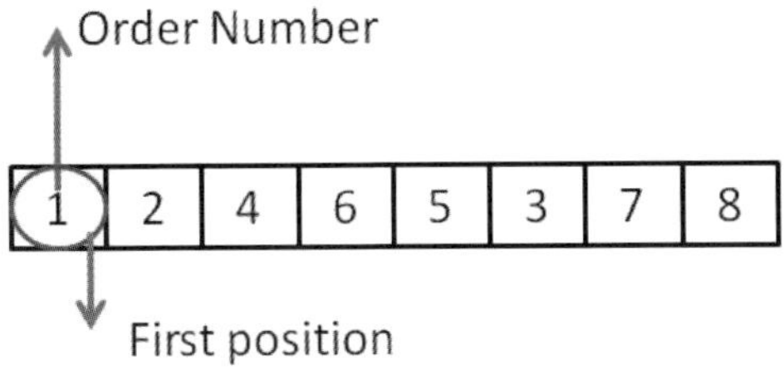

Figure 1. Initial solution.

Step 2: Evolution. New solutions are generated, from the initial solutions. The first solutions set are constructed by a genetic algorithm. These techniques employed the processes of genetic combination 99% and/or genetic mutation 1%, implement any measures necessary to set in the optimization or sub optimization of the problem desired.

The second solutions set are generated by a random algorithm. These techniques are based in the following theory: Each point, in the solution space can be generated with equal probability. If a large solutions number are generated, the probability to find the optimum solution tends to one.

The above actions will cover the solution spaces in order to achieve the best optimization possible.

Note: The proposed problem will be solved by the following intelligence techniques: genetic algorithms, randomized algorithms and genetic-random algorithm, etc.

Step 3: Fitness and Stop. For each of the solutions found in the previous step, evaluate the quality of the answer found. Under the following functions calculated (Fitness):

$$X_{ij} = \begin{cases} 1 \ \textit{if the solution is between the location } i \textit{ and location } j \\ \qquad 0 \ \textit{in other cases} \end{cases} \qquad \text{eq. (1)}$$

$$Min \ z = \ \sum_i \sum_j C_{ij} X_{ij} \qquad \text{eq. (2)}$$

subject to:

$$\sum_{i=1}^{N} X_{ij} = 1 \ \ for \ j = 1,2,3,4 \dots N \qquad \text{eq. (3)}$$

$$\sum_{j=1}^{N} X_{ij} = 1 \ for \ j = 1,2,3,4 \dots N \qquad\qquad \text{eq. (4)}$$

$$U_i - U_j + NX_{ij} \leq N - 1$$
$$For \ I <> j \ i = 1,2,3, \dots N; j = 1,2,3 \dots N \qquad\qquad \text{eq. (5)}$$

Equation (2) represents the total distance of arches, the constraint equation (3) allows only to pass once through each location, the constraint equation (4) ensures that each location is left behind only once, the constraint equation (5) ensures: a) Not including sets X_{ij} that include a subtour. b) Any set X_{ij} that forms a tour is feasible, i.e. U_j exists and satisfies the equation (5), where U_j is the position where the order will be attended j. Additionally, N represents the number of orders, C_{ij} is the cost of picking up an order from location i in location j, when $C_{ij} = M$, there is no possible route between locations i and j. [16]. The last two steps, are performed until not be possible to obtain a better solution.

Step 4: Approximation. To analyze the approximation of the solutions regarding the optimal or suboptimal solution, it has been calculated the best and the worst solution to the problem. The latter will determine the range in which the solutions move, giving the rate of approximation of the solutions on this range. This allows to establish the effectiveness of the proposed methodology.

Step 5: Variance analysis. In order to certify the consistency of the methodology, it is necessary to repeat the methodology for any number of times (treatments or other techniques to solve the problem). In each of the treatments, the ten best results on the fitness functions are taken as reference. In order to determine if the results correspond statistically to similar or different treatments, an analysis of variance under the following model is done: $y_i = \mu + T_i + \varepsilon_i$, where Y_i represents the response variables, T_i , the effects caused by the ith y ε_i, treatment, and i^{th} is the experimental error. At this point, it is important to verify that the information collected agree the requirements of independence and normality statistical, which allow to applying the required tests. The figure 2, Show this methodology.

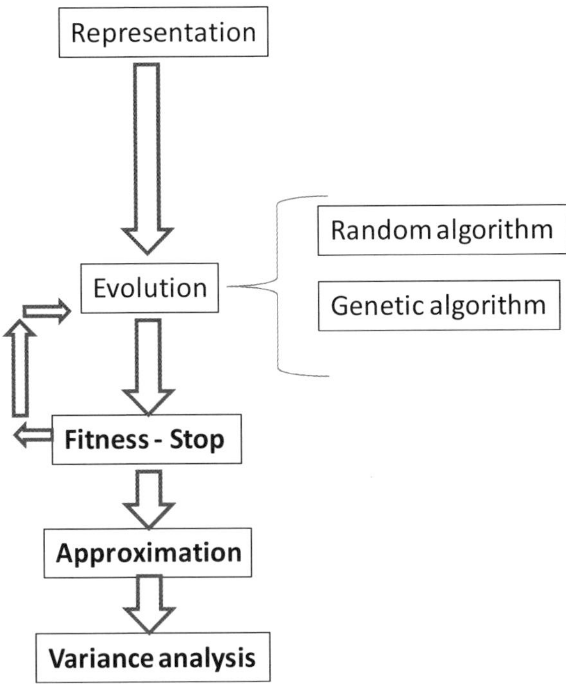

Figure 2. Proposed Methodology.

3. Experimentation

An analysis of Table 1 shows the number of possibilities, which are figure out for a number of orders N, where $7 <= N <= 18$.

Table 1. Number of possibilities.

Order N	Possibilities N!
7	5.040
8	40.320
9	362.880
10	3.628.800
11	39.916.800
12	479.001.600
13	**6.227.020.800**
14	87.178.291.200
15	1.307.674.368.000
16	20.922.789.888.000
17	355.687.428.096.000
18	6.402.373.705.728.000

Table 1 shows that computationally, it is only possible to calculate the optimum in reasonable time, for values of N >= 13. However, as experimentation, a problem with N = 18, show in Table 2.

Given the design of the problem (see Table 2) it can be deduced that this presents an optimum of 190, with the following sequence [1, 2, 3, 4, 5, 6, 7, 8, 9, 10, 11, 12, 13, 14, 15, 16, 17, 18]. Similarly, it can deduce the worst solution of the problem: [1 18 2 17 3 16 4 15 5 14 6 13 7 12 8 11 9 10] at a cost of 1550. Consequently the cost of the solutions of the problem will move in a range between 0 and 1360. The last value will use as a reference, showing the effectiveness of the proposed algorithm.

Table 2. Problem object of the study. 36.402.373.705.728.000 Possibilities

N	1	2	3	4	5	6	7	8	9	10	11	12	13	14	15	16	17	18
1	M	30	40	50	60	70	80	90	100	110	120	130	140	150	160	170	180	190
2	30	M	10	20	30	40	50	60	70	80	90	100	110	120	130	140	150	160
3	40	10	M	10	20	30	40	50	60	70	80	90	100	110	120	130	140	150
4	50	20	10	M	10	20	30	40	50	60	70	80	90	100	110	120	130	140
5	60	30	20	10	M	10	20	30	40	50	60	70	80	90	100	110	120	130
6	70	40	30	20	10	M	10	20	30	40	50	60	70	80	90	100	110	120
7	80	50	40	30	20	10	M	10	20	30	40	50	60	70	80	90	100	110
8	90	60	50	40	30	20	10	M	10	20	30	40	50	60	70	80	90	100
9	100	70	60	50	40	30	20	10	M	10	20	30	40	50	60	70	80	90
10	110	80	70	60	50	40	30	20	10	M	10	20	30	40	50	60	70	80
11	120	90	80	70	60	50	40	30	20	10	M	10	20	30	40	50	60	70
12	130	100	90	80	70	60	50	40	30	20	10	M	10	20	30	40	50	60
13	140	110	100	90	80	70	60	50	40	30	20	10	M	10	20	30	40	50
14	150	120	110	100	90	80	70	60	50	40	30	20	10	M	10	20	30	40
15	160	130	120	110	100	90	80	70	60	50	40	30	20	10	M	10	20	30
16	170	140	130	120	110	100	90	80	70	60	50	40	30	20	10	M	10	20
17	180	150	140	130	120	110	100	90	80	70	60	50	40	30	20	10	M	10
18	190	160	150	140	130	120	110	100	90	80	70	60	50	40	30	20	10	M

4. Discussions and Results

Step 1-4: Although the best solutions found, with these three techniques, are quite good (see Table 3), they are slightly separate from the optimal solution. According to the effectiveness of the solutions it is important to point out that the scale of the solution is in a range between 0 and 1360, therefore, it is necessary to adjust each of the solutions found in this range. This is achieved by subtracting the value of the optimal cost (190) from each of the solutions generated. Then, the approximate percentage of this last value is calculated, in the new range (0 - 1360), where zero represents the optimum and 1360 the worst solution (See Table 3).

Table 3. Solutions found, with these techniques. Approximate optimal solution

Ruta																		Costo	Referencia 0 -1360	% Aproximación
1	2	3	4	5	6	7	8	9	10	11	15	18	17	16	14	13	12	250	60	95.58%
1	2	3	4	5	6	7	8	9	10	11	16	17	18	15	14	13	12	250	60	95.58%
1	2	3	4	5	6	7	8	9	10	15	18	17	16	14	13	12	11	260	70	94.48%
1	2	3	4	5	6	7	8	9	14	16	18	17	15	13	12	11	10	260	70	94.48%
1	2	3	4	5	6	7	8	9	10	14	15	13	11	12	16	17	18	270	80	94.11%
1	5	6	4	2	3	7	8	9	10	11	12	13	14	15	16	17	18	270	80	94.11%

Step 5: Finally, an analysis of Table 4 shows the treatment with the algorithms such as: genetic algorithms, random algorithms and genetic - random algorithm. They show similar results, which establishes those proposed algorithms are similar. In addition, Table 4 shows that solutions are consistent. They do not show great variability.

Table 4. Analysis of variance

T proceso	Repeticiones										Sum
	1	2	3	4	5	6	7	8	9	10	
Alg. Genet	250	250	260	260	270	270	250	250	250	260	2369
Alg. Aleat	240	250	250	260	270	250	240	250	260	260	2530
Alg Gen - Ale	260	260	250	270	290	240	250	250	250	300	2620

Fuente Varia	GL	SC	CM	Fcal	F Tabla
Sum C Total		47188,97			
Tratamiento	2,00	3234,07	1617,03	0,99	3,35
Error Exper	27,00	43954,90	1627,96		
Total	29,00	47188,97	3244,99		
EL MODELO NO ES SIGNIFICATIVO					

5. Conclusions

According to an analysis of variance, the different solutions found by these artificial intelligence techniques show that there are no significant differences among results found in different kinds of the algorithms: Genetic algorithm, random algorithm, and the combination of both. Thus, this new technique analyzed allows found average solutions with an approximation, respecting to the optimal solution of 94.72%, according to the variable studied. As a future line of research it is proposed that the behavior of the parameters of the evolutionary algorithm can be studied in order to improve its effectiveness.

References

1.   H. Wang, H. WeiHsu. A closed-loop logistic model with a spanning-tree based genetic algorithm. Computers & Operations Research, 37, 2010, 376–389.
2.   José RM. La función de la logística en la empresa. Consultado de: http://www.barandilleros.com/la-funcion-de-la-logistica-en-la-empresa.html. Revisado Septiembre 2009.

3. K. de Ruyter, M. Wetzels, J. Lemmink, et al. The dynamics of the service delivery process: A value-based Approach. International Journal of Research in Marketing 14, 1997, 231–243.

4. F. Lasserre. Logistics and the Internet: transportation and location issues are crucial in the logistics chain. Journal of Transport Geography 12, 2004, 73–84.

5. D. Rondinelli, M. Berry. Multimodal Transportation, Logistics, and the Environment: Managing Interactions in a Global Economy. European Management Journal. 18, 4, 2000, 398–410.

6. E. Kutanoglu, D. Lohiya. Integrated inventory and transportation mode selection: A service parts logistics system. Transportation Research Part E, 44, 2008, 665–683.

7. S. Bock. Real-time control of freight forwarder transportation networks by integrating multimodal transport chains. European Journal of Operational Research, 200, 2010, 733–746.

8. Z. Pan, J. Tang, R. Y.K. Fung. Synchronization of inventory and transportation under flexible vehicle constraint: A heuristics approach using sliding windows and hierarchical tree structure. European Journal of Operational Research, 192, 2009, 824–836.

9. S.H. Zegordi, M.A. Beheshti. A multi-population genetic algorithm for transportation scheduling. Transportation Research Part E 45, 2009, 946–959.

10. T.G. Crainic, M. Gendreau, J. Potvin. Intelligent freight-transportation systems: Assessment and the contribution of operations research. Transportation Research Part C 17, 2009, 541–557.

11. J. Huang, M. Yao. On the coordination of maintenance scheduling for transportation fleets of many branches of a logistic service provider. Computers and Mathematics with Applications. 56, 2008, 1303–1313.

12. R. Zhang, W. Young Yun, I. Moon. A reactive tabu search algorithm for the multi-depot container truck transportation problem. Transportation Research Part E 45, 2009, 904–914.

13. X. Wang, T.C.E. Cheng. Logistics scheduling to minimize inventory and transport costs. International Journal Production Economics, 121, 2009, 266–273.

14. Adam Redmer. Optimisation of the exploitation period of individual vehicles in freight transportation companies. Transportation Research Part E 45, 2009, 978–987.

15. 16.B.Q. Rieksts, J.A.Ventura. Two-stage inventory models with a bi-modal transportation cost. Computers & Operations Research, 37, 2010, 20–31.

16. W.L. Wynston. Investigación de operaciones. Aplicaciones y algoritmos. Thomson Editores. México 2005.

A PERSONNEL SELECTION MODEL WITHIN THE STRATEGIC HUMAN RESOURCES MANAGEMENT PROCESS USING THE GALOIS GROUP THEORY

ARAS KEROPYAN, ANNA MARIA GIL-LAFUENTE

Department of Economics and Business Organization, University of Barcelona
Avinguda Diagonal, 690
08034 Barcelona, Spain

In this paper, we propose a personnel selection model based on the comparison between the qualifications of prospective candidates and established characteristics of the offered position within the human resources recruitment process. The model based on the Galois group theory will allow us to group different candidates depending on the common characteristics that meet a certain level. The result will enable us to select the most proper candidates who meet those prioritized characteristics that are set by the company for the offered job.

Keywords: Personnel Selection, Galois Group Theory, Human Resources Management, Recruitment, Galois Lattices

1. Introduction

Human factor is getting even more important for the companies which want to be distinguished among their rivals, ensure their existence in the competitive market conditions and increase their profits. In order to achieve these goals, companies intend to select the most adequate candidates for them and hire the best employees to be in front of their competitors in the market and achieve their high financial goals.

To settle the most adequate employee in his rightful place is not always an easy task. Job assignment demands perfect knowledge of personal qualities and activities. On the other hand, the rapid evolution of science and techniques requires permanent dynamism in adaptation to jobs, which should satisfy both the company objectives and the employee.

Considering the rapid changing factors in the business world and the increase of the importance of human factor in companies, we think that some mathematical models can be applicable to improve personal selection process inside the human resources activities.

2. Human Resources and Strategic Human Resources Management

The Human Resources (HR) and Strategic Human Resources Management (SHRM) concepts are widely confused. The field of SHRM is different from traditional HR management research in two distinctive forms. First of all, SHRM focuses on organizational performance rather than individual performance. In the second place, strategy of human resources focuses on the role of HR management systems as solutions to business problems rather than individual HR management practices. But the word "strategic" refers more than to systems focuses and financial performances. 'Strategy is about building sustainable competitive advantage that in turn creates above-average financial performance. The simplest depiction of the SHRM model is a relationship between a firm's HR structure and firm performance. The HR architecture is composed of the systems, practices, competencies, and employee performance behaviors that reflect the development and management of the firm's strategic human capital'. (B. Becker and M. Huselid, 2006)

We believe that if the human resources process is optimized then a strategy for the HR management can be developed. A good managed HR strategy is important because it is widely accepted that it can make major contributions to a firm's financial performance. (Wright, Dunford and Snell, 2001) In this study we are going to focus on the variables within the HR recruitment process and our model aims optimizing a personal selection procedure. Once HR processes are improved then a proper strategy can be developed and firm's performance may be increased.

3. The Model

3.1. *Introduction to the model*

The model that we build aims to modernize the methods used before in the personal selection process. Once our model is applied to recruitment it can also be applied to different areas that appear in human resources departments such as, training of employees, organization development, performance management, qualifications of employees, the possible task changes, permanent training in new activities, the reduction of employment, part-time work, social promotion, salary and benefits, harmony between employees, leadership, etc.

In our model, we make a transition from verbal semantics to the corresponding numerical semantics in order to be able to hire the most adequate candidate, according to the match between their abilities and the required characteristics for the offered position.

The adequacy of the model is very important in terms of measuring well the characteristics of the candidates and determining if these characteristics match with expected features of the offered job.

The characteristics are not always objective. The model we propose lets us to introduce subjective characteristics for certain special cases where measurement is possible. Although there may exist some objective characteristics we have to accept the fact that the transition from verbal semantics to numerical semantics is subjective for those special cases that could have been measured. (J. Gil-Lafuente, 2002).

3.2. *Galois Group Theory and Galois Lattices*

3.2.1. *Introduction to the Theory*

Galois Theory is a connection between the field theory and the group theory. Certain problems in field theory can be reduced to group theory using Galois Theory. This allows us understanding the problems easier and solving them in a simpler way. In the beginning, Galois used permutation groups to explain how the various roots of a given polynomial equation were related to each other. (H.M. Edwards, 1984).

Galois Theory is based on a remarkable correspondence between subgroups of the Galois group of an extension E/F and intermediate fields between E and F.

If $G = \text{Gal }(E/F)$ is supposed to be the Galois group of the extension E/F. If H is a subgroup of G, the fixed field of H is the set of elements fixed by every automorphism in H, that is:

$$F(H) = \{x \in E: \sigma(x) = x \text{ for every } \sigma \in H\}.$$

If K is an intermediate field, that is, $F \leq K \leq E$, define

$$G(K) = \text{Gal}(E/K) = \{\sigma \in G: \sigma(x) = x \text{ for every } x \in K\}.$$

In other words fixing group of K for G(K), since G(K) is the group of automorphisms of E that leave K fixed. Galois Theory is about the relation between fixed fields and fixing groups. (H.M. Edwards, 1984), (E. Artin, 1998).

3.2.2. *Definitions of the Theory*

Definition 1: A lattice is a partially ordered set in which two any elements have a least upper bound (lub) and a greatest lower bound (glb). A complete lattice is a lattice where any set has a lub and a glb.

Definition 2: A context K is a triple (O,F, ζ) where O is a set of objects, F is a set of attributes and ζ is a mapping from O×F into {0, 1}.

Definition 3: Given a context K = (O,F, ζ) let us define two mappings from P(O) into P(F) and from P(F) into P(O) using the same notation ´ by the formula:

$$\forall A \subset O, A´ = \{f \in F \mid \forall o \in A, \zeta(o, f) = 1\}$$

$$\forall B \subset F, B´ = \{o \in O \mid \forall f \in B, \zeta(o, f) = 1\}$$

A´ is called the dual of A, similarly B´ is called the dual of B.

Definition 4: Given a context K = (O,F, ζ), the pair C = (A, B) is called a concept of K if and only if A´ = B and B´ = A.

Definition 5: A is called the extent of the concept C and B is called its intent.

This is denoted by A = extent(C) and B = intent(C).

Considering an order relationship defined through inclusion of intents, one may

define a Galois lattice or concept lattice:

Definition 6: The complete lattice L(K) of concepts of the context K is called (general) Galois lattice or concept lattice.

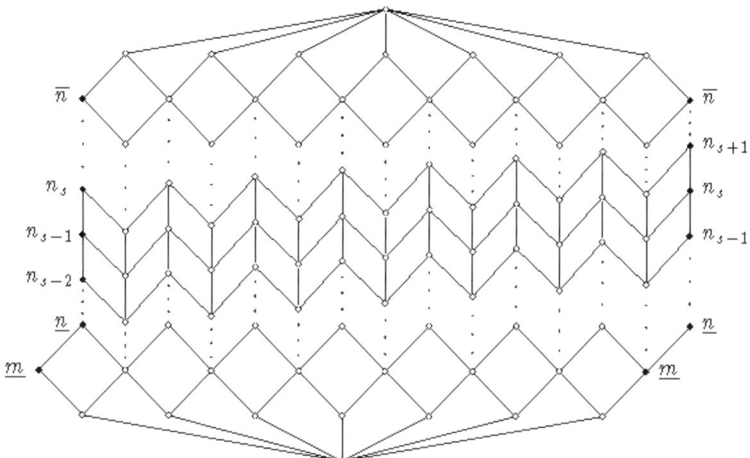

Figure 1: J. B. Nation's counter example to the finite height conjecture[*]

According to the figure 1 lattice is infinite and indirectly irreducible but the variety it generates contains only finitely many other varieties, refuting an old conjecture. If this lattice is imagined as wrapped as around a cylinder then the elements at the sides with the same labels can be identified. The middle part of this diagrams moves up when going from left to right so that when it is wrapped around the cylinder it is helical.

Although the lattice is infinite in figure 1 we can limit it to the variables that we are going to analyze and apply it to our model. As we mentioned in the introduction part of this paper we would like to improve the traditional methods used in the personal selection process. In this study we are going to analyze variables related to recruitment process but our model can be applied to other topics within the HR process such as training of employees, organization development, performance management, qualifications of employees, the possible task changes, permanent training in new activities, the reduction of employment, part-time work, social promotion, salary and benefits, harmony between employees, leadership.

4. Application

In this study we propose following five set of semantics to point if prospective candidate's qualifications cover the company's requirements or not. The

---

[*] *Available at: http://www.math.hawaii.edu/LatThy/*

characteristic represented by VP covers the requirement totally while a characteristic represented by VB doesn't cover the requirement at all.

- VP = Candidate is very proper = (5)
- P = Candidate is Proper = (4)
- E = Candidate is not very proper nor not very proper = (3)
- B = Candidate is not proper = (2)
- VB = Candidate is not proper at all = (1)

Let's suppose that in a determent moment a company is faced with certain personal character requirements in its personal selection process that are represented by the following R set:

$$R = \{R_1, R_2, R_3, R_4\}$$

where:

$R_1 = $ Very high education background

$R_2 = $ Several spoken languages

$R_3 = $ Very extrovert personality

$R_4 = $ At least 5 years job experience in consultancy

is required.

From here we assume that company has different 5 candidates for that position who have different backgrounds for the required properties.

$$P = \{P_1, P_2, P_3, P_4\}$$

where:

$$P_1 = \{a_1, b_1, c_1, d_1\}$$
$$P_2 = \{a_2, b_2, c_2, d_2\}$$
$$P_3 = \{a_3, b_3, c_3, d_3\}$$
$$P_4 = \{a_4, b_4, c_4, d_4\}$$
$$P_5 = \{a_5, b_5, c_5, d_5\}$$

Here $\{a_i, b_i, c_i, d_i; i=1, 2, ..., 5\}$ values represent each characteristic of every candidate as it was explained before. For example if first candidate has a very high education level then $a_1 = \text{VP} = 5$. If he speaks some languages required then his b_1 characteristic would be E = 3. If he is a very introvert person his c_1 semantic would be represented by VB = 1. Finally if he has 3 years working experience in consultancy his d_1 characteristic would be proper which is showed by P = 4 in this study. After taking into account all these characteristics for this candidate he would be represented by $P_1 = \{VP, E, VB, P\} = \{5,3,2,4\}$. Once this analysis is made for all candidates, a matrix between the candidate's personal characteristics and the required qualifications for a job position can be created as shown in table 1.

Table 1: Cross matrix between required and carried personal characteristics

	R_1	R_2	R_3	R_4
$P_1 =$				
$P_2 =$				
$P_3 =$				
$P_4 =$				
$P_5 =$				

5. Conclusion and Further Research

In this study, we are proposing a personal selection model based on the comparison between the determined characteristics of an employment offer and qualifications of prospective candidates for that job inside the human resources recruitment process. Our model is based on the Galois group theory and it allows us to group different candidates depending on their common characteristics. In table 1, we present a matrix that refers to the correlations of each candidate's characteristics and the required qualifications. In further studies, the required characteristics $R = \{R_1, R_2, R_3, R_4\}$ can be defined for a real job position. After doing that, for every candidate their qualifications $P_i = \{a_i, b_i, c_i, d_i\}$ can be determined and a matrix like shown in table 1 can be created. In the end, HR manager can select the most adequate candidate according to its overall results that meet the certain level for the required characteristics. The model we are presenting in this study can be applied to various HR processes and it may allow optimizing those processes. In the end, due to the optimizations done in the processes, a better SHRM can be handled by the company.

References

1. G. Birkoff, *American Mathematical Society Colloquim Publications*, Lattice Theory, **Vol 25**, (1991).
2. E. Zenou and M. Samuelides,. *Journal of Universal Computer Science*, Galois Lattice Theory for Probabilistic Visual Landmarks, **Vol. 10, No. 8,** (2004).
3. B. Becker and M. Huselid, *Journal of Management*, Vol **32, No. 6, 892** (2006).
4. E. Artin, *Dover Publications*, Galois Theory, (1998).
5. H. M. Edwards, *Springer-Verlag*, Galois Theory, (1984).
6. D. Dubois and H. Prade, Operation on fuzzy numbers, *International Journal of Systems Service* **9,** 613, (1978).
7. L.A. Zadeh, *Fuzzy set, Information and Control.* **8,** 338 (1965).
8. J. Gil Aluja, *Kluwer Academic Publishers, Dordrecht,* The Interactive Management of Human Resources in Uncertainty, (1996).
9. J. Gil Aluja, A.M. Gil-Laufente, A. Klimova, Elementos técnicos para la obtención de las afinidades. Reticulos de Galois, (2007).
10. J. Gil-Laufente, *Algoritmos Para La Excelencia*. Claves para el éxito en la gestión deportiva. Editorial Milladoiro, Vigo, Spain, (2002).
11. P. M. Wright, B.B. Dunford and S. A. Snell, *Journal of Management*, Human resources and the resource based view of the firm, **27(6): 701**, (2001).

METHODS OF PROXIMITY FOR PERSONNEL SELECTION THROUGH COMPETITIONS

ROSARIO GARZA RÍOS[*], ILEANA PÉREZ VERGARA,
CARIDAD GONZALEZ SANCHEZ

Instituto Superior Politécnico "José Antonio Echeverría"
Ciudad de La Habana, Cuba

There are different models of personnel's selection, including the personnel's selection through competitions, this model allows to obtain the objectives in the organizations, guaranteeing to have a personnel that carries out their work with good levels of efficiency, comfort, satisfaction and security, however none of the models considers that this decision presents the characteristics of a problem multicriteria where it is necessary to evaluate each one of the competitions (that will denominate criteria) and considering the opinions of experts, that makes multicriterial techniques are not used in the process of the personnel's selection through competitions. The present work shown how should be carried out personnel's selection using multicriterial techniques, in particular the fuzzy set.

1. The personnel's selection in the management of competitions

The personnel's selection through competitions tries to approach the competitions from the candidate to the competitions of the work station.

For this, it is necessary to define the profile of competitions of the work station and their ideal profile.

Taking into account that from the own definition of competitions the problem is multicriterial, the authors propose the use of fuzzy proximity methods that support the process of personnel's selection using this focus.

---

[*] E mail: rosariog@ind.cujae.edu.cu

1.1. *Elaboration of the ideal profile of the competitions of the work station*

The elaboration of the ideal profile can be based on the opinion of a single expert or in the opinion of several of them, which complicates the problem, but it is this case that will study in this work.

To collect the information, authors propose the realization of a inquiry to the expert group with the objective of obtain the ideal value for each competitions of the work station, this constituted in "the ideal profile of competition". This will be a descriptor where the desired values of each one (competitions) will appear to be considered in the problem, for each expert, which will be designated with the capital letter D. The authors recommend using a semantic scale endecadaria, to obtain a quantification that allows to value with more accuracy the criteria, like the following:

$$
\begin{aligned}
&1: \text{excellent} \\
&0.9: \text{very good} \\
&0.8: \text{quite good} \\
&0.7: \text{almost good} \\
&0.6: \text{rather good} \\
&0.5: \text{regular} \\
&0.4: \text{rather bad} \\
&0.3: \text{quite bad} \\
&0.2: \text{bad} \\
&0.1: \text{very bad} \\
&0: \text{terrible}
\end{aligned}
$$

This scale it is a recommendation and it is susceptible to changes according to the habits, customs and interesting of the experts dedicated to the activity. In the fuzzy sets, the Greek letter μ [1] it is used to express the representative evaluations of the level or weight of each criterion. For the characteristic C_1, C_2, ..., C_m will be levels 1, 2,....,m respectively. In general:

$$\mu i \in [\,0,1\,], i = 1,2,.....m$$

the descriptor of the ideal alternative would be:

	C_1	C_2	C_3	C_m
$\underline{D_j}$ =	μ_1	μ_2	μ_3	μ_m

for j = 1,... n

where:
n: number of experts.

The global ideal profile for the group of experts, can be obtained through one of two methods:

> The repetition of each expert's ideal profile.
> The global valuation considering the opinion of experts.

If is used

> The repetition of each expert's ideal profile:

$$\underline{D}_{1,\ldots,n} = \begin{array}{|c|c|c|c|c|c|c|c|c|} \hline C_1 & C_2 \ldots & C_m & C_1 & C_2 \ldots & C_m & C_1 & C_2 \ldots & C_m \\ \mu_1^1 & \mu_2^1 \ldots & \mu_m^1 & \mu_1^2 & \mu_2^2 \ldots & \mu_m^2 & \ldots & \mu_1^n & \mu_2^n \;\; \mu_m^n \\ \hline \end{array}$$

where:

μ_i^j : evaluation of the criterion i emitted by the expert j

Being elaborated the ideal profile of the work station.

> **The global evaluation considering the opinion of experts**

In this case, the authors propose the ideal profile using the results of the ideal profiles expressed by each expert.

For this, there are different methods considering the evaluations given by the experts such as:

1. Rating [1], [2]
2. Arithmetical Mean [3]
3. Mode (in case more than a value will repeat the same quantity of times (multimode), another method should be selected to determine the weights).

This ideal profile is then:

$$\underline{D} = \begin{array}{|c|c|c|c|c|} \hline C_1 & C_2 & C_3 \ldots & & C_m \\ \mu_1 & \mu_2 & \mu_3 & & \mu_m \\ \hline \end{array}$$

$\underline{D}$ = ideal model
μ_i = global value of the competition i obtained of the opinion of the experts
being i = 1,..., n
n = quantity of competitions.

1.2. *Elaboration of the profile of the candidate of the competitions of the work station*

To determine the candidate's profile can be used the characteristical techniques of personnel's selection. For them the candidates are subjected to different test, interviews, etc. being necessary to make a standardization of the results to be able to use the proposed endecadaria scale.

The authors propose some recommendations according to the used scales.

> Standardization of qualitative values to adjusted quantitative values to the semantic endecadaria scale. It proposes the use of the scale in the Table 1.

Table 1: Standardization of the results of qualitative values

Value qualitative result of the test	Value of the semantic endecadaria scale
Excellent	1
Very well	0.9
Well	0.6 – 0.8
Regular	0.3 – 0.5
Bad	0 – 0.2

> Standardization of the quantitative values to values of the semantic endecadaria scale. It proposes the use of the scale that is shown in the Table 2.

Table 2: Standardization of the results of quantitative values.

Quantitative value, result of the test (by percent)	Value of the semantic endecadaria scale
100 %	1
90 -99 %	0.9
80 - 89%	0.8
70 - 79%	0.7
60 - 69%	0.6
50 59 %	0.5
40 - 49%	0.4
30 – 39%	0.3
20 – 29%	0.2
10 – 19 %	0.1
0 – 9 %	0

> Standardization of the results in tests of correct and incorrect answers. It proposes the use of the scale that is shown in the Table 3.

Table 3. Standardization of the results in tests of correct and incorrect answers.

Result of the test	Value of the semantic endecadaria scale
Good	1
Not good	0

To create each candidate's profile, are assigned to each competition the values obtained in the tests and those are standardized, conforming to a fuzzy set for each candidate. This result is represented through a denominated descriptor P.

$$\underline{P_k} = \begin{array}{|c|c|c|c|c|} \hline \mu_1 & \mu_2 & \mu_3 & \cdots\cdots & \mu_m \\ \hline \end{array}$$

with columns $C_1 \quad C_2 \quad C_3 \quad \cdots\cdots \quad C_m$

for k = 1,..., r
where:
r: quantity of alternative.

The global profile of the group of experts for each candidate can be obtained according to the two methods described previously for the global ideal profile.

1.3. *The candidate's selection among a group*

To select the candidate that better is adjusted to the ideal model created by the experts, the authors propose the use of the fuzzy set in particular the methods "Minimum Level and Maximum" and "Distance of Hamming."

Method of the Minimum and Maximum Level

Index of maximum and minimum level σ (Dj, Pk) is expressing the grade of proximity among the global ideal profile of competitions and the global profile that it describes to each candidate, it's used this method for their simplicity and easiness for calculating that make it very operative, obtaining the same one by the expression 1.

$$\sigma(\underline{D_j}, \underline{P_k}) = \frac{\Sigma \, | \mu_D(x) - \mu_P(x) | + \Sigma \, 0 \vee [\, \mu_D(x) - \mu_P(x)\,]}{\text{card } u + \text{card } v} \tag{1}$$

where:

u: group of the criterion that cannot be exceeded.

v: group of the criterion that can be exceeded.

This method specifies the definition of each criterion for which it is not convenient that will be exceeded the ideal profile of the competitions and the criterion that exceeding the ideal profile doesn't have bigger transcendency.

- To determine for each criterion that cannot be exceeded:

$$| \mu_D(x) - \mu_P(x) | \tag{2}$$

- To determine for each criterion that can be exceeded

$$0 \vee [\mu_D(x) - \mu_P(x)] \tag{3}$$

In the case of personnel's selection through competitions are applied that always the aspirants overcome the competitions of the work station. Such as index of maximum and minimum level is expressing the similarity between the ideal profiles, the more as the distance less interesting will be studied alternative, for that reason, the alternative whose index is smaller, will be selected.

Hamming Distance

The method of the Distance of Hamming [4], allows in a simple way to obtain the consents of the group of experts in the best candidate's selection, The authors propose a combination of the same one with the use of fuzzy sets. The concept of Hamming Distance manifests the grade of proximity among the ideal profile and the profile that it describes to each candidate, the one that is determined using the expression 2:

$$\delta(D,Pj) = (1/m^*n) \; \Sigma \; |\mu D1,...n - \mu P1,2...n \, j| \tag{4}$$

where:

n: expert's number.

m: number of considered criterion.

As the distance show the grade of proximity of the ideal profile, is expressing the similarity between the ideal profiles, the more as the distance, less interesting will be the studied alternative, for what the alternative will be selected whose index is smaller.

The use of these proximity methods for the personnel's Selection through management of competition provides to organizations of a simple and potent tool.

2. Application of the proximity methods for the selection of a production coordinator in an Industrial Complex

Competitions that are considered for the work station of a coordinator of production of a company are: leadership, autocontrol, initiative, autonomy, behavior before adverse situations, self-criticism, organizational capacity, capacity of management of problems, management of resources, and work in team, authority and communication.

For the elaboration of the ideal profile of the competitions of production coordinator's work station, it is conformed a team of 9 experts those that gave their evaluations for the 12 competitions.

For obtaining the global ideal profile for the group of 9 experts it used the median and the result obtained for the position of coordinator's of production of the company was:

	C_1	C_2	C_3	C_4	C_5	C_6	C_7	C_8	C_9	C_{10}	C_{11}	C_{12}
$\underline{D}$	1	0.9	0,8	0,8	1	1	1	0,9	0,8	0.9	1	1

The profiles of each one of the 6 candidates, once made the corresponding tests were:

	C_1	C_2	C_3	C_4	C_5	C_6	C_7	C_8	C_9	C_{10}	C_{11}	C_{12}
$\underline{P_1}$	0.8	0.9	0.85	0.75	0.6	0.9	1	1	1	0.95	0.85	0.85
$\underline{P_2}$	0.85	0.7	0.85	0.9	0.95	0.9	1	1	0.95	0.75	1	1
$\underline{P_3}$	0.85	0.75	0.6	0.8	0.7	0.7	0.7	0.75	0.55	0.95	0.6	0.85
$\underline{P_4}$	0.65	0.65	0.65	0.85	0.75	0.75	0.6	0.65	0.85	0.7	0.6	0.75
$\underline{P_5}$	1	0.7	0.8	0.8	0.9	0.8	0.55	0.7	0.9	0.95	0.85	0.75
$\underline{P_6}$	0.85	0.85	0.6	0.7	0.9	0.95	1	1	0.95	0.75	0.8	0.75

The values of the indexes obtained by each method and the classification of the candidates are shown in the Table 4.

Table 4. Classification of the values of the index of the candidates.

Ranking	Index of the minimum and maximum level	Ranking	Hamming Distance index
Candidato 2	0.02	Candidato 2	0,00972
Candidato 1	0.07	Candidato 6	0,01111
Candidato 6	0.1	Candidato 1	0,01157
Candidato 5	0.1166	Candidato 5	0,01295
Candidato 3	0.1916	Candidato 3	0,02129
Candidato 4	0.2219	Candidato 4	0,02546

As it is appreciated in the table 4, the candidate 2 is the most competent to take the position of production coordinator's work, with independence of the used method.

References

1. J Gil, *Seminario Internacional de Gestión Empresarial en la Incertidumbre.* Ciudad de La Habana, Cuba. (2001).
2. M Tabucanon, *Multiple Criteria Decision Making in Industry*, Studies in Production and Engineering Economics, Elserver. Amsterdam - Oxford - New York, Tokyo (1988).
3. P. Aragonés, *Técnicas de ayuda a la toma de decisiones en Proyectos.* Universidad Politécnica de Valencia. (2003).
4. R. Garza, *Procedimiento multicriterio para la planificación de rutas de distribución.* Tesis para optar por el grado científico de Doctor. Ciudad de La Habana, Cuba. (2001).

LEVEL OF INFLUENCE OF THE VARIABLES IN THE PROCESS OF THE KNOWLEDGE MANAGEMENT: A QUANTIFICATION OVER THE THEORY OF UNCERTAINTY

GERARDO GABRIEL ALFARO CALDERÓN

Universidad Michoacana de San Nicolas de Hidalgo
Morelia, Michoacán, 58030, Mexico

In the present paper we apply the fuzzy theory in the linguistic labels approach in order to measure the variables that ensemble the knowledge management. This theory is based on is based on the fuzzy sets theory, applicable when the variables that are present in the problem are from a linguistic character. We focus on the Small and Medium manufacturing enterprises (SMEs) from the city of Morelia, Michoacan, Mexico.

1. Introduction

The challenges that the directors from enterprises face are continuously growing, the globalization that is present in almost all the representative business activities, has had as result a bigger intensity and diversity of competence, which has made a great uncertainty for enterprises and in a bigger scale for the small and medium manufacturing business (SME´s), that's why these enterprises has to search for new alternatives in order to get competitive advantages in respect to their competitors.

Argvris, Scön (1998), Nonaka 1999, Kogut & Zander 1992, Grant 1996, Davenport & Prusak 1998 affirmed that the knowledge represents one of the most critic values to achieve sustainable success in any organization. In the same way Dogson (1993), expresses that in order to face the highly competitive environment such as the actual, it is necessary to acquire the capacity of receive information, transform it into knowledge, incorporate it, share and put it in practice, when, where and how it is necessary.

One of the critical factors in order to evaluate the process of knowledge management is without a doubt the intangibility of the variables to research, for the past statements we present this idea, the use of this theory of uncertainty as a tool useful for this work.

The objectives of the paper are the following. First, we want to apply the theory of uncertainty or Fuzzy Logic in a linguistic approach in order to measure the level of importance of the variables that ensemble the process of knowledge management in the SMEs of the city of Morelia Michoacán México. And second, make a comparison between the theory of uncertainty vs. the classic models in the measurement of the variables of the process of knowledge management in the Small and Medium enterprises.

2. Theoretical Framework

2.1. *Knowledge Management*

In the existing literature over the present job and specially in this matter we start form two concepts, administration of knowledge and knowledge management, we have chosen knowledge management based on Koontz (1995), who defines management as the "process in which we obtain, display or use a variety of basic resources in order to support the objectives of the organization", in this case the resource is knowledge.

Hence, knowledge management must achieve this purpose, understanding as one of the resources to the knowledge. There are, in the literature, a lot of definitions such the ones from: Wiig (1997), Hibbard (1997), Bedrow y Lane (2003), Berkeley (2001) Kim (2000), Duffy (2000), Trepper (2000), Chyi y Yang (2000), O´Dell y Garyson (1998); Parish, (2001), Horwitch y Armacost (2002), and form them we come through with: the knowledge management is a dynamic and interactive process made in order to detect, generate, encode, transfer capture and use the knowledge to achieve the objectives and resolve the problems that the organization faces, also the generation of competitive advantages (Alfaro C. 2007).

2.2. *Objectives of the Knowledge Management*

Some of the objectives that are pursued by the knowledge management are the following:

- The organizations can only acquire and maintain competitive advantages by the correct use of knowledge (Grant, 1991, Quinn 1992, Prusak 1997, Nahapiet y Ghoshal 1998 Nonaka y Byosiere 2000 Bueno 2000, Drucker 2000).

- Create an environment in which the knowledge and the information available in the organization can be accessible and can be used to stimulate the innovation and make possible the improvement in the decision making.
- Monitor and evaluate the achievements obtained by the application of knowledge.
- Reduce the times and cycles in the development of new products, improving the existing ones and optimizing the time of solution to problems that may appear.
- Reduce costs associated to the repetition of errors and duplicity of efforts.
- Potentiate the abilities competences and knowledge of the people that integrate the organization.
- Create a culture of self-knowledge and socialization of knowledge.
- Make the existent knowledge be part of the work routine, and create new knowledge to get better results in the organization.

2.3. *Models of Knowledge Management*

In order to obtain a new model of knowledge management (KM) that was applicable to the manufacturing SMEs from the city of Morelia Michoacán México the next models were analyzed: Process of knowledge creation (Nonaka & Takeuchi), Andersen Model (Arthur Andersen), Knowledge Management Assessment Tool (KMAT), Model of knowledge management from KPGM Consulting (Tejedor & Aguirre), Model of knowledge growth (Kogut & Zander 1992), that will establish the pace to follow for the application of a KM system organization, such as the implied agents , the ones compound the basis for the model generation in the study. Fig (1).

2.3.1. Model of Knowledge Management for Manufacturing SMEs

This model is a product of an investigation for the manufacturing SMEs from the city of Morelia Michoacán México, in which, the elements, Culture, management style, structural capital, relative capital that incentivize the human capital, that makes a maximization from the process of KM which in fact is integrated by the variables, detection, generation, codification, transference, capture and use of knowledge, just as it is showed in Figure 1.

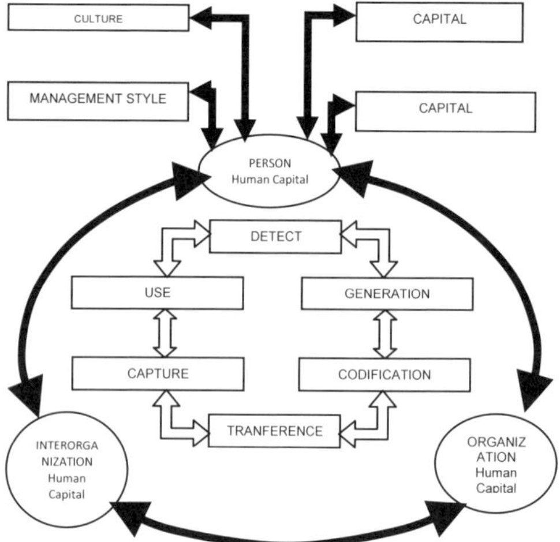

From: Alfaro Calderón (2007)

Fig. 1. Proposed model for the Knowledge management for manufacturing SME's.

2.4. *Knowledge Management Process*

"Dynamic and interactive process made in order to detect, generate, encode, transfer capture and use the knowledge to achieve the objectives and resolve the problems that the organization faces, also the generation of competitive advantages" (Alfaro, 2007). This model has a systemic approach, because it allows the interaction from the elements that are in the process of the knowledge management, observing that these are not independent, but connected between each other.

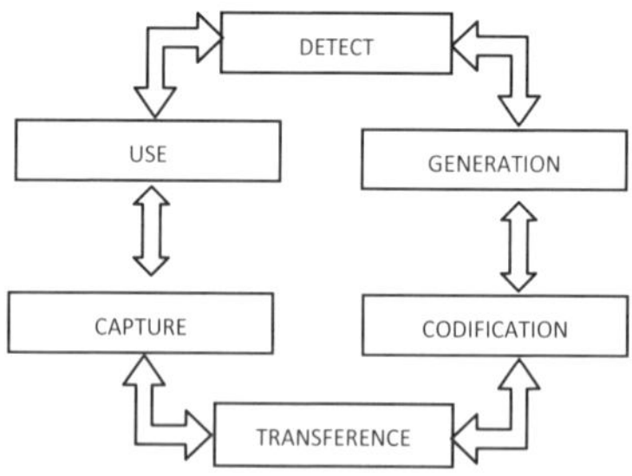

Fig. 2. Knowledge Management Process.

From the model that we presented before in which one observes that is fundamental for the knowledge management as a whole, the process of knowledge management, we present the analysis of influence with classic theory and uncertainty theory.

3. Methodology of Analysis with Linguistic Labels

Just as it is shown by Lizardi (2006), the classic models of decision making can have just a few things in common with the real life events. In a lot of real decision making processes, the objectives, restrictions and the way of action are not certainly known. The individuals that participate in the problem have difficulty in expressing with a numerical value, the exact level of preference when choosing an alternative. Under those circumstances, a more realistic approximation consists on expressing the opinions from experts, under linguistic terms, rather than exact numerical values. This under the understanding that the dominance from the variables that are involved is a group of linguistic terms bounded in a set.

This way of approach from the decision making is based on the fuzzy sets theory and it receives the name of linguistic approach. It is applied, when the involved variables are qualitative (Zadeh, 1975; Tong y Bonissone, 1980; Delgado, Verdegay y Vila 1993; Herrera y Herrera-Viedna, 2000). In this way, we can represent the information from the individuals, in am more precise way, thus the information tends to be almost always imprecise. The fuzzy approach has been applied with success in several problems that has qualitative aspects, evaluated by linguistic terms.

A linguistic term defines a numerical variable in which the values that can be taken are not in a big range, rather, they are words or sentences form a natural or artificial language (Zadeh 1975).

In a linguistic model the decision making assumes the existence from an appropriate set of terms or labels, according with the dominance of the problem, under the basis, that the individuals express their preferences.

One must remember the level of distinction in which the uncertainty wants to be expressed, or the granularity from the set of labels (Zadeh 1975) and the semantics of the labels as well, defining an intermediate, "approximately 0.5", that represents a neutral state and the other distributed symmetrically around it. The semantics of the terms set is usually given by fuzzy numbers, in the interval $[0,1]$ defined by the functions of pertinence, this as a result that the linguistic labels are linguistic approximations owned by the individuals (Zadeh, 1979; Tong and Bonissone, 1984).

In this work we use the set of labels in the interval $[0, 1]$, $L=\{l_i\}, i \in H=\{0,...,t\}$, from odd cardinal, finite and totally sorted in the usual line (Zadeh, 1979, Bonissone y decaer, 1986; Delgado, Verdegay y Vila, 1993). The label from the center represents uncertainty from approximately 0.5 and the rest is distributed semantically in both ways. Any linguistic label represents a possible value from a linguistic variable, a restriction or defined property in $[0, 1]$.

4. Evaluation of the Process of Knowledge Management under the Fuzzy Theory Applying Linguistic Labels

In order to evaluate the level of importance from an attribute we will use a set of 5 linguistic labels L={l0,l1,l2,l3,l4}.The semantics from the labels will be given by the NBT from the interval [0, 1], that are observed in table 1, expressed by the four real numbers that characterize them:

	Linguistic label	NBT
l_4	Always	(0.8,0.9,1.0,1.0)
L_3	Almost always	(0.5,0.7,0.8,0.9)
L_2	Sometimes	(0.3,0.45,0.55,0.7)
L_1	Almost never	(0.1,0.2,0.3,0.45)
L_0	Never	(0.0,0.0,0.1,0.2)

The added opinion from all the surveyed individuals regarding each one of the variables, regarding the process of knowledge management, are expressed by a fuzzy middle number, hence, for each variable we will obtain a fuzzy middle number from the NBT set, corresponding to the linguistic labels that express the estimation or the level of importance of the surveyed individuals. The process made for each of the process variables in the knowledge management is presented next:

KNOWLEDGE DETECTION

FRECUENCY			INTERVALS					OPERATION				
0	(	0	0	0.1	0.2	)	=	(	0	0	0	0	)
11	(	0.1	0.2	0.3	0.45	)	=	(	1.1	2.2	3.3	4.95	)
38	(	0.3	0.45	0.55	0.7	)	=	(	11	17	21	26.6	)
30	(	0.5	0.7	0.8	0.9	)	=	(	15	21	24	27	)
7	(	0.8	0.9	1	1	)	=	(	5.6	6.3	7	7	)
				SUM				(	33	47	55	65.6	)
				MEAN				(	0.4	0.5	0.6	0.76	)

Obtaining the next trapezoidal fuzzy number:

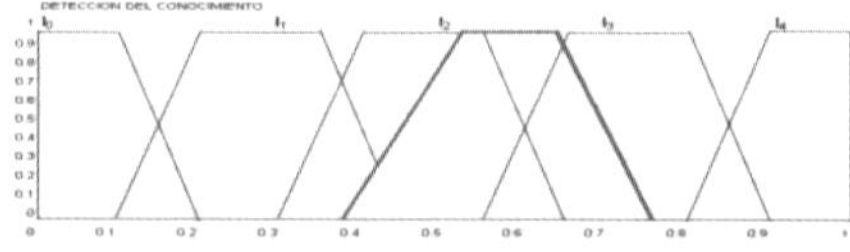

In which one can observe that the detection of the knowledge in the SMEs is made by mayor incidence in the linguistic label of "Sometimes", in the other side the statistic descriptive analysis observed a tendency to "Almost always", which make us take a better decision regarding this variable.

KNOWLEDGE GENERATION

Obtaining as a result the next trapezoidal fuzzy number:

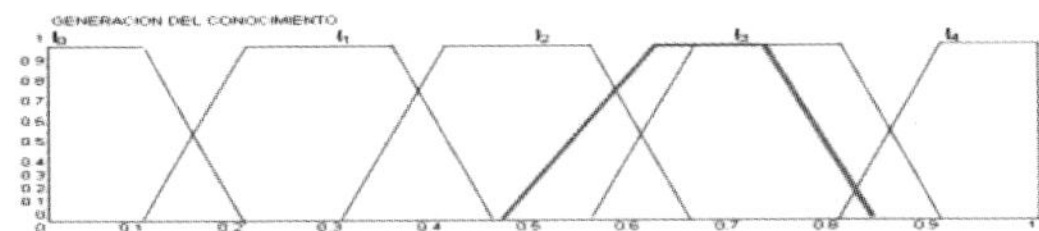

The results in this area show that the generation of knowledge is made "Almost always" in the manufacturing SMEs, this associated to the classic theory.

CODIFICATION OF KNOWLEDGE

Obtaining the next trapezoidal fuzzy number:

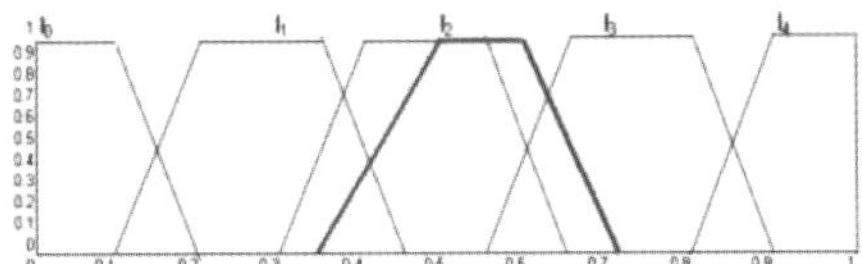

Showing us that the codification of the SMES relies in the label of "Sometimes", while in the classic theory it is shown that follows an "Almost always" tendency.

KNOWLEDGE TRANSFERENCE

Obtaining as a result the next fuzzy number:

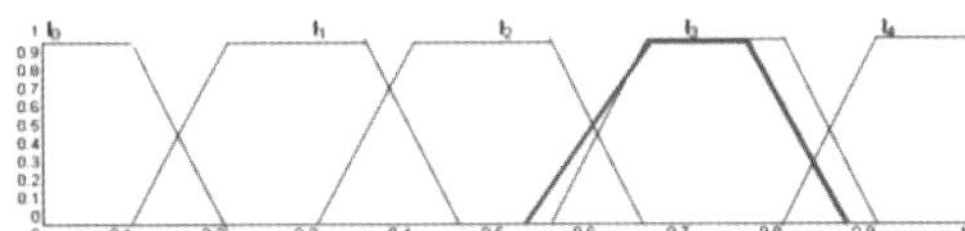

KNOWLEDGE CAPTURE

Giving the next trapezoidal fuzzy number:

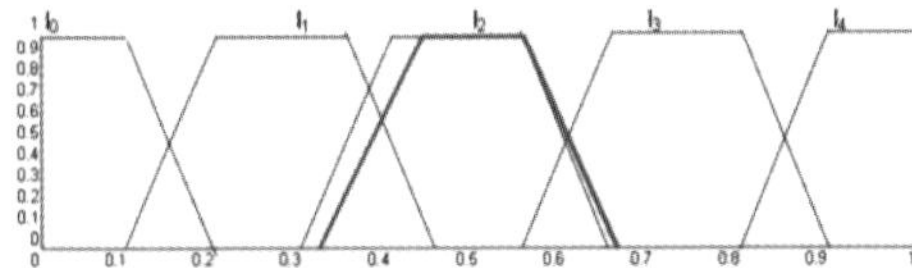

In which we observe that the Capture of knowledge is given in a sporadically form, while in the classic theory it is shown that has a tendency to go to "almost always".

USE OF KNOWLEDGE
Obtaining the next:

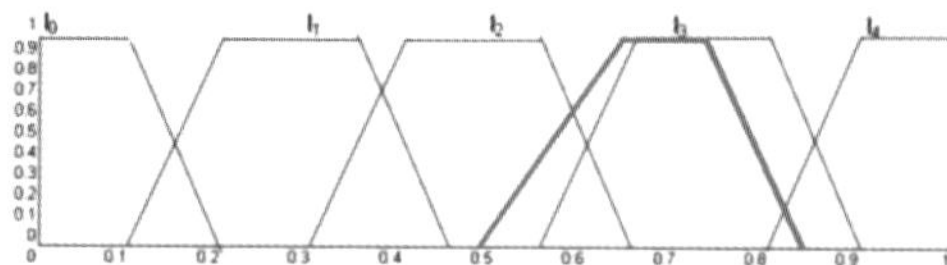

So we say that "Almost always" the knowledge generated is used in the manufacturing SMEs.

5. Conclusions

The implied variable analysis in the process of knowledge management with the utilization of linguistic labels, allow us to have a bigger spectre of decision, than with the use of punctual measures shown in the classic theory.

The linguistic fuzzy approach has been applied with success to a several number of real life problems, because it allows to represent the information available, when it is not precise in a more appropriate way, and the decision maker can express in a much more conventional language, with the use of linguistic variables. Also the linguistic approach simplifies the convergence of the language to shared meanings.

References

1. Alfaro C. G. (2007), "Modelo de Gestión del Conocimiento para PyMES", Ed. Morevallado. Méx.
2. Andersen A. (1999), "El Mangement en el siglo XXI" ED.Granica Buenos Aires
3. Andersen A. (1999), "KMAT (Knowledge Management Assessment Tool) Andersen A. Study London
4. Argyris C. (1999), "Conocimiento para la acción: Una guía para superar obstáculos del cambio en la organización", ed. Granica México
5. Bonissone P.P. Decker (1986), Selecting uncertanty calculi and granulary: An experiment in trading-off precision and complexity", en Kanal, L.H. Lemmer, J.F. (edits) Amsterdam.

PART 4:
MARKETING, SPORTS AND TOURISM

THE SELECTION OF THE PILOT PRODUCT BEST SUITED TO A TARGET SEGMENT

JAIME GIL-LAFUENTE
JULIO ROJAS-MORA

Dpt. of Business Economics and Organization, University of Barcelona
Av. Diagonal, 690. 08034 Barcelona, Spain

The continued innovation that companies must undertake is a strategic resource of great value against the competition, although it involves what might account to a big investment which, if little commercial success, can impact negatively. For this reason, many companies use probes like "test of concepts", "test products" or "trial runs" trying to minimize investment failure in the development and launch of a product from a new idea. We present a tool for the selection of pilot product best suited to a particular market segment based on the concept of distance between fuzzy subsets.

1. Introduction

Currently, companies that commercialize a wide variety of products, sometimes with high product rotation, tend to have departments specializing in consistently providing technically viable and economically feasible ideas.

The "bank of ideas" that such organizations have or should have, generate a multitude of reference points for the delivery of new goods or services (Gil-Lafuente [1]). Virtually any previously screened idea, may be of commercial interest. However, many of the failures in its commercialization may result either from presenting it to the wrong kind of client, or if the ideal client is found, he did not need it at that moment.

By means of the theory of fuzzy logic created by Zadeh [2], we can determine the best among a group of candidates, when information is subjective in nature, or statistical information should be filtered through experts. As an example of this line of research, we can observe all the important works of Kaufmann and Gil-Aluja [3], Chen and Wang [4] and its application to the search for the perfect home [5], the application to databases developed by Yang *et al.* [6], the process carried out by the International Olympic Committee for the selection of the venue of the 1st Summer Youth Olympic Games [7], or the model created by Rojas-Mora and Gil-Lafuente [8] for the hiring process of professional sports teams.

Our contribution is based on this same line of research, using fuzzy sets to model uncertain information on products that are candidates to be released as a "pilot test" for a particular market segment. Among them, one will fit better and should be selected for further testing.

2. Fuzzy subsets and fuzzy numbers

In cases when information is not only uncertain, but also subjective or provided by an expert, the theory of fuzzy subsets can help in the construction of a model that helps the decision maker evaluate the alternatives. A fuzzy subset $\tilde{A}$ is a set of pairs with elements from a universal set such that:

$$\tilde{A} = \{(x, \mu_{\tilde{A}}(x)) \mid x \in X \,,\, \mu_{\tilde{A}}(x) \in [0,1]\} \,. \tag{1}$$

For the purpose of this work, a fuzzy number $\tilde{M}$ is a fuzzy subset for which:
1. $x \in [0,1]$, i.e., the domains of the fuzzy numbers are normalized.
2. $\mathrm{hgt}(\tilde{M}) = 1$, i.e., there is at least one element, called the maximum of presumption, for which $\mu_{\tilde{M}}(x) = 1$.
3. $\tilde{M}$ is convex.

We will define four kinds of fuzzy numbers which will be used throughout this paper. A fuzzy singleton is a fuzzy number whose support is a single value $\bar{x}$. When uncertainty only lets the maximum of presumption to be enclosed in an interval between x_1 and x_2, we call this fuzzy number an interval of confidence $\tilde{M} = [x_1, x_2]$. When an expert can give a maximum of presumption in a point x_2, but uncertainty covers a triangular region with minima in x_1 and x_3, the assessment takes the shape of a triangular fuzzy number (TFN) $\tilde{M} = [x_1, x_2, x_3]$. Finally, if the maximum of presumption of this triangle covers an interval x_2 and x_3, then the shape is that of a trapezoidal fuzzy number (TrFN) $\tilde{M} = [x_1, x_2, x_3, x_4]$.

For practical reasons, we can represent each of the previously defined fuzzy numbers as TrFN. A fuzzy singleton would be $[\bar{x}, \bar{x}, \bar{x}, \bar{x}]$, an interval of confidence would be $[x_1, x_1, x_2, x_2]$ and a TFN would be $[x_1, x_2, x_2, x_3]$.

3. Description of the target market segment

The first thing that needs to be defined is a mathematical descriptor that numerically and accurately reflects the market segment that the Marketing Department is interested in reaching.

A hypothetical dairy company wants to introduce a new product for the a particular market segment defined by the following characteristics:
- Health-conscious consumer.
- With an age above 50 years.
- Willing to pay a high price for healthier diary product.
- Interested in new technology driven products, but not a totally technology devoted consumer.
- Looking for a product that can be carried around and consumed at any time.

Given this information, the marketing department models the target segment with the fuzzy set $\tilde{S} = \{\tilde{s}_i\}$, $\forall i \in \{1, \ldots, 5\}$, as we can see in Table 1.

Table 1: Target segment modeled as a fuzzy set.

	c_1	c_2	c_3	c_4	c_5
$\tilde{S} =$	[0.7 , 1]	[0.6, 1]	(0.5, 0.8, 1)	(0.7, 0.8, 0.9)	[0.8, 1]

Each fuzzy number $\tilde{s}_i$ represents an assessment of the ideal level that the target segment has on each one of the characteristics in the set $C = \{c_i\}$. The characteristics, as well as the meaning of the assessments given to this particular segment, are defined as:
- c_1- Health-consciousness: A consumer is regarded as health-conscious if at least 70% of his food purchases are done with health in his mind.
- c_2- Maturity: A consumer is considered mature if he has already lived more than 60% of his life expectancy.
- c_3- Price level: In this case, the consumer prefers to buy products in the top 50% of the price scale, with a maximum preference for products in the 80%.
- c_4- Novelty of organoleptic or technological characteristics: the consumer prefers to buy between 70 and 90% of the times, with a maximum of 80%, a new product if new flavors or properties are also involved.
- c_5- Easiness of transportation and consumption: when a consumer buys a product he prefers the top 80% in easiness of transportation and consumption, meaning he wants a product that can be carried around with no worries of spillage or spoilage, and that needs almost no additional procedures beyond opening its package for its consumption.

Each category has been equally weighted as there is no information on which one has more importance on the decision.

4. Description of the candidates for the pilot test

The R&D of the company has decided that the pilot test should be run with one of the following five products from the set $\mathfrak{P} = \{\tilde{P}_j\}$, $j \in \{1, \ldots, 5\}$:

• $\tilde{P}_1$- Fructose sweetened soy yogurt with fruits: It has been assessed as a product with above the average healthy properties, without a defined age group, an average price, no real novelty in flavor or in technology, and with no more or less limitations in transportability and consumption that most products.

• $\tilde{P}_2$- Inulin sweetened Greek yogurt enriched with calcium: Being a Greek yogurt means this is a fatty product, although this is compensated with the substitution of complex sugars with inulin, so this product is in the middle of the pack in healthiness, although with some uncertainty. Nonetheless, by enriching it with calcium, the age group targeted is definitely mature. Price, as well as its technological appeal due to the novelty of inulin, ranges in the middle upper echelon. Of course, a Greek yogurt is a product to keep refrigerated and eaten with a spoon, which limits its transportability.

• $\tilde{P}_3$- Aspartame sweetened, fat free chocolate pudding enriched with Omega-3: By removing fat while adding Omega-3 and aspartame, this product can be considered very healthy. Age groups from young adulthood to elderly will be equally attracted to consume it. The price is above average but not the most expensive. However, this is not a technologically driven product as all its characteristics are found in many products. This product has the same problems of transportability described for the Greek yogurt.

• $\tilde{P}_4$- Digestion helping, cucumber yogurt soup with *Lactobacillus casei*: A yogurt soup that designed to aid digestion is regarded as an almost perfect element of a healthy diet. Age groups for this product go from middle aged people to consumers entering maturity, as flavor is not a favorite of younger groups and the introduction of external bacteria might cause problems to older groups. Price is top of the line as this is considered a *gourmet* food. Even if technologically speaking there is nothing new in this product, the flavor and the concept are good enough to put this product above average in preferences of people looking for new products with new flavors. Finally, easy consumption is not really feasible with a soup.

• $\tilde{P}_5$- Energy boosting tropical fruits flavored smoothie, enriched with amino acids and taurine: This product might only be considered healthy in the group of people that has an active night life, as well as those that practice sports. This makes it more suitable for age groups ranging from young adulthood to early maturity. It is in the most expensive level, has a high impact in people looking for technology oriented foods and is the easiest product to use, although it is recommended to consume it cold.

Thus, each $\tilde{P}_j = \{\tilde{\mu}_{ij}\}$ is a fuzzy set with the same cardinality as $\tilde{S}$, whose elements, $\tilde{\mu}_{ij}$, are fuzzy numbers. Each product is modeled according to the information gathered as shown in Table 2.

Table 2: Assessments made by the company experts on the new products.

	c_1	c_2	c_3	c_4	c_5
$\tilde{P}_1=$	$(0.5, 0.6, 0.7)$	$[0.1, 1]$	0.5	$[0, 0.1]$	0.5
$\tilde{P}_2=$	$(0.4, 0.5, 0.6)$	$[0.7, 1]$	$[0.7, 0.8]$	$[0.7, 0.9]$	0.4
$\tilde{P}_3=$	$[0.8, 1]$	$[0.3, 1]$	0.8	0.7	0.4
$\tilde{P}_4=$	$[0.8, 0.9]$	$[0.4, 0.7]$	1	$[0.5, 0.7]$	0.1
$\tilde{P}_5=$	$[0.2, 0.4]$	$[0.3, 0.7]$	1	1	0.9

5. The notion of distance

A distance function is a map $d : \varepsilon \times \varepsilon \to R$ that measures the separation of two points of the set ε. A metric is a distance function such that:

1. $d(x, y) \geq 0$ and $d(x, y) = 0 \iff x = y$.
2. $d(x, y) = d(y, x)$.
3. $d(x, z) \leq d(x, y) + d(x, z)$.

A hemimetric is a distance function that fails to satisfy the second condition. In [6] we can find a hemimetric that is used to measure the separation between two fuzzy numbers, but that considers a special case when the first fuzzy number is partially or totally contained by the second. This hemimetric measures the separation only the region of the first fuzzy number not overlapped by the second, modeling the situation when a characteristic reaches a desired level but does not exceed it. A combination of the separations in each category produces a mean hemimetric that we will use in our case:

$$\delta(\tilde{P}_j, \tilde{S}) = \frac{\sum_{i=1}^{n} d(\tilde{\mu}_{ij}, \tilde{s}_i)}{n} \tag{2}$$

where n is the number of caracteristics evaluated.

6. Final results

We now proceed to calculate the distance between the target segment and each one of the new products proposed for a test run. The product closest to the target segment will be the one selected for this test.

$$\delta(\tilde{P}_1, \tilde{S}) = \frac{\sum_{i=1}^{5} d(\tilde{\mu}_{i1}, \tilde{s}_i)}{5}$$

$$\delta(\tilde{P}_1, \tilde{S}) = \frac{0.115 + 0.5 + 0.173 + 0.702 + 0.3}{5} = 0.358$$

$$\delta(\tilde{P}_2, \tilde{S}) = \frac{0.208 + 0 + 0.058 + 0.058 + .4}{5} = 0.145$$

$$\delta(\tilde{P}_3, \tilde{S}) = \frac{0 + 0.3 + 0 + 0.058 + .4}{5} = 0.152$$

$$\delta(\tilde{P}_4, \tilde{S}) = \frac{0 + 0.2 + 0.115 + 0.183 + .7}{5} = 0.240$$

$$\delta(\tilde{P}_5, \tilde{S}) = \frac{0.412 + 0.3 + 0.115 + 0.153 + 0}{5} = 0.196$$

As we can see, the closest product is the Greek yogurt, a product that meets most of the requirements even if transportability if not a distinguished feature. The chocolate pudding is quite close to the Greek yogurt, but seems that it would need a good marketing campaign to introduce it in the age group of the target segment.

The worst suited is the soy yogurt, maybe because it is a generic product that can be used as a baseline to check how well targeted are other products.

We can present the results in terms of preference using the precedence operator:

$$\tilde{P}_1 \prec \tilde{P}_4 \prec \tilde{P}_5 \prec \tilde{P}_3 \prec \tilde{P}_2$$

This means that the Greek yogurt is the product best suited for a test run, but in case it is not possible, the chocolate pudding should be picked, then the energy boosting smoothie, the cucumber yogurt soup and the soy yogurt, respectively.

7. Conclusions

In this work we have presented a methodology based on fuzzy subsets theory for the evaluation of new products that are candidates for a test run in a particular target segment. This methodology allows the comparison of products with different features, some close to the target segment and some others far from it, and take a decision accordingly. A product test run might be an expensive affair, and as such a decision on which product launch has to be as fully supported as possibly. A good feature of this methodology is that statistical information, adequately transformed or processed by experts, can be used together with subjective information, usually disregarded by statistical methods, to get a more comprehensive view of the situation and give better help to the decision maker.

References

1. J. Gil-Lafuente, *Marketing para el nuevo milenio. Nuevas técnicas para la gestión comercial en la incertidumbre*, Ed. Pirámide, Madrid (1997).
2. A. Kaufmann and J. Gil-Aluja, *Introducción de la teoría de los subconjuntos borrosos a la gestión de las empresas*, Ed. Milladoiro, Vigo (1986).
3. L. A. Zadeh, Fuzzy sets. *Information and Control*, 8(3):338–353 (1965).
4. S. H. Chen and C. C. Wang, Representation, ranking, distance and similarity of fuzzy numbers with step form membership function using k-preference integration method. In the *Proceedings Joint 9th IFSA World Congress and 20th NAFIPS International Conference*, 2:801–806 (2001).
5. S. H. Chen and C. C. Wang, House selection using fuzzy distance of trapezoidal fuzzy numbers. In the *Proceedings of the Sixth International Conference on Machine Learning and Cybernetics*, Hong Kong (2007).
6. M. S. Yang, W. L. Hung, and S. J. Chang-Chien, On a Similarity Measure between LR-Type Fuzzy Numbers and Its Application to Database Acquisition. *International Journal of Intelligent Systems*, 20(10):1001–1016 (2005).
7. IOC Panel of Experts, *1st Summer Youth Olympic Games in 2010*. Technical report, IOC (2007).
8. J. Rojas-Mora and J. Gil-Lafuente, The signing of a professional athlete: Reducing uncertainty with a weighted mean hemimetric for Φ-fuzzy subsets. *In the Proceedings of the ICEIS 2009 Conference,* Milan, (2009).

THE USE OF EXPERTONS FOR COMPLAINT HANDLING IN A CRM STRATEGY

ANNA M. GIL-LAFUENTE, CAROLINA LUIS BASSA

*Faculty of Economics and Business, University of Barcelona,
Av. Diagonal 690, 08034 Barcelona, 08025, Spain*

The aim of this paper is, using the semantic scale, creating a response model based on the theory of *Experton* that helps companies to have a good complaint handling to fit customer needs.

Keywords: Complaint Handling, Cutomer Loyalty, Expertons, Relational Marketing, CRM, Customer Relationship Management

1. Introduction

Customer Relationship Management, also known as CRM in the commercial world, is taken as the strategic process undertaken by companies to achieve the loyalty of their most valuable customers. (Parvatiyar and Sheth, 2001)

The keys to this strategy are related to the company's ability to detect and respond to the needs and preferences of customers at all times (Cabanelas, Cabanelas & Paniagua, 2007). This means for the company to be in a continual state of "active listening" to what customers say, claim, think and even feel about the experience with the product or service.

On the other hand, is not only heard but also document the listened, analyze it and assimilate it, to respond to the client about his message, track customer reaction to the answer and then notify the entire company on what they learned with this interaction and how to act in a similar situation at the next opportunity. This is the subtle point that companies must carefully observe and which most probably will be not only the technological tools that help them do that, but a clear understanding by all partners of the firm's value offered by this form of listener-response in the relation, because is a vision where everyone wins. (Cabanelas, Cabanelas & Paniagua, 2007).

The *Customer Knowledge* is a business's competence, and they are embedded in the cognitive activities of the organization and are not easily observable from the outside (Campbell, 2003).

One of the most common ways to listen, understand and respond to customer expectations is through the complaint handling. Most companies are not well informed about how to successfully manage the gaps in services or the impact of claims management strategies and suggestions. The presence of emotional aspects in the interpersonal treatment that the client receives from the company, especially to that in complaint handling, is directly related to the degree of satisfaction and therefore the level of customer loyalty that keeps with the company. Employees who act in an empathic and caring way, coupled with a clear intention to solve the problem, help to soften the anger of customers in most of the incidents of complaint handling, while, if the employee behaves rudely, the customer malaise is exacerbated (Tax, Brown & Chandrashekar, 1998).

Complaint Handling is part of after sales services offered by companies, especially Service Companies.

A usual way to gather the opinions and complaints from our customers is through questionnaires and satisfaction surveys. Many of these questionnaires fail to collect the real message the client wants to convey with their answers. For example in the hospital business, decisions are often based on information from the customer surveys. But who fills these polls? Any customer is a candidate to fill these surveys but not all do it. This is what is known as *nonresponse bias*, and is one of the most classical statistical errors. (Barsky & Huxley, 1992)

According to Garcia (1997), there are two basic ways of encode information: an analogical and a digital form. He claims that, to describe a process in which an information unit is converted from analogical form to digital form, is to describe a process that necessarily involves a loss of information, and that this is because we went from a larger information structure to a lower content. The digital conversion is a process in which irrelevant information units have been pushed aside. Thus, says Garcia, the contrast between analogical encoding systems and a digital encoding of information is useful to differentiate between sensory processes and cognitive processes. Cognitive activity is the conceptual manipulation of information received, while the feeling, what the popularly is called *the look* (or sound, or taste) of things, and what psychologists call *percept*, is informational profuse and specific. Knowledge, unlike is selective and exclusive.

It is possible that, in the case of surveys and questionnaires to measure customer satisfaction, it is losing important sensory information that conveys the overall perception of customers towards a product or service. The questionnaires and satisfaction surveys are developed in order to conceptualize the ideas of customers and are encoded in digital, simple and concrete units.

This article presents a collecting information method on opinions or complaints and suggestions from customers, using the semantic scale to design questionnaires with sufficient alternatives to provide adequate levels of truth that provide more complete information about what the client wants to convey. Once results are obtained, we will use the concept of *Experton* to value the answers and calculate the representative mathematical expectation of the group that has completed the questionnaire.

2. Tools for information processing

CRM strategies have traditionally been measured only from a financial dimension using quantitative indicators (KPIs) such as sales, customer acquisition and retention, reducing costs and length of service, but when evaluating a CRM strategy must take into account the behavioral dimension (behavioral) that includes elements such as service attitude, understanding of client expectations, perceptions of quality, etc.. These attitudinal factors are those that fill the gap between economic goals of business and these efforts to build relationships, which has been the result of associating only with economic indicators CRM (Kim & Kim, 2008)

For example, companies are not well informed about how to successfully manage the gaps in services or the impact of strategies for complaints handling (Tax, Brown & Chandrashekar, 1998)

In the study by Parasuraman, Berry, Zeithaml in 1991 they detail the basic nature of the expectations of customers; they expect that firm's supposed they have to do: customers expect simplicity and not complexity, compliance and not empty promises. The more experience customers have with the product or service purchased, the greater the expectation. The customer relationships are centered on the principle of exceeding their expectations. It is an intensive process that requires a responsive service, safe and empathic over time. The genuine relationships with customers are created on the basis of equality, genuine efforts to understand and help the customer, and continuous communications and custom-service attributes that are demonstrated at the delivered (Parasuraman, Berry, Zeithaml, 1991).

The adequate level of service is one that the client finds acceptable, and determines a "Zone of tolerance" which varies according to customer expectations. If customers perceive that there are several choices of providers, their zone of tolerance decreases. The expectation level rises and the tolerance level falls, when the client's situation is urgent (Parasuraman, Berry, Zeithaml, 1991).

Moreover, customers want to have long term relationships with service companies. They want the company's contact them before initiating contact. They want to have a "partner", someone who knows them and take care of them. Unfortunately, customers seeking this type of long-term relationship are generally disappointed. Despite the apparent interest in relationship marketing for many companies, the study by Parasuraman, Berry, Zeithaml in 1991, said that this is not true. (Parasuraman, Berry, Zeithaml, 1991)

One aspect, that most affects long-term relationship between companies and customers is complaints handling. The presence of emotional aspects in the interpersonal treatment that the client receives from the company, particularly in complaints handling, is directly related to the degree of satisfaction and therefore the level of customer loyalty that keeps the company. Employees who act in an empathic and caring, coupled with a clear intention to solve the problem, help to soften the anger of customers in most of the incidents of complaints and suggestions, while, if the employee behaves rudely, the customer malaise is exacerbated (Tax, Brown & Chandrashekar, 1998). In practical terms, means that in case of an inadequate complaints handling, there is a high degree of losing customers, even those who were previously very satisfied (Homburg & Fürst, 2005).

For the case, how the client handles their complaints is another aspect to deepen as a possible cause of the gap between customer expectations and service delivery. The information collected on complaints and suggestions from our customers is the key to a quality management task as it can be used to correct problems within the company. From a process perspective, the complaints handling may be seen as a sequence of events in which to procedures start when the complaint is communicated, spawns a process of interaction through which decisions and results are generated. (Tax, Brown & Chandrashekar, 1998)

Homburg & Fürst (2005) used the term "Complaint Satisfaction" to describe the customers perception degree of how they perceived the company handles complaints and suggestions and how this management meets or exceeds expectations. The authors also define the term "Customer loyalty after the complaint" to refer to the degree to which a client continues its relationship with the company after the complaint, and the degree of intention to do so in the future. In the case of an ineffective handling of the complaint, there is a high risk of losing even those customers who were previously satisfied. In other words, a prior customer satisfaction does not give the firm a guarantee against the consequences of mishandling claims and suggestions.

Curiously, those customers with greater emotional connection to the company, tend to feel betrayed when a fault occurs in the service and that is why it is extremely important a special care in handling the complaints and suggestions. (Mattila, 2004)

Correctly understanding of what customers want to say when they issue their opinion about a product or service, is therefore a fundamental factor for companies to apply corrective and immediate action to rectify the fault.

In this article we propose a method for expanding the choices that customers have to give their opinion; flange companies a broader range of answers to a better understanding of the client's message when issuing their opinions.

3. Introducing the *scale of eleven terms* for questionnaires management

Despite the disadvantages of questionnaires caused by inadequate sample selection, research design, or a limited market, managers are paying close attention to information from the surveys. (Barsky & Huxley, 1992)

Barsky & Huxley (1992) conducted their study to see the usefulness of questionnaires to measure service hotels. They found that many of the instruments for measuring customer opinion are not entirely valid to measure what is supposed to measure. For example, generally the purpose of the cards to know the opinion of guests aims, have the purpose of showcasing the degree of satisfaction in order the hotel improved when the guest returns. But the typical questions and measurement scales provided by these instruments do not reflect the true level of guest satisfaction. The objective scales, common in the questionnaires provided only a small part of customer satisfaction. A classic example is: "Evaluate your level of satisfaction with food" (1 = Poor, 4 = excellent). Information gathered after this question is still insufficient to truly understand the level of guest satisfaction.

These authors as well as others have developed new models of questionnaires that seek to improve the quality and usefulness of the information collected.

In this paper we propose the use of semantic scale of eleven terms, by Kaufmann & Gil Aluja (1993). This scale provides two advantages: first allowed by the semantic transformation (Table 1), transform fully the views of respondents in numerical values. Secondly, the eleven terms scale values, allow a better adaptation and processing of concepts discussed, because our brain is very used to working in decimal scale. As a result of various experiences through consultation with experts and executives, the authors conclude that the 11 levels are extremely welcome and provide enough variation in the scale without these excessive.

Table 1. Scale of eleven terms

Scale of eleven terms	
0	False
1/10	Mostly false
2/10	Almost false
3/10	Fairly false
4/10	More false than true
5/10	Neither true nor false
6/10	More true than false
7/10	Quite true
8/10	Almost real
9/10	Virtually real
1	True

The *scale of eleven terms* scale provides levels of truth with one decimal place for all levels, facilitating the calculation to perform what is known as a *valuation*. A valuation is an expression of the true level, a level which takes its values of the confidence interval [0,1]. In the binary field a valuation is expressed in {0,1}. (Kaufmann & Gil Aluja, 1993)

Once we have the information, we proceed to its development and treatment. This requires an *aggregation* process. That is, the information directly from the sample would not be useful, but need to be developed to meet their tendency (Gil Lafuente, 2005). This is because firms adopt policies in accordance with the trend shown by the surveys. In this sense, it must have a suitable instrument for aggregating the information contained in the questionnaires and, in addition, show the trend and distribution. Fortunately we have more techniques designed to achieve these objectives. Thus, Experton (Kaufmann & Gil Aluja, 1993), is an instrumental that allows a level of generality and flexibility that makes it suitable to solve any problem of aggregation.

The property of monotone no decreasing horizontal and vertical of an Experton makes has the distributive lattice configuration for $\wedge$ and $\vee$ for. Thus:

1. $\forall \alpha \in [0,1] a_1(\alpha) \leq a_2(\alpha) en[a_1(\alpha), a_2(\alpha)]$

$$(1)$$

2. $\forall \alpha, \alpha' \in [0,1] \ (\alpha' > \alpha) \Rightarrow [a_1(\alpha) \leq a_1(\alpha'), a_2(\alpha) \leq a_2(\alpha')];$

$(\alpha = 0) \Rightarrow (a_1(\alpha) = 1, a_2(\alpha) = 1)$

The use of accumulated laws specific to the Expertons makes that operators used in these mathematical tools are included in so-called "triangular rules" or τ-norms (T-norms and T-conorm) and satisfy properties such as:

1. Commutativity: $\tilde{a}(\wedge)\tilde{b} = \tilde{b}(\wedge)\tilde{a}$

2. Associativity: $(\tilde{a}(\wedge)\tilde{b})(\wedge)\tilde{c} = \tilde{a}(\wedge)(\tilde{b}(\wedge)\tilde{c})$

3. Idempotency: $\tilde{a}(\wedge)\tilde{a} = \tilde{a}$

4. Distributivity: $\tilde{a}(\wedge)(\tilde{b}(\vee)\tilde{c}) = (\tilde{a}(\wedge)\tilde{b})(\vee)(\tilde{a}(\wedge)\tilde{c})$ $\qquad (2)$

5. Involution: $\overline{\overline{\tilde{a}}} = \tilde{a}$

6. Operations with 0 and 1: $\quad \tilde{a}(\wedge)0 = 0 \qquad \tilde{a}(\vee)0 = \tilde{a}$

$$\tilde{a}(\wedge)1 = \tilde{a} \qquad \tilde{a}(\vee)1 = 1$$

7. De Morgan Theorem: $\overline{\tilde{a}(\wedge)\tilde{b}} = \overline{\tilde{a}}(\vee)\overline{\tilde{b}}$

$$\overline{\tilde{a}(\vee)\tilde{b}} = \overline{\tilde{a}}(\wedge)\overline{\tilde{b}}$$

8. Principle of contradiction: $\tilde{a}(\wedge)(\tilde{a}(\wedge)\tilde{b}) = \tilde{a}$

4. Conclusions

In this work we have had the opportunity to raise that, the correct collection and treatment of information provided by customers is essential for businesses to take action to improve their loyalty.

In this regard we have proposed the use of the eleven terms semantic scale for the process of gathering information on where it originates. So, who transcribed the information is responsible for implementation of semantic processing, leaving the respondent complete freedom to express their opinion in terms that are more comfortable and avoiding distorting the information content.

After gathering the information, it proceeds to its aggregation with the model of Experton. The results allow, aside from knowing the final value-added, knowledge of the distribution in relative terms of the views based on the value of the characteristic function of belonging.

This process will allow the company to receive more information and representative results of the customers' opinions without the process followed in the treatment has been distorted. With this, companies would be in a position to take the decisions that they deem more appropriate.

References

1. Barsky J.; Huxley S.; A customer-survey tool: Using the "quality sample" , *The Cornell Hotel and Restaurant Administration Quarterly*, Volume 33, Issue 6, Pages 18-25. (1992)

2. Cabanelas J., Cabanelas P., Lorenzo J.; La gestión de las relaciones con los clientes como característica de la alta rentabilidad empresarial; *Revista Europea de Dirección y Economía de la Empresa*. Vol. 16, No. 3, 133-148. (2007)

3. Campbell, A. Creating Customer Knowledge Competence: Managing Customer Relationship Management Programs Strategically; *Industrial Marketing Management*. Vol. 32, 375-383. (2003)

4. Gil Lafuente, A.M., Fuzzy Logic in Financial Analysis, España, Springer-Verlag, (2005)

5. Kaufmann, A; Gil Aluja, J. *Técnicas especiales para la gestión de expertos*. Santiago de Compostela (España): Editorial Milladoiro. ISBN 84-404-3657-2. (1993)

6. Kim, H.-S., & Kim, Y.-G. A CRM Performance Measurement Framework: Its Development Process and Application; *Industrial Marketing Management*. (2009) doi:10.1016/j.indmarman.2008.04.008

7. Mattila, A. The Impact of Service Failures on Customer Loyalty; *International Journal of Service Industry Management*. Vol.15, No. 2, 134-149. (2004)

8. Parasuraman, A; Berry, Ll; Zeithaml, V. Understanding, Measuring, and Improving Service Quality - Findings From a Multiphase Research-Program; *Service Quality*. págs. 253-268. (1991)

9. Parvatiyar, A., & Sheth, J. N. Customer Relationship Management: Emerging Practice, Process, and Discipline; *Journal of Economic and Social Research*. Vol. 3, No. 2, 1-34. (2001)

10. Sirbiladze, G., Gachechiladze, T., Restored fuzzy measures in expert decision-making, *Information Sciences*, Volume 169, Issues 1-2, Pages 1-187. (2005)
11. Tax, Ss; Brown, Sw; Chandrashekaran, M. Customer Evaluations of Service Complaint Experiences: Implications for Relationship Marketing; *Journal of Marketing*. Vol. 62, No. 2, 60-76. (1998)

A MODEL FOR JUNIOR FOOTBALL PLAYERS' VALUATION

JOSÉ M. BROTONS

*Department of Economic and Financial Studies, Miguel Hernandez University,
Avda. del Ferrocarril, s/n, 03292, Elche, Spain*

The need to value sports management of the trainers, coaches and the people in charge of the junior players of football teams has led us to develop a general valuation model for football players. We propose a methodology that allows us to achieve that objective; starting from the point that the existence of objective figures is not enough for valuation to be determined. The fact that the valuation of football players presents a high level of subjectivity and fuzziness, has led us to propose a new methodology based on a questionnaire that will be presented to experts on this subject.

1. Introduction

Although Fried, Shapiro, & De Schriver (2003) consider that the study of sport finance is in its infancy, there are many papers which focus on the study of sports finance. Kedar-Levy & Bar-Eli (2008) present a theoretical model that assesses athletes' valuation, which is based on the Asset Pricing Model (CAPM). That paper focuses on the return of the investment, not on the valuation of the athletes. The marginal Revenue Product (MRP) has been used by several authors like Krautmann (1999) or Zimbalist (1992a, 1992b) .

One of the most interesting methodologies applied to value football players is the one developed by Pujol & García-del-Barrio (2008) and Pujol, García-del-Barrio, & Elizalde (2007). They estimated the intangible notion of media value by two complementary elements: popularity and reputation.

Despite the information available and the studies carried out, in this paper, we have presented a new methodology, in which we try not to determine the suitability of the price paid for the player (because the price is something that cannot be changed), but to propose a system to determine the price of the players, basically junior players who still have not been transferred and consequently their price is unknown. Our methodology differs from others such as that of Pujol & García-del-Barrio (2008), because we consider the market price of the transferred football players as an input.

This methodology is based on the fact that experts already have all the data and the objective information about characteristics of both the team players and the transferred players, and the prices of the latter.

Therefore, the experts questioned know the reality and the data, so that information is introduced in the model through their knowledge. From that point they must give their opinions knowing that what we want to estimate is the market value of the junior players (uncertainty) based on the valuation of a group of qualities to which there is no set of objective measures (subjectivity). We are working with the problem of assigning values to the variables that dispense with the requirement of exclusivity and about which it is possible to comment in an ambiguous way.

In short, the main objectives of the present paper are:

- The valuation of junior football players, who have not been on the market before and for which there is no reference price.
- Prior to the valuation of the junior football players we need to value their characteristics. Our purpose is to value characteristics like the vision of the game through expressions like good, very good, bad, very bad, etc.
- The formation of homogeneous groups of football players that have similar characteristics. A homogeneous group is the set of football players that are interchangeable for a particular position.

Consequently, the structure of the paper is as follows: the next section analyze the psychosocial, physical and technical elements of the players on the market to form groups that have similar characteristics and are interchangeable, as well. Each group must be analyzed in order to get the relation between the price of each player and their distance from the group, and finally we allocate our player to one of the former groups to get the theoretical value of the market. A discussion of the paper and a proposal of further research are presented in the last section.

2. The valuation of football players' characteristics

In order to begin the description of our model, we will start by describing the characteristics that a football player must fulfill. Knowing that each position requires different qualities, according to Gil-Lafuente (2002), three sections are considered: psychosocial elements, or inherent to a person and to their training; physical elements, or the result of their physical condition; and training and technical elements, either innate or acquired, and the most important are shown in Table 1.

Table 1. Football player qualities.

Psychosocial elements	Physical elements	Technical elements
• Winner Behavior.	• Resistance to physical pain.	• Speed without ball.
• Good relations in the locker room.	• Physical resistance.	• Speed with ball.
• Good relations with external people.	• Average speed.	• Ability to play against another.
• Intellectual level.	• Level of acceleration.	• Risk in attack, successfully.
• Cultural and civic level.	• Strength and forcefulness.	• Way of centering a foul.
• Quality of habits, hobbies, …	• Bone strength.	• Left leg kicking power.
• Mental Strength.	• Tendency to common diseases.	• Right leg kicking power.
• Level of discipline and seriousness.	• Muscle power.	• Vision of game.
• Leadership skills.	• Level of recovery after effort.	• Speed in getting rid of the ball.
• Ability to adapt to country's culture.	• Rapid appearance of tiredness.	• Power with head.
• …	• …	• …

Firstly, we have to choose the characteristics that our football player must fulfill, which may be different depending on the position that the player has in the field. It is clear that the characteristics of a goalkeeper are different from those of an attacking player, and the latter differs from the centre forward. Let's suppose that we have chosen a player C with n characteristics $C = \{C_1, C_2, ..., C_n\}$. We know that it is difficult to value each of those qualities economically, so each expert has to value each quality with expressions like: perfect, good, average, bad, etc. We particularly recommend using the following scale: 1, perfect; 0,9, very good; ….; 0.2 pretty bad; 0.1, very bad, and 0, awful. These valuations represent the level or degree that a football player presents with regard to a characteristic through the letter μ. In our model we suppose that every characteristic presents the same weight, but they can be adjusted by a particular weight represented by $\omega_i, i = 1, ..., n / \sum_{i=1}^{n} \omega_i = 1$,

To proceed with the organization of the players, as with the further valuation, we need to know the distance or difference that exists between two players. To do so, we will use the Hamming distance. Assuming that we start from two sets, M and N, which n characteristics, the relative Hamming distance:

$$\delta(M, N) = \frac{1}{n} \sum_{i=1}^{n} \left| \mu_M^i - \mu_N^i \right| \tag{1}$$

Where μ_M^i is the degree that a football player M presents with regard to a characteristic i. In order to calculate the distance, it is possible to assign different weights to each characteristic according to their importance.

3. Football players market

A fundamental aspect for valuing our players is a detailed analysis of the football players market, for this, we need to have a database of football players that includes all the players transferred in a particular period. To do so, it is necessary to:

- Compile the prices of each of the players to be transferred in the period to be considered,
- Make a detailed analysis of the psychosocial, physical and technical characteristics, through an expert survey,
- Create groups in which all the football players are interchangeable, because their contribution to the team is similar, from the previous information and according to the methodology that we present below.

Assuming that we have a football player that is perfectly valuable with four characteristics (in fact, we need many more, but we take only four in order to simplify the presentation of the model. The practical implementation of it with computing applications will help us to introduce all the desired variables: A, physical resistance; B, vision of the team; C, ability to play against another, and D, risk in defense, successfully.

And assuming that J players have been transferred, a table can show the number of experts that have answered each valuation for each characteristic of a transferred player on the market (for instance for player a, and for level 0, n_0^a). Column n shows the number of people that have answered the question for that player (for player a, n^a), which we call referential, and finally, column μ shows the degree or level of each evaluated characteristic, by taking the arithmetic mean that represents the membership function of that quality, which takes values from zero to one.

	0	0,1	...	1	n	μ
Player a	n_0^a	$n_{0,1}^a$	...	n_1^a	n^a	μ_A^a
...		...	...	...	...	...

For instance, the membership function for player a is obtained as $\mu^a = \sum_{s=0}^{1} s.n_s^a / n^a$, where n_s^a is the number of answers for player a and quality

s, $s = 0$, $0,1$, ..., $0,9$, 1. We have assumed that all the experts have the same information and their opinions are considered equally important, but a different weight can be assigned to each expert (Hsi-Mei & Chen-Tung, 1996).

To sum up, we can state that we have two sets, the players set to order, which is called $E_1 = \{a, ..., J)\}$, and the characteristics set, that is represented by $E_2 = \{A$ (Physical resistance), B (Vision of the team), C (Ability to play against another), D (Risk in defense, successfully)$\}$. Consequently, we proceed to join the former valuations into a fuzzy relation expressed in the matrix $[\tilde{R}]$, whose values express the degree of importance assigned to each characteristic of a player. In order to be able to compare players with each other, we proceed to get the relative distance between them (J_i, J_j), expressed thought a disimilarity matrix (we divide by four, because we are considering four characteristics only).

$$\overline{\delta}_{i,j} = \overline{\delta}(J_i, J_j) = \frac{1}{4}\sum_{S=A}^{D}\left|\mu_S^i - \mu_S^j\right|, \; i, j = a, ..., J \tag{2}$$

Now, we can find the dissimilarity matrix, or the distance between two players. So, higher values of $\overline{\delta}_{i,j}$ mean that players present less similarities and, what is more, they are less replaceable with each other. Data can be collected in a dissimilarity matrix [D], remembering that the distance between a player and himself (elements of the diagonal of the matrix) is zero. Anyway, as we want to know the similarity between two players, we have to take the complementary to one $\delta_{i,j} = 1 - \overline{\delta}_{i,j}$, which is the similarity matrix [S].

From matrix S, and in order to get a more operative matrix, for each element, we take,

$$a_{ij}(\alpha) = \begin{cases} 1, & si \; \mu_{ij} \geq \alpha \\ 0, & si \; \mu_{ij} < \alpha \end{cases} \tag{3}$$

So, from matrix [S] we take the α-cut [S_α], in which all the elements, according to (4) are zeros or ones ($a_{ij} \in \{0,1\}$).

From all the previous information, our objective is to find groups of interchangeable players. In this way, we will have homogeneous groups of transferred players which we can apply the present study to, and assign our junior players to. To do so, the Pitach algorithm (Pitach, 1970) is used.

Once, the algorithm has been used, we can find that there are players that only belong to one group, which indicates a certain inelasticity. Anyway, other players belong to more than one group, who are interchangeable between them. Anyhow, we want to emphasize that the only players that are interchangeable with each other are those belonging to one group.

Thus, transferred players can be grouped. We want to call attention to the fact that the main task for a correct performance of the present model is precise knowledge about transferred players in a year, and in addition, their prices and a valuation of their characteristics, and furthermore, the valuation of the characteristics of the junior players. The first one, 'prices', can be obtained from the news published about the signing up market, whereas for the second we need the participation of a set of experts. In the following section we will introduce 'price' into our model.

4. Player groups in the market

Let's assume that, according to the information available, J players have been transferred, whose prices are denoted by $P_i, i = 1, ..., J$. Furthermore, assuming that G groups have been made up from former players, denoted by $G_g, g = 1, ..., G$, each group holding n_{G_g} players.

For group G_i with n_{G_i} players, the value of the membership function for the characteristic A of the player j is $\mu_A^{n_{Gi}, G_i}$.

Even though we present an example with only four characteristics, it is evident that a complete study will deal with many more. In order to find the relation between characteristics and price we must work out an added value, as an average (weighted, if we consider a suitable weighted factor) of the levels of each characteristics. So, the weighted value of characteristics A is:

$$\mu_A^{G_i *} = \frac{1}{n_{G_i}} \sum_{j=1}^{n_{G_i}} \mu_A^{j, G_i} \tag{4}$$

We proceed in a similar way for the rest of characteristics, obtaining as added values $\mu_*^{G_i *} = \left(\mu_A^{G_i *}, ..., \mu_D^{G_i *} \right)$.

Next, we work out the distances between each element of each group and their added values, using the Hamming distance to do so. For instance, to work out the distance between the player r and its added values:

$$\delta_r^* (G_i) = \frac{1}{4} \sum_{j=A}^{D} \left| \mu_j^r - \mu_j^{G_i *} \right| \tag{5}$$

In this way, we get the distance to the added value from each element of the group G_i.

One of the main advantages of this detailed study is the fact that it refers only to homogeneous groups of players, that is, players who are interchangeable with each other, and furthermore, it is possible to know the distance to what we might call the core of the group.

In the next stage, we go on to find the relation between the absolute difference between a player's price and the average price of the group, and their distance to the group. The regression between each characteristic of the player and their price could be considered, but apart from making the model much more complex, it is possible to find situations where it is impossible to find the parameter estimators because the number of observations are lower than the number of parameters to be estimated, furthermore, what is really important is the group which the players belong to and the distance to the core of the group.

$$p_j^{G_i} = b_0^{G_i} + b_1^{G_i} \delta_j^*(G_i) + e_j \tag{6}$$

$p_j^{G_i}$ being the deviation of the price of player j of group G_i with regard to the average of the group. In this way, a regression is estimated for each group between the absolute difference of the price and the distance of the player's characteristics to the core of the group.

5. Value of a junior player

In order to get the valuation of our junior players, their characteristics must be valued in the same way as for the transferred players, independent experts must value each characteristic with expressions like good, very good, etc. Once all these valuations have been collected, they must be added. Let's suppose that our junior player z presents added value μ_A^z, μ_B^z, μ_C^z and μ_D^z for their characteristics.

The next step is the assignation of our junior player to one of the homogeneous groups, which could be defenders, midfielders, forwards, etc, but within these groups we can make different subgroups. In order to do this, we work out the distance of our player to each group, using the Hamming distance. This process is repeated for each junior player that we have to value. So, the distance to player z from each player of group i (player 1, ..., player G_i) must be calculated as:

$$D_{1,z} = D(Player\ 1, z) = \sum_{j=A}^{D} \left| \mu_j^{player1} - \mu_j^z \right| \tag{7}$$

...

So we have the distances of each player to group G_i from our junior player z. The global distance to that group, if all of the players of this group have the same importance, we will work out the average of the players.

$$\overline{D}_{G_i,z} = D(group\ \mathbf{G}_i, z) = \frac{1}{n_{G_i}} \sum_{j=1}^{n_{G_i}} D_{j,z} \tag{8}$$

Once we have found the relative distance between the player to every group, we will be able to conclude that the best group for the junior player is the one that minimizes the distance. Let's assume the best one is group Gi. It is easy to get the monetary value of the junior player, just by applying the regression corresponding to group $\mathbf{G}_i$: $P_z = b_0^{G_i} + b_1^{G_i}\ \overline{D}_{G_i,z}$

We have valued a junior player from their psychosocial, physical and technical characteristics, through a method of valuation which allows anticipation of the market, because when a junior player becomes well known, their price rockets. It is a tool which permits subjectivity and deals with it properly.

6. Discussion and further research

In this paper we develop a model to estimate the price of junior players from the opinion of football experts like trainers, coaches, sports managers, sports journalists, etc. about subjective characteristic like leadership skills, rapid appearance of tiredness, or vision of the team. In our opinion, the appropriate selection of characteristics is the most important factor for the correct implementation of the model.

The use of this methodology means, firstly, that we can make a valuation of each of the football players transferred and secondly, and more importantly, that we can analyze the differences between them and make interchangeable player groups. As a result, prices of the interchangeable football players are comparable, and finally, even though it is not our objective, we can detect the existence of low-priced football players (this fact is not really important for other people but it is very important for people who deal with the price of the players). Anyway, in the model, the price paid has been considered as an input because it is the best information for valuing other football players. The groups have been made using the abovementioned Pichat algorithm. Performance evaluation (appraisal) is a central issue in management (Robbins, 2005) including sports management (Byers, 2004).

The present model of football players' valuations can be applied to other team sports, and with small changes, to individual sports. Nowadays, we are working on the implementation of the present model in one of the most important clubs of the Spanish football league in order to value their junior players, by considering the price of the transferred players throughout the last year and their characteristics. In any case, it is my wish to conclude the present paper by considering the model that we have presented in this paper as complementary to the others that we have quoted, because in order to get a suitable value, the median value, the CVM and others like that of Kedar –Levy should be considered.

References

1. T. Byers, Managing sport operations, quality and performance, in J. Beech & S. Chadwick (Eds.). The business of sport management. New York: Prentice Hall (2004).
2. G. Fried, S.J. Shapiro and T.D. DeSchriver, Sport finance. Champaign, IL: Human Kinetics (2007).
3. J. Gil-Lafuente, Algoritmos para la excelencia, claves para el éxito en la gestión deportiva. Barcelona: Futbol Club Barcelona (2002).
4. H. Hsi-Mei and C. Chen-Tung, *Fuzzy Set. Syst.* **79**, 279-285 (1996).
5. H. Kedar-Levy and M. Bar-Eli, *J. Sport Manage.* **22(1)**, 50-81 (2008).
6. A.C. Krautmann, *Econ. Inq. 37*, 369-381 (1999).
7. E. Pitach, Contribution a l'algorithmique non numerique dans les ensembles ordonées. Tesis doctoral de Ciencias. Universidad de Grenoble (1970).
8. F. Pujol, P. García-del-Barrio, *Report on media value in football.* ESIrg Universidad de Navarra, www.unav.es/econom/sport (2008).
9. F. Pujol, P. García-del-Barrio and J. Elizalde, Report on media value in football. ESIrg Universidad de Navarra, www.unav.es/econom/sport (2007).
10. S.P. Robbins Organizational behavior (11th ed.). Upper Saddle River, NJ: Prentice Hall (2005).
11. Zimbalist, Baseball and billions. New York: Basic Books (1992a).
12. Zimbalist, Salaries and performance: Beyond the Scully model, in P.M. Sommers (Ed.) Diamonds are forever, (109-133). Washington, DC: The Brookings Institution (1992b).

CHOICE OF MARKET ENTRY MODE INTO A FOREIGN MARKET: THE CASE OF BALEARIC HOTEL CHAINS IN THE CARIBBEAN REGION AND GULF OF MEXICO

ONOFRE MARTORELL CUNILL, CARLES MULET FORTEZA,
ANTONIO SOCÍAS SALVÁ

*Deparment d'Economa de l'Empresa, University of Balearic Islands, Ctra. de
Valldemossa, Km 7.5. Campus UIB. Edificio Jovellanos. Palma de Mallorca, Spain*

The region formed by the Caribbean and Gulf of Mexico is currently the top destination chosen by Balearic hotel chains in their international expansion strategies. These hotel chains can choose from among a variety of different entry modes. This study attempts to pinpoint the factors that play a decisive role in the decision process of Balearic hotel chains when choosing a growth strategy for expansion into the Caribbean or Gulf of Mexico The conclusions show that to analyse the choice of entry mode, the transaction cost theory (TCT) must be modified, incorporating factors of an institutional and cultural nature.

1. Introduction

When a company expands into a foreign market, one important decision that must be made is the choice of entry mode, choosing between equity and non-equity modes. The main aim of this study is to identify factors that play a key role in the choice of entry mode by Balearic hotel chains when expanding internationally into the Caribbean and Gulf of Mexico. This paper therefore focuses on the hotel sector: a particularly appropriate sector when analysing choices of entry modes into international markets, since non-equity modes are just as widespread, if not more so, than equity-based ones (Contractor and Kundu, 1998).

2. Sample Mathematical Text

In this study, we take a syncretic approach to the choice of entry mode (in other words, we do not just take into account factors specific to the host country, but also factors relating to the companies wishing to penetrate these markets and corporate strategic planning and control-related factors), like that used by Contractor (1990).

Our analysis is based on information obtained from primary and secondary sources. The secondary information is taken from a review of literature on entry modes by international companies, particularly companies from the service sector, and the primary information was taken from a survey of each of the 10 Balearic hotel chains present in the Caribbean and Gulf of Mexico in early 2007. The survey was answered by 8 of the 10 companies, accounting for 80% of the total sample. The two companies that did not answer the survey have a low presence in the region, since the 8 chains used in our study account for 90% of the total number of hotels and 97% of all rooms run by Balearic chains in the Caribbean and Gulf of Mexico. In short, the sample that we use in this study covers a total of 139 hotels, which in turn represent 60,111 rooms. Our empirical research was also based on a Delphi analysis, performed using executives in charge of the expansion of some of the Balearic Islands' most prestigious chains, like Sol Meliá, Barceló Hotels & Resorts, Iberostar Hotels & Resorts, and Riu Hotels. In the Delphi analysis, the executives were asked to rate the perceived importance given to certain strategic factors (analysed in continuation) when a hotel chain engages in a process of international expansion, using a scale ranging from 1 (not very important) to 5 (very important).

In line with most research on the choice of entry mode (Kogut and Zander, 1993; Contractor and Kundu, 1998; Pan and Tse, 2000; Luo, 2001 etc), our dependent variable is a categorical one. Given the characteristics of the investment modes that can be used in the Caribbean, we developed a qualitative variable with three categories: M=1 if the hotel is run under a management contract, M=2 if it is run under a leasehold, and M=3 if it is run by the owner. Thus the dependent variable is a polytomous ordinal measure. The higher the variable, the higher the amount of capital invested by multi-national investors and the tighter their control over the foreign company, allowing the parent company to consolidate itself internationally.

Given the nature of the dependent variable, logistic regression (or logit) model were used to verify our hypotheses. Since there were more than two categories involved, a multinomial logit model was applied.

3. Theoretical Review and the Formulation of Hypotheses

3.1. *Country-specific variables*

a) The country's level of risk (political, economic and financial). High volatility in the external environment of the host country, i.e., high country risk, has been demonstrated to promote the use of shared-control arrangements. In high-risk countries, firms must possess the necessary flexibility to shift to a different mode of operation should the original mode be rendered inefficient by unpredictable changes in the environment. Integrated modes are associated with high switching costs and, as a result, are not generally recommended in these environments. Low-control modes, on the other hand, offer the necessary flexibility and are characterized by low switching costs.

H1: M (a dependent variable that shows increases in the level of control and shareholder involvement) is negatively related with the country's political and/or economic level.

b) Cultural Gap. On the one hand, a series of studies argue that the greater the cultural gap, the smaller the shareholding that will be held in the company and the greater the prevalence of collaborative alliances in growth strategies. Others authors claim, however, that when different cultures are involved, companies prefer to expand through ownership, thus imposing their own management methods. In an unknown environment, a company does not fully trust local management methods and will prefer to run the hotel itself. Whatever the discrepancy in the impact of the cultural differences, the transaction cost theory suggests that the two visions are correct. The second hypothesis to test is as follows:

H2: M is negatively associated with cultural differences between the investor country and host country.

c) Level of economic development. According to a study of the hotel industry by Dunning and McQueen (1981, 1982a, b) participation in the share capital of a hotel business is positively related with the level of economic development of the host company, and so the hypothesis that we have formulated is as follows:

H3: M is positively related with the economic development of the place where the hotel is located.

d) Existing foreign investment into the local economy. The study of the hotel industry by Dunning and McQueen (1981) proposes that, holding all else constant, hotels will tend to choose a growth strategy that involves shareholder control. As a result, since our study focuses on the hotel industry, our hypothesis is as follows:

H4: M is positively related with the level of foreign investment into a particular host country.

3.2. *Structural factors of the company*

e) The size of the company. That most studies show that as the size of a company grows, it is more likely to opt for direct investment through ownership (Argarwal and Ramaswami, 1992; Yu, 1990; Osborne, 1996, Campa and Guillén, 1999; Rialp et al., 2002), whilst smaller companies with more limited resources and/or skills in investing in foreign markets will prefer shared modes of control (Erramilli and Rao, 1993). Given the substantial investment that is required in the hotel trade, we propose the following hypothesis:

H5: There is a positive relationship between the size of the companies and M.

f) International experience. According to Welch and Luostarinen (1988), if the firm has already been involved in FDIs in several countries, the firm will have accumulated capabilities and know-how concerning such a mode of entry, which may be used in other destinations, and even allow the firm to bypass intermediate stages. In this context, those firms with higher investment abroad also possess a higher level of accumulated distinctive competencies, which allow them to overcome what Zaheer (1995) has called 'the liability of foreignness', i.e. the additional costs incurred by firms operating in foreign markets, which would not be incurred by a local firm. In this respect, Contractor and Kundu (1998) and Randoy and Dibrell (2002) have detected a positive correlation between the scope of a firm's international operation (number of FDIs in different countries) and its degree of investment commitment.

The following hypotheses have been formulated for testing:

H6: M is directly related with the company's international experience.

H7: M and the number of countries in which the company is present are directly related.

3.3. *Strategic factors and control factors of the company*

g) The perceived importance of economies of scale. Some literature insists that to achieve economies of scale, companies must maintain a high level of control, and so they will tend to use equity-based growth strategies. At the same time, another opposing vision insists that to achieve a worldwide presence, companies must accept numerous local partners in several different markets.

Nevertheless, it has been suggested that, in the case of the Spanish hotel sector, there is a certain cost involved in the transfer of specific know how, generated by possible market errors. As a result, our hypothesis is as follows:

H8: The perceived importance of the scale of a hotel's global (worldwide) operations is positively related with M.

h) The perceived strategic importance of the size of a company's global operations. We propose that, in the specific case of the hotel industry, when priority is given to larger-scale global operations, hoteliers will tend to invest more direct capital in ownership, holding all else constant. Thus our hypothesis is as follows:

H9: M is positively related to the perceived importance of a company's size.

i) The perceived strategic importance of an international booking system and trade name or brand. In the hotel industry, a worldwide booking system and brand name are both considered to be strategic advantages, which the parent company normally owns and controls (Dunning and McQueen, 1981). These advantages also boost the possibility of successful alliances (Contractor and Kundu, 1998). Thus companies with well-known trade names and important booking systems tend to increase the number of franchise operations and management contracts they use. Consequently, our hypotheses are as follows:

H10: The perceived importance of a booking system is negatively associated with M.

H11: The perceived importance of a brand name is negatively associated with M.

j) The perceived strategic importance of investment into training. Companies that invest heavily in training tend to choose equity-based growth strategies such as ownership, because the profits that can be reaped from staff training are better put to use under systems that guarantee stricter control. Consequently:

H12: The perceived strategic importance of investment into training is positively related with M.

k) The perceived strategic importance of management controls and quality controls. Our analysis of this variable shows that companies that do not consider it to be very important prefer to use growth strategies based on shareholder investment. Consequently:

H13: M is positively associated with the perceived importance lent to management controls and quality controls.

l) The perceived strategic importance lent to diversifying operations. To define this variable, the executives were asked to rate how important it is to be able to diversify operations or, in other words, reconvert a hotel into another business (like a condo-hotel or timeshare businesses). Our analysis shows that chains that consider this variable to be very important use shareholder-based growth strategies. Consequently:

H14: M is positively related to the perceived importance lent to diversifying operations.

m) The perceived strategic importance of a company's skill at centralizing and decentralizing its operations. Our analysis shows that those chains that consider this variable to be very important prefer to use non-equity growth strategies. Therefore:

H15: M is negatively related to the perceived importance lent to a company's capacity to centralize and decentralize its operations.

4. Results and Conclusions

Before outlining the results of the multinomial logit analysis, a series of comments should be made. Firstly, a synthetic index was drawn up to test the assumptions concerning the qualitative variables. The synthetic index was created in order to avoid problems of multicollinearity with some of these variables. This synthetic index groups together all the qualitative variables, with the exception of variables relating to the perceived importance of economies of scale and the perceived importance of a hotel chain's capacity to centralize and decentralize its operations. For this reason, the results have been presented in two different models. Model 1 excludes the qualitative variables that did not prove to be significant when the synthetic index was drawn up. In contrast, model 2 includes these two variables separate from the synthetic index. Likewise two different adjustments were made, introducing 6 hotels from the sample run under leaseholds by Spanish hotel chains operating in the Caribbean and Gulf of Mexico in regression A and not including them in regression B. It is interesting to see that the obtained results were consistent in both cases.

All the regressions were significant ($p<0.001$) and their goodness of fit was acceptable for this type of model ($0.27<$Pseudos-R2<0.37), confirming that the syncretic theory can be applied in the case of the Balearic hotel industry. That is, the theory that includes specific factors relating to the host country and company, plus strategic corporate planning and control-related aspects when choosing an entry mode into a foreign country. Additionally, the results of Table 4 show a high level of significance for the chi-square value.

Table 1. Estimates regression multinomial logistic ordinal.

	Regression A (with hotels on lease)		Regression B (without leased hotels)	
Variable	**Model 1**	**Model 2**	**Model 1**	**Model 2**
RI_i	0.105 (0.135)	0.085 (0.118)	0.093 (0.121)	0.078 (0.111)
CUL_{IJ}	-1.677 (0.609)**	-0.831 (0.647)	-1.345 (0.585)**	-0.723 (0.605)
$GDPcap_i$	-0.001 (0.000)*	-0.001 (0.000)*	-0.001 (0.000)*	0.000 (0.000)
FDI/GDP_i	0.168 (0.058)**	0.119 (0.052)**	0.136 (0.052)**	0.101 (0.046)**
$SIZE_j$	0.000 (0.000)	0.000 (0.000)	0.000 (0.000)	0.000 (0.000)
IEX_j	-0.203 (0.686)	-3.400 (2.0133)*	-0.243 (0.688)	-3.131 (1.879)*
NCP_i	0.357 (0.191)*	0.540 (0.334)*	0.315 (0.187)*	0.400 (0.301)
Synthetic index	2.820 (0.631)***	6.827 (2.156)**	2.378 (0.586)***	5.657 (1.648)***
ISE		6.905 (3.381)**		5.422 (2.477)**
ICENTRAL		1.835 (1.122)		1.274 (0.848)
Prob>K^2	**0.000**	**0.000**	**0.000**	**0.000**
Pseudo-R^2	**0.276**	**0.374**	**0.267**	**0.309**
Chi-Square	**64.517 *****	**87.407*****	**49.156*****	**56.929*****
No observations	**139**	**139**	**133**	**133**

It is important to note that the results of the regression differ from those obtained by Contractor and Kundu (1998) and Ramón (2002), mainly due to the fact that our study is directed at a very specific tourist destination, while the aforementioned studies focus on internationalization in a broader sense, since they cover all international destinations.

The factors that have been most decisive in equity-based growth strategies, which allow for greater control over hotels, are:

- A secure investment.
- Uncertainty with regard to the transfer of specialist know how.
- Training costs.
- The importance of economies of scale.

The factors that have been most decisive in encouraging strategies based on collaborative alliances are:

- The importance of the hotel chain's booking system and brand names.
- Countries those are culturally different from the hotel chain's own country.
- The evolution of the profit-earning capacity of the original investment.
- An interest in increasing the size of the hotel chain.

References

1. J. Campa and M. Guillén. *The Internalization of Exports: Firm- and Location- Specific Factors in a Middle-Income Country. Management Science*, **13**: 181-201 (1999).
2. F. Contractor. *Contractual and cooperative forms of international business: Towards a unified theory of modal choice. Management International Review*, **30** (1): 31-54 (1990).
3. F. Contractor and S. Kundu. *Modal Choice in a world of alliances: Analyzing organizational forms in international hotel sector. Journal of International Business Studies*, **29** (2), 325–358 (1998).
4. J. Dunning and M. McQueen. Transnational corporations in the international tourism. New York: UNCTC (1981).
5. J. Dunning and M. McQueen. The eclectic theory of the multinational enterprise and the international hotel industry. In A. M. Rugman (Ed.), New theories of multinationals. London: Croom Helm (1982a).
6. J.Dunning and M.McQueen. *Multinational corporations in the international hotel industry. Annals of Tourism Research*, **9**: 69-90 (1982b).
7. M.K. Erramilli and C. Rao, C. *Service firms' international entry mode choice: A modified transaction-cost analysis approach. Journal of Marketing*, **57**: 19-38 (1993).
8. B. Kogut and U. Zander. *Knowledge of the firm and the evolutionary theory of the Multinational Corporation. Journal of International Business studies*, **24:** 625-645 (1993).
9. Y. Luo . *Determinants of Entry in an Emerging Economy: A Multilevel Approach. Journal of Management Studies*, **38**: 443-447 (2001).
10. K. Osborne. *The Channel Integration Decision for Small-to Medium-Sized Manufacturing Exporters, International Small Business Journal*, **14** (3): 40-56 (1996).
11. Y. Pan and D. Tse. *The Hierarchical Model of Market Entry Modes. Journal of International Business Studies*, **31** (4): 535-554 (2000).
12. T. Randoy and C. Dibrell. *How and Why Norwegian MNCs Commit Resources Abroad: Beyond Choice of Entry Mode. Management International Review*, **42**: 119-140 (2002).
13. A. Rialp, C. Axinn and S. Thach. *Exploring Channel Internalization among Spanish Exporters. International Marketing Review*, **19** (2): 133-155 (2002).
14. L. Welch and R. Luostarien. *Internationalisation: Evolution of a Concept. The Journal of Industrial Economics*, **XXVI** (2): 177-191 (1988).
15. C. Yu. *The Experience Effect and Foreign Direct Investment. Weltwirtschaftliches Archiv*, **126** (4): 561-580 (1990).
16. S. Zaheer (1995). *Overcoming the Liability of Foreignness. Academy of Management Journal*, **38**: 341-363 (1995).

MODEL FOR THE ESTIMATION OF VARIABLES THAT TAKE PART IN THE DECISION MAKING PROCESS OF THE POPULATION TOWARDS ATTITUDES OF SOCIAL COMMITMENT

ANNA MARIA GIL-LAFUENTE[†], Mª LUISA SOLÉ MORO

Department of Economics and Business Administration, University of Barcelona, Avda. Diagonal 690, 08034 Barcelona, Spain

The objective of this paper is to analysis the behaviour of individuals with the purpose of establishing the policies and strategies of investment in more suitable and efficient resources to promote social commitment through altruistic attitudes. Our investigation find those elements that bring about certain behaviours and attitudes as well as all the conditions that make it possible with the last aim to direct the financial resources towards those elements that are more efficient to secure the proposed objectives. In this sense cause-effect the relationship will become the development of a model based on the processing of the incidence relations whose origins are in the models of structural equations. The model that is going to be implemented presents some variants that are going to allow the processing of subjective causal relations as well as the combinatory processing of all incidences that are going to show some elements on others, about causes or effects.

1. Introduction

The interest of companies and institutions jeopardizes the different aspects that affect to the social commitment is in the fact of being able to have a sufficiently global model, flexible and adaptive being able to tackle the problems derived from the evolution of the social behaviours in a certain context. The objective is based on being able to have the maximum information at the time of destining its investments with the purpose of obtaining the maximum yield in the form of social benefit. At times of economic activity slowing down, it is made

---

[†] Corresponding author: Tel: +34 93 402 19 62; Fax: +34 93 402 45 80.
   E-mail addresses: amgil@ub.edu (A.M. Gil), mlsolesole@ub.edu (M.L. Sole).

indispensable to have instruments that allow to take advantage of maximum expression of resources, as well as to be able to offer the greater benefit to social level. For the east company project until now, represented a step forward with respect to all the processed works and information since it raised for them a new platform to obtain results.

On the other hand, when defining the indirect effects, the own directors or people in charge of the institutions have to reconsider the appreciation that have of the answer of the citizen to the stimuli and propose actions.

The process of continuous change in the form and the objectives to arrive to the citizen causes that key elements eg: take letter from protagonist in the studies in the scope of the social commitment experiences and previous personal situations of each individual, context or atmosphere in which lives, works and is related the individual and own sensitivity, among others many factors.

The present work is framed in a line of investigation based on the analysis of the processing of the uncertainty. At the moment, the techniques applied to the realised studies to date have concentrated in the statistical scope. In spite of having obtained some interesting results, the majority of the models only partially explain the different behaviours in the contemplated process.

Our proposal must like objective complement statistical the traditional models through the use of mathematical techniques for the processing of the uncertainty. In this way we offer different instruments that will allow it to better management in the decision making in the processes of selection and implication in the social commitment. Given the process of existing globalisation in the economies of all the countries it becomes essential to establish some mechanisms that allow working with all the information, as much of an objective type as of a subjective type, with the objective of making forecasts that approach most possible the reality. It is precise, for it, to have some tools able to allow the obtaining of excellent information and decisive in relation to these processes that not always are evident and whose implications through direct relations of causality are masked by the intervention of other interposed elements that not always are in the open and, therefore, are not contemplated.

The objective of being able to make decisions with all the possible information is vital for the processes of previsual analysis of social implication of each one of the different population segments, in which most of the cases numerous investments in resources, time are realised and effort that not always provide the maximum efficiency. The mechanisms that need in these cases must count on the adaptation of some technical sufficiently flexible and general at the same time as they are able to incorporate all the possible eventualities that can be produced.

In 1988 professors Kaufmann and Gil Aluja had already done some experimental studies leaning towards the proposal of modelling that we try to implement in this work.

Thus, the interest of this work is the one of being able to count on some tools apt for the prediction and promotion of the individual behaviours towards altruistic attitudes and of social commitment and will allow to optimize the resources to invest as well as being able to raise the decision making adapted around the strategies and tactics to use at every moment and based on the proposed objectives. Nowadays either many methods of analyses based on statistical methods exist and always ex post, that is to say, contemplating the results occurred. But the new development on that we try to investigate is in the fact of being able to anticipate the behaviour of the citizens and therefore the institution will be able to direct to its resources and investments towards those elements that will provide major projection and yield from the economic and social perspective.

To show the operation of the theory of the forgotten effects we will raise briefly its methodological foundations. If we have two assemblies of elements:

$$A = \{a_i \mid i = 1,2,...,n\}$$
$$B = \{b_j \mid j = 1,2,...,m\}$$

We will say that there is an incidence of a_i on b_j if the value of the function characteristic of property of the pair (a_i, b_j) it is estimated in $[0,1]$, that is to say:

$$\forall (a_i, b_j) \Rightarrow \mu(a_i, b_j) \in [0,1]$$

The assembly of pairs of estimated elements will define the one that we called "matrix of direct incidence", which shows the relationship between cause-effect in the different degrees that are produced enters the elements of assembly A (causes) and the elements of the joint B (effects):

$$
\underset{\sim}{M} = \begin{array}{c} \\ a_1 \\ a_2 \\ a_3 \\ a_4 \\ a_5 \\ \vdots \\ a_i \end{array} \begin{array}{cccccc} b_1 & b_2 & b_3 & b_4 & \cdots & b_j \\ \mu_{a_1 b_1} & \mu_{a_1 b_2} & \mu_{a_1 b_3} & \mu_{a_1 b_4} & \cdots & \mu_{a_1 b_j} \\ \mu_{a_2 b_1} & \mu_{a_2 b_2} & \mu_{a_2 b_3} & \mu_{a_2 b_4} & \cdots & \mu_{a_2 b_j} \\ \mu_{a_3 b_1} & \mu_{a_3 b_2} & \mu_{a_3 b_3} & \mu_{a_3 b_4} & \cdots & \mu_{a_3 b_j} \\ \mu_{a_4 b_1} & \mu_{a_4 b_2} & \mu_{a_4 b_3} & \mu_{a_4 b_4} & \cdots & \mu_{a_4 b_j} \\ \mu_{a_5 b_1} & \mu_{a_5 b_2} & \mu_{a_5 b_3} & \mu_{a_5 b_4} & \cdots & \mu_{a_5 b_j} \\ \vdots & \vdots & \vdots & \vdots & \vdots & \vdots \\ \mu_{a_i b_1} & \mu_{a_i b_2} & \mu_{a_i b_3} & \mu_{a_i b_4} & \cdots & \mu_{a_i b_j} \end{array}
$$

The assembly of incidences that show the relationship between cause-effect to us that take place between two assemblies of elements represents the matrix of direct incidence (or of first order). If it appears a third assembly of elements C formed by elements that act like effects of the joint B, that is to say:

$$
C = \{ c_k / k = 1, 2, \ldots, z \}
$$

$$
\underset{\sim}{N} = \begin{array}{c} \\ b_1 \\ b_2 \\ \vdots \\ b_m \end{array} \begin{array}{cccc} c_1 & c_2 & \cdots & c_z \\ \mu_{b_1 c_1} & \mu_{b_1 c_2} & \cdots & \mu_{b_1 c_z} \\ \mu_{b_2 c_1} & \mu_{b_2 c_2} & \cdots & \mu_{b_2 c_z} \\ \cdots & \cdots & \cdots & \cdots \\ \mu_{b_m c_1} & \mu_{b_m c_2} & \cdots & \mu_{b_m c_z} \end{array}
$$

We will obtain two relations of incidence that will have the elements of the joint B common, that is to say:

$$
\underset{\sim}{M} \subset A \times B \quad i \quad \underset{\sim}{N} \subset B \times C
$$

The mathematical operator who allows to connect the incidence of A exceeds C is the composition max-min. When three uncertain relationships of incidence consider its composition defines the causality relationship enters the elements of the first assembly and the elements of third assembly C the intensity or degree that it estimates to have considered the elements that belong to the joint B.

$$\forall (a_i, c_z) \in A \times C:$$

$$\mu(a_i, c_z) \underset{\sim}{M} \circ \underset{\sim}{N} = \forall_{bj} (\mu M(a_i, b_j) \wedge \mu N(b_j, c_z))$$

2. Relation of direct and indirect causalities

We begin our exposition with the existence of a relation of direct incidence, that is to say, a first uncertain cause-effect defined by two assemblies of elements:

$A = \{a_i / i = 1, 2, ..., n\}$, that acts like causes

$B = \{b_j / j = 1, 2, ..., m\}$, that acts like effects

And a causality relation $\underset{\sim}{M}$ defined by the matrix:

$$[\underset{\sim}{M}] = \{\mu_{a_i b_j} \in [0,1] / i = 1, 2, ..., n; j = 1, 2, ..., m\}$$

Being $\mu_{a_i b_j}$ the functions characteristic of property of each one of the elements of the matrix $[M]$ (formed by the rows corresponding to the elements of the assembly A - cãuses - and the columns corresponding to the elements of the assembly B - effects). We could say, then, that the matrix $[M]$ it is composed by the estimations realised around all the effects that the˜ elements of the assembly A they exert on the elements of the assembly B. The more significant the relationship of incidence, the more elevated the estimate assigned to each one of the elements of the matrix will be. Our objective is based on obtaining a new matrix of incidences but that reflects, not only the direct relations of causality, but those that in spite of being evident do not exist already, are fundamental for the appreciation of this phenomena.

In order to reach this objective it is necessary to establish the devices that make it possible, the fact that different causes can at the same time have effect on themselves and, to consider that certain effects can also give rise to incidences themselves. Therefore it will be necessary to construct two relations of additional incidences which will on the other pick up the possible effects that are derived to relate causes to each other, on the one hand, and effects to each other. These two auxiliary matrices are defined:

$$[A] = \{\mu_{a_i a_j} \in [0,1]/i,j=1,2,...,n\}$$
$$[B] = \{\mu_{b_i b_j} \in [0,1]/i,j=1,2,...,m\}$$

The matrix $[A]$ picks up the relationship of incidence that can be produced between each one of the elements that we acted like causes and the matrix $[B]$ it does respectively between the elements that act like effects. As much $[A]$ as $[B]$ they agree in the fact that both are first reflective, that is to say:

$$\mu_{a_i a_j} = 1/i,j=1,2,...,n$$
$$\mu_{b_i b_j} = 1/i,j=1,2,...,m$$

In counterpart nor $[A]$ nor $[B]$ they are first symmetrical, that is to say:

$$\mu_{a_i a_j} \neq \mu_{a_j a_i},i,j=1,2,...,n$$
$$\mu_{b_i b_j} \neq \mu_{b_j b_i},i,j=1,2,...,n$$

Once constructed the matrices $[M]$, $[A]$ and $[B]$, it has to come to the establishment from direct and indirect incidences, that is to say, incidences in which, simultaneously, some cause or interposed effect takes part. For it we will come to the composition max-min from the three matrices:

$$[A] \circ [M] \circ [B] = [M^*]$$

The obtained result will be a new matrix $[M^*]$ that it picks up the incidences between causes and effects of second generation, that is to say, the initial causal relations affected by the possible interposed incidence of some cause or some effect. The difference between the matrix of the effects of second generation and the matrix of direct incidences will allow us to know the degree in which some relations of causality have been forgotten or avoided:

$$[O] = [M^*](-)[M]$$

The result allows us to know, from the degree of forgetfulness of some incidence, the element, is cause or effect, that for of connection. It is possible to say, finally, that at the most elevated it is the value of the function characteristic of property of the matrix $[O]$ more elevated it is the degree of forgetfulness produced in the relation of initial incidence.

3. Conclusions

One of the basic aspects of the exposition is to identify the quantitative agents and organizations that could be involved in the development of the civic commitment with the purpose of applying the qualitative elements and what defines it. This work tries to make a model for the prediction, incentive and promotion of civic behaviours. A question that has to date not been obtained with the classic instruments of modelling.

At present there are many and varied methods of analysis but none whose objective is the prediction or at least not in the sufficiently general and flexible terms like the precise reality. The model is based on the recovery of hidden effects, that is to say, elements that really exists and is fundamental in all relation of causality, but that in different circumstances is not considered. In this way, to not only make arise these elements essential in motivating civic behaviours in the population, but to choose those activities on the part of companies and institutions that with smaller investment in resources provide a greater approach to the raised and persecuted objectives.

Basically this investigation tries to look for those elements that turn out keys to develop directed activities to increase, in absolute and relative terms, the attitudes that foment the social and civic commitment of the citizens. The results will allow establishing the policy of investments necessary to reach the goal to achieve. The model that already has been implemented successfully in different studies tries to present the key elements in maximizing the inverted resources at the time of reaching the raised objectives. One is which with minimum economic grants the maximum yield in the scope of the social commitment can be obtained.

References

1. Boehm, A, (2009) Business Social Responsibility: Perspectives of Businesses and Social Workers, Journal of Social Service Research, Volume: 35 Issue: 3.
2. Canto-Mila, N; Lozano, JM, (2009) The Spanish Discourse on Corporate Social Responsibility, Journal of Business Ethics, Volume: 87.
3. Dalmoro, M; Venturini, JC; Pereira, BAD, (2009) Green Marketing: integrated social and environmental responsibility in the marketing environment, Rev. Brasileira de Gestao de Negocios, Vol. 11, Is. 30.

4. Gil Lafuente A. (2005), Fuzzy logic in financial analysis. Ed. Springer-Verlag.

5. Kaufmann, A.; Gil Aluja, J. (1988), Modelo para la investigación de efectos olvidados. Ed. Milladoiro.

6. Jorgensen, A; Hauschild, MZ; Jorgensen, MS, et al., (2009). Relevance and feasibility of social life cycle assessment from a company perspective, International Journal of Life Cycle Casements Volume: 14 Issue: 3.

7. Jegatheesan, V.; Liow, J.L.; Shu, L., et al., (May 2009) the need for global coordination in sustainable development , Journal of Cleaner Production.

8. Lamsae, AM; Vehkaperae, M; Puttonen, T, et al., (2008) Effect of business education on women and men students' attitudes on corporate responsibility in society, Journal of Business Ethics, Volume: 82 Issue: 1.

9. Muñoz, MJ; Rivera, JM; Moneva, JM, (2008) Evaluating sustainability in organisations with a fuzzy logic approach, Industrial Management & Data Systems, Volume: 108   Issue: 5-6.

10. Rothstein, R; Jacobsen, R, (2009) Measuring Social Responsibility, Educational Leadership, Volume: 66 Issue: 8.

11. Petrini, M; Pozzebon, M, (2009) Managing Sustainability with the Support of Business Intelligence Methods and Tools, Conference Information: 3rd International Conference on Information Systems, Technology, and Management, Date: MAR 12-13, 2009 Ghaziabad INDIA.

12. Preuss, L; Haunschild, A.; Matten, D, (2009) The rise of CSR: implications for HRM and employee representation, International Journal of Human Resource Management, Volume: 20 Issue: 4.

13. Saarni, SI; Hofmann, B; Lampe, K, et al., (2009) Ethical analysis to improve decision-making on health technologies, Bulletin of The World Health Organisation, Volume: 86 Issue: 8.

14. Sanchez, JLF; Sotorrio, LL, (2007) The creation of value through corporate reputation, Journal of Business Ethics, Volume: 76.

15. Selgelid, MJ, (2008) Improving global health: Counting reasons why, Conference Information: Workshop on Poverty and Medicine, Date: Jan, 2006 Univ. Melbourne, Ctr Appl Philos & Publ Ethics Melbourne AUSTRALIA, Developing World Bioethics, Volume: 8 Issue: 2.

16. Vilanova, M; Lozano, JM; Arenas, D, (2009) Exploring the Nature of the Relationship Between CSR and Competitiveness, Journal of Business Ethics, Volume: 87.

17. Weidenbaum, M, (2009) Who will Guard the Guardians? The Social Responsibility of NGOs, Journal of business Ethics, Volume: 87.

18. Wising, F, (2009). Political and Economic Arguments for Corporate Social Responsibility: Analysis and a Proposition Regarding the CSR Agenda, Journal of Management, Volume: 86 Issue: 4.

IMPACT OF CAMPAIGNS FOR THE PREVENTION OF ALCOHOL ABUSE IN ADOLESCENCE

AGUSTÍ CASAS ROMEO, RUBÉN HUERTAS GARCÍA, ESTER SUBIRÀ LOBERA

Departament d'Economia i Organització d'Empreses; Universitat de Barcelona
Av. Diagonal 696, 08034 Barcelona. Spain
acasas@un.edu, rhuertas@ub.edu, esubira@ub.edu

Many studies have used an experimental design to evaluate the characteristics of effective communication and to attempt to identify relationships between specific controllable variables (factors such as the source and the message) and outcome variables (such as attention, comprehension, and attitudes, which affect willingness to purchase). The novelty of this study lies in the characteristics of the message content assessed: the "regulatory focus to the message," as proposed by Higgins (1997). In addition, we used a novel fractional factorial design that has three levels and is distributed in blocks. This is based on subset designs and uses the efficiency criterion D (D-optimal). The goal was to assess whether there were differences in responses to variations in the message and source between genders.

1. Introduction

Despite numerous campaigns to reduce alcohol consumption in adolescents, young people continue to drink in excess. In Spain, as in many countries, government departments have designed campaigns to prevent alcohol abuse, but have failed to achieve their goal. Therefore, a crucial issue for the public and for advertising agencies is how to create effective communication campaigns for teenagers.

Adolescents are considered a profitable target for advertising. Early prevention of alcohol abuse advertising campaigns emphasized the negative physical consequences of drinking, particularly these promoted by Dirección General de Tráfico (Spanish authority that manages traffic). This was a definite step in the right direction but proved to be an inefficient means of discouragement, especially among adolescents.

Higgins' (1997) regulatory approach has emerged as a powerful theory for predicting the persuasiveness of adverts. This theory suggests that there are two types of consumers with different motivational orientations: promotion-focused consumers and prevention-focused consumers. This approach suggests that persuasiveness of a message might depend on the characteristics of the receiver[*] and whether he/she is motivated to achieve the goals or to avoid random behaviour. Researchers have proposed (under the regulatory approach) that the persuasiveness of advertising could also depend on the characteristics of the message[†].

The aim of this study is to analyze the characteristics of effective communication and determine the role of the regulatory approach in improving the persuasiveness of a campaign to prevent alcohol consumption among adolescents. In addition, the goal is to verify, by means of discrete choice experiments, whether there are significant differences in the type of regulatory approach among female and male adolescents.

2. Discrete choice models

Discrete choice modelling can be used to assess the choice of an ad from a sample of various advertisements. This is a family-based method for modelling preference surveys for a particular property, in which the samples have been described or presented in terms of attributes and levels of intensity. The interviewees are presented with alternatives and are asked to rank them or assign them values according to their preferences. The way in which respondents make their assessment (lexicography, elimination by aspect, or other heuristics) is a complicated topic and it is out from our study.

The conceptual framework underlying discrete choice models is the theory of characteristic value. This theory assumes that the utility to consumers of purchasing goods can be broken down into the utility of each characteristic of the goods. Such models have been widely used in market research.

To select the source variables, we conducted a literature search and consulted experts in the field of advertising. Once we had preselected the variables, we coded them, as shown in Table 1.

Table 1. Variables making up the factorial design 3^4

	Variables	-1	0	+1
X1	Ethnic characteristics of the sources	Very pronounced	Mixed	Not pronounced
X2	Approach to message	Preventive negative	Neutral	Promotional positive
X3	Age of source (joint)	Mature	Mixed	Youth
X4	Source gender	Male	Mixed	Female

In experimental design standard texts, such as those by Myers and Montgomery (2002), provide examples of various applications, but focus on experiments

---

[*] Called "regulatory approach to the receiver".
[†] Called "regulatory approach to the message".

involving chemical processes. In these processes the use of block techniques is less important than, for example, in biological experiments because the high variability of behaviour of the alive beings. We considered that experiments with individuals will generate a high variability similar to biological experiments.

In this work we propose a novel methodology, in the field of marketing, to set out experiments. The process involves three steps:

(1) Determine the number of experiments to be performed.

(2) Design the procedure for selecting the number of experiments that meet a set of desirable properties.

(3) Group experiments in blocks so as to maintain the desirable properties of the selection process.

To determine the number of experiments conducted, we used the resource equation. This equation (1) requires at least n experiments in blocks of size n_b

$$n = \frac{n}{n_b} + \frac{q(q+3)}{2} + n_{lof} + n_{pe}, \tag{1}$$

where q is the number of variables, n_{lof} is the number of degrees of freedom (typically between 5 and 10) required to estimate the principal terms, and n_{pe} is a small number (typically between 5 and 10) which reflects the degrees of freedom required to estimate the pure error.

In this work, the number of variables is four, $q = 4$, and the blocks are of six experiments, $n_b = 6$. Fifteen degrees of freedom were required to estimate the principal terms and the pure error, $n_{pe} + n_{lof} = 15$ (the same value was used by Gilmour and Trinca, 2006). Therefore, the resource equation is 34.8.

Secondly, we needed to determine the number of experiments with desirable properties. We aimed to fit a second order polynomial model to the responses. The standard experimental design procedures, as in Myers and Montgomery (2006), would require a high number of experiments to be established efficiently, in addition to the degrees of freedom required to fit the model and to estimate the pure error.

Gilmour (2005) introduced a very interesting class of designs for factors with three levels, called subset designs (SD). Designs with three factors or variables have three levels and can be encoded as follows -1, 0 and 1. SDs are formed by subsets of factorial designs derived from the factorial 3^q. They were described by Hoke (1974) as follows: S_r, $r = 1$, ..., q is a subset of points of a factorial design in 3^q, given a hyper sphere of radius $\sqrt{r}$ around the centre point, S_o. Thus, S_r contains all the points that are r factor values with value ± 1 and the remaining $q - r$ factor with a value of 0.

Hoke (1974) also proposed a combination of designs to obtain efficient models with the fewest possible experiments. Gilmour (2005) studied combinations of these designs to produce different subsets of S_r. Therefore, a design formed by

414

subsets of S_r is defined by $c_{r1} S_{r1} + C_{r2} S_{r2} + \ldots$ and $c_r S_r \ldots$ means that the points in the subset will be replicated C_r times.

In a subsequent paper, these were matched to the D-optimal designs (4). Some SDs allow you to adjust a second order polynomial model. The following requirements must be met:

> • $c_r > 0$ for at least two r, and $c_r > 0$ for at least one r with $1 \leq r \leq q - 1$. All parameters can be estimated.

> • $c_r > 0$ for at least one $r \leq 2$. All interactions can be estimated.

Each subset S_r contains $\begin{pmatrix} q \\ r \end{pmatrix} 2^r$ points, including a 2^r factorial design for levels -1 and 1 for each combination of r factors, while the other $q - r$ factor value is 0.

In this paper, we consider four factors (variables) of three levels (values) each (Experiment 3^4). From the four factors, we can extract four subsets: *S1, S2, S3, S4*, and a central point S_o. In addition, the subset S_3 contains 32 experiments, the subset S_4 has 16 sub-experiments, S_2 has 24 experiments, S_1 has 8 experiments and S_0 has 1 experiment.

The S_r composition of each subset contains all the points that are r factor with values ± 1 and the remaining $q - r$ factors with a value of 0. For example, S_4 is *4* factors with values ± 1 and the remaining *4-4= 0*-factor with a value of 0. S_3 has *3* factors with values ± 1 and the remaining *4-3 = 1* factor with values of 0.

According to the *resource equation*, the minimum number of experiments is 34.8. We rounded this number up to 36 experiments, in order to study four factors. Various combinations of the subsets are required to consider the four factors in a second order polynomial model

> • $c_r > 0$ for at least two *r*, i.e. at least two subsets, and $c_r > 0$ for at least one *r*, with $1 \leq r \leq 4 - 1$, i.e. at least one that is replicated from one to three times. All quadratic parameters can be estimated.

> • $c_r > 0$ for at least one $r \geq 2$, i.e. at least one subset should be replicated twice, so that all interactions can be estimated.

In this case we need at least two subsets. Examples of SDs are: $S_3 + 4S_0 = 36$ experiments, $S_4 + 2S_1 + 4S_0 = 36$ or $S_3 + 4S_0 = 36$. We used the D-criteria to assess the efficiency of each design. The determinant (2) of the matrix of time has been calculated as follows:

$$|\mathbf{M}| = \frac{|\mathbf{X'X}|}{N^p} \tag{2}$$

where p is the number of parameters in the model and N is the number of experiments. Following the D-criteria, the best designs are $S_3 + 4S_0$ and $S_4 + 2S_1 + 4S_0$. The second design was chosen.

Third, the items should be divided into small blocks to facilitate sorting by the respondents. The theory of aliases and the confusion of the partial factorial design arise in experimental designs, but these problems can be solved in many situations (4). But in other situations this one is not a good solution.

In this paper, we considered 36 announcements, which were to be presented to the interviewees in six blocks of six and classified by them. In a block design system, each block usually has an orthogonal design. However, this is not possible when the variance of estimates increases with respect to the orthogonal design. Therefore, the loss of information should be minimized to preserve the characteristics of the design before it is configured in blocks. Several criteria can be used to select the best block design. In this paper, following the recommendations of Trinca and Gilmour (2000), we use a block design to minimize the S matrix, which is also called "basic scores". The S matrix shows the distribution of the loss of accuracy between the different variables to be estimated and, therefore, can be used to select the most suitable design. For example, if the interpretation of quadratic effects is not relevant for some qualitative variables, a design can be selected that focuses on the loss of efficiency in quadratic variables, rather than in the main variables and interactions.

If we consider the following model (3) for the design blocks and assume that the effect of the blocks is fixed:

$$y = B\alpha + X\beta + \varepsilon \tag{3}$$

where $y\ (n \times 1)$ is the response vector, $\alpha\ (b \times 1)$ is the vector of parameters that reflect the effect of the block, B is a matrix $(n \times b)$ whose columns are the indicator's lock, $X\ (n \times p)$ is the extended matrix of combinations of treatments for the polynomial model in order to incorporate q factors, $\beta\ (p \times 1)$ is the vector of the parameters to be estimated, and $\varepsilon\ (n \times 1)$ is the vector of random error. We define the model's efficiency (4) at estimating the parameters βi as:

$$EF(\hat{\beta}_i) = \frac{V_*(\hat{\beta}_i)/\sigma_*^2}{V(\hat{\beta}_i)/\sigma^2} \times 100\% \tag{4}$$

Where $V_*(\hat{\beta}_i)$ and σ_*^2 are the variance of $\hat{\beta}_i$ and the error respectively for the design with no block, while $V(\hat{\beta}_i)$ and σ^2 are the variance of the $\hat{\beta}_i$ and the error when the block design is used. However, as σ_*^2 and σ^2 are unknown before the experiment, we can transform the above expression as follows (5), by isolating variances relative to the betas:

416

$$EF\,(\hat{\beta}_i)\,\frac{\sigma_*^2}{\sigma^2} \;=\; \frac{V_*\,(\hat{\beta}_i)}{V\,(\hat{\beta}_i)}\;\times\;100\,\% \tag{5}$$

The variance $\hat{\beta}_i$ (6) of the design with blocks is:

$$V\,(\hat{\beta}) \;=\; \left[(X'X)^{-1} \;+\; SA^{-1}S'\right]\sigma^2, \tag{6}$$

where $S = (X'X)^{-1}X'B$ and

$A = \left[B'B + n_b\,n_b' - B'X(X'X)^{-1}X'B\right]$ is the variance $\hat{\beta}_i$ of the design without blocks (7):

$$V\,(\hat{\beta}) \;=\; (X'X)^{-1}\sigma^2, \tag{7}$$

It is clear that the matrix S, called the matrix of "basic scores", plays a decisive role in the efficiency of the model. Following Trinca and Gilmour (2000), an s_{ij} is the background score of the parameter i in block j $(i = 1, 2, .., p, j = 1, 2, ..., b)$. When the elements of S are zero, apart from the first row, no information is lost as a result of the block design. A different result indicates that information has been lost in estimating the betas that generated the block design. In this respect, the "basic scores" show where information has been lost as a result of the block design, and therefore the researcher can assess the suitability of the information loss as a result of the exchange of rows between one design and another.

The selected design is shown in Table 2. In this design, the loss of information due to the block design mainly occurred in the quadratic variables, given that their interpretation when the variables are qualitative does not make sense.

We also had to determine the criteria to be used by interviewees to assess their preferences. There are basically three criteria: choose the best option, rank the six options or assign a score to each of the options. But, each one of these options has consequences in its analysis and the models used for its adjustment. Some authors recommend using the criteria and models that require the lowest number of possible scenarios.

Finally, we had to specify the model we would use to adjust the results and the procedure for their estimation. We selected the second-order polynomial model (9) and the ordinary least squares or maximum likelihood method for the estimations:

$$\mu = \beta_0 + \sum_{i=1}^{q}\beta_i x_i + \sum_{i=1}^{q}\beta_{ii} x_i^2 + \sum_{i=1}^{q-1}\sum_{j=i+1}^{q}\beta_{ij} x_i x_j, \tag{9}$$

Table 2. Design of 36 announcements in six blocks of six each

Factors									
Blocks	X1	X2	X3	X4	Blocks	X1	X2	X3	X4
1	-1	-1	-1	-1	4	-1	-1	1	1
	1	-1	1	-1		-1	1	1	-1
	-1	0	0	0		1	-1	-1	-1
	0	1	0	0		1	1	-1	1
	0	0	-1	0		0	0	0	0
	0	0	0	1		0	0	0	0
2	-1	-1	-1	1	5	-1	1	-1	-1
	1	-1	1	1		-1	1	1	1
	1	0	0	0		1	0	0	0
	0	1	0	0		0	-1	0	0
	0	0	1	0		0	0	1	0
	0	0	0	-1		0	0	0	-1
3	-1	-1	1	-1	6	1	1	-1	-1
	-1	1	-1	1		1	1	1	1
	1	-1	-1	1		-1	0	0	0
	1	1	1	-1		0	-1	0	0
	0	0	0	0		0	0	-1	0
	0	0	0	0		0	0	0	1

3. Fieldwork and results

We used 6 blocks of six scenarios each replicated 257 times (136 girls and 121 boys). The questionnaires were completed during class time with the collaboration and supervision of school teacher. Parental consent was obtained.

Students were asked to order the 6 scenarios from best to worst and then give them a score of 1-10. A score of one was given to announcements that did not preferred and 10 to those that was perfectly preferred. Once the results had been obtained, they were adjusted by the ordinary least squares model.

The results are showed in Table 3, they explain about 30% of the variability. These results are in line with others obtained by similar works that only try a partial explanation of the reality.

Table 3. Results

	Girls		Boys	
Effect	Estimation	Sig.	Estimation	Sig.
(constant)	6.576	0.000	6.337	0.000
X1 (ethnic trait)	0.162	0.117	0,158	0.187
X2 (regulatory approach)	0.227	0.028	0.266	0.030
X3 (age)	0.514	0.000	0.202	0.095
X4 (gender)	0,023	0.824	-0.037	0.761
X1 × X2	0.189	0.111	0.040	0.766
X1 × X3	0.038	0.776	-0.036	0.814
X1 × X4	-0.212	0.062	-0.073	0.571
X2 × X3	0,178	0,117	0.147	0.268
X2 × X4	0.386	0,001	0,005	0,971
X3 × X4	-0.165	0,202	-0.267	0.071
$X1^2$	- 0.779	0.000	- 0.613	0.012
$X2^2$	0.876	0.000	1.092	0.000
$X3^2$	-0.334	0.087	-0.312	0.198
$X4^2$	0.033	0.867	0.287	0.241

$$R^2 = 0,387 \qquad R^2 = 0,274$$

Two of the four main factors, X2 (regulatory approach to the message) and X3 (age), were significant and positive in both subsamples, between 90 to 99% significance level. However, where the main differences are observed are in interactions. For the subsamples of female students there are two significant interactions: X1 × X4 (ethnic traits with gender) with negative sign and X2 × X 4 (regulatory approach to gender) with positive.

As for male students only one of the interactions, X3 × X4 (age and gender) with negative sign, had a 90% significance level. These results were as expected. The attractiveness of the source is related to the similarity or familiarity that it arouses in the receiver, due to the appearance of the issuer, and other personal traits. Such attractiveness involves the ability to generate belief in the receiver, through the process of identification (8).

4. Conclusions

Although the development of marketing literature on methods for the design of experiments and analysis has evolved significantly (6), the application of such methods to empirical work is progressing more slowly. Designs are frequently simple and focus on the analysis of the main factors. This paper presents a design model based on subsets (SD), applied to a problem of social marketing. The results show a complex situation, which could not have been determined using simple models based only on the main factors.

References

1. T. HIGGINS, "Beyond Pleasure and Pain," American Psychologist, Vol. 52, N° 12, pp. 1280-1300. (1997).

2. H. MYERS & D. C. MONTGOMERY, Response Surface Methodology, John Wiley & Sons, Inc. (2002).

3. S.G.GILMOUR, "Response Surface Designs for Experiments in Bioprocessing" Biometrics, Vol. 62, (June), pp. 323-331. (2005).

4. G GILMOUR & L. A. TRINCA "Response Surface Experiments on Processes with High Variation" in KHURI, A. I. (2006): Response Surface Methodology and Related Topics, World Scientific Publishing Co. (2006).

5. A. TRINCA, & S. G. GILMOUR, "An algorithm for arranging response surface designs in small blocks" Computational Statistics & Data Analysis, Vol. 33, pp. 25-43. (2000).

6. TOUBIA & J. R. HAUSER, "On Managerially Efficient Experimental Designs" Marketing Science, (Nov.-Dec.) Vol. 26, pp. 851-858. (2007).

7. A.T. HOKE, "Economical second order designs based on irregular fractions of the 3^n factorial" Technometrics, Vol. 16, pp. 375-384. (1974).

8. E. BELCH & M. A. BELCH, Publicidad y Promoción (6ª edición), Ed. Mc Graw Hill. (2004).

MODEL OF HIERARCHIAL STRUCTURING VARIABLES OF EXPORTING COMPANIES

JOEL BONALES VALENCIA[*]

Institute of Economic and Enterprise Investigations
Universidad Michoacana de San Nicolás de Hidalgo
Morelia, Michoacán, México

JUAN GAYTÁN CORTES
JOSÉ SÁNCHEZ GUTIÉRREZ

University Center of Economic-Administrative Sciences
Universidad de Guadalajara,
Guadalajara, Jalisco, México

This research is based upon the study of the competitiveness of twenty-five export companies of avocado with available information about their organization, objectives, production, problems, and ability to efficiently export into the US. The documentary research focused towards the knowledge of the main theories on International Commerce. All this, in order to know the origin of company competitiveness (main objective of this study), and to get as a result its conceptualization, measurement and the variables that affect it – quality, price, technology, training and distribution channels -, as well as, the independent variables dimensions and indicators, in order to produce the research instrument. In order to determine the relevance between the variables considered in this investigation, the Technique of Analytical Hierarchial Structuring was used, which is used to evaluate the importance of the posed problems or the causes of he same. The method consists of realising comparisons by pairs between each one of the alternatives that in this case are variable and, by means of a previously specific scale, to evaluate the magnitudes of preference, among them, based on the objective that is persecuted to make the comparison.

1. Background

The documentary investigation focused to the knowledge of the main theories on International Commerce, Competitiveness and Uncertainty, as well as, the situation of the market of this product at world-wide level. As result of this 5 explanatory variables were identified that are: the quality, price, technology, qualification and channels of distribution.

---

[*] This work investigated the competitive factors of 25 avocado exporting companies located in Uruapan, Michoacán (Mexico). This cradle in a census of the twenty-five exporting companies, which its organization, its objectives and its problematic production could be known.

The opening of the U.S. market in November 1997 to the commercialization of Mexican avocado production was an excellent opportunity to develop a market in a culture that tended to consume natural foods, of good quality; within that a considerable amount of Mexican customary incorporating the avocado in its diet is included. Mexico's State of Michoacan. The Uruapan municipality, is the largest producer of "Hass" avocados in the world. Proximity to the large U.S. market of 300 million inhabitants with high spending power was a unique business opportunity to take advantage of the efficient network of dealers with experience in the handling of the avocado.

Problematic of the industrial sector the radical process of commercial opening adopted by Mexico as of the decade of 80's, generated challenges and opportunities for several Mexican companies but I question of blow competitive problems in customary companies to work in protected markets. These distortions with serious social effects are related directly to the competitiveness. One critical issue for the Mexican avocado industry has been U.S. import regulations that have often denounced as "green barriers". These regulations concern agricultural pesticide use as well as quality and maturity standards. In spite of the NAFTA, the U.S. has continued to impose a six cents per pound tariff avocado imports from Mexico but not on avocado imports from countries such as Chile and the Dominican Republic. With the entry of Mexico into the General Agreement On Tariffs and Commerce (GATT) in 1986, the export of Michoacan's avocados has experienced a number of diverse problems. Noncompetitive intermediaries have assumed greater control over avocado commercialization and distribution. Strong U.S. policies protecting the U.S. California avocado industry have continued.

The Mexican avocado sector is underorganized with production automation and commercialization having fallen behind that of other avocado producing countries such as Chile, Israel, the U.S., and Spain. There has been very little research on the competitive success factors of Mexican firms, by identifying the competitiveness factors for Mexican avocado exporting firms, this study will advance current knowledge about competitive factors for organizations in the Mexican agricultural sector that are dependent on exports to the U.S.A.

2. Theory and Hypotheses

International trade is of critical importance in theoretical models of competitiveness. According to Porter's (1991) theory of comparative advantage, a nation need not produce all its own goods and services and can increase its competitiveness by only producing goods and services for which it holds a comparative advantage. Although there is a lack of consensus on the definition of "competitiveness" [need reference], international competitiveness is most commonly associated with greater productivity as measured by penetration in international markets, investment flows, and workforce unit costs. Derived from the Latin words "cum" (con) and "petere" (to ardently wish, to request), competitiveness implies not only a willingness to compete against others for a desired prize but also possessing the capacity to take action to establish, protect, and expand market positions. Although a literature review revealed over 100 difference competitiveness models, the following eight are the most relevant to this study.

In agreement with Worldwide Report on Competitiveness, competitiveness exists at the country level, the sector level, and the company level (Aguilar, 1995: 35). The extent to which national sociopolitical and economic conditions are favorable to business is the primary determinant of country level competitiveness. Sector level competitiveness is the degree to which an industrial sector has the potential to grow and to produce attractive yields on investment. Company level competitiveness is determined by an organization's ability to design, produce, and commercialize goods and services that are more attractive than those of market competitors.

Competitiveness is a relative concept with not all nations, sectors or companies being able to be equally competitive in global markets. Widely competitive a national atmosphere for a business can not be it for another one. The Mexican Secretariat of Commerce (SECOFI) identified the following factors in their competitiveness model: (1) atmosphere with clear and permanent rules; (2) economies of scale; (3) economies of specialization (particularly important for small and medium companies; (4) flexible and fast adoption of the most appropriate technology (including processes of shared production); and (5) markets operating correctly. Nevertheless, this model has been criticized because it does not consider factors such as the development of qualified human resources, communications and transportation infrastructures, regulatory clarity, and the presence of a comprehensive and high priority industrial policy for long term investment in science and technology.

1. Porter (1991: 855) defined competitiveness as the production of goods and services that are of higher quality and lower prices than those of domestic and international competitors. National competitiveness results in real income growth for a country's population. Porter's model identified four generic attributes of a nation that determine its competitive environment: (1) Related conditions of the factors, (2) market demand conditions; (3) industries and government support; and (4) the strategy, structure and rivalry of the company. These attributes measure the degree to which national environments are supportive of sector competition. Porter's "Diamond" reflects the many diverse elements of a nation, measures the manner by which nations create competitive forces and influence organizations, as well as identifying the need strategies and instruments for enhancing competitive advantage.

2. The Presidential Commission on Industrial Competitiveness of the United States (1985) concluded that national competitiveness is the basis for a standard of life that maintains and increases real income. Reason why it is from fundamental importance for the expansion of the use and the international fulfillment of obligations.
3. The World Economic Forum (1995) of the OECD used 330 indicators to measure eight basic factors that distinguish between the "soft side" (entry distribution, quality of the environment, and cultural values) and "hard facts" (GDP, economic growth, inflation, and balance of trade) of competitiveness

3. Quality

The quality is a significant variable that it influences in the competitiveness of the companies. According to the models of competitiveness of: The European Union, the Technological Institute of Massachussets, the OECD, BANCOMEXT, Michael And Porter, Carlos Wagner, Alexander Serralde, Sergio Hernandez, Alexander Lerma, Ricardo Arachavela and Vicente Felgueres. From the industrial point of view, the word quality means: lo better to satisfy desires and tastes with the consuming public. (Francisco J. Ortiz 1991, 23). All the products have quality and, depending if they satisfy or not the consuming public, traditionally the systems of quality control have settled down to assure minimum norms quality related to the necessities and tastes of the consumers.

The norms or specifications of quality are the pattern against which the characteristics of quality of the products are moderate that make or produce and, for that reason, are the first dimension that is due to know, if it is tried to get to control the quality. The second dimension of the quality is to have the system quality control that allows to correct the differences detected in the inspection of the products that take place. The last dimension of the variable quality, is to design the inspection systems, that is to say, the forms in which the characteristics of quality of products against the norms and specifications will be compared. These ideas take us hypothesis to our first of work:

Hypothesis 1: The application of the quality norms, the improvement of the system of control of quality and a readecuación of the system of inspection in the exporting companies from avocado to the United States of America, will bring like consequence a greater competitiveness.

Price

This variable form leaves from the models of the OECD, the Technological Institute of Massachussets, BANCOMEXT, Michael And Porter, Thomas J. Peters, Carlos Wagner, Safe Julio, Ricardo Arachavela and Vicente Felgueres.

The price is the only element of the marketing mixture that is generating of income; all the others are costs: therefore, it must be an active instrument of the strategy in the main areas of the decision making of marketing. The price is an important competitive tool to face and to overcome to the rivals and products near substitutes. Frequently the competition will force to reduce the prices, whereas the financial considerations intra-company produce an opposite effect. The prices next to the costs, will determine the long term viability of the company (Michael Czinkota 1996, 292).

The function of the analysis of the market in relation to the determination of the prices of export consists of establishing a maximum limit to the corresponding decision, from the demand of the product and the characteristics of the competitors. In the countries developing it is the situation of the market that determines the range of prices of exportation.

Reason why, one sets out:

> Hypothesis 2: When determining a better price of the avocado, indicated by means of the market that supplies, its production costs and costs of commercialization; a greater competitiveness of the exporting companies from avocado will be maintained to the United States of America.

4. Technology

Form leaves from the models of the OECD, the Technological Institute of Massachussets, Bancomext, Michael And Porter, Alfonso Cebreros, Henry Mintzberg, Ricardo Arachavela and Vicente. It is a determining variable that influences in the competitiveness of the companies. A thorough study of the variable technology was made to deduce its real definition, its dimensions and indicators.

The technology has been always point used in the speeches of the Mexican Government of an opportunistic and deceptive way. To thus they demonstrate to the National Plan of Desarrollo (PND) and the National Program of Technological Development and Científico it (PRONDETYC). The PND mentions that the competitiveness will depend crucial on the technological modernization of the country. (PND 1995, 91).El world of the words has crashed with the reality. The cost in science and technology is the plus under the emergent countries and comparativily inferior to Economies like the similar Spanish and Korean economic powers (CONACYT 2001).

Different concepts from technology exist. The Japanese say that it is a survival exercise, because thanks to the technology the Japanese town that faces manifold natural restrictions, has been able to emphasize in the world-wide concert. They add that in the coming years, the technological administration will be key of the success of the companies everywhere of the world (Akio Morita 1986, 255). The technology is defined as the knowledge organized for production aims, that are built-in in the force of work (abilities), in the equipment, or loose knowledge. The technology comprises of trinomio science-technology-production. Due to it, the following hypothesis sets out:

> Hypothesis 3: To greater use of technology a greater competitiveness of the exporting companies from avocado to the United States of America is guaranteed.

5. Training

Qualification Including in the models of the OECD, the Technological Institute of Massachussets, BANCOMEXT, Michael And Porter, Thomas J. Peters, Carlos Wagner, Alfonso Cebreros and Vicente Felgueres; it is a variable that influences in the competitiveness of the companies.

> Hypothesis 4: The qualification, based by means of the organization and the investment helps to obtain a greater competitiveness of the exporting companies from avocado to the United States of America.

6. Channels of the Distribution

Including in the models of the OECD, the Technological Institute of Massachussets, BANCOMEXT, Michael Porter, Miller, Alexander Serralde, Alexander Lerma, Ricardo Arachavela and Vicente Felgueres; the distribution channels are a variable that influences in the competitiveness of the companies. The administration of the distribution channel and its relation with the distribution channel are comparable with a marriage, as soon as it reunites to two independent organizations with shared goals. So that the relation works, each part must be clear with respect to its expectations and to openly communicate the changes perceived in the behavior of the other part, that could be opposite to the contract. Between narrower it is the relation with the distributor, is more probable that the success of marketing is materialized. The relation must be handled with the objective to reach the long term. Reason why, their indicators are the contract that is had with the intermediaries, the knowledge of the intermediaries and the distribution channels that handle the competition takes to the following hypothesis:

> Hypothesis 5: To better selection of the channels of distribution, interpreted by means of the design and administration of the distribution channel and the boarding; a greater competitiveness of the exporting companies from avocado to the United States of America is obtained.

7. Hierarchial Structuring Variables

They were five variables that emerge from the theoretical framework of competitiveness, to interact and determining the assumptions to prove or disprove as the result of the collection, processing and interpretation of data obtained from the field study.

To determine the relevance between variables considered in this investigation, we used the analytic hierarchy technique, which is used to assess the significance of the problems or the cause thereof. The method involves making pairwise comparisons between each of the alternatives in this case are variable and, on a scale previously specifically assess the magnitude of preference between them, depending on the purpose intended to make the comparison.

Market mentions that the problem statement assumes that all variables and objectives can be divided into different subsets and that there is order among them, so that the elements of a set have higher or lower priority than another.So, the problem is summed to determine the importance of each of the variables considered, so one must know the scale of values associated with each of them, ie what is the best or worst in terms of variable how they contribute to a greater or lesser degree to the achievement of each of the objectives set for analysis.

. The structure of the problem requires the division level objectives, which in this case the general aims of competitiveness and both can be divided into the layers of processing the product, marketing and business as a whole. The method first compares the importance of each of the variables together, based on comparison to one of the objectives of the next higher level. Thus, comparing in each stratum, the items were identified as targets. In summary, the method provides the relative importance of each variable in each of the levels using the following theorem:

$$W = \left[V_1^5 V_2^5 V_3^5 V_4^5 \,\middle|\, V_1^4 V_2^4 V_3^4 \,\middle|\, V_1^3 V_2^3 \,\middle|\, V_1^2 \right]$$

Subject:

W = Total relevance
V = Independent variable

The fact that the evaluation of each variable is made by a person implies that there is some bias opinion occurred, but to subdivide the original problem in a large number of subproblems and the error is minimized.

428

Table 1. Hierarchy of objetives and variables, based in the results of the theoretical framework of documentary research.

Competitive				
Product		Marketing		Company
Quality	Price	Technology	Training	Distribution channels

To solve the problem, first raised the different strata in which the targets were located and the variables considered, and relations between them according to the model mentioned above. Thus the following table is constructed with three levels where the first is the main objective of competitiveness study, in the second level are three objectives for the application of this technique are considered the product, marketing and business. Finally, the third layer, are the variables considered in the study.

Table 2. Significance of the independen variable, based on the results of field research.

Objetives	Quality	Price	Technology	Training	Distribution channels	Total
Product	41.9%	25.6%	14.9%	9.0%	8.6%	100%
Marketing	42.2%	25.8%	11.3%	12.1%	8.6%	100%
Company	42.7%	23.3%	12.2%	8.3%	13.5%	100%
Total	42.2%	25.1%	12.9%	9.9%	9.9%	100%

Solving the matrix system as required by Theorem "Saaty", and applying the estimates of importance of objectives and variables whose scale is presented in the rating scale of activities, obtain the results shown in the table below, which shows that the total sum to relevances hundred percent.

According to this technique, it appears that the overall importance of the variables is given in the following order: quality, price, technology, training and distribution channels. The results indicate the main objective with a 38.8% product, marketing with a 36.6% and the company with a 24.7%. This is the importance given to the analysis of competitiveness through the variables considered.

References

1. M. Alvarez, "Estrategias Efectivas para Incrementar su Posición Competitiva", (1999).
2. V. Barraba and G. Zaltman, "La voz del mercado: La ventaja competitiva a través del uso creativo de la información del mercado", (2002).
3. G. W. Bohrnstedt, "Evaluación de la confiabilidad y validez en la medición de actitudes", (1998).
4. T. Burns and G. Stalker, "The Management of innovation", (1991).
5. F. David, "Conceptos de Administración Estratégica", (2004).
6. G. García, "Esquemas y Modelos para la Competitividad", (2003).
7. F. Kerlinger, "Investigación del Comportamiento", (2002).
8. E. Mercado, "Productividad base de la Competitividad", (2002).
9. F. Ortíz, "Metodología para el Análisis de la Competitividad Internacional de la Empresa", (1998).
10. M. Porter, "The competitive advantage of nations", (1991).
11. F. Reyna, "Ventajas comparativas y dotación de factores", (2003).
12. B. Yavitz and W. Newman, "Estrategia en Acción: Ejecución, Políticas y Resultados de Planeación Comercial", (1995).

THE OPTIMIZATION OF INVESTMENT IN POS ADVERTISING THROUGH A FUZZY MODEL BASED ON THE APPLICATION OF NEUROMARKETING TECHNIQUES

JAIME GIL-LAFUENTE
JOSEP MARIA TORTOSA VIDAL
JORDI AYMERICH MARTINEZ

Dpt. of Business Economics and Organization, Marketing Area
University of Barcelona
Av. Diagonal, 690. 08034 Barcelona, Spain

There have been a lot of discussions on the possibilities of neuroscience being applied to Marketing, but few are their applications to the business world and even fewer is the modeling of the results obtained in these applications. The majority of the data exploitations obtained in studies carried out with neuromarketing techniques are only descriptive and their value is found on the comparison of the results obtained with the benchmark data of similar studies. Our intention is to present a model based on diffused logic for optimizing investment in POS (Point-Of-Sale) advertising of an advertiser from the information obtained in a study on consumer behavior in the point of purchase. The reaction of the consumers is measured *neurometrically* taking into account different stimuli, media and the formats of advertisement in a perfumery.

1. Introduction

It is on the whole complicated to measure the effectiveness of different materials (formats and media) which are used for advertising products in the point of sales since there are no similar tools as the ones used for massive outdoor advertising in television, radio or newspapers.[*] Often companies and brands decide their advertising budgets in the point of sales based on experience and habits, and on the recommendation that the retailer provides to the manufacturer.

Therefore, the only way to find out the effectiveness of different materials used for optimizing investment in the point of sales is to measure the response of the consumer to the materials used in terms of sale or their preferences. We propose, along this line, to measure the response of the consumer taking into account the different stimuli of POS advertising, but not in terms of sale or preferences but in

---

[*] Studies on advertising effectiveness like those published by Infoadex, Study of television audience of Sofres Audimetria or the Estudio General de Medios (EGM).

432

more "emotional" terms, because the different formats and media have an impact on the consumer, although not necessarily predispose the sale. It is about measuring the emotional response of the consumer before the different materials of POS advertising and finding a model which would allow us to determine which of those materials have a higher impact on the consumer, with the objective that the companies can optimize their investment in advertising in the point of sale.

We have found in Zadeh's [1] theory of fuzzy sets the perfect formulation for establishing a model which would permit the optimization of investment in POS advertising from the data obtained measuring the neurometric parameters of the consumer, mentioned by Carl Senior *et al* [2] in the face of different elements of POS advertising.

2. The measurement of the consumer's response through neuromarketing

The measurement of neurometric parameters of the interviewed subjects in front of the scenes to be evaluated and in front of the different communicated elements of the point of sale will be necessary. The interpretation of the measurements in terms of cognitive activity, intensity, emotional quality and activation/interest/ motivation will be used for establishing which emotions are awaken by which elements and in which sense build the global process of purchase to, ultimately, isolate which elements are more susceptible to be the trigger for purchase [3].

The measurement through neuromarketing technique [4] consists of the registration of 4 neurobiological variables (brain activity, cardiac activity, muscular tension and electrical conductance of the skin) which provide the knowledge of cognitive and emotional activation produced by the stimuli of the point of sale in relation to a base line (resting state) [5].

1. Measurement of the brain activity
Before introducing the stimulus the values of the brain activity in the resting state will be recorded. During the test the frequencies of different areas of the brain will be registered, and afterwards, the two records will be compared. If the values are higher than the basal values, it would indicate a high processing of information, a cognitive focus. If the basal values are below, it indicates high mental imagery, significant perception of images and sensations.

2. Measurement of cardiac activity
After establishing the rest the changes in cardiac rhythm (Cardiac Interbeat) and the coherence are taken into consideration. The deviations of the basal value during the stimulation show that high values mean positive emotions, pleasure,

happiness, and low values negative emotions, displeasure. One of the pioneers in this area is the American Institute Heartmath[*], which specializes in mathematical measurement of different elements of the cardiovascular system and its relation with emotions.

3. Measurement of muscular tension

Before the test we measure the muscular tension during rest, and afterwards we present the stimulus and measure the reactions so as to compare them with that of the resting state. The deviations of the basal value during stimulation indicate the presence of emotional expression if high values (high tension) are observed and the absence of emotional expression if the values are low (low tension).

All this is based on the Facial Action Code (FAC) developed by Ekman and Friesen [6], which allows us to codify the muscles which are activated during the expression of emotions.

4. Measurement of the electrical conductance of the skin

Before presenting the stimulus we measure the subject's resting state so as to measure later the reactions during the test and compare the data. The duration of the impact of the stimuli is approximately 20-30 seconds. The deviations of the basal value during the stimulation indicate an increase of the motivation and interests if the values are high, and a decrease in motivation and lack of interests if the values are low.

This is a measurement in use since 1888, discovered by Feré [7] and Tarchanoff [8]; it measures the level of mental activation or *arousal* through electrodes placed on the hands which register changes in the skin's conductivity (GSR). The changes of the skin's electrical activity are produced by the exocrine sweat glands.

The GSR is related to the autonomic nervous system (ANS) since it is sensible to the changes of temperature and sweating. This is a measurement which indicates attention, orientation, arousal, emotionality and stress of a subject. It has been validated and can predict the results of sale in the advertising and marketing field according to LaBarbera, Tucciarone [9], and shows a high correlation with motivational tests.

3. Study in a perfumery with 14 POS advertising elements

A perfumery in a big city centre (Madrid) is selected. Information of 60 subjects was collected during their visit to this shop. The group consists of equal number of men and women between 25 and 50 years old, who are regular buyers and users of selective fragrances.

---

[*] Institute of HeartMath, 14700 West Park Ave., Boulder Creek, California 95006.

The procedure of the measurement follows the following stages:

1. The following sensors are placed on the subject:
    - EEG electroencephalograph to measure the brain's electrical activity (***mind***)
    - ECG electrocardiogram, plethysmograph in the middle finger, to measure the cardiac rhythm, interbeat interval and spectrum power (***heart***)
    - EMG surface electromyograph, placed in the corrugator muscle of the eye to measure the muscular tension (***eyes***)
    - GSR Galvanic skin response, to measure the electrical conductibility of the skin (***hands***)
2. The parameters obtained from the subject during the resting state (base line or basal state) are recorded.
3. The parameters during the exposure of the subject to different stimuli are recorded (14).
4. The parameters obtained during exposure to stimulus are compared with those during the resting state.

The stimuli tested are different POS advertising media, formats and brands which are listed as follows:

1. PRD Tester Shelf
2. PRD Counter Tester
3. CH y PR M Tester Shelf
4. PR W Tester Shelf
5. PR Góndola
6. CH Shelf
7. CH Banner Outpost
8. CH Anty-robbery
9. CH Shelf Decoration
10. CH Screen
11. CH Window
12. CH Tester Fountain
13. CH Tester stand & Gloriffier Table
14. CH Column

The measurement at rest indicates that the brain registers an activity of 23 Hz *High-Beta*; this type of activity is associated with the presence of thinking directing to calculation, concentration, and problem solving. The registered cardiac rhythm during rest was 82 pulsations per minute; the index of variability between pulsations was 35%. This is characterized as moderate anxiety. The emotions are neutral. Muscular tension registered was 13 microvolts during rest, the subjects did not show any emotional tension, and the skin conductivity during rest was 17 microsiemens, this orients the subjects towards apathy.

The results of the comparison of the basal values with those during exposure to the stimulus are shown below:

Table 1. Differences between the values of the subject before the stimulus with respect to the basal values.

	A.Brain	A.Cardio	T.Muscular	Elec.Skin
1.PRD Tester Shelf	-23	7	-46	24
2. PRD Count. Tester	-44	6	-73	35
3. CH y PR M Test Shelf	-33	4	-18	12
4. PR W Tester Shelf	-11	10	-27	-5
5. PR Góndola	-12	8	48	-1
6. CH Shelf	-20	5	8	15
7. CH Banner Outpost	-45	2	-28	25
8. CH Anty-robbery	-45	5	-24	20
9. CH Shelf Decoration	-43	10	-27	-24
10. CH Screen	-10	10	-35	-6
11. CH Window	-20	5	-38	24
12. CH Tester Fountain	-18	5	-35	18
13. CH Tester stand & Gloriffier Table	-12	5	-5	-16
14. CH Column	-38	11	-35	30

4. Modeling by means of fuzzy subsets to determine the impact and effectiveness of the materials tested

We conclude the process of final decision making by the information obtained from expert analysts of the totality of the data gathered.

As we have mentioned, we will take into account:

$$C = \{C_1, C_2, C_3, C_4\}$$

- C_1: Brain Activity
- C_2: Cardiac Activity
- C_3: Muscular Tension
- C_4: Skin Electrical Conductance

It should be noted that it is not only possible, but also recommended to consider each of these factors. In this case, we consider very useful working with convex weights.

$$\upsilon_{C1} = 0.9;$$

$$\upsilon_{C2} = 0.7;$$
$$\upsilon_{C3} = 0.5;$$
$$\upsilon_{C4} = 0.7.$$

Taking into account that: $\omega_1 = \dfrac{\upsilon_1}{\sum\limits_{i=1}^{n} \upsilon_i}$, $\omega_2 = \dfrac{\upsilon_2}{\sum\limits_{i=1}^{n} \upsilon_i}$,..., $\omega_m = \dfrac{\upsilon_m}{\sum\limits_{i=1}^{n} \upsilon_i}$.

We obtain:

$$\omega_1 = \frac{\upsilon_1}{\sum\limits_{i=1}^{n} \upsilon_i} = \omega_1 = \frac{0.9}{2.8} = 0.3214; \quad \omega_2 = 0.25; \quad \omega_3 = 0.1786; \quad \omega_4 = 0.25.$$

Then, the experts will proceed to describe the totality of the materials depending on the levels in which each of them fulfils each of the factors mentioned. These "valuations"[*] will be performed, equally given for each of the values conceived in *[0, 1]*.

Following the example at hand, we will consider these 14 materials as object of analysis:

$$P = \{M_1, M_2, M_3, M_4, M_5, M_6, M_7, M_8, M_9, M_{10}, M_{11}, M_{12}, M_{13}, M_{14}\}$$

- M_1: PRD Tester Shelf
- M_2: PRD Counter Tester
- M_3: CH y PR M Tester shelf
- M_4: PR W Tester Shelf
- M_5: PR Góndola
- M_6: CH Shelf
- M_7: CH Banner Outpost
- M_8: CH Anty-robbery
- M_9: CH Shelf Decoration
- M_{10}: CH Screen
- M_{11}: CH Window
- M_{12}: CH Tester Fountain
- M_{13}: CH Tester Stand & Gloriffier Table
- M_{14}: CH Column

---

[*] A valuation is a subjective numerical assignment.

The description is made, then, by means of fuzzy subsets [10]:

$$\tilde{M}_n = \begin{array}{|c|c|c|c|} C_1 & C_2 & C_3 & C_4 \\ \hline \mu_{C1}{}^{(m)} & \mu_{C2}{}^{(m)} & \mu_{C3}{}^{(m)} & \mu_{C4}{}^{(m)} \end{array}$$

$$, m = 1, 2, \ldots 14$$

In the case at hand, we would have the followings:

$$\tilde{M}_1 = \begin{array}{|c|c|c|c|} C_1 & C_2 & C_3 & C_4 \\ \hline 0.46 & 0.63 & 0.22 & 0.81 \end{array}$$

$$\tilde{M}_2 = \begin{array}{|c|c|c|c|} C_1 & C_2 & C_3 & C_4 \\ \hline 0.88 & 0.54 & 0 & 1 \end{array}$$

$$\tilde{M}_3 = \begin{array}{|c|c|c|c|} C_1 & C_2 & C_3 & C_4 \\ \hline 0.66 & 0.36 & 0.46 & 0.61 \end{array}$$

$$\tilde{M}_4 = \begin{array}{|c|c|c|c|} C_1 & C_2 & C_3 & C_4 \\ \hline 0.22 & 0.09 & 0.38 & 0.32 \end{array}$$

$$\tilde{M}_5 = \begin{array}{|c|c|c|c|} C_1 & C_2 & C_3 & C_4 \\ \hline 0.24 & 0.72 & 1 & 0.39 \end{array}$$

$$\tilde{M}_6 = \begin{array}{|c|c|c|c|} C_1 & C_2 & C_3 & C_4 \\ \hline 0.4 & 0.45 & 0.67 & 0.66 \end{array}$$

$$\tilde{M}_7 = \begin{array}{|c|c|c|c|} C_1 & C_2 & C_3 & C_4 \\ \hline 0.9 & 0.18 & 0.37 & 0.83 \end{array}$$

$$\tilde{M}_8 = \begin{array}{|c|c|c|c|} C_1 & C_2 & C_3 & C_4 \\ \hline 0.9 & 0.45 & 0.41 & 0.74 \end{array}$$

$$\tilde{M}_9 = \begin{array}{|c|c|c|c|} C_1 & C_2 & C_3 & C_4 \\ \hline 0.86 & 0.9 & 0.38 & 0 \end{array}$$

$$\tilde{M}_{10} = \begin{array}{|c|c|c|c|} C_1 & C_2 & C_3 & C_4 \\ \hline 0.2 & 0.9 & 0.32 & 0.3 \end{array}$$

$$\tilde{M}_{11} = \begin{array}{|c|c|c|c|} C_1 & C_2 & C_3 & C_4 \\ \hline 0.4 & 0.45 & 0.29 & 0.81 \end{array}$$

$$\tilde{M}_{12} = \begin{array}{|c|c|c|c|} C_1 & C_2 & C_3 & C_4 \\ \hline 0.36 & 0.45 & 0.29 & 0.71 \end{array}$$

$$\tilde{M}_{13} = \begin{array}{|c|c|c|c|} C_1 & C_2 & C_3 & C_4 \\ \hline 0.24 & 0.45 & 0.57 & 0.14 \end{array}$$

$$\tilde{M}_{14} = \begin{array}{|c|c|c|c|} C_1 & C_2 & C_3 & C_4 \\ \hline 0.76 & 0.99 & 0.32 & 0.91 \end{array}$$

Once the fourteen descriptions of the fourteen materials of the point of sale are done, the experts elaborate the fuzzy subsets, considered as ideal:

$$\tilde{I} = \begin{array}{|c|c|c|c|} \hline C_1 & C_2 & C_3 & C_4 \\ \hline 1 & 1 & 1 & 1 \\ \hline \end{array}$$

5. Brief reference to the notion of distance

To establish a coherent ordination it would be necessary to use an operator, who would show us the levels of "nearness" or, in its defect, of the "distance" between each of them [11]. We consider suitable, in this case, to work with "Hamming Relative Distance with Convex Weight". Thus, assuming two fuzzy subsets:

$$\tilde{I} = \begin{array}{|c|c|c|c|c|} \hline C_1 & C_2 & \cdots & C_{m\text{-}1} & C_m \\ \hline \mu^{(1)}{}_{C1} & \mu^{(1)}{}_{C2} & \cdots & \mu^{(1)}{}_{Cm\text{-}1} & \mu^{(1)}{}_{Cm} \\ \hline \end{array}$$

and

$$\tilde{M}_1 = \begin{array}{|c|c|c|c|c|} \hline C_1 & C_2 & \cdots & C_{m\text{-}1} & C_m \\ \hline \mu^{(2)}{}_{C1} & \mu^{(2)}{}_{C2} & \cdots & \mu^{(2)}{}_{Cm\text{-}1} & \mu^{(2)}{}_{Cm} \\ \hline \end{array}$$

m being the number of factors to keep in account, we will get its "Hamming Relative Distance with Convex Weight" [12] by means of:

$$\delta(\tilde{I}, \tilde{M}_1) = \frac{\sum_{i=1}^{m} \left| \mu_{P_1}(x_i) - \mu_{P_2}(x_i) \right|}{m}$$

Therefore, if we have:

$$\tilde{I} = \begin{array}{|c|c|c|c|} \hline C_1 & C_2 & C_3 & C_4 \\ \hline 1 & 1 & 1 & 1 \\ \hline \end{array}$$

and

$$\tilde{M}_1 = \begin{array}{|c|c|c|c|} \hline C_1 & C_2 & C_3 & C_4 \\ \hline 0.46 & 0.63 & 0.22 & 0.81 \\ \hline \end{array}$$

We will be able to find out the indices of separation by calculating:

$\delta(\tilde{I}, \tilde{M}_1) = 0.3214 |1 (\text{-}) 0.46| (+) 0.25|1 - 0.63| (+) 0.1786|1 - 0.22| (+) 0.25|1 - 0.81| = 0.4516075$

Following the same steps, we will reach all the distances:

$\delta(\tilde{I}, \tilde{M}_1) = 0.4516075;$

$\delta(\tilde{I}, \tilde{M}_2) = 0.33273457;$

$\delta(\tilde{I}, \tilde{M}_3) = 0.46387363;$

$\delta(\tilde{I}, \tilde{M}_4) = 0.55554628;$

$\delta(\tilde{I}, \tilde{M}_5) = 0.46703297;$

$\delta(\tilde{I}, \tilde{M}_6) = 0.47357495;$

$\delta(\tilde{I}, \tilde{M}_7) = 0.39166667;$

$\delta(\tilde{I}, \tilde{M}_8) = 0.339347;$

$\delta(\tilde{I}, \tilde{M}_9) = 0.43013631;$

$\delta(\tilde{I}, \tilde{M}_{10}) = 0.57810616;$

$\delta \tilde{I}, \tilde{M}_{11}) = 0.50398845;$

$\delta(\tilde{I}, \tilde{M}_{12}) = 0.53774056;$

$\delta(\tilde{I}, \tilde{M}_{13}) = 0.67537158;$

$\delta(\tilde{I}, \tilde{M}_{14}) = 0.22345062$

These results show that the majority of the materials offer a performance far from the optimum (ten of them with distances superior to 43%). Nevertheless, it is clear that the material M_{14} is the one closest to the ideal.

The order of preference would be as follows:

$$M_{14} \succ M_2 \succ M_8 \succ M_7 \succ M_9 \succ M_1 \succ M_3 \succ M_5 \succ M_6 \succ M_{11} \succ M_{12} \succ M_4 \succ M_{10} \succ M_{13}$$

When observing the distances, conveniently ordered,

1. $(\tilde{I}, \tilde{M}_{14}) = 0.22345062;$
2. $(\tilde{I}, \tilde{M}_2) = 0.33273457;$
3. $(\tilde{I}, \tilde{M}_8) = 0.339347;$
4. $(\tilde{I}, \tilde{M}_7) = 0.39166667;$
5. $(\tilde{I}, \tilde{M}_9) = 0.43013631;$
6. $(\tilde{I}, \tilde{M}_1) = 0.4516075;$
7. $(\tilde{I}, \tilde{M}_3) = 0.46387363;$
8. $(\tilde{I}, \tilde{M}_{51}) = 0.46703297;$
9. $(\tilde{I}, \tilde{M}_6) = 0.47357495;$
10. $(\tilde{I}, \tilde{M}_{11}) = 0.50398845;$
11. $(\tilde{I}, \tilde{M}_{12}) = 0.53774056;$

12. $(\tilde{I}, \tilde{M}_4) = 0.55554628;$

13. $(\tilde{I}, \tilde{M}_{10}) = 0.57810616;$

14. $(\tilde{I}, \tilde{M}_{13}) = 0.67537158.$

we can determine visually that the stimuli with distances superior to 0,5 are not recommended POS elements to be used in a shop, and as a result, of doubtful ROI. Hence, the elements M_{14}, M_2, M_8, M_7, M_9, M_1, M_3, M_5, M_6 are the materials which should be present in the perfumery and the materials M_{11}, M_{12}, M_4, M_{10}, M_{13} should be withdrawn and not to be invested in.

6. Conclusions

The optimization of investment in POS advertising materials in a retail shop is possible due to the attainment of a model which prioritizes and determines those materials which are close to the ideal stimulus. Through this ordination it is possible to know which is the format, media and brand that has major effectiveness and generate more impact on the consumer in the purchase process in a shop or establishment. All this is possible due to the model based on the theory of fuzzy subsets from the valuations carried out by experts after the analysis of data obtained in a measurement of neurometric constants of the consumers (brain activity, cardiac activity, muscular tension and electrical resistance of the skin), both during rest and when in face of each stimulus during a purchase process in a point of sale.

References

1. L. A. Zadeh, Fuzzy sets. Information and Control, 8(3):338–353 (1965).
2. Carl Senior, Hannah Smyth, Richard Cooke, Rachel L. Shaw, Elizabeth Peel. Mapping the mind for the modern market researcher. Qualitative Market Research: An International Journal. V:10, i:2, p. 153–167 (2007).
3. Sven Braeutigam. Neuroeconomics—From neural systems to economic behaviour. Brain Research Bulletin. V.67, I.5. P 355–360 (2005).
4. Braidot, N. Neuromarketing: neuroeconomía y negocios. Madrid: Puerto Norte-Sur, 2005.
5. Masanes, P.; Apicella, A. "Las nuevas tecnologías para la investigación de mercados. Neurobiomarketing" Actas del 22º Seminario de TV de AEDEMO. Madrid, 2006, p. 151.
6. Ekman, Paul and Wallace Friesen: Unmasking the Face. A Guide to recognizing emotions from facial expressions. Prentice-Hall, Englewood Cliffs, 1975.

7. Fere, C. Note sur les modifications de la r6sistance dlectrique sous l'influence des excitations sensorielles et des emotions. *Comtes Radus de la Société de Biologie, 40,* 217–219 (1888).
8. Tarchanoff, J. Uber de galvanischen orscheinunger an der haut des menschen bei reizung der sinnesorgane und bei verschieden formen der psychyschen tatig keit. *Ptlgers m c h . fzcr die gesamtephysiologie, 46,* 46–55 (1890).
9. P. LaBarbera and J.D. Tucciarone. GSR Reconsidered: A Behavior-Based Approach to Evaluating and improving the sales potency of dvertising. Journal of Advertising Research 35 p. 33–35 (1995).
10. Kaufmann A. and Gil Aluja, J.: "Introducción a la teoría de los subconjuntos a la gestión de las empresas". Ed. Milladoiro, 3ª edición, 1993.
11. Kaufmann, A. and Gil Aluja, J.: "Técnicas de gestión de empresas. Previsiones, decisiones y estrategias". Ed. Pirámide. Madrid, 1992, p. 285 a 295.
12. Gil Lafuente, J.: "Marketing para el nuevo milenio. Nuevas técnicas ara la gestión comercial en la incertidumbre" Ed. Pirámide. Madrid, 1997, p. 142 a 145.

BUSINESS MODELLING FOR ECRM SYSTEMS: APPLYING UML SPECIFICATIONS

CĂLIN GURĂU

GSCM –Montpellier Business School, 2300 Avenue des Moulins
34185 Montpellier, France

The implementation of a customer-oriented approach in online business requires careful planning of the interaction between various operational systems and actors. A clear representation of the eCRM system using business modelling languages can significantly facilitate this complex restructuring operation. This paper attempts to identify the specific requirements of implementing eCRM systems in terms of business modelling and to analyze the specific advantages of the Unified Modelling Language (UML) for this operation.

1. Introduction

The World Wide Web has allowed companies to reach customers in previously inaccessible markets, and to compete efficiently with the traditional store based retailers[1]. However, the low entry barriers, the market size and the relatively low costs of online business activities have created a situation of intense competition. The most effective answer to hyper-competition is to enhance customers' long-term loyalty using a reputable brand name and value-added customer services.

The adoption of a customer-oriented strategy is referred to as Customer Relationship Management (CRM). In the online environment the introduction and maintenance of CRM requires a complex process of planning, analysis, strategy design and implementation. This paper discusses the importance of business   odeling for this process in the digital environment and advocates the use of Unified Modelling Language (UML) as a standard   odeling language to support web business process   odeling and re-engineering.

2. Customer Relationship Management

The successful implementation of eCRM systems requires a specific bundle of IT applications that support the classic domains of the CRM concept (marketing, sales and service). In this context, personalization systems play a key role in delivering consistent customer satisfaction. The bases of the personalization process are customer profiles containing a holistic view of the customer. Through continuous accumulation and analysis of customer data, the eCRM becomes an organizational learning system structured in a closed-loop architecture.

The implementation of an eCRM system requires the restructuring of all institutional structures and processes, at organizational, informational and managerial level. Considering the dynamic and the interactive nature of eCRM systems, the business process represents the most appropriate unit of analysis. A business process can be defined as a collection of activities designed to produce a specific output for a particular customer or market. On the other hand the process implies a specific ordering of work activities across time and place, with a beginning, an end, and clearly defined inputs and outputs: a structure for action.

The eCRM system comprises a number of business processes, inter-linked in a logical succession:

1. Market segmentation: the collection of historical data, complemented by information provided by third parties (such as marketing research agencies), is segmented on the basis of customer life-time value criteria, using data mining applications.

2. Capturing the customer: the potential customer is attracted to the web site of the firm through targeted promotional messages, diffused through various communication channels.

3. Customer information retrieval: The information retrieval process can be either implicit or explicit. When implicit, the information retrieval process registers the web behavior of customers, using specialized software applications, such as cookies. On the other hand, explicit information can be gathered through direct input of demographic data by the customer (using online registration forms or questionnaires). Often these two categories of information are connected at database level, linking the demographic profile of customers with their web behavior.

4. Customer profile definition: the information collected about customers are analyzed in relation with the target market segments identified through data mining, and a particular customer profile is defined. The profile can be enriched with other data, e.g. external information from marketing information providers. This combination creates a holistic view of the customer regarding his/her needs, interests and behavior.

5. Personalization of firm-customer interaction: The customer profile is used to identify the best customer management campaign (CMC), which is applied to personalize the company-customer online interaction. The completed transaction results in profits for the firm,

increased satisfaction for customer, as well as information, which is integrated in the transaction history of that particular customer.

6. Resource management: the company-customer transaction initiate complex resource management operations, which are partially managed automatically, through specialized IT-applications such as Enterprise Resource Planning (ERP) or Supply Chain Management (SCM), and partly through the direct involvement and co-ordination of operational managers.

The challenges raised by the complexity of eCRM systems can be solved through a logical process of planning,   odeling and implementation. The aim of the   odeling exercise is to develop an appropriate *abstraction* of the business. The business model cannot and should not contain all the details of a business system. A model that attempts to provide a complete representation of the real system becomes too complex to understand and analyze. On the other hand, some business details cannot be represented because of the specific limitations of   odeling languages. A good business model should focus on the core business processes and key operations. In order to achieve the coherence of the model, a clear leading concept should be established from the beginning – such as the main orientation of the business organization (customer-orientation, profit-orientation, sales-orientation or manufacturing-orientation).

3. The Business Modelling Language

The starting point for selecting and applying a good modelling language is the analysis of the specific characteristics and requirements of the eCRM implementation process:

1. eCRM is an Internet-based system, therefore the modelling language should be able to represent web processes and applications;
2. the interactive nature of eCRM systems requires a clear representation of the interaction between customers and company's web applications, as well as between various business processes within the organization;
3. eCRM systems are using multiple databases, which interact with various software applications; the modelling language should therefore support data modelling profiles and database representation;
4. the necessity for resource planning and control requires a clear representation of each business process with its inputs, outputs, resources and control mechanisms;
5. the implementation and management of an eCRM system requires the long-term collaboration of various specialists, such as business and operational managers, programmers and web designers, which are sometimes working from distributed locations; the modelling language should therefore provide a standard, intuitive representation of the

eCRM system and business processes, in order to facilitate cross-discipline interaction and collaboration;

6. the complexity of the eCRM system requires a modelling language capable to present both the organizational and the functional architecture of the system, at the level of system, process, software applications and resources; this will facilitate the multi-user, multi-purpose use of the same business model, although the detail of representation might differ depending on the required perspective.

The online environment introduces new rules of interaction, and the traditional approaches to business or software are no longer valid. This online environment can be described as[2]:

- *Distributed*: information is distributed all over the world, located in many different places.

- *Concurrent*: activities are decentralized and simultaneous. Neither business decision-making nor software programs can perform with a single thread of control.

- *Connected*: an action in one place can produce effects in various other locations.

Responding to these specific requirements of the digital environment, more and more companies are integrating critical operations in systems distributed across the enterprise. Such systems are increasingly developed using object-oriented technology – the term Enterprise Distributed Object Systems is often used to describe such systems. These object-oriented systems contain distributed servers and databases that are connected to support highly concurrent business operations. Increasingly, industries must inter-operate in real time to do business efficiently.

Concurrent, distributed systems have complex interactions that are difficult to understand and predict[2]. Vague system specifications and wrong model designs represent major problems for their performance. In the past, the specification of a centralized, local system, affected only that system since the effects were limited to just one business system or operation. Now, a business system may have to inter-operate with another system located in an entirely different part of the world, and often both are designed and implemented by people who have never heard of each other. A failure to follow specifications can introduce errors that propagate internationally[3].

The robustness of the distributed system is also an important issue. The distributed system needs to be resilient to the failure, error, or data corruption, of one or more of its components. Most online business organizations are, or integrate in their structure, real-time systems. Exact timing is therefore required to interact efficiently with customers and partners. Finally, the performance of complex systems is often nonlinear and cannot be predicted by a simple extrapolation of the present situation.

The UML is the notation presented in this paper to support the business process modelling activity. The UML is well suited to the demands of the online environment – it has an object-oriented approach, and was designed to support distributed, concurrent, and connected models[2].

4. The Unified Modelling Language (UML)

The UML was developed in 1995 by Grady Booch, Ivar Jacobson, and Jim Rumbaugh at Rational Corporation, with contributions from other leading methodologists, software vendors, and users. Rational Corporation chose to develop UML as a standard through the Object Management Group (OMG). The resulting co-operative effort with numerous companies led to a language specification adopted by OMG in 1997.

In comparison with other modelling languages, UML has a number of advantages:

1. **Simplicity of notation:** The notation set is very simple and intuitive.
2. **Standard:** The fact that the UML notation has achieved a standard through the OMG gives confidence to modelers that there is some control and consideration given to its development.
3. **Support:** A significant level of support is available to modelers in using the UML. This support takes many forms:
    a. text books that describe the UML notation as well as consider specific application areas[4].
    b. papers in journals and publications/resources on the Internet help spread knowledge of the UML (refer to links to Rational Resource Center and UML Zone as examples).
    c. software tools, often referred to as Computer Aided Software Engineering (CASE) tools are available. These provide support for documentation of UML diagrams, such as *Rational Rose, argoUML, Objects By Design* and *Enterprise Modeler*. Training courses are available which instruct in the use of the core notation, as well as general modelling concepts and use of associated CASE tools.
4. **Uptake:** The UML notation has quickly gathered momentum. This is driven by the need for such notation, though greatly assisted by the support mechanisms identified above. The more the UML is used, the wider the knowledge pool becomes, which leads to a wider dissemination of information concerning the benefits and pitfalls of its use.
5. **Methodologies:** The development of methods or methodologies that provide support and guidelines of how to use the UML in a particular situation is widespread. A good example is the Rational Unified Process.

6. **Extensible:** The UML has a number of standard extension mechanisms to make the notation flexible. These are: stereotypes, tagged values and constraints.

7. **Living Language:** It is important to recognize UML as a living language – the standard is constantly developing, though in a controlled manner. The development of the UML standard is maintained by the OMG[5]. The OMG works with representatives from various companies to clarify and address problems in the UML specification as well as considering recommendations for extensions to the language.

The UML is used to model a broad range of systems (software systems, hardware systems, databases, real-time systems and real-world organizations). By sharing a common notation across system and business boundaries, the business analysts and system analysts can better communicate their needs, being able to build a system that solves the customers' problems. In addition, UML is developing in three main directions that are of interest for this paper:

- **Data Modelling:** One or more databases are a component of almost all e-business applications, including CRM. Coordinating programming languages and databases has long been a difficult problem in system development, because each used a different method to declare data structure, leading to subtle inconsistencies and difficulties in exchanging information among programs and databases. UML addressed this problem by introducing a Data Modelling profile, which includes an additional set of notations to capture the data modelling and database connectivity aspects of modelling[6].

- **WWW System Modelling:** The development of businesses and systems for the WWW has lead to an extension of UML for modelling web based systems. This capability is provided as a UML profile that enables modelers to represent various elements that compose a Web application - client pages, server pages, forms, frames, etc. The profile contains a set of stereotypes for different elements and their relationships[7].

- **Business Process Modelling:** Important extensions to UML concern notation to support business modelling. More specific extensions to the UML notation are suggested to describe more fully the processes, goals and rules of business[8,9].

5. Concluding Remarks

Customer relationship Management (CRM) is increasingly found at the top of corporate agendas[10]. Online retailing companies in particular are embracing CRM as a major element of corporate strategy, because online technological applications permit a precise segmentation, profiling and targeting of customers, and the competitive pressures of the digital market require a customer-centric corporate culture. The implementation of CRM systems in online organizations determines a complex restructuring of all organizational elements and processes.

The development of effective business models can be critical to the understanding and evaluation of a company's business procedures. In this context, the Unified Modelling Language (UML) can be used for specifying, visualizing, constructing, and documenting business models and associated software systems. The utility of the UML for business modelling in the online environment is manifold:

1. UML can be used to represent the workflow processes within the organization, and especially the flow of information process, which is essential for online retailers. The design of a business model is a first step for Business Process Re-structuring, changing the product orientation into a customer-centric strategy.

2. UML can provide a neutral platform for designing the database architecture. The database represents the most important asset of a company engaged in relationship marketing. UML offers a complete semantics for database design, and can provide a powerful neutral platform for multi-user databases[11].

3. UML can be used to represent the interaction between the digital company and different types of customers, helping the operational managers to identify the areas/activities of value creation and those of value destruction. Once defined, these areas can be addressed with specific strategies designed to increase the customer lifetime value.

4. UML provides the basis for designing and implementing suitable information systems that support the business operations. The models can also be used to identify and specify the requirements of those systems. The use of UML both for software description and for business modelling offers the possibility to map large sections of the business model directly into software objects[3]. The increased automation of many online business processes increases the utility of this feature - automated customer interaction, customer data collection, marketing data processing, customer profiling and automated suppliers management can be represented as business processes using UML, and then the same model can be used for object-oriented programming.

5. UML can provide a protocol neutral modelling language to design the interface between co-operating virtual organizations. For online retailers, networking and outsourcing are essential features. The standard digital organization is highly specialized, focusing on its main competitive advantage. The remaining business processes and operations are outsourced from other digital and/or physical organizations. In this situation the digital retailer becomes the centre as well as the member of multiple business networks which require a complex design and co-ordination of interface interactions and information flows.

The UML establishes a means for addressing problems, finding solutions and improving systems via an industry-standardized modelling language. The restructuring of the business represented in the model has the potential of creating differential competitive advantage and stronger customer loyalty. The UML cannot guarantee success in online retailing enterprises, but establishes a consistent, standardized and tool-supported modelling language that provides a framework in which practitioners may focus on delivering value.

References

1. M. De Kare-Silver, *E-Shock*. Macmillan Business (1998).
2. J. Rumbaugh, *http://www.therationaledge.com/content/dec_00/f_uml.html* (2000).
3. G. Booch, *http://www.rational.com/products/whitepapers/285.jsp* (2001).
4. P. Stevens and R. Pooley, *Using UML Software Engineering with Object and Components*, Pearson Education Limited (2000).
5. S. S. Alhir, *http://home.earthlink.net/~salhir/applyingtheuml.html* (1998).
6. Rational, *http://www.rational.com/products/whitepapers/101516.jsp* (2000a).
7. J. Conallen, *Building Web Applications with UML*. Addison Wesley Longman (2000).
8. H.-E. Eriksson and M. Penker, *http://www.therationaledge.com/rosearchitect/mag/archives/fall99/f5.html* (1999).
9. H.-E. Eriksson and M. Penker, *Business Modelling with UML: Business Patterns at Work*. John Wiley & Sons (2000).
10. A. Payne, *http://www.bt.com/insight-interactive/browse/ii_content.jsp?contentKey=00352* (2002).
11. Rational, *http://www.rational.com/products/whitepapers/411.jsp* (2001b).

MEDIA AUDIENCES PREDICTION: A MODEL

ANNA MARIA GIL-LAFUENTE

Department of Economics and Business Administration,
University of Barcelona, Avda. Diagonal 690, 08034 Barcelona, Spain
amgil@ub.edu

LUIS AMIGUET MOLINA

Journalism Department, University Rovira i Virgili,
Av. Catalunya 35, 43002 Tarragona, Spain
lamiguet@lavanguardia.es

The consumer judgement of each newspaper, website, radio or tv station is the result of aggregation and composition of certain subjective estimates, which are also different in each individual, and on certain qualities or characteristics that that media is suposed to possess. One of our main objectives is to find, directly or indirectly, those items that consumers, whether consciously or unconsciously, seek and desire in the mass media they choose so that way companies and media corporations can focus their resources on enhancing investment in those qualities expected by citizens. This can be achieved by undertaking certain actions aimed at influencing the public in its assessment of the qualities of the media in varying degrees or levels. It is, in short, to establish causal mechanisms, through a combinatorial approach any cause-effect relationships between different actions or measures to make them reach the population, and characteristics of the most valued by consumers.

1. Introduction

Most studies carried out by marketing to measure and predict audiences usually consider only the direct causal relationships between the characteristics of each media and the qualities expected by the public. But in the complex system of social, family, and professional relationships we should look at how, to some extent, some causal relationships interact as such on other causes or effects, which in turn can feed back the process. If you really want to know how efficient are the researchers that measure people's perceptions of the different qualities of the media you will have to resort to an analysis of causality in which the combinatorial treatment of all elements willdetermine what effect is a cause by itself and what effect through other cause-effect relationship, so that all of the animation effect obtained through an indirect route to an item brought.

Too often we stop the process of causality in order to achieve a direct impact on this whole web of interconnections of elements. This means that such information is no longer considered valuable because it was not obvious or direct observation, therefore those data are automatically discarded. In a world in which the complexity of the phenomena causes an interdependence between cause and effect is basic to recover the so-called forgotten effect, a name which has led to a theory born out of the hands of teachers Kaufmann and Gil Aluja and is called Effects Forgotten Theory (Kaufmann and Gil Aluja, 1988).

The proposed technique for the recovery of forgotten effects in the field of communication, specifically in increasing the audience of media, acquires a special interest because of the need to allocate more resources in a more efficcient way.

Moreover, the fact of having access to those hidden elements which bridge a causal link provides valuable information that can be used to modify or ratify the original expectations.

Moreover, to separate the indirect effects, the high executives in media corporations can challenge their previous conceptions with the citizen's response to stimuli and actions portrayed by the model proposed.

The process of continuous change in the form and objectives of reaching the consumer does take center stage in studies in the field of communication as key elements are: image of the media, channels or means of distribution and consumption rate.

A prediction model of audiences should also determine to what extent the quality of content increases the audience or if, instead, chooses not much for the quality but because of those media products that best suit your needs.

This work is part of a line of research based on the analysis of the treatment of uncertainty in the context of control of audiences. Currently, the techniques applied have focused on statistics and in all multivariable models application (Carlos A. Guerrero Seron, 1992; Sanchez Carrion CIS, 1992). But despite having achieved some interesting results, most models only partially explains the different behaviors in the process contemplated.

More innovative suggestions will appear in inquiries from multidisciplinary fields such as "Television audience predicted by neural networks" (E. Parra Bootes, University of Malaga, 1993) or those of Brachman (Brachman et al, 1996) applied later by British Broadcasting Corporation (BBC) that covers the use of neural networks and decision trees applied to historical data of the chain thereby performs a filtering process that allows inferences and predictions. Our proposal aims to complement the traditional statistical models through the use of mathematical techniques for treating uncertainty. This offer various tools that allow better management decisions in the process of selecting and processing media. Given the existing process of globalization on the economies of all countries is essential to establish mechanisms for working with all information, both objective and type of subjective, for the purposes of making forecasts that are as close as possible to reality. It is necessary to this end have some tools that can enable the production of relevant and decisive in relation to these processes that are not always clear and direct causal relations which are masked by the intervention of other elements that are not always brought to discovered and therefore not covered.

The objective decisions can have all the information possible is vital to the process of audience analysis in most cases made very substantial investments in resources that do not always work at maximum efficiency. The mechanisms that are needed in these cases require the adaptation of a sufficiently flexible and general techniques while being able to incorporate all possible eventualities that may occur during the process.

2. Model Approach

In the usual variables in studies of hearing, (EGM or shares of Nielsen by audiometry) and systematized sufficiently addressed in the manuals on the use (Vidosa González 1990, Martínez Ramos 1992 or Soler, Perdiguer 1992) this paper seeks to add those who are not easily quantifiable, but no doubt a decisive influence on the size and composition of the audience of a medium whose variables have not been systematized so far.

Elements that influence the consumer:
1. Time of advertising.
2. Accessibility and quality of reception.
3. Interest of contents.
4. Level of empathy generated.
5. Exclusivity and/or novelty of the content.
6. It is part of the consumer's leisure time.
7. Generates regular monitoring.
8. Identification with social and political ideals of the media.
9. Diversity of content to different segments of the population.
10. Media Image.
11. Feed-Back capability of the media the accuracy with which collects consumer response to its proposals for content and how it accommodates it.

Elements affecting media companies:

1. Investment in infrastructure.
2. Campaigns to retain consumers.
3. Resources to reward customer loyalty.
4. Relations with political actors, economic and social.
5. Tradition of the media and the value of his tradition/historical background.
6. Value of prescription/recommendation.
7. Circulation/territorial distribution.
8. Quality writers/presenters/participants and the rest of investment made in talent.
9. Preconceived image Consolidation.

Variables that influence, in turn, the audience analysis of the media:
1. Extent of knowledge of the people concerning the mark in the middle.
2. Reception quality or ease of purchase.
3. Monitoring frequency.
4. Monitoring frequency in the last month.
5. Number of people who follow the media.
6. Number of people who have followed the media in the last month.
7. Average time spent on the consumption of the media.
8. Average time commited in the last month.
9. SHARE and total daily viewing hours (data).
10. SHARE and total daily viewing hours (data from last month).
11. Knowledge of the media name by sex and age.
12. Monitoring frequency by sex and age.
13. Daily devoted time by sex and age.
14. Time of daily dedication of his listeners by sex and age.
15. Distribution of the audience during the day.

16. Distribution of the audience during the week.
17. Progression of the audience.

The concept of incidence could be associated with the idea of function. In any sequential process naturalesa where incidents are transmitted is usual to omit chained voluntarily or involuntarily some stage. Each results in oblivion spillover effects throughout the network of advocacy into a kind of combinatorial process.

If we have two sets of elements:

$$A = \{a_i \, / \, i = 1, 2, \ldots, n\}$$

$$B = \{b_j \, / \, j = 1, 2, \ldots, m\}$$

say that there is an incidence of about bj ai if the value of the characteristic function of belonging of the pair (ai, bj) is valued at, ie:

$$\forall (a_i, b_j) \Rightarrow \mu(a_i, b_j) \in [0, 1]$$

The set of pairs of matrix elements define the direct impact

$$
M =
\begin{array}{c|ccccc|c}
 & b_1 & b_2 & b_3 & b_4 & \cdots & b_j \\
\hline
a_1 & \mu_{a_1 b_1} & \mu_{a_1 b_2} & \mu_{a_1 b_3} & \mu_{a_1 b_4} & \cdots & \mu_{a_1 b_j} \\
a_2 & \mu_{a_2 b_1} & \mu_{a_2 b_2} & \mu_{a_2 b_3} & \mu_{a_2 b_4} & \cdots & \mu_{a_2 b_j} \\
a_3 & \mu_{a_3 b_1} & \mu_{a_3 b_2} & \mu_{a_3 b_3} & \mu_{a_3 b_4} & \cdots & \mu_{a_3 b_j} \\
a_4 & \mu_{a_4 b_1} & \mu_{a_4 b_2} & \mu_{a_4 b_3} & \mu_{a_4 b_4} & \cdots & \mu_{a_4 b_j} \\
a_5 & \mu_{a_5 b_1} & \mu_{a_5 b_2} & \mu_{a_5 b_3} & \mu_{a_5 b_4} & \cdots & \mu_{a_5 b_j} \\
\vdots & \vdots & \vdots & \vdots & \vdots & \vdots & \vdots \\
a_i & \mu_{a_i b_1} & \mu_{a_i b_2} & \mu_{a_i b_3} & \mu_{a_i b_4} & \cdots & \mu_{a_i b_j}
\end{array}
$$

Now suppose you see a third set of elements:

$$C = \{c_k \, / \, k = 1, 2, \ldots, z\}$$

formed per elements that act as effects of the whole, ie:

$$N = \begin{array}{c|c|c|c|c|}
 & c_1 & c_2 & \cdots & c_z \\
\hline
b_2 & \mu_{b_1 c_1} & \mu_{b_1 c_2} & \cdots & \mu_{b_1 c_z} \\
\hline
b_2 & \mu_{b_2 c_1} & \mu_{b_2 c_2} & \cdots & \mu_{b_2 c_z} \\
\vdots & & & & \\
b_m & \mu_{b_m c_1} & \mu_{b_m c_2} & \cdots & \mu_{b_m c_z} \\
\end{array}$$

Obtain two incidence relations with the common elements of the set:

$$M = \begin{array}{c|c|c|c|c|}
 & b_1 & b_2 & \cdots & b_m \\
\hline
a_1 & \mu_{a_1 b_1} & \mu_{a_1 b_2} & \cdots & \mu_{a_1 b_m} \\
\hline
a_2 & \mu_{a_2 b_1} & \mu_{a_2 b_2} & \cdots & \mu_{a_2 b_m} \\
\vdots & & & & \\
a_n & \mu_{a_n b_1} & \mu_{b_m c_2} & \cdots & \mu_{b_m c_z} \\
\end{array}$$

$$N = \begin{array}{c|c|c|c|c|}
 & c_1 & c_2 & \cdots & c_z \\
\hline
b_2 & \mu_{b_1 c_1} & \mu_{b_1 c_2} & \cdots & \mu_{b_1 c_z} \\
\hline
b_2 & \mu_{b_2 c_1} & \mu_{b_2 c_2} & \cdots & \mu_{b_2 c_z} \\
\vdots & & & & \\
b_m & \mu_{b_m c_1} & \mu_{b_m c_2} & \cdots & \mu_{b_m c_z} \\
\end{array}$$

That is, we have two incidence relations:

$$M \subset A \times B \text{ i } N \subset B \times C.$$

The mathematical operator that allows to know the impact on the max-min composition:

$$M \subset A \times B, \ N \subset B \times C, \ P \subset A \times C$$

$$M \circ N = P$$

where the symbol represents precisely the max-min composition. The composition of two uncertain relations is such that:

$$\forall \left(a_i, c_z\right) \in A \times C:$$

$$\mu\left(a_i, c_z\right)_{M \circ N} = \underset{bj}{V} \left(\mu_M(a_i, b_j) \wedge \mu_N(b_j, c_z)\right)$$

We can say that the incidence relation P define the causal relationships between elements of the first set i the elements of the third set to the extent that presupposes having considered the elements belonging to the set.

We intend to propose a methodology to learn the cause-effect relationships that are hidden when a new study of these features. We began the study with two sets of elements:

$$A = \left\{a_i / i = 1, 2, ..., n\right\}, \text{ That act as causes}$$

$$B = \left\{b_j / j = 1, 2, ..., m\right\}, \text{ Which act as effects}$$

And a causal relationship M defined by the matrix:

$$[M] = \left\{u_{a_i b_j} \in [0, \ 1] / i = 1, 2, ..., n; j = 1, 2, ..., m\right\}$$

being the $\mu_{a_i b_j}$ characteristic functions belonging to each of its elements. We could say that the matrix $[M]$ is composed of the estimates made around the effects that the elements of A cause in the elements of B.

Our goal is to find an array of incidents that reflect the total causality, ie, direct plus indirect dimension fully appreciate the appreciation of the causal relationships between phenomena. This requires building two auxiliary matrices that list the possible effects of cause and effect between each other. These matrices are defined as:

$$[A] = \left\{ \mu_{a_i a_j} \in [0,\ 1] / i, j = 1, 2, ..., n \right\}$$
$$[B] = \left\{ \mu_{b_i b_j} \in [0,\ 1] / i, j = 1, 2, ..., m \right\}$$

The matrix $[A]$ lists the incidence relations that can occur between each of the elements that act as causes and the matrix $[B]$ respectively does among the elements that act like effects. Both matrices $[A]$ and $[A]$ are reflexive, ie:

$$\mu_{a_i a_j} = 1 / i, j = 1, 2, ..., n$$

$$\mu_{b_i b_j} = 1 / i, j = 1, 2, ..., m$$

In contrast neither $[A]$ nor $[B]$ are symmetric matrices, ie:
$$\mu_{a_i a_j} \neq \mu_{a_j a_i}$$

$$i, j = 1, 2, ..., n$$

$$\mu_{b_i b_j} \neq \mu_{b_j b_i}$$

$$i, j = 1, 2, ..., m$$

Once constructed the matrices, $[M]$, $[A]$ and $[B]$, we must proceed with the establishment of all possible combinations of direct and indirect impacts, ie, incidents in which, in turn, acts brought some cause or effect. To do so proceed to the max-min composition of the three matrices:

$$[A] \circ [M] \circ [B] = [M^*]$$

The result $[M^*]$ will be a new array that collects the occurrences in i causes second generation effects, ie the initial causal relationships affected by the possible impact brought by some cause or an effect. In this regard we have:

$$\underset{[A]}{\begin{array}{c|cccc} & a_1 & a_2 & \cdots & a_n \\ \hline a_1 & 1 & \mu_{a_1a_2} & \cdots & \mu_{a_1a_n} \\ a_2 & \mu_{a_2a_1} & 1 & \cdots & \mu_{a_2a_n} \\ \vdots & \vdots & \vdots & \ddots & \vdots \\ a_n & \mu_{a_na_1} & \mu_{a_na_2} & \cdots & 1 \end{array}} \circ \underset{[M]}{\begin{array}{c|cccc} & b_1 & b_2 & \cdots & b_m \\ \hline a_1 & 1 & \mu_{a_1b_2} & \cdots & \mu_{a_1b_m} \\ a_2 & \mu_{a_2b_1} & 1 & \cdots & \mu_{a_2b_m} \\ \vdots & \vdots & \vdots & \ddots & \vdots \\ a_n & \mu_{a_nb_1} & \mu_{a_nb_2} & \cdots & 1 \end{array}} \circ \underset{[B]}{\begin{array}{c|cccc} & b_1 & b_2 & \cdots & b_m \\ \hline b_1 & 1 & \mu_{b_1b_2} & \cdots & \mu_{b_1b_m} \\ b_2 & \mu_{b_2b_1} & 1 & \cdots & \mu_{b_2b_m} \\ \vdots & \vdots & \vdots & \ddots & \vdots \\ b_m & \mu_{b_mb_1} & \mu_{b_mb_2} & \cdots & 1 \end{array}} =$$

$$= \underset{[M^*]}{\begin{array}{c|cccc} & b_1 & b_2 & \cdots & b_m \\ \hline a_1 & \mu^*_{a_1b_1} & \mu^*_{a_1b_2} & \cdots & \mu^*_{a_1b_m} \\ a_2 & \mu^*_{a_2b_1} & \mu^*_{a_2b_2} & \cdots & \mu^*_{a_2b_m} \\ \vdots & \vdots & \vdots & \vdots & \vdots \\ a_n & \mu^*_{a_nb_1} & \mu^*_{a_nb_2} & \cdots & \mu^*_{a_nb_m} \end{array}}$$

3. Conclusions

The difference between the matrix of effects of second-generation i the matrix of direct impact we will reveal the extent to which some causalitdad relations have been forgotten or overlooked:

$$[O] = [M^*](-)[M]$$

$$[O] \;=\; \begin{array}{c|c|c|c|c}
 & b_1 & b_2 & \textrm{I} & b_m \\
\hline
a_1 & \mu^*_{a_1 b_1} - \mu_{a_1 b_1} & \mu^*_{a_1 b_2} - \mu_{a_1 b_2} & \textrm{I} & \mu^*_{a_1 b_m} - \mu_{a_1 b_m} \\
a_2 & \mu^*_{a_2 b_1} - \mu_{a_2 b_1} & \mu^*_{a_2 b_2} - \mu_{a_2 b_2} & \textrm{I} & \mu^*_{a_2 b_m} - \mu_{a_2 b_m} \\
\vdots & \textrm{I} & \textrm{I} & \textrm{I} & \textrm{I} \\
a_n & \mu^*_{a_n b_1} - \mu_{a_n b_1} & \mu^*_{a_n b_2} - \mu_{a_n b_2} & \textrm{I} & \mu^*_{a_n b_m} - \mu_{a_n b_m}
\end{array}$$

It is also possible to know, apart from the degree of neglect of any incident, the element, whether cause or effect, making bond. To do this just follow the steps taken from the max-min composition of the parent listed above.The higher the membership characteristic function of the matrix $[O]$ the higher the degree of neglect in the relationship of initial impact. This means that the implications of some incidents that have not seen or considered in its proper intensity may lead to some actions wrong or at least poorly estimated.

References

1. Gil Lafuente A. Fuzzy logic in financial analysis. Ed. Springer-Verlag, (2005).
2. Guerrero Serón, Carlos A. Determinación de Audiencias; Una aplicación multivariable. Ed. Universidad de Sevilla, (1992).
3. Kaufmann, A.; Gil Aluja, J. Modelo para la investigación de efectos olvidados. Ed. Milladoiro, (1988).

4. Parra Boyero, Eloy. Predicción de Audiencia de Televisión mediante redes neuronales. Tesis doctoral Fac. Informática de la Universidad de Málaga, (1991).

5. Sánchez Carrión, J.J. Análisis de Tablas de Contingencia. Ed S.XXI-CIS, Madrid, (1992).

PART 5:
ECONOMICS AND POLITICS

IMPRECISE PROBABILITY FOR ESTIMATED FORECASTING VARIANTS OF THE ECONOMICAL DEVELOPMENT

G.C. IMANOV, H.S. ALIYEVA, R.A. YUSIFZADE

Fuzzy Economics Department, Cybernetic Institute of NAS, Baku, Azerbaijan

In this paper we investigate the possibility of application of fuzzy conditional information granulation theory, Sugeno metrics and Choquet integral for evaluation forecasting variants of the economical development.

1. Introduction

The problem of uncertainty of the socioeconomic system is the subject of the fuzzy economics. Problems economical uncertainty and their solution by methods of fuzzy logic widely described in the investigates by professor J.Gil-Aluja [1], [2]. Between problems economical uncertainty very important meaning have problem not only economical information uncertainty and also forecasting problem of economical event and process

Economical are being grounded in the human intuition. Intuitive opinions are fundamental for the hypothesis, which is being used in the forecasting of economical events and processes.

Nowadays, methods of mathematical statistics, probability theory and fuzzy logic are widely used for forecasting. All these methods applicable only when we have preliminary hypotheses. Last time for forecasting and predict different events and processes very widely methods imprecise possibility used.

Framework of imprecise probability includes measures of fuzziness, possibility, upper and lower probabilities.

In the report by L.Zadeh, R.Aliev *et al* [3], for the solution of the problem of the decision-maker in uncertain situation some models of the imprecise probability proposed. These models were applied for different economical processes.

In this paper we do certain attempts to apply some methods of imprecise probability (conditional fuzzy granulation, Sugeno metrics, Choquet integral) for evaluation of forecasted variants of the economical development of the country.

2. Estimated forecasting variants by conditional fuzzy granulation

In the first stage fuzzy logic model has been used for forecasting of the economic development. Input parameters of the model are as follows: price of 1 barrel of oil in the world market (WOB), growth rate of the world economy (WEG), foreign investment (FIN), level of inflation in the country (INF).
Output parameters – growth of GDP (GDP) rate.

Using fuzzy logic inference we calculated three variants A, B, C for 2009-2013 years, which are demonstrated in the table 1.

Table 1. Forecasting values of the economic gross rate.

Variants	2009	2010	2011	2012	2013
A	3.58	3.58	3.58	11.20	11.20
B	3.58	11.20	11.20	21.30	21.30
C	11.20	16.25	16.25	21.30	21.30

Variant A corresponds to the price of 1 barrel of oil in the world market, which equal to 70 USD and low rate of the growth of the world economy.
Variant B corresponds to 100 USD and average rate of growth of the world economy.
Variant C corresponds to 125 USD and high rate of growth of the world economy.

In the second stage for the definition of conditional probability for every variant we have used theory fuzzy sets and information granularity, which was proposed by L.Zadeh [5]. For solution of this problem we have chosen following input parameters: price of the 1 barrel of oil in the world market (WOB), growth rate of the world economy (WEG), variant forecasting, which we get on the previous stage.

Output parameters are: conditional probabilities of occurrence of the A, B and C events, which are expressed by words with granules correspondingly low, average and high. To low granules corresponding interval is $0 - 0.33$ of probability, average $0.33-0.66$ and high $0.66-1.00$.

For construction of logical rules we have taken into account the reality, which is in the world economy and oil market, in other words, price for 1 barrel of oil taken for 70 USD and corresponding value of rate of growth. In connecting with above mentioned we have constructed following rules:

R1: *IF* the price for 1 barrel of oil in the world market equals to 70 USD and rate of growth of the world economy is average and proposed variant of forecasting development A, *THEN* the probability of occurrence of A events is high;

R2: . *IF* the price for 1 barrel of oil in the world market equals to 100 USD and rate of growth of the world economy is average and proposed variant of forecasting development B, *THEN* the probability of occurrence of B events is high;

R3: *IF* the price for 1 barrel of oil in the world market equals to 125 USD and rate of growth of the world economy is high and propose variant of forecasting development C, *THEN* the probability of occurrence of C events is low.

The solution of this problem for every year of the forecasted period using fuzzy logic inference method is given in following table 2.

Table 2. The values of input parameters and results of forecasting.

Variants	Years	2009	2010	2011	2012	2013
A	WOP	80	70	70	70	70
A	WEG	1.4	1.9	2	2.2	2.5
A	GDP	36.48	37.78	39.14	43.52	48.39
A	PRO	0.718	0.718	0.718	0.663	0.495
B	WOP	100	100	100	100	100
B	WEG	1.4	4	4	4	4
B	GDP	36.48	40.56	45.11	54.71	66.37
B	PRO	0.385	0.330	0.330	0.248	0.165
C	WOP	125	125	125	125	125
C	WEG	1.4	5	5	5	5
C	GDP	39.16	45.53	52.92	64.20	77.87
C	PRO	0.275	0.165	0.165	0.165	0.165

Further for defining left and right bounder of conditional probability we use conditional fuzzy granulation., which describe in [5]. The conditional fuzzy granulation represents a conditional probabilistic relation between variable in the left side, X and right side Y, abovementioned rules. Let us denote it as $\Pi_{(Y|X)}$. Moreover, the probability distribution of X is defined as well: P_X thus we can define the set of granules as follows:

$$E = \left\{ P_X , \Pi_{(Y|X)} \right\} \tag{1}$$

Let us assume that is necessary to evaluate the probability P(Y *is* Q). As was mentioned before [5], the value is interval, the upper bound is called *expected possibility* EΠ(Q), the lower bound is called *expected certainty* EC(Q), which can be calculated as follows:

$$E\Pi(Q) \overset{\Delta}{=} E_X \, Poss\{Y \text{ is } Q|X\} = \sum_i p_i \, \sup\left(Q \cap G_i \right), \tag{2}$$

$$EC(Q) = 1 - E\Pi(Q') \tag{3}$$

where $G_i = \Pi_{(Y|X)}$ operator "sup" is supremium of the intersection of two fuzzy sets. Intersection operation can be defined as the minimum of membership values:

$$\left(A \cap B \right)(x) = \min[\, A(x),\, B(x)\,] \tag{4}$$

and Q' is complement of fuzzy set Q, defined as:

$$A'(x) = 1 - A(x) \tag{5}$$

For estimation of forecast variants by fuzzy granulation methodology, which was noted above, we use results of the solution, which we have obtained in the first stage (fig.1). This figure demonstrates the cumulative fuzzy forecasting numbers A,B,C variants.

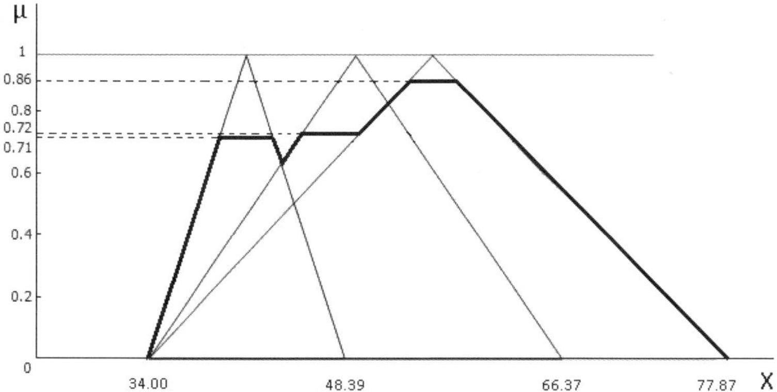

Figure 1. Cumulative fuzzy forecasting numbers variants A, B, C.

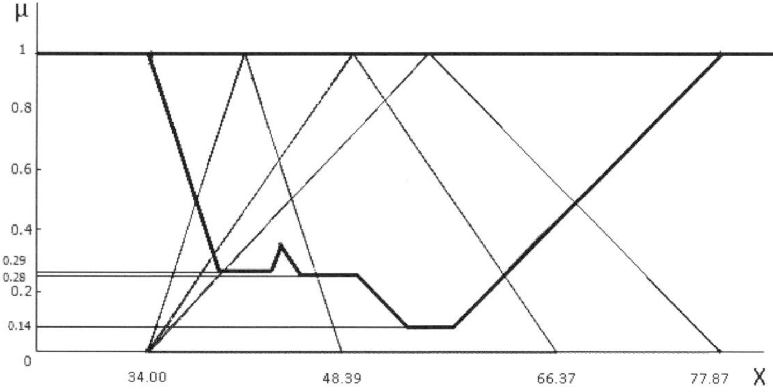

Figure 2. Complement of the cumulative fuzzy forecasting numbers variants A, B, C.

Value of the forecast parameters GDP and corresponding membership degree and probability given in table 3.

Table 3. Forecasting value of GDP, $\mu(GDP)$ and **PRO**.

	A			B			C		
GDP	39.11	43.29	43.96	43.96	45.65	49.79	52.86	59.00	77.87
μ(GDP)	0.710	0.710	0.620	0.620	0.720	0.720	0.860	0.860	0.000
PRO	0.029	0.046	0.071	0.018	0.029	0.110	0.072	0.363	0.919

Using formulas (2) and (3), we have calculated upper bound of the expected possibility and lower bound is called expected certainty:

470

*EΠ$_A$=(0.000*0.385+0.710*0.718+0.620*0.700)=0.944;*
*EΠ$_B$=(0.615*0.330+0.720*0.330+0.720*0.330)=0.678;*
*EΠ$_C$= (0.720*0.165+0.860*0.165+0.860*0.165+0.000*0.165)=0.403;*

*EC$_A$=1-((1-0.000)*0.385+(1-0.710)*0.718+(1-0.620)*0.700)=0.141;*
*EC$_B$=1-((1-0.615)*0.330+(1-0.720)*0.330+(1-0.720)*0.330)=0.557;*
*EC$_C$= 1-((1-0.511)*0.270 +(1-0.720)*0.165+(1-0.860)*0.165+*
*(1-0.860)*0.165+(1-0.274)*0.169+(1-0.5)*0.172+(1-0.000)*0.165)=0.401;*

As it is seen from calculation the best variant of the forecast is A, with the upper probability 0,944 and the lower probability 0,141.

3. Estimate forecasting variants by Choquet integral

In this part for estimation of the forecast variant we apply fuzzy Sugeno metrics and Choquet integral. The specification for the general fuzzy measures requires the values of a fuzzy measure for all subsets in X. Sugeno has developed the λ-additive axiom [6] in order to reduce the difficulty collecting information. Let (X, β, g) be a fuzzy measure space λ: $\lambda \in (-1,+\infty)$. If $A \in \beta, B \in \beta$; and $A \cap B = \emptyset$, and

$$g(A \cup B) = g(A) + g(B) + \lambda * g(A) * g(B) \tag{6}$$

If this holds, then fuzzy measure g is λ-additive. This kind of fuzzy measure is named λ-*fuzzy* measure, or the Sugeno measure.

λ is calculated by the following equations:

$$\lambda + 1 = \prod_{i=1}^{n}(1 + \lambda g^{i}) \tag{7}$$

where, g^{i} is the density of fuzzy measure. In our case g^{i} is chosen from the results of the solution, which we get in first stage (table.4).

Table 4. Values g^i for forecasting periods.

Years	Variant A g^i_A	Variant B g^i_B	Variant C g^i_C
2010	0.718	0.330	0.165
2011	0.718	0.330	0.165
2012	0.663	0.248	0.165
2013	0.495	0.165	0.165

For every forecasting variant values of λ were calculated, using information of table 4 and formula (7):

$$\lambda^A = -0.9842; \quad \lambda^B = -0.1779; \quad \lambda^C = 1.7322$$

On the next stage Sugeno measures were constructed

Table 5. Sugeno measures.

	Variant A	Variant B	Variant C
g(x1)	0.718	0.330	0.165
g(x2)	0.718	0.330	0.165
g(x3)	0.663	0.248	0.165
g(x4)	0.495	0.165	0.165
g(x3,x4)	0.835	0.406	0.377
g(x2,x3,x4)	0.963	0.712	0.650
g(x1,x2,x3,x4)	1	1	1

On the final stage for estimation of the forecasting variants we have applied Sugeno measure and Choquet integral:

$$C_{(g)}(x) = \sum_{i=1}^{n} [f(x_i) - f(x_{i-1})] * g(\{x_i, x_{i+1}, ..., x_n\}) \quad (8)$$

or

$$C_{(g)}(x) = \sum_{i=1}^{n} f(x_i) * [g(A_i) - g(A_{i-1})] \quad (9)$$

where, $0 \le f(x_1) \le f(x_2) \le ... \le f(x_n) \le 1$; $f(x_0) = 0$;

$A_i = \{x_i,...,x_n\}$ and $A_{n+1} = \emptyset$, $(i=1,2,...,n)$

Using Choquet integrals variants of forecast: Variant A – 0.75; Variant B – 0.42; Variant C – 0.51 were estimated.

As it is seen from the calculation Choquet integral best are variant A. Results of the estimation of the variants by conditional fuzzy granulation and Choquet integral are demonstrated in the table 6.

Table 6. Comparison of the methods of estimation forecasting variants.

Forecasting variants / Methods	Fuzzy granulation	Choquet integral
A	0.141 – 0.944	0.75
B	0.557 – 0.678	0.46
C	0.401 – 0.403	0.51

4. Conclusion

Reseach has illustrated that methods of fuzzy information granulation and Choquet integral give an opportunity to evaluate variants of the goal-forecasting for the development of the economy of the country, depending on the economical situation arisen in the world economy. In the future at the forecasting stage application of the fuzzy logic type 2 is desired.

References

1. Gil-Aluja, J. (ed.), (2001) Handbook of management under uncertainty, Kluwer Academic Publishers, Dordrecht, Netherlands, 804p.
2. Gil-Aluja, J. (2003) Introduction to the uncertainty theory in enterprises management. Vigo-Barcelona, Milladoiro-Academy of Doctors.
3. L.A.Zadeh, R.A.Aliev. (2009) (Report) Decision Theory with Imprecise Probabilities. Contract on"Application of Fuzzy Logic and Soft Computing to communications, planning and management of uncertainty". Berkeley-Baku. http://www.raliev.com/report.pdf.
4. George J. Klir. (2006) Uncertainty and information, Foundations of Generalized Information Theory, Wiley Interscience, 499p.
5. Zadeh, L.A. (1979) "Fuzzy Sets and Information Granularity", in: M.M.Gupta, R.K.Ragade et al. (eds), Advances in Fuzzy Set Theory and Applications, North-Holland Publishing Company,pp. 3-18.
6. Sugeno, M. and Terano, T. (1997) "A model of learning based on fuzzy information", *Kybernetes*, **Vol. 6**, No 26 pp.157-166.

MODELLING OF ECONOMIC RISK AND UNCERTAINTY IN LARGE INFRASTRUCTURE PROJECTS

HANS SCHJÆR-JACOBSEN

Copenhagen University College of Engineering, 15 Lautrupvang
DK-2750 Ballerup, Denmark

The Danish Ministry of Transportation has formulated new requirements to budgeting and risk and uncertainty management of large infrastructure projects. This paper proposes an approach that complies with some of the central requirements. An appropriate cost model is developed that allows for tracking of uncertain impacts caused by risk events in terms of unit prices, quantities, and resulting cost change of activities as well as the total project cost. Uncertainty is modelled in accordance with the two basic principles of possibility and probability, methods of calculation are proposed, and computational evidence is produced based on a numerical example.

1. Introduction

By issuing of the document [1] the Danish Ministry of Transportation instigated a new approach to budgeting of large infrastructure projects. This initiative was prompted by the experience of a number of large infrastructure projects that had seriously overrun the budgets at unacceptable levels and caused political unease in the central administration. The political initiative was followed by a paper [2] that put forward a number of requirements that would have to be met in future projects in order to avoid, or at least reduce, cost overruns. The Ministry is pioneering the new approach in large project of developing and installing a new signaling and security system to be implemented by the Danish railway authorities.

Alternative approaches to modeling of economic uncertainty can be divided in two distinctive different categories, namely methods based on possibilities and probabilities, respectively, [3]-[8]. In this paper we use triple estimates and triangular probability distributions.

2. New requirements

We focus on some of those new requirements in [2] that are specifically central to risk and uncertainty management and calls for new approaches:

1. The project budget should be explicitly made in terms of unit prices and quantities. Unit prices and quantities are estimated based on experience from comparable projects.
2. Budget control is done by standardized budgets and logging of follow-up results. At the end of all project phases, a budget version is logged. Explanations on any difference between actual and earlier budgets are made available.
3. Risk and uncertainty management is conducted during the entire project. IT-supported database of all risk and uncertainties is maintained. Continuous reporting on development of risks and uncertainties is done.

The rough budget estimate in the first phase of the project is based on estimates of unit prices, quantities, and particular risks. An additional experience based supplementary budget of one third of 50% of the rough budget is allocated in order to arrive at the *anchor budget*, whereas the remaining two thirds are paid to a central reserve fund to cover the aggregated risk of the total portfolio of ongoing projects.

3. An appropriate cost model

3.1. *The anchor budget*

For the purpose of this paper, we will focus on the project life cycle from the anchor budget onwards. In order to keep track of the way cost is developing during the project period under consideration we calculate the anchor budget at the time $t = 0$. Any subsequent modification to the anchor budget is marked by the time t of modification, so that comparison with the anchor budget, modifications previously made, and/or realised cost can be established at any time wanted.

It is a central requirement that project budgets are kept in terms of unit price and quantities. Let the entire project be described by n activities A_i, $i = 1,\ldots,n$. For the cost of the i'th activity of the project an estimated volume q_i at the estimated unit price p_i is needed resulting in the cost at the time $t = 0$

$$C_i = p_i \cdot q_i. \quad (1)$$

With a total of n activities this gives the total cost function $C\,(t = 0)$ of the anchor budget

$$C = p_1 \cdot q_1 + p_2 \cdot q_2 + \ldots + p_i \cdot q_i + \ldots + p_n \cdot q_n. \quad (2)$$

For the sake of simplicity, we assume in this paper that the cost of an activity is adequately described by only one set of unit price and quantity.

However, the principles and results presented can easily be generalised to comprise the more realistic situation with any number of sets per activity.

Notice that some of the quantities may be equal to zero. This is because subsequent risk analyses may create new types of activities compared to those contained in the anchor budget. For the sake of simplicity we let n denote the total number of activities relevant for the completed project. This means that the value of n may not be formally known at the time t = 0 of the anchor budget with a number of activities probably smaller than n.

3.2. *Analysis of risk event impacts*

By nature, risk analyses may turn out differently at different times during the project lifetime. This is due to the fact, that attempts may have been made to reduce the risk and new knowledge has been acquired (may be at an additional cost). In addition, change of design specifications during the project is a frequent cause of new activities and derived costs. Consequently, it is advisable to keep track of the time dimension in all calculations in order to be able to establish a timeline of references to changing conditions and judgments as the project is approaching completion. Naturally, if an activity is completed, the realised unit price and quantity is introduced in the calculations since they are no more subject to risk or change.

An analysis at the time $t = \tau$ of m possible risk events E_j, $j = 1,\ldots,m$ during the project results in impacts that will influence the n activities more or less according to a thorough analysis. In general, any risk event may influence all of the activities concerning both unit price and quantity. Considering the j'th risk event it will influence the i'th price by the amount Δp_{ij} and the i'th quantity by the amount Δq_{ij}. The deltas may be positive or negative, representing an increase in unit price and quantity or a decrease, respectively.

Considering the situation where all m risk events are occurring we can write for the modified estimation of the i'th unit price p_i^τ at the time $t = \tau$

$$p_i^\tau = p_i + \Delta p_{i1} + \Delta p_{i2} + \ldots + \Delta p_{ij} + \ldots + \Delta p_{im}. \quad (3)$$

(For simplicity of notation, the symbol τ is omitted for the deltas). Correspondingly, we have for the modified estimation of the i'th quantity q_i^τ

$$q_i^\tau = q_i + \Delta q_{i1} + \Delta q_{i2} + \ldots + \Delta q_{ij} + \ldots + \Delta q_{im}. \quad (4)$$

For the i'th activity, we then get the modified estimated cost C_i^τ at time τ by multiplication of (3) and (4)

$$C_i^\tau = (p_i + \Delta p_{i1} + \Delta p_{i2} + \ldots + \Delta p_{ij} + \ldots + \Delta p_{im}) \cdot (q_i + \Delta q_{i1} + \Delta q_{i2} + \ldots + \Delta q_{ij} + \ldots + \Delta q_{im})$$
$$= C_i + p_i \cdot (\Delta q_{i1} + \Delta q_{i2} + \ldots + \Delta q_{ij} + \ldots + \Delta q_{im}) + (\Delta p_{i1} + \Delta p_{i2} + \ldots + \Delta p_{ij} + \ldots + \Delta p_{im}) \cdot q_i$$
$$+ \Delta p_{i1} \cdot (\Delta q_{i1} + \Delta q_{i2} + \ldots + \Delta q_{ij} + \ldots + \Delta q_{im})$$

$$+\Delta p_{i2}\cdot(\Delta q_{i1}+\Delta q_{i2}+\ldots+\Delta q_{ij}+\ldots+\Delta q_{im})$$
$$+\ldots$$
$$+\Delta p_{ij}\cdot(\Delta q_{i1}+\Delta q_{i2}+\ldots+\Delta q_{ij}+\ldots+\Delta q_{im})$$
$$+\ldots$$
$$+\Delta p_{im}\cdot(\Delta q_{i1}+\Delta q_{i2}+\ldots+\Delta q_{ij}+\ldots+\Delta q_{im}). \quad (5)$$

By closer inspection, (5) can be rearranged and interpreted to show the contributions ΔC_{ij}^{τ} to the cost of the i'th activity from the individual risk events and contributions from the interaction with all other risk events ΔC_i^{τ}:

The change of the cost ΔC_{ij}^{τ} of the i'th activity due to the j'th risk event alone consists of three contributions, namely the original unit price multiplied by the increase of volume, the increase of unit price multiplied the original volume, and the increase of unit prices multiplied by the increase of volume. We write

$$\Delta C_{ij}^{\tau} = p_i \cdot \Delta q_{ij} + \Delta p_{ij} \cdot q_i + \Delta p_{ij} \cdot \Delta q_{ij}. \quad (6)$$

This change of cost is calculated as if the j'th risk event is the only one occurring. However, when other risk events are occurring as well, the price and volume changes created by the j'th risk event will generate additional contributions to the cost of the i'th activity due to interactions with the changes created by those other risk events. We can write for the change of cost for the i'th activity A_i due to interactions between risk events

$$\Delta c_i^{\tau} = \quad \Delta p_{i1}\cdot(\quad \Delta q_{i2}+\Delta q_{i3}+\ldots+\Delta q_{ij}+\ldots+\Delta q_{im})$$
$$+\Delta p_{i2}\cdot(\Delta q_{i1} \quad +\Delta q_{i3}+\ldots+\Delta q_{ij}+\ldots+\Delta q_{im})$$
$$+\Delta p_{i3}\cdot(\Delta q_{i1}+\Delta q_{i2} \quad +\ldots+\Delta q_{ij}+\ldots+\Delta q_{im})$$
$$+\ldots$$
$$+\Delta p_{ij}\cdot(\Delta q_{i1}+\Delta q_{i2}+\Delta q_{i3}+\ldots \quad +\ldots+\Delta q_{im})$$
$$+\ldots$$
$$+\Delta p_{im}\cdot(\Delta q_{i1}+\Delta q_{i2}+\Delta q_{i3}+\ldots+\Delta q_{ij}+\ldots \quad). \quad (7)$$

Note that this cost change cannot be ascribed to any specific risk event. It is the result of all risk events interacting and the resulting cost change Δc_i^{τ} can only be ascribed to the i'th activitity.

We may now sum up the total change of the cost of the i'th activity due to the occurrence of all m risk events and get (equivalent to (5)):

$$C_i^{\tau} = C_i + \sum_{j=1}^{m} \Delta C_{ij}^{\tau} + \Delta c_i^{\tau}. \quad (8)$$

3.3. *The risk budget*

The results of the above impact analyses together with the anchor budget are appropriately organised in a convenient calculation format in order to allow for easy communication with professionals from economics as well as mathematics, see Table 1. The impacts on unit price, quantity, and cost are summed over all activities and events, respectively. This gives a complete picture and a good decision base for initiating additional risk analyses or risk mitigation activities. Focus should be on the risk events and activities producing the highest relative or absolute increases of cost. The risk budget is structured similarly to the anchor budget in order to facilitate direct budget control for all activities at any given time. Using the data of the impact matrix the unit prices, quantities and cost per activity are updated so the actual risk analyses contained in the event impact matrix is reflected in the actual risk budget.

Table 1. Appropriate set-up for risk and uncertainty calculations, n=5, m=3.

| Activity | Anchor Budget at t = 0 | | | Event Impact Matrix at $t = \tau$ | | | | | | | | | Inter-action | Sum | Risk Budget at t = τ | | |
| | | | | E_1 | | | E_2 | | | E_3 | | | | | | | |
	p	q	Cost	Δp	Δq	ΔCost	Δp	Δq	ΔCost	Δp	Δq	ΔCost	ΔCost	ΔCost	p	q	Cost
A_1	p_1	q_1	C_1	Δp_{11}	Δq_{11}	ΔC_{11}^{τ}	Δp_{12}	Δq_{12}	ΔC_{12}^{τ}	Δp_{13}	Δq_{13}	ΔC_{13}^{τ}	Δc_1^{τ}	ΔC_1^{τ}	p_1^{τ}	q_1^{τ}	C_1^{τ}
A_2	p_2	q_2	C_2	Δp_{21}	Δq_{21}	ΔC_{21}^{τ}	Δp_{22}	Δq_{22}	ΔC_{22}^{τ}	Δp_{23}	Δq_{23}	ΔC_{23}^{τ}	Δc_2^{τ}	ΔC_2^{τ}	p_2^{τ}	q_2^{τ}	C_2^{τ}
A_3	p_3	q_3	C_3	Δp_{31}	Δq_{31}	ΔC_{31}^{τ}	Δp_{32}	Δq_{32}	ΔC_{32}^{τ}	Δp_{33}	Δq_{33}	ΔC_{33}^{τ}	Δc_3^{τ}	ΔC_3^{τ}	p_3^{τ}	q_3^{τ}	C_3^{τ}
A_4	p_4	q_4	C_4	Δp_{41}	Δq_{41}	ΔC_{41}^{τ}	Δp_{42}	Δq_{42}	ΔC_{42}^{τ}	Δp_{43}	Δq_{43}	ΔC_{43}^{τ}	Δc_4^{τ}	ΔC_4^{τ}	p_4^{τ}	q_4^{τ}	C_4^{τ}
A_5	p_5	q_5	C_5	Δp_{51}	Δq_{51}	ΔC_{51}^{τ}	Δp_{52}	Δq_{52}	ΔC_{52}^{τ}	Δp_{53}	Δq_{53}	ΔC_{53}^{τ}	Δc_5^{τ}	ΔC_5^{τ}	p_5^{τ}	q_5^{τ}	C_5^{τ}
Sum			C			$\Delta C_{.1}^{\tau}$			$\Delta C_{.2}^{\tau}$			$\Delta C_{.3}^{\tau}$	Δc^{τ}	ΔC^{τ}			C^{τ}

4. Introducing risk and uncertainty in the cost model

Whereas we include any risk event in the analysis according to relevance criteria, there is still the problem of assessing and representing the size of the impact of the risk event, which is not normally done in any of the known standard procedures. In this paper, we take the approach that such impacts can only be estimated by uncertainty depending on the body of knowledge and experience available to the decision maker. Any such estimation will have to be expressed in terms of changes of unit price and quantity for the already known cost items or, alternatively, unit price and quantity for new cost items to be introduced in the risk budget. Actually, even the anchor budget may be expressed in terms of uncertain unit prices and quantities if, for any reason, uncertainty is prevailing at the time t = 0, when the anchor budget is set up.

Obviously, by nature a risk event is characterised by the fact that it may or may not occur. We assume that the risk events are independent and that the j'th risk event occurs with the probability pr_j. The estimation of probabilities of occurrence is an intricate process and it is not expected to be done with high precision, [8], [9].

5. Calculating risk and uncertainty by alternative approaches

The uncertain impacts are modelled by triangular representations [7], i.e. triple estimates of the form [a; c; b] and triangular probability distributions of the form $\{\mu; \sigma\}$, with expected value $\mu = (a + b + c)/3$ and variance $VAR = \sigma^2 = (a^2 + b^2 + c^2 - a{\cdot}b - a{\cdot}c - b{\cdot}c)/18$. In both cases the anchor budget of Table 2 is used.

Table 2. Anchor Budget without uncertainty.

Acti-vity	Anchor Budget at t = 0		
	p	q	Cost
A_1	100	1.000	100,000
A_2	50	10,000	500,000
A_3	200	500	100,000
A_4	500	150	150,000
A_5	-	-	-
Sum			850,000

The uncertain impacts are estimated by:

Event E_1: Δp_{11}=[18; 20; 25], Δq_{11}=[95; 100; 125], Δp_{31}=[25; 30; 45].

Event E_2: Δq_{12}=[21; 25; 31], Δq_{42}=[7; 10; 16].

Event E_3: Δq_{23}=[-210; -200; -175], Δp_{53}=[145; 150; 165], Δq_{53}=[280; 300; 350].

The resulting risk budget is shown in Table 3 by using appropriate fuzzy calculation methods [7] in order to obtain correct results and in Table 4 using Monte Carlo simulation [10], assuming independent variables. By comparing the tables, it is easily seen that although the input variables are numerically identical, the triple estimate costs are considerable wider than the corresponding costs by (independent) probabilities.

Table 3. Risk Budget using triple estimate representation [a; c; b].

Acti-vity	Risk Budget at t = τ		
	p	q	Cost
A_1	[118; 120; 125]	[1,116; 1,125; 1,156]	[131,688; 135,000; 144,500]
A_2	50	[9,790; 9,800; 9,825]	[489,500; 490,000; 491,250]
A_3	[225; 230; 245]	500	[112,500; 115,000; 122;500]
A_4	1,000	[157; 160; 166]	[157,000; 160,000; 166,000]
A_5	[145; 150; 165]	[280; 200; 350]	[40,600; 54,000; 57,750]
Sum			[931,288; 945,000; 982,000]

Table 4. Risk Budget using triangular probability representation $\{\mu; \sigma\}$.

Acti-vity	Risk Budget at $t = \tau$		
	p	q	Cost
A_1	{121.0; 1.47}	{1,132; 6.87}	{137,012; 1,851}
A_2	50	{9,805; 7.36}	{490,250; 368}
A_3	{233.3; 4.25}	500	{116,667; 2,125}
A_4	1,000	{161.0; 1.87}	{161,000; 1,871}
A_5	{153.3; 4.25}	{310.0; 14.7}	{47,534; 2,619}
Sum			{952,462; 4,305}

Now we introduce possibilities of occurrence of the risk events and the corresponding distributions of the total costs are displayed in Table 5. Strictly speaking, the table shows the distribution for c (for the triple estimates) and μ (for the probabilities).

Table 5. Distributions of C^τ for representations by triple estimates and probabilities.

E_1	E_2	E_3	Probabilities of occurrence		Cost C^τ	Cost C^τ
$pr_1=0.6$	$pr_1=0.3$	$pr_3=0.2$	pdf	cdf	[a; c; b]	$\{\mu; \sigma\}$
no	no	no	0.224	0.224	850,000	850,000
no	yes	no	0.096	0.320	[859,100; 862,500; 869,100]	{863,567; 1,882}
no	no	yes	0.056	0,376	[880,100; 885,000; 899,000]	{887,783; 2,642}
yes	no	no	0.336	0.712	[891,710; 897,000; 913,125]	{900,573; 2,810}
no	yes	yes	0.024	0.736	[889,200; 897,500; 918,100]	{901,350; 3,251}
yes	yes	no	0.144	0.880	[901,188; 910,000; 933,000]	{914,679; 3,380}
yes	no	yes	0.084	0.964	[921,810; 932,000; 962,125]	{938,356; 3,853}
yes	yes	yes	0.036	1.000	[931,288; 945,000; 982,000]	{952,462; 4,305}

Based on Table 5 various observations of the risk and uncertainty of the total cost can be made, for example:

- Triple estimate representation: With probability 0.736, the most possible cost will be equal to or less than 897,500 corresponding to E_2 and E_3 occurring. For this combination of events, the worst-case cost will be 918,100 and the best-case cost will be 889,200.
- Probability representation: With probability 0.736, the expected cost will be equal to or less than 901,350 corresponding to E_2 and E_3 occurring. The standard deviation of cost is 3,251.

6. Conclusion

Contributions to the mathematical core of risk and uncertainty management in compliance with the new requirements of the Danish Ministry of Transportation have been made. It has been of special importance to develop a specific way of setting up the calculation procedure in order to obtain ease of communication and traceability of changes throughout the entire project life cycle in terms of unit prices, quantities, and cost. Further, a clear presentation of the risk and uncertainty impacts per activity, per risk event, and for the whole project as well, has been obtained. The approach developed allows for application of alternative modelling of risk and uncertainty. It should be emphasised that the alternatives of possibility and probability represent alternative kinds of uncertainty. The former covers uncertainty in the form of lack of knowledge, the latter uncertainty of a statistical nature. Consequently, that representation should be chosen that most closely reflects the actual uncertainty present in the problem at hand.

References

1. *Document No. 16*, Document communicated to the Finance Committee from the Minister of Transportation, Denmark, (October 24, 2006). (In Danish).
2. Ministry of Transportation, *New Budgeting in the Ministry of Transportation, including model of financial control and risk management for construction projects*, Copenhagen, Denmark (November 14, 2008). (In Danish, under revision).
3. H. Schjær-Jacobsen, A new method for evaluating worst- and best-case economic consequences of technological development, *International Journal of Production Economics*, **46-47**, 241-250 (1996).
4. H. Schjær-Jacobsen, Modeling of economic uncertainty, *Fuzzy Economic Review* **9**, 49-73 (2004).
5. H. Schjær-Jacobsen, Possibility and probability in modelling of economic uncertainty, in: G. Savoiu (Ed.), *Exploratory Domains of Econophysics*, 89-109, Editura Universitara, Bucharest (2009).
6. H. Schjær-Jacobsen, Comparison of probabilistic and possibilistic approaches to modelling of economic uncertainty, *Proceedings of the 8th Workshop on Uncertainty Processing*, 213-225, Liblice, Czech Republic (2009).
7. H. Schjær-Jacobsen, Numerical calculation of economic uncertainty by intervals and fuzzy numbers, *Journal of Uncertain Systems*, **4**, 47-58 (2010).
8. Project Management Institute, Inc., *A guide to the project management body of knowledge/PMBOK*, Newton Square, Pennsylvania (2000).
9. US Department of Defense, *Risk Management Guide for DOD acquisition*, 6th Edition, Version 1.0 (2006).
10. Palisade Corporation, *@Risk 5.0, Monte Carlo simulation add-in module for MS Excel*, www.palisade.com/risk/ (2008).

LINGUISTIC APPROACH FOR EVALUATING BASIC NEEDS DISSATISFACTION[*]

LUISA L. LAZZARI

CIMBAGE, Facultad de Ciencias Económicas, Universidad de Buenos Aires,
Av. Córdoba 2122, Ciudad de Buenos Aires, C1120AAQ, Argentina

MARÍA J. FERNANDEZ

CONICET/CIMBAGE, Facultad de Ciencias Económicas, Universidad de Buenos Aires,
Av. Córdoba 2122, Ciudad de Buenos Aires, C1120AAQ, Argentina

Fuzzy sets theory and linguistic models are a bridge connecting the mathematical and the language-oriented economists. The direct method more widely used for measuring poverty is known as the "Unsatisfied Basic Needs". This method consists in checking whether the households have met a number of requirements previously defined. The fuzzy approach to measure poverty allows to capture its different levels without loosing information. In this paper we present a linguistic model for evaluating the degree of dissatisfaction of certain basic needs. It is based on a new approach for linguistic framework and linguistic aggregation operators which compute with words directly defined by Xu.

1. Introduction

The gap between mathematical and language-oriented economists is due to the different methodologies each side thinks should be applied in dealing with economic problems. Some economists tried to use the so-called inductive approach to economic problems and tried to utilize standard mathematical tools like linear equations, matrix algebra or calculus. These precise mathematical tools did not contribute as much as expected to a better understanding of economics. The kind of precision of the mathematical tools used is sometimes inadequate because they bear little resemblance to the real world economic phenomena. They are pseudo precise and incapable of forming the kind of concepts needed in Economics. However, there are tremendous advantages in using mathematics to analyze that kind of phenomena [1].

---

[*] This work is supported by the Secretaría de Ciencia y Técnica de la Universidad de Buenos Aires, Proyecto UBACyT E018 and by the Consejo Nacional de Investigaciones Científicas y Técnicas, Argentina.

The concepts and relations in mathematical theories have so far been crisp and exact, whereas language-oriented economists have been using linguistic variables and linguistic descriptions of relations between them. These linguistic variables and relations are in general imprecise and fuzzy and often more correct in respect to the underlying economic phenomena [1]. According to this author, the gap is due to the fact that both sides are using very different tools which are appropriate in some respect, but the overall result is quite often frustrating. Fuzzy sets theory and linguistic models are a bridge connecting the two sides.

From a language-oriented economist's point of view, fuzzy sets are used to express mathematically the type of concepts which are typical in language and most valuable in dealing with complex systems like an economy [1].

In Economics, attribute values of concepts are mostly expressed by numbers, and fuzzy numbers would be useful instead if appropriate. However, some attribute values are linguistic and could be handled by a linguistic model. An attribute value is the linguistic description of the actual appearance of a property. A qualitative property is a property where there is no generally accepted and unique sequence according to which the property values can be ordered [1]. In this case, it can be described and modeled by means of linguistic attribute values. According to [2], the fuzzy sets theory allows to measure each household relative level of poverty or deprivation to estimate the average poverty index of households' population and to measure the relative deprivation and poverty corresponding to each component or attribute included. When poverty is considered a matter of degree, in contrast with the dichotomy poor / not poor, it should be considered to use other tools such as linguistic labels and the different aggregation methods.

Alkire and Foster [3] consider that much attention has been paid to the aggregation step in poverty measurement through which the data is combined into an overall index. Less attention has been given to the identification step, being a very important component in the methodology of poverty analysis.

The fuzzy approach to measure poverty allows to capture the gradualities without loosing information using crisp, fuzzy, random and hybrid variables.

In principle, all individuals in a population are subject to poverty or deprivation, but at different degrees. We say that each individual has a certain propensity to poverty or deprivation [4]. However, the degree of fuzziness and imprecision will be functional, depending on the required and achievable precision, and the trade-off that is willing to pay, which should be analyze in each case.

In this paper we present a linguistic model for evaluating the degree of dissatisfaction of certain basic needs.

The paper is organized as follows. In Section 2 a review of the direct method for measuring poverty is presented; in Section 3 we introduce a linguistic framework presented by Xu [6] to define the LWAA operator. A linguistic model of evaluation of the basic needs dissatisfaction of each household is introduced in Section 4 and in Section 5 an illustrative example of the proposed approach is showed. Finally, in Section 6 some concluding remarks are pointed out.

2. Basic Needs

The identification of target populations is relevant when implementing social policies that prioritize their intervention in the most vulnerable groups of society. Nationally representative living-standard surveys are now common in both rich and poor countries [7].

In practice, two methods are used: the direct one and the indirect one. The indirect method that is used primarily is the poverty lines based on household income. It is argued that this is a limited concept of welfare and that it would be better to use various *non income* indicators [7]. The direct method more widely used for measuring poverty is known as the "Unsatisfied Basic Needs". This method consists in checking whether the households have met a number of requirements previously defined and considers that a household is poor if they have not succeeded in accomplishing one of them. The range of attributes that it describes explores the social, demographic and housing of the population. It is a basic source for understanding the living conditions of households [8].

It usually uses indicators related directly to four areas of people's basic needs (shelter, sanitation, basic education and minimum income), and it is available in population and housing's census.

This method requires the definition of minimum levels that indicate a subjective valuation of the different degrees of satisfaction of the needs considered as basic at some stage of society's development [8]. Poor households are classified if they fail to meet some of their needs and welfare is directly related to the satisfaction of the basic need. The indicators provide detailed information about the kind of shortages that they have and they are useful when identifying target groups for social policies [8]. One of the disadvantages of this method is that synthesizing into a single indicator the diverse needs and the degree of how they are met, requires a lot of subjectivity when setting the "cut" level of each variable [8]. The basic needs (BN) and its indicators used in Argentina and in this paper are shown in Table 1.

Table 1. Basic Needs in Argentina

Components	Indicators	Components	Indicators
Overcrowding	Households with three or more persons per room	**Sanitary conditions**	Accessibility to safe drinking water. Bathroom or latrine and its exclusivity. WC with water discharge.
Housing	Type of housing. Material of the floors. Material of the outer walls. Outside cover of the roof . Ceiling. Place for cooking with water installation. Cooking fuel. Home and/or ground ownership.	**School attendance**	School attendance of children between 6 and 12 years.
		Ability of subsistence	More than four people per occupied member. Head of household without third year of primary school complete.

3. Fuzzy Linguistic Approach

The fuzzy linguistic approach is an appropriate technique to deal with qualitative aspects of problems [9]. Following a Xu [6, 10] we consider a finite and totally ordered label set $S = \{ s_\alpha / \alpha = -t, ..., -1, 0, 1, ..., t \}$, which cardinality value is odd, and t is a positive integer. Each term s_α represents a possible value for a linguistic variable [6, 10] and it must have the following characteristics:

i) $s_\alpha > s_\beta$ iff $\alpha > \beta$.

ii) There is the negation operator: $\text{neg}\,(s_\alpha) = s_{-\alpha}$; mainly $\text{neg}\,(s_0) = s_0$.

The mid linguistic label s_0 represents an assessment of "indifference" and the rest of labels are defined around it symmetrically.

To preserve all the given information, Xu [6] extended the discrete linguistic label set S to a continuous linguistic label set $\bar{S} = \{ s_\alpha / \alpha \in [-q, q] \}$, where $q\,(q > t)$ is a sufficiently large positive integer.

If $s_\alpha \in S$, then s_α is called an original linguistic label, otherwise, s_α is called a virtual linguistic label. Generally, the decision maker uses the original linguistic terms to evaluate attributes and alternatives, and the virtual linguistic labels can only appear in calculations [10].

Considering any of the two linguistic terms $s_\alpha, s_\beta \in \bar{S}$, and $\lambda \in [0, 1]$, Xu [6] introduces two operational laws of linguistic variables as follows:

$$\blacksquare \quad s_\alpha \oplus s_\beta = s_\beta \oplus s_\alpha = s_{\alpha+\beta} \,. \tag{1}$$

$$\blacksquare \quad \lambda.s_\alpha = s_{\lambda\alpha} \,. \tag{2}$$

Based on (1) and (2) Xu [6, 10] developed various linguistic aggregation operators, which compute with words directly.

In this section we present the linguistic weighted arithmetic averaging (LWAA) operator due to the fact that it will be the linguistic operator used in our model.

Definition [6]: Let $LWAA : \bar{S}^n \to \bar{S}$. If

$$LWAA_w \left(s_{\alpha_1}, s_{\alpha_2}, ..., s_{\alpha_n}\right) = w_1 s_{\alpha_1} \oplus w_2 s_{\alpha_2} \oplus ... \oplus w_n s_{\alpha_n} = s_{\bar\alpha} \tag{3}$$

Where $\bar\alpha = \sum_{j=1}^{n} w_j.\alpha_j$, $w = (w_1, w_2, ..., w_n)$ is the weight vector of the linguistic label

s_{α_j} , $j = 1, ..., n$, $w_j \in [0,1]$ and $\sum_{j=1}^{n} w_j = 1$, then LWAA is called the linguistic

weighted arithmetic averaging operator.

If $W = (1/n, 1/n, ..., 1/n)$, then the LWAA operator is reduced to a linguistic averaging operator. The fundamental aspect of the LWAA operator is that it computes the linguistic labels taking into account the importance of the information [6].

4. Linguistic Model for Evaluating the Basic Needs Dissatisfaction

According to the direct approach of poverty measuring, also called basic needs dissatisfaction or unmet basic needs poverty measurement it is possible to use a linguistic approach [11]. It consist in valuing the household's needs by means of linguistic labels rather than exact numerical values, assuming that the domain of the variables involved is a set of linguistic terms.

In this paper the linguistic term set used to value the degree of dissatisfaction of each BN is:

$$S = \{\, s_{-3} = \text{null (N)}, \; s_{-2} = \text{very low (VL)}, \; s_{-1} = \text{low (L)}, \; s_0 = \text{middle (M)}, \; s_1 = \text{high (H)},$$

$$s_2 = \text{very high (VH)}, \; s_3 = \text{absolute (A)}\}$$

The basic needs considered for each household will be those that are shown in Table 1. To obtain the degree of dissatisfaction of each BN of each household, the interviewer will express the valuations of each indicator for each component using a linguistic label of set S.

The degree of dissatisfaction of each basic need is firstly obtained for each household and then a global index that expresses the aggregated degree of dissatisfaction is calculated. In general, the relative importance of each indicator for each component and each basic need is not considered equally[*]; experts are consulted to determine the degree of relative importance of each one. With these values the respective weighting vectors will be constructed.

4.1. Degree of Dissatisfaction of Each Component for Each Household

Step 1. Indicator's importance
The most important indicator of each component is selected and a value of 1 (maximal) is assigned. Then the others indicators are compared with this one and a value to each r_j, $j = 1,...,n$ is allocated so that $\max\{r_1,\cdots,r_n\} = 1$ and $\min\{r_1,\cdots,r_n\} > 0$. Each element of the weighting vector is given by the degree of importance (w_j) of the indicator I_j that is obtained:

$$w_j = r_j / \sum_{j=1}^{n} r_j, \; j = 1,\cdots,n; \;\; w_j \in [0,1], \; \sum_{j=1}^{n} w_j = 1 \tag{4}$$

If all indicators are equally important, the weights are equal:
$$w_1 = w_2 = \cdots = w_n = 1/n \tag{5}$$

Step 2. Degree of dissatisfaction of each component
If n is the quantity of proposed indicators of the component considered and m the amount of components, the degree of dissatisfaction (g_i) of the component c_i is obtained by means of the application of (3).

$$g_i = LWAA_{c_i}\left(s_{\alpha_1}, s_{\alpha_2}, ..., s_{\alpha_n}\right) = s_{\overline{\alpha}_i} \;\;\;\; i = 1,...,m \tag{6}$$

Where $\overline{\alpha}_i = \sum_{j=1}^{n} w_j \alpha_j$, w_j is the degree of importance of indicator I_j obtained in the S*tep* 1 and $s_{\overline{\alpha}_i} \in \overline{S}$ is the linguistic label that indicate its degree of dissatisfaction.

4.2. Global Index of Each Household's Dissatisfaction

Step 1. Basic needs' importance
It can be obtained in a similar way as in *Step* 1 of section 4.1.
$v_i = u_i / \sum_{i=1}^{m} v_i$, $i = 1,\cdots,m$; $v_i \in [0,1]$, $\sum_{i=1}^{m} v_i = 1$.

Step 2. Degree of dissatisfaction of each household
If m is the quantity of proposed components and t the amount of households, the relative level of poverty or deprivation (P_k) of each household (h_k) considered is obtained by means of the application of (3).

$$P_k = LWAA_{h_k}\left(s_{\alpha_1}, s_{\alpha_2}, ..., s_{\alpha_m}\right) = s_{\overline{\alpha}_k} \;\;\;\; k = 1,...,t \tag{7}$$

---

[*] The value of the weights may vary according to the relevance of each component, which is linked to cultural factors, regionalities, climatic conditions, etc.

Where $\overline{\alpha}_k = \sum_{i=1}^{m} v_i \alpha_i$, v_i ($i=1,...,m$) is the degree of importance of the component obtained in the *Step* 1 and $s_{\overline{\alpha}_k} \in \overline{S}$ is the linguistic label that indicates its degree of dissatisfaction. If $s_{\overline{\alpha}_k}$ is the virtual label obtained, the approximation to a label of the set S that shows the degree of dissatisfaction of the household's basic needs h_k is acquired by means of the rounding operation commonly used.

5. Application

In this section, the level of poverty or deprivation of a household is obtained as an illustrative example of the approach proposed.

5.1. Components Evaluation

As an example of the calculation of the degree of dissatisfaction of the components, we will obtain it for C_5 : *"Ability of subsistence"*.

Indicators must be evaluated I_1 : *Amount of people per occupied member* (Table 2) and I_2 : *Educational level of the head of household* (Table 3)..

Table 2. Evaluation of People per Occupied Member

1. Amount of people per occupied member	degree of dissatisfaction
1	null
2	very low
3	low
4	middle
5	high
6	very high
7 or more	absolute

Table 3. Evaluation of Head of Household

2. Educational level of the head of household	degree of dissatisfaction
Tertiary or higher	null
High school completed	very low
High school incompleted	low
Primary school completed	middle
Up to 5th. grade of primary level	high
Up to 3rd. grade of primary level	very high
Any education	absolute

Step 1. The degree of importance of each indicator is obtained as follows:
If $r_1 = 0.5$ and $r_2 = 1$ then, by (4) $w_1 = 0.5/1.5$ and $w_2 = 1/1.5$.

488

Step 2. If the valuation for indicators is I_1 : s_1 and I_2 : s_0 .

By means of (6) the dissatisfaction of the component C_5 , to the household h_1 is:
$\overline{\alpha}_5 = 0.5/1.5 \times (1) \oplus 1/1.5 \times (0)$, $\overline{\alpha}_5 = 0.33$. This means that $C_5 = s_{0.33}$.

5.2. Household's Evaluation

Step 1. In this case the weights are defined as follows:
If $u_1 = 0.7$, $u_2 = 0.8$, $u_3 = 0.9$, $u_4 = 0.7$ and $u_5 = 1$, then by (4) $v_1 = 0.7/4.1$
$v_2 = 0.8/4.1$, $v_3 = 0.9/4.1$, $v_4 = 0.7/4.1$ and $v_5 = 1/4.1$.

Step 2. Degree of global dissatisfaction of the household analysed
It is assumed that the household h_1 surveyed found the following valuations for each component: $C_1 = s_{-1.10}$, $C_2 = s_{1.92}$, $C_3 = s_{2.31}$, $C_4 = s_{-3}$ and $C_5 = s_{0.33}$.

The degree of dissatisfaction to household h_1 is:
$$\overline{\alpha}_1 = \frac{0.7}{4.1} \times (-1.10) \oplus \frac{0.8}{4.1} \times (1.92) \oplus \frac{0.9}{4.1} \times (2.31) \oplus \frac{0.7}{4.1} \times (-3) \oplus \frac{1}{4.1} \times (0.33) = 0.2596$$

Then $P_1 = s_{0.2596}$. Using the usual rounding operation gives an approximation to the label s_0 that indicates that the degree of dissatisfaction of the basic needs of household h_1 is *middle*.

6. Conclusions

This paper offers a new linguistic approach to evaluate the basic needs dissatisfaction of the households and global index of dissatisfaction. This approach allows to capture the its different levels without loosing information and may operate with these inaccuracies without discarding any data or phenomena considered relevant.

Once the valuation of all households surveyed has been obtained, it is possible to make an affinity grouping by overall dissatisfaction or by components [11].

References

[1]   A. Pfeilsticker, *Fuzzy Sets and Systems* **6**, 209 (1981).

[2]   C. Dagum, *Analysis and measurement of Poverty and Social Exclusion using Fuzzy Set Theory. Application and Policy Implications* (University of Bologna, Bologna, 2002).

[3]   S. Alkire and J. Foster, *30th. General Conference of the International Association for Research in Income and Wealth*, http://www.iariw.org (2008).

[4]   G. Betti, B. Cheli, A. Lemmi and V. Verma in A. Lemmi and G. Betti (Edits.) *Fuzzy Set Approach to Multidimensional Poverty Measurement*, 115 (Springer, New York, 2006).

[5]   G. Betti, B. Cheli, A. Lemmi and V.Verma in N. Kakwani, J. Silber (eds.) *Quantitative Approaches to Multidimensional Poverty Measurement*, 30 (Palgrave Macmillan, New York, 2008).

[6]   Z. Xu in H. Bustince, F. Herrera and J. Montero (eds.), *Fuzzy Sets and Their Extensions: Representation, Aggregation and Models*, 163 (Springer-Verlag, Berlin, 2008).

[7]   M. Ravallion, *The Economic Journal* **106** n. **438**, 1328 (1996).

[8]   J. C. Feres and J. Mancero, *Serie estudios estadísticos y prospectivos* (2001).

[9]   L.A. Zadeh, Part I, *Information Sciences* **8**, 199. Part II, *Information Sciences* **8**, 301. Part III, *Information Sciences* **9**, 43 (1975).

[10] Z. Xu, *Group Decision and Negotiation* **15**, 593 (2006).

[11] L. Lazzari, M. J. Fernandez, *Fuzzy Economic Review* **XIII n. 2**, 37 (2008).

CAUSAL STRUCTURE AND SYSTEMIC APPROACH IN ECONOMICS

PABLO SEBASTIAN GARCIA

Universidad de Buenos Aires/CONICET de Argentina

From a systemic point of view, linear causality is rejected because of its inadequacy. In fact, the model "A causes B" should be abandoned because of its naïve simplicity, much far away from complexity of economic and, in general, social systems. On the contrary, structure is a notion that can give an account of that complexity, without denying the two fundamental features of efficacy and asymmetry, as we shall try to defend in the present paper. In economic analysis, the question about the direction of causal influence between prices and money is a clear example of this problem.

1. Introduction

In previous papers [1], [2] and[3], we have analyzed the notion of causality presented by Kevin Hoover in his *Causality in Macroeconomics* [5], examining its connections with scientific explanations and its ontological consequences. In the present paper we shall examine the adequation of the notion of "causal structure" proposed by Hoover to explain causality in social processes, specially in economic processes, from a systemic point of view.

As Hoover says, Hume and his successors struggled with the two most characteristic features of causality: causes are efficacious, that is, they make things happen; and causes are asymmetrical, that is, efficacy runs from cause to effect and never from effect to cause. But, in Hoover's opinion, Hume is wrong to believe that all we experience, and the onlyl source of our ideas, are sensations. In fact, causal relations, though they may be misapprehended and are corregible, are part of the ordinary experiences of life: there is no genuine doubt that this is so, Hoover says, and we would find it hard to conduct our lives without causal knowledge, but it is evidente that causes are, in general, neither necessary nor sufficient for their effects. Hoover analyzes the conditional account of causality proponed by John Mackie [4], and connects it with Herbert Simon's account of causal direction, to develop an account of causal structure adequate to the problems of efficacy and asymmetry.

492

From a systemic point of view, linear causality is rejected. The model "A causes B" is abandoned because of its naive simplicity, much far away from complexity of social systems. Structure, on the contrary, is a notion that can give an account of that complexity, without denying the two fundamental features of efficacy and asymmetry, as we shall try to deffend in the present paper.

2. Humean concept of causality

As Hoover says, Hume's interest in a causal account of the economiy is both that of the philosopher (or scientist) and of the would-be policy advisor for whom causal knowledge "may frequently be of use". For him, causation is a process, although he refers to the time order of causes before effects relatively infrequently. And he thought cause is also asymmetrical. In the language of the modern statistician, correlation is not causation for Hume. In fact, causes are often hidden below their surface manifestations in Hume's account: an apparent correlation between two variables is explained often by a common third cause, and both are the effects of the same hidden cause.

Causes are efficacious too: Hume rarely reasons from a correlation, a repeated conjunction, to an effect. Instead, Hume starts with a prior or commonsense understanding of elementary causal connections and composes them into a larger causal structures in which effects can be reliably expected to follow causes. For Hoover, the implicit message of Hume's famous thought experiments is that causation is counterfactual and compositive, that is, causes can be linked together to connect to effects in ways that are indirect and not obvious: causes are implicitly defined by their efficacy in producing effects, and this property of connecting what-is with what-is-not-yet underwrites inference beyond experience and connects Hume's positive análisis of economy with his normative interests, in the sense that causal understanding may permit us to guide future outcomes according to our goals and desires.

As we can see, the empiricist sensibility embodied in the received view of the philosophy of science, represented by logical positivism and Karl Popper, Willard Quine, and Imre Lakatos, is the background often unacknowledged to the portrait of the economist as scientist, which economists typically paint when they engage in methodological reflections on their discipline: the received view is one line of descent from Hume's empiricism, presented in his essential philosophical work, *A Treatise of Human Nature* (1739) and *Enquiry Concerning Human Understanding* (1777). In fact, Hume's empirical philosophy is an economical construction animated by a single premise that sustains that all human perceptions derive from sense impressions, and the ideas, which form the other variety of perceptions, are a variety of sense impression, so that every idea is ultimately resolvable into sense impressions.

So, the idea of cause is no different than any other idea. Hume relieves that the idea of one billiard ball striking another and causing it to move resolves into thee elements: (1) the cause is spatially contiguous with the effect, that is, one billiard ball causes another to move when it touches it; (2) the cause precedes the effect, that is, the ball that moves first is the cause, and the other is the effect; and (3) the cause must be necessarily connected to its effect, that is, the action of the first ball reliably sets the second to motion. Hume considers the idea of "necessary connection" to encompass what others mean when they refer to causes as "productive" or as having "efficacy". The first two elements of the idea of cause are given in sense experience, but we do not directly perceive necessary connection. Then, after considering a varierty of alternative sources for the empirical basis of the idea of necessary connection, Hume concludes that it could only be the experience of the "constant conjunction" of cause and effect that gives us the idea of a necessary connection between them. The necessity is the "custom" of the mind, resulting of frequent repetition, to connect the cause with the effect rather than a property of the objects that are causally related: the customary conjunction of cause abd effect is truly constant for Hume. In fact, for him, laws of nature codify the exceptionless regularities between particular observables that constitute scientific knowledge, so there is no chance in the world, only ignorance of real causes, Hoover says [4].

3. Causality as constant conjunction

Hoover sustains that Hume has been read as dismissing necessary connection in favor of constant conjunction, so that cause becomes a mere honorific title for "law-governed regularity". But in that case the problem of inductive warrant undermines Hume's own account of causality: Hume wants to use the constant conjunction of cause and effect in the past to reason from causes to effects in the future, yet there can be no demonstration that the conjunction will remain constant. The philosophical tradition that includes logical positivism has taken Hume to have dismissed necessary connection and replaced it with constant conjunction, but the problem of induction has remained: he does not deny that there are powers at work behind sense impressions, but he does deny that we can know anything about them. And he argues that we should not let the vague idea of them lead us astray from the clear ideas we do posses. For Hume, knowledge is either knowledge of the empirically observable or of the logical and mathematical relations among ideas: his inquiry into the foundations of knowledge, which began with sense impressions as the source of all knowledge, terminates in complete intellectual skepticism. His uncompromising empiricism inspired generations of philosophers. It is evident in the logical positivist distinctions between sense and nonsense and in the interest of Popper and Lakatos in the criterion that demarcate science from nonscience.

The constant conjunction of cause and effect is the source of the idea of causal necessity, andi t cannot be analyzed further: "It never gives any insight into the internal structure or operating principle of objects, but only accustoms the mind to pass from one to another" (Hume, 1739: 169). It is not the irreducible impression of constant conjunction, but the idea of necessary connection that it conveys, that gives causal knowledge its utility: even if constant conjunction fails to provide insight into internal structures, causes compound to form complex structures, which are knowable through análisis, Hoover remarks. In discovering the origin of the impression of causal necessity in the constant conjunction of a cause to its effect, Hume does not seek to deny the reality of necessary connection or to replace it with the notion of "regularity". For it is the necessity with which effects follow causes that permits us to know, and to control, the future. The constancy of the conjunction is essential to project it into the future: a relationship that sometimos held and sometimos did not would not warrant this projection. Hume argues that such a relationship involves chance, and chance is the antithesis of causality, because chance is pure ignorance and causality is knowledge.

Many modern accounts of causality, meant to be Humean in spitit, have relied nonetheless upon the criterion of constant conjunction: these may be referred, Hooves says, as "regularity accounts". The most important regularity account for economics is the probability account. Crudely, A causes B on probabilistic accounts if $P(B/A) > P(B)$, where "$P(X)$" means "the probability of X" and "X/Y" means "X conditional on Y". The probabilistic theory of causality in its simplest form is faced with a formidable difficulty: $P(B/A) > P(B)$ implies that $P(A/B) > P(A)$; that is, if A causes B, then B causes A. This paradox led to accept that not every A such that $P(B/A) > P(B)$ is regarded as a cause of B: a workable probabilistic account must recognice that A and B might have common causes, or that third causes might intervene between them, or that probabilities might be calculated with respect to nonhomogeneous reference clases, and so forth. Much of the effort in developing probabilistic theories of causality is spent in elucidating the refinements necessary for preventing probabilistic relations like *prima facie* cause from getting it wrong. But this is partly a matter of causal intuitions. And, what are these "causal intuitions" intuitions of? It would appear that there is an implicit notion of causal structure involved in setting the agenda for probabilistic causality, Hoover says [4]: a probabilistic analysis is judged adequate only when it corresponds to the structure of the hypothetically true causal mechanism. The primacy of these mechanisms is implicit in the very notion that probabilistic account should resolve the various problems that they describe. The central thesis of Hoover is that what is implicit in the strategy of the probabilistic approach ought to be explicitly embraced, that is, that causal structures are fundamental. In fact, probabilistic accounts are misrepresented when they are seen as elucidating the concept of causality: they are useful not for conceptual analysis, but as part of the epistemology of inferring causal structure from observations.

On the contrary, the structural approach asserts that physical, social, and economic structures are real: they exist externally and independently of any human mind, as Uskali Mäki sustains in his [7].

These structures posses causal powers and transmit causal efficacy. They give an account for the human experience of manipulation and control, as well as for the characteristic asymmetry of causal relations.

Hume's objection that terms like "power" and "efficacy" are merely names with no more meaning than "scarlet" has for a blind man (Hume, 1739: 168) is based, Hoover says, on his implausible first premise that sense impression alone is the source of all ideas: the blind man may learn much about scarlet from its role in the complex of his knowledge, from the electromagnetic spectrum, for instance. We have no sense experience of the color ultraviolet, but we do not doubt its reality. Equally we know "power", "efficacy", "agency", "energy", "necessity", "connection", and "productive quality", to cite the complete list of synonyms in Hume, from their functions: they are not placeholders for I-know-not-what, but placeholders for particular claims about physical and social experience, directly observed or not.

Structural accounts reject the view that probability relations are useful in defining the concept of cause, although they may be important in the epistemology of inferring causal structure from observations. A structural account must define the concept of cause differently. Causes have been regarded as necessary conditions for their effects, but this is not acceptable since the same effect might be achieved from different causes, even simultaneously occurring different causes, like in the case known as "causal overdetermination". Causes have been regarded as sufficient for their effects, but it is not right in its simple form: the match is the cause for the explosion but only in conjunction with other factors like the explosive, the right humidity conditions, and so forth.

496

4. Conditional account of causality

Any variation on criteria of sufficiency or necessity appeals to the logic of condicional statements: "if p, then q", Hoover observes. Such conditionals are known as "counterfectuals" because "if p, then q" may be trae even when p is false. And to assert a counterfactual is to assert the existence of a disposition, that is, to assert that the nature of the situation is such that q is disponed to occur when p does. Such dispositions need not be deterministic: q may occur only with some probability. Nevertheless, invariance is implicit in couterfactuals: a counterfactual cannot be rightly asserted if, when its antecedents are fulfilled, it does not entails the same consequence. So, invariance of this sort underwrites the intuitively appealing notion that causes are efficacious in bringing about their effects. A causal structure can then be seen as a network of counterfactual relations that maps out the underlying mechanisms through which one thing is used to control another: the structural account makes the empirical claim that there is something more in the objects then Hume's associative notion of causality allows. Then, "A causes B" is an empirical claim that there is a real relationship through which A can be used to control B. Hume is correct in asserting that the reality is not read off the experience: our knowledge of reality consists of empirically based conjectures, and then is necessarily corregible.

5. Direct and indirect causes

The probabilistic account of causality raises the conceptual problem of defining what a cause is and the epistemological problem of inferring causes from evidence, but it does so in order to avoid making any ontological commitment to what causes are "in the objects". For instance, causes have been defined by the procedure, that is, by conditional probabilities, through which they are inferred. After Hume, the usual approach to the analysis of causality was to reduce the causal relation to something else, probabilistic relations, interpreted as deterministic versions of natural laws. The thesis of structural account of causality is that cause is not reducible, but is a fundamental building block of our understanding of the world: "cause" is the name that we give to our experience of "directed influence", that is, the hidden power that connects the actions of one thing to another. Hume is correct, Hoover remarks, that we cannot observe these connection immediately, but nonetheless we can infer them, conjecture their existence and check our conjectures, as well as we infer anything in ordinary life or in science that lies beyond our direct sense experience. In the science of systems, we talk about living organisms that "fit" with their environment, but we point out that such an adaptation is not the effect of any particular cause. The structural account can explain this adaptation. And in the same way structural account describe the social phaenomena, including economic ones. To understand this we have to clarify the notion of "direct" and "indirect" cause.

A "direct cause" is one that is unmediated: A directly causes C if and only if there is some causal path connecting A to C in which there is no B that is, at once, an effect of A and a cause of C. The direction of direct causation, that is, its causal asymmetry, is part of the essential notion of causality as a dispositional property, andi s reflected in the analysis of the causal relationship in terms of counterfactual conditionals: this conditional nature permits causal relationships to be used to control further events. The direction of "indirect" causation arises from the relationships of direct causes. In that way, the structural account explains complex and indirect causal relationships preserving its asymmetry in the frame of a system of influences, like those prevaling between the organism and its environment.

Finally, we want to remark, following Hoover, that causality is about how things get determined to occur. So, in many fields, including economics, determinism seems to be incomplete, and relationships are beter understood as probabilistic. Butt he structural view accounts for probabilistic outcomes by accepting random variables and analyzing their causal relationships with reference to the parameters that govern their probability distribution, that is, as almost all explanations we are used to find in economic literacy are formulated in terms of probabilisties, those explanations can, in its turn, be included in the major framework of structural explanations.

6. Results in economics: the causal direction between money and prices

The debate in economics over the causal direction between money and prices goes back at least to Hume. In modern times it had seemed settled in favor of the view that money causes prices, but recent interest in real Business cycle models has reopened the question. The question of interest could be, for instance: supposing the Federal Reserve can control the stock of money, can it thereby also control the level of prices? As Hoover points out, new classical economists are often seen as successors to monetarism, but some of them now doubt the causal efficacy of money over income and prices, and have argued that a large portion of the money stock, bank deposits ("inside money"), responds passively to independent changes in economic activity, and that prices are determined almost completely by the amount of currency and central bank reserves in circulation ("outside money"): it seems that all real activity is determined

498

without reference to monetary variables. And, examining the behavior of money, prices, and interest rates in the United States from 1950 to 1985, Hoover says, we can say that the evidence supports the view that prices cause money, and not money causes prices. [5, 277] Only a structural analysis, i.e., an approach to the question about causal direction between prices and money from a systemic point of view, can bring us an answer in a particular case, in a particular system of related components which includes all relevant variables. In each case, and in a particular causal structure, price can cause money, but in a different causal structure prices are caused by money, without denying the principles of efficacy and causal asymmetry.

References

1. García, P.S. (2005) "Causality in macroeconomics: the probabilistic approach and its ontological consequences", F. González Santoyo *et alia* (eds.): Techniques and methodologies for modeling and simulation of systems, Morelia (México): AMSE, pp. 183-185.
2. García, P.S. (2005) "On causal explanation: statistical approach, fuzzy logics and supervenience", F. González Santoyo *et alia* (eds.): Techniques and methodologies for modeling and simulation of systems, Morelia (México): AMSE, pp. 22- 24.
3. García, P.S. (2006) "Causal and statistical explanations in economics", F.B. Abdelaziz (ed.): Optimization techniques: Fizziness and nonlinearity for management and economy, Hammamet (Tunisia): LARODEC, pp. 403-407.
4. Mackie, J.L. (1980) The Cement of the Universe: A Study in Causation, Oxford: Clarendon Press.
5. Hoover, K. (2001) Causality in Macroeconomics, Cambridge: Cambridge University Press.
6. Mäki, U. (1992) "On the Method of Isolation in Economics", Poznan Studies in the Philosophy of Science and the Humanities, vol. 25: 289-310.
7. Mäki, U. (1996) "Scientific Realism and Some Peculiarities of Economics", R.S. Cohen *et alia*: Realism and Anti-realism in the Philosophy of Science, Dorrecht: Kluwer, 427-447.
8. Morgan, M. (1990) The History of Econometric Ideas, Cambridge: Cambridge University Press.
9. Morgan, M. (1997) "The Technology of Analogical Models: Inving Fischer's Monetary Worlds", Philosophy of Science 64(4), 304-314.

PRESENTATION BASED ON MACROECONOMIC SYSTEMS EVOLUTION

LEONID A. KUZNETSOV

Head of the Department of Automated Systems Control, Lipetsk State Technical University, 30, Moskovskaya str., Lipetsk, 398600, RUSSIA.
E-mail: Kuznetsov@stu.Lipetsk.RU

The existing theoretical descriptions of macroeconomic systems include inter-relations between system parameters taken from interpretation of retrospective information and applicable for statement and explanation of facts taken place in the past. These inter-relations and results are linked with fixed timing or space in the past and are static in nature expressed by absolute numbers. They do not allow analyzing outlooks in case the conditions change. The proposed description of market macroeconomic systems is based on presentation of production and consumption as developing processes in time and allows reflecting both the static and evolution of the system.

Keywords: inflation, macroeconomic system, market, evolution

1. Preamble. State-of-the-art

Topical issue of the economy study is the analysis of cost of capital formation and forecast of inflation rate. Both cost of capital value and inflation are quantitative categories. They produce not only scientific, but practical interest as well, as they define the economic system situation. There are some theories to explain inflation causes, but they miss any formal, quantitative representations, on the basis of which one might forecast development of events in macroeconomic system more or less accurately. Mathematics is not used by them.

Going back on mathematical basis which adequately reflects specifics of macroeconomic system is a pre-requisite for a possibility to apply formal mathematical methods to analyze its behavior. Only such an approach can result in development of methods of actual status analysis and forecast of future statuses of macroeconomic system taking into account possible change in internal and external factors with reference to the system influencing its evolution. Development of such approach is set forth in the paper.

500

2. Basic representation used

Formal description of any processes and systems might lead to development of practically useful and efficient mathematical models, only when they are based on accumulated experience in the area under investigation, on aggregate of all available theoretical and practical results. Theoretical description of macroeconomic market system relies on commodities flow, which reflects volume of commodities and services produced in the country in money terms, and income flow, which reflects total volume of funds which can be directed to consumption of commodities and services. Formula [1] is given which defines the money velocity, which, as it was said there, "is valid in all cases":

$$V \equiv \frac{NNP}{M} \equiv \frac{PQ}{M}. \tag{1}$$

The formula uses the following designations:

NNP – net national product which is different in US from gross national product (GNP) by depreciation expenses, however, these details do not have any principal meaning for further explanations and NNP can be replaced by GDP,

P – level of prices which can be indexed in case of inflation,

Q – real GNP defined by recalculation of NNP taking into account price indices,

M – amount of money.

The same formula, accurate within the designations, is given in Russian textbooks [2, 3]. The formula (1) is often rewritten as:

$$VM = PQ. \tag{2}$$

In the left (2) income flow stands, in the right – commodity flow expressed in current prices. A possibility to change prices in the right part (2) has a principal meaning and will be used further on. The expressions (1), (2) rely upon the assumption that consumption equals to production. Such condition of the economy can be called as balanced: purchase power of income flow corresponds exactly to the value of flow of commodities that can be bought. The flows are interbalanced. In life situations income can mismatch expenses. Deficit or less frequently surplus can be included into a national budget.

Macroeconomic system is dynamic, it evolves all the time and its status changes in time, but it is not taken into account in (2). Variables being changed in time are represented not by fixed numbers which are used in (2), but by time functions or processes.

3. Flows presentation

A commodity flow is all commodities and services which are produced in a country. They are reflected in money terms by summing up of all values of all commodities and services for some elapsed time periods: months, quarters, years. For practice it is important to be able to forecast production and consumption rates in the future. For forecasting such representation of flows is not applicable, as there are no variables which stand for future values.

Formulas (1), (2) use natural fixed value of variables in money terms. Lots of problems can be fixed, when arguments, changing in time according to the actual conditions, can reflect actual values of variables characterizing macroeconomic system status, production and consumption rates in particular, can be used instead of fixed numbers like P, Q, etc. Besides, it makes sense to replace relative variables in scale of known values of macroeconomic indices for natural values of variables used in (2), which are difficult to define due to inflation in many cases.

Instead of PQ current volume of production can be used (commodity flow) $X(t)$ by the point of time t expressed in scale of gross domestic product (GDP) to be calculates in money terms of the currency of a corresponding country. Let us designate $X(t_0) = $ GDP for the previous year, where t_0 – indicates that beginning of a year will be a starting point for the study, and GDP of the previous year will be the initial value and scale unit.

Let designate the relative value of commodity flow by a small letter $x(t)$ and define it as:

$$x(t) = X(t)/ X(t_0). \tag{3}$$

As a consequence it is better to take t_0, trying to (3) $t = t_0$, as the reference point (starting point) we have:

$$x(t_0) = X(t_0)/ X(t_0) = 1, \tag{4}$$

i.e. $x(t_0) = 1$ – flow value for the previous year – is accepted as initial relative value of commodity flow for the current year in case of such trying.

The reverse transformation from relative variables to natural variables is done upon the following expression:

$$X(t) = x(t) \times X(t_0). \tag{5}$$

The current value of commodity flow $X(t)$ can be represented as two addends:

$$X(t) = X(t_0) + \Delta X(t), \tag{6}$$

where $X(t_0)$ – production of the last year taken as a scale unit of relative variables, $\Delta X(t)$ – production in the year under study for the period of $\Delta t = t - t_0$.

Flow value (6) in relative units will be:

$$x(t) = X(t_0)/X(t_0) + \Delta X(t) /X(t_0) = 1 + \Delta x(t), \tag{7}$$

where $\Delta x(t) = \Delta X(t) /X(t_0)$ – total production in the current year for the period of $\Delta t = t - t_0$ in relative units (in GDP shares for the previous year).

Periods Δt are usually months, then values $\Delta x(t)$ can be compared with production in corresponding periods of the last year which gives 1 GDP in the aggregate. In some tasks of the analysis and the forecast it is convenient to use increments in natural units as $\Delta X(t)$, in some – relative units as $\Delta x(t)$.

Income flow can be described similarly. The difference lies in the fact that income is initially evaluated in money terms. To make comparison possible, it is expedient to use a single scale unit $X(t_0) =$ GDP. Let $Y(t)$ be a natural value of income flow. Then its value in units $X(t_0) =$ GDP will be:

$$y(t) = Y(t)/X(t_0). \tag{8}$$

Value of income flow in the previous year can be designated as $Y(t_0)$. Then income flow can be represented, similarly to (3), as:

$$Y(t) = Y(t_0) + \Delta Y(t) \tag{9}$$

or in relative values similar to (4):

$$y(t) = Y(t_0)/X(t_0) + \Delta Y(t)\ /X(t_0) = y(t_0) + \Delta y(t), \tag{10}$$

where $y(t_0)$ – relative value of income flow expressed in commodity flow units.

When a balance of flows is achieved upon the expired year results, then $y(t_0) = x(t_0)$; if the flows are not equal as of the current year beginning $y(t_0) \neq x(t_0)$, then $y(t_0)$ value can be represented as $y(t_0) = (1+\alpha)\ x(t_0)$, where α takes into account the difference between $y(t_0)$ and $x(t_0)$.

4. Cost of capital

The initial value of cost of capital, let us designate it as $z(t_0)$, can be defined as a value which reflects "materialistic" content of one money unit, its actual "main point" as of the year beginning. It will be equaled to the variable reciprocal of GDP. The following designation $X(t_0) =$ GDP has been introduced before. So, initial cost of capital will be $z(t_0) = 1/\ X(t_0)$ or $z(t_0) = 1/$GDP. Money expression of commodity flow value $X(t)$ will equal to:

$$x(t) = X(t)\times z(t_0) = X(t)\times(1/\ X(t_0)) = X(t)/\ X(t_0), \tag{11}$$

i.e. it coincides with (3).

Cost of money unit can change in time and its current value $z(t)$ in any point of time $t > t_0$ can de represented as:

$$z(t) = z(t_0) + \Delta z(t), \tag{12}$$

where $z(t_0)$ – cost of a money unit at the beginning of the year,

$\Delta z(t)$ – positive or negative increment of money unit cost for the time of $\Delta t = t - t_0$.

Money unit cost can be changed due to stable, univalent mismatch between commodity and income flows:

$$\Delta z(t) = x(t) - y(t) = X(t)/X(t_0) - Y(t)/X(t_0) = [X(t) - Y(t)]/X(t_0) = \Delta Z(t)/X(t_0). \tag{13}$$

In (13) $\Delta Z(t)$ variable characterizes the difference between generalized production and generalized consumption in intrinsic units. When $X(t) > Y(t)$, excess of commodity flow over income flow takes place, i.e. some surplus of commodities $\Delta Z(t)$. As a result the cost of capital grows:

$$z(t) = z(t_0) + \Delta z(t) = 1/ X(t_0) + \Delta Z(t)/X(t_0) = [1 + \Delta Z(t)]/X(t_0) > z(t_0). \quad (14)$$

It is evident that when $x(t) < y(t)$ from (13), it means $\Delta Z(t) < 0$, and there is a commodity shortage in the volume of $\Delta Z(t)$ to cover income flow. Therefore, cost of capital will go downward:

$$z(t) = z(t_0) + (- \Delta z(t)) = 1/ X(t_0) - \Delta Z(t)/X(t_0) = [1 - \Delta Z(t)]/ X(t_0) < z(t_0). \quad (15)$$

The option (15) illustrates the inflation as surplus of money not secured by commodities and services can be compensated only by increase of their prices.

As long as cost of capital changes, commodity flow value in any point of time (as of any date) $t > t_0$ can be represented as a sum of addends, which show components of flow change. It comes, when flow expression of (6) is used in (11) and current cost of capital (12) substitutes for constant cost of capital:

$$x(t) = X(t) \times z(t) = [X(t_0) + \Delta X(t)] \times [z(t_0) + \Delta z(t)] = X(t_0) \times z(t_0) + \Delta X(t) \times z(t_0)$$
$$+ X(t_0) \times \Delta z(t) + \Delta X(t) \times \Delta z(t)$$

or

$$x(t) = 1 + X(t_0) \times \Delta z(t) + \Delta X(t) \times z(t_0) + \Delta X(t) \times \Delta z(t). \quad t \geq t_0. \quad (16)$$

In the right part of the expression (16) there are four addends which are summed in money term of commodity flow in current prices. The first addend reflects year-to-date GDP when cost of capital is $z(t_0)=1/\text{GDP}$. The second addend reflects increment of cost estimate of GDP at the expense of cost of capital change. The third addend reflects evaluation of the current year GDP for the period $\Delta t = t - t_0$ provided cost of capital is kept at the level of the beginning of the year. The forth addend reflects change in GDP evaluation for the period $\Delta t = t - t_0$ of the current year due to change of cost of capital. Due to using relative variables and one scale unit elements $2 - 4$ in (16) are comparable with the first element, i.e. with a unit reflecting production for the expired year.

5. Description of market economy evolution

Commodities flow can be represented as $x(t) = X(t)/X(t_0)$ (4), where $X(t)$ is a sum of two addends: commodity flow for the past year $X(t_0)$ and increment $\Delta X(t)$ in the current year. Due to the fact that $x(t)$ is a relative variable in scale $X(t_0)$, its initial value is $x(t_0)= X(t_0)/X(t_0)= 1$, and increment $\Delta x(t) = \Delta X(t)/X(t_0)$ features increase of commodity flow in shares (or per cents) to the last year.

In the simplest forecast the dynamics of commodities flow as compared to GDP of the previous year can be described by the following equation:

$$\frac{dx(t)}{dt} = k_x \, x(t) , \ x(t_0) = x_0, \quad (17)$$

where $x(t)$ – current value of commodities flow mark-up in t point of time,
$dx(t)/dt$ – rate of $x(t)$ flow change;

$t \geq t_0$ – current time which can be expressed in a specific task in ay scale (day, month, year, etc.),

t', t_a – fixed points of time – numbers, similarly $x(t')$, $x(t_a)$ – numbers, $x(t)$ value in t', t_a points of time;

k_x – parameter which defines rate of GDP growth – commodities flow $x(t)$ defined below,

$x(t_0) = x_0$ – initial value of flow $x(t)$ as of the date t_0.

The level achieved within the previous year can be taken as initial value of flow x_0 resulted in $x_0 = 1$.

Income flow change in time can be described by similar difference equation:

$$\frac{dy(t)}{dt} = k_y\, y(t), \quad y(t_0) = y_0. \tag{18}$$

where variables meaning is similar to their meaning in equation (17).

Cost of capital change (inflation or deflation), arisen due to difference of income and commodity flows, reflected in (13), can be described by the following difference equation:

$$\frac{dz(t)}{dt} = k_z z(t) + k_u [x(t) - y(t)], \quad z(t_0) = z_0, \tag{19}$$

where z_0 – cost of capital as of the beginning of time period under consideration,

k_z – coefficient which characterizes natural inflation rate,

k_u – coefficient which characterizes inflation rate due to income and commodity flows mismatch.

$x(t)$, $y(t)$, $z(t)$ variables characterize, by accumulated total from the initial point of time, the macroeconomic system status – changes of its key indices: production, consumption and inflation. As of the initial point of time t_0 is taken at random, but in economic development studies t_0 is usually the beginning of a month, quarter, year, etc. In fact $x(t)$, $y(t)$, $z(t)$ variables are key parameters and so they allow to judge about the whole system condition. When production and consumption growth rates are close to one another, inflation is at negligibly low level, the system is balanced and no economic cataclysms threaten it. When production (commodities flow) rate $x(t)$ is behind consumption (income flow) rate $y(t)$, inflation comes around, the development rate of which depends on the current difference $x(t) - y(t)$. In this case the system might be out of stable balance and develops to volatility.

6. Example. Application of the model (21) to forecast

Let us take quite simple example to illustrate application of the model (21) to forecast production, consumption and inflation indices changes for the next period depending on various assumed development rates of commodities and income flows. Let us assume that there is a necessity to verify development of the system upon three scenarios defined by 3 options of parameter values given in Table 1.

Table 1. Values of parameters taken for forecast of commodity flow, income flow and inflation dynamics in a year.

Option	Commodities			Income		
	Runup η %/y	K_x, (t-t_0=1 year)	k_x, (t-t_0=12 months)	Runup γ %/y	K_y, (t-t_0=1 year)	k_y, (t-t_0=12 months)
1	10	0.09531	0.007943	2	0.019803	0.00165
2	3	0.029559	0.002463	4	0.039221	0.003268
3	2	0.019803	0.00165	10	0.09531	0.007943

In Table 1 capital letters K_x and K_y designate parameters which correspond to time change with increment of 1 year, while small letters k_x and k_y designate their values which correspond to time change with increment of 1 month. These values are defined upon (23) rate of commodity flow change η %/y and income flow change γ %/y, given also in Table 1.

Table 2 gives result of forecast values calculation for changes of commodity flow, income flow and difference between them, which determines inflation with increment of 1 month for a period of 1 year.

Table 2 demonstrates that when commodity flow exceeds income flow only by 1 %, slight inflation occurs. Options 1, 3 reflect the opposite situations. Option 1 shows development of inter-relation between demand and offer, when commodity flow outdistances income flow, oversupply accumulates, commodity prices might go down while cost of capital can go up.

Vice versa, option 3 reflects the opposite development of the situation, when inter-relation between demand and offer is defined by more intensive development of income flow as compared to commodity flow. Upon conditions used in that example there is a dramatic break-off of income flow from commodity flow resulted in rapid decrease of cost of capital.

It is clearly seen that the model (20) allows making a simple forecast upon specified assumed rate of production and consumption development.

Table 2. Forecast results upon (16) additions by months of flows and changes in cost of capital for the options of parameters given in Table 1 which characterize the dynamics

Month	Commodity flow, %			Income flow, %			Inflation[*], %		
	Option 1	Option 2	Option 3	Option 1	Option 2	Option 3	Option 1	Option 2	Option 3
1	100.79	100.24	100.16	100.16	100.32	100.79	0.31	-0.04	-0.31
2	101.60	100.49	100.33	100.33	100.65	101.60	0.63	-0.08	-0.63
3	102.41	100.74	100.49	100.49	100.98	102.41	0.95	-0.12	-0.94
4	103.22	100.99	100.66	100.66	101.31	103.22	1.26	-0.16	-1.26
5	104.05	101.23	100.82	100.82	101.64	104.05	1.58	-0.20	-1.57
6	104.88	101.48	100.99	100.99	101.98	104.88	1.89	-0.24	-1.89
7	105.71	101.73	101.16	101.16	102.31	105.71	2.21	-0.28	-2.21
8	106.56	101.98	101.32	101.32	102.64	106.56	2.52	-0.32	-2.52
9	107.41	102.24	101.49	101.49	102.98	107.41	2.84	-0.36	-2.84
10	108.26	102.49	101.66	101.66	103.32	108.26	3.15	-0.40	-3.15
11	109.13	102.74	101.83	101.83	103.66	109.13	3.47	-0.44	-3.47
12	110.00	103.00	102.00	102.00	104.00	110.00	3.79	-0.48	-3.79

7. Conclusion

The paper shows principles of formal description of macroeconomic market system which opens up a possibility to get quantitative characteristics of such systems status in the form generally accepted in the system theory and management theory, i.e. a possibility of macroeconomic mathematical models development, for analysis of which vast and effective armory of mathematical management theory might be used. Certainly, the paper uses simple to the limit presentations which can be significantly detailed upon content and time rules of their composition.

References

1. Paul A. Samuelson. *Economics*, Fifth Edition, McGraw-Hill Book Company, INC (1961).
2. Bulatov A.S. *Economics: Textbook. 3rd edition revised and enlarged*, Moscow: Yurist, (2002).
3. Zhukov E.F., Zelenkova N.M., Eriashvili N.D. *Money. Credit. Banks: Textbook for higher education institution students, economic faculties. – 4th edition revised and enlarged*, Moscow.: UNITY-DANA (2009).
4. John J. Hampton. *AMA Management handbook*. Amacom (1995).

---

[*] When economics follow the first option, production (commodities) overbalances consumption (income), so inflation comes around – cost of capital grows; the second and the third options assume excess of income over commodities resulted in relatively lowering of cost of capital.

CHAOTIC DYNAMICS AND MACROECONOMICS SHOCK AMPLIFICATION[*]

ESTEBAN OTTO THOMASZ[†]

*Faculty of Economic Sciences, University of Buenos Aires, Córdoba 2122
Ciudad Autónoma de Buenos Aires, ZIP: 1120 AAQ, República Argentina*

MARIA TERESA CASPARRI

*Centro de Investigación en Métodos Cuantitativos aplicados a la Economía y la Gestión,
Córdoba 2122
Ciudad Autónoma de Buenos Aires, ZIP: 1120 AAQ, República Argentina*

The aim of this paper is to summarize one application of chaotic dynamics to macroeconomic analysis. In this opportunity, we will focus on the idea of shock propagation, meaning the persistence and even amplification of an exogenous perturbation as the system evolves in the long run. This may explain certain dynamics observed in emerging economies, where the impact of external-exogenous crisis seem to amplify its effects due to certain characteristics of economy-structure, changing the qualitative dynamics of the system.

1. Introduction

The aim of this paper is to summarize one application of chaotic dynamics to macroeconomic analysis. In this opportunity, we will focus on the idea of shock propagation, meaning the persistence and even amplification of an exogenous perturbation as the system evolves in the long run. This may explain certain dynamics observed in emerging economies, where the impact of external-exogenous crisis seem to amplify its effects due to certain characteristics of economy-structure, changing the qualitative dynamics of the system.

In the first section some definition of chaotic dynamics are presented. In the second we display three simulations to show the idea of shock amplification. In

---

[*] This work is supported by PICT 2006 N° 770 and UBACyT E008 (2008-2010), both under direction of Dr. Casparri.

[†] Work partially supported by PICT 2006 N° 770 of the National Agency of Scientific and Technological Promotion (*Agencia Nacional de Promoción Científica y Tecnológica*).

the third we present a conceptual application of the latter to macroeconomics. Last, the characteristics and properties of the model are summarized.

2. Chaotic Dynamics

A chaotic system is a deterministic nonlinear dynamical system which is bounded and has sensitive dependence on initial conditions.

These systems tend to be totally aperiodic even in the long run and unstable with respect to perturbations or modifications of small amplitude. To understand the latter more properly, we transcript the following paragraph (Maneville, 2004):

> *(…) when compared to the real world, any abstract implementation is intrinsically blurred with numerous approximations and its control parameters are not determined with infinite precision. Accordingly, in order to be of help, the analytical model must be robust, i.e. its predictions must not be too sensitive to these different sources of inaccuracy. This property indeed fails at bifircation points where the system experiences qualitative changes of behavior. At such points one says that it is structurally unstable: the nature of the state depends sensitively on the perturbation.*

In chaotic models, this is related to one distinct property, the *sensitive dependence on initial conditions*, what make that long term predictions be totally inaccurate even in a deterministic model.

Summarizing some characteristics' of chaotic systems are: deterministic, nonlinear, asymtocally aperiodic, unstable and bounded trajectories and sensitive dependent to initial conditions.

A more formal definition is due to Devaney (1989): A map of a set into itself, $f:V \rightarrow V$, is chaotic if: 1) it exhibits sensitive dependence on initial conditions, 2) is topologically transitive, and 3) periodic points are dense in V.

Conceptually speaking, chaotic dynamics can be seen as part of a broader family of models, the so called complex. According to Day (1994), a nonlinear dynamical model is complex if for nonstochastic reasons it does not go to either a fixed point, to a limit cycle, or explode. This implies that it must be a nonlinear system, although not all nonlinear systems are complex, e.g. the exponential function. It also implies that the dynamics are bounded and endogenously generated[*]. If to the latter the property of sensitive dependence on initial conditions is added, we should arrive to a chaotic model definition.

In the following section we present a set of simulations to display the difference between stable and chaotic dynamics, focusing in the model's response to an exogenous perturbation. The objective is to show the idea of shock amplification.

3. Simulations

In this section three simulations are presented. For simplicity, we have chosen the logistic[†] equation to perform the simulations. The procedure is the following: an exogenous shock is introduced onto the flow, and the new flow is iterated to explore the persistence of the initial shock. For each simulation, three figures are presented: Figure "a" represents the original flow, figure "b" the perturbed flow and figure c the difference between "a" and "b".

Simulation 1: A traditional steady state is presented. In the 27th lag a perturbation is introduced. As is seen in figure 1.b., the shock is totally transient, as the flow rapidly returns to the original path.

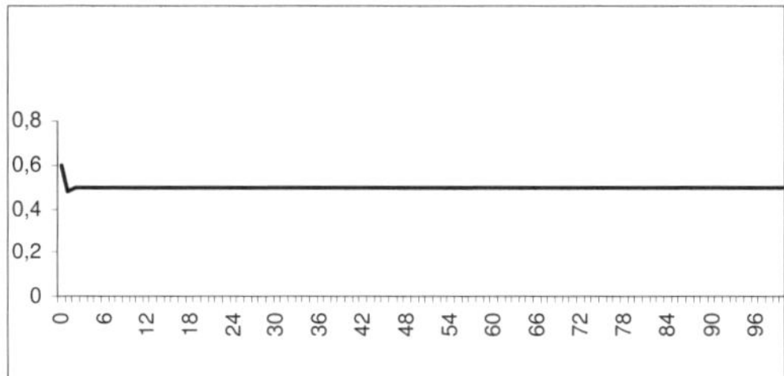

Figure 1.a. Steady State

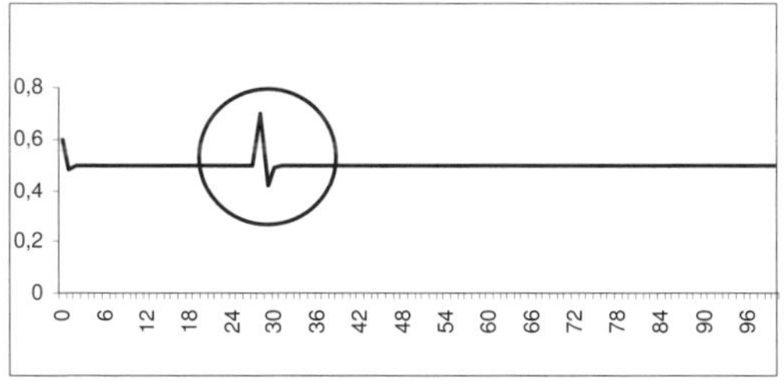

Figure 1.b. Steady State – Exogenous shock

---

[*] The definition can be found in Rosser (2000, p. 55).

[†] $x_t = kx_t(1 - x_{t-1})$, with normalizad values of x_t .

510

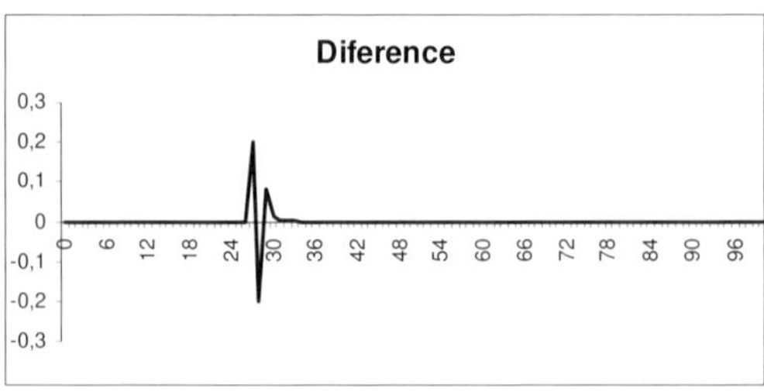

Figure 1.c. Difference

Simulation 2: A traditional limit cycle is presented. In the 27th lag a perturbation is introduced. As is seen in figure 1.b., the shock is also transient, as the flow again returns to the original path. However, in this case the shock persists in the system a bit longer, but, as can be seen in figure 2.c., it tends to disappear in the long run, being also a transient behavior.

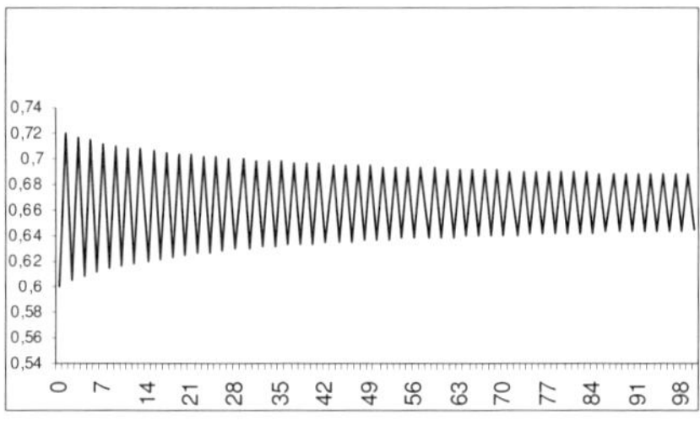

Figure 2.a. Cycle

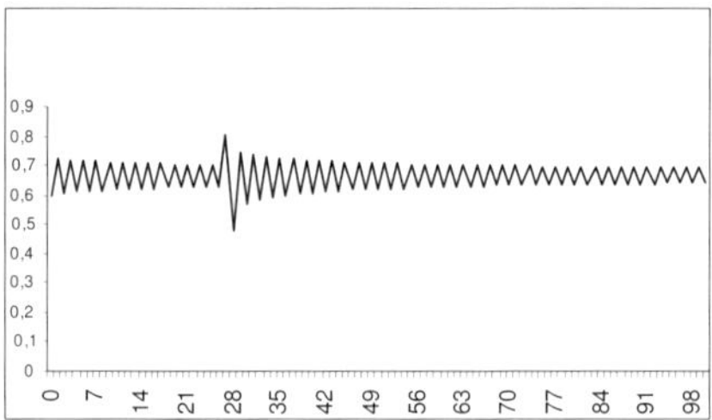

Figure 2.b. Cycle – Exogenous Shock

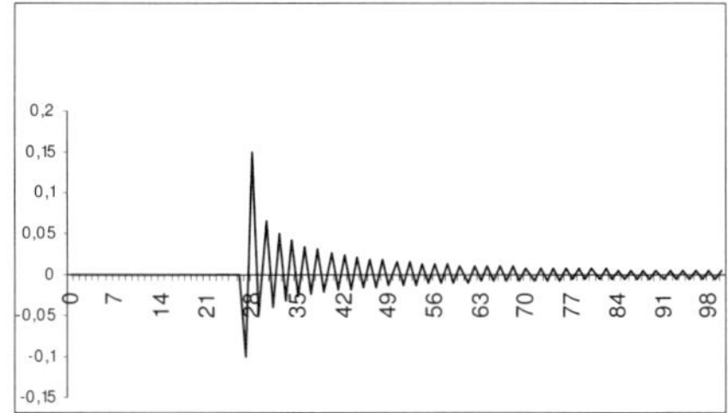

Figure 2.c. Difference

Simulation 3: In this case, a non-stable aperiodic –chaotic- flow is presented. Note that after the perturbation the system change its trajectory. In this case, the shock persists as the system evolves in the long run. In other words, the shock is permanent.

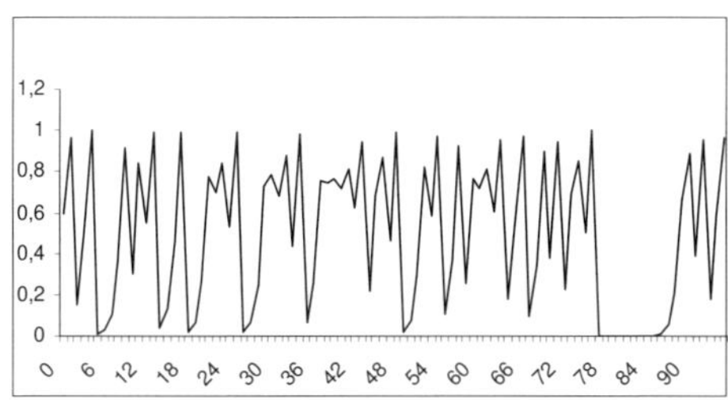

Figure 3.a. Non-Stable Path

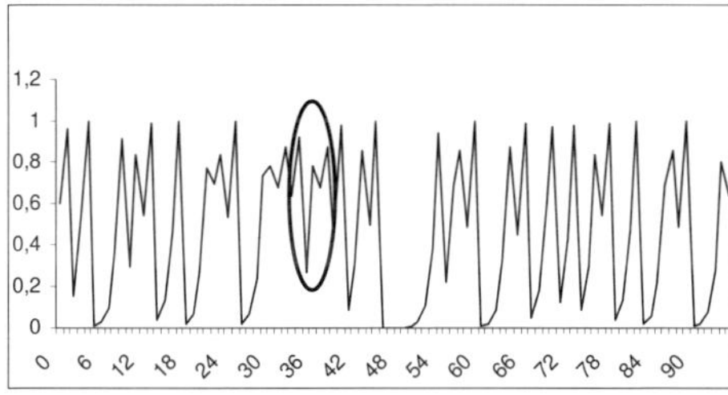

Figure 3.b. Non-Stable Path with exogenous shock

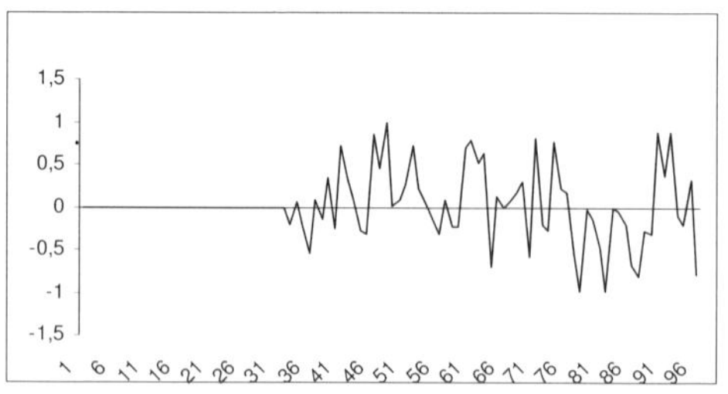

Figure 3.c. Difference

The following table summarizes the results.

Table 1. Simulations results

	Simulation 1	Simulation 2	Simulation 3
Equation Dynamcis	Steady-State	Limit Cycle	Chaotic
Shock	Transient	Transient	Permanent

However, another way to read the previous results is to consider the forcing process. For example, to generate a total aperiodic behavior in the fist simulation (the steady state), a sequence of random aperiodic perturbations must be introduced. If the sequence happens to be regular, the output will be a periodic flow. However, this is not necessary in the third simulation (the chaotic flow). In this case, only a slight perturbation is needed to change the qualitative dynamics of the flow, being the lack of periodicity an endogenous dynamic.

Table 2. Forcing mechanism and system´s response

	Linear Systems	**Nonlinear Systems**
Constant Forcing	Regular response	May generate varaible response (Lorenz, 1963)
Variable Forcing	Random response	Variable response

In all, to generate a total irregular flow in linear systems, it must be forced in a total irregular way. But this is not the case if the equations governing the system are nonlinear. In the words of Lorenz (1936), *if the equations contain terms representing advection (…) a constant forcing can lead to a variable response.* That is why we are interested in the upper left cell of the previous table, which corresponds to the non-stable path shown in figure 3. If, apart from exhibiting aperiodic behavior those equations are sensitive dependent on initial conditions, the shock not only generates the irregular patter but also amplifies the initial signal as the system evolves in the long run.

In the following section, we present a conceptual analogy to this behavior in the area of macroeconomics.

4. Macroeconomic Interpretation

Traditionally business cycle modeling treats fluctuations as deviations from a steady state caused by exogenous "shocks" like fiscal and monetary policy changes, changes in technology, or any other perturbation – such as exogenous crisis of any kind -.

This means that the vision of the economy corresponds to the mathematical model presented in simulations one and two, which derives from stable equations where the fluctuations are the result of the perturbations introduced.

However, policy-makers face one certain fact in economics: uncertainty regarding the results of the measures applied. However, traditional economic modeling shows the convergence of the system to a steady state after the (stochastic) shock.

The same idea is apply to an external crisis: the exogenous shock would force the system out the steady state performing a fluctuation, but the nature of the economy will sooner or later make the system return to the previous path. However, this is not the case in every economy, or at least in emerging markets such as Latin America. Moreover, there are certain characteristics of these economies that make them sensitive to external perturbations:

- Commercial shock amplification due to sensitivity of tributary structure to the external sector
- Financial constriction, due to flight to quality effect
- Less effect of fiscal policy, because of:
    - Lack of automatic stabilizers
    - Reduction of the fiscal program's multiplier effect, due to credibility problems concerning discretionality and funding – chance of negative multipliers -

These points are the ones that generate that certain external shocks such as a financial crisis tend to <u>amplify</u> its initial effects in Latin American economies. In the words of Cespedes *et all* (2005) *alternative policy reactions and policy setups may dampen or amplify the consequences of these shocks.*

Another way to see this, according to table 1, is if the shock is transient (traditional view) or permanent[*] (complex or chaotic view).

The distinction in economic modeling is that now we posses a set of equation that can emulate the idea of shock amplification, such as the chaotic flow presented in section 3. However, this doesn't mean that the economy must be chaotic, it means that there are a set of simple deterministic equations that allows us to describe certain behavior of the economic system in a more accurate way than the steady state perspective. In this way, we agree with Barnet (1997) *et al*:

> *It is well known, for example, that deterministic chaotic systems can generate output qualitatively similar to the actual economic time series. However, none of these broad considerations can be used as a conclusive argument that business fluctuations are actually the output of chaotic deterministic systems. They do, however, strongly suggest that, in order to describe complex dynamics mathematically, one does not necessarily have to make recourse to exogenous, unexplained shocks. The alternative option - the deterministic description of irregular fluctuations - provides economists with new research opportunities undoubtedly worth exploiting.*

5. Conclusions

The main properties and characteristics of the model presented are:
- No need to use the recourse of exogenous shocks to explain fluctuations
- Persistence of external shocks, even in the long run
- Qualitative changes in dynamics (bifurcation points)
- Amplification of initial shocks
- Account for systems that evolve far from equilibrium
- Difficulties in prediction

Concerning macroeconomics applications, if at certain interval of time the system can be seen as complex (in the Day (1995) definition) or even chaotic, the traditional stabilization policies –such as monetary expansion or increasing fiscal expenditure, among others- may not have the expected effect, and there's even the chance of being contra productive. Thus, the emphasis of stabilization policies must be placed in acting in the *parameters* of the model, in order to reach a bifurcation point that settles back the economy into a new dynamical equilibrium.

---

[*] To acquire a deeper insight about macroeconomic consequences of transient or permanent shock read Fanelli (2009) page 89.

References

1. P. Maneville, *Instabilities, Chaos and Turbulence*. Imperial College Press, (2004).
2. J. Barkley Rosser, *From Catastrophe to Chaos: A General Theory of Economic Discontinuities: Mathematics, Microeconomics, Macroeconomics, and Finance*. Kluwer Academic Publishers, (2000).
3. E. Lorenz, *Journal of the Atmospheric Science*. **V20**, (1963).
4. W. Barnett, A. Medio and A. Serletis, *Econometrics*. **9709001**, EconWPA, (1997).
5. P. Anderson, K. Arrow, D. Pines and EDITOR *"The Economy as an Evolving Complex System (Santa Fe Institute Studies in the Sciences of Complexity Proceedings)*, Westview Press (2003).
6. J. Jimenez, *Crisis, Volatilidad, Ciclo y Política Fiscal en América Latina*, CEPAL, LC/L.3038.
7. J. Fanelli, *La política económica fuera del corredor. Reflexiones sobre la crisis global y la experiencia latinoamericana*, Ensayos Económicos **53/54**: 73-105 – Banco Central de la Repùblica Argentina (2009).
8. L. Céspedes, I. Goldfajn, R. Valdés, *Policy Responses to External Shocks: The experiences of Australia, Brazil and Chile*, Central Bank of Chile Working Papers N° **321** (2005).

APROXIMATION TO THE THEORY OF AFFINITIES TO MANAGE THE PROBLEMS OF THE GROUPING PROCESS[*]

ANNA MARIA GIL-LAFUENTE, ANNA KLIMOVA

Department of Economics and Business Organization, University of Barcelona, Diagonal 690, Barcelona 08034, Spain

Perhaps more than ever, new economic and enterprise needs have increased the interest and utility of the methods of the grouping process based on the theory of uncertainty. We represent a brief analysis of the concepts such as a theory of affinities, uncertain pretopology and a Galois lattice that constitute a basis for the processes of fuzzy grouping. An illustrative example of the homogeneous grouping process of the economic areas of Russia is made.

1. Introduction

The intelligibility of the universe for each person depends on his aptitude to group or classify different objects. The analysis of the process of group making is fundamental nowadays for understanding the complex engineering processes and different economic and company management systems.

At the beginning Boolean logic has appeared as one of the most powerful mathematical tools able to make different groups giving the adequate solutions. Then some difficulties that occurred in these processes lead to a new manner of thinking. Fuzzy logic along with a theory of fuzzy sets gave a new model of groping process characterized as a more detailed mode to classify the elements.

The concept of affinity between the elements has been considered as an "angular stone" of fuzzy segmentation process.

In this work a brief analysis of the main themes that form a theoretical basis of the process of fuzzy grouping is made. The themes are the following: a theory of affinities, an uncertain pretopology and a Galois lattice considered as an effective tool for structuring the obtained results.

An illustrative example of the homogeneous grouping process is made.

---

[*] This work is supported by Ana Maria Gil Lafuente and Anna Klimova.

2. The theory of affinities

The theory of affinities represents a generalization of the relations of similarity extending the field of their performance to the field of the rectangular matrices. It makes possible to apply this theory in the multitude of the problems of economics and company management.

An attempt to generalize the notion of similarity was initiated in the eighties by the scientists Jaime Gil Aluja and Arnold Kaufmann. The theory of affinities turned out to be a successful result of this work.

"We determine the affinities as those homogeneous orderly structured groups limited to the established levels which join all elements of two sets of different nature. These two sets are related between themselves by the own essence of the phenomenon which represent them" [11].

3. Axioms for an uncertain pretopology

There are two elements such as a finite referential E and a "power set" $P(E)$ that have a different nature. Let us define uncertain pretopology [2,10-14].

Definition 1. A mapping Γ of $P(E)$ in $P(E)$ is uncertain pretopology of E if, and only if, the following axioms are given:

1. $\Gamma\varnothing = \varnothing$.

2. $\forall \underset{\sim}{A}_k \in P(E): \underset{\sim}{A}_k \subset \Gamma\underset{\sim}{A}_k$ (where $\Gamma E = E$ and $\underset{\sim}{A}_k$ is a fuzzy subset).

Using the same terms as usual in determinism, a mapping Γ for all elements of $P(E)$ will be called as an "adherent mapping" or "adherence". It is also possible to associate Γ with an "inner mapping" or "inner" δ, defined by:

$$\forall \underset{\sim}{A}_k \in P(E): \quad \delta\underset{\sim}{A}_k = \overline{\Gamma\overline{\underset{\sim}{A}_k}} \quad \text{(where } \overline{\underset{\sim}{A}_k} \text{ is a complement of } \underset{\sim}{A}_k\text{).} \tag{1}$$

Definition 2. $\underset{\sim}{A}_k$ is closed set for an uncertain pretopology if $\underset{\sim}{A}_k = \Gamma\underset{\sim}{A}_k$.

Definition 3. $\underset{\sim}{A}_k$ is open set for an uncertain pretopology if $\underset{\sim}{A}_k = \delta\underset{\sim}{A}_k$.

We considered the widest notion of uncertain pretopology. If new axioms are added then new uncertain pretopological spaces appear with characteristics of special interest for the treatment of the problems of economic systems.

Definition 4. A mapping Γ of $P(E)$ in $P(E)$ is uncertain isotone pretopology of E if, and only if, the following axioms are carried out:

1. $\Gamma\varnothing = \varnothing$.

2. $\forall \underset{\sim}{A}_k \in P(E): \underset{\sim}{A}_k \subset \Gamma\underset{\sim}{A}_k$, *extensivity.*

3. $\forall \underset{\sim}{A_k}, \underset{\sim}{A_l} \in P(E): \left(\underset{\sim}{A_k} \subset \underset{\sim}{A_l}\right) \Rightarrow \left(\Gamma\underset{\sim}{A_k} \subset \Gamma\underset{\sim}{A_l}\right),$ *isotony.*

Let us pay attention to one of the uncertain isotone pretopologies that satisfies the property, which is idempotency, and can be represented as the fourth axiom.

4. $\Gamma\left(\Gamma\underset{\sim}{A_k}\right) = \Gamma\underset{\sim}{A_k},$ *idempotency.*

With these four axioms, we get Moore's closure which, moreover, has the property $\Gamma\varnothing = \varnothing$, not required in the axiomatic of this closure.

Moore's closure is of special importance in the development of the algorithms capable of dealing with segmentation problems. So it is necessary to establish ways for obtaining Moore's closures on the basis of the concepts that could easily be found in the information supported by institutions.

4. Obtaining a Moore's closure

On the basis of previous practice, we have found two concepts that seem to adapt well to the exposed necessities. These are the notion of a Moore's family and a graph or fuzzy relation, see [1,9,11,16].

5. Axiomatic of Moore's family.

Definition 5. Let one family be determined through $F(E) \subset P(E)$. If there are two axioms:

1. $E \in F(E)$.

2. $(\underset{\sim}{A_k}, \underset{\sim}{A_l} \in F(E)) \Rightarrow (\underset{\sim}{A_k} \cap \underset{\sim}{A_l} \in F(E)),$.

then this is Moore's family.

Moore's closure is obtained by the following way:

a) Once the family $F(E)$ is available it is necessary for each element $\underset{\sim}{A_k} \in P(E)$ to find a subset of elements of $F(E)$ that contain $\underset{\sim}{A_k}$ and will be referred to as $F_{\underset{\sim}{A_k}}(E)$.

b) For each $F_{\underset{\sim}{A_k}}(E)$ its intersection $\bigcap\limits_{F \in F_{\underset{\sim}{A_k}}(E)} F$ is obtained.

c) A mapping $M\underset{\sim}{A_k}$ is determined by the mode that $\bigcap\limits_{F \in F_{\underset{\sim}{A_k}}(E)} F$ will be corresponded to each element $\underset{\sim}{A_k}$, that is to say: $M\underset{\sim}{A_k} = \bigcap\limits_{F \in F_{\underset{\sim}{A_k}}(E)} F$.

So, Moore's closure was found using one family. There is only one closure for each family.

3. The concept of relation is at the basis of a majority of algorithms of non-numerical mathematics of uncertainty, considered by Zadeh [15] and Kaufmann [9]. To formalize this relation there are two graphs that can be used represented either in matrix form or arrowlines.

Let us consider a fuzzy relation $[\underset{\sim}{R}]$ between the elements of a referential $E = \{y_1, y_2, ..., y_n\}$, such as $[\underset{\sim}{R}] \subset E \times E$.

4. With this information a Boolean graph is determined, taking a threshold α as follows:

$$[R_\alpha] = \{(y_i, y_j) \subset E \times E / \quad \mu_R(y_i, y_j) \geq \alpha\}, \quad \alpha \in [0,1] \tag{2}$$

5. Predecessors and successors of y_i limited to the level α are determined as:

$$\left. \begin{array}{l} y_j \text{ is a sucessor of } y_i \\[2mm] y_i \text{ is a predecessor of } y_j \end{array} \right\} \text{ if: } (y_i, y_j) \in [R_\alpha] \tag{3}$$

These concepts allow us to find the connection to the right $R_\alpha^+ \underset{\sim}{A}_k$ and to the left $R_\alpha^- \underset{\sim}{A}_k$.

Definition 6. A connection to the right $R_\alpha^+ \underset{\sim}{A}_k$ or, a mapping R_α^+ of $P(E)$ in $P(E)$ such that for all $\underset{\sim}{A}_k \in P(E)$, R_α^+ is a subset of elements of E that are successors, limited to the level α, of all element that belong to $\underset{\sim}{A}_k$, expressed as:

$$R_\alpha^+ \underset{\sim}{A}_k = \{y_j \in E / (y_i, y_j) \in [R_\alpha], \forall y_i \in \underset{\sim}{A}_\alpha\}, \text{ with } R_\alpha^+ \varnothing = E \tag{4}$$

Definition 7. A left connection $R_\alpha^- \underset{\sim}{A}_k$ or, a mapping R_α^- of P(E) in P(E) such that for all $\underset{\sim}{A}_k \in P(E)$, R_α^- is a subset of the elements of E that are predecessors, limited to the level α, of all elements that belong to $\underset{\sim}{A}_k$. It is expressed as:

$$R_\alpha^- \underset{\sim}{A}_k = \{y_i \in E / (y_i, y_j) \in [R_\alpha], \forall y_j \in \underset{\sim}{A}_k\}, \text{ with } R_\alpha^- \varnothing = E \tag{5}$$

6. The right connection $R_\alpha^+ \underset{\sim}{A}_k$ and the left one $R_\alpha^- \underset{\sim}{A}_k$ can be found directly by simple reading of the relation $[R_\alpha]$, in the following way:

$$\forall y_i \subset \underset{\sim}{A}_k \in P(E): \quad R_\alpha^+ \underset{\sim}{A}_k = \bigcap_{y_i \subset \underset{\sim}{A}_k} R_\alpha^+ \{y_i\} \quad \text{and} \quad R_\alpha^- \underset{\sim}{A}_k = \bigcap_{y_i \subset \underset{\sim}{A}_k} R_\alpha^- \{y_i\}. \tag{6,7}$$

7. Two Moore's closures corresponding to the fuzzy relation $[R_\alpha]$ or to the graph, limited to level α, are obtained by the maxmin convolution R_α^- with

R_α^+ and R_α^+ with R_α^-. It is written:

$$M_\alpha^{(1)} = R_\alpha^- \cdot R_\alpha^+ \quad \text{and} \quad M_\alpha^{(2)} = R_\alpha^+ \cdot R_\alpha^-. \tag{8,9}$$

where $M_\alpha^{(1)}$ and $M_\alpha^{(2)}$ are the two Moore's closures.

Two concepts, such as a family and a graph, can be used to obtain Moore's closures which are considered to be important for a wide rang of economic approaches.

5. Moore's closed sets as maximum groups

As for any pretopology, a set of Moore's closed sets is formed by the elements that comply with the following condition:

$$\forall A_{\sim k} \in P(E) : A_{\sim k} = MA_{\sim k}. \tag{10}$$

Let us determine a subset of closed sets of $P(E)$ corresponding to Moore's closure $M_\alpha^{(2)}$ as $C(E, M_\alpha^{(2)})$. As $R_\alpha^- A_{\sim k}$ is a closed of $P(E)$ for $M_\alpha^{(2)}$, which can be written as follows:

$$C(E, M_\alpha^{(2)}) = \bigcup_{A_{\sim k} \in P(E)} R_\alpha^- A_{\sim k}. \tag{11}$$

and, $R_\alpha^+ A_k$ is a closed for $M_\alpha^{(1)}$ and we determine the subset of closed sets of $P(E)$ corresponding to Moore's closure $M_\alpha^{(1)}$ as $C(E, M_\alpha^{(1)})$, we get:

$$C(E, M_\alpha^{(1)}) = \bigcup_{A_{\sim k} \in P(E)} R_\alpha^+ A_{\sim k}. \tag{12}$$

Both families $C(E, M_\alpha^{(1)})$ and $C(E, M_\alpha^{(2)})$ are isomorphic and dual for each other. They are also antitone. Therefore, we get:

$$A_{\sim k} \in C(E, M_\alpha^{(1)}) \Rightarrow (A_{\sim l} = R_\alpha^- A_{\sim k} \in C(E, M_\alpha^{(2)}) \text{ and } R_\alpha^+ A_{\sim l} = A_{\sim k}). \tag{13}$$

$$A_{\sim l} \in C(E, M_\alpha^{(2)}) \Rightarrow (A_{\sim k} = R_\alpha^+ A_{\sim l} \in C(E, M_\alpha^{(1)}) \text{ and } R_\alpha^- A_{\sim k} = A_{\sim l}). \tag{14}$$

These families of closed sets can be associated to each other and each of the families forms a finite lattice [9]. As a result of the maxmin convolution, both families of closed sets provide the groupings with the greatest possible number of elements of the referential E. In the formation of groups, the groupings of the elements of one family of the closed sets are accompanied by the other groupings of the other family of closed sets related to them.

6. Galois lattice and its importance in the process of segmentation

There is a fuzzy rectangular relation $[\underset{\sim}{R}] \subset E_1 \times E_2$. In this case the necessary properties obtained for only one referential are kept [3]. Only one lattice is obtained after two lattices were joined and where each vertex represents the relation of the groupings of elements of set E_1 with the groupings of elements of set E_2 taking into consideration a previously established level α. If this happens then there is affinity between the groups of the elements limited to the correspondent level. This lattice determines a structure for these relations [4-8].

If, when the upper end of the lattice is different to $(E_2, \quad)$ and the lower end is different to $(\quad, E_1)$, we add these vertices, then we have a Galois lattice that shows up two sets of Moore's closed sets that have the previous relations $(E_2, \quad)$ and $(\quad, E_1)$ as the upper and lower ends.

7. Illustrative example

We have participated in the process of formation of economic homogeneous groups of the regions of Russian Federation.

We selected 7 regions and their 6 more significant social and economic attributes. There are two sets of the regions and their indicators:

$$E_1 = \{a,b,...,g\} \text{ and } E_2 = \{A,B,...,F\}.$$

So we have the following relation:

	A	B	C	D	E	E
a	75.328	14.620	10.895,5	8,2	58.301	8.436
b	244.352	38.362	58.407,2	34,2	100.218	10.553
c	254.965	81.399	61.400,8	64,7	319.501	9.630
d	125.971	58.760	31.771,8	32,3	121.827	7.252
e	746.141	37.033	86.969,8	117,5	401.294	14.243
f	148.447	42.607	35.523,8	38,5	213.552	10.317
g	11.344	13.835	22.202,4	29,6	41.872	9.389

The data of this matrix is normalized.

The average values for each column of the indicators are calculated. These values are considered as the presumption levels of homogeneity α from which the homogenous groups are determined. The level for A is 0,308, for B - 0,503; ... for F - 0,700. So, the fuzzy relation is turned to a Boolean matrix, see below:

	A	B	C	D	E	E
a	0	0	0	0	0	0
b	1	0	1	0	0	1
c	1	1	1	1	1	0
d	0	1	0	0	0	0
e	1	0	1	1	1	1
f	0	1	0	0	1	1
g	0	0	0	0	0	0

The right connection B^+ and the left connection B^- are established.

$$B^+\varnothing = E_2, \; B^+\{a\} = \varnothing, \; B^+\{b\} = \{A,C,F\}, \; B^+\{c\} = \{A,B,C,D,E\}, \; ...,$$

$$B^+\{a,b,c,d,f\} = \varnothing, \; ..., \; B^+\{a,b,c,d,e,f,g\} = \varnothing.$$

$$B^-\varnothing = E_1, \; B^-\{A\} = \{b,c,e\}, \; B^-\{B\} = \{c,d,f\}, \; B^-\{C\} = \{b,c,e\}, \; ...,$$

$$B^-\{A,B,C,D,E\} = \{c\}, \; .., \; B^-\{A,B,C,D,E,F\} = \varnothing.$$

Then, Moore's closures $M^{(1)} = B^- \cdot B^+$ and $M^{(2)} = B^+ \cdot B^-$ are obtained.

In the next step the families of closed sets relative to the Moore's closures $M^{(1)}$ and $M^{(2)}$ are formed:

$$f(E, M^{(1)}) = \left\{\varnothing, \{B\}, \{E\}, \{F\}, \{A,C\}, .., \{A,B,C,D,E\}, \{A,C,D,E,F\}, E_2\right\}.$$

$$f(E, M^{(2)}) = \left\{\varnothing, \{c\}, \{e\}, \{f\}, \{b,e\}, ..., \{b,e,f\}, \{c,d,f\}, \{c,e,f\}, E_1\right\}.$$

The families of closed sets which represent the isomorphic lattices are associated to each other, see Figure 1, giving a Galois lattice, see Figure 2.

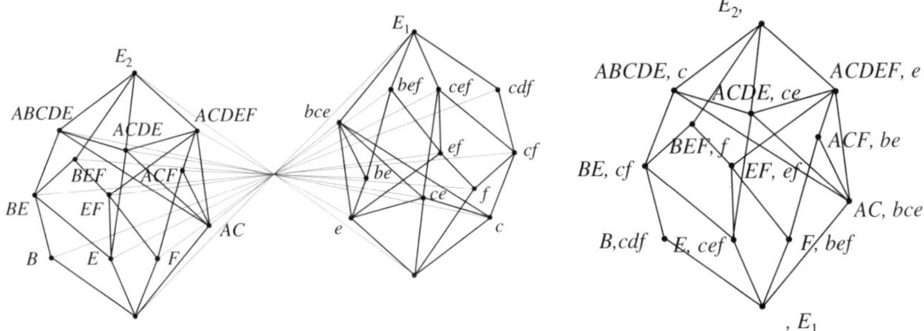

Figure 1. Isomorphic lattices　　　　　*Figure 2. Galois lattice*

The following similar groupings of elements of two sets which are the set of regions and the set of attributes have been obtained.

$$\varnothing \leftrightarrow E_2, \; \{c\} \leftrightarrow \{A,B,C,D,E\}, \; \{e\} \leftrightarrow \{A,C,D,E,F\}, \; \{f\} \leftrightarrow \{B,E,F\},$$

$$\{b,e\} \leftrightarrow \{A,C,F\}, \; \{c,e\} \leftrightarrow \{A,C,D,E\}, \; ..., \{b,c,e\} \leftrightarrow \{A,C\},$$

$$\{b,e,f\} \leftrightarrow \{F\}, \; \{c,d,f\} \leftrightarrow \{B\}, \; \{c,e,f\} \leftrightarrow \{E\}, \; E_1 \leftrightarrow \varnothing.$$

8. Conclusion

- Generalization of the notion of similarity by using the theory of affinities.
- Transition from one axiomatic to the other in pretopologies.
- Obtaining the strictest uncertain pretopology determined as uncertain pretopology of Moore.
- Process for obtaining maximum groupings in the cases of fuzzy rectangular relations by using a Moore's closure and Moore's closed set.
- Practical verification of the theoretical concepts is made. Galois lattices show the advantages of the mathematical methods considered above.

References

1. N. Bourbaki, Eléments de Mathématique.III. Hermann & Cie., Paris (1940).
2. J. Gil Aluja, La pretopología en la gestión de la incertidumbre, Discurso de investidura, Universidad de León (2001).
3. J. Gil Aluja, Interactive management of human resources in uncertainty. Kluwer Academic Publishers, London, Dordrecht (1998).
4. A. M. Gil Lafuente, Nuevas estrategias para el análisis financiero en la empresa. Ariel, Barcelona (2001).
5. J. Gil Lafuente, Proceedings of Congress M.S. China, 332-335 (2001).
6. J. Gil Lafuente, Algoritmos para la excelencia. Claves para el éxito en la gestión deportiva. Milladoiro, Vigo (2002).
7. U. Höhle, Many valued topology and its applications. Kluwer Academic Publisher, Dordrecht (2001).
8. U. Höhle, S. Rodabaugh and A. Sostak, Fuzzy and Sets Systems **73** (1995).
9. A. Kaufmann, Introduction à la thèorie des sous-ensambles flous à l'usage des ingénieurs, 4. Masson, Paris (1977).
10. A. Kaufmann, Prétopologie ordinaire et prétopologie floue. Note de Travail 115. La Tronche (1983).
11. A. Kaufmann and J. Gil Aluja, Proceedings of XI Euro O. R. Congress, Aachen, Germany (1991).
12. C. Ponsard, Un modèle topologique d'equilibre économique. Dunod, Paris (1969).
13. S. Rodabaugh, Topology Applications **11**, 319-334 (1980).
14. A. Sapena, Applications of General Topology **2**, 63-76 (2001).
15. L. Zadeh, Information and Control **12**, 94-102 (1968).
16. L. Zadeh, Information Sciences **3**, 177-200 (1971).

MODELLING OF SELECTED ECONOMIC TIME SERIES USING THE N-REGIME MODELS[*]

ANNA PETRIČKOVÁ[†], JANA LENČUCHOVÁ

PhD students, Department of Mathematics, Faculty of Civil Engineering, Slovak University of Technology, Radlinského 11, 813 68 Bratislava, Slovakia

In this paper we will discuss regime-switching models with regimes determined by observable variables (SETAR, LSTAR and ESTAR) and by unobservable variables – MSW models. These models have a nonlinear character. The goal of this work is to provide a brief overview of the problem and to describe these classes of models. We estimate all the examined real economic time series with more types of switching models and compare them using certain goodness-of-fit criteria.

1. Introduction

One of the features of many real time series is their variable variance. In process of time series the phases with higher and lower dispersion alternate, these periods are short, sometimes longer. Practical analysis of financial time series shows that the autocorrelation in time series of yield in stock prices depends on their volatility [6]. Autocorrelation tends to rise during periods of lower volatility and tends to decline during periods of higher volatility. This character of the relationship is logical, since higher volatility indicates the presence of relatively stronger non-systematic component (and relatively weaker systematic component). The change of volatility, respectively autocorrelation of time series can be understood as the change of regime in the behaviour of time series. This change may be due to the several factors. Some of them are well identified, others hardly or even never.

In recent years there were proposed many time series models, which formalize the idea of the existence of different regimes of behavior in time series. Here belong, for example, models that can be used for modelling of time series financial yields, hydrological and geodetic time series, and so on ([1], [4], [8]). These models have nonlinear character. These include, for example,

---

[*] This work was supported by Slovak Research and Development Agency under contract No. LPP-0111-09.
[†] Corresponding author

regime-switching models with regimes determined by observable variables and regime-switching models with regimes determined by unobservable variables.

In this article will deal with 3 classes of regime-switching models with regimes determined by observable variables (SETAR, LSTAR and ESTAR) and 1 class with regimes determined by unobservable variables - MSW models.

2. Overview of nonlinear regime-switching models

In the real life we often meet time series that exhibit strong non-linear features, because linear models are not in general always suitable for use. In this paper we focus on the class of regime-switching models, which are well to interpret and are also very suitable for modeling a lot of real data. The basic feature of these models is their „control" with one or more variables.

2.1. *Regime-switching models with regimes determined by observable variables*

Typical models belonging to this class are TAR models ("Threshold **A**uto**R**egressive"). They form the basis of regime-switching models with regimes determined by observable variables and were designed by Tong ([11], [12]). These models assume that any regime in time t can be given by any observed variable q_t (*indicator variable*). Values of q_t are compared with *threshold value* c. In case of 2-regimes model the first regime applies if $q_t \leq c$, the second if $q_t > c$.

2.1.1. *Model SETAR*

We have a special case, when the variable q_t is taken to be a lagged value of the time series itself, that is $q_t = X_{t-d}$ for a certain integer $d > 0$. The resulting model is called a **S**elf-**E**xciting **T**hreshold **A**uto**R**egressive (SETAR) model ([3]). For example 2-regime model SETAR with AR(p) in both regimes has form

$$X_t = \left(\phi_{0,1} + \phi_{1,1}X_{t-1} + \cdots + \phi_{p,1}X_{t-p}\right)\left[1 - I\left(X_{t-d} > c\right)\right] + \\ + \left(\phi_{0,2} + \phi_{1,2}X_{t-1} + \cdots + \phi_{p,2}X_{t-p}\right)I\left(X_{t-d} > c\right) + a_t \tag{1}$$

where $\{a_t\}$ is the strict white noise process with $E[a_t] = 0$, $D[a_t] = \sigma_a^2$ for all $t = 1, ..., n$ and I[A] is the *indicator function* with values I[A] = 1 if the event A occurs and I[A] = 0 otherwise. For more details on SETAR models see, e.g. ([2], [3], [11], [12]).

2.1.2. *Model STAR*

If we replace the indicator function $I[X_{t-d} > c]$ by a continuous function $F(q_t, \delta, c)$ (so called *transition function*), which changes smoothly from 0 to 1 as X_{t-d} increases, the resultanting model is called **S**mooth **T**ransition **A**uto**R**egressive (STAR) model ([2], [3]). For example 2-regime model STAR with AR(p) in both regimes and indicator variable $q_t = X_{t-d}$ has form

$$X_t = \left(\phi_{0,1} + \phi_{1,1}X_{t-1} + \cdots + \phi_{p,1}X_{t-p}\right)\left[1 - F\left(X_{t-d},\delta,c\right)\right] + $$
$$+ \left(\phi_{0,2} + \phi_{1,2}X_{t-1} + \cdots + \phi_{p,2}X_{t-p}\right)F\left(X_{t-d},\delta,c\right) + a_t \tag{2}$$

If the transition function $F(q_t; \delta, c)$ is the logistic function

$$F\left(q_t;\delta,c\right) = \frac{1}{1 + \exp\left(-\delta\left(q_t - c\right)\right)}, \qquad \delta > 0, \tag{3}$$

the resulting model is called a Logistic STAR (LSTAR) model. If the transition function $F(q_t; \delta, c)$ is the exponential function

$$F\left(q_t;\delta,c\right) = \left(1 - \exp\left(-\delta\left(q_t - c\right)^2\right)\right), \qquad \delta > 0, \tag{4}$$

the resulting model is called an Exponential STAR (ESTAR) model. For more details on STAR models see, e.g. ([2],[3],[9]).

2.2. *Regime-switching models with regimes determined by unobservable variables*

This class of models goes out from assumption that a regime is determined by any unobservable stochastic process, which can be labeled as $\{S_t\}$. It follows that separate regimes can not be identified exactly, but only with some probability. In case of 2 regimes process $\{S_t\}$ can take only values 1 and 2. If we work on a model AR(p), the regime-switching model with regimes determined by unobservable variables is

$$X_t = \phi_{0,S_t} + \phi_{1,S_t}X_{t-1} + \ldots + \phi_{p,S_t}X_{t-p} + a_t \text{ for } S_t = 1,2 \tag{5}$$

2.2.1. *Markov switching models (MSW models)*

An MSW model belongs to the class of regime-switching models with regimes determined by unobservable variables.

The class of MSW models is based on the assumption that a regime is determined by the discrete ergodic first order Markov process, hence important is only the actual and the previous state:

$$P\left(q_t = S_j \mid q_{t-1} = S_i, q_{t-2} = S_k, \ldots\right) = P\left(q_t = S_j \mid q_{t-1} = S_i\right) = p_{ij} \; 1 \le i, j \le N \tag{6}$$

where $p_{ij} \ge 0$, $\sum_{j=1}^{N} p_{ij} = 1$ and p_{ij} is a state transition probability (transition from the state S_i at time $t-1$ to the state S_j at time t in Markov chain), $t = 1, 2, \ldots,$ n are

528

time instants associated with state changes and q_t is actual state at time t. For details on MSW models see, e. g.[3], [4], [5].

2.2.2. *The relation between conditional and unconditional central moments of MSW model*

State-dependent *p-th order* autoregressive MSW model with normally distributed increments is

$$X_t = \phi_{0,q_t} + \phi_{1,q_t} X_{t-1} + \ldots + \phi_{p,q_t} X_{t-p} + a_t \tag{7}$$

where X_t, t = 1, ..., n is examined time series, $q_t = 1,2,\ldots,N$ is (unobservable) state variable, generated by ergodic *N*-state Markov process, $q_t \in M = \{1, 2, \ldots, N\}$ are real constants and a_t is a zero-mean random variable which is identically and independently distributed over time (i.i.d. process). We assume that the number of states N is finite and coefficients ϕ_j , j = 1, ..., p are state dependent (coefficients of autoregressive model may be different in each regime), $\boldsymbol{\pi} = (\pi_1,\pi_2,\ldots,\pi_N)'$ is the N-vector of steady-state (ergodic) probabilities that solve the system of equations $\mathbf{P}'\boldsymbol{\pi} = \boldsymbol{\pi}$, where $\mathbf{P} = \begin{pmatrix} p_{11} & \cdots & p_{1N} \\ \vdots & \ddots & \vdots \\ p_{N1} & \cdots & p_{NN} \end{pmatrix}$ is transition probability matrix of type N x N. The vector $\boldsymbol{\pi}$ represents unconditional probabilities, applying to the N states.

In general for N-states *k-th order central moment* of $\{X_t\}$ is

$$\mu^k = E\left[(X_t - \mu)^k\right] = \sum_{i=1}^{N} E\left[(X_t - \mu)^k | q_t = i\right] \cdot P[q_t = i] =$$

$$= \sum_{i=1}^{N} E\left[(X_t - \mu)^k | q_t = i\right] \pi_i = \sum_{i=1}^{N} \mu_i^k \pi_i = \boldsymbol{\pi}' \cdot \begin{pmatrix} \mu_1^k \\ \vdots \\ \mu_N^k \end{pmatrix} \tag{8}$$

where π_i is unconditional probability of state i, μ^k is unconditional k-th order central moment and μ_i^k , i = 1, ..., N is k-th order central moment for i^{th}-regime of the stochastic process $\{X_t\}$. For example, mean is in the form (for p = 1)

$$\mu = \boldsymbol{\pi}' \cdot \begin{pmatrix} \mu_1 \\ \vdots \\ \mu_N \end{pmatrix} = \boldsymbol{\pi}' \cdot (\mathbf{I_N} - \Phi \cdot \mathbf{B})^{-1} \cdot \begin{pmatrix} \phi_{0,1} \\ \vdots \\ \phi_{0,N} \end{pmatrix}, \text{ where } \mathbf{I_N} \text{ is the N x N identity matrix,}$$

$$\Phi = \begin{pmatrix} \phi_{1,1} & 0 & \cdots & 0 \\ 0 & \phi_{1,2} & \cdots & 0 \\ 0 & 0 & \cdots & 0 \\ 0 & 0 & \cdots & \phi_{1,N} \end{pmatrix}$$ is the diagonal matrix of autoregressive coefficients

and **B** is the "backward" transition probability matrix of type N x N.

2.3. *Empirical specification procedure for nonlinear models*

In the process of the empirical specification of nonlinear models, the following steps are recommended (see, e.g. [2], [3])

1. specify an appropriate linear AR(p) model for the time series considered

2. test the null hypothesis of linearity against the alternative regime-switching nonlinearity

3. estimate the parameters in the selected nonlinear model

4. evaluate the model using diagnostic tests

5. modify the model if necessary

6. use the model for descriptive or forecasting purposes.

When we test the null hypothesis of linearity against the alternative of SETAR and MSW –type nonlinearity, we need to know estimates of parameters of the nonlinear model. Therefore, in this case we start a specification procedure for the model with estimation of parameters.

3. Application

We focused at the application of previously mentioned modelling procedures to real data, in our case 20 time series. Modelling of the time series can be (generally) used for any real data. In this paper we focused on macroeconomic indicators, exchange rates and other economic time series. We worked particularly with the Slovak data, but also within V4 countries, we also used U.S. data and data of the European Union. Some data were seasonally adjusted, some were not, and we also used monthly as well as quarterly data. All data used in this paper can be downloaded from the pages of National Bank of Slovakia (www.nbs.sk) and European Central Bank (www.ecb.int), which takes some data directly from Eurostat (www.ec.europa.eu / Eurostat).

The first section summarizes the results of estimates of optimal parameter values of regime-switching models - concretely SETAR, LSTAR, ESTAR (regime-switching models with regimes determined by observable variables) and MSW (regime-switching models with regimes determined by unobservable variables). For each model, we consider 2 and 3 regimes. We tested linearity of the model to detect, whether a linear or a nonlinear model is better and then, if hypothesis of linearity was rejected, we tested the remaining nonlinearity to detect, which of two model types is more suitable for our data: 2-regimes or 3-regimes time series model. We tested also the autocorrelation of residuals.

In the second part we engaged to the prediction of values. The analysis of time series was realized only on the part of data. The last 5 data we used to compare with the predictions given with models. This way we found out (with prediction errors RMSE and MAE) prediction properties of individual models.

For modelling of time series, we used the comp. syst. *Mathematica*, vers. 6.

3.1. *The best of the models*

For each time series we choose the best model for descriptive purposes. The main criteria are standard deviation of residuals σ_{rez} and information criterion BIC^*. Selected the best models are written bold.

Table 1. Selected the best models.

	SETAR	LSTAR	ESTAR	MSW
data	σ_{rez}	σ_{rez}	σ_{rez}	σ_{rez}
HUF	3.18992	3.73904	3.6476	**1.7241**
SKK	0.379069	0.3494	0.32066	**0.2045**
PLN	0.0714825	0.07561	0.0847207	**0.04624**
CZK	0.395944	0.31698	0.279932	**0.172545**
SVK nezam	0.389888	0.4016	0.408823	**0.229316**
SVK inflácia	0.577351	0.5898	0.564074	**0.39583**
DoS USA	0.560333	0.5764	0.593941	**0.365027**
GDP HUF	0.0056863	0.00495	0.0049641	**0.00339**
GDP SVK	**0.0331243**	0.08367	0.0816442	0.0827
GVA agri	**0.0224458**	0.05421	0.0541416	0.02694
GVA constr	0.0392516	0.06914	0.0455781	**0.037535**
GVA fin	0.05792	0.0627	0.0635908	**0.034292**
GVA industry	0.112423	0.07994	0.0899662	**0.048653**
GVA other	0.0520568	0.05924	**0.051921**	0.07327
NofB10 SVK	**0.0091872**	0.0113	0.0100063	0.0153717
NofB100 SVK	0.0198671	0.03611	0.018785	**0.01541**
CAP. GOODS	0.683058	0.69453	0.699761	**0.31864**
EMPLOY SVK	0.0242428	0.02059	**0.0181273**	0.025826
UNEMPLOY	0.219382	0.15396	0.149922	**0.11426**
TRANSPORT SVK	0.958404	0.933265	0.879461	**0.506225**

---

*Bayesian information criterion for *N*-state MSW: $BIC_N = 2\ln L\left(\hat{\theta}_{ML}|\Omega_n\right) + d_N \ln(n)$

In the Table 1 we can see, that for 15 from 20 considered time series are the best models from the class MSW models (9 two-regimes, 6 three-regimes). Models from the class SETAR are the best for 3 and ESTAR for 2 time series.

3.2. *Predictions*

In the previous section we have chosen the best models for description of real time series from SETAR, LSTAR, ESTAR and MSW class of models. For each time series we choose here the best models for prediction. The main criteria are prediction errors RMSE[*] and MAE[†]. In the following table (Table 2) the best predictions for our time series are presented (they are written bold).

Table 2. Selected the best models for forecasting purpose.

	SETAR		LSTAR		ESTAR		MSW	
dáta	MAE	RMSE	MAE	RMSE	MAE	RMSE	MAE	RMSE
HUF	**27.0034**	**29.905**	32.2411	35.4209	28.866	31.9405	27.745	30.486
SKK	0.0237	0.02972	0.90024	1.10128	**0.0136**	**0.01739**	0.05384	0.0727
PLN	0.4945	0.59874	0.5321	0.6484	0.5757	0.66814	**0.3393**	**0.40842**
CZK	1.8767	2.30835	48.391	65.853	2.3097	2.76181	**1.0311**	**1.0706**
SVK nezam	0.2369	0.284	0.23438	0.26254	**0.14262**	**0.2208**	0.2187	0.27982
SVK infl	0.7871	0.82114	**0.14497**	**0.162**	0.2286	0.28468	0.25997	0.32995
DoS USA	1.8284	2.2414	1.2138	1.5594	2.08424	2.4987	**0.7826**	**1.28017**
GDP HUF	1.2025	2.01185	0.7033	0.8185	**0.007546**	**0.009228**	0.025	0.03552
GDP SVK	0.36026	0.38431	0.4516	0.47464	**0.261984**	**0.304438**	3.1447	5.2265
GVA agri	**0.0783**	**0.11114**	0.20684	0.2386	98.913	197.79	0.15274	0.16877
GVA constr	0.1482	0.18596	1.3572	1.4275	881.62	1758.76	**0.1173**	**0.21465**
GVA fin	**0.1722**	**0.2511**	0.59942	0.8199	0.17376	0.25853	0.18711	0.26296
GVA industry	0.5387	0.75576	0.59942	0.8199	**0.49297**	**0.7033**	0.632	0.6811
GVA other	**0.15135**	**0.16403**	12.316	20.468	4.91322	5.65359	0.33511	0.54571
NofB10 SVK	0.01463	0.017079	0.01194	0.0152	**0.007287**	**0.008177**	0.01084	0.01211
NofB100 SVK	**0.02479**	**0.02803**	0.02707	0.03348	0.064783	0.104212	0.04515	0.0539
CAP. GOODS SVK	0.19626	0.2334	0.2421	0.28848	**0.1316**	**0.1462**	0.58255	0.68643
EMPLOY SVK	0.07515	0.08337	0.07903	0.0844	**0.0417**	**0.04595**	0.059	0.06821
UNEMPLOY očist	0.36349	0.29185	**0.2694**	**0.3286**	0.212	0.26771	0.40453	0.49664
TRANSPORT SVK	**2.167**	**2.3903**	2.7394	3.0264	4.12363	4.57536	3.8322	4.3276

[*] root mean squared error
[†] mean absolute error

The best predictive properties for considered time series have models from the class ESTAR (8 from 20 time series). The subsequent order (based on predictive properties) is: models from class SETAR (6), MSW (4) and LSTAR (2).

4. Conclusion

In this work we discussed the class of regime-switching models with regimes determined by unobservable variables – Markov-switching models and we compared estimations of all the examined real time series with models with regimes determined by observable variables (SETAR, LSTAR a ESTAR).

15 from 20 considered time series are best described by models from the class MSW models (9 two-regimes, 6 three-regimes). Model from the class SETAR are the best for 3 and ESTAR for 2 time series.

The best predictive properties for considered time series have models from the class ESTAR (8 from 20 time series). The subsequent order (based on predictive properties) is: models from class SETAR (6), MSW (4) and LSTAR (2).

Because autocorrelation function isn't suitable for description of residual dependence of regime-switching models, we want to examine description of this dependence with 'auto-copula', which is cumulative distribution function of time lagged value random variables that generate time series.

References

[1]   B. Akintug and P. F. Rasmussen, *Water Resour.* Res. **41** (2005).
[2]   J. Arlt and M. Arltová, Grada Publishing a.s., (2003).
[3]   P. H. Frances and D. van Dijk, *Cambridge University Press*, Cambridge, (2000).
[4]   J. D. Hamilton, *Econometrica* **57**, 357 – 384 (1989).
[5]   J. D. Hamilton, *Princeton University Press.* (1994).
[6]   B. LeBaron, *Journal of Business* **65**, 199 – 219 (1992).
[7]   Z. Psaradakis and M. Sola, *Journal of Econometrics* **86**, 369 – 386 (1997).
[8]   Sean D. Campbell. *Department of Economics*, Brown University, (2002).
[9]   T. Teräsvirta, T. *Journal of American Statistical Association* **89**, 208 – 218 (1994).
[10] A. Timmermann, *Journal of Econometrics* **96**, 75 – 111 (2000).
[11] H. Tong, *C. H. Chen (ed.)*, Amsterdam, 101 – 141 (1978).
[12] H. Tong, *Oxford University Press*, Oxford. (1990).
[13] A. Petričková, 2009. MSc. thesis, Comenius University, Bratislava, (2009).

MACROECONOMIC FLOWS IN CEFTA COUNTRIES

MILICA BULAJIC, DRAGANA KRAGULJ, SANDRA JEDNAK

Faculty of Organizational Sciences, University of Belgrade
Jove Ilica 154, Belgrade, Serbia

Western Balkan countries are in transition and late process of European integration. They are putting their efforts to build market structure, institutions and macroeconomic stability. The key to economic recovery and regional stability in Southeast Europe (especially Western Balkans) economies is creating a free trade area. The aim of the paper is to analyse regional integration processes in the Western Balkan Countries (CEFTA) as well as their economic objectives and results. Data on economic flows in the Western Balkan countries will be used as the basis for the I-distance classification. The result of such classification can be considered a measure of the achieved degree in the transition process.

1. Introduction

Western Balkan countries are still in the transition process and in a late period of integration into the European Union. Their most important aim is the access to the European Union. However, in order to achieve this, it is necessary to implement economic and political reforms and to adopt basic economic principles of the European Union. In 2000, the Council of Europe notified for the first time the possibility of total integration into the European Union of the Western Balkan countries. This prospect was repeated in Copenhagen in 2002. In March 2003 in Brussels, the Council of Europe confirmed that "the future of Western Balkan countries lies within the European Union". The European Union offered European Union partnership to the Western Balkan countries on the European summit conference in Thessaloniki in June 2003. The main priority of the European Union is to prepare these countries for the integration into the European structure. In order to make their way toward creation and joining the other modern democratic market economies, the Western Balkan countries should strengthen regional integration and CEFTA agreement membership – the unique multilateral free trade agreement in Southeast Europe, the so-called CEFTA 2006 agreement.

2. Free Trade Zone in Southeast Europe

Although the name CEFTA (The Central European Free Trade Agreement) refers to an agreement among countries in Central Europe, today (in 2007) it is the agreement which defines the free trade zone of Southeast Europe. CEFTA agreement was signed on 21 December 1992 in Krakow by Poland, Hungary and Czechoslovakia, and the signed agreement came into force on 1 March 1993. The members of CEFTA became Slovenia (on 1 January 1996), Romania (on 1 July 1997), Bulgaria (on 1 January 1999), Croatia (on 1 March 2003) and Macedonia (in 2006). By the the European Union enlargement in 2004 and 2007, Poland, Hungary, Czech Republic, Slovakia, Slovenia, Romania and Bulgaria left this form of trade integration. Nowadays, CEFTA is a trade agreement between Albania, Bosnia and Herzegovina, Macedonia, Moldova, Serbia, UNMIK on behalf of Kosovo and Metohia, Croatia and Montenegro. CEFTA has served as a preparation for the final aim of all countries - EU membership. Since the 1990s, European Union has been trying to stimulate certain countries to join and become a part of the EU. The European Union made its first effort with regional cooperation within CEFTA (Central European Free Trade Area) and BFTA (Baltic Free Trade Area). Thereafter, it has continued through the Stabilisation and Accession process that will lead countries to the European Union integration. Nowadays, EU insists on closer mutual economic cooperation of Western Balkan countries.

The establishment of Southeast free trade zone was preceded by the signing of the Memoradum of Understanding on Trade Liberalisation and Facilitation on 27 June 2001 in Brussels in the framework of the Stability Pact for South Eastern Europe by Serbia and Montenegro, Romania, Bulgaria, Croatia, Bosnia and Herzegovina (B&H), Macedonia (FYRM), Albania and later Moldova. These countries were obliged to make bilateral free trade agreements by 31 December 2002 which would be based on principles according to the World Trade Organization standards. According to those standards, the entire trade between those countries would be without quantitative limits and customs duties. Although thirty-one bilateral free trade agreements were signed by the end of 2005, many of the agreements were not operative. In order to improve economic cooperation in the West Balkan region and preparation for the European Union integration, the decision was made on forming the unique multilateral free trade agreement in Southeast Europe, that would practically substitute all the bilateral agreements. This new single FTA (Free Trade Agreement) - known as CEFTA 2006 agreement, was initiated on 9 November, and it was signed on 19 December 2006 in Bucharest.

CEFTA 2006 offers great possibilities and advantages to the countries of the region. Common market, operating according to 31 bilateral free trade agreements signed by the countries of the region during the previous years, becomes the single regional trade agreement characterized by:

- Further liberalization and all quantitative restrictions (except for arms, weapons and other goods for military purposes);
- The rule of non-discrimination (which means that all products are equally treated);
- The rule of origin (which means that CEFTA product is treated as domestic product when it is exported to foreign markets);
- Introduction of diagonal cumulation (which means that the products produced in one member state of Agreement are considered to be domestic products, no matter whether they are partially or wholly produced in that country);
- General safeguards and compensatory measures are defined according to World Trade Organization rules and national legislations;
- The special attention is paid to the protection of intellectual property rights.

3. Economic Characteristics of the Region of Southeast Europe

All West Balkan countries have very similar characteristics. In that sense, they create market based economies, implement structural and institutional reforms and macroeconomic stability. Despite the improved situation, these small economies are uncompetitive due to inadequate harmonization with European and international standards. Macroeconomic imbalances – current account and fiscal deficits, are present across the region. High inflation rate and particularly high unemployment rate are the most serious challenges for most countries.

By forming West Balkan Free Trade Zone, numerous positive economic and political effects are expected in the economies of the countries in the region. The most important ones are:

- Enabling free flow and movements of goods, people, capital and services within the countries in the region;
- Increasing exchange of goods among the countries in the region and improving export and import structure;
- Productivity and efficiency increase due to greater competition;
- Improvement of productive cooperation among the countries in the region in order to find the third markets for goods;
- Utilization of economies of scale;
- Attracting foreign direct investments, especially greenfield investments;

- Investment stimulation among the countries in the region, and also, joint investments in the third countries;
- Significantly easier and cheaper access to higher-quality products for all consumers;
- Harmonizing legislation in the countries of the region;
- Political stability in the region and positive effects on the security of Balkans etc.

4. Estimation of Macroeconomic Performances

In the economic theory four most common macroeconomics objectives are singled out. These are categories which measure and estimate macroeconomic performance of a national economy:

1. Stable growth of gross national product;
2. Stable level of prices;
3. High employment levels;
4. Stable (equal) balance of payments.

For achieving these objectives several macroeconomic instruments are used. These are, in fact, instruments by which creators of economic policy influence the pace and direction of economic activities. The four most important macroeconomic instruments are:

1. Fiscal policy,
2. Monetary policy
3. Income and price policies and
4. International economic policy.

Every country faces the problem of choice while defining economic policy: the accomplishment of priority objectives. An ideal economic condition would exist if domestic and foreign equilibriums were achieved, that is, a condition which can be expressed through equality of the sum of production and imports, on the one hand, and consumption and exports, on the other.

In this paper we will present some results of the statistical analysis made on data regarding objectives of macroeconomics for Western Balkan Countries and Moldavia.

The goal of the analysis was to see how the countries would be classified on the bases of achieved objectives of macroeconomics. Ranking based on several indicators can be performed in different ways, but technique used in this paper is I-distance, method of multivariate statistical analysis, developed by Ivanović [2] during his research on countries and regions ranking, based on development level, in the period from 1950 to 1970. Many socio-economical development indicators were considered and the problem was how to use all of them to calculate a single synthetic indicator which will represent the rank. The ranks based on I-distance method can be compared to ones obtained in ranking processes based on other methodologies. Data Envelope Analysis (DEA), as a leading method for performance evaluation, in terms of the number of published research papers, as well as in the number of applications is one of methodologies whose results can be compared to ones based on I-distances [5], but such comparison will not be presented in this paper. Here will be presented the results of the analysis based only on I-distance method.

Selection of indicators is the first and one of the most important steps in the ranking procedure. Statistical methods, such as correlation analysis, can be used in order to define the set of the indicators relevant for the analysis. Calculated I-distance depends on the order of the chosen indicators. It was suggested that the indicators should be ranked according to their importance. The first attribute is the most important, while the last one has the smallest influence.

Let $X = \{x_{1s}, x_{2s}, \dots, x_{ks}\}$ be the set of indicators, ordered by their importance, for the unit P_s. I-distance for the units P_r and P_s, is is given by:

$$D(r,s) = \sum_{i=1}^{k} \frac{|d_i(r,s)|}{\sigma_i} \prod_{j=1}^{i-1} (1 - r_{ji.12\dots j-1}) \tag{1}$$

where $d_i(r,s) = x_{ir} - x_{is}$, $i \in \{1, \dots, k\}$ is discriminate effect, e.g. difference between values of attribute x_i for P_r and P_s. σ_i is standard deviation of x_i, and $r_{ji.12\dots j-1}$ is partial correlation coefficient for x_i and x_j, $(j<i)$.

I-distance is calculated through the following steps:

- Calculate the value of discriminate effect of attribute x_1, (the most significant indicator);
- Add value of *discriminate* effect of x_2 *which* is not covered by x_1;
- Add value of *discriminate* effect of x_3 which is not covered by x_1 and x_2
- Repeat the procedure for all indicators.

Squared I-distance, defined by (2), is used in order to eliminate negative values of partial correlation coefficients.

$$D(r,s) = \sum_{i=1}^{k} \frac{\left| d_i^2(r,s) \right|}{\sigma_i} \prod_{j=1}^{i-1} (1 - r^2_{ji.12...j-1})$$
(2)

In order to rank the elements in the observing set using I-distance methodology, it is necessary to fix one unit as a referent. A unit with minimal value for each indicator, or some fictive maximal or average values unit, can be set up as the referent unit. Ranking of the units in the set is based on the calculated distance from the referent unit.

In this paper I-distance method will be used in order to rank CEFTA members according to achieved degree of their macroeconomic goals. Software used in order to calculate I-distance is SPSS. Data for tree years period (2005-2007) used in the analysis are:

GDP - Gross domestic product *(Percentage change over the preceding year);*
BUDBAL - Budget balance *(Per cent of GDP);*
CPI - Consumer prices *(Percentage change over the preceding year);*
UNEMPL - Standardized unemployment rates *(Per cent of civilian labour force).*

Data on observed macroeconomic indicators, as well as corresponding I-distances and ranks, are given in Table 1. for the year 2005, Table 2. (2006) and Table 3. (2007).

Table 1. Data on macroeconomic flows[6] , standardized I-distance and rank for the year 2005

Country	GDP	BUDBAL	CPI	UNEMPL	I-distance	Rank 2005
Albania	5.7	-8.7	2.4	14.1	0.1047	3
B&H	3.9	-17.5	3.8	42.0	-0.9180	7
FYRM	4.1	-2.7	0.5	37.3	0.3579	2
Moldova	7.5	-8.1	12.0	6.4	0.6969	1
Montenegro	4.2	-8.6	2.3	20.6	-0.2386	6
Serbia	6.3	-8.4	16.5	32.4	0.0010	4
Croatia	4.3	-6.3	3.3	12.3	-0.0040	5

Standardized values of I-distance are used as the bases in ranking process of the countries. Differences in ranks from year to year for the countries indicate their performance in transition process.

Ranks based on I-distances have changed from year to year. Moldova, 1st country in 2005, is the last one in 2007, while Bosnia and Herzegovina had rank 7 in 2005 and 1 in 2007. Montenegro was ranked 1st in 2006, but 5th in 2007and so on.

Table 2. Data on macroeconomic flows[6], standardized I-distance and rank for the year 2006

Country	GDP	BUDBAL	CPI	UNEMPL	I-distance	Rank 2006
Albania	5.5	-5.6	2.4	13.8	0.3184	2
B&H	6.9	-8.4	6.1	44.8	-0.0993	5
FYRM	4.0	-0.9	3.2	36.0	-0.1816	6
Moldova	4.8	-11.7	12.8	7.4	-0.0974	4
Montenegro	8.6	-24.1	2.1	20.6	0.4271	1
Serbia	5.2	-10.6	12.7	33.2	-0.4959	7
Croatia	4.7	-6.7	3.2	10.5	0.1286	3

Table 3. Data on macroeconomic flows (estimates)[6], standardized I-distance and rank for the year 2007

Country	GDP	BUDBAL	CPI	UNEMPL	I-distance	Rank 2007
Albania	6.3	-9.1	2.9	13.2	0.1077	3
B&H	6.8	-12.7	1.5	44.0	0.3014	1
FYRM	5.9	-7.2	2.3	34.9	0.1183	2
Moldova	3.0	-15.2	12.3	5.1	-0.4535	7
Montenegro	10.7	-29.3	3.5	16.8	0.0185	5
Serbia	6.9	-15.3	6.5	18.1	-0.1967	6
Croatia	5.5	-7.6	2.9	9.6	0.1042	4

I-distance values obtained for the countries and specific year can be analyzed in order to perceive similarities and differences in macroeconomic performances of CEFTA members on their way to European Union. Small difference in I-distance values for the countries, indicate similarity in their performances. From the data in the tables it is clear that the differences in I-distance values became less from year to year, what indicates the fact that differences in transition processes in the analyzed countries are decreasing as the countries are approaching the European Union.

5. Conclusion

Regional cooperation among Southeast European countries on the economic and political development plan is powerfully supported by the European Union. Establishing the West Balkan Free Trade Zone is a necessary precondition for trade liberalization between the EU and countries of this region. Although the unique multilateral free trade agreement in Southeast Europe – CEFTA 2006 agreement is a reality, the export performance of these countries to the EU market will continue to present a difficulty. Differences in achieving macroeconomic objectives can be observed among the countries of the region and some of them are analysed in this paper. I-distance method was used in order to compare performances of the countries' economies in less complicate way, throw one synthetic indicator, calculated on the basis of several macroeconomic indicators.

References

1. European Economy, European Commission, enlargement papers, No 23 – dec 2004, The Western Balkans in Transition.
2. Ivanović B., *Teorija klasifikacije*, Institut za ekonomiku i industriju, Beograd, 1977.
3. Kragulj D., Jednak S., *Investment Climate in the South East European Countries*, 2nd International Conference on Business, Economics and Management, Yashar University, Izmir, Turkey, Jun 2006., ICBME Proceedings, p. 55-60.
4. Kragulj D., Jednak S., Bulajić M., *Investment climate and Foreign Direct Investments in New Members States and South East European Countries*, The World Bank and Ministry of Economy and Finance of Greece, conference "Structuring Regulatory Frameworks for Dynamic and Competitive South Eastern European Markets", Athens, Greece, december 2006.
5. Mihailovic N., Bulajić M., Savic G., *Ranking of Banks in Serbia*, YUJOR, Vol. 19(2009), No 2, p 323-334, Belgrade 2009.
6. Transition Report, IMF, World Economic Outlook.

DECISION MAKING WITH THE GENERALIZED PROBABILISTIC WEIGHTED AVERAGING DISTANCE OPERATOR

JOSÉ M. MERIGÓ, MONTSERRAT CASANOVAS

Department of Business Administration, University of Barcelona,
Av. Diagonal 690, 08034 Barcelona, Spain

We develop a new decision making model that uses subjective and objective information in the same formulation. For doing so, we introduce the generalized probabilistic weighted averaging distance operator. It is a new distance aggregation operator that unifies the probability and the weighted average in a general model that considers the degree of importance that each concept has in the aggregation. The main advantage of this approach is that it includes a wide range of distance aggregation operators that use the probability or the weighted average such as the probabilistic weighted averaging distance operator, the probabilistic weighted quadratic averaging distance operator, the weighted Minkowski distance and the generalized probabilistic distance. We study some of its main properties and develop a decision making application in political management.

1. Introduction

Distance measures [2-5] are a very useful type of aggregation operator [1,5,8] for comparing different elements. In the literature, we find a wide range of distance measures. For example, we can use a distance measure that uses the weighted average or the probability in the normalization process. Another type of distance measure that can be used is those that use generalized aggregation operators such as the Minkowski distance. For more information of other types of distance measures, see for example [2-5].

Recently, Merigo [5-6] has suggested a new aggregation operator that unifies the weighted average and the probability in the same formulation considering the degree of importance that each concept has in the aggregation. He called it the probabilistic weighted averaging (PWA) operator. The main advantage of this aggregation operator is that it is able to consider subjective and objective information at the same time. The PWA operator can be generalized by using generalized and quasi-arithmetic means, obtaining the generalized PWA (GPWA) operator [7].

542

The objective of this paper is to present the generalized probabilistic weighted averaging distance (GPWAD) operator. It is a new aggregation operator that uses generalized distance aggregation operators in a unified framework between the probability and the weighted average. That is, it uses generalized means in distance measures. Moreover, it also uses the PWA operator. Thus, it is able to consider the degree of importance that each concept has in the aggregation. We study some of its main properties and a wide range of particular cases such as the weighted Minkowski distance, the generalized probabilistic distance, the normalized Minkowski distance, the weighted Hamming distance, the weighted Euclidean distance, the PWA distance, the quadratic PWA distance (PWQAD), the geometric PWA distance (PWGAD), the harmonic PWA distance (PWHAD) and the cubic PWA distance (PWCAD).

We further generalize this approach by using quasi-arithmetic means. The result is the Quasi-PWAD operator. The main advantage of this approach is that it is more general because it includes the GPWAD operator as a particular case.

We also develop an application in a decision making problem concerning political management. We analyze a problem where the government is looking for its optimal fiscal policy. We see that the results may vary depending on the particular type of GPWAD operator used.

This paper is organized as follows. In Section 2, we review the PWA operator and the generalized probabilistic distance. Section 3 present the GPWAD operator and Section 4 analyzes several particular cases. Section 5 introduces a further generalization by using quasi-arithmetic means and Section 6 develops an application in a decision making problem. In Section 7 we end the paper summarizing the main conclusions of the paper.

2. Preliminaries

In this section we briefly review the PWA operator and the generalized probabilistic distance.

2.1. *The Probabilistic Weighted Averaging Operator*

The probabilistic weighted averaging (PWA) operator [5-6] is an aggregation operator that unifies the probability and the weighted average in the same formulation considering the degree of importance that each concept has in the aggregation. It is defined as follows.

Definition 1. A PWA operator of dimension n is a mapping $PWA: R^n \to R$ such that:

$$PWA\,(a_1, \ldots, a_n) = \sum_{j=1}^{n} \hat{v}_i a_i \tag{1}$$

where the a_i are the argument variables, each argument a_i has an associated weight (WA) v_i with $\sum_{i=1}^{n} v_i = 1$ and $v_i \in [0, 1]$, and a probabilistic weight p_i with $\sum_{i=1}^{n} p_i = 1$ and $p_i \in [0, 1]$, $\hat{v}_i = \beta p_i + (1-\beta)v_i$ with $\beta \in [0, 1]$ and $\hat{v}_i$ is the weight that unifies probabilities and WAs in the same formulation.

2.2. *The Generalized Probabilistic Distance*

The generalized probabilistic distance [5] is a distance measure that uses probabilities and generalized aggregation operators in the analysis. Thus, we can consider objective information under risk environments in the calculation of distances and a generalized framework that includes a wide range of particular cases such as the probabilistic Hamming distance and the probabilistic Euclidean distance. It can be defined as follows for two sets $A = \{a_1, \ldots, a_n\}$ and $B = \{b_1, \ldots, b_n\}$.

Definition 2. A generalized probabilistic distance of dimension n is a mapping GPD: $[0, 1]^n \times [0, 1]^n \rightarrow [0, 1]$ that has an associated weighting vector W of dimension n with $\sum_{j=1}^{n} w_j = 1$ and $w_j \in [0, 1]$, such that:

$$GPD\,(A, B) = \left(\sum_{i=1}^{n} w_i \mid a_i - b_i \mid^{\lambda} \right)^{1/\lambda} \tag{2}$$

where a_i and b_i are the ith arguments of the sets A and B respectively, and λ is a parameter such that $\lambda \in (-\infty, \infty)$.

3. The Generalized Probabilistic Weighted Averaging Distance

The generalized probabilistic weighted averaging distance (GPWAD) operator is a distance measure that uses the WA and the probability in the same formulation considering the degree of importance that each concept has in the aggregation. Moreover, it also uses generalized means providing a more complete representation of the aggregation process. It can be defined as follows for two sets $X = \{x_1, x_2, \ldots, x_n\}$ and $Y = \{y_1, y_2, \ldots, y_n\}$.

Definition 3. A GPWAD operator of dimension n is a mapping *GPWAD*: $R^n \times R^n \rightarrow R$ that has an associated weighting vector P such that $\hat{v}_i \in [0, 1]$ and $\sum_{i=1}^{n} \hat{v}_i = 1$, according to the following formula:

$$GPWAD\ (\langle x_1, y_1 \rangle, \langle x_2, y_2 \rangle, \ldots, \langle x_n, y_n \rangle) = \left(\sum_{i=1}^{n} \hat{v}_i \mid x_i - y_i \mid^{\lambda} \right)^{1/\lambda} \tag{3}$$

where each argument (individual distance) $|x_i - y_i|$ has an associated weight (WA) v_i with $\sum_{i=1}^{n} v_i = 1$ and $v_i \in [0, 1]$, and a probabilistic weight p_i with $\sum_{i=1}^{n} p_i = 1$ and $p_i \in [0, 1]$, $\hat{v}_i = \beta p_i + (1 - \beta) v_i$ with $\beta \in [0, 1]$, $\hat{v}_i$ is the weight that unifies probabilities and WAs in the same formulation and λ is a parameter such that $\lambda \in (-\infty, \infty)$.

Note that the GPWAD can also be formulated separating the part that strictly affects the probability and the weighted average. This representation is useful to see both models in the same formulation.

Definition 4. A GPWAD operator is a mapping *GPWAD*: $R^n \times R^n \rightarrow R$ of dimension n, if it has an associated weighting vector P, with $\sum_{i=1}^{n} p_i = 1$ and $p_j \in [0, 1]$ and a weighting vector V that affects the WA, with $\sum_{i=1}^{n} v_i = 1$ and $v_i \in [0, 1]$, such that:

$$GPWAD\ (\langle x_1, y_1 \rangle, \ldots, \langle x_n, y_n \rangle) =$$

$$= \beta \left(\sum_{i=1}^{n} p_i |x_i - y_i|^{\lambda} \right)^{1/\lambda} + (1 - \beta) \left(\sum_{i=1}^{n} v_i |x_i - y_i|^{\lambda} \right)^{1/\lambda} \tag{4}$$

where $|x_i - y_i|$ are the individual distances, $\beta \in [0, 1]$ and λ is a parameter such that $\lambda \in (-\infty, \infty)$.

Note that if the weighting vector is not normalized, i.e., $\hat{V} = \sum_{i=1}^{n} \hat{v}_i \neq 1$, then, the GPWAD operator can be formulated as follows:

$$GPWAD \left(\langle x_1, y_1 \rangle, \langle x_2, y_2 \rangle, \ldots, \langle x_n, y_n \rangle\right) = \left(\frac{1}{\hat{V}} \sum_{i=1}^{n} \hat{v}_i \mid x_i - y_i \mid^\lambda \right)^{1/\lambda} \tag{5}$$

Note that $GPWAD \left(\langle x_1, y_1 \rangle, \langle x_2, y_2 \rangle, \ldots, \langle x_n, y_n \rangle\right) = 0$ if and only if $x_i = y_i$ for all $i \in [1, n]$. Note also that $GPWAD \left(\langle x_1, y_1 \rangle, \langle x_2, y_2 \rangle, \ldots, \langle x_n, y_n \rangle\right) = PWAD \left(\langle y_1, x_1 \rangle, \langle y_2, x_2 \rangle, \ldots, \langle y_n, x_n \rangle\right)$.

The GPWAD operator is bounded, monotonic and idempotent. It is bounded because the GPWAD aggregation is delimitated by the minimum and the maximum. That is, $\mathrm{Min}\{|x_i - y_i|\} \leq GPWAD \left(\langle x_1, y_1 \rangle, \langle x_2, y_2 \rangle, \ldots, \langle x_n, y_n \rangle\right) \leq \mathrm{Max}\{|x_i - y_i|\}$. It is monotonic because if $|x_i - y_i| \geq |s_i - t_i|$, for all $|x_i - y_i|$, then, $GPWAD \left(\langle x_1, y_1 \rangle, \langle x_2, y_2 \rangle, \ldots, \langle x_n, y_n \rangle\right) \geq GPWAD \left(\langle s_1, t_1 \rangle, \langle s_2, t_2 \rangle, \ldots, \langle s_n, t_n \rangle\right)$. It is idempotent because if $|x_i - y_i| = |x - y|$, for all $|x_i - y_i|$, then, $GPWAD \left(\langle x_1, y_1 \rangle, \langle x_2, y_2 \rangle, \ldots, \langle x_n, y_n \rangle\right) = |x - y|$. for all $|x_i - y_i|$, then, $GPWAD \left(\langle x_1, y_1 \rangle, \langle x_2, y_2 \rangle, \ldots, \langle x_n, y_n \rangle\right) = |x - y|$.

4. Families of GPWAD Operators

The GPWAD operator includes a wide range of particular cases [5-8]. For example, if we analyze the parameter β, we get the following:

- The weighted Minkowski distance: When $\beta = 0$.
- The generalized probabilistic distance: When $\beta = 1$.

Note that if one of the sets of the GPWAD operator is empty, then, we get the generalized probabilistic weighted averaging (GPWA) operator [7].

And if we analyze the parameter λ, we can obtain the following special cases of the GPWAD operator:

- The PWAD operator: When $\lambda = 1$.
- The maximum distance: $\lambda \to \infty$.
- The minimum distance: $\lambda \to -\infty$.
- The quadratic probabilistic weighted quadratic averaging distance (QPWQAD) operator (the Euclidean case): When $\lambda = 2$.
- The geometric probabilistic weighted geometric averaging distance (GPWGAD) operator: $\lambda \to 0$.
- The harmonic probabilistic weighted harmonic averaging distance (HPWHAD) operator: $\lambda = -1$.
- The cubic probabilistic weighted cubic averaging distance (CPWCAD) operator: When $\lambda = 3$.

5. The Quasi-PWAD Operator

The Quasi-PWAD operator is a further generalization of the GPWAD operator by using quasi-arithmetic means. It can be defined as follows.

Definition 5. A Quasi-PWAD operator of dimension n is a mapping $QPWAD$: $R^n \times R^n \to R$ that has an associated weighting vector W of dimension n with $\hat{v}_i \in$ [0, 1] and $\sum_{i=1}^{n} \hat{v}_i = 1$, such that:

$$QPWAD\ (\langle x_1, y_1 \rangle, \langle x_2, y_2 \rangle, \ldots, \langle x_n, y_n \rangle) = g^{-1}\left(\sum_{j=1}^{n} \hat{v}_j g\left(D_{(j)}\right) \right) \tag{6}$$

where each argument (individual distance) $|x_i - y_i|$ has an associated weight (WA) v_i with $\sum_{i=1}^{n} v_i = 1$ and $v_i \in$ [0, 1], and a probabilistic weight p_i with $\sum_{i=1}^{n} p_i = 1$ and $p_i \in$ [0, 1], $\hat{v}_i = \beta p_i + (1 - \beta) v_i$ with $\beta \in$ [0, 1], $\hat{v}_i$ is the weight that unifies probabilities and WAs in the same formulation and g is a strictly continuous monotonic function.

As we can see, when $g(b) = b^\lambda$, then, the Quasi-PWAD becomes the GPWAD operator.

Note that all the properties and particular cases commented in the GPWAD are also applicable in the Quasi-PWAD operator.

6. Application in Political Management

In the following, we are going to develop a numerical example of the new approach concerning political decision making problems.

Assume a country is planning the fiscal policy for the next year and they consider three possible alternatives.

1) A_1: Develop an expansive fiscal policy.
2) A_2: Do not develop any change.
3) A_3: Develop a contractive fiscal policy.

After careful review of the information, the government establishes the following general information about the fiscal policies. They consider that the results of the fiscal policy taken will depend on the economic situation of the next year, being S_1 = Very good economic situation, S_2 = Good economic situation, S_3 = Normal economic situation, S_4 = Bad economic situation, S_5 = Very bad economic situation. Note that the results are evaluations between [0, 1] about the benefits obtained with each strategy. The results are shown in Table 1.

Table 1. Characteristics of the fiscal policy.

	S_1	S_2	S_3	S_4	S_5
A_1	1	0.8	0.6	0.5	0.2
A_2	0.8	0.8	0.7	0.6	0.3
A_3	0.4	0.5	0.7	0.8	0.8

According to the objectives of the government, they establish the following ideal fiscal policy. The results are shown in Table 2.

Table 2. Ideal fiscal policy.

	S_1	S_2	S_3	S_4	S_5
I	1	1	0.9	0.9	0.8

With this information, it is possible to develop different methods for selecting a fiscal policy. In this example, we consider the normalized Hamming distance (NHD), the weighted Hamming distance (WHD), the probabilistic distance (PD) and the PWAD operator. We assume that the weights are: $W =$ (0.1, 0.3, 0.2, 0.2, 0.2) and $P =$ (0.1, 0.2, 0.4, 0.2, 0.1). Note that the weighted average has a degree of importance of 60%. The results are shown in Table 3.

Table 3. Aggregated results.

	NHD	WHD	PD	PWAD
A_1	0.3	0.32	0.3	0.312
A_2	0.28	0.28	0.25	0.268
A_3	0.28	0.27	0.26	0.266

As we can see, with the WHD and the PWAD, the best alternative is A_3 because it has the lowest distance. With the PD the optimal choice is A_2 and with the NHD either A_2 or A_3 are optimal.

7. Conclusions

We have presented the GPWAD operator. It is a new distance aggregation operator that uses the probability and the weighted average in the same formulation and considering the degree of importance that each concept has in the aggregation. Moreover, it also uses generalized means providing a more complete representation that includes a wide range of particular cases such as the PWAD, the QPWQAD, the CPWCAD, the weighted Minkowski distance and the generalized probabilistic distance.

We have further generalized the GPWAD by using quasi-arithmetic means obtaining the Quasi-PWAD operator. We have seen that the GPWAD operator is included in this formulation as a particular case.

We have also studied the applicability of the GPWAD operator in a decision making problem regarding the selection of fiscal policies. We have seen that the GPWAD operator permits to consider a wide range of scenarios and select the one that is in accordance with our interests.

In future research we will develop further developments to this approach by using more general formulations and looking for other types of applications.

Acknowledgements

Support from the projects "JC2009-00189" and "MC238206" is gratefully acknowledged.

References

1. G. Beliakov, A. Pradera, T. Calvo, *Aggregation functions: A guide for practitioners* (Springer-Verlag, Berlin-Heidelberg, 2007).
2. R.W. Hamming, Error-detecting and error-correcting codes, *Bell Systems Technical J.* **29**, 147 (1950).
3. N. Karayiannis, Soft learning vector quantization and clustering algorithms based on ordered weighted aggregation operators, *IEEE Trans. Neural Networks* **11**, 1093 (2000).
4. A. Kaufmann, *Introduction to the theory of fuzzy subsets*, (Academic Press, New York, 1975).
5. J.M. Merigó, *New extensions to the OWA operators and their application in decision making* (PhD thesis (in Spanish), Department of Business Administration, University of Barcelona, 2008).
6. J.M. Merigó, The probabilistic weighted averaging operator and its application in decision making. In: *Operations Systems Research & Security of Information* (The International Institute for Advanced Studies in Systems and Cybernetics, Canada, pp. 55-58, 2009).
7. J.M. Merigó, The generalized probabilistic weighted averaging operator and its application in strategic decision making. In: *Proc. of the SIGEF 2009 Conference*, Lugo, Spain, pp. 422-435, 2009.
8. J.M. Merigó and A.M. Gil-Lafuente, The induced generalized OWA operator, *Inform. Sci.* **179**, 729 (2009).

SIMULATION APPROACH TO TESTING REGIME-SWITCHING MODELS FOR SLOVAK ALPINE RIVER FLOWS[*]

MAGDA KOMORNÍKOVÁ AND DANUŠA SZÖKEOVÁ

*Faculty of Civil Engineering, Slovak University of Technology, Radlinského 11,
813 68 Bratislava, Slovakia*

JOZEF KOMORNÍK

*Faculty of Management, Comenius University, Odbojárov 10, P.O.BOX 95,
820 05 Bratislava, Slovakia*

In this paper the application of several nonlinear regime-switching time series models (SETAR, LSTAR and MSW) for annual river flows in the Tatra region is presented and their fitting and forecasting capabilities are compared.

1. Introduction

The aim of this paper is to point out the effectiveness of simulation-base complex testing procedures for multiple-state time series models in the classes SETAR, STAR, MSW models and apply them in analyses of yearly average outflows (for 71 years) of seven Slovak alpine rivers that have a considerable impact on Slovak economy and tourism. Five of the studied rivers (Biely Váh, Boca, Belá, Revúca and Ľubochnianka) are alpine type tributaries of the principal Slovak river Váh. Their flows have been measured at the sites located close to their mouths. The measurement sites for larger rivers Váh and Poprad are located in places where their alpine characters change.

2. Theoretical foundations

2.1. *General form of the models*

For each individual time series X_t under consideration and each selected class of models we assume the sequence of relations

---

[*] The research was partly supported by the Grants APVV- 0012-07 and LPP-0111-09

$$X_t = F(\Omega_{t-1}, \theta) + \varepsilon_t, \quad t = 1,\ldots,n, \tag{1}$$

where Ω_{t-1} contains a finite set of past values, F is a so-called *skeleton* of the model (specific for each model class) and determined up to a vector of unknown parameters θ that are supposed to be fitted and tested using the actual values of data. The residuals ε_t are supposed to be independent on Ω_{t-1}, centered ($E(\varepsilon_t) = 0$) and homoscedastic ($D(\varepsilon_t) = \sigma_\varepsilon^2$). We suppose that linear AR model describes the dynamic behaviour of the time series adequately in each regime. In the following sections we discuss representations of the different regime-switching models, parameter estimation and testing methods for the presence of regime-switching effects in the time series.

2.1.1. *Threshold autoregressive (TAR) models*

Tong (13) initially proposed the (m-regime) *Threshold Autoregressive* (TAR) model (see also 2, 3, 5, 6, 14), which assumes that the regime that occurs at a time *t* can be determined by an observable *threshold variable* q_t relative to a *threshold value* which we denote as *c*.

Suppose that the observed data are $(X_1, \ldots, X_n)$, where n is the total number of observations in a time series (the *length* of the time series). We are going to formalize the introduction of 2-regime threshold autoregressive models for the values X_t of the time series in integer times t (using different autoregressive coefficients $\left(\phi_{0,i}, \phi_{1,i}, \cdots, \phi_{p_i,i}\right)$ for regimes i = 1, 2). Let us denote $Y_{t,i} = (1, X_{t-1}, \ldots, X_{t-p_i})$ and $\Phi_i = \left(\phi_{0,i}, \phi_{1,i}, \cdots, \phi_{p_i,i}\right)^T$ for i = 1,2; I[A] is an indicator function with I[A] = 1 if the event A occurs and I[A] = 0 otherwise; q_t is the transition variable and ε_t is i.i.d.$(0,\sigma^2)$. Then 2-regime TAR model is given by

$$X_t = Y_{t,1}\, \Phi_1 \left(1 - I[q_t > c]\right) + Y_{t,2}\, \Phi_2\, I[q_t > c] + \varepsilon_t \tag{2}$$

where ε_t, t = 1, $\ldots$, n are (white noise) residuals of the model.

Self-Exciting TAR (SETAR) models is a special case of TAR models where the threshold variable q_t is taken to be a lagged value of the time series itself, $q_t = X_{t-d}$ for a certain integer $d > 0$ (3, 6).

2.1.2. *Smooth transition AR (STAR) models*

A more gradual transition between the different regimes can be obtained by replacing the indicator function $I[q_t > c]$ in (2) by a continuous at least twice continuously differentiable function $G(q_t; \gamma, c)$, which changes smoothly from 0 to 1 as q_t increases (so-called *transition function*). STAR model was introduced in 12 and popularized by (7).

A formal representation of a 2-regimes STAR model is

$$X_t = Y_{t,1}\,\Phi_1\,(1 - G(q_t; \gamma, c)) + Y_{t,2}\,\Phi_2\,G(q_t; \gamma, c) + \varepsilon_t \,. \tag{3}$$

Logistic STAR (LSTAR) model is a STAR model with the *logistic* transition function

$$G_L(q_t; \gamma, c) = \frac{1}{1 + exp(-\gamma(q_t - c))}\,, \tag{4}$$

where γ is the *smoothness* parameter. The parameter γ determines the *smoothness* of the change in the value of the logistic function and thus the transition from one regime to the other. For more details see (6).

2.1.3. *Markov – Switching (MSW) model*

MSW models described by (8, 9) represent the class of the regime switching models with the regime switching determined by unobserved state (or regime) variable s_t that takes only values $1,2,\dots,m$. The state variable s_t is assumed to follow m−state Markov chain described by a transition probability matrix $\mathbf{P}$ with elements $p_{i,j} = \Pr\{s_t = j \mid s_{t-1} = i\}$, i, $j = 1,2,\dots,m$. Thus, $p_{i,j}$ is equal to the probability that the Markov chain moves from state i at time $t-1$ to state j at time t. Also of interest in the MSW models are the unconditional probabilities that the process is in each of the regimes $\Pr(s_t = i)$ for $i = 1,2,\dots,m$.

The m-regime MSW model with an AR(p) specification in all regimes is given by

$$X_t = \phi_{0,s_t} + \phi_{1,s_t} X_{t-1} + \cdots + \phi_{p,s_t} X_{t-p} + \varepsilon_t \,,\ t = 1,2,\dots,n,\ s_t = 1,2,\dots,m. \tag{5}$$

2.2. *Modeling cycles for multi-regimes models*

The considered construction of nonlinear models is in general based on the principle "from simple to more complex" (6, 7). For each considered class of models the linear simplifications are tested against nonlinear alternatives. The standard modeling cycle has the following structure:
- Estimate an optimal autoregressive model AR(p).
- Calculate a test statistics for testing the linear model against the nonlinear alternatives in the selected model class (for models in SETAR and MSW model classes using extensive simulations computation).
- If the linear model is rejected, complete the parameter specification of the optimal nonlinear model.
- Perform diagnostic tests of the resulting nonlinear model.

- Modify the selected model if it is desirable.
- Use the resulting model for description and prediction purpose.

2.3. Linearity testing

The first step in the construction of multi-regime models is to compare the quality simple linear model against models with more regimes. From the formal point of view, we test the hypothesis that the linear model is suitable against the alternative that more regimes are adequate to the data. In case of a 2-regime alternative we test the hypothesis H_0 of equality of autoregressive coefficients for both regimes. In case of these test types the alternative hypothesis requires identification of more parameters than H_0. These extra parameters are called "nuisance" parameters. Consequently, the likelihood ratio test statistics have nonstandard distributions that can be often found only by using simulation procedures (SETAR, MSW). The basic structure of a simulation procedure is that one generates a large number (at least 5000) of artificial time series according to the model that holds under the null hypothesis. Next one estimates both AR and selected nonlinear models for each artificial time series and computes the corresponding test statistic.

The problem of testing the linearity against STAR alternatives was described and modified in 6. It suggests approximating the transition function $G(q_t; \gamma, c)$ with Taylor approximation around $\gamma = 0$ and to use a Lagrange Multiplier statistic which has an asymptotic χ^2 distribution.

2.4. Parameter estimation

Estimation of the parameters can be obtained by minimizing the residuals variance. For more details see (8, 9, 11, 12, 14).

2.5. Diagnostic checking

2.5.1. Testing for the serial correlation

The STAR model skeleton $F(\Omega_{t-1}, \theta)$ is at least twice continuously differentiable function. An *LM* test of kth order serial dependence in ε_t can be obtained as nR^2, where R^2 is the coefficient of determination for the regression of $\hat{\varepsilon}_t$ on $\partial F(\Omega_t, \hat{\theta})/\partial\theta$ and k lagged residuals $\hat{\varepsilon}_{t-1},\ldots,\hat{\varepsilon}_{t-k}$. The above test statistics has asymptotically $\chi^2(k)$ distribution under the null hypothesis of serial independence. The SETAR model skeleton is discontinuous therefore the LM-statistic for serial correlation cannot be applied to the residuals of an estimated SETAR model. Hence we approximate the SETAR model by a LSTAR model setting γ equal to some large value. The test of the serial correlation MSW model is LM type test and is based on so called score function $h_t(\theta)$ defined as the derivative of the log of conditional density $f(X_t|\Omega_{t-1},\theta,\rho)$ with respect to the parameter vector θ (for more details see 6, 9).

2.5.2. *Testing for the remaining nonlinearity*

The approach is similar as in the linearity testing, but the null hypothesis is a 2-regime model against alternative of a 3-regime model.

2.6. *Prediction procedures*

Assume that the data satisfy a (nonlinear) model of the form (1). Then a least-squares prediction of X_{t+h} based on the information in Ω_t is $X_t(h) = E(X_{t+h} \mid \Omega_t)$. In a contrast to the linear case we can not expect that the operator E and the functional F commute. This problem can be partially overcome by the use of Monte-Carlo or Bootstrap methods (for details see e.g. 6, 9).

3. Application to the real data modeling

The Tatra alpine mountain region belongs to the internal part of the West Carpatian belt. The neighbouring Beskyds have witnessed several summer seasons with extremely heavy rains and consequent devastating. On the other hand the West Carpatian region had to struggle with frequent extremal snow poor winters with severe consequences for tourism and shortages of water in the reservoirs. This provides intuitive justification for the application of nonlinear regime-switching time series models. For this study seven rivers in Tatra region were selected. The length of observations in all individual catchments was 71 years $(1931 - 2001)^*$. Sixty-six years were used for model identification and parameter estimation of annual data. The rest of the data was used for verification and model forecasting performance comparison. We proceeded according to the methodology of chapter 2 and received for all rivers the best models in all considered classes (SETAR, LSTAR and MSW).

Table 1 presents P-values for testing linearity against the alternative of a regime-switching model for individual rivers in each of the considered model classes (critical values of the test-statistic for SETAR and MSW models have to be determined by simulation of 10 000 artificial time series). The null hypothesis can be rejected at conventional significance levels (for all 7 rivers and all model classes). The best models in individual classes were chosen based on the

---

* The data can be found at http://www.shmu.sk (presently payable).

554

minimal P-values and on minimal values of BIC information criterion (see e.g. 1, 6, 9).

Concerning the diagnostic checking the residuals were tested for serial correlation and remaining non-linearity. From Table 2 it is evident that for all considered models (except MSW model for Poprad river) P-values of serial correlation test are not significant at the 5% significance level. In Table 2 there are presented also P-values for testing the remaining non-linearity (critical values of the test-statistic for SETAR and MSW have to be determined by simulation of 10 000 artificial time series). It is evident that for all rivers the best selected models have three states corresponding to dry, average and wet years (in SETAR and MSW model classes) but in LSTAR class are 2-regime models suitable (except Belá and Lubochnianka rivers).

Table 1. P-values for linearity testing against the alternative of a regime-switching model

	SETAR	LSTAR	MSW
Belá	0,010	0,0006	0,001
Biely Váh	0,011	0,0221	0,002
Boca	0,002	0,0116	0,007
Lubochnianka	$< 10^{-3}$	0,0029	0,001
Poprad	0,001	0,0364	0,005
Revúca	0,002	0,0198	0,003
Váh	0,003	0,0088	0,008

Table 2. P-values for the diagnostic checking of estimate models

	The serial correlation test			**The remaining nonlinearity test**		
	SETAR	LSTAR	MSW	SETAR	LSTAR	MSW
Belá	0,087	0,1719	0,068	$< 10^{-3}$	0,0016	0,004
Biely Váh	0,241	0,1781	0,128	$< 10^{-3}$	0,1590	$< 10^{-3}$
Boca	0,331	0,1494	0,383	$< 10^{-3}$	0,1371	$< 10^{-3}$
Lubochnianka	0,174	0,1473	0,184	$< 10^{-3}$	0,0020	$< 10^{-3}$
Poprad	0,072	0,1470	0,046	$< 10^{-3}$	0,2001	0,002
Revúca	0,225	0,0998	0,297	$< 10^{-3}$	0,5165	0,007
Váh	0,069	0,2970	0,087	$< 10^{-3}$	0,5024	0,009

In Table 3 we present descriptive qualities of the optimal models (for each river and each considered class SETAR, LSTAR and MSW) characterized by the sums of squares of residuals (and their relative reductions in comparison to AR models). We see that the best descriptive qualities have in all cases MSW model.

Table 3. The sums of residual squares and their relative reductions
$(SSR_0-SSR_1)/SSR_0$ (bold is used for the best models)

River (66 years)	AR	SETAR		LSTAR		MSW	
	SSR_0	SSR_1	rel. reduc	SSR_1	rel. reduc	SSR_1	rel. reduc
Bela	27,34	16,27	0,411	22,905	0,162	4,782	**0,825**
Biely Vah	7,69	5,30	0,311	7,187	0,065	1,121	**0,854**
Boca	18,71	11,39	0,438	13,718	0,267	2,574	**0,862**
Lubochnianka	11,08	8,17	0,356	8,988	0,189	1,352	**0,878**
Poprad	50,95	28,08	0,485	39,302	0,229	7,861	**0,846**
Revuca	66,09	38,96	0,410	31,990	0,516	10,904	**0,835**
Vah	865,52	425,71	0,508	792,632	0,084	219,938	**0,746**

For each river and the corresponding best model in all model classes we have computed 1-step-ahead forecasts for 5 years and the prediction errors MSE (Mean Square Error) and MAE (Mean Absolute Error). The Table 4 presents forecasting errors for all rivers and considered model classes. We see that in this case the best predictions for different rivers provide various model classes.

Table 4. The prediction errors for 1-step-ahead forecasts for 5 annual
data (bold is used for the best models)

River	Model					
	SETAR		LSTAR		MSW	
	MSE	MAE	MSE	MAE	MSE	MAE
Bela	**0,252**	**0,446**	0,327	0,511	0,288	0,462
Biely Vah	0,081	0,087	0,104	0,302	**0,008**	**0,061**
Boca	0,118	0,271	**0,045**	**0,185**	1,805	1,208
Lubochnianka	**0,025**	**0,155**	0,051	0,168	0,350	0,563
Poprad	0,999	0,730	0,730	0,617	**0,319**	**0,409**
Revuca	**0,307**	**0,326**	0,608	0,469	0,533	0,623
Vah	7,359	2,557	9,369	3,247	**1,367**	**0,736**

4. Conclusions

We applied the presented modeling procedures (that are substantially based on utilization of simulation techniques) to annual river data flow. The best descriptions for all rivers were attained by models in the MSW class while the best forecasts were provided for different rivers by models from various model classes. Reasons for this fact may be several however it is believed that differences in underground storages formed by the quarternary sediments and of accumulated glacial, glaciofluvial, fluvial and proluvial sediments strongly influence the runoff regime in the particular rivers. These storages clearly influence the variability of the series and their memory properties however the extent and effect of this influence should be further investigated.

Concerning the further development of the mathematical models we consider an especially promising direction of research applications of multidimensional Markov switching models MSW (with common states for a group of modelled hydrological variables). This would enable to apply uniform classifications of dry, medium and wet years with respect to all considered rivers. New nontrivial challenges for appropriate simulation techniques will have to be creatively solved.

References

1. B. Akintug and P. F. Rasmussen, *Water Resour. Res.* **41(9)**, W09424.1 (2005).
2. A. Amendola and M.Niglio, *Statistical Methods & Applications* **13**, 3 (2003).
3. A. Amendola and G. Storti, *Proceedings of SCO'99*, 179 (1999).
4. K. S. Chan and H. Tong, *Journal of Time Series Analysis* **7**, 179 (1986).
5. V. Fortina, L. Perreaulta and J. D. Salas, *Journal of Hydrology* **296**, 135 (2004).
6. P. H. Franses and D. van Dijk, *Cambridge University Press* (2000).
7. C.W.J. Granger and T. Teräsvirta, *Oxford University Press* (1993).
8. J. D. Hamilton, *Econometrica* **57**, 357 (1989).
9. J. D. Hamilton, *Princeton University Press* (1994).
10. B. E. Hansen, *Journal of Applied Econometrics* **7**, S61 (1992).
11. B. E. Hansen, *Econometrica* **68 (3)**, 575 (2000).
12. T. Teräsvirta, *Journal of Amer. Statistic. Assoc.* **89**, 208 (1994).
13. H. Tong, *Springer Verlag* (1983).
14. H. Tong, *Oxford University Press* (1990).

PART 6:
APPLICATIONS IN ENGINEERING

DECISION SUPPORT MODEL FOR EARLY ALERT OF METEOROLOGICAL SEVERE EVENTS

ALAÍN CALZADILLA RIVERO

Center for Atmospheric Physics, Institute of Meteorology (INSMET),
Loma de Casa Blanca, Regla, La Habana, Cuba,
alain.calzadilla@insmet.cu

JOSÉ A. DÍAZ BATISTA

Facultad de Ingeniería Industrial, Instituto Superior Politécnico J.A. Echeverría
(CUJAE), Ave. 114 # 11901, Marianao, La Habana, Cuba, diaztony@tesla.cujae.edu.cu

The geographic situation of Cuban island makes it vulnerable to different meteorological events that occur in that region. Some of these events happen on a local scale in short time intervals, causing important human and material damages. Although, meteorological numerical models are mainly a tool for the weather forecast, and particularly of severe weather events, software tools are not enough to support the early forecast of these events. It is proposed the use of the method of case-based reasoning (CBR) and fuzzy logic to achieve the design of a computer model that allows intelligent and joint use of numerical weather forecast models, in this case meso-scale alpha (MM5) and gamma (ARPS) with the support of Information Technology and Telecommunications (IT).

1. Introduction

Numerical models of weather forecasts do not represent the state of the atmosphere continually, but there are systems that solve the equations of motion by finite difference methods, working in three-dimensional grid of points that represents the region of the atmosphere where it is done prognosis. As the capacity of computing resources is limited, you cannot make a prediction for an arbitrarily large region with a resolution (number of grid points per unit volume or area) far too high. The strategy that has been used to face this problem is to divide the models into three general categories, where covering a larger area it is necessary a lower resolution.

The aim of this work is oriented to use intelligent techniques in numerical modeling to predict atmospheric weather meso-scale and design an intelligent computer model for early warning of severe weather events. It has to be able to link intelligent numerical models of meso-scale alpha and gamma, which were not originally designed to be interconnected. This helps to provide early warning of severe local storms occurrences (TLS), promote the use of numerical models applied to the meteorological conditions in Cuba and to achieve better accuracy about the local weather forecasting.

There are no universal criteria for what events should be considered severe, in some cases it is necessary to impose thresholds of severity to decide whether or not the event is classified as severe. For example, the National Weather Service of the United States, defines a thunderstorm as severe if it occurs with a linear winds magnitude higher than 25 m/s, the occurrence of hail with a diameter greater than 1.9 cm (three-quarters inch), or if the storm produces tornadoes. Storms only need one of these conditions to be severe. Moreover, Alfonso (1994) in his chronology of severe local storms in Cuba [1], defined as any local storm (meso-scale range of Orlanski [2]), usually electric, which has one or more of the following events, considered as severe: tornado, linear wind gusts of 25m/s or more, not directly associated with a tornado, hail of any size, waterspout and heavy rain.

Defense measures against severe weather events in Cuba increase its efficiency continually, and the number of victims of hurricanes and other synoptic systems, predictable in time, are decreasing. The TLS is today the greatest danger to national security by natural events, due to its difficult forecast and its destructive character.

The literature searched reveals that in the world has been made a lot of researches about TLS predictions. Some of these investigations as [3], [4], [5], [6] use a technique known as "nowcasting" or immediate forecast, to detect and/or locate TLS taking mainly the radar data. This is a precise technique for a prediction term from several minutes to an hour or two. Wilson in his article [7] reveals that the uses of intelligent techniques is essential for detecting and/or locate local severe events in a longer period. In the article the author speculates about creating a sort of hybrid approach linking short-term forecast techniques, where models play the principal role, and some techniques of Artificial Intelligence (AI) as fuzzy logic, neural networks and expert systems, among others. However, the main difficult of this hybrid approach is the automatic detection and monitoring of severe local events.

2. The decision support model's base

To achieve an effective early warning of severe weather events has been developed a computational model that allows an intelligent and combined use of numerical forecast models of weather meso-scale atmospheric alpha and gamma. Taking into consideration previous researches done in INSMET by specialists involved in numerical modeling ([8],[9]), the Meso-scale Model of Fifth Generation (MM5) with a resolution of 9km and the scale model of storms Advanced Regional Prediction System (ARPS) with a resolution of 500m were selected as basis for prediction. Since the ARPS is a more detailed model of the atmosphere physics it is pretended to feed it with the output data of MM5, as from a prior intelligent selection of the regions where interest events may occur.

The process to run higher resolution models from other data that cover larger areas is called "nesting" and it is the most efficient way to achieve effective forecasts in specific regions. Nesting means selecting regions to run numerical models of storm scale in terms of probability of severe local weather events occurrence. It is given by an analysis of the output data of numerical models of meso-scale alpha or beta in order to not to consume excessive resources and time predicting with high resolution in regions or localities that are not of interest.

Although the MM5 lacks adequate resolution to reproduce in detail the formation of severe local weather events and the ARPS provide better resolution to detect these events, the ensemble use of these two models allows giving accurate alerts at the selected regions.

Each type of model characterizes a set of events associated with the spatial scale of work, from synoptic events of thousands of kilometers and periods of days, until meso-scales events with a scale of kilometers and periods of hours. Table 1 shows the meteorological scales for different types of numerical models developed by Orlanski [2].

Table 1. Scales of meteorological models.

Type of model	Scale	Atmospheric events
Macro-a	15000km	General circulation, long waves
Macro-b	5000km	Depressions and anticyclones
Macro-g	500km	Fronts, hurricanes
Meso-b	100km	Breezes, mountain waves, low-level jets, convective complexes, heat island
Meso-g	5km	Storms, rain
Meso-d	500m	Cumulus, tornadoes, winds katabatic
Micro-b	50m	Tufts, steles, waterspouts, dust storms
Micro-g	2m	Sound waves, turbulence

Convective rainfall in MM5 outputs was considered as an initial entrance to begin the identification of TLS, and it also used some elements presented by Martínez [10], where the author identifies the favorable thermodynamic conditions for the tornadoes occurrence.

A CBR was designed to identify severe weather local events from a database of cases where its characteristics (thermodynamic) were similar to the present case, to make an analysis of the ARPS runs according to the event detected, then set the run of the ARPS that better fits to the event and finally learn about the current case to improve the efficiency of solutions in order to be applied in future similar cases.

Fuzzy logic is then used to identify and detect the occurrence of TLS, it also provides the CBR to identify and evaluate relevant characteristics that help to determine, for priority levels and weights, which are the most appropriate solutions (runs of ARPS) in a determined case (TLS). In addition, it also helps determining which runs are the most important and how much runs should the ARPS has to make according to available resources.

3. Results

Integration proposal between artificial intelligence and numerical forecast modeling of local weather follows the idea of improving the local forecast of the weather warning. It also rationalizes and increases numerical models use and decrease costs of computers and their peripherals. Figure 1 depicts a general scheme of the proposal design and the potential to be gained from the application of grid technology[*] [11].

---

[*] Grid technology is a type of distributed system which allows sharing, selecting and adding distributed resources.

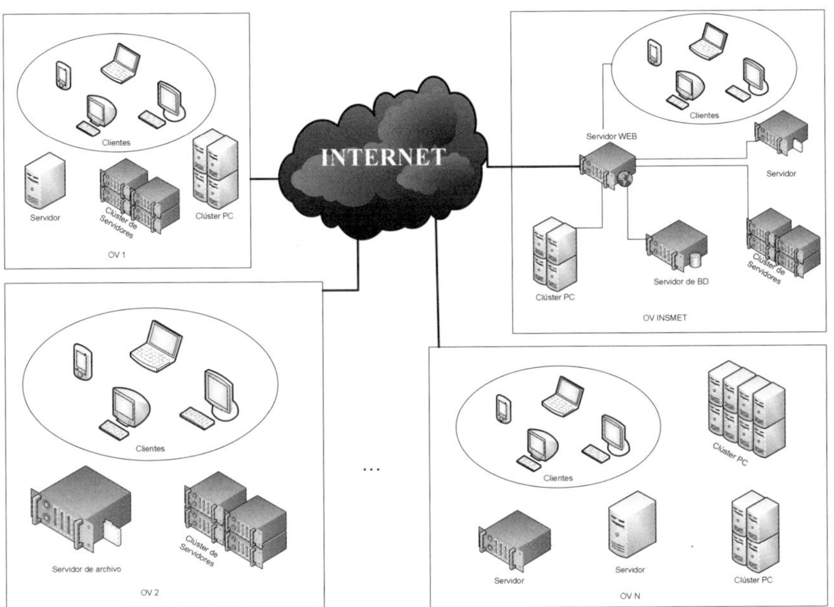

Figure 1. General scheme of the proposal design.

The intelligent software product comprises four key components. The download subsystem provides the information to run MM5 and must be installed on a file server with Linux operating system in any version, because it is developed as a bash script. This script downloads data from the Global File System (GFS) model from the web site http://nomad3.ncep.noaa.gov. These data are downloaded from the operational runs that are conducted twice a day with the MM5, at 00 hours and again at 12 hours.

The subsystem of configuration and run of the MM5 is divided into two main variants. One is a tool that enables to interact with the model through user-friendly interfaces that allow users to manage the data necessary to run MM5 and select the best resource that is available on the grid without extensive knowledge about model or operating system that receives them. The other alternative is to implement a set of scripts that allow the operating runs of MM5 model that are performed automatically.

The reasoning subsystem implements the method of detection and identification of TLS. It consists on several main modules, the first module is a data acquisition software product that can store in detail TLS records (cases) that occurred in Cuba, and was designed to interact with climatic database of INSMET to obtain the necessary data of the thermodynamic variables to facilitate the detection of future events (knowledge base). The second module is the identification of local severe weather events based in MM5 model outputs data.

This last module determines the favorable condition that leads the emergence of severe weather local events using the results of a previous research project developed by the INSMET, which describes the behavior of some thermodynamic indices that suggest favorable conditions for deep convection, severe weather and atmospheric instability like are the called CAPE, CINE, SI, TT, K, LI, SWEAT & PP. These indices, although are not a diagnosis method, suggest favorable conditions for the atmospheric severity.

The method is being designed to work in a grid with a 9km resolution above fields on the surface convective rainfall, wind speed and direction, temperature, dew point, relative humidity at different levels (surface, 200, 500, 700, 850hPa), surface pressure and geopotential height, plus instability indices discussed above. The initial search locate the regions of convective rainfall and in these regions perform a second search to locate potential areas of occurrence of severe local reactions based on threshold temperatures and high relative humidity above 87%, and vertical instability between moderate and high with conditions:

a) $CAPE - CINE > 1500J/Kg$,
b) $TT > 40$,
c) $K > 40$,
d) $LI < -2$,
e) $SI < 0$ y
f) $SWEAT > 300$;

As well as the location of wind convergence in low and middle levels, less than 500hPa usually associated with meso-cyclones and the occurrence of tornadoes. Once the severe weather local events are identified, CBR and fuzzy logic are applied to detect the types of events identified. Then it is necessary to verify the amount of resources available and define the events to be modeled by ARPS. Continuously an analysis of ARPS run configurations is realized according to the detected events, thus a possible solution is defined and a configuration proposed for each analyzed case. Although it must have a generic ARPS configuration that can be used for any event, it is necessary that these solutions must be previously registered in the CBR by a specialist. Then it prepares the subsystem of configuration and run of the ARPS to implement and execute each of the solutions proposed above.

This last component performs the model runs for those regions previously identified and allows deeper observation of the development of TLS detection.

Developed tools, based on free software, were used to design these components, besides with the Linux operating system to maximize the advantages of processing and memory management that it offers. The technological benefits that support Java technology to provide a higher quality service to end users were used as well.

4. Conclusions

- The decision support model, using fuzzy logic and case-based reasoning, explores a new way to obtain more accurate forecast in early warning of severe weather events, which helps to preserve human life and economical resources.
- The model developed represents an innovation because allows the use of models MM5 and ARPS, which were no designed to work together, to identify more precisely the presence of TLS.
- The proposed hybrid approach gives a solution to the identification and detection of TLS, based on AI techniques.

References

1. A. P. Alfonso, *Climatología de las tormentas locales severas de Cuba. Cronología*, Editorial Academia, La Habana (1994).
2. I. Orlanski, *A rational subdivision of scales for atmospheric processes. Bull. Amer. Meteor. Soc.*, **56**, 527 (1975).
3. J. W. Wilson and W. E. Schreiber, *Initiation of Convective Storms at Radar-Observed Boundary-Layer Convergence Lines. Mon. Wea. Rev.*, **114**, 2516 (1986).
4. J. W. Wilson, G. B. Foote, N. A. Cook, J. C. Fankhauser, C. G. Wade, J. D. Tuttle, C. K. Mueller and S. K. Krueger, *The Role of Boundary-Layer Convergence Zones and Horizontal Rolls in the Initiation of Thunderstorms: A Case Study. Mon. Wea. Rev.*, **120**, 1785 (1992).
5. A. R. Moller, C. A. Doswell, M. Foster and G. R. Woodall, *The Operational Recognition of Supercell Thunderstorm Environments and Storm Structures. Wea. Forecasting*, **9**, 327 (1994).
6. S. Novo, *Pronóstico inmediato del movimiento y crecimiento de radioecos de precipitación sobre cuba. aplicación al seguimiento de áreas convectivas extensas*, Tesis doctoral, Instituto de Meteorología (2009).
7. J. W. Wilson, N. A. Crook, C. K. Muller, J. Sun and M. Dixon, *Nowcasting Thunderstorms: A Status Report. Bull. Amer. Meteor. Soc.*, **79**, 2079 (1998).
8. A. Bezanilla, *Influencia de los Procesos de Fase Sólida en la Simulación de una Tormenta Convectiva sobre Camagüey*, Tesis doctoral, Instituto de Meteorología (2001).

9. D. R. Pozo, *Simulación numérica de la formación y evolución de sistemas nubosos convectivos de meso-escala sobre Camagüey con ayuda de un modelo tridimensional*, Tesis doctoral, Instituto de Meteorología (2003).

10. G. A. Martínez, G. G. Aguilar and M. Carnesoltas, *Condiciones termodinámicas favorables para la ocurrencia de tornados sobre Camagüey*, Instituto de Meteorología (2009).

11. D. F. Slezak, C. L. Carri, E. Mocskos and P. Turjanski, *Tecnología Grid Mito o Realidad?*, Nex IT Specialist, 20 (2006).

SYMBOLIC COMPUTATIONS IN DESIGN AND MODELLING OF NONLINEAR CONTROL

A.A. DYDA, E.V. LUBIMOV

Department of Automatic and Information Systems, Maritime State University,
Vladivostok, 690059, Russia

S. DI GENNARO

Department of Electrical Engineering, University of L'Aquila, Monteluco Di Roio,
67040 L'Aquila, Italy

This paper is devoted to the problem of the design procedure automatization for nonlinear control systems on the basis of symbolic computations and such well-known technique as exact linearization via nonlinear feedback. Developed software realizes the synthesis of control laws in symbolic form that is convenient for further analysis, modelling, and practical implementation of the system. Examples of the software applications to induction motor, robot manipulator, and underwater vehicle are given and discussed.

1. Introduction

Important features of large-scale systems are high dimension, nonlinearity, and often uncertainty. To overcome the difficulties of large-scale systems research, the decomposition methods and appropriate computer soft wear as effective tools are traditionally used. The notion "decomposition" can be considered, on one hand, as a procedure of splitting the large system into subsystems of lower dimensions. On other hand, decomposition can be desired result of control system design when susbsystems dynamics are independent and demonstrate prescribed behaviour.

A number of modern methods which are used to solve the problem of control systems synthesis exploit an idea of linearization. Among them the exact linearization of the controlled object dynamics via nonlinear feedback seems to be one of the most popular techniques. This approach, comprehensively given by A.Isidori, H. Nijmeijer and A. van der Schaft and other researchers, last two decades was extended and applied to adaptive control, variable structure control etc [1]-[4]. The main advantages of the nonlinear feedback linearization (NFL) method consist in its strong formalization and possibility to make decomposion of large system, to decouple controlled subsystems and to provide them reference (as a rule, linear) transient dynamics. Unfortunately, when the dimensions of state, control, and output vectors are large, the control system designer faces huge difficulties associated with complicated computations.

To deal with such systems, modern software for symbolic calculations can be applied. Moreover, as it will be demonstrated, the single procedure of the full system synthesis based on the NFL approach can be often implemented.

The aim of this paper is to develop the softwear for control law design and full control system modelling with usage of NFL method and symbolic computations.

The paper is organized as follows. In Section II a necessary background on NFL method is given. Section III briefly describes main features of algorithms and program realization of symbolic synthesis according to the NFL method. In Section IV the mathematical models of such dynamical objects as induction motor, robot manipulator, and underwater vehicle are presented. In order to demonstrate the effectiveness of approach to symbolic synthesis, developed software was applied to design the control systems for them. Results of computer synthesis are derived as symbolic expressions describing nonlinear control laws. Examples of system processes are shown. Section V contains discussion and final comments and touches possible directions of future development of the approach.

2. The Method of Nonlinear Feedback Linearization: Brief Background

To begin with, we briefly review necessary concepts of feedback linearization, following [1]. The mathematical model of dynamical control object is supposed to be described by the equations

$$\dot{x} = f(x) + g(x)u$$
$$y = h(x) \tag{1}$$

where

$$x = (x_1, \ldots x_n)^T,$$

$$u = (u_1, \ldots u_m)^T,$$

$$y = (y_1, \ldots y_m)^T$$

are the state, control, and output vectors, respectively.

According to the method of feedback linearization [1], the control should be formed as follows

$$u = A^{-1}(x)(w - \Gamma(x)) . \tag{2}$$

The decomposition matrix $A(x)$ and vector $\Gamma(x)$ are calculated by formulas

$$A(x) = \begin{bmatrix} L_{g_1} L_f^{r_1-1} h_1(x) & .. & .. & L_{g_m} L_f^{r_1-1} h_1(x) \\ L_{g_1} L_f^{r_2-1} h_2(x) & .. & .. & L_{g_m} L_f^{r_2-1} h_2(x) \\ .. & & .. & .. & .. \\ L_{g_1} L_f^{r_m-1} h_m(x) & .. & .. & L_{g_m} L_f^{r_m-1} h_m(x) \end{bmatrix}, \tag{3}$$

$$\Gamma(x) = \begin{bmatrix} L_f^{r_1} h_1(x) \\ L_f^{r_2} h_2(x) \\ ... \\ L_f^{r_m} h_m(x) \end{bmatrix}, \tag{4}$$

where $r = (r_1, ... r_m)^T$ the relative degree vector,

$w = (w_1, ... w_m)^T$ the new control input.

By the definition, the derivative of function $h_j(x)$ along vector $f(x)$ is the following

$$L_f h_j(x) = \sum_{i=1}^{n} \frac{\partial h_j(x)}{\partial x_i} f_i(x) . \tag{5}$$

The feedback control (2) transforms a nonlinear system (1) into m decoupled chains of r_i cascade-connected integrators and, as consequence, the input-output behavior of the system satisfies the linear equations

$$y_i^{(r_i)} = w_i . \tag{6}$$

Obviously, the choice of the new control in the form

$$w_i = y_{di}^{(r_i)} + k_1 e_i^{(r_i-1)} + ... + k_{r_i} e_i , \tag{7}$$

where $y_d(t)$ is the desirable trajectory of the system and error

$e(t) = y_d(t) - y(t)$, provides asymptotically stable tracking.

570

If the equality $r_1 + ... + r_m = n$ takes place, the system is full-state linearizable, otherwise, it has unobservable subsystem with its own dynamics, or zero dynamics (for more details see [1], [2]).

3. Computer Symbolic Design of Control Laws

In the case when one needs to design the control system for the nonlinear dynamical object of relatively low dimension, the usage of the formulas (2)-(7) is rather simple. But with increasing of dimension which characterizes large-scale systems, number of inputs and outputs, the computational complexity soon arises.

Meanwhile, for research purposes, it is symbolic form of control that is most valuable and preferable. Naturally, symbolic expressions of control laws are convenient for further analysis, modelling, and practical realization.

Complicated work on deriving the control expressed in symbolic form and based, in particular, on the NFL method can be essentially facilitated by means of modern software systems such as Maple, MATEMATICA, MATLAB, MATHCAD etc. They have built-in functions for symbolic differentiation, vector and matrix operations, and many others.

In this research the computer program for the NFL-based symbolic synthesis and modeling of nonlinear control system was developed in the environment of Maple and MATLAB. Principal modules of the software are following:

- The description of variables (vectors of state, control and output);
- The description of the desirable system trajectory $y_d(t)$;
- The input of dynamical object model in symbolic form;
- The deriving of expressions for function $f(x)$ and matrix $g(x)$;
- The determination of relative degree vector;
- The input of coefficients which determine desirable transients;
- The symbolic calculations of decomposition matrix $A(x)$ and vector $\Gamma(x)$;
- The generation of symbolic expressions for control u and new control w;
- The forming of full closed-loop control system model by substitution of generated control laws into object model;
- The input of control object parameters;
- Control system modeling.

The user of developed program just input a description of control object in symbolic form and necessary parameters which computer demands. The program, in its turn, generates control laws that provide (at least, partial [1]) decomposition and reference dynamics for subsystems. If one needs, the program simulates the designed control system and presents the processes in it.

4. Examples of Symbolic Control Synthesis and System Modelling

To demonstrate the effectiveness of the approach and developed software, consider the examples of symbolic control synthesis and simulations for three dynamical objects. These are induction motor, robot manipulator, and underwater vehicle.

4.1. *The induction motor*

The model of induction motor can be written as following equations [5]:

$$\dot{\phi} = -\alpha\phi + p\omega\xi\phi + \alpha L_m I$$
$$\dot{I} = \alpha\beta\phi - p\beta\omega\xi\phi - \gamma I + U/\sigma , \tag{8}$$
$$\dot{\omega} = \mu I^T \xi\phi - T_L / J$$
$$\dot{\theta} = \omega$$

where θ, ω are the rotor angular position and velocity; $\phi = (\phi_a, \phi_b)^T$, $I = (i_a, i_b)^T$ are the rotor flux and the stator current vectors; $U = (u_a, u_b)^T$ the control input voltage; T_L the load torque; $\alpha = R_r / L_r$, $\beta = L_m /(\sigma L_r)$,

$$\xi = \begin{pmatrix} 0 & -1 \\ 1 & 0 \end{pmatrix} \qquad \gamma = \frac{L_m^2 R_r}{\sigma L_r^2} + \frac{R_s}{\sigma}$$

$$\sigma = L_s - \frac{L_m^2}{L_r} \qquad \mu = \frac{3 L_m p}{2 JL_s} \quad .$$

R_s, R_r the stator and rotor resistance; L_r, L_s, L_m the rotor, stator and mutual inductances; p the number of pole pairs.

The output and desirable trajectory of the system are chosen as following

$$y = \begin{bmatrix} \omega \\ \phi^T\phi \end{bmatrix}, \qquad y_d = \begin{bmatrix} c_1 \sin(c_2 + vt) \\ c_3 \end{bmatrix}.$$

The results of the computer-based symbolic control synthesis are obtained (given in the Maple format), particularly,

$$U_1 = 2*Rr*(-x2*Lm^2*Rr*Fbi-x1*Lm^2*Rr*Fai-2*x2*Rr*Lm^3*x4-2*Rr*x2^2*Ls*Lr-2*Rr*x1^2*Ls*Lr+x2*Lm*x4*Rs*Lr^2+Lm^3*x4*p*x5*x1*Lr+x1*Lm*x3*Rs*Lr^2-Lm^2*x4^2*Rr*Ls*Lr-Lm*x4*p*x5*x1*Lr^2*Ls+3*x2*Rr*Lm*x4*Ls*Lr+2*Rr*x2^2*Lm^2-Lm^3*x3*p*x5*x2*Lr-Lm^2*x3^2*Rr*Ls*Lr+3*x1*Rr*Lm*x3*Ls*Lr-2*x1*Rr*Lm^3*x3+Lm*x3*p*x5*x2*Lr^2*Ls+2*Rr*x1^2*Lm^2+Lm^4*x4^2*Rr+Lm^4*x3^2*Rr)/Lr^2/(-Ls*Lr+Lm^2);$$

$$U_2 = 1/6*(4*Rr*x1*w2*J*Lr^3*Ls-4*Rr*x1*w2*J*Lr^2*Lm^2+6*Rr^2*x1^2*Lm*p*x4*Ls*Lr+6*Rr*x1^2*Lm*p^2*x3*x5*Lr^2*Ls-6*Rr*x1^2*Lm^3*p^2*x3*x5*Lr+6*Rr*x1*Lm^2*p^2*x2^2*Lr*x5-6*Rr^2*x1^2*Lm^2*p*Fbi+6*Rr*x1^3*Lm^2*p^2*Lr*x5+6*Rr*x1^2*Lm*p*x4*Rs*Lr^2+18*x2^2*p*Rr^2*Lm*x4*Ls*Lr+3*x2*p*w1*Lr^3*Ls-3*x2*p*w1*Lr^2*Lm^2+12*x2*p*Rr^2*x1^2*Lm^2+6*x2*p*Lm^4*x3^2*Rr^2+6*x2*p*Lm^4*x4^2*Rr^2+6*x2^2*p*Rr*Lm*x4*Rs*Lr^2+6*x2^2*p^2*Rr*Lm*x3*x5*Lr^2*Ls-6*x2^2*p^2*Rr*Lm^3*x3*x5*Lr-6*x2*p*Lm^2*x4^2*Rr^2*Ls*Lr-6*x2*p*Lm^2*x3^2*Rr^2*Ls*Lr-6*x2^2*p*Rr^2*Lm^2*Fbi+12*x2*p*x1*Rr^2*Lm*x3*Ls*Lr-12*x2*p*Rr^2*x1^2*Ls*Lr-12*x2*p*x1*Rr^2*Lm^3*x3-12*x2^3*p*Rr^2*Ls*Lr-12*x2^2*p*Rr^2*Lm^3*x4+12*x2^3*p*Rr^2*Lm^2)/p/Lr^2/Lm/Rr/(x1^2+x2^2);$$

$$w_1 = (C2-x1^2-x2^2)*ki11+(-2*x1*(-Rr*x1-p*x5*x2*Lr+Rr*Lm*x3)/Lr-2*x2*(-Rr*x2+p*x5*x1*Lr+Rr*Lm*x4)/Lr)*ki12;$$

$$w_2 = (C1*sin(v*t)-x5)*ki21+(C1*cos(v*t)*v-1/2*(-3*Lm*p*x3*x2+3*Lm*p*x4*x1-2*Tl*Lr)/J/Lr)*ki22-C1*sin(v*t)*v^2.$$

In the given formulas the following variables are used:

$$x1 = \phi_a, x2 = \phi_b, x3 = i_a, x4 = i_b, x5 = \omega, x6 = \theta$$

After deriving the symbolic expressions for controls, the program substitutes them into the object model and simulates the whole system. Some processes are shown on Fig.1. – Fig.3.

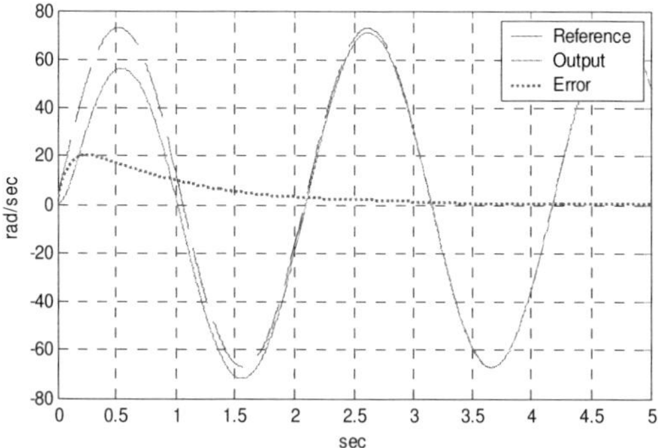

Fig. 1. The desired reference and real angular velocities.

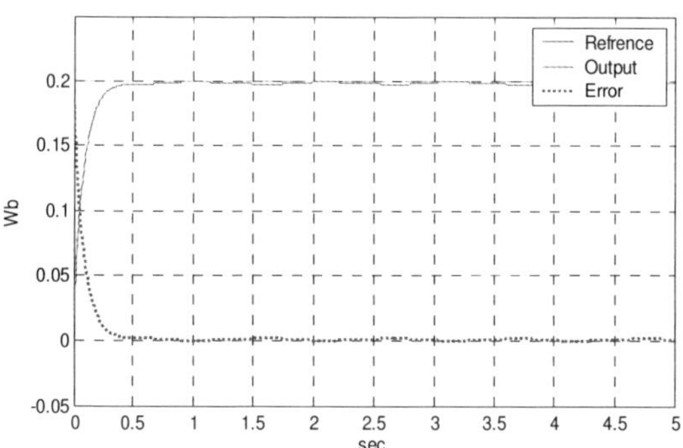

Fig. 2. The rotor flux square modulus output and reference.

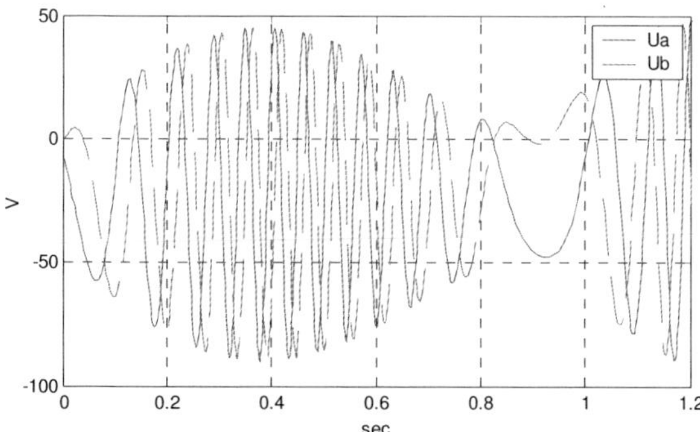

Fig. 3. Control input voltage vector

As seen, synthesized control input is bounded and provides asymptotically stable tracking of reference trajectory $y_d(t)$.

4.2. *The robot manipulator*

Next example of dynamical object to which we will apply the developed software is the robot manipulator UMS-2 [6]. Its dynamics are described by the equation

$$D(q)\ddot{q} + B(\dot{q},q)\dot{q} + G(q) = U,$$

where $U \in R^3$, $q \in R^6$ are the control the generalized coordinates vectors. The matrices are determined as follows

$$D(q) = \begin{bmatrix} I_1 + I_2 + I_3 + m_3(q_3 + l_3)^2 & 0 & 0 \\ 0 & m_2 + m_3 & 0 \\ 0 & 0 & m_3 \end{bmatrix},$$

$$B(\dot{q},q) = \begin{bmatrix} 2m_3(q_3 + l_3)\dot{q}_3 & 0 & m_3(q_3 + l_3)\dot{q}_1 \\ 0 & 0 & 0 \\ -m_3(q_3 + l_3)\dot{q}_1 & 0 & 0 \end{bmatrix}$$

$$G(q) = \begin{bmatrix} 0 & (m_2 + m_3)g & 0 \end{bmatrix}^T.$$

The order of the system is n=6, the number of inputs is m=3. The variables are redefined as $x_1 = q_1, x_2 = \dot{q}_1, x_3 = q_2, x_4 = \dot{q}_2, x_5 = q_3, x_6 = \dot{q}_3$:

Undefined parameters are supposed to be constant.

The outputs of the system are the coordinates of the manipulator grasp in task space

$$h_1 = (x_5 + l_3)\sin(x_1),$$
$$h_2 = (x_5 + l_3)\cos(x_1),$$
$$h_3 = x_3$$

Desired trajectory $y_d(t)$ is chosen to provide the movement of the grasp along the spatial circle

$$y_{d1} = R\sin(\alpha t),$$

$$y_{d2} = c_1,$$

$$y_{d3} = c_2 - R\cos(\alpha t)$$

The program generates the following symbolic expressions for control:

$$U = \begin{bmatrix} \dfrac{w_1 m_3 x_5^2 \cos x_1 + (2m_3 x_5 l_3 + m_3 l_3^2)(w_1 \cos x_1 - w_2 \sin x_1)}{x_5 + l_3} + \\[2mm] + \dfrac{(w_1 \cos x_1 - 2x_2 x_6 - w_2 \sin x_1)I}{x_5 + l_3} \\[2mm] (m_2 + m_3)(w_3 + G) \\ \dfrac{m_3(x_2^2 + w_2 x_5 \cos x_1 + w_2 l_3 \cos x_1 + 2x_2^2 x_5 l_3}{x_5 + l_3} + \\[2mm] + \dfrac{x_2^2 l_3^2 + x_2^2 x_5^2 + x_5 w_1 \sin x_1 + l_3 w_1 \sin x_1)}{x_5 + l_3} \end{bmatrix}$$

$$w = \begin{bmatrix} (R\sin\alpha t - (x_5 + l_3)\sin x_1)k_{11} + (R\alpha\cos\alpha t - x_6 \sin x_1 - \\ -(x_5 + l_3)x_2 \cos x_1)k_{12} - R\alpha^2 \sin\alpha t \\ (c_1 - (x_5 + l_3)\cos x_1)k_{21} + ((x_5 + l_3)x_2 \sin x_1 - x_6 \cos x_1)k_{22} \\ (c_2 - R\cos\alpha t - x_3)k_{31} + (R\alpha\sin\alpha t - x_4)k_{32} + R\alpha^2 \cos\alpha t \end{bmatrix}$$

Fig.4 - Fig.7 show the transient processes obtained in the simulation of the whole control system.

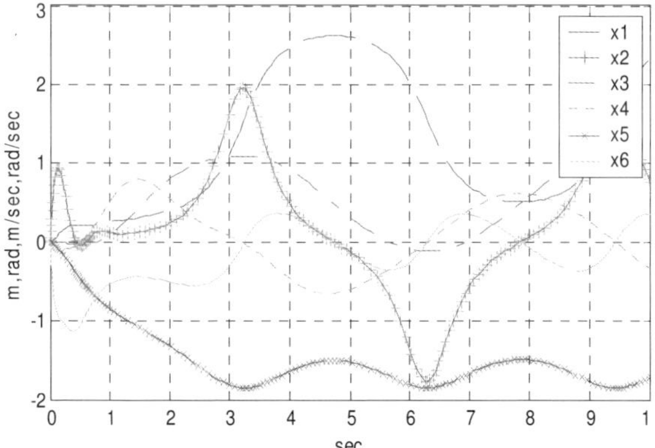

Fig. 4. The evolution of the state vector components.

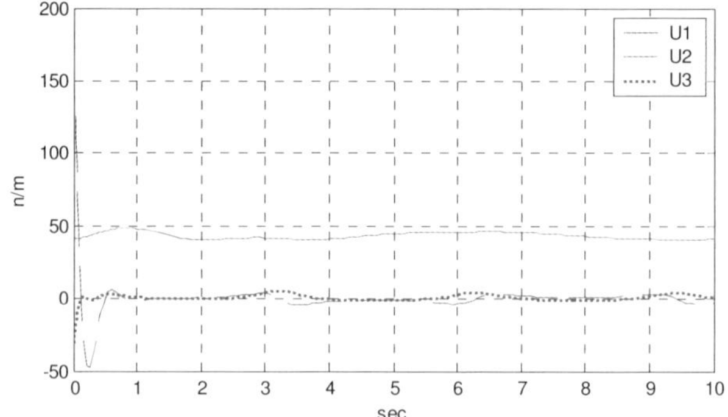

Fig. 5. The control vector components.

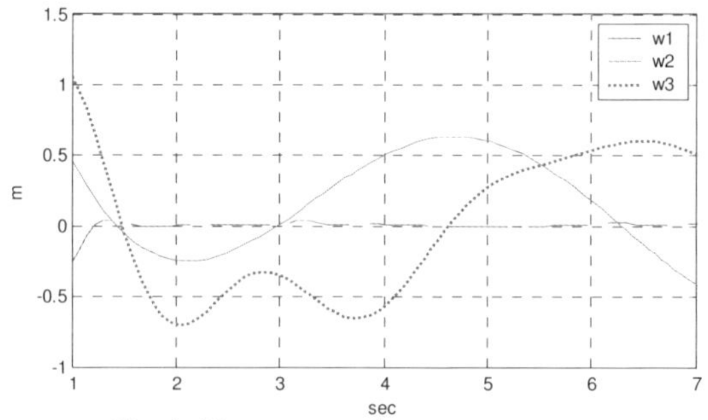

Fig. 6. The new control vector components.

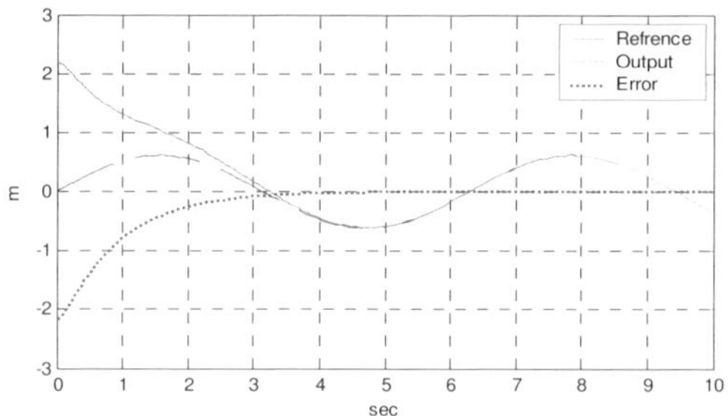

Fig. 7. First output, reference, and error.

To save a space in the paper, only first output, reference and error is given (Fig.7). The simulations confirm that the derived control forces the tracking errors to tend asymptotically to zero.

4.3. *The underwater vehicle*

To finish the illustration of the developed software for symbolic synthesis of control system, consider the model of underwater vehicle (UV) [7]. It consists of 12 differential equations that describe the UV kinematics and dynamics:

$$\frac{d\theta}{dt} = \omega_x - \frac{(\omega_y \cos\theta \sin\zeta + \omega_z \sin\psi \sin\theta)}{\cos\psi}$$

$$\frac{d\varphi}{dt} = \frac{(\omega_y \cos\theta + \omega_z \sin\theta)}{\cos\psi}$$

$$\frac{d\psi}{dt} = \omega_z \cos\theta + \omega_y \sin\theta$$

$$\frac{dx}{dt} = V_x \cos\varphi\cos\psi - V_y \cos\varphi\cos\theta\sin\psi + V_y \sin\varphi\sin\theta +$$
$$+ V_z \cos\varphi\sin\psi\sin\theta + V_z \cos\theta\sin\varphi$$

$$\frac{dy}{dt} = V_x \cos\psi + V_y \cos\psi\cos\theta - V_z \cos\psi\sin\theta$$

$$\frac{dz}{dt} = -V_x \cos\psi\sin\varphi + V_y \cos\varphi\sin\theta + V_y \cos\theta\sin\varphi\sin\psi +$$
$$+ V_z \cos\varphi\cos\theta - V_z \cos\varphi\sin\psi\sin\theta$$

$$(M + \lambda_{11})\dot{V}_x - My_c\omega_z + (M + \lambda_{33})V_z\omega_y - (M + \lambda_{22})V_y\omega_z +$$
$$+ My_c\omega_x\omega_y + P_l \sin\psi = F_x$$
$$(M + \lambda_{22})\dot{V}_y + (M + \lambda_{11})V_x\omega_z - (M + \lambda_{33})V_z\omega_x -$$
$$- My_c(\omega_z^2 + \omega_x^2) + P_l \cos\psi\cos\theta = F_y$$

$$(M + \lambda_{33})\dot{V}_z + (M + \lambda_{22})V_y\omega_x + My_c\dot{\omega}_x -$$
$$- (M + \lambda_{11})V_x\omega_z +$$
$$+ My_c\omega_y\omega_z - P_l \cos\psi\sin\theta = F_z$$

578

$$(J_x + \lambda_{44})\dot{\omega}_x + ((J_z + \lambda_{66}) - (J_y + \lambda_{55}))\omega_z\omega_y +$$

$$+My_c\dot{V}_z + (\lambda_{33} - \lambda_{22})V_zV_y - My_c(V_x\omega_y - V_y\omega_x) +$$

$$+My_cg\cos\psi\sin\theta = M_x$$

$$(J_y + \lambda_{55})\dot{\omega}_y + ((J_x + \lambda_{44}) - (J_z + \lambda_{66}))\omega_x\omega_z +$$

$$+(\lambda_{11} - \lambda_{33})V_xV_z = M_y$$

$$(J_z + \lambda_{66})\dot{\omega}_z + ((J_y + \lambda_{55}) - (J_x + \lambda_{44}))\omega_x\omega_y -$$

$$-My_c\dot{V}_x + (\lambda_{22} - \lambda_{11})V_xV_y + My_cg\sin\psi -$$

$$-My_c(V_z\omega_y - V_y\omega_z) = M_z$$

where θ, φ, ψ are Euler's angles; $(x, y, z)^T$ is the coordinates vector, $(\omega_x, \omega_y, \omega_z)^T$, $(V_x, V_y, V_z)^T$ are angular and linear velocities vectors; $F_x, F_y, F_z, M_x, M_y, M_z$ are components of the control vector; other parameters are constant.

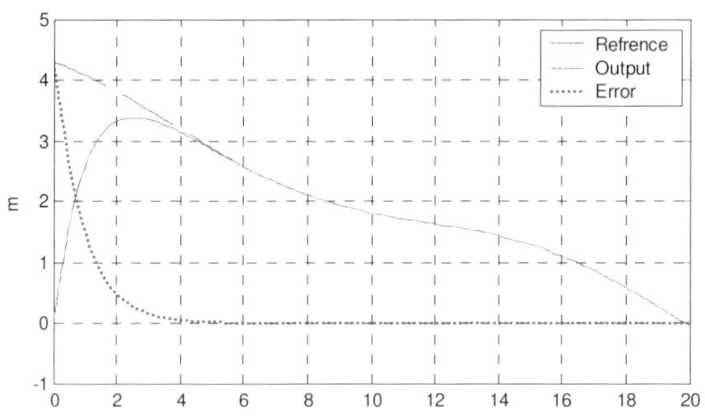

Fig. 8. Third output, reference, and error.

The control law generated by the program is very large and not presented here, but the simulation of the system had confirmed its correctness. As illustration, on Fig. 8 the third output of the system is shown with desirable function

$$y_{d3} = 4 + 0.3\cos(0.4t) - 0.2t$$

As seen from simulation results, asymptotically stable tracking of reference trajectory of UV is achieved with derived control law.

5. Discussion and Final Comments

The software developed in this work can effectively support the procedure of control system design in symbolic form. Clearly, the bigger the dimension of the object model, the longer and more complicated symbolic expressions will be obtained. For example, one can expect that the program will generate very large expressions describing the control laws for different flexible structures, such as given, for instance, in [8], when dynamics are approximated by a finite multi–dimensional model. The software helps to designer to solve the problem of the synthesis of nonlinear control systems and to simulate them easily. Practical implementation of derived control laws in regulators is also facilitated, because the control is expressed in explicit form and can be directly used in appropriate hardware or software.

Derived control laws can be of particular interest. Their symbolic presentation makes possible further analysis, optimization, simplification etc. If designer uses full nonlinear model of the dynamical object, evidently, the regulator of the system will be more complex than in the case of simplified model. The computer program presented here lets to designer fast to compare different regulators and to choose the perspective one.

The NFL has been taken as example to show the effectiveness of the symbolic computations. Nevertheless, other well-formalized methodologies can be considered. Future development of the approach and software for symbolic synthesis and modelling is supposed to be oriented to output feedback nonlinear, adaptive and robust control.

References

1. A. Isidori, *Nonlinear Control Systems.* Berlin: Springer-Verlag, 1995.
2. H. Nijmeijer, A. van der Schaft, *Nonlinear Adaptive Feedback Linearization of Systems.* New York: Springer-Verlag, 1990.
3. C.I. Byrnes, F.D. Priscoli, A. Isidori, *Output Regulation of Uncertain Nonlinear Systems.* Boston: Birkhauser, 1997.
4. P.V. Kokotovic, I. Kanellakopoulos, A.S. Morse *Adaptive Feedback Linearization of Nonlinear Systems //* P.V. Kokotovic (ed.) Foundation of Adaptive Control. Berlin: Springer-Verlag, 1991.
5. B. Castillo-Toledo, S. Di Gennaro, A.G. Loukianov, J. Rivera "On the disrete-time modelling and control of induction motor with sliding modes," in *Proc. American Control Conf.*, Boston, Massachusetts, 2004, pp. 2598-2604.
6. M. Vucobratovic, N. Kircansky, *Scietific Fundamentals of Robotics* Vol.1-3 . Berlin: Springer-Verlag, 1982-1985.

7. A.A. Dyda, S. Di Gennaro, "Adaptive trajectory control for underwater robot," in *Proc.OCEANS-94 Osates,* Brest, 1994.

8. S. Di Gennaro, A.A. Dyda, "Attitude control of a satellite with damping compensation of the flexible beam," in *Proc. European Control Conf.,* Groningem, 1993, pp. 1656-1661.

FUZZY AND PID CONTROLS OF FES-ASSISTED WALKING WITH BODY WEIGHT TRANSFER: SIMULATION STUDIES

R. JAILANI[1,2], M.O. TOKHI[1] AND S.C. GHAROONI[1]

[1]*Department of Automatic Control and System Engineering, University of Sheffield, UK*
[2]*Faculty of Electrical Engineering, Universiti Teknologi MARA, 40450 Shah Alam,
MALAYSIA*
Email: r.jailani@sheffield.ac.uk

This paper presents a simulation of bipedal locomotion to generate stimulation pulses for activating muscles for paraplegic walking with wheel walker using functional electrical stimulation (FES) with body weight transfer (BWT). The study is carried out with a model of humanoid with wheel walker using the Visual Nastran (Vn4D) dynamic simulation software. The humanoid model is designed based on anthropometric data. Stimulated muscle models of quadriceps and hamstrings are developed for knee extension and flexion. Proportional-integral-derivative (PID) and fuzzy logic control (FLC) are designed in Matlab/Simulink to regulate the muscle stimulation pulse-width required to drive FES-assisted walking gait and the computed motion is visualised in graphic animation from Vn4D. The body weight transfer (BWT) technique is introduced to improve the paraplegic walking performance. The results show that body weight transfer can reduce torque and stimulation pulses required for FES-assisted paraplegic walking with wheel walker. FLC is found to perform slightly better than PID in terms of torque and stimulation pulses required for the walking with BWT.

1. Introduction

Paraplegic is impairment in motor and/or sensory function of the lower extremities. It is usually the result of spinal cord injury (SCI) which affects the neural elements of the spinal canal. Sisto et al. [1] reported that more than 200,000 people in the United States (US) suffer from SCI and each year 10,000 new cases occur. Brown-Triolo et al. [2] in their study found that 51% of SCI subjects defined mobility in terms of life impact and autonomy, and gait was found to be perceived as the first choice in possible technology applications. Their subjects also indicated willingness to endure time intensive training and undergo surgery operation if mobility is guaranteed. Therefore, solutions to mobility loss were seen as an exciting prospect to these patients.

The main objective in rehabilitating SCI patients is to help them become as much independent as possible. One way to accomplish this task is to provide them with assistive devices, such as crutches [3-4], walker [5-8], braces [9], orthosis [10-12] and walk trainer [13].

FES has been shown to improve impaired function and muscle deterioration in paralyzed limb of SCI patients. However, one of the major limitations is that the stimulated muscles tend to fatigue very rapidly, which limit the role of FES [14]. Similar to other hybrid FES activity, the performance of FES-assisted walking gait can be enhanced through the implementation of an efficient control strategy. Suitable electrical stimulation to the muscle is required in achieving a smooth and well coordinated walking gait.

Many researchers have investigated various control strategies to address the variability and nonlinearities of the musculoskeletal system, muscle conditioning and fatigue in many different FES-activities [15,16]. Control has been a great challenge in paraplegic mobility research due to the highly non-linear, time-varying nature of the system involved. Conventional control has been used, but knowledge-based control such as neural networks [17, 18], fuzzy logic [18-21] and genetic algorithm [22] is still the practical choice in most current mobility control systems. Feng and Andrews [20] used adaptive fuzzy logic control (FLC) to control functional electrical stimulation (FES) for swinging leg. They found that the controller can customize a general rule-based controller and adapt to the time-varying parameters due to muscle while Yu-Luen et al. [18] found that fuzzy control solves the non-linear problem by compensating for the motion trace errors between neural network control and actual system. One of the possible methods is the use of closed-loop adaptive control technique that measures the output and alters the muscle stimulation for better control. This paper presents the effectiveness of two main approaches; body weight transfer and control strategy to enhance the performance of walking gait and reduce stimulation pulses required to drive FES-walking manoeuvre.

2. Description of the Model

2.1. *Humanoid model*

Humanoid model is built up using anthropometric data. Therefore, the quality and completeness of the anthropometric data are very important in this study. The anthropometric data considered in this study is based on Winter's work [23]. Human body is characterized by three main planes and directions with planes crossing in the centre of the body gravity. The length and mass of each body segment is expressed according to the overall weight and height of the humanoid model. The humanoid model developed in this work is based on a human body with height 1.73m and weight 80kg.

2.2. *FES-assisted walking with wheel walker model*

The wheel walker model is developed using Visual Nastran (Vn4D) software based on the design of a wheel walker sold by youreableshop^{TM}. The model developed incorporated all the basic parts of the real machine. For the wheel walker considered in this paper, the material, dimension and weight are duplicated from real wheel walker that is available in the market [24].

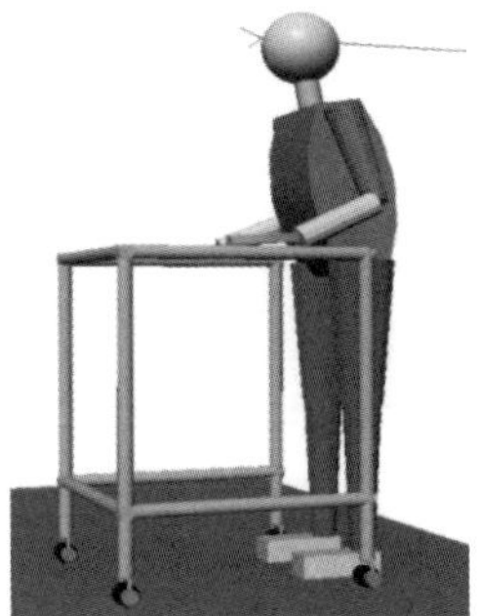

Figure 1: Humanoid model with wheel walker

The final stage of the development of the humanoid with wheel walker model incorporated is the combination of both models. It is important to make sure that the humanoid model is attached to the wheel walker model at the right position and right joint. The complete model of the humanoid with wheel walker using Vn4D is shown in Figure 1.

2.3. *ANFIS muscle model*

In order to simulate FES, a physiological based muscle model is constructed with adaptive neuro-fuzzy inference system (ANFIS) based on previous work [25, 26]. A series of experiments using FES with different stimulation frequencies, pulse width and pulse duration to investigate the impact on muscle output torque are conducted. The data that is obtained is used to develop the paraplegic muscle model. 500 training data and 300 testing data set are used in the development of muscle model. The muscle model developed is validated with experimental data from one subject having T2/T3 incomplete lesion for 29 years. Further explanation can be obtained in previous publications [25, 26].

2.4. *Body weight transfer*

In this paper, body weight transfer technique is applied to reduce stimulation pulses. It is assumed that paraplegic can compensate for the changes by volitional activity of the trunk and upper extremities acting over the wheel walker on the ground. Figure 2 shows the walking cycle considered in this paper. In this technique, while the left leg is in the swing phase, the upper body will tilt to the right and transfer the upper body weight on the right leg. This will reduce the pressure and weight to the left leg and furthermore the torque required will also decrease. The same procedure is used with the left leg in the stance phase. The shaded area in Figure 2 shows the maximum body weight position during one complete walking cycle.

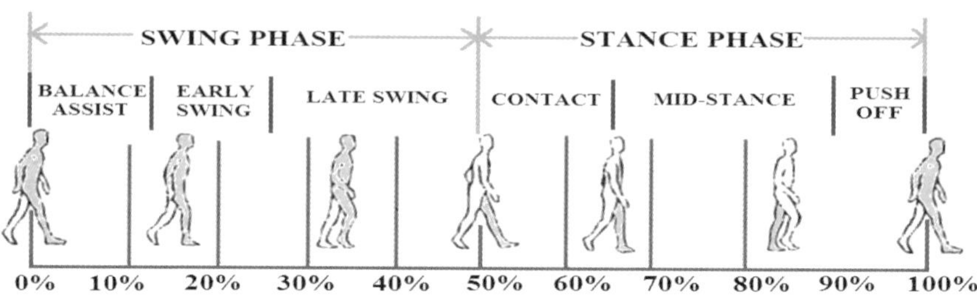

Figure 2: Walking cycle

3. Implementation of Control Strategy

The total joint moment generated by the muscle model to drive the walking gait depends on stimulated pulse width as the frequency is fixed to 33Hz. A specific control strategy is required to regulate the stimulated pulse width in order to obtain smooth walking gait. In this study, fuzzy logic and PID controllers are designed to control knee extensor and flexor for both legs to perform smooth walking gait. The walking cycle is divided into 4 gait phases; stance, heel-off, heel strike and swing. Predefined walking trajectory is used as a reference trajectory for the both controllers.

3.1. *Fuzzy logic controller*

A block diagram of FLC system is shown in Figure 3. There are two inputs to the controllers, the error (difference between actual knee trajectory measured from Vn4D simulation output and reference knee trajectory) and change of error. The controller output is the stimulated pulse width. Five Gaussian (bell-shaped) type membership functions are used for each input and output. The inputs and output are normalised from 0 to 1 and the scaling factors used in left leg FLC are 0.1, 0.0025 and 70 while in the right leg FLC are 0.055, 0.0025 and 70 for error, change of error and output respectively. The stimulation pulse width from fuzzy controller will feed into the muscle model and produce muscle torque that drives the Vn4D model to follow the walking gait. Then the error and change of error are fed back to the fuzzy controller to adjust stimulation pulse-width to the optimum level.

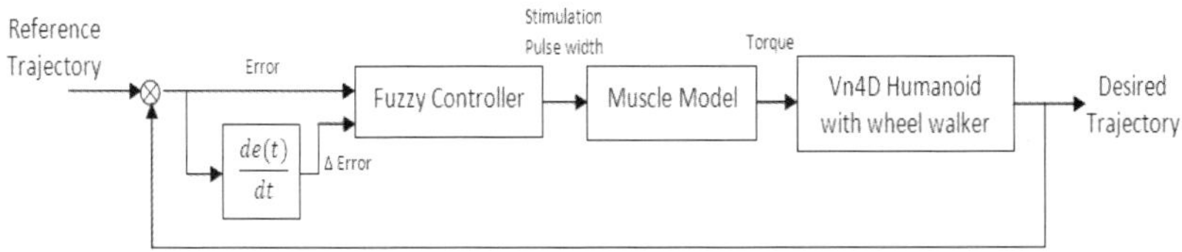

Figure 3: Block diagram of the fuzzy control system

3.2. *Proportional integral derivative (PID) control*

PID control is a widely used in industrial control systems. The PID control algorithm involves three different parameters; the proportional (P), the integral (I) and derivative (D) values. Generally, the PID control can be used in closed-loop to make it more robust to changes in the system. The proportional value determines the reaction to the current error, the integral value determines the reaction based on the sum of current errors, and the derivative value determines the reaction based on the rate at which the error has been changing. The weighted sum of these three actions is used to adjust the process via a control element, which in this case are stimulation pulses. The PID control can be written as:

$$u(k) = k_p e(k) + k_I \frac{e(k)}{1 - Z^{-1}} + k_D (1 - Z^{-1}) e(k)$$

In this paper, two PID controllers are used, one for each leg. For left knee PID controller, the parameter values used are 3.6, 0.02 and 0.05 while for right knee PID controller parameter values are 3, 0.01 and 0.025 for P, I and D respectively. Figure 4 shows a block diagram of the PID controller applied to the walking system. The PID controller input is an error between the system output and the reference while the output is stimulation pulse-width.

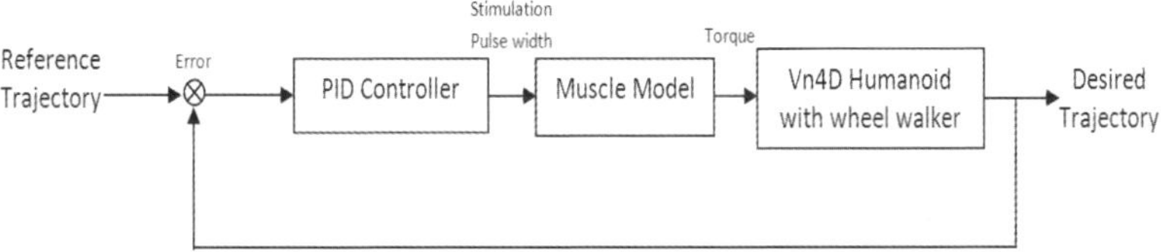

Figure 4: Block diagram of the PID control system

4. Simulation Results

The control strategy was implemented in Matlab/Simulink with incorporation of humanoid with wheel walker model in Vn4D to illustrate the effectiveness of the control scheme in FES-assisted walking with wheel walker. The control objective is to regulate the level of stimulated pulse width for muscle stimulation to perform smooth walking gait by following the reference trajectory. The knee trajectories for walking gait from PID and FLC are shown in Figure 5 and Figure 6. Figure 5 shows the result of left knee trajectory while Figure 6 shows the results of right knee trajectory from PID and FLC. Due to various perturbations and limited strength of the hip and knee flexor and extensor muscles, the shank and thigh may not perfectly track the reference trajectory.

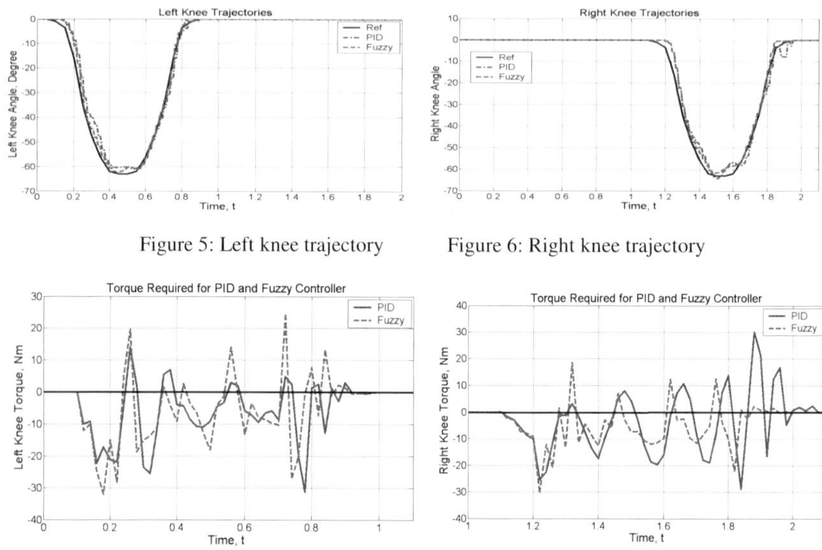

Figure 5: Left knee trajectory   Figure 6: Right knee trajectory

Figure 7: Left knee torque   Figure 8: Right knee torque

The accuracy of these two techniques in terms of walking gait is similar but for FLC, the total torque required is less. Therefore, the stimulation pulse width required in FLC will also be reduced and muscle fatigue can be minimized. Figure 7 shows the torque for left knee while Figure 8 shows the torque for right knee. These torques were generated from muscle model that received input from PID and fuzzy logic controller. The negative torque is the torque required for quadriceps muscle to produce knee extension while positive torque is the torque required for hamstring muscle to produce knee flexion. The torque required for PID is reduced by 9.9% for the left leg but increase by 28.74% for the right leg compared to the FLC. This means that total torque required for one complete gait using FLC was 18.84% less than total torque required using PID control. The percentage of reduction or increment is calculate by taking the difference between integral of both techniques over the initial value, in this case integral from without BWT is the initial value.

5. Conclusion

The advantage of FLC to minimise stimulation pulse width and torque required in FES-assisted walking with wheel walker has been demonstrated. The results show that in one complete walking cycle, there is more than 18% reduction in torque required for walking with FLC as compared with the torque required for walking with PID. It is also concluded that PID and FLC have been successfully implemented to regulate the level of stimulation pulse-width used to stimulate the knee extensor and flexor muscle for FES-assisted walking with wheel walker. Based on the control strategy, a stable walking gait has been achieved.

References

1. S. A. Sisto, G. F. Forrest, and P. D. Faghri, Technology for Mobility and Quality of Life in Spinal Cord Injury, Analyzing A Series of Options Available, in *IEEE Engineering in Medicine and Biology* 2008, pp. 56-68.
2. D. Brown-Triolo, R. Triolo, and P. Peckham, Mobility Issues and Priorities in Persons with SCI : A Qualitative Investigation, Second *Annual IFESS Conference*, 1997.
3. M. Zefran, T. Bajd, and A. Kralj, Kinematic modeling of four-point walking patterns in paraplegic subjects, *Systems, Man and Cybernetics, Part A, IEEE Transactions on*, vol. 26, pp. 760-770, 1996.
4. T. Bajd, A. Kralj, and T. Karcnik, Unstable states in four-legged locomotion, Proceedings of the IEEE/RSJ/GI Intelligent Robots and Systems '94. 'Advanced Robotic Systems and the Real World', IROS '94. 1994.
5. X. Zhaojun, W. Dahai, M. Dong, and W. Baikun, New Gait Recognition Technique Used in Functional Electrical Stimulation System Control, *The Sixth World Congress on Intelligent Control and Automation*, WCICA 2006, 2006.
6. Y. Hu, D. Ming, Y. Z. Wang, Y. W. Wong, B. K. Wan, K. D. K. Luk, and J. C. Y. Leong, Three-dimensional dynamical measurement of upper limb support during paraplegic walking, *26th Annual International Conference of the IEEE Engineering in Medicine and Biology Society*, IEMBS '04, 2004.
7. A. Scheiner, D. C. Ferencz, and H. J. Chizeck, The effect of joint stiffness on simulation of the complete gait cycle, *Proceedings of the 16th Annual International Conference of the IEEE in Engineering Advances: New Opportunities for Biomedical Engineers.*, 1994.
8. M. R. Popovici, V. Dietz, T. Keller, I. Pappas, and M. Morar, Grasping and Walking Neuroprostheses for Stroke and Spinal Cord Injured Subjects, *American Control*, San Diego, 1999.
9. E. B. Marsolais and J. M. Mansour, Hip and trunk stability in paraplegic electrically augmented gait, *Engineering in Medicine and Biology Magazine, IEEE*, vol. 11, pp. 64-67, 1992.
10. P. Jaspers, W. Van Petegem, G. Van der Perre, and L. Peeraer, Design of an automatic step intention detection system for a hybrid gait orthosis, *Proceedings of the 18th Annual International Conference of the IEEE*, 1996.
11. M. Solomonow, R. Baratta, M. Harris, and R. D'Arnbrosia, Activities Of Daily Living Available To Paraplegics Using the LSU-FES Powered Walking Orthosis, Engineering in Medicine and Biology Society, 1992. vol. 14. *Proceedings of the Annual International Conference of the IEEE*, 1992.

12. D. M. Hendershot and C. A. Phillips, Improvement of efficiency in a quadriplegic individual using an FES-RGO system, 1988. *Proceedings of the Annual International Conference of the IEEE in Engineering in Medicine and Biology Society,*, 1988.

13. M. Bouri, Y. Stauffer, C. Schmitt, Y. Allemand, S. Gnemmi, R. Clavel, P. Metrailler, and R. Brodard, The WalkTrainer: A Robotic System for Walking Rehabilitation, *IEEE International Conference on Robotics and Biomimetics, ROBIO '06*, 2006.

14. S. Gharooni, S. Sareh, and M.O. Tokhi. Development of FES-rowing machine with quadriceps stimulation and energy storing device, *12th Annual Conference of the International FES Society*, USA, 2007.

15. H. J. Chizeck, Adaptive and nonlinear control methods for neural prosthesis, in *Neural Prostheses: Replacing Motor Functional After Disease or Disability*, R. B. Stein, P. H. Peckham, and D. B. Popovic, Eds. New York: Oxford Univ. Press, 1992, ch. 14, pp. 298–328.

16. H. J. Chizeck, R. Kobetic, E. B. Marsolais, J. J. Abbas, I. H. Donner, and E. Simon, *Proc.* IEEE Control of functional neuromuscular stimulation systems for standing and locomotion in paraplegics, vol. 76, pp. 1155–1165, 1988.

17. D. Graupe and H. Kordylewski, Neural network control of FES in paraplegics for patient-responsive ambulation, *IEEE Int. Symp. on Circuits and Syst. ISCAS '94*, 1994.

18. Y.-L. Chen, S.-C. Chen, W.-L. Chen, C.-C. Hsiao, T.-S. Kuo, and J.-S. Lai, Neural Network and Fuzzy Control in FES-Assisted Locomotion for The Hemiplegic, *Medical Engineering & Technology*, vol. 28, pp. 32-38, 2004.

19. N. Sau Kuen and H. J. Chizeck, Fuzzy vs. non-fuzzy rule base for gait event detection, *Proceedings of the 16th Annual International Conference of the IEEE Engineering in Medicine and Biology Society, Engineering Advances: New Opportunities for Biomedical Engineers*, 1994.

20. W. Feng and B. J. Andrews, Adaptive fuzzy logic controller for FES-computer simulation study, *Proceedings of the 16th Annual International Conference of the IEEE Engineering in Medicine and Biology Society, Engineering Advances: New Opportunities for Biomedical Engineers*, 1994.

21. R. Davoodi and B. J. Andrews, Fuzzy logic control of FES rowing exercise in paraplegia, *Biomedical Engineering, IEEE Transactions on*, vol. 51, pp. 541-543, 2004.

22. R. Davoodi and B. J. Andrews, Optimal Control of FES-assisted Standing Up in Paraplegia Using Genetic Algorithms, *Medical Engineering & Pysics*, vol. 21, pp. 609-617, 1999.

23. D.A.Winter, Biomechanics and motor control of human movement, 2nd ed. *New York: Willey-Interscience*, 1990.

24. Where services and care matters, Mobility Smart, retrieve at *http://www.mobilitysmart.cc/progress-closed-cuff-cruth-p-452.html?p=product*

25. R. Jailani, M. O. Tokhi, S. C. Gharooni, Z. Hussain, A Novel Approach in Development of Dynamic Muscle Model for Paraplegic with Functional Electrical Stimulation, *Journal of Engineering and Applied Science*, Medwell Journals, vol. 4, no. 4, pp 272-276, 2009. ISSN: 1816-949x

26. R. Jailani, M.O. Tokhi, S.C. Gharooni, and Z. Hussain, Development of dynamics muscle model with functional electrical stimulation. *Proc. International Conference on Complexity in Engineering (COMPENG2010)*, 22–24 February, Roma, Italy.

MODELING, SIMULATION AND POWER MANAGEMENT OF A STAND-ALONE WIND/PHOTOVOLTAIC ENERGY SYSTEM[*]

DJAMILA REKIOUA[†]

University of Bejaia, Electrical Department, Bejaia, 06000, Algeria

TOUFIK REKIOUA

University of Bejaia, Electrical Department, Bejaia, 06000, Algeria

A power management control (PMC) for a hybrid system that comprises wind and photovoltaic generation subsystems, a battery bank, and an ac load is developed in this paper. The objectives of the power control are, primarily, to satisfy the load power demand and, second, to maintain the state of charge of the battery bank to prevent blackout and to extend the life of the batteries. For these purposes, the system controller determines the operation mode of both generation subsystems, switching from power regulation to maximum power conversion. Decision criteria for PMC based on measurable system variables are presented. Finally, the performance of the PMC is extensively assessed through computer simulation using Matlab Simulink package. The simulation results are presented and show the effectiveness of the proposed method.

1. Introduction

Due to the development of renewable energy systems, sustainable development issues (pollutant emission, rarefaction of fossil energy resources), hybrid systems are one efficient solution for electrical energy generation, especially for isolated sites or for a micro-generation unit connected to weak AC grid [1-5]. The hybrid systems combine several conventional or renewable energy sources interconnected via a DC bus. For remote area, the association of an electrochemical storage with the hybrid system allows eliminating the diesel generator (which is commonly required in generation systems based on a single renewable energy source). In this context, we define a hybrid generation system obtained by combining photovoltaic panels and wind turbines (taking advantage of their complementary nature) with storage batteries to overcome periods of scarce generation and for the system control. Many topologies are available for

---

[*] This work is supported by the laboratory LTII-University of Bejaia.

[†] Electrical department.

hybrid systems, depending on interface converters between sources and the interconnection method [6-11]. Our investigation concerns the interconnection of the sources with maximum energy transfer, optimum control and energy management. The simulation calculations are achieved using the MATLAB®-SIMULINK® package under variable atmospheric condition.

2. Description of the Studied System

Stand-alone hybrid generation systems are usually used to supply isolated areas or locations interconnected to a weak grid. They combine several generation modules, typically assimilating different renewable energy sources. The application of these hybrid topologies reduces the probability of energy supply shortage and, with the incorporation of energy storage; it allows to eliminate the background diesel generator (which is commonly required in generation systems based on a single renewable energy source). In this context, many autonomous electric generation hybrid systems (EGHS) frequently combine solar and wind energy sources (taking advantage of their complementary nature) with a lead-acid battery bank (to overcome periods of scarce generation). The topology of the hybrid system under consideration in this paper is represented in Figure. 1.

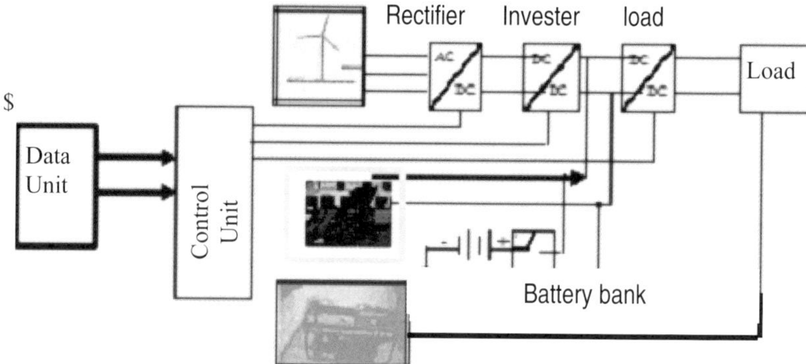

Figure 1. Hybrid system description

3. Hybrid Installation Size

We have data file of wind speed and solar irradiation recorded every month in the meteorological station of a coastal region Bejaia during a period of ten years. Bejaia is a coastal city of north east of Algeria (see Figure 2.). The wind turbine and PV power outputs are matched to a given load demand and to verify the equality between the generated energy and the power consummation.

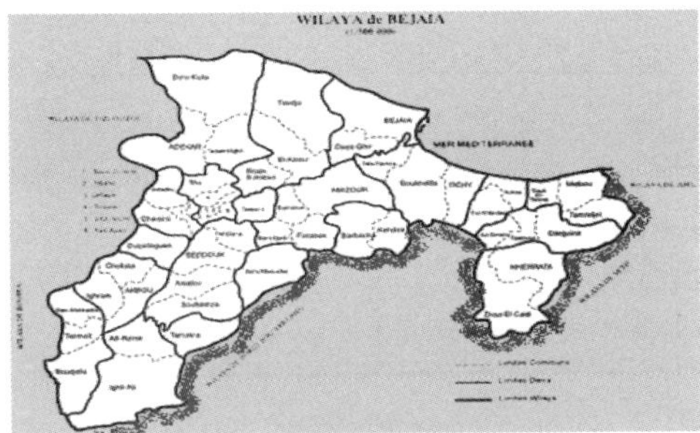

Figure 2. Area of Bejaia (Algeria)

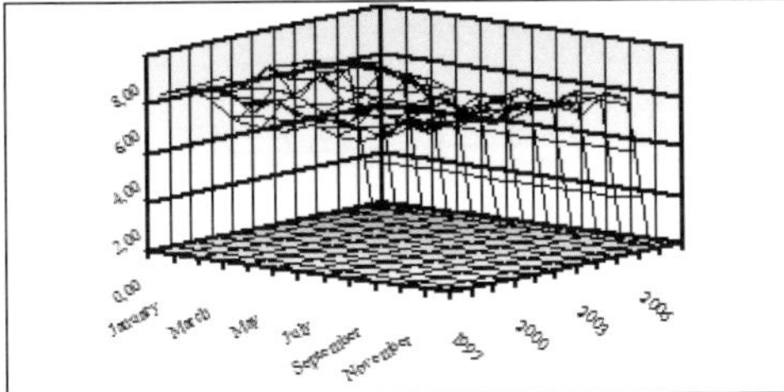

Figure 3. Average variation of the wind speed for a period of ten years in Bejaia

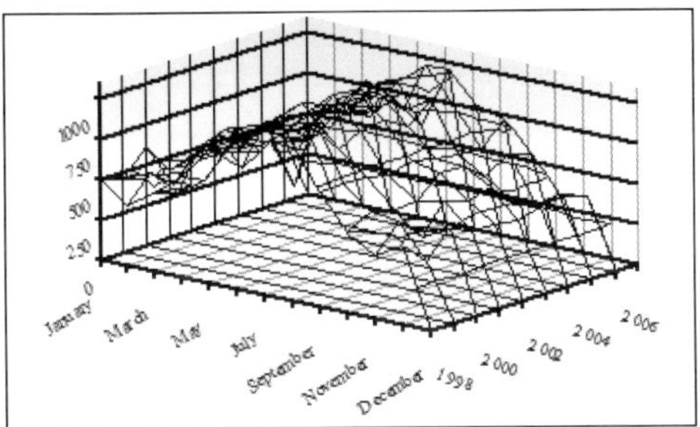

Figure 4. Yearly variations of solar irradiation in Bejaia

4. Modeling of the Proposed System

4.1 Model of PV Array

Various mathematical models of photovoltaic generators were developed to represent their nonlinear behavior which results from the semiconductors junctions which are at the base of their realization. In our work, we choose the following model [8-10]:

592

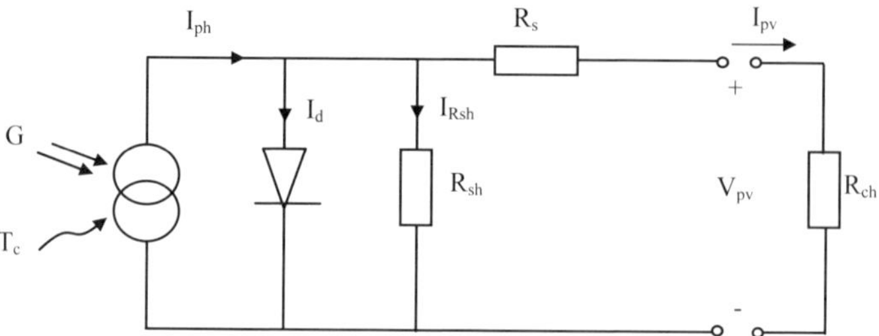

Figure 5. Equivalent circuit of solar cell

The PV array equivalent circuit current Ipv can be expressed as a function of the PV array voltage Vpv:

$$I_{pv} = I_{sc}\left\{1 - K_1\left[\exp K_2 V_{pv}^m - 1\right]\right\}$$ (1)

Eq(1) is only applicable at one particular irradiance level G, and cell temperature T_c, at standard test conditions (STC) (G_{STC}=1000 W/^{m2}, T_{STC}=25°C). When insolation and temperature vary, the parameters change according to the following equations:

$$\Delta T_c = T_c - T_{stc}$$ (2)

$$\Delta I_{pv} = \alpha_{sc}\left(\frac{G}{G_{stc}}\right)\Delta T_c + \left(\frac{G}{G_{stc}} - 1\right)I_{sc,stc}$$ (3)

$$\Delta V_{pv} = -\beta_{oc}\Delta T_c - R_s\Delta I_{pv}$$ (4)

The curves power-voltage $P_{pv}(V_{pv})$ and current-voltage $I_{pv}(V_{pv})$ of the photovoltaic panel, are carried out by varying the load's resistance for three levels of irradiance and temperature (see Figure.6,a.b). The experimental characteristics obtained are compared with the simulation characteristics for the same operating conditions (G=450W/m², T_c=25°C; G=650W/m², T_c=33°C; G=900W/m², T_c=35°C). From the current and power characteristics the non-linear nature of the PV array is apparent. Thus, an MPPT algorithm must be incorporated to force the system to always operate at the maximum power point (MPP).

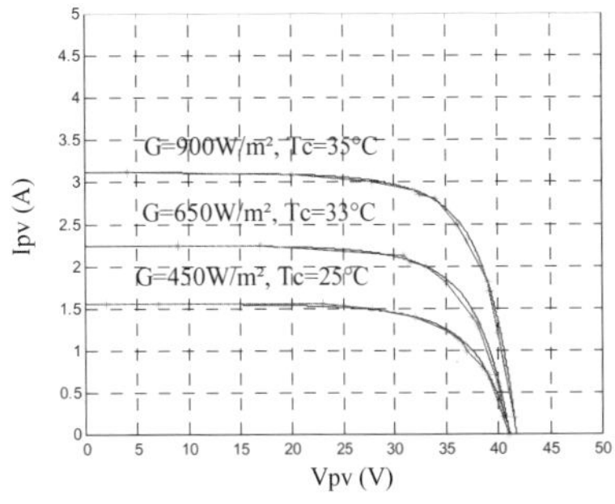

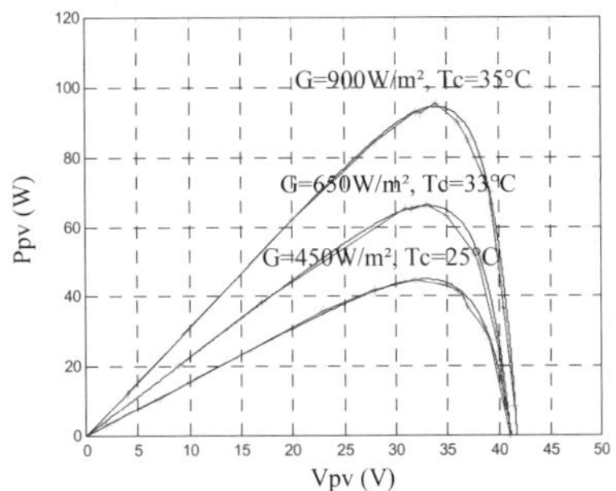

Figure 6.a. Experimental and simulation curves   Figure 6.b. Experimental and simulation curves

4.2 Modeling of the Battery

The battery is necessary in such a system because of the .fluctuating nature of the output delivered by the PV arrays. Thus, during the hours of sunshine, the PV system feeds directly the load and the excess electrical energy is stored in the battery. During the night, or during a period with low solar irradiation, energy is supplied to the load from the battery. The terminal voltage of the battery is given by:

$$U_{batt} = E_b - r_b I_{batt} - K_b \int \frac{I_{batt}\, dt}{Q_o} \tag{5}$$

Where: U_{batt}: Terminal battery voltage, E_b: Open circuit voltage of the battery.

4.3 Wind System Model

The wind turbine model used in this work is [11]. The power coefficient is:

$$Cp = \frac{2 * P_{wind}}{\lambda * S * V_{wind}^{3}} \tag{6}$$

We can calculate the output power and torque of the wind turbine by the following equations:

$$P_{wind} = \frac{1}{2} Cp\,(\lambda) * \rho * S * V_{wind}^{3} \tag{7}$$

$$T_{wind} = T_{mec} = \frac{1}{2} \frac{Cp\,(\lambda) * \rho * R * S * V_{wind}^{2}}{\lambda} \tag{8}$$

Where: S is the area swept by the rotor blades (m^2), ρ the air density, R is the radius of the rotor (m), V_{wind} is the wind speed (m/s), λ is the tip speed ratio.

594

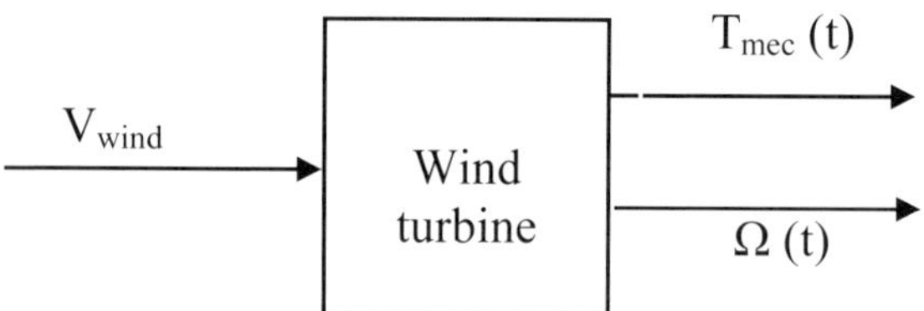

Figure 7. Wind turbine Model

The permanent magnet synchronous machine model used is described by the following equations:

$$\begin{bmatrix} V_d \\ V_q \end{bmatrix} = \begin{bmatrix} R & -\omega L_c \\ \omega L_c & R \end{bmatrix} \begin{bmatrix} i_d \\ i_q \end{bmatrix} + L_c \frac{d}{dt} \begin{bmatrix} i_d \\ i_q \end{bmatrix} + \begin{bmatrix} e_d \\ e_q \end{bmatrix} \tag{9}$$

The electromagnetic torque is given by:

$$T_{em} = \frac{p}{\omega}(e_q \cdot i_q) = p \cdot \Psi_f \cdot i_q \tag{10}$$

The MATLAB/SIMULINK simulation model of the wind turbine is represented in Figure 8.

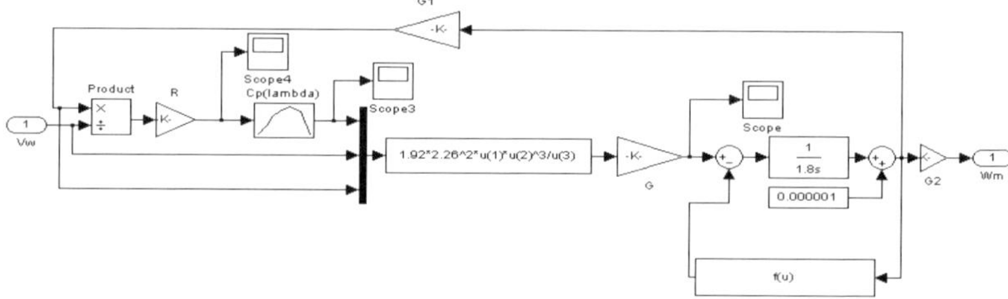

Figure 8. Simulink model of the wind turbine

5. Power Management of the Hybrid Wind/Photovoltaic Energy System

The system is controlled automatically by a source reverser, between the three systems which is ordered by a temporisation witch orders the switch on and the switch off according to the weather conditions to manage the energy transfer of different sources, the hybrid system must be largely instrumented of sensors which allow us to obtain the meteorological conditions

6. Numerical Simulation

We introduce the data input of solar irradiation and wind speed. Different cases are studied. Firstly, we take two consecutives winter days (See Figure 9.a) and then we considered two consecutives summer days (See Figure 9.b). We can notice that the system control works exactly according to the functions described previously, and the voltage battery varies between two predefined minimal and maximal values.

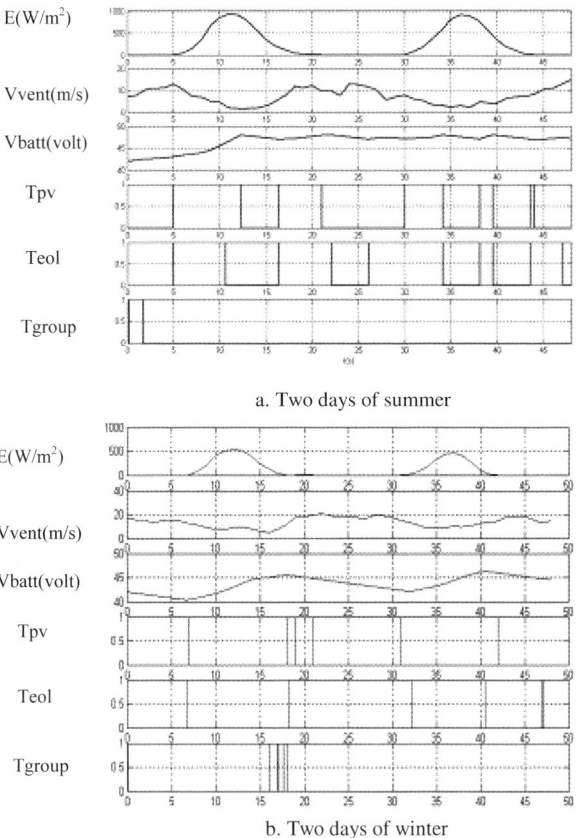

a. Two days of summer

b. Two days of winter

Figure 9. Hybrid operation

7. Conclusion

In this paper, the modelling and simulation of a wind-solar energy conversion is presented. The numerical simulation results show good performances and permits us to conclude that this combination permits to get electrical production continuity in the case of users not connected to the network and in the case of an isolated power station. We can also conclude that the region of Bejaia is a potentially favourable site to achieve a wind-solar energy conversion system, but it would be interesting to associate a generator to assure production continuity better, without interruption and to get a more reliable system.

596

References

1   N. Kato, K. Kurozumi, N. Susuki and S. Muroyama, *Hybrid power-supply system composed of photovolataic and fuel-cell systems*, Conference INTELEC (2001).

2   O. Gergaud, *Modélisation énergétique et optimisation économique d'un système de production éolien et photovoltaïque couplé au réseau et associé à un accumulateur, thèse de doctorat de l'ENS de Cachan France* (2002).

3   A. Tomilson J. Quaicoe, R. Gosine, M. Hinchey, N. Bose, *Modeling and autonomous wind-diesel system using simulink, Conference CCECE'97*, (1997).

4   A. Schmidhofer, H. Weis, *Optimisation of power electronics for small stand alone wind power stations, Conference EPE*, Toulouse, France (2003).

5   J. Sevensson, *A comparaison between electrical systems for variable speed operation of wind turbines, Association Conference and exhibition* (EWEC'94), Thessaloniki, Greece, 10-14 Octobre (1994).

6   M. A. S. Masoum, S. M. Mousavi Badejani, and Ewald F. Fuchs, *Microprocessor- Controlled New Class of Optimal Battery Chargers for Photovoltaic Applications, IEEE tran. on energy conversion*, Vol. 19, No. 3, (2004).

7   Hansen D, Sorensen P, Hansen Lars H, Henrik B, *Models for a stand-alone PV system*. Rio-R-1219 (EN)/, SEC-R-12, (2000).

8   Sukamongkol Y, Chungpaibulpatana S, Ongsakul W, *A simulation model for predicting the performance of a solar photovoltaic system with alternating current loads*, Renewable Energy (2002).

9   O. Gergaud, B. Multon, H. Ben Ahmed, *Analysis and Experimental Validation of Various Photovoltaic System Models, 7th International ELECTRIMACS Congress*, Montréal, (2002).

10 W. Durisch and J. C. Mayor, *Application of a generalized current voltage model for module solar cells to outdoor measurements on a siemen SM110, 3rd World Conference on Photovoltaic Energy Conversion*, (2003).

11 F. Giraud and Z. M. Salameh, *Steady-state Performance of a Grid Connected Rooftop Hybrid Wind-Photovoltaic Power System with Battery Storage, IEEE Trans. Energy Conv.*, Vol. 16, No. 1, (2001)

12 A. Mellit, M. Benghanem, S. A. Kalogirou, *Modeling and simulation of a stand-alone photovoltaic system using an adaptive artificial neural network: Proposition for a new sizing procedure, Renewable Energy* 32 (2007).

13 V. M. Pacheco, L. C. Freitas, J. B. Vieira Jr, A. A. Coelho, V. J. Farias, A dc/dc converter adequate for alternative supply system applications, Power Electronics Conference and Exposition APEC'02, Vol. 2, (2002).

TOWARDS A FRAMEWORK FOR ROAD NETWORK VULNERABILITY ASSESSMENT

SJOERD MEVISSEN, EDWIN DADO

Faculty of Military Science, Netherlands Defense Academy,
Hogeschoollaan 2, Breda, The Netherlands

The vulnerability of road networks in emergency situations is a subject of increasing importance. In general, the identification of vulnerable spots in the network is important to identify the needs for network maintenance and for the allocation of emergency services. Although it is of crucial influence on the success of acute evacuation, the vulnerability of the road network for acute mass-evacuation, is often ignored. It can help to increase the insight in the consequences of link failure on the evacuation process. Furthermore, the use of the available evacuation time can be optimized by using the road network as long as possible. This paper introduces a framework for evacuation modeling on disrupting networks using the MaDAM dynamic traffic assignment algorithm including route choice and aims to derive the importance of links in the network.

1. Introduction

Research in the field of determining road network vulnerability has gained more interest recently. One of the main instigators for this increased interest are the financial resources of local and national governments. In order to better prioritize investments in road infrastructure or to allocate emergency services, with respect to emerging situations, local and national authorities should be able to determine the vulnerable spots in the road infrastructure. However, a commonly accepted scientific basis for this determination is still lacking.

Although some effort has recently been made into the development of vulnerability assessment methods for preventive evacuation situations [1, 2], the development of vulnerability assessment methods related to acute mass-evacuation situations is largely ignored. This application, however, is essential to be able to analyze the feasibility of acute evacuation and to identify vulnerable spots in the road network that obstruct or hamper such an evacuation.

In this paper, we present ongoing work on developing a macroscopic tool for analysis and planning. This mathematical model and support tool can be used express the vulnerability of (parts of) a road network and furthermore to examine the feasibility of acute evacuation plans with respect to the degradation of a road infrastructure which is under direct threat of a hazard.

2. Road Network Vulnerability Under Emergency Conditions

Several road network vulnerability assessment methods are available but the most-often found method in literature is to determine the change in total generalized travel cost due to the failure of a link (road) in the network [1, 3, 4]. By using the travel time increase as a measure of vulnerability, one has a good indicator for the consequences of road failure in a network and hence for evacuation [2]. Therefore, the identification of failing links with high consequences on the traffic flow pattern (e.g. a severe increase in travel times or a failure that leads to unsatisfied demand) is required to take effective measures.

Although this method is designed and used for normal social economic conditions in which road failure is inflicted by accidents or road maintenance, it can be used for evacuation situations [2]. Because of the variety of evacuation types, the application of a vulnerability method will differ between these types. This paper will focus on *acute evacuation*. Acute evacuation is characterized by the immediateness of its execution. The evacuation will be executed *during* a disaster and is forced to start immediately (acute) because a disaster has occurred and the effects will manifest themselves shortly. This kind of evacuation is expected to work in relatively slow proceeding disasters only, such as river floods and if it is executed according a predefined plan known by the population [5].

For road networks that are subject to the effects of such a disaster (steady disruption of the road network and hence diminishing the evacuation routes) the above indicated vulnerability method is quite applicable. Especially for disasters where the probability of occurrence (moment, location, and course) can be determined with a relatively high degree of accuracy, it is easier to select the failing links for vulnerability assessment. Having gained insight in the vulnerability of the road network, authorities concerned with evacuation planning can change their evacuation strategy or improve the road network making it more robust against the effects of the disaster. Therefore, a dynamic planning tool for an acute evacuation process is needed which is able to deal pro-active to changes in a network over time and express the consequences of the change.

3. Evacuation Model

To measure vulnerability of a network under disaster conditions the change in total travel time between several network states has to be computed. The evacuation models that have been developed in the last few years are meant for preventive evacuation [6], using a steady network and are not able to simulate acute evacuation. Hereto a model for acute evacuation is developed by the first author of this paper. This model, as a planning tool, must provide information of the consequences of the disruption of the road network e.g. the change in total travel time and the decline of available routes.

The main objectives of the evacuation model are:
1. To optimize the usage of the available evacuation time, by using the road network as long as possible, in order to maximize the number of evacuated people.
2. To determine the link failure and its consequences on the evacuation process.

In order to meet the first objective, some principles are applied. The first is to consider the evacuees as a homogenous group, making rational decisions to optimize the individual situation. Secondly, the evacuees possess real time, en-route, and future information on the traffic conditions and state of the networks. This principle prevents people from getting confronted with network changes while being en route, hence their number of route alternatives decreasing. Evacuees are expected to plan their route and destination anticipating on upcoming events (link failures, expected congestions), based on a network that will change in time during the evacuation. Although this behavior of evacuees is unrealistic in real life, it is acceptable for planning purposes to find optimal use of evacuation routes.

The model framework determines the optimal routing scheme for all states in a disrupting network and makes a comparison between them. The optimal states are found using dynamic network and dynamic route choice mechanisms in an iterative fashion. The global process includes some preprocessing and a series of simulations for each network state. The entire process is build upon functionalities from the OmniTRANS transport planning software package, using the StreamLine dynamic assignment framework.

For measuring the consequences of link failure (second objective), previous research has shown that the vulnerability methodology presented by Jenelius provide some opportunities [2]. As expression for single link vulnerability he introduced a demand weighted change in generalized cost and named it importance [4]. This approach is used in the model framework as a basis for expressing the consequences of link failure.

3.1. *Routing Methodology*

Due to flooding, the study area suffers from a disrupting network over time. A flood scenario means that failing links lead to a series of network states. A simulation is performed for each network state. The aim of the algorithm is to have an optimal routing strategy for the network state. Since the routing mechanism is based on instantaneous route choice (at time of departure), multiple dynamic runs are performed for a single network state. Iterations take place until the change in routing strategy is insignificant, meaning that the impedances used to determine route fractions are practically equal to the resulting impedances from this choice.

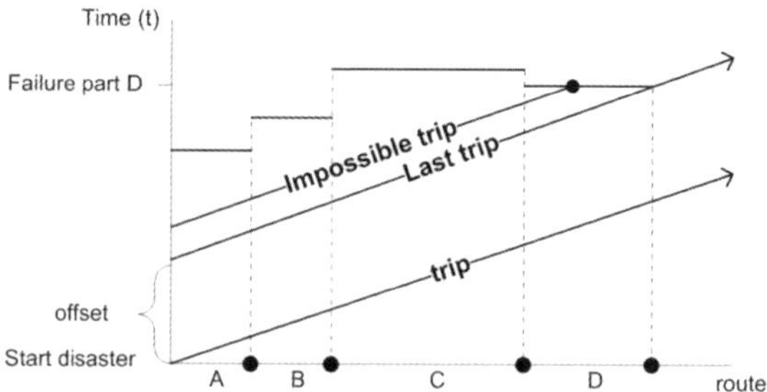

Figure 1. Determining LMD over a specific route

One core element in the framework is the optimal usage of links until failure. For failing links, the dynamic results from the simulations are used to determine the Last possible Moment of Departure (LMD). Figure 1 shows the concept using an example for a combination of a failing link (D) on a specific route (A-B-C-D). The Last trip is determined to establish until what departure time the route is available (the 'offset'). Results from previous runs (although aggregated in blocks of several minutes) are used for this purpose, by developing a backward trajectory for a vehicle entering the failing link at the time of failure. Once the moment of last departure has been determined for all routes, the framework assigns the travel demand to the network, thereby only using available routes. So with the disruption of the network and the increase of time, the availability of routes decreases, leading to a decrease of network performance.

Several time dimensions are distinguished in the framework. First, simulation time, which is semi-continuous (time step of 1 second). The propagation of traffic through the network takes place at this time scale. Secondly, there is a time dimension for route choice intervals. Since MaDAM[a] is a macroscopic dynamic model, the assignment takes place as a flow of vehicles; therefore, route choice does not take place at the level of the individual traveller, but for a group of travellers. This model framework uses stochastic route choice to assign a group of travelers between the same origin and destination over multiple routes at once. These groups are combined from route choice intervals, indicated by the symbol l. Thirdly, there is a time dimension for the aggregation of results.

3.2. *Data Preparation*

Before the simulation starts, data is prepared. This mainly includes the preparation of the network and the generation and filtering of routes.

A network is derived from a nationwide network including zones with socio data such as the number of residents. From flood simulation packages, such as SOBEK[b], the degradation process of the road network can be evoked. Routes will be generated and filtered using a discrete choice model (Multinomial Logit). This requires a finite set of alternative routes to be identified before the simulation starts. A set of candidate routes is first generated using an accelerated Monte Carlo simulated Dijkstra algorithm. These candidates are then filtered to remove routes that have large overlap ratios or unfeasible detour ratios [7]. The dynamic travel demand is represented in demand matrices (time based on departure) that apply to an interval (departures take place equally over time within an interval).

3.3. *Traffic Assignment*

The first run performed by the simulation framework is a static assignment for each interval. This way, a first indication is obtained for the travel times on the network, which are needed to apply the route choice model. The static assignment is followed by a dynamic assignment for the reference situation, see Figure 2. In this situation the optimal routing strategy takes place as if the area is not at risk of flooding. The reason this assignment takes place, is to be able to compare the first disrupted network state. At the end of the iteration process (loop 2 in Figure 2) a table with travel times, over all routes and intervals, is

---

[a] MADAM is OmniTRANS' implementation of a macroscopic dynamic assignment model
[b] SOBEK is a powerful 1D and 2D instrument for flood forecasting, Delft hydraulic software

stored. After the reference run a new run will start for every network state in time (loop 1 in Figure 2). Every network state will produce its one cost table.

Because of the simulation approach used in the modeling framework, little is known about the existence of a unique, global optimal routing strategy. The degrees of freedom for the assignment problem are such that the optimal strategy cannot be expressed mathematically. Local optima might exist and it is possible that the starting strategy has a significant influence on the solution found for a network state. One approach to deal with this could be to use the same starting point for each network state, for example by assuming route choice for all intervals to be based on free flow travel conditions. However, this approach would always require at least three iterations to get towards a stable state. Therefore, another approach is used: the first iteration routing scheme is based on the dynamic network conditions of the last iteration of the previous network state (previous run). This can be done because the disruption of the network is cumulative: once a link has failed, it is unlikely that it becomes available again at a later time during the evacuation.

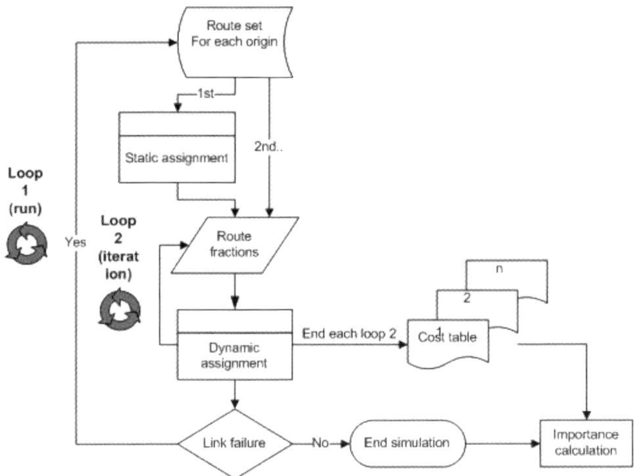

Figure 2. Model framework

4. Link Importance

When a link becomes unavailable, the conditions on the network do not have to aggravate by definition, which is known as Braess' Paradox [8]. However, due to the high amounts of traffic for evacuation scenarios, it is believed that removing a link from the network will always lead to a less optimal circulation pattern. This reduction in network performance is due to two factors. First, there are the vehicles that can no longer travel on the failing link and, therefore, have to switch towards another, longer route. Secondly, due to these `new travelers', the alternative routes will be more heavily loaded and travel conditions will aggravate on these links. These higher order effects are especially likely to occur in congested situations. Hence, for acute evacuations, the failure of a single link might have significant impact on a large portion of the network.

The cost tables produces at the end of each run are used to make a comparison between the resulting flow patterns for all network states. In general, the increase in vehicle time can be taken as a measure of impact. In this study, link importance is defined by:

$$I_n = \frac{TTT^{(n)} - TTT^{(n-1)}}{TTT^{(0)}} \tag{1}$$

$$TTT^{(n)} = \sum_l \sum_{ij} \sum_{r \in R^{ij}} x_{nlr}^{ij} \cdot c_{nlr}^{ij} \tag{2}$$

$TTT^{(n)}$ is the Total Travel Time for run n, x_{nlr}^{ij} is the number of vehicles for network state n travelling from zone i to zone j, starting in interval l and using route r. Symbol c_{nlr}^{ij} refers to the corresponding travel time.

Formulae 4 and 5 are based on the idea that link importance cannot be expressed by an absolute number. Instead, to express the `value' of a failing link, the importance equation is based on the relative increase in car-minutes between two network states relative to the car-minutes in the reference situation, $TTT^{(0)}$. By measuring all network states to the reference case, values are comparable among network states. Moreover, the importance values can be summed to get a 'cumulative' importance for a series of network states to express the increase in car-minutes.

5. Conclusion and Remarks

The research described in this paper aims for the proposal of a planning and analysis tool as being the first step towards computing road network vulnerability for a feasible acute evacuation strategy. Evacuating people during the course of slowly proceeding disasters is possible by optimizing the usage of the available time before the disaster affects the road network. This requires good understanding of the availability and location of routes and insight in the consequences of link failure for the evacuation flow. For this purpose a dynamic evacuation model is built in OmniTRANS using the StreamLine Framework (MaDAM propagation model). The model incorporates dynamic traffic assignment based on `real-time' and future information about the road network conditions, multi-routing, and exhibits a link vulnerability approach based on demand weighted time increase. The results from preliminary runs show 'realistic' optimizing travel behavior, however, complete and full runs of a 'real' case are not yet available but are ongoing at the moment of writing.

References

1. L. Issacharoff, S. Lämmer, V. Rosato and D. Helbing, Critical Infrastructures Vulnerability: The Highway Networks. Managing Complexity: Insights, Concepts, Applications. Springer Berlin/Heidelberg (2008) pp. 201-216.
2. S.A.N. Mevissen and M.v. Maarseveen, Vulnerability and Link Importance of a Road Network during Mass Evacuation - Proposal for a new approach for emergency situations. 10th TRAIL Congress and Knowledge Market 2008, Rotterdam (2008).
3. J. Husdal, Reliability and vulnerability versus costs and benefits. European Transport Conference 2004, Strasbourg (2004).
4. E. Jenelius, T. Petersen and L.-G. Mattsson, *Transportation Research Part A: Policy and Practice*, Vol. 40, No. 7, Importance and exposure in road network vulnerability analysis. 2006, pp. 537-560.
5. S.A.N. Mevissen and P. Kant, Acute Evacuation on Disrupting Networks. International Conference on Evacuation Modeling and management, The Hague (2009).
6. M.J.P. Mens, M. v.d. Vat and D. Lumbroso, A comparison of evacuation models for flood event management Application on the Schelde and Thames Estuaries. In: Samuels, P., Huntington, S., Allsop, W.andharrop, J. (eds.): Flood Risk Management: Research and Practice. Taylor & Francis Group, London (2009) pp.
7. M.S. Fiorenzo-Catalano, *Choice Set Generation in Multi-Modal Transportation Networks*. Delft University of Technology/TRAIL, Delft (2007).
8. D. Braess, *Unternehmensforschung*, Vol. 12, Uber ein Paradoxon aus der Verkehrsplanung. 1969, pp. 258-268.

DIGITAL CONTROLLER MODELING, SIMULATION AND DESIGN USING LOGIC NEURAL NETWORKS

MONICA LEBA, EMIL POP

System Control, Applied Informatics and Computer Engineering Department,
University of Petrosani, Str. Universitatii, 20 Petrosani, 332006, Romania

In this paper a new approach on digital controller modeling, simulation and design using logic neural networks is presented. First the logic neuron and its logic function are introduced. Then, there is written the logic equation for the logic neural network, which allows the easy modeling, simulation and design of any digital controller directly from the truth table. This solution is validated through MatLab Simulink modeling and simulation and then is presented the possibility to be implemented in a VLSI chip using VHDL hardware description language. This method has the advantages of simplicity and flexibility and represents an easy to use modern solution for both modeling-simulation and design.

1. Introduction

A digital control system is described by truth tables or logic and timing functions. For example, a logic function with 3 variables called u_0, u_1 and u_2 has the truth table of $2^3=8$ lines that generate eight logic terms as shown in figure 1.a. The terms selection is made through other logic variables x_i, i=0.7, for which the output y=1. In figure 1 the output y is given by the equation (1), where "·", "+" and "‾" represent the AND, OR and NOT logic operators.

$$y = \overline{u_2} \cdot \overline{u_1} \cdot u_0 + \overline{u_2} \cdot u_1 \cdot u_0 + \overline{u_2} \cdot \overline{u_1} \cdot \overline{u_0} \tag{1}$$

Analyzing the truth table there can be noticed that each column achieves a logic commutation from 0 to 1 with increasing frequencies from 2^0 to 2^2. This commutation can be represented using bi-positional switches, as presented in figure 1.b. According to the truth table results the diagram from figure 1.c. This diagram can be simplified if there are switches with the same value of inputs, as shown in figure 1.d.

606

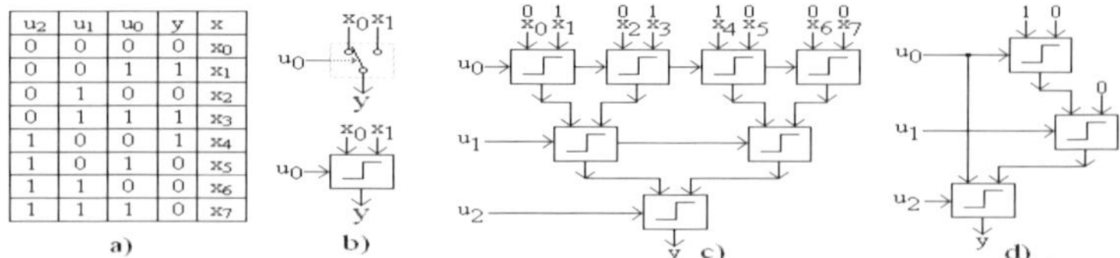

Figure 1. Commutation diagram: a) truth table; b) neuron representations; c) logic neuron network; d) simplified network

From figure 1.c and figure 1.d there can be noticed that these diagrams are similar to the neural networks, where each switch is a logic neuron with one output and three inputs, two used for learning and one for control, but the commutation is done by a logic equation.

The neuron was defined by McCulloch-Pitts as an element having n inputs x_1, x_2, ..., x_n and one output y characterized by the real values: w_1, w_2, ..., w_n as weights, a threshold function θ for firing and the time periods t_1, t_2 ,..., t_n for operation [3].

The neuron is fired if:

$$\sum_i x_i \cdot w_i \geq 0 ; \quad y(t + t_i) = \theta\left[\sum_i x_i \cdot w_i\right] \tag{2}$$

Generally, the inputs $x_i=1$ (i=1,2,...,n), the weights w_i (i=1,2,...,n) are positive for neuron activation and negative for inhibition. A neural network is a connection between a number of neurons having several inputs and several outputs. In figure 2 are presented some examples of neural structures.

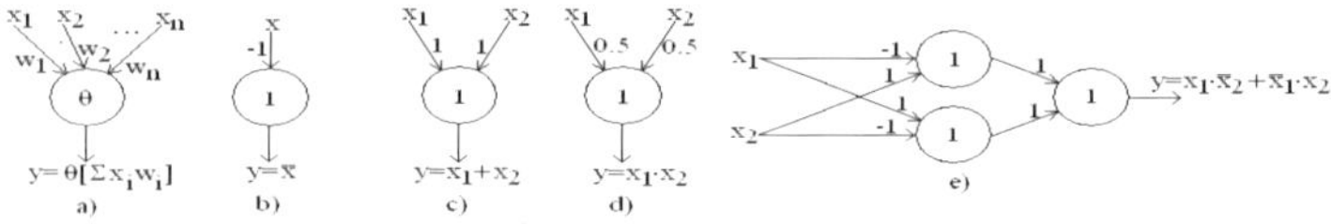

Figure 2. Neural structures: a) neuron; b) NOT; c) OR; d) AND; e) network for XOR

If we consider the threshold function as a step distribution, as follows:

$$\theta : K^m \to R; \qquad \theta[\varphi(x)] = \begin{cases} 1; & \varphi(x) \geq 0 \\ 0; & \varphi(x) < 0 \end{cases} \tag{3}$$

then, the classical neuron becomes the logic neuron presented above. So, the logic neuron models the bi-positional switch and has the logic function:

$$y = \bar{u} \cdot x_0 + u \cdot x_1 \tag{4}$$

Further in this paper, this element will be called logic neuron.

Depending on the input values x_0, x_1 and u_0 there can be obtained elementary logic functions, as shown in figure 3.a.

Considering the n control inputs neural network from figure 3.b, the logic function for this is [4]:

$$y = \overline{u_n} \cdot [\overline{u_{n-1}} \cdot \ldots \cdot \left(\overline{u_0} \cdot x_0 + u_0 \cdot x_1\right) + u_{n-1} \cdot \ldots \cdot \left(\overline{u_0} \cdot x_{2^{n-1}-2} + u_0 \cdot x_{2^{n-1}-1}\right)] +$$
$$+ u_n \cdot [\overline{u_{n-1}} \cdot \ldots \cdot \left(\overline{u_0} \cdot x_{2^{n-1}} + u_0 \cdot x_{2^{n-1}+1}\right) + u_1 \cdot \ldots \cdot \left(\overline{u_0} \cdot x_{2^n-2} + u_0 \cdot x_{2^n-1}\right)] \tag{5}$$

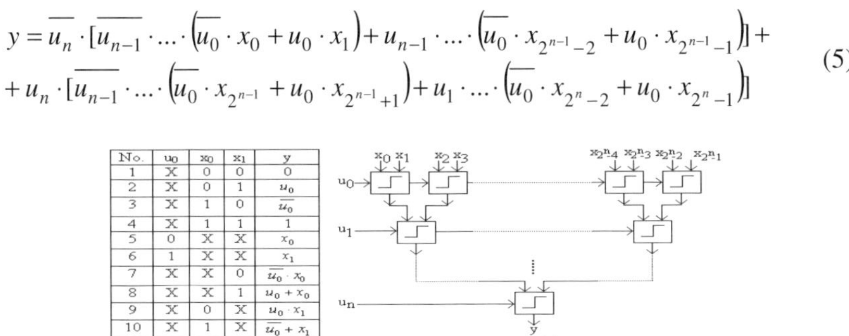

No.	u_0	x_0	x_1	y
1	X	0	0	0
2	X	0	1	u_0
3	X	1	0	$\overline{u_0}$
4	X	1	1	1
5	0	X	X	x_0
6	1	X	X	x_1
7	X	X	0	$\overline{u_0 \cdot x_0}$
8	X	X	1	$u_0 + x_0$
9	X	0	X	$u_0 \cdot x_1$
10	X	1	X	$\overline{u_0} + x_1$

a)   b)

Figure 3. a) Elementary logic functions; b) Neural network

The main advantages of this method are generality, flexibility and simplicity. This approach allows designing any logic structure, modeling, simulating and implementing using a hardware description language and a VLSI device.

2. Modeling, simulation and VHDL implementation of combinatorial systems

In this section, we will do the modeling, simulation and VHDL implementation of the bidirectional drive control. The classic circuit is shown in figure 4.a and the logic functions are:

$$KL = \overline{O} \cdot \left(PL + KL\right) \cdot \overline{KR}$$
$$KR = \overline{O} \cdot \left(PR + KR\right) \cdot \overline{KL} \tag{6}$$

These are necessary to build the simplified neural network diagram from figure 4.b.

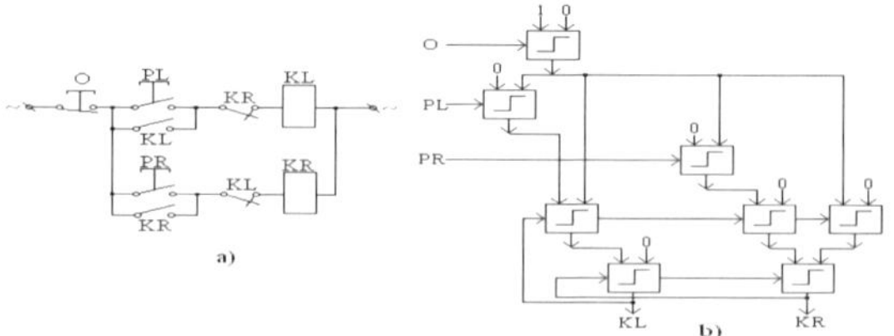

Figure 4. Bidirectional control of an electrical drive system: a) Classic diagram; b) Corresponding neural network

Next, the corresponding logic neural network from figure 4.b is modeled and simulated in MatLab-Simulink. In the model from figure 5.a, each logic neuron was separately implemented as a block diagram and then all the neurons were interconnected to build up the logic network. In figure 5.b are presented the simulation results.

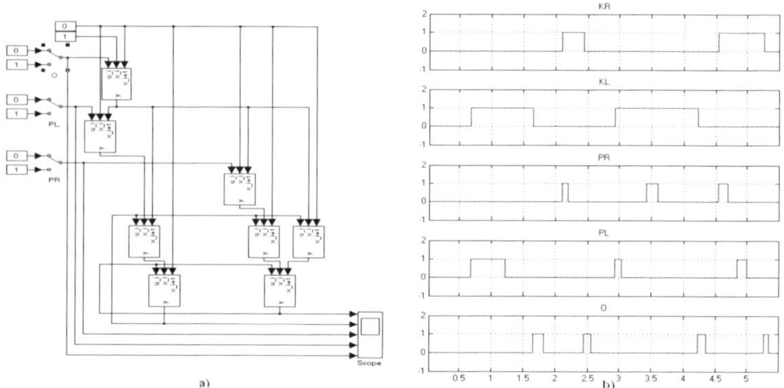

Figure 5. Bidirectional control: a) neural model; b) simulation results

From the simulation model there can be noticed the simple way of logic network achievement by a tree network of identical blocks. This represents a big engineering advantage for the VHDL hardware description language structural implementation [5].

Next, there is presented the VHDL implementation of the bidirectional drive control based on logic neural network principle.

The program has the structure elements declared as neur0, having one input, and neur1, having two inputs, as can be seen also from the RTL schematic diagram from figure 7.

```vhdl
library IEEE;
use IEEE.STD_LOGIC_1164.ALL;
entity neur0 is
    Port ( u0 : in STD_LOGIC;
           x0 : in STD_LOGIC;
           x1 : in STD_LOGIC;
           y0 : out STD_LOGIC);
end neur0;
architecture neur0 of neur0 is
begin
y0<=(not u0 and x0) or (u0 and x1);
end neur0;

library IEEE;
use IEEE.STD_LOGIC_1164.ALL;
entity neur1 is
    Port ( u0 : in STD_LOGIC;
           u1 : in STD_LOGIC;
           x0 : in STD_LOGIC;
           x1 : in STD_LOGIC;
           x2 : in STD_LOGIC;
           x3 : in STD_LOGIC;
           y1 : out STD_LOGIC);
end neur1;
architecture neur1 of neur1 is
begin
y1<=(not u1 and((not u0 and x0) or (u0 and
x1)))or (u1 and((not u0 and x2) or (u0 and x3)));
end neur1;

library IEEE;
use IEEE.STD_LOGIC_1164.ALL;
entity bidi0 is
    Port ( o : in STD_LOGIC;
           pl : in STD_LOGIC;
           pr : in STD_LOGIC;
           kl : out STD_LOGIC;
           kr : out STD_LOGIC);
end bidi0;

architecture structural of bidi0 is
component neur0 is
Port ( u0 : in STD_LOGIC;
       x0 : in STD_LOGIC;
       x1 : in STD_LOGIC;
       y0 : out STD_LOGIC);
end component;
component neur1 is
Port ( u0 : in STD_LOGIC;
       u1 : in STD_LOGIC;
       x0 : in STD_LOGIC;
       x1 : in STD_LOGIC;
       x2 : in STD_LOGIC;
       x3 : in STD_LOGIC;
       y1 : out STD_LOGIC);
end component;

signal a,b,c,d,e,f,g,h: std_LOGIC;
begin
a<='1';
b<='0';
uo:neur0 port map(o,a,b,c);
u1:neur0 port map(pl,b,c,d);
u2:neur0 port map(pr,b,c,e);
u3:neur0 port map(g,d,c,f);
u4:neur1 port map(g,h,e,b,c,b,h);
u5:neur0 port map(h,f,b,g);
kl<=g;
kr<=h;
end structural;
```

Figure 6. VHDL code for bidirectional drive control

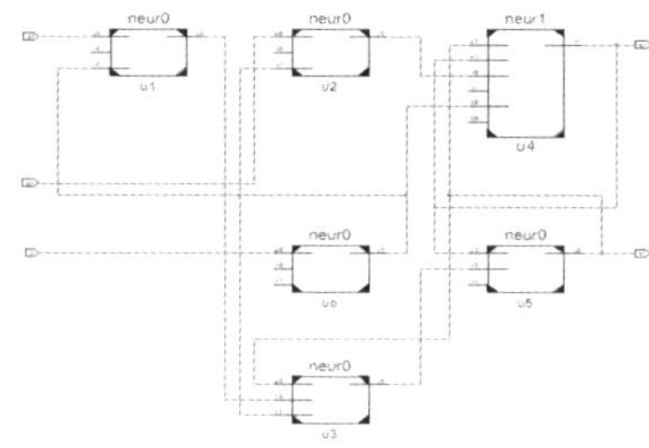

Figure 7. RTL schematic of the VHDL logic neural network

In figure 8 are presented the simulation results for the VHDL implementation of the logic neural network.

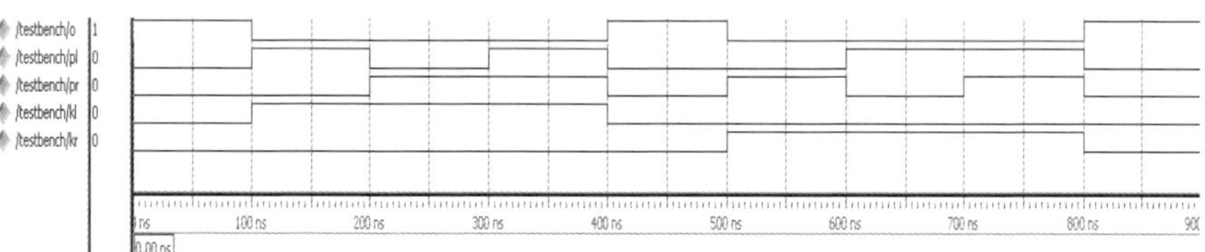

Figure 8. VHDL implementation simulation results

610

3. Modeling, simulation and VHDL implementation of sequential systems

In order to design complex controllers it is necessary to use sequential logic functions. For this reason we have to introduce the time dependent logic functions in the logic neural networks [2]. In this approach, the timing functions will be achieved using a two states state machine, as presented for the normal opened-timing on closing (NOTC) relay in figure 9.

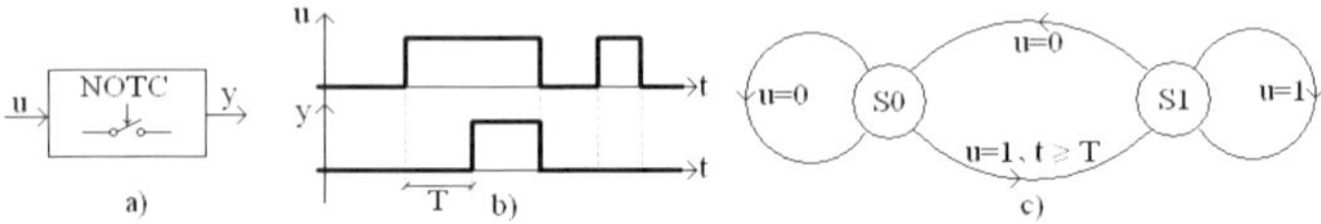

Figure 9. NOTC relay: a) block diagram; b) timing principle; c) state machine

Using the same principle it is possible to design the normal closed-timing on opening relay (NCTO), by simply inverting the output of NOTC relay. Also, based on the state machine principle there can be designed the normal closed-timing on closing (NCTC) relay and the complementary normal opened-timing on opening (NOTO) relay. Next, in figure 10 are presented the simulation waveforms for the NCTO and NOTC relays in VHDL.

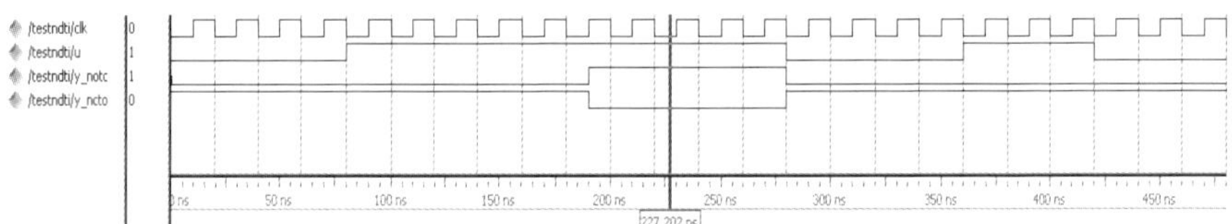

Figure 10. VHDL simulation waveforms

Next, we will implement a complex application using the neural approach for bidirectional star-delta drive control [6]. Using the push button O there is stopped the drive and using the push buttons PL and PR can be chosen the drive movement direction in star connection for a preset time. Next, the delta connection is establishes after braking the star connection for several milliseconds. The logic equations for the star-delta bidirectional control are [1]:

$$KL = \overline{O} \cdot (PL + KL) \cdot \overline{KR} \tag{7}$$

$$KR = \overline{O} \cdot (PR + KR) \cdot \overline{KL} \tag{8}$$

$$RTS = KL + KR \tag{9}$$

$$RTD = RTS \cdot RTS \downarrow \tag{10}$$

$$STAR = RTS \cdot \overline{RTS} \uparrow \tag{11}$$

$$DELTA = RTS \cdot RTD \downarrow \tag{12}$$

There can be noticed that the star-delta connection needs the use of timing NOTC ($RTS \downarrow$ and $RTD \downarrow$) and NCTO ($\overline{RTS} \uparrow$) relays. In figure 11.a is presented the MatLab-Simulink neural model of the star-delta bidirectional controller and in figure 11.b the simulation results.

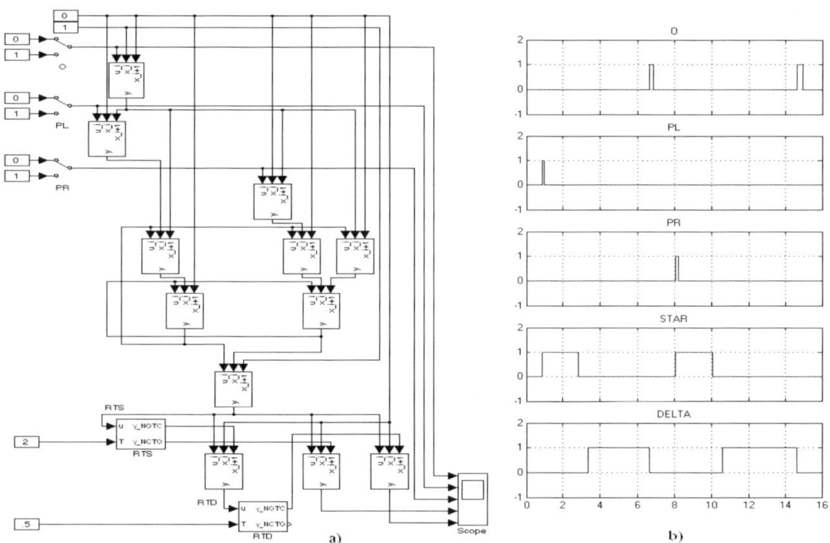

Figure 11. Star-delta control: a) neural model; b) simulation results

Next, there was implemented the star-delta bidirectional drive control as a logic neural network in VHDL language. In figure 12 are presented the simulation waveforms for the VHDL project.

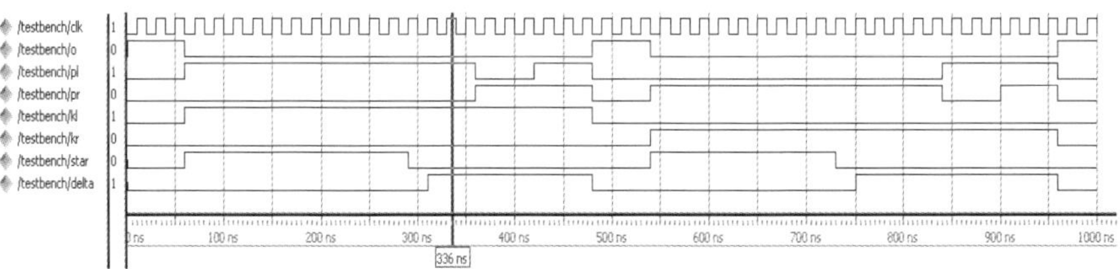

Figure 12. Simulation waveforms

4. Conclusions

First in this paper it is defined the neuron logic function as a particular case of the classic neuron. Then, is defined the general logic neural network as a tree structure. This structure is suitable for logic controller design and also for VHDL implementation. Next, there are presented through examples the possibilities to VHDL implement the combinatorial and sequential systems based on neural networks. As combinatorial example was presented the bidirectional drive controller and as sequential example the star-delta bidirectional drive controller. All the proposed solutions are validated through modeling and simulation first in MatLab-Simulink environment and then in VHDL ModelSim. This new method of logic neural networks controllers design is simple to use and ensures generality, flexibility and reliability.

References

1. E. Pop and M. Leba, Microcontrollers and PLC. *EDP*, Romania (2003).
2. E. Pop, Systems Theory. *EDP*, Romania (1983).
3. M. Arbib, The Handbook of Brain Theory and Neural Networks, *MIT Press*, USA (2003).
4. E. Pop and M. Leba, Digital Controller Design Based on Logic Neural Networks. *Proceedings of IFAC Workshop DESDES'09*, Gandia, Spain, pp. 186-191 (2009).
5. E. Pop, M. Leba, M. Pop, B. Sochirca and A. Badea, Software Based on Logic Neural Networks for Digital Controllers design. *Proceedings of the 8th WSEAS International Conference on CIRCUITS, SYSTEMS, ELECTRONICS, CONTROL & SIGNAL PROCESSING*, Puerto de la Cruz, Spain, ISBN 978 960 474 139 7, ISSN 1790 5117, pp. 168-173 (2009).
6. E. Edelhauser and A. Ionica, Software Solutions for the Romanian Underground Coal Mining, *Freiberger Forschungshefte Reihe C 526 - Geoingenieurwessen*, ISBN 978-3-86012-340-6, ISSN 0071-9404, pp. 31-38, Freiberg, Germany (2008).

THE INFLUENCE OF BARREL RIFLING TWIST ON THE STABILITY OF A PROJECTILE

IYD EQQAB MAREE

Department of Mechanical Engineering,
Erbil Technical College/Iraq Kurdistan Region
E-mail: aiyed67@yahoo.com

Most guns used today spin-stabilized projectiles. Spinning a projectile promotes flight stability. Spinning is obtained by firing the projectiles through a rifled tube. The projectile engages the rifling by means of a rotating band normally made of copper. The rotating band is engaged by the lands and grooves. In this paper we can prove that the stability of projectile is inversely proportional to rifling twist. To do this work a 105mm projectile is considered, first calculate the aerodynamics coefficient for projectile 105mm, then find the relation between the gyroscopic stability and the rifling twist. The rifling twist for projectile 105mm is 1/18 twist of rifling. The effect of rifling twist on gyroscopic stability was obtained by assuming a theoretical rifling twist rate, we note that with increasing the rifling twist the spin rate is decreased and this leads to a decrease in the projectile gyroscopic stability.

Keywords: projectile gyroscopic stability, spin rate and barrel rifling twist.

1. Introduction

The stability of projectile differs from the stability of aircraft and missile. The stability of a projectile is concerned with its motion following a disturbance from an equilibrium condition. In the vast majority of cases there is a distinct requirement for a projectile to be stable in flight so that it never deviates too greatly from its intended flight path following a disturbance. This has the benefit of reducing drag (yaw-depending drag) and also a reduction in dispersion of fire. We now need to be able to understand which physical characteristics determine whether a projectile is statically stable, unstable or neutral. Stability may be conferred on a projectile through the use of spin rather than fins, using a gyroscopic phenomenon known as a precession.

2. Spin Rate Effect

The spin rate of a spinning projectile is determined from the internal ballistics phase characterized by the number of turns per caliber, the barrel length, and the muzzle velocity [2]. In addition, the factors that affect how a projectile processes along the trajectory depend on the weight distribution of the projectile, its geometry and the location of the CG as shown in fig. (1) [3]. The amount of spin rate for a stabilized projectile is bounded by both the upper and lower bounds of the amount of spin which can be employed. The lower bound refers to the small amount of spin employed which consequently causes the projectile to tumble in flight when there is a disturbance. This is due to a rapid increase in precession causing the projectile to be unstable. On the other hand, when the upper bound is employed, the projectile spins too fast to resist any attempts to perturb it. It precesses so slowly that the nose does not follow the trajectory causing the projectile to land base first. In addition, using spin rates at both the upper and lower bound results in a shorter range. The effects of the spin rate can be seen in Figure (2).

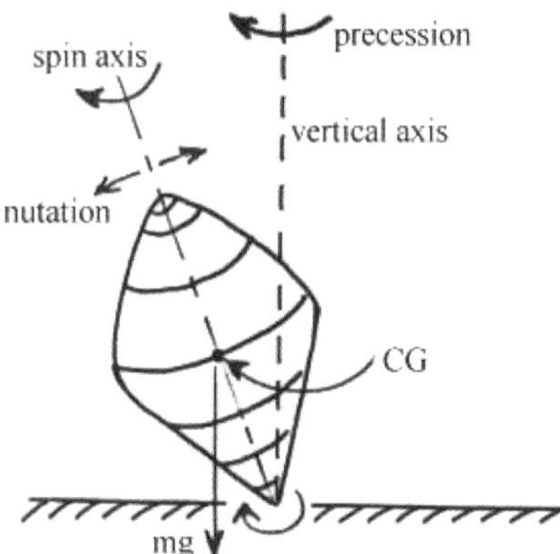

Figure 1. Gyroscopic Stabilization on a Spinning Top [see ref. 7]

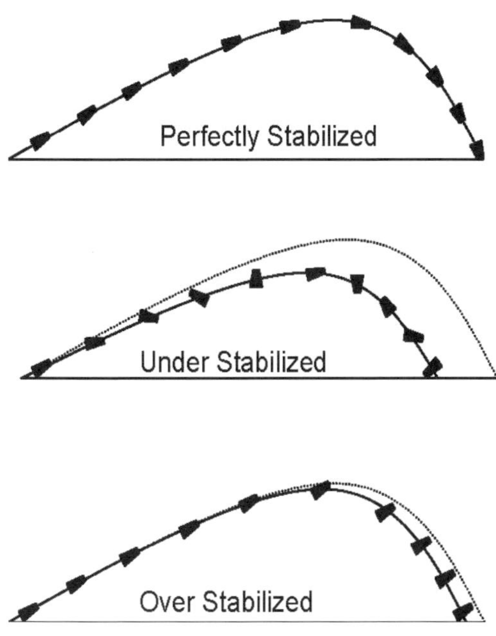

Figure 2. Spin Rate Effect on Stabilization

3. Initial Spin Rate Estimation

In order to have a statically stable flight for spin-stabilized projectile trajectory motion, the spin rate (p) prediction at the gun muzzle in the firing site us important. According to McCoy definitions, [1] the following form is used:

$$p = 2\pi V / nD \qquad (1)$$

Where
p : spin rate (rad/sec)
V : is the projectile velocity (m/sec)
n : the rifling twist rate at the gun muzzle(calibers per turn),
D: the reference diameter of the projectile type (m).

4. Prediction of Aerodynamic Coefficients

The aerodynamic characteristics of the 105mm shell have probably been studied more intensely than those of any other spin-stabilized artillery shell. Data at

616

small angles of attack were published [5] in 1955. Free flight measurement of the aerodynamic forces and moments were made in 1971-72, at angles of attack up to 35 degrees at subsonic speeds and up to 25 degrees at supersonic speeds. Also wind tunnel measurements of the aerodynamic forces and moments at subsonic speeds have been made [6] at various ratios of axial spin to forward velocity for all angles of attack up to 180 degrees. The aerodynamic properties used in present study are given in Table (1).

5. Gyroscopic Stability Simulation

Classical exterior ballistics [4] defines the gyroscopic stability factor Sg in the following generalized form:

$$S_g = \frac{I_{XX}^{\,2}\, p^2}{2\rho I_{YY} S_{ref} D V^2 C_{m\alpha}} \qquad (2)$$

Substitute equation (1) in equation (2) gives:

$$S_g = \frac{I_{XX}^{\,2}\, (2\pi V)^2}{2\rho I_{YY} (nD)^2 S_{ref} D V^2 C_{m\alpha}} \qquad (3)$$

Or

$$S_g = \frac{2 I_{XX}^{\,2}\, (\pi)^2}{(n)^2 \rho I_{YY} S_{ref} D^3 C_{m\alpha}} \qquad (4)$$

Since

$$S_{ref} = \frac{\pi}{4} D^2$$

So

$$S_g = \frac{8\pi I_{XX}^{\,2}}{(n)^2 \rho I_{YY} D^5 C_{m\alpha}} \qquad (5)$$

5.1 Simulation and Results

Equations (1) – (5) give the mathematical model for Stability of the projectile. The gyroscopic stability for projectile 105mm has been simulated for the following data with constant launch velocity 493 m/sec   and take the aerodynamic coefficient is taken from Table (1).

DATA

I_{YY}= 0.23118 kg.m^2 , D = 104.8 mm $\rho = 1.206\ kg/m^3$,   V = 493m/sec

I_{XX}= 0.02326 kg.m^2 $C_{m\alpha} = 3.75$

n = 17, 18,19,20,21,22,23,24,25 calibers per turn

The magnitudes of Gyroscopic stability factor calculated by eq. (5) and the magnitudes of spin rate are calculated by eq. (1). The magnitudes of Gyroscopic stability factor and spin rate are tabulated in Table (2). The effect of rifling twist on the gyroscopic stability factor and on a spin rate is shown in Figs. (A-1) and (A-2). From Fig(A-1) we note with increasing the rifling twist the Gyroscopic stability factor is decrease because we note from equation (5) the relation between them is inversely proportional. From Fig. (A-2) we note with increasing the rifling twist the projectile spin rate is decrease because the spin rate is proportional inversely with rifling twist according to equation (1).

Table 1. Tabulated Gyroscopic stability factor and spin rate of the105mm, Ml Projectile

n(calibers per turn)	p(rad/sec)	S_g
17	1738	3.5
18	1642	3.1
19	1555	2.789
20	1477	2.517
21	1407	2.283
22	1343	2.08
23	1285	1.903
24	1231	1.748
25	1182	1.61

Table 2. Aerodynamic Characteristics of the 105mm, Ml Projectile

Mach no.	0.46	0.61	0.78	0.925	1.09	1.5	2.5
C_{Do}	0.124	0.124	0.124	0.15	0.415	0.375	0.276
$C_{m\alpha}$	3.55	3.76	3.92	4.85	3.83	3.75	3.75
$C_{L\alpha}$	1.63	1.63	1.43	1.78	1.57	1.97	2.5

GYROSCOPIC STABILITY CALCULATION FOR 105mm PROJECTILES

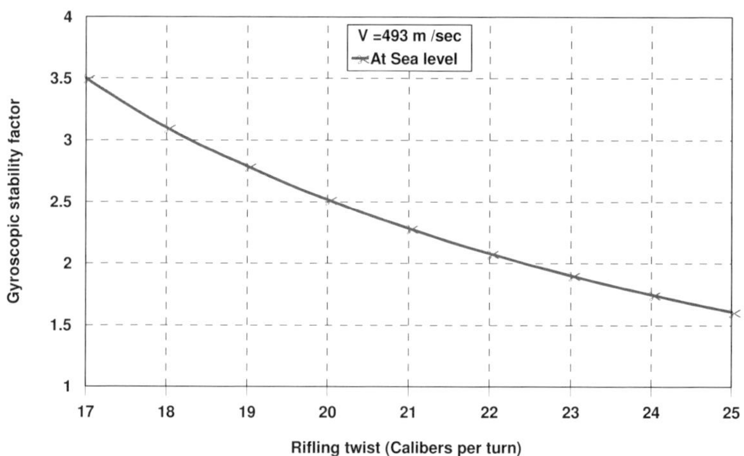

Figure (A-1) Gyroscopic Stabilty Factor VS. Rifling Twist

GYROSCOPIC STABILITY CALCULATION FOR 105mm PROJECTILES

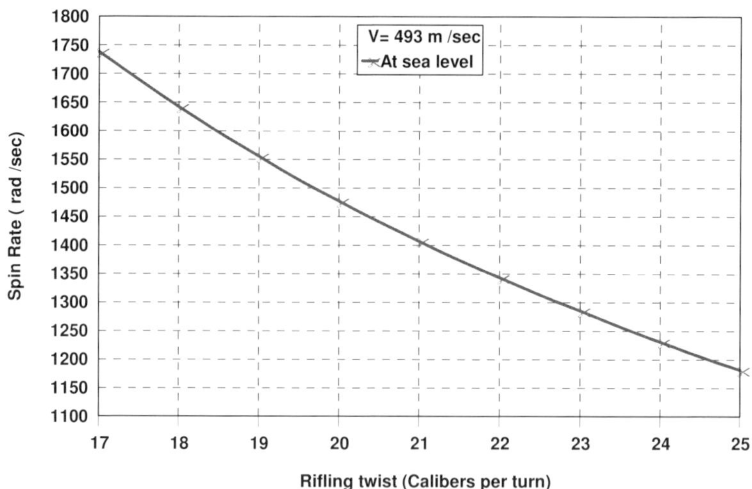

Figure (A-2) Spin Rate VS. Rifling Twist

6. Conclusions

- With increasing the barrel rifling twist the projectile spin rate will be decreased.
- With increasing the barrel rifling twist the projectile Gyroscopic stability will be decrease.
- A spinning projectile is made stable by static stability parameter $1.5 < S_g < 3.5$ Therefore we note from figure (A-1) the best barrel rifling twist for projectile 105mm is 18 twist because at barrel rifling twist 17 the projectile is in critical stablility.
- Many parameters affect the design of cannon barrel, one of them is rifling twist, therefore theoretically we can choose the best barrel rifling twist that satisfies the optimum gyroscopic stability ($1.5 < S_g < 3.5$) from Equations (1) – (5) that will be needed in the design of the cannon barrel.

References

1. McCoy, R. L. Modern exterior ballistics, Schiffer Publishing Ltd., Atglen, PA 19310, China, 1999. pp. 32-40.
2. Jankovic, S. (1979). *Aerodynamika Projektila*. "Aerodynamics of Projectiles" Masinski Fakultet, Univerziteta u Beogradu, Belgrade.
3. Rheinmetal GmbH, Dusseldort (1982) Handbook on Weaponry.
4. Dr. Slobodan Jankovic, S. (1977) SPOLJNA BALISTIKA, Univerziteta u Beogradu, Belgrade.
5. Braun, W. F., "Aerodynamic Data for Small Arms Projectiles," Ballistic Research Laboratories Report No. 1630, 1973.
6. McCoy, R. L., "The Aerodynamic Characteristics of .50 Ball, M33, API, M8, and APIT, M20Ammunition," Ballistic Research Laboratory Memorandum Report BRL-MR-3810, 1990.
7. Bray, Derek. "External Ballistics". Cranfield University, Shriven ham, accessed December 1, 2006.

THE EFFECT OF SPACE ENVIRONMENTS FACTORS ON SPACECRAFT STRUCTURE

SAFEEN YASEEN EZALDEEN

Assistant Professor
Mech. Eng. Department
University of Salahaddin / Iraq-Erbil

This work covers the investigation of the effects of the space environments factors on the spacecraft structure. The satellite operates on a low earth orbit at circular (500,500) km, and subjected to different torques in space environments. The purpose of this paper is to develop the satellite structure design and tested to obtain the mechanical behavior of structure. The satellite used so far is spin – stabilized, is rotating about one axis in 3rpm. A configuration to the structure is suggested to be octahedral. The dimension of structure is 110cm in diameter and 85cm high. The general static & dynamics tested of the system are verified, and analyzed to find the (stress, strain, and vibration) on the structure.

1. Introduction

A satellite structure must fulfill various requirements. First of all, must resist the loads induced by the lunch environment (acceleration, acoustics thermal). Met all the functional performances required on orbit such as dimensional stability for example. The concept must be compatible with the standard manufacturing process and use standard components (sheet-iron, tube,) every time it is possible. The spacecraft structure is a complex shape and cannot be described with the mathematical analysis. The use of finite element analysis software package such as NASTRAN makes it possible to model structures mathematically in detail.

The finite element analysis can sometimes lead to errors up to 40% in dynamic models. So the structural testing required to qualify an assembly for launch is often accomplished by subjecting a prototype to static and dynamic loads in excess of those anticipated for flight and actual unit is subjected to near flight levels. The experimental work is the best way to verify the theoretical models that will be developed in the other types. In the open literature there are several experimental setups and procedures for such task. [1, 2, 3, 4, 5, 6] are investigated these experimental setups and procedures of measurements.

The test rig constructed is an engineering model that built for a quarter scale flight model. The raw materials used for subsystem are tested, qualified, and accepted for low earth orbit Satellite. After system assembly, experiments were held to find the strain & stresses characterized were obtained by the strain test.

The natural frequency, amplitude, mode shape and transient response characterize the mode of vibration were obtained by the dynamic test.

2. Development Testing

The objective of he development tests is to assure that testing of critical items at all levels of assembly is sufficient to validate the design approach. A structural development test is also needed to verify the stiffness properties of the space vehicle and to measure member load and stress distribution and deflections in structures with redundant load paths.

2.1 *Structural Static Load Test*

This test demonstrates the adequacy of the structure to meet requirements of strength or stiffness, or both, with the desired design margin when subjected to simulated critical environments, such as temperature and loads, predicted to occur during its service life. The structural configuration materials and manufacturing processes employed in the qualification test specimens shall be identical to these of flight articles. Static loads representing the design limit load and the design ultimate shall be applied to the structure, and measurements of the strain and deformation shall be recorded. Strain and deformation shall be measured before loading, after removal of the limit loads, and at several intermediate levels up to limit load for post-test diagnostic purposes.

The test conditions include the combined effects of pressure, per loads and temperature. These effects can be simulated in the test conditions as long as the simulations envelop the failure modes and design margins. For example temperature effects, such as material degradation and additive thermal stresses can often be accounted for by increasing mechanical load [1].

2.2 *Dynamic Test*

This section presents the outline functions and the detailed procedure of the measurement techniques and instrumentation required for determining the experimental natural frequencies and the mode shapes of the developed test models. This test demonstrates the ability of space vehicle to withstand or, if appropriate, to operate in the design level vibration environment, which is the maximum level, imposed in flight plus a design margin.

Vibration shall be applied at the base of the adapter via fixture in each three orthogonal directions, one direction being parallel to the thrust axis. [1]. Also transient response tested in this research by changing the load with variable time. The vibration characteristics of the linear elastic structure (frequency and amplitude) can be described by means of the frequency response function. Which may be expressed in terms of magnitude, real or imaginary parts and phase angle? In this work, the two kinds of the testing methods: the steady state (pure sine or random) and the transient, had been used to measure the natural frequencies of the test structural model.

3. Structural Subsystem

The full duplex deployment simulation results can be achieved between full-scale prototype and a proper scale model if a PI-Number is derived throughway from the governing representative quantity [7]. The geometrical-similarity between the model and the prototype is achieved in this work.

The structural subsystem is responsible for construction of the (Beam, plates, tube) and joining them with (hinges, clamped) the structural subsystem consists of the following items are shown in figure (1). And table (1). Show the materials and dimensions of different parts.

Structural parts designed to remain rigid. The experimental data stet represented the characteristics of one continuous structure, which was manufactured and assembled with certain tolerances and tested under certain environmental conditions. Electrical motor of (3 rpm) is using to rotating the structure along the test, to simulate the satellite spinning. It's jointed to the structure at two positions in tube at medium and lower plates by two bolts in each position.

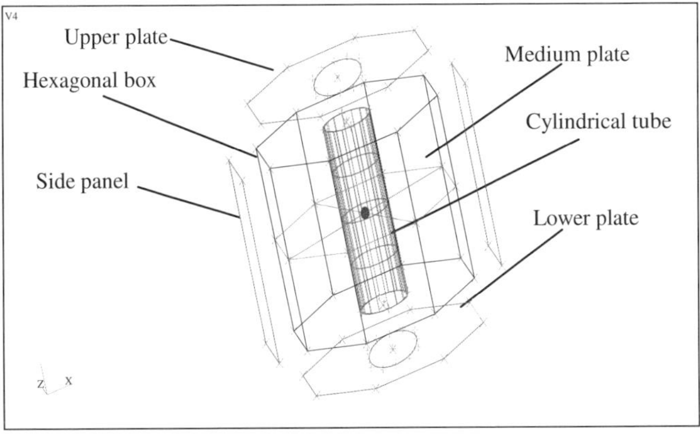

Figure (1) Detailed design of the satellite structure

		Dimension			Properties			
		Length*width	t	ρ	E	G	υ	σy
Material	Type	mm	mm	Kg/cm^2	Kg/cm^2	Kg/cm^2		Kg/cm^2
AL 7075.T6	Plate	275x275	1	2.82	700000	260000	0.33	1050
AL 7075.T6	Plate	110x215	1	2.82	700000	260000	0.33	1050
AL 2012	Beam	15x15x110	1	2.82	700000	260000	0.33	1050
AL 2021	Tube	78x215	1	2.82	700000	260000	0.33	1050

624

4. Mathematical Model for Experimental

In this work the general equation of the model were used for calculating the strain, stress, vibration and all other deployment parameters. The strain is recorded by strain gage and analyzed using mathematical model developed from system characteristics. In this mathematical model, all static parameters were related directly to the strain. The dynamic characteristics at deployment were measured in two methods by frequency response and transient response. To build the complete mathematical model for experimental calculations many parameters affecting operation have been considered as follows:

(A) Static Load

The equivalent torque Te is given by

$$Te = Tg + Ts + Taer. + Tmag. \qquad (1)$$

Where:

$$Tg = gravitonal\ \ torque$$

$$Ts = Solar\ \ pressure\ \ torque$$

$$Tare. = Aerodynami\ c\ torque$$

$$Tmag. = Magnatisum\ \ torque$$

The total torque is less than one Newton per meter. The torque (1 N.m) is subjected to all parts of structure. The force that applied to the structure from thruster load is 10N, where subject to the structure in vertical and horizontal direction.

(B) Dynamic Load

The loads that applied to the structure are variable with time at transient analysis and depend on the change of satellite position in space during rotation about earth, where effects the solar pressure and geomagnetic are changed. In the frequency response analysis, the forces depend on the variable of frequency was effects on the structure were subject the structure to the range of frequency (0-25 Hz) depended on the theory analysis.

5. Test Models

The experimental programmed carried to investigate the static and dynamic behavior. Two various test set-ups were used. The first model is Static instrumentation as shown in figure (2) for measuring the strain of the structure at different parts. The second model is Vibration instrumentation, for measuring the transient response and frequencies response of the structure at variable loads with time and variable frequencies. The experimental apparatus used for the measurement of the free resonant frequencies and mode shapes, of the developed structure model, is shown schematically in fig. (3).

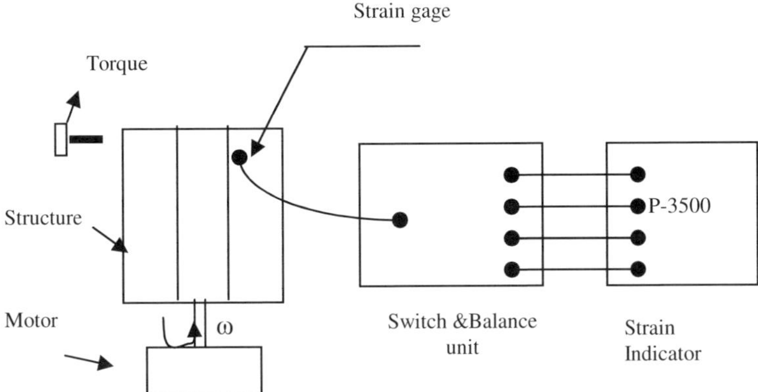

Figure (2) The test setup for the static measurement

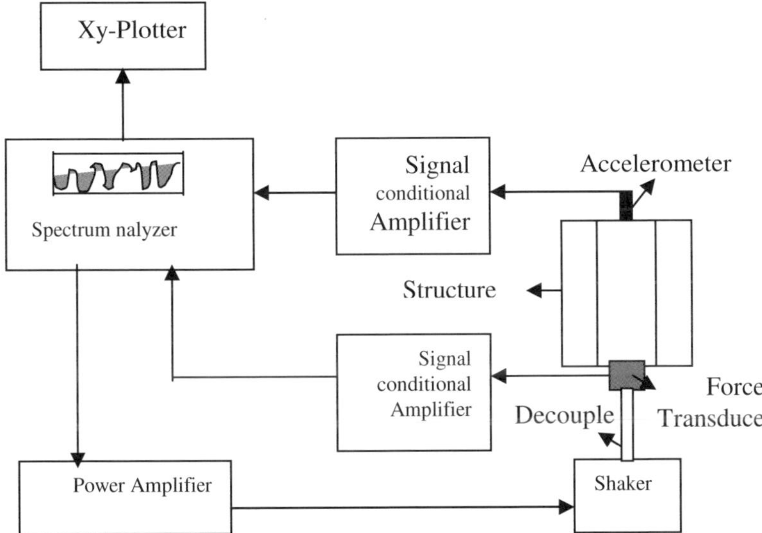

Figure (3) Block diagram of the testing instrumentation and apparatus applied for the steady-state and transient methods

5.1 *Test Procedure and Experimental Results*

The objective of this section is to give a test procedure adopted to give accurate values of the strain, stress, natural frequencies of the prepared structure model. The procedure required that the structure, under test, be excited by a loads and the response at various points be measured. In order that all test results may be compared meaningfully, the test procedure must establish homogeneous conditions throughout all stages of the work. Thus, the method used for supporting the structure, during each turn of the experiment, should be simple to set up and reproducible.

5.2 *Static Test*

The first case is the test by the torque activated by weight attached to beam and joined with the structure by bolts. The change of the weight gives the variable torques at deployment. Strains are recorded and Von Misses stresses computed in the same manner as for static analysis. Figure (4) shows the Von Misses stress at different positions when the structure is subjected to a torque (1N.m).

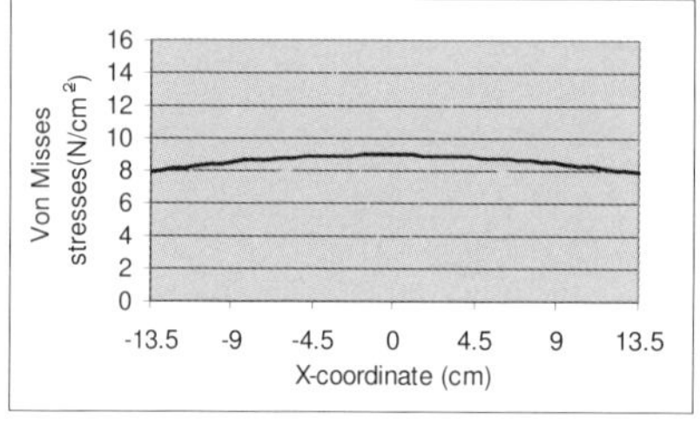
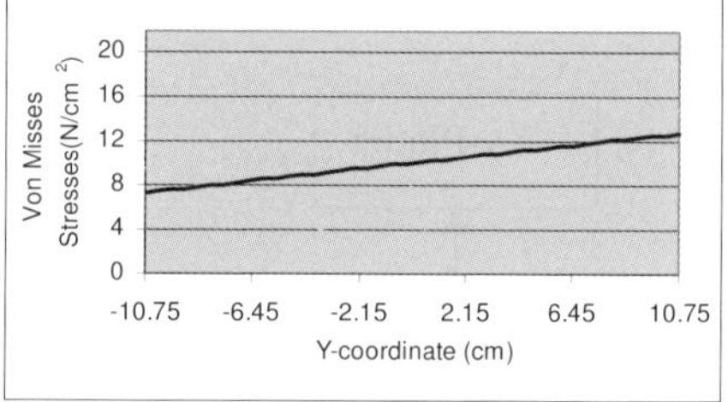

Figure (4) Von Misses stress along X and Y coordinate at subjected to torque (1N)

Second case is activated by weight attached directly to the structure to represent the thruster force in horizontal and vertical directions the strain gauges are connected to all parts of structure.

Figure (5) shows the Von misses stresses at different positions in horizontal & vertical directions of structure when the structure is subjected to the thrust load (10N) in X-direction. Figure (6) shows the Von misses stresses at different positions in horizontal & vertical directions when the structure is subjected to the thrust load (10N) in Y-direction.

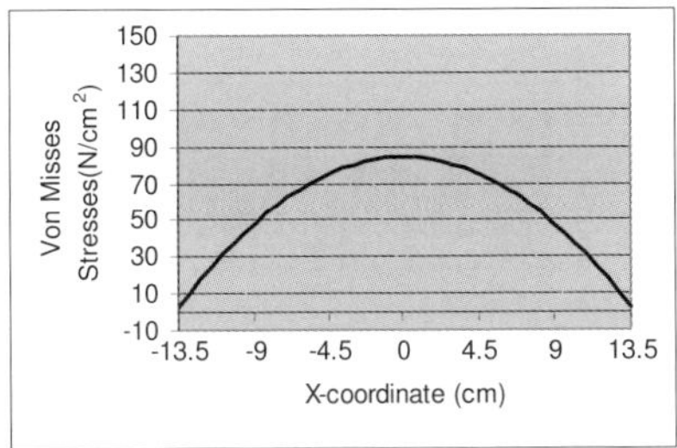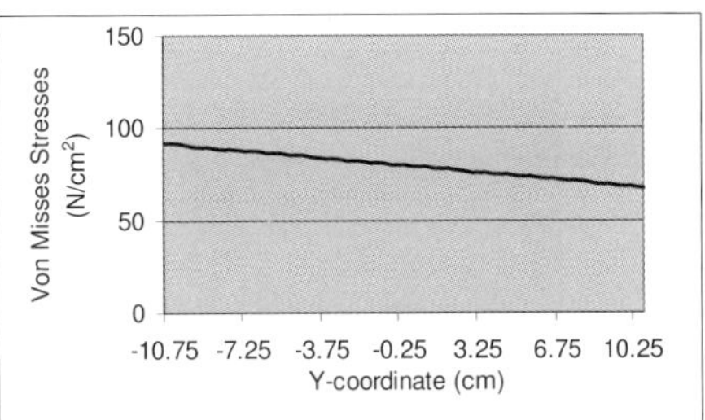

Figure (5) Von Misses stress along X and Y coordinate at thrusts load subjected in X direction

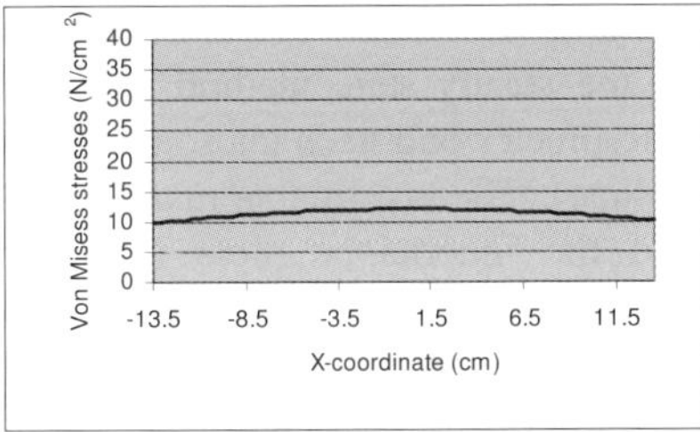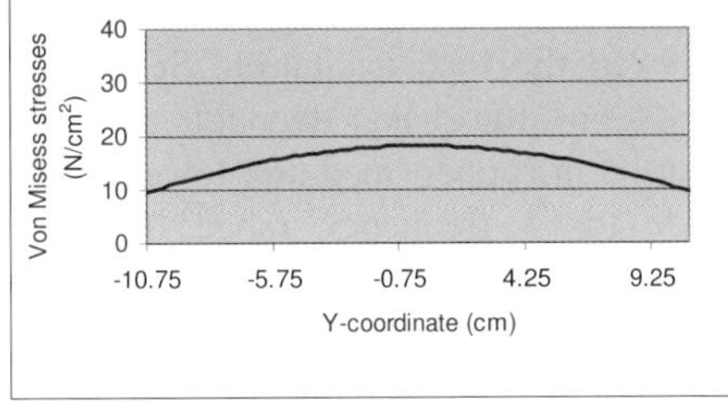

Figure (6) Von Misses stress along X and Y coordinate at thrusts load subjected in Y direction

5.3 *Dynamic Test*

The objective of this section is to introduce a test procedure adopted to give accurate values of the natural frequencies of the prepared structural model. The procedure required that the structure, under test, be excited by a force and the response at various points be measured. In order that all test results may be compared meaningfully, the test procedure must establish homogeneous conditions throughout all stages of the work. Thus the method used for hinged structure, during each turn of the experiment. An arbitrary choice of the point of excitation could lead to difficulties in producing the resonant condition. Exciting the structure at a nodal point (where the vibration amplitude vanishes) would result in missing out the peak in the inheritance plot (magnitude or imaginary Vs frequency).

At first, the test was carried out to verify the spectrum plot, imposed by transient excitation (Impulse force) at location and two different positions in (upper, medium, lower and side plane) of the response accelerometer. The entrance (magnitude and force excited) of selected positions on the upper and side plane of structure as varied within a selected time as shown in figure (7).

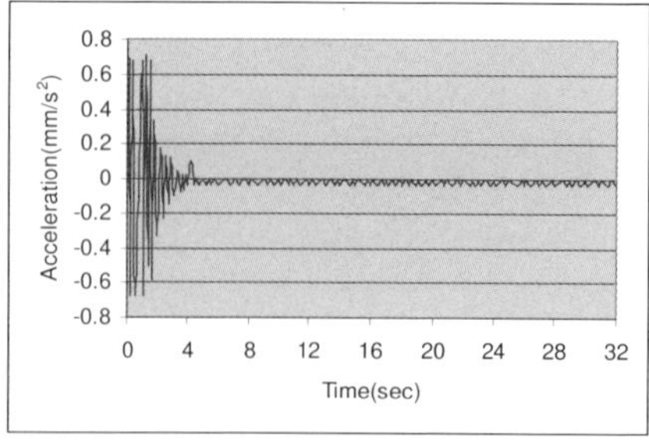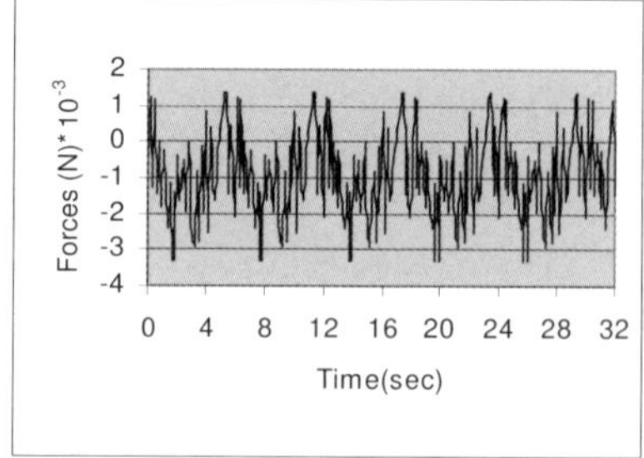

Figure (7) Transient Response and excitation force for structure

It is clear that the acceleration is at time impulse domain and to be vanished after removed the load excitation. Second, using the steady state method (random excitation), the shaker decouple and the accelerometer had been chosen to be at location in (upper, medium, lower and side plane). The test by this manner was made for a frequency range (0-25Hz) and the inheritance plots (absolute magnitude, imaginary) had been acquired, as shown in figures (8-A, B, C, and D). It is clear at all positions that be tested is the some of shape and small different in value in some parts but they are different with other parts.

6. Results and Discussion

From the stress levels at subjected torque (1N.m) at deployment configuration the upper plate suffers higher stress levels than another plates and beams. The critical areas were at hinge position; a (15) N/cm^2 stress was detected for Von misses stresses, a level of (-3.5) N/cm^2 was observed at side plate. When the structure is subjected to thruster force in x-coordinate, maximum stress occurs at the medium plat is (146) N/cm^2 and minimum at upper plate is (-49) N/cm^2.

When the structure is subjected to thruster load in y-coordinate, max. Stresses occur at side plane is (34) N/cm^2 and min. at bar is (-8) N/cm The stresses distribution in horizontal and vertical direction is different when the structure is subjected to (1N.m) the stresses from edge increases in horizontal-direction to mid plate, and return to the same shape in the other side, Such as sine shape. But in the vertical-direction the stresses is increased exponentially from bottom to top of structure.

When the structure is subjected to the thruster load in horizontal coordinate the stresses in the horizontal-direction takes the sine shape. But in vertical-direction the curve decreases exponentially from bottom to top of structure. When the structure is subjected to the thruster load in vertical coordinate the stresses in the horizontal-direction is the curve take approximate linearly.

When the structure is subjected to the transient force, the value of acceleration shown on the upper and side plate of structure is equal to $(0.7mm/s^2)$. The transient response in all structural parts is the same because it depends on the force excitation, mass and stiffness of structure. When the structure is subjected to vibration excitation, the acceleration of structure increases and became max. At frequency of 12Hz, and decreases to zero.

7. Conclusions

Structural design does not only encompass materials selection and configuration but must also include analyses and verification testing as part of the process, with an increasing reliance being placed upon analytical methods as experience grows.

1-The max. Stress occurs on center of upper plate when the structure subjected to 1N.m, and max. Stress occurs at center of medium plate when the structure subjected to thruster load in x-direction. And when the structure subjected to the thruster load in y-direction, the max. Stress occurs at side plane. The main characteristics obtained are to estimate the strain and stress at different parts and positions on the structure.

2-When the structure is subjected to transient load, the acceleration is changed with the excitation period and to be vanished after removed the load excitation. This change is not clear at different damping ratios because the impulse domain is very short time.

3-When the satellite is subjected to vibration excitation the resonance occurs approximately at 12Hz, and acceleration decreases to zero after this frequency. This indicates that the effect of low frequency is very important, and the vibration test must be conducted with this small range.

4-It was found that the magnitude is the same at all points on the same element (upper plate, medium plate, lower plate and side plate), but it differs from that measured another elements.

References

1. Military Standard "Test Requirements foe space vehicles" Department of Air force, Washington, D.C 20301, October (1982).
2. Report of NASA space vehicle design criteria (structures) qualification testing NASA sp-8044, pp 1-22 May (1970).
3. Report of NASA space vehicle design criteria (structures) qualification testing NASA sp-8045, pp 1-22. May (1970).
4. Hobbs A.J., Moore M.A., "Assembly integration and test report of British aerospace", PIC. CH20, PP 1-56.
5. Michael K., "Asoft 6-axis active vibration isolation", by spans, et al, presented at (1995) ACC.

630

6. Frank L. Knight, "The space Test program APEX mission Flight Results", (1996).
7. D.J schuning, "scale models in engineering" cal span corporation pergamon preset, (1977).

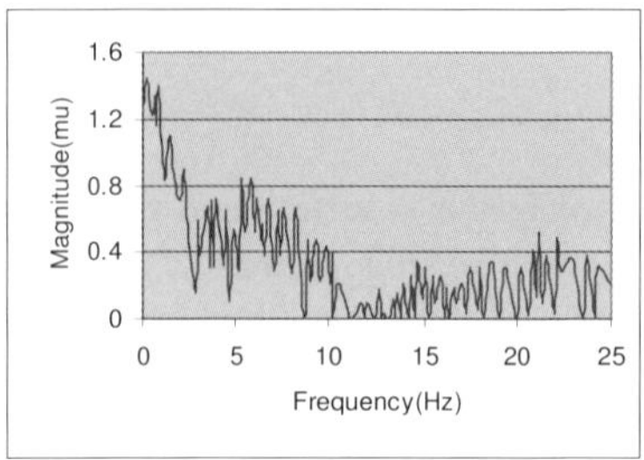
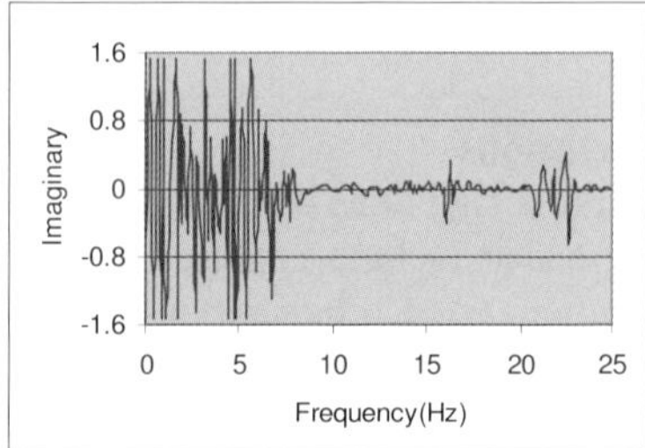

Figure (8-A) Frequency Response on the upper plate

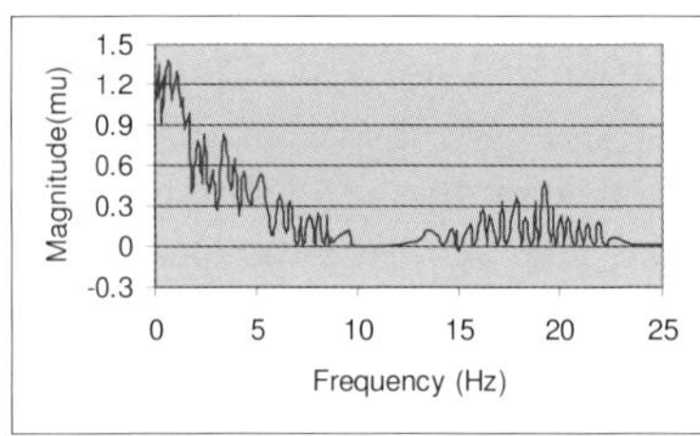
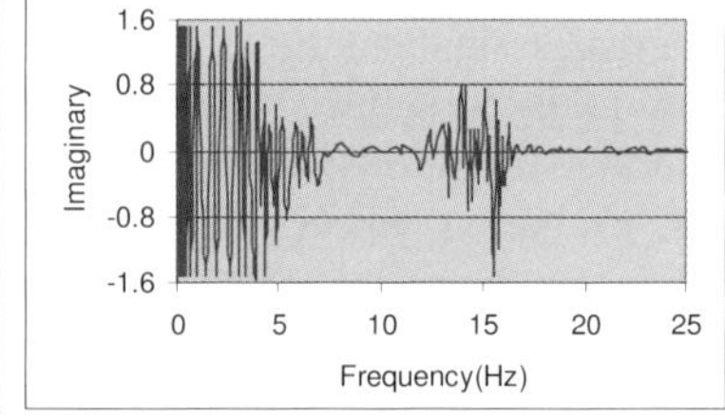

Figure (8-B) Frequency Response on the side plane

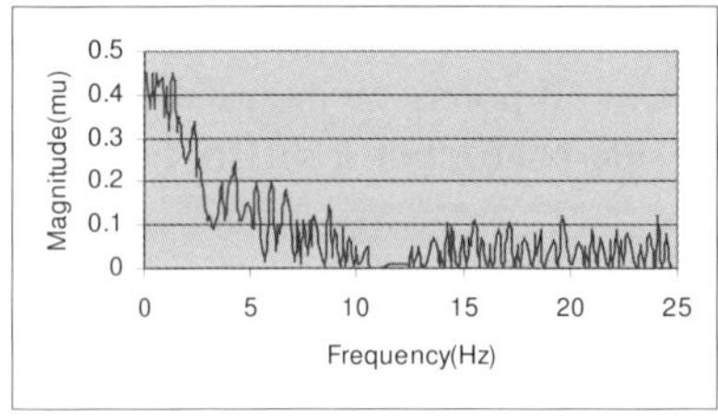
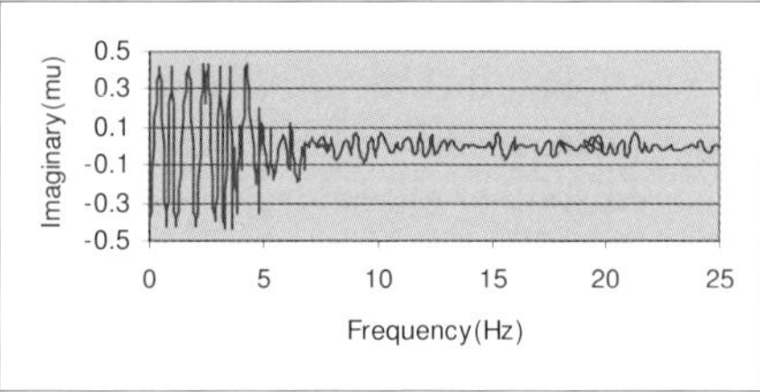

Figure (8-C) Frequency Response on the medium plate

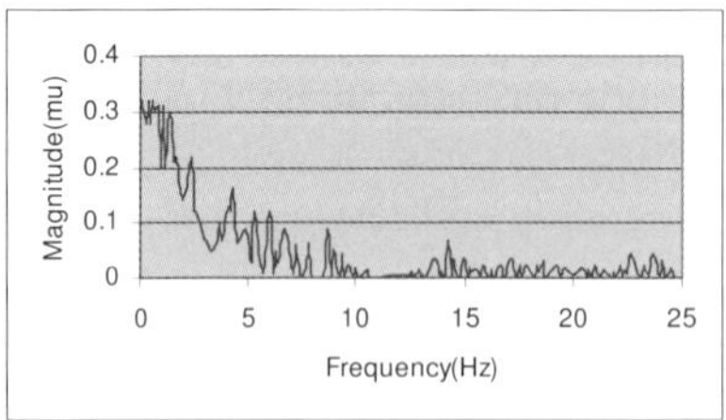
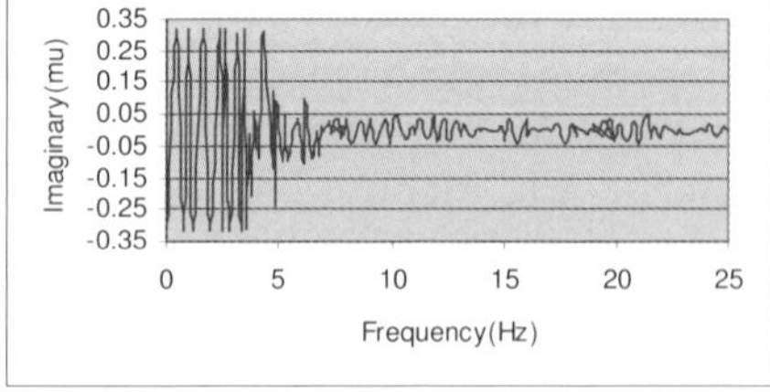

Figure (8-D) Frequency Response on the lower plate

THERMOMECHANICAL TREATMENT 0F 7020 Al ALLOY

SHAWNIM R. JALAL

College of Engineering, University of Salahaddin,
Erbil, Iraq

The effects produced by TMT on mechanical microstructural and stress corrosion resistance of 7020 Al alloys have been investigated. Choice of initial condition, the amount of deformation (0-5-10-15-20-25%) and temperature of deformation (room Temp., 170-190-210 °C) and the time and Temperature of the final age hardening sequence were found to be crucial in producing material with optimum properties. In general it was found that alloys should be age hardened to the peak hardness condition before deformation at an elevated temperature in order to promote homogeneous slip. Results of this study demonstrate that TMT of 7020 Al can generate a metal with YS and UTS equivalent to peak hardness condition and SCC resistance equivalent to the over aged T7 condition. With great improvement in KIC and optimum properties of the alloy was T6 +20% def at 190 °C + Age 160 °C for 3 hrs.

1. Introduction

Recently, considerable progress has been made in the development of some light materials, such as Al, but many difficulties have been encountered in their subsequent processing. Those difficulties usually arise due to the lack of knowledge of the behavior and properties of the material under the conditions encountered in the processing operation and heat treatment [1].

In the period beginning with the industrial revolution continuing well into 20th century, the various technological processes involving deformation and temperature were categorized according to the temperature of deformation, i.e. hot, warm, or called work. [2].

TMT is one of the most powerful tools of the alloy designer and that its full potential is yet to be realized. It means achieving high strength with good toughness and exfoliation corrosion resistance this treatment involves the simulation application of heat and a deformation process to an alloy, in order to change its shape, modify the microstructure and develop texture [2, 3]. In order to achieve this and even multi – staged heat treatment combined with mechanical deformation have been used with (deformation strain, aging time, and temp. were varied to optimize the size, shape and distribution of over aged precipitates [4].

632

Many studies[5-6-7-8-9-10-11-12] show that the properties of 7000 series Al alloys are obtained through a complex thermo-mechanical treatment, which starts with a solution treatment, quench, a plastic deformation to relieve quench stresses and followed with a multi – step aging treatment. This treatment combine plastic deformation with heat treatment, the purpose is to increase the dislocation density and to stabilize this configuration by precipitates that are nucleated along the lines of dislocations. The combination of precipitation and substructure hardening may enhance the strength and toughness with good SCC resistance of some alloys and this was the purpose of this research. However no report on the main mechanisms responsible for the relations between composition, formability and resulting properties has been published [13].

2. Experimental Procedure

Al alloy (7020) with chemical composition (0.35 Si, 0.20 Cu, 1.2 Mg, 4.5 Zn, 0.33 Mn, 0.40 Fe, 0.25 Cr, 0.05 Zr, Al Bal) used in this research. At the start it was important to select the solution annealing temperature which should be as high as possible but not too high to be in the vicinity of recrystallization temperature. So annealing temperature of this alloy is in the range of (470-500) [14]. Samples prepared from 7020 Al plate (10mm) thickness with dimension (25*130*10) mm annealed at 500°C then solution heat treated at 480°C for 30 min within the single phase regions (α) then quenched and aged at 120°C for 24 hrs. to reach peak hardness (T6) followed by deformation at different %(10,15,20,25%) at (room temperature, 170, 190, 210°C) and then aging at 160°C for 3 hrs, deformation occur by using small rolling machine(rolling is common thermo-mechanical treatment, which plays an important part in the processing of various compositions of many steels and Al) [3] .

Samples for tensile tests were prepared from annealed, quenched, aged, and deformed % as show in figs. (1, 2, 3) in a direction parallel to the rolling direction according to ASTM standard [15]. Brinell hardness HB5 of the samples for all conditions was measured fig.4. Also the notched bar impact test samples were prepared. The purpose of these test to assess the toughness of a material .The notched bar impact test (Charpy impact test) used since the magnitude of impact work is dependent upon the shape of sample.

The value of this result change slightly with deformation % and temperature as shown in fig. (6). the result of impact value used to calculate fracture toughness (KIC) by using the following empirical relation [16].

$$\left(\frac{KIC}{\delta_{ys}}\right)^2 = 0.64\left(\frac{CVN}{\delta_{ys}} - 0.01\right)$$

Where KIC ($Mpa\sqrt{m}$) is the plain-strain fracture toughness. CVN (Joul) is the Charpy v notched impact test value and δ_{ys} (MPa) is yield strength. The results of this test are shown in fig (7). It is reduced at (Room temperature, 170°C) deformation and increased with increasing deformation temperature (190, 210°C). Microstructure analysis along the rolling direction was examining also micrographs (1-2-3).

3. Result and Discussion

The result indicate that yield and tensile strengths of this alloy decreased with increasing deformation % as show in figs. (1, 2, 3) at high deformation temperature such as 170°C, 190°C, 210°C while it increased with low temp. such as (R.T). Because room temperature deformation after artificial aging increases the strength further but without sacrifice in ductility. Fig. (5). Deformation introduces a large density of dislocations in the material which can alter the precipitation sequence in a number of ways, either by heterogeneous precipitation on dislocation sites or by modification of bulk precipitation kinetics. Dislocations are always favorable nucleation sites for precipitates and short-circuit diffusion paths for solutes. This results in faster and coarser precipitation on dislocations. Moreover precipitation on structural defects naturally promotes the stable rather than the metastable phases, increasing deformation rate increases dislocation density which will enhance precipitation kinetics and consequently coarsen precipitation particle size]. The net result is a reduction in the mechanical properties i.e, yield, tensile strength and hardness. This reduction is pronounced when deformation at 210°C was applied and to less extent at 190°C.

At high deformation temperature particularly at 210°C overaging occurs much more rapidly and the metastable equilibrium does not persist, this is thought to indicate that the η stable phase is no longer able to survive so the yield and tensile strength, and hardness are reduced rapidly figs. (1-2-3), with improving ductility fig.(5). In this context, Deschamps et al [17] studied the influence of deformation on peak hardening and found out that it is negligible. This results mainly from the mixing law for adding the precipitates and dislocations contributions to the flow stress. This means that larger precipitates lay on dislocations does not influence the achievable peak strength because the volume fraction concerned is too small. The influence of deformation on precipitate coarsening appears to be a faster decrease in yield strength for 190°C deformation. This acceleration of precipitate coarsening is faster as the amount and temperature of deformation are increased.

Room temperature deformation slightly hardens this alloy. Hardness values appear to fall in a scatter band that shows an approximately linear increase, fig. (4), for hardness at intermediate temperature such as 170°C. The trend was less variation with deformation %. However for 190°C and 210 °C the curve indicates a more rapid fall off. Lu and WeIssmann [4] shows that if the alloy was deformed at a temperature below the GP solvus temperature (140 °C) for example, at room temperature, the deformation became highly localized resulting in an inhomogeneous distribution of dislocations characterized by widely spaced slip bands. In contrast, deformation above the GP, solvus temperature resulted in a homogeneous distribution of dislocations throughout the alloy, including regions adjacent to the grain boundaries and these dislocations and vacancies were effectively introduced in all grains of the specimen. The uniform dislocation structure was stabilized by the post–aging step. In this way, the process of nucleation of precipitation in denuded zones was accelerated and consequently, soft regions at grain boundaries and in the grain interior were removed. Thus the specimens treated by TMT contained a uniform stabilized dislocation structure. Figs. (6-7) indicates that increasing in deformation % at room temperature reduced impact value and fracture toughness with an increase in yield strength because the precipitation would be heterogeneous so the material more brittle due to stress concentrations at the boundaries a head of localized slip bands which favors crack nucleation and easy propagation.

In this context Deschamps et al. [18] showed that the presence of heterogeneous precipitation on slip bands also decrease the energy dissipated for intragranular failure. At high deformation temperatures (170, 190, 210°C) coarse intragranular precipitates probable inhibit the formation of macroscopic planar slip bands and thus decrease the proportion of brittle fracture mode.

It has to be emphasized that this fracture mode is ductile and dissipative since large local plastic deformation are involved. Thus it is not surprising to find the highest values of toughness shown in Fig. (7). when the alloy is deformed 20% at 190°C, micrograph (1).

In this context Dumont et al. [19] studied the relationship between microstructure, strength, and toughness. They found that, toughness is confirmed to be minimum at peak strength (T6) and modified for over aged condition. Also they described the evolution of toughness as a function of microstructure parameters, such as the volume fraction of precipitates (course or fine) on grain boundaries and the value of yield strength. The evaluation of fracture toughness is complex. However very little data is available, which contains simultaneously a detailed quantitative analysis of the microstructure and the associated mechanical tests in a wide range of process parameter situations [19, 20].

The main result of this investigation shows in Fig. (8) which indicate diagrammatically the sequence used for thermo-mechanical processing of this alloy. The dotted curve shows the normal aging response of Al alloys. The metal is used in the peak hardness T6 (micrograph 2) condition where stress corrosion cracking resistance is not required. For good stress corrosion cracking resistance the metal must be over aged to the T7 condition (micrograph3) where the yield stress is much lower but the large non-coherent precipitates promote good stress corrosion cracking resistance. The solid upper curve demonstrates the hardening response of the thermo-mechanically processed material. The, deformation step introduced at the T6 condition must occur at an elevated temperature in order to promote homogeneous slip as described. This deformation introduces an increment of strength which, upon further aging, is partially lost. In doing so the large non-coherent precipitates required for good stress corrosion cracking resistance are developed while the high dislocation density is retained, giving an increment of strength sufficient to maintain the T6 or the equivalent of T6 hardness or yield strength. It will be noted that the aging time to achieve an equivalent precipitate size is much less after deformation than without the deformation. Resulting in a much shorter aging time for thermo-mechanically processed materials.

4. Conclusion

1. The combined strengthening effect of the precipitates (from aging) and the high dislocation density (from deformation) during TMT added increment of strengths reach 6% to the already peak hardened material (T6 in 7020 Al alloy).
2. To avoid planer slip and impart homogeneous deformation to the, deformation can be performed at elevated temperature (warm working), in the peak hardness condition. The precipitates remaining from prior aging treatment are sufficient to pin the dislocations during subsequent aging .This prevents recovery and loss of dislocation density required to impart good properties to the TMT product.
3. The optimum temperature for the warm deformation treatment has been found to be at or just above the G.P. solvus temperature (190 $^{\circ}$C) where a transition from planer to random slip occurs.
4. It will be noted that the post aging time to achieve an equivalent precipitate size equal to T7 is much less after TMT process , it was 3hrs at 160 $^{\circ}$C, as compared to 24 hrs at 160 $^{\circ}$C for T7 condition for 7020 Al.
5. The optimum properties such as yield and tensile strength with good SCC resistance for the alloy was: T6+20%def. at 190 $^{\circ}$C +age 160 $^{\circ}$C for 3 hrs.
6. The effect of deformation on the precipitation is complex and depends on the amount and temperature of this deformation.

References

1. M. Gargali, B. Aksakal, (Effect of various nomoge. Sation treatment othe hot workability of ingot Aluminum alloy AA 2014), Materials science and Engineering, **A 254** (1998), PP. 189-199.

636

2. V. Zachay, (Thermomechanical processing). Materials science and engineering, **25** (1976), PP. 247-261.

3. P. Chandramohan, K. Manikanda Subramanian, P. Chandrasekar, (Rolling process with ohsas texture formation- Areview,) Engineering Science and Technology, **Vol. 4, No. 1** (2009), pp. 1-19.

4. L.P. Troeger, Edge A. starker, (New process produces superplastic aerospace / Automotive Al alloy), Advanced engineering materials, 2 (2000), PP. 802-806.

5. M.C. Lu, S. Welssmann, (The influence of aging and thermomechanical treatment on the fatigue properties of an Al – 6.55 Zn alloy). Materials science and Engineering, **32** (1978), PP. 41-53.

6. N.E Paton, A.W Sommer, (Influence of thermomechanical processing treatments on properties of Al alloys), proceeding of third international conference on the strength of metals and alloys, vol. 1 Cambridge, England, 20-35 August (1973) pp. 101-107.

7. D.S. Thampson, S. Levy, (Thermomechanical aging of Al alloys). Third international conference on the strength of metals and alloys, Vol. 1, Cambridge, England, 20-25 August (1973), pp. 119-123.

8. John M. Papazian, (The effect of warm working on Al alloy 7075 – T651), materials science and engineering, **51** (1981), pp. 223-230.

9. A. Deschamps. F. Livet, Y. Brechet, (Influence of pre-deformation on aging in an Al – Zn – Mg alloy – 1- microstructure evaloution and mechanical properties), Acta mater, **Vol. 47** (1999), pp. 281-292.

10. G.S. Murty and M.J. Koczak, (Investigation of region I of a super plastic Al – Zn – Mg – Cu – Mn alloys), materials science and Engineering, **96** (1987), pp. 117-124.

11. C.M. Wan, M.T. Jahn, T.Y. Chen, L. Chang, (The precipitation behavior in a thermomechanically treated Al – Zn – Mg alloy), materials science, **13** (1978), pp. 2059-2060.

12. A. Deschamps, M. Niew czas, F Bley, Y. Brechet, J. D Embury, L. Lesing, (Low temperature dynamic precipitation in a super saturated Al – Zn – Mg alloy and related strain hardening), published in : phil. Mag. **A. 79** (10), (1999), pp. 2485-2504.

13. M.J. Starink, N. Gao, N. Kamp, S.C. Wang, (Relation between microstructure, precipitation, age- formability and damage tolerance of Al-Cu-Mg-Li(Mn,Zr,Sc)alloys for age forming), Mater science Engineering, **A, Vol. 418**, 2006, pp. 241-249.

14. A. Deschamps, D. Solas m Y. Brechet, (Modeling of microstructure evolution and mechanical properties in age – hardening Aluminum alloys), published in microstructure, mechanical properties and processes, proceedings of Euromat 99, **Vol. 3,** munchen, Germany, (2000), pp. 121-132.

15. Annual book of ASTM standards, (Metallography, Nondestructive testing) part 11. (1978), pp. 49-50.

16. S. Missori, A. Sili, (Mechanical behavior of 6082 – T6 Al alloy welds), metallurgical science and technology 18 (2000), pp. 12-18.

17. A. Deschamps, Y. Brechat, (Nature and distribution of quench- induced precipitation in An Al– Zn – Mg – Cu alloy), scripta materialia, vol. 39. No. 11. (1998), pp. 1517-1522.

18. A. Deschamps, D. Dumont, Y. Brechet, C. Sigli, B. Dubost, (Process modeling of age – hardening Al alloys, from microstructures evolution to mechanical and fracture properties), published in proceedings of the James T. staley honorary symposium on Al alloys, Nov. (2001), pp. 298-305. Indianapolis, USA.

19. D. Dumont, A. Deschamps, Y. Brechet, (On the relationship between microstructure strength and toughness in AA7050 Aluminum alloy), materials science and Engineering, **A00**, (2003), pp. 1-11.

20. Joseph S. Santenez, (A study of fracture in high purity 7075 Al alloys), metallurgical transactions, A, (1978), pp. 769-779.

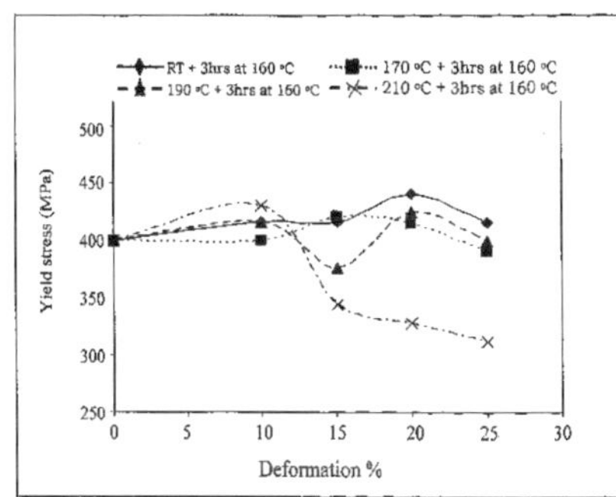

Fig. 1

The relation between yield stress & Def.% in 7020 Al alloys

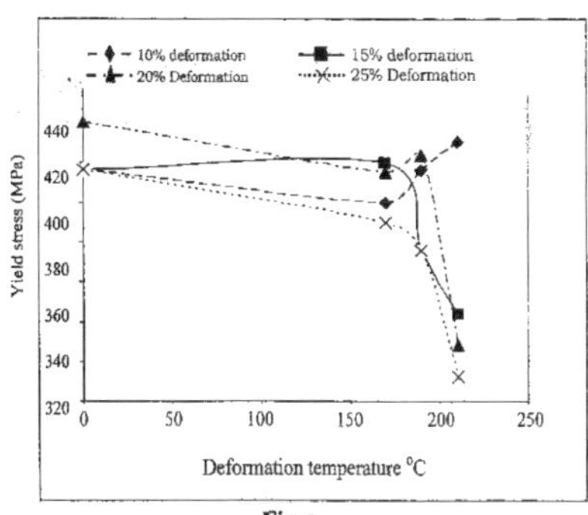

Fig .2

The relation between yield stress & Def. temperature °C in 7020 Al alloy

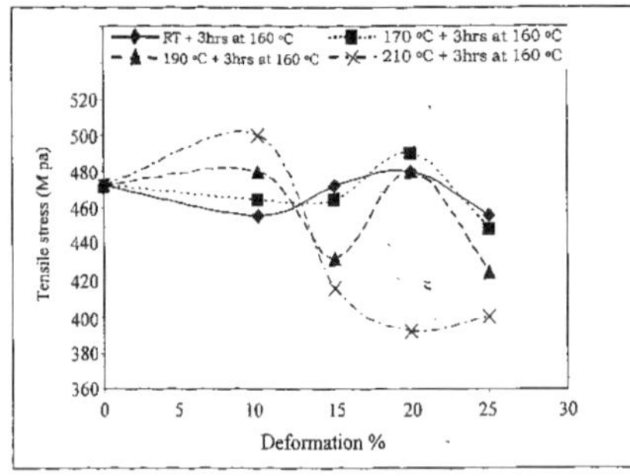

Fig. 3

The relation between tensile stress & Def.% in 7020 Al alloys

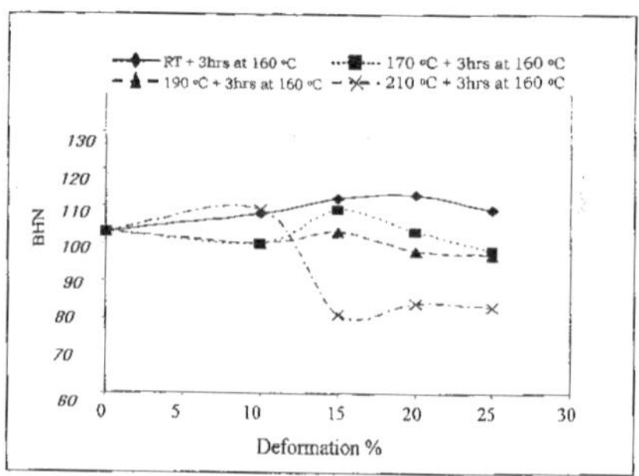

Fig .4

The relation between BHN & Def. %in 7020 Al alloy

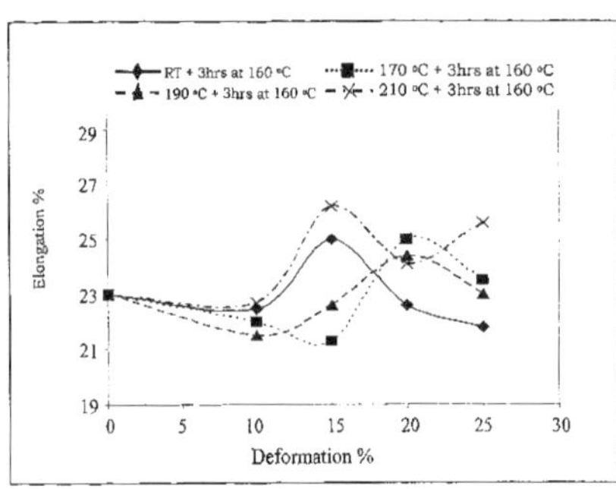

Fig .5

The relation between Elongatin %& Def. % in 7020 Al alloys

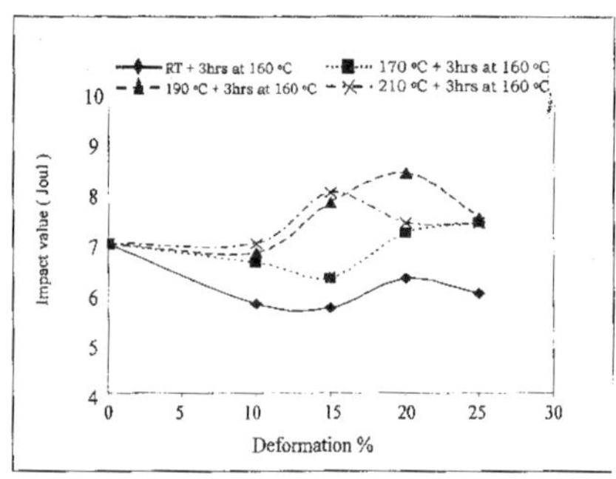

Fig .6

The relation between impact value & Def.% in 7020 Al alloy

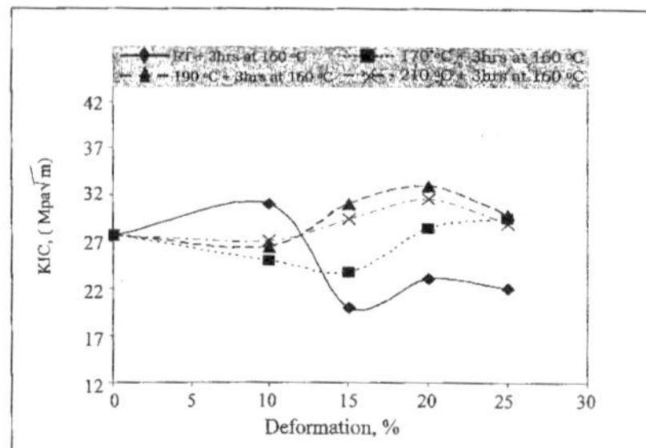

Fig . 7

The relation between KIC & Def.% in 7020 Al alloys

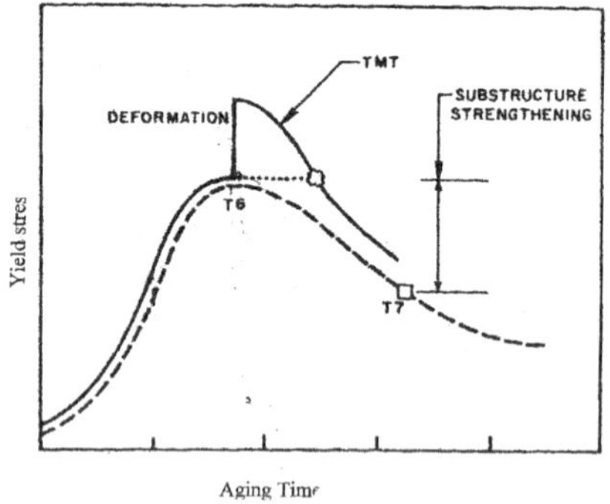

Fig . 8

Schematic Representation of TMT of Al alloys

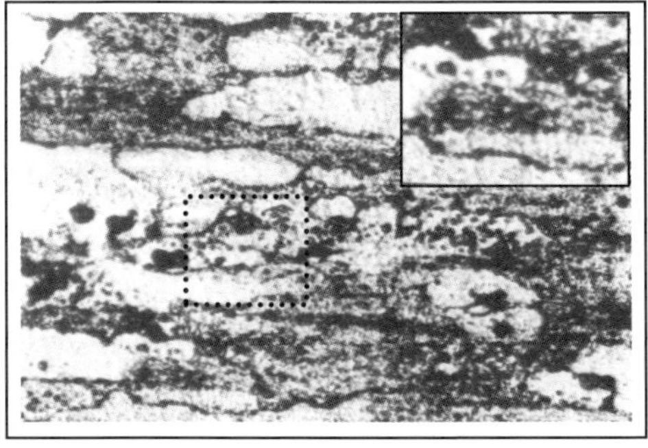

Micrograph (1)

7020 Al alloy at (20% def. at 190°C + age at 160°C for 3hrs.) causes grain growth with elongated grains, large black particles of insoluble element. 150X

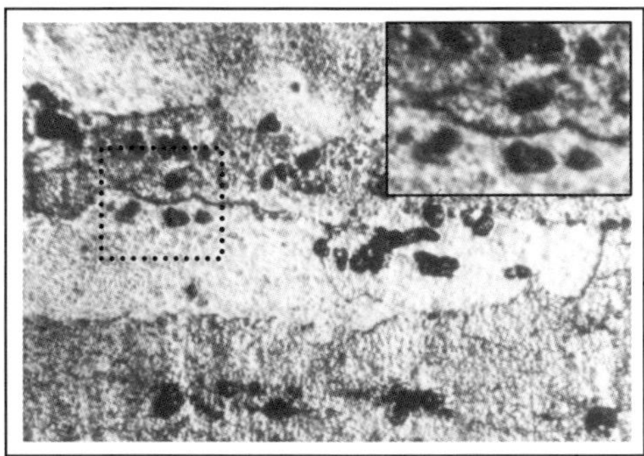

Micrograph (2)

7020 Al alloy in T6 condition (S.T at 480°C + W.Q + aged at 120°C for 24hrs. Grains are elongated, large particles are insoluble. Lack of grain contrast. 150X

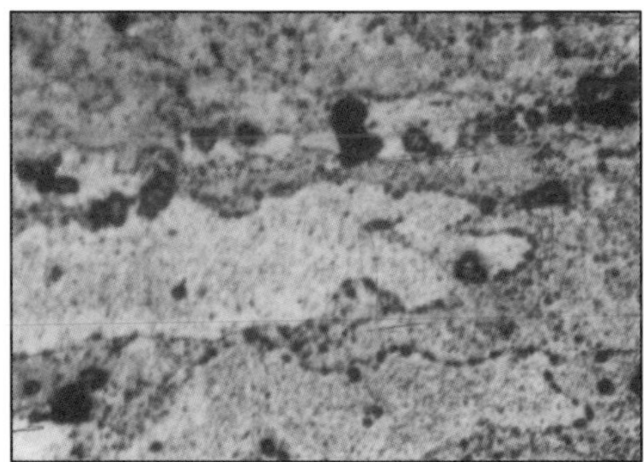

Micrograph (3)

7020 Al alloy at T_7 (over aged structure) large grains compared with previous photo (3-13), $MgZn_2$ has precipitated on grain boundary, large particles are insoluble phases. 150X

AGENT-BASED TEMPERMOD APPROACH FOR APPLICANT'S CHARACTER RECOGNITION

IEVA LAUBERTE, EGILS GINTERS

Sociotechnical Systems Engineering Institute, Vidzeme University of Applied Sciences, Cesu Street 4, Valmiera, LV-4200, Latvia

More and more researchers use agent-based simulation in various fields of social science, because agent-based modeling is a most natural way for describing and analyzing humans including their behavior, traits and emotions. One of this type models is TemPerMod, which is developed by Sociotechnical Systems Engineering Institute at Vidzeme University of Applied Sciences, and its purpose is to determine temperament type and mode of perception of applicant.

1. Introduction

More and more social psychologists use agent-based simulation. It is an alternative approach to theory building or third way of doing science in addition to traditional deductive and inductive reasoning [1].

The term "agent-based" refers to a particular type of simulation. Agent-based simulations have two essential components, agents, and environment [2]:

- An agent's behaviour is the result of rules based on local interactions.
- The environment has certain autonomy, i.e. it has a certain level of independence from what the agents do, but it can also be influenced by the agents' behaviour.

Agents-based simulation is one of the most exciting practical developments in modeling [3]. It can better capture the complex, dynamic, and interactive processes that are important in the real world [4].

Agent-based modeling has been gaining growing acceptance in various fields of social science, because offers a most natural way for describing and analyzing humans. Human behavior is complex emergent phenomena, therefore describing by mathematical equations is difficult. Agent-based modeling allows studying the outcome of the bargain in context close to the context of the market, considering heterogeneous agents characterized by evolving decentralized beliefs about their environment [5].

Daria Bartineva, Luis Paul Reis and Nuno Lau [6] proved that teams of the agents with different temperaments have different performances in the same simulation scenario. They used teams with 9 agents and analyzed homogeneous teams of Choleric, Phlegmatic, Sanguine and Melancholic agents and heterogeneous teams with different temperamental agents in the same team. To perform their test, they evaluated the agent's performance only depending of individual temperamental (physiological) configuration. They concluded that the temperamental decision mechanism strongly influences system performance.

Similarly to previous, Juan Martinez-Miranda and Juan Pavon [7] also used agent-based modelling for testing team's performance based on set of human characteristics. They proposed agent-based model TEAKS, which can assist project manager during the decision-making process for the configuration of work team. The virtual team can be configured using the characteristics of the real persons. The agent-based model TEAKS generates the possible performance of the team-members. Agents can be added or removed from the team. Once these modifications are introduced, new simulations can be executed to analyze the consequences and observe which team presents a better performance [7].

Apart from previous models, Michiaki Iwazume, Yuichiro Kato, Akihito Kanai [8] proposed a multi-agent model for analyzing recognition process of advertising information. They analyzed customer's recognition process of TV commercials from the viewpoints of audio-visual rhetoric and cognitive science. The multi-agent model makes clear the interaction between elements of customer's knowledge structure and the rhetorical characteristics of audio-visuals [8]. The model consists of sensory agents, monitoring agents, a working memory, high-order recognition agents and long-term memory agents.

Similarly to group work, also in e-learning systems it is important to know temperament and perception type of trainee, because it affects the results of training process and expected outlay. One of the methods to determine temperament type and mode of perception is agent-based model TemPerMod [9, 10], which is developed by Sociotechnical Systems Engineering Institute of Vidzeme University of Applied Sciences. It differs from the methods mentioned above, because the type of temperament and perception of trainee is recognized by agent-based simulation model instead of using traditional questionnaires like Keirsey Temperament Sorter (KTS-II) or Jung Typology test.

2. Agent-based Simulation Model TemPerMod

The model TemPerMod is created in NetLogo environment. NetLogo [11] is a multi-agent programmable modeling environment for simulating natural and social phenomena.

Agent-based simulation model TemPerMod is created for determining person's temperament type. Of course many different ways exist how to recognize the type of personality, temperament and mode of perception. Apart from traditional tests – questionnaires in written form, there are also other ones, such as [9]: color tests, painting tests, picture tests, figure tests, scenario test, handwriting analysis and even card game. However, usually people take questionnaires, but they are very long and irritating. Besides, applicant can manipulate with answers based on his/her mood. Therefore the elaboration of TemPerMod was launched.

The benefit of agent-based simulation is possibilities of estimation the all factors simultaneously reducing the chance of the applicant to manipulate with the answers [10].

For TemPerMod designing the following background is used:

- Galen's and Hippocrates (personality types) [12];
- Kersey's taxonomy (temperament types) [13,14];
- Susan Dellinger (psychogeometric) [15];
- Bandler and Grinder (Neuro-Linguistic Programming) [16].

The most popular classification of temperament, which is also the oldest one, was introduced by Greek physicians Galen's and Hippocrates. The four basic temperament groups $\langle T \rangle$ are sanguine, phlegmatic, choleric and melancholic. Other classification done by Keirsey [13, 14], who introduced the new types of temperament: artisan, rational, idealist and guardian, more emphasising professional suitability of the person, but the modern interpretation of temperament theory were introduced in 1984 by the Drs Phyllis and Richard G Arno[17]. They recognized one more temperament type – supine.

Every temperament type has its own specific colour $\langle C \rangle$ [18]:

- Sanguine – Yellow {c1} (the colour of adventure and artistry);
- Phlegmatic – Blue {c2} (the colour of cold clear: thought, logic and perception);
- Choleric – Magenta {c3} (the colour of intuition and transcendent);
- Melancholic – Red {c4} (the colour of authority and stability);
- Supine – Gray {c5} (the colour of neutrality and steadiness).

$$\langle C \rangle = \left(c_j \right) \text{ and } j=1,\ldots, 5 \tag{1}$$

According to Dr.Susan Dellinger, 83% of the time the shapes $\langle F \rangle$ you have just chosen will represent your primary and secondary personality [19]. These shapes are circle {f1}, square {f2}, triangle {f3}, rectangle {f4} and squiggle {f5}. Circle represents harmony, unity and balance. At the workplace circles tend to act more as stabilizers than leaders and they are happy to help resolving problems [20]. Square represents the structure. They are the most organized of all shapes and they are very tidy, logical and practical, focused and detailed. They are very slow decision makers [21]. Triangle represents ambition and high achievement. Triangles are goal setters, high achievers and decision makers. They are leaders, because they want to be in control and one of their strengths is the ability to delegate work to others [21]. Squiggle represents high energy, animation, sense of humor and creative intelligence. These kinds of persons are very creative, flamboyant, witty, but they are the messiest and least organized of all shapes [21]. Rectangle represents change and inner growth or transition. Similar as squiggle persons, they are incredibly messy and they have lack of focus. Rectangles are inquisitive and they often try new things, but they are not certain about their future [21].

The activity $\langle Act \rangle$ of the person is attributing of each type of the personality. Activities can be measured from static to very active and even chaotic.

$$\langle Act \rangle = \left(act_n \right) \text{ and } n=1,\ldots, 5 \tag{2}$$

The most important factor in training is perception $\langle P \rangle$ of the applicant. In conformity with the ideas of Bandler and Grinder (70-ties) related with Neuro-Linguistic Programming [16] at least three types exist – visual, auditory and kinesthetic. Visual {p1} person perceive information better from images, graphs and tables. Auditory {p2} person perceive information best by listening. Kinesthetic {p3} is a person with predominant sense. Of course, it is most difficult case of training.

$$\langle P \rangle = \left(p_m \right) \text{ and } m=1,\ldots, 3 \tag{3}$$

As mentioned above, people can be classified by type of personality or temperament $\langle T \rangle$. Each group has appropriate behaviour or activity $\langle Act \rangle$, corresponds to predefined colour $\langle C \rangle$ and form of the favourite objects $\langle F \rangle$. Also there are two favourite sayings $\langle S \rangle$ for each temperament group. Mottos $\langle S \rangle$ – Choleric person favourite sayings are "I always say that I think" and

"Win at any cost", but sanguine – "Here and now!" and "All the world's stage and the sun is my spotlight". Phlegmatic favorite sayings are "Peace at all costs" and "Let's be friends.", but melancholic – "Artist-Poet in search of kindred souls…" and "You have the problem, not me". The fifth temperament type supine slogans are "I answer to a higher authority" and "I will do anything in the world for you as long as you do not mistreat me":

$$\langle S \rangle = \left(s_i \right) \text{ and } i = 1,\dots, 10 \tag{4}$$

We can suppose that activity, colour, form and motto combine the set of attributes $\langle A \rangle$. Therefore the goal of the agent-based simulation model TemPerMod is recognizing the type of the personality $\langle T \rangle$ and the kind of perception $\langle P \rangle$:

$$\langle T, P \rangle \leftarrow A(C, F, Act, S) \tag{5}$$

The modeling desktop has the form of a pentagon. It is divided in five frames, where in each frame at the beginning of simulation cycle is equal amount of the agents, which have the same shape $\langle F \rangle$ and colour $\langle C \rangle$. Inside large pentagon has a smaller one. Each frame has the door to the inner pentagon. During the simulation cycle agents move with different speed of motion and step by step they can get in to smaller pentagon through the doors. The agent colour, form and activities are not critical for filling the inner pentagon, which is a random process. One simulation cycle is 100 ticks long. The length of the simulation session is 125 cycles, where one modeling cycle continues 8-10 seconds. Agents change shape, colour, behavior and position in every cycle.

3. Evaluation of Agent-based TemPerMod Approach

Like to other modeling techniques, the agent-based model TemPerMod has some restrictions:

- The model has only one purpose: to determine applicant temperament type and mode of perception;
- TemPerMod requires serious computing resources (otherwise there will be twitching while the simulation runs);
- The agent-based model TemPerMod is quite long (125 cycles in total), therefore is difficult to hold attention to simulation, especially for choleric ones.

646

The agent-based model TemPerMod was validated by Jung Typology test as one of most popular.

The testing sample involved 47 respondents [9]. The Jung typology test results showed that the most of respondents are melancholic ones, but the less sanguine. Otherwise, TemPerMod given the same result related with melancholic, but instead of sanguine prefers choleric as occasional. The TemPerMod matched with Jung Typology test identifying phlegmatic persons for 75% and testing melancholic persons for 71%. The comparison did not fit for sanguine and choleric groups.

4. Conclusion

The term "agent-based" refers to a particular simulation type, which have two essential components: agents and environment. Agents have certain autonomy. They can interact with other agents and they have capability to respond to the environment.

The TemPerMod model is created in the NetLogo environment and aimed to determining the type of person's personality, because traditional questionnaires are long and irritating.

The TemPerMod further will be improved focusing on reducing the session time and adding some more parameters. In the TemPerMod will be added some audio information, while the simulation runs, but removed some attributes thus reducing simulation time. The new colour map by Don Lowry [22] will be introduced. The TemPerMod will be validated for bigger amount of respondents.

In future version of the TemPerMod it will be possible to create and tune the custom agents of any temperament type and use them in simulation games stored in libraries of scenarios.

References

1. R.Axelrod, *Simulation Social Phenomena*, 21 (1997).
2. I.Lauberte, *Annual Proceedings of Vidzeme University College: ICTE in Regional Development*, 99 (2005).
3. C.M.Macal, M.J.North, *Proceedings of the 2007 Winter Simulation Confernece*, 95 (2007).
4. R.E.Smith, R.F.Conrey, *Personality and Social Psychology Review*, **11**, 87, (2007).
5. S.Moulet, J.Rouchier, *Post-Proceedins of the AESCS International Workshop 2005: Agent-based approaches in Economic and Social Complex Systems IV*. 33 (2007).

6. D.Barteneva, P.L.Reis, N.Lau, *Proceedings 21st European Conference on Modelling and Simulation*, 181 (2007).
7. J.Martinez-Miranda, J.Pavon, *International Symposium on Distrobuted Computing and Artificial Intelligence 2008*, 80 (2009).
8. M.Iwazume, Y.Kato, A.Kanai, *IEIC Technical Report*, **101**, 49 (2001).
9. I.Lauberte, E.Ginters, A.Cirulis, *Proceedings of the 11th WSEAS International Conference on Automatic Control, Modelling and Simulation*, 489 (2009).
10. I.Lauberte, E.Ginters, L.Novitsky L, *Proceedings of the 4th WSEAS/IASME International Conference on Educational Technologies: Education and New Educational Technologies*, 116 (2008).
11. Netlogo. http://ccl.northwestern.edu/netlogo/ (Accessed on 07.11.2009).
12. T.Chamorro-Premuzic, Personality and Individual Differences, BPS Blackwell (2007).
13. Wikipedia, Keirsey temperament sorter. http://en.wikipedia.org/wiki/Keirsey_Temperament_Sorter (Accessed on 16.11.2009).
14. D.Keirsey, Please Understand Me II: Temperament, Character, Intelligence, 1st Ed., Prometheus Nemesis Book Co. (1998).
15. S.Dellinger, Communicating Beyond Our Differences: Introducing the Psycho-Geometrics System, Jade Ink; 2nd edition (1996).
16. R.Bandler, J.Grinder, Frogs into Princes: Neuro Linguistic Programming, Moab, UT: Real People Press (1979).
17. Wikipedia, Five Temperaments. http://en.wikipedia.org/wiki/Five_Temperaments#cite_note-9 (Accessed on 15.11.2009).
18. R.Religa, Temperament Colors System. http://www.jedigirl.com/www/personality_types/temperament/index.html (Accessed on 06.11.2009).
19. S.Dellinger, Communicating Beyond Our Differences: Introducing the Psycho-Geometrics System, Jade Ink; 2nd edition (1996).
20. S.Dellinger, The Circle person. http://www.psychometricshapes.co.uk/circle.php (Accessed on 11.11.2009).
21. S.Dellinger, The Box person. http://www.psychometricshapes.co.uk/box.php (Accessed on 11.11.2009).
22. True Colors, What is True Colors. http://www.true-colors.com/whatistruecolors.htm (Accessed on 30.12.2009).

5 Gb/s LOW-NOISE AND HIGH BANDWIDTH 0.35 μm CMOS TRANSIMPEDANCE AMPLIFIER

ESCID HAMMOUDI[†], ATTARI MOKHTAR

Houari Boumediene University of Sciences and Technology,
Instrumentation Laboratory, BP.32, Bab Ezzouar 16111, Algiers, Algeria,
hescid@yahoo.f, attari.mo@gmail.com

Abstract: A low-noise and high-bandwidth transimpedance amplifier for 2.75 GHz has been implemented in 0.35 μm CMOS technology. The designed amplifier is configured on three identical stages that use an active load. This structure operates at 3.3V power supply voltage, displays a transimpedance gain of 531 Ω, exhibits a gain bandwidth product of 1.46 THzΩ and a low-noise level of about 12,764 pA/Hz$^{0.5}$, while operating with a photodiode capacitance of 0.4 pF. The predicted performance is verified using simulations tools with 0.35 μm CMOS AMS parameters.

Keywords: Transimpedance amplifiers; CMOS technology; low-noise amplifier; optical receiver; negative feedback.

1. Introduction

As motivated by the huge data transmission capacity for multimedia communications, optical communication systems, such as LAN (Local Area Networks) and FTTH (Fiber-To-The-Home), are booming today. The performance of the optical interconnection system depends on the receiver's gain, bandwidth, power consumption, and noise. These four parameters tend to trade-off with each other [1]. The front-end component of typical optical receiver generally is an amplifier. The typical amplifier generally requires a low-noise characteristic in order to achieve a good noise performance of overall receiver system. And the amplifier should operate a high of an input signal as possible without being saturated. To meet the noise requirement, two different types of amplifier architectures are available [2]. One is high input impedance amplifier for low noise, and the other is transimpedance amplifier using resistive shunt-shunt feedback (Figure 1.). The high impedance amplifier can provide lower noise, but bandwidth can be reduced significantly due to the longer input RC time constant, and therefore, another circuit like equalizer to compensate the bandwidth reduction. In contrast, the transimpedance amplifier has more noise due to feedback resistance but wide bandwidth and the design is simple. Furthermore, the transimpedance amplifier has wide dynamic range due to the higher saturation limit. Thus, transimpedance amplifier (TIA) architecture is widely used in optical receiver systems.

[†] Work partially supported by grant 2-4570.5 of the Swiss National Science Foundation.

650

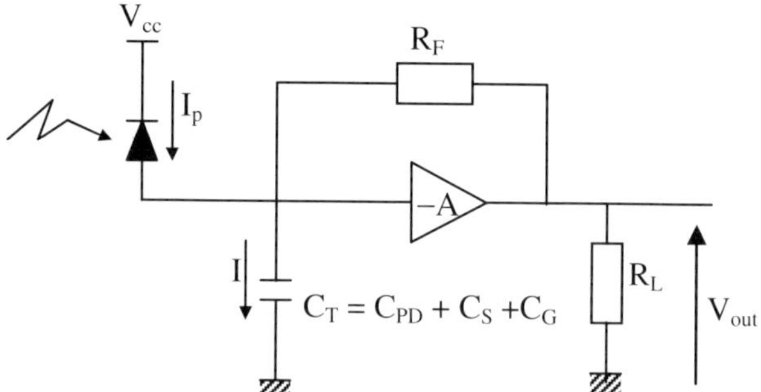

Figure 1 Closed loop transimpedance amplifier used in an optical receiver

Though the traditional TIA is designed using more expensive IC technologies such as silicon bipolar or GaAs MESFET, there has been an increasing interests in CMOS based implementation because of the demand for the lower cost and greater integration with digital circuits.

2. Design and optimization of the transimpadance amplifier

A push–pull inverter at the input is used to maximize the transconductance of the amplifier and increases its gain bandwidth product (GBP) [5]. An improved CMOS implementation of the transimpedance amplifier is presented in Figure 2.

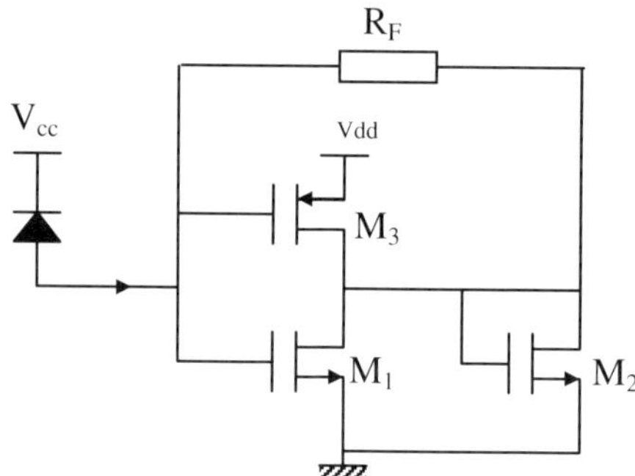

Figure 2 The proposed CMOS transimpedance amplifier

The transimpedance amplifier takes a current from the input and converts it into a voltage signal. The transistors M_1 and M_3 form the inverter while M_2 is added to increase the bandwidth and minimize the Miller effect. To design such an amplifier, by knowing that the gain can be approximated by the value of the feedback resistor, we evaluate R_F while estimating C_T. These two parameters will be used as starting point in the design. The gain of the inverter will be exploited in addition to the negative feedback, which will impose an increase in the gain. Thus, from the small signal model, the expression of the gain will be:

$$A_0 = \frac{V_{out}}{V_{in}} = \frac{g_{m1} + g_{m3}}{g_{m2}} \qquad (1)$$

The cut-off frequency at -3 dB is increased by the transconductance of M_2 as long as the gain is simultaneously reduced. The signal should be amplified through subsequent amplifiers because of the low-gain of the single amplifier stage. Then, we will have:

$$A_0 = \alpha + \sqrt{\frac{\mu_p}{\mu_n} \beta (1 + \alpha)} \qquad (2)$$

where : $\qquad \alpha = \frac{W_1 L_2}{W_2 L_1} \quad$ et $\quad \beta = \frac{W_3 L_2}{W_2 L_3}$

The complete improved transimpedance amplifier (Figure 3.) consists of three identical cascaded stages. We can use a resistor as a feedback or a PMOS transistor as an active feedback resistor biased by the voltage source V_G [10]. The feedback resistor will be determined using:

$$R_F = \frac{1}{\frac{W}{L} \mu C_{ox} (V_{GS} - V_T)} \qquad (3)$$

The bandwidth of the transimpedance is approximately equal to:

$$f_{-3dB} = \frac{1 + A}{2 \pi R_F C_T} \qquad (4)$$

The stability of the system is related to A, and the total gain of the system must be strictly controlled. It is equal to $A = A_0^3$, where A_0 is the open loop gain of one stage.

A conceptual optimization has been considered by taking the gain of a single stage of the transimpedance amplifier. An analysis has been carried out by introducing the different intrinsic capacitances at the level of each MOS transistor (Figure 4.).

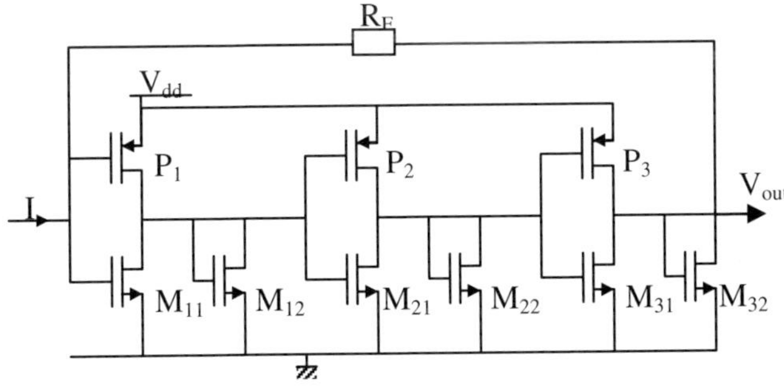

Figure 3 The proposed transimpedance amplifier with three identical cascaded stages

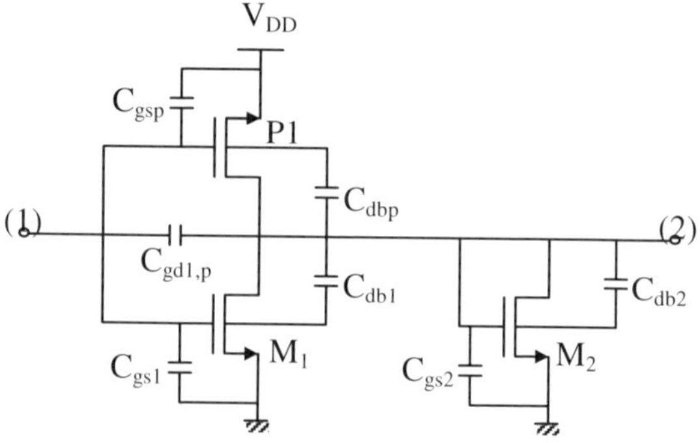

Figure 4 Different capacitances involved in the amplifier stage

The gain of each stage of our structure has the following expression:

$$A_0 = \frac{g_{m1} + g_{mp}}{2\pi(\gamma+1)NX_A C_1 f} \tag{5}$$

Where X_A is a factor ranging between 2 and 3 [10], $\gamma = C_2/C_1$, and N represents the number of stages.

Indeed, from Eq. (2). and using that giving Γ (the PMOS / NMOS mobility ratio of the Push-Pull inverter), we estimate the lower limits of the dimensions of the transistors constituting the inverter Push-Pull. After development, we get:

$$\frac{W_{n1}}{W_{n2}} = \frac{A_0^2}{1 + 2A_0} \tag{6}$$

and:
$$\frac{W_p}{W_{n2}} = \frac{\Gamma A_0^2}{1 + 2A_0} \tag{7}$$

To have the widest bandwidth possible, the transistor constituting the charge must has the smallest size possible. This requires us to choose W_{n2} in the limit of 0.35 µm process technology.

3. Noise analysis of the transimpedance amplifier

The equivalent noise power at the input node are given respectively by Eq. (8).

$$<i_{tot}^2> = 2qI_{obs}B + \frac{4KT}{R}B + 2qI_G B + \frac{8KT}{3}\frac{1}{g_m}\left[\frac{B}{R_e^2} + (2\pi C_T)^2 B^3\right] \tag{8}$$

where q is the electron charge, K is Boltzmann's constant, T is the absolute temperature, I_{obs} is the dark current of the photo detector, I_G is the dark current, C_T is the total input capacitance, and B indicates the useful bandwidth. If we use a PMOS transistor as a feedback we eliminate the factor *4KTB/R*. In addition to this advantage it reduced considerably the surface during the integration of the active resistance. The last term is the more prominent then the noise power, depends mainly on B^3 and C_T^2/g_m. This last term gives the absolute minimum noise that can occur at the input, assuming R_F extremely high. However, the noise performance is close to the optimum when [4]:

$$0.2\,(C_{PD}+C_S)<(C_{gs}+C_{gd})<2(C_{PD}+C_S) \tag{9}$$

An increase in the capacitance $(C_{gs} + \beta C_{gd})$ in extreme lower cases enables us to carry out this optimization. This is obtained with a definite number M of transistors connected in parallel. Thus, the capacitance of the transistors of attack will be equal to $M(C_{gs}+\beta C_{gd})$; the total transconductance however, will be equal to Mg_m: This allows us to assess C_{gs}, C_{gd}, and g_m translated by their respective relationship. In assessing $M(C_{gs}+\beta C_{gd})$ at around the minimum value (So that $C_T = C_{PD}+C_S+M(C_{gs}+C_{gd})= 1\text{pF}$). Thus the value of M is given by the following equation [3]:

$$M = \frac{\delta}{\delta+1}\,\frac{C_{tot}+C_1}{C_1} \tag{10}$$

Where δ is a factor which reflects the inequality given in (Eq. 9), it varies between 0.1 and 2.0.

4. Simulations results

The TIA shown in Figure 1 is implemented with 0.35µm CMOS technology, and the power dissipation is 53.5 mW with 3.3V supply voltage.. As can be seen in Figure 5, By using a photodide with a capacitance of 0.4 pF, the transimpedance gain is a 531 Ω and the bandwidth is 2.75 GHz, which makes the amplifier suitable for 5 Gb/s application.

The simulated noise at the input of the proposed topology is depicted in Figure 6, which shows a maximum at low frequencies, then it falls and tends to zero at high frequencies along the desired frequency range.

A DC analysis giving the output voltage versus the photocurrent is shown in Figure 7. This characteristic shows a good linearity of the amplifier as well as a high dynamic range along a high input current range. This proposed topology allows the detection of a photocurrent ranging from 0.5 µA to 5 µA. A layout of the proposed transimpedance amplifier has been drawn using 0.35 µm CMOS technology (Nwell, one-poly and three-metal layers). We obtain a chip size of 1251.9 µm2

5. Conclusion

A low noise and high bandwidth transimpedance amplifier has been designed and simulated in a standard 0.35 µm technology, The proposed TIA achieve 2.75 GHz-3 dB bandwidth, wich give 5 Gb/s of transmission speed, 54.5 dBΩ transimpedance gain, with 53.5 mW of power dissipation from a 3.3 supply voltage.

The analytical illustrations as well as different simulation results given by PSPICE tool, show that the designed amplifier, displays good optimized performance that offers considerable gain, good dynamic range and, particularly, a relatively low-noise level at the input, required in most of the communication standards, which makes more feasible to achieve a higher transmission speed.

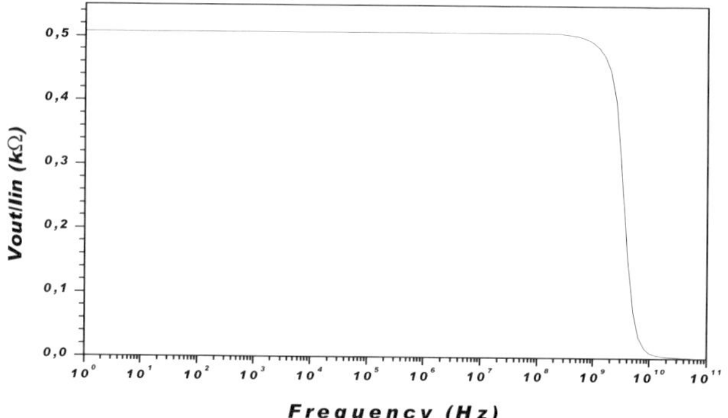

Figure 5 Transimpedance gain versus frequency

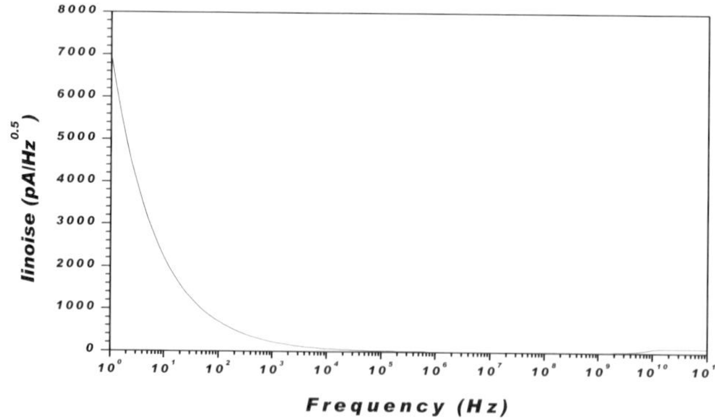

Figure 6 Input noise current of the transimpednace

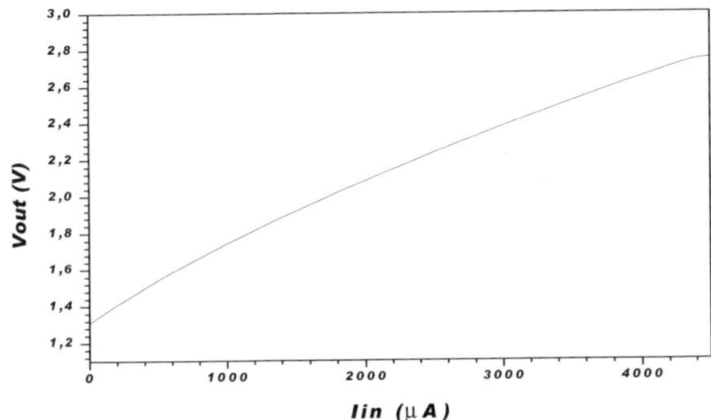

Figure 7 Output voltage versus Input photo-current

Table 1. Summarizes the results of our design and give different results given in the literature

Reference	Technology	C_{PD} pF	BP GHz	Gain dbΩ	Noise $pA/\sqrt{Hz}$	Power mW
[7]	CMOS 0 ,35 µm	1.5	1.9	65	9.7	17 under 3.3V
[8]	CMOS 0 ,5 µm	0.6	1.2	64	0,6	115 under 3.3V
[9]	CMOS 0 ,18 µm	0.2	1.8	58.7	13	47 under 1.8V
This work	CMOS 0 ,35 µm	0.4	2.75	54.5	12,764	53.5 under 3.3V

References

1. M. Nakamura, N. Ishihara, Y. Akazawa, and H. Kimura, "An Instantaneous Response CMOS Optical Receiver IC with Wide Dynamic Range and Extremely High Sensitivity Using Feed-Forward Auto-Bias Adustment," IEEE J. Solid-State Circuits, September 1995.

2. S. M. Park and C. Toumazou, "Gigahertz Low Noise CMOS Transimpedance Amplifier," IEEE International Symposium on Circuits and Systems, 1997, pp. 209-212.

3. J. E. Franca and Y. Tsividis, Design of Analog Digital VLSI Circuits for Telecommunications and Signal Processing, Chap. 5 (Prentice-Hall, Englewoods Cliffs, N.J., 1994).

4. A. Abidi, On the noise optimum of gigahertz FET transimpedance amplifier, IEEE J. Solid-State Circuits 22 (1987) 1207–1209.

5. D. M. Pietruszynski. J. M. Steininger and E. J. Swanson, A 50Mbit/s CMOS monolithic optical receiver, IEEE J. Solid-State Circuits 23 (1988) 1426–1433.

6. Huang, Beiju, Zhang Xu, and ChenHongda, 1 Gb/s zero pole cancellation CMOS transimpednace amplifier for Gigabit Ethernet applications, Journal of Semiconductors vol.30, N° 10, October 2009.

7. Sunderarajan S. Mohan, Maria del Mar Hershenson, Stephen P. Boyd, and Thomas H. Lee, Bandwidth Extension in CMOS with Optimized On Chip Inductors, IEEE Jornal Of Solide–State Circuits, Vol. 35, NO 3, March 2000, pp. 346–355.
8. Beaudoin, F. El-Gamal, M. N., A 5-Gbit/s CMOS optical receiver frontend, Circuits and Systems, 2002. MWSCAS-2002., Vol. 3, pp. 168–171.
9. C. D. Motchenbacher and J. A. Connelly, Low Noise Electronic System Design (John Wiley and Sons, Inc., New York, 1993).
10. M. Ingels, M. Steyaert, A 1Gb/s, 0.7 µm CMOS Optical Receivers With Full Rail to Rail Output Swing, IEEE Journal of Solid State Circuits, Vol 34, July. 1999.

SUPPORT VECTOR MACHINE FOR MODELLING DESIGN PARAMETERS IN CIRCULAR AND TRIANGULAR MICROSTRIP PATCH ANTENNAS

M. CACCIOLA, G. MEGALI, S. CALCAGNO, M. VERSACI, F.C. MORABITO

Department of Informatics, Mathematics, Electronics and Transportation (DIMET),
University Mediterranea of Reggio Calabria
Via Graziella Feo di Vito, Reggio Calabria, I-89100, Italy

In telecommunication, there are several types of microstrip antennas, also known as printed antennas. The most common of which is the microstrip patch antenna or patch antenna. Common microstrip antenna radiator shapes are square, rectangular, circular and elliptical, but any continuous shape is possible. Microstrip antennas are really cheap and mostly exploited for UHF communication. Since their ability to have polarization diversity, the ease and precision in their design is really important and challenging.

In this work, a fast method for the design of circular and equilateral triangular microstrip antennas, based on a Support Vector Machine, is presented. Numerical results obtained by using this technique agree quite well with the results of Method of Moments. The proposed technique can therefore be fruitfully used in microwave and millimeter wave CAD applications.

1. Introduction

Low profile antennas are usually required in high-performance microwave and millimeter-wave spacecraft or satellite applications, where size, weight, cost, performance, ease of installation, and aerodynamic profile are constraints.

A patch antenna is a narrowband, wide-beam antenna fabricated by etching the antenna element pattern in metal trace bonded to an insulating dielectric substrate with a continuous metal layer bonded to the opposite side of the substrate which forms a groundplane. Common microstrip antenna radiator shapes are square, rectangular, circular and elliptical, but any continuous shape is possible. Some patch antennas eschew a dielectric substrate and suspend a metal patch in air above a ground plane using dielectric spacers; the resulting structure is less robust but provides better bandwidth. Because such antennas have a very low profile, are mechanically rugged and can be conformable, they are often mounted on the exterior of aircraft and spacecraft, or are incorporated into mobile radio communications devices.

Microstrip antennas are also relatively inexpensive to manufacture because of the simple 2-dimensional physical geometry. They are usually employed at UHF and higher frequencies because the size of the antenna is directly tied to the wavelength at the resonance frequency. A single patch antenna provides a maximum directive gain of around 6-9 dBi.

An advantage inherent to patch antennas is the ability to have polarization diversity. Patch antennas can easily be designed to have Vertical, Horizontal, Right Hand Circular (RHCP) or Left Hand Circular (LHCP) Polarizations, using multiple feed points, or a single feedpoint with asymmetric patch structures [1].

In addition, by adding loads between the patch and the ground plane, such as pins and varactor diodes, adaptative elements with variable resonant frequency, impedance, polarization and pattern can be designed [2]. Among various possible geometries, circular and the equilateral triangular have been received a great attention in the technical literature (see Figure 1). In fact, in the past some numerical and analytical models for evaluating the resonant frequency and the input impedance of these antennas have been developed [3-5]. However, between these methods, the Integral Equation model in conjunction with Method of Moments (MoMs) plays the major role to provide rigorous and accurate solutions for microstrip printed antennas. But, as well know, this technique requires considerable computational effort and it is very time consuming [2].

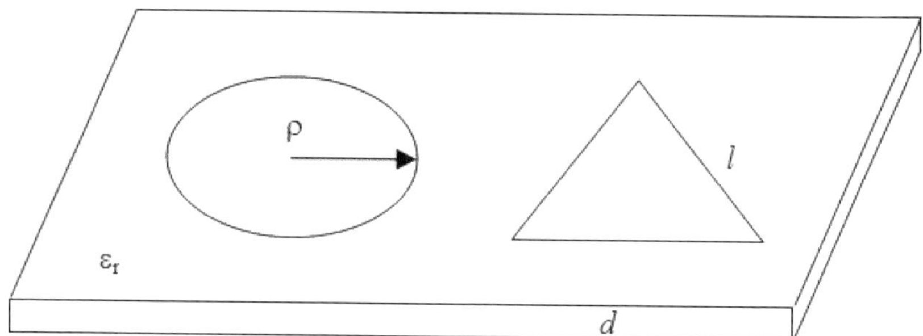

Figure 1. Circular and triangular microstrip antennas.

Pastly, Artificial Neural Networks (ANNs) [6] and Neuro-Fuzzy Networks (NFN) [7] approaches have been exploited to microwave and millimeter wave area as a fast and flexible vehicle to design devices and circuits. Significant speed-up of CAD by using neural models in place of classical electromagnetic models resulted in a drive to develop advanced neural modelling techniques [8,9]. In this paper we propose an alternative approach for the design of microstrip antennas, based on the use of a Support Vector Regression Machine (SVRM), focusing our attention to design of circular and equilateral triangular patch antennas. In fact, ANNs and NFNs have some drawbacks, e.g., effective methods to determine the number of hidden layers and hidden nodes are not available. Furthermore, ANNs have difficulties with generalization, in many cases producing models which can overfit the data. This is a consequence both of the optimization algorithms used for parameter selection and of the statistical measures used to select the "best model". Nowadays SVRM developed by Vapnik [10] are gaining popularity due to many attractive features capable to overcome the limitations connected to ANNs. This is due to the Structural Risk Minimization (SRM) principle embodied by SVRMs, which has been demonstrated to be more effective than the traditional Empirical Risk Minimization (ERM) principle exploited by ANNs [10]. This different philosophy equips SVRMs with a greater ability to generalize, if compared with ANNs. The paper is organized as follows: section 2 presents a brief introduction on the design problem at hand. Section 3 describes the basics on SVRM approach. In section 4 it is shown the performances of the realized SVRM and finally, section 5 illustrates the conclusions.

2. Problem Formulation

As well known, the design of a microstrip antennas is a trial and error process. It is usually performed as follows: firstly, specified the dielectric grounded substrate parameters, we define a work frequency for the patch. Generally, this frequency correspond to resonant frequency on the antenna's dominant mode. Next, starting from these data, the physical dimensions for the antenna are determined using at this purpose a simplified model for the patch, as a transmission line model or a cavity model. Finally, it is necessary to verify that the designed antenna works on assigned frequency. This is a critical step, because a patch antenna work well only close to the specified resonant frequency. This step can be realized employing an integral equation model as EFIE [11]:

$$\iint_{\Sigma} \mathbf{G} \cdot \mathbf{J} dS = \mathbf{E} \tag{1}$$

where $\mathbf{G}$ is the dyadic Green's function of the grounded dielectric slab, $\mathbf{J}$ is the unknown surface current on patch and $\mathbf{E}$ is the electrical field produced by feed. The standard procedure for solving Eq. (1) is based on the MoM. The surface current $\mathbf{J}$ is expanded over a set of basis functions:

$$\mathbf{J} = \sum_{k=1}^{N} I_k \mathbf{J}_k \tag{2}$$

where I_k is the unknown coefficient to be determined for the nth expansion function. Substituting the Eq. (2) into Eq. (1) and taking the inner products of the resulting equation with each basis function, we obtain the following matrix equation:

$$[Z]\, I = V \tag{3}$$

where I is the vector containing the unknown coefficients in Eq. (2), $[Z]$ is the impedance matrix and V is excitation vector.

Since the resonant frequency is defined to be the frequency at which the field and the current can sustain themselves without an external source, no driving terms exists in Eq. (1) [15]:

$$\iint_{\Sigma} \mathbf{G} \cdot \mathbf{J} dS = \mathbf{0} \tag{4}$$

and the Eq. (3) becomes as:

$$[Z]\, I = 0 \tag{5}$$

Therefore, for the existence of nontrivial solution in (5), the determinant of the $[Z]$ matrix must be zero, i.e.:

$$\det[Z] = 0 \tag{6}$$

which occurs only at the resonant frequencies of the printed antenna. If the fundamental resonant frequency is found major or minor with respect to the design frequency, the design process must be repeated adjusting the initial geometrical dimensions accordingly to the information obtained by computed resonant values.

3. Theoretical Overview of SVRMs

Support Vector Machines (SVMs) are heuristic structures able to solve classification, regression and estimation problems. They have been introduced within the Statistical Learning Theory by Vapnik [12]. Subsequently, SVMs have been applied to regression problems, where they were named as SVRMs. In order to explain the mathematical framework in which SVRMs are defined, let us consider the problem to approximate the set of data $D = \left\{ (\mathbf{x}_1, y_1), ..., (\mathbf{x}_n, y_n) \right\}, \mathbf{x} \in X, y \in \Re$ by a linear function

$f(\mathbf{x}) = \langle \mathbf{w}, \mathbf{x} \rangle + b$ where $\langle , \rangle$ denotes the inner product in X, i.e., the space of the input patterns. This problem can be solved selecting the optimal regression function as the minima of the following functional [13]:

$$\Phi(\mathbf{w}, \xi) = \frac{1}{2}\|\mathbf{w}\|^2 + C\sum_i \left(\xi_i^- + \xi_i^+ \right) \tag{7}$$

where C is a user-defined value, and ξ_i^-, ξ_i^+ are slack variables representing upper and lower constraints on the output of the system. However, the set D often is not linearly separable: the separation can be obtained by means of a suitable nonlinear mapping that projects D into a high-dimensional space where the linear regression can be carried out. This nonlinear mapping is accomplished by a *kernel function* $K(\mathbf{x}_i, \mathbf{x}_j)$ [14]. Loosely speaking, in the above problem, like in the standard regression problem, it is supposed that the relationship between the independent and dependent variables is given by a function $f(\mathbf{x})$. The task is to find a functional form for $f(\mathbf{x})$ which gives to the SVRM the right prediction accuracy: this can be achieved by training the SVRM on a suitable data set associated with the problem under analysis.

4. Numerical Results

In the design problem at hand, the SVRM inputs are the permittivity of the substrate ε_r, its thickness d, the antenna's geometry and its dominant mode resonant frequency f, while the SVRM output is the antenna dimension a, where a is the radius ρ in the case of circular patch, or the side length l in the case of equilateral triangular patch. A training data set is obtained by numerical simulations using a MoM code based on the analysis described in Section 2. Furthermore, to validate the performances of the exploited SVRM, a new set of MoM simulations are realized and presented to the network.

Table 1. Range of input parameters for all the geometries under study.

Input Parameters	Range data Set	Range Test Set
ε_r	2.32, 3, 78, 10.5	2.55
h	0.0781, 0.159, 0.312 [cm]	0.259 [cm]
f	*min*= 0.5 [GHz] *max*= 40 [GHz]	*min*= 2 [GHz] *max*= 20 [GHz]

Table 1 gives the range of the physical parameters employed to obtain the data sets.

In order to implement a SVRM-based estimator, a loss function must be used. In what follows, we used the Vapnik ε-insensitive loss function:

$$L_\varepsilon(y) = \begin{cases} 0 & for \left| f(\mathbf{x}) - y \right| < \varepsilon \\ \left| f(\mathbf{x}) - y \right| & otherwise \end{cases} \tag{8}$$

performing a tuning, carried out according to [15], in order to obtain an acceptable setting for C and ε. Moreover, we evaluated the performances of linear, polynomial and Radial Basis Function based kernels. Figure 2 shows the estimated results by SVRM versus MoM ones. Different try and test evaluations have been carried out, considering the Root Mean Squared Error (RMSE) between actual and SVRM estimated values, to reach at a suitable choice of these parameters. It requires a small computational time to reach at a suitable choice of defined parameters with our data set. Best performances have been obtained with a 2-degree polynomial kernel, setting C=12 and ε=0.01. The linear profile having 45° slope, points out the good agreement between estimated and evaluated MoM antenna's size in all the range of the considered input parameters.

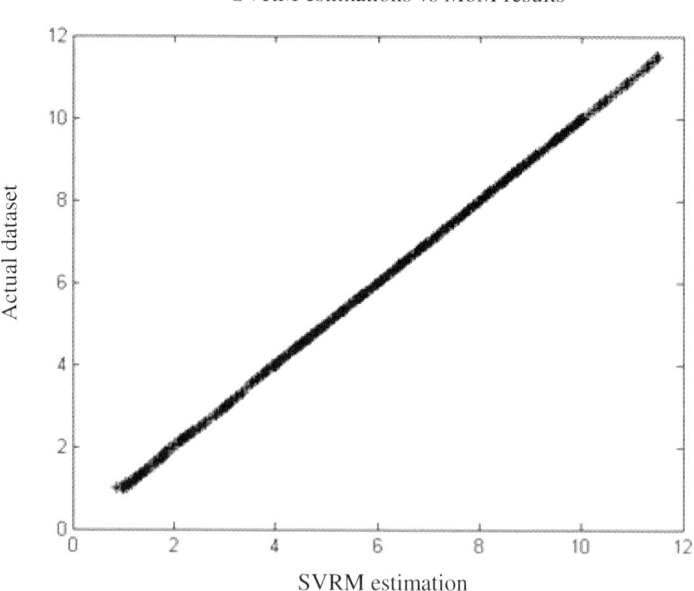

Figure 2. SVRM estimation vs. MoM resonant dimensions (Test Set case) for all the geometries under study. (All the dimensions are in [cm]).

The scatter plot draws the performances of our SVM estimator in calculating and assessing the main design parameter of patch antennas. Please, let us remark that, for a perfect estimator, the plot of SVRM estimated values of a vs. the value calculated by MoM are placed along the perpendicular bisector of I and III quadrants. In our case, the performances are very good, and our SVRM based estimator could be considered as a good tool for designing microstrip patch antennas, starting from well known electrical and geometrical quantities and resulting the radius ρ in the case of circular patch, or the side length l in the case of equilateral triangular patch. Table 2 summarizes the characteristics of SVRM based estimator and the performances in terms of RMSE. As shown, the obtained root mean square error is acceptable for most design applications.

Table 2. Performances of the developed SVRM model.

Input	4
Output	1
Size of Training Database	400
RMSE	0.85%

5. Conclusions

Microwave and Millimeter-wave CAD requires a full-wave model in order to predict accurately the performances of printed antennas. In this paper a SVRM model for design a circular and a equilateral triangular patch antennas, has been proposed. Very good agreement between the MoM computed resonant dimensions and the SVRM model is found, revealing the effectiveness of the proposed approach. Furthermore, the SVRM reduces dramatically the design time. Accordingly, this approach can be very useful for the development of fast CAD models.

6. Acknowledgment

Authors gracefully thanks Dr. Giovanni Angiulli, University Mediterranea of Reggio Calabria, DIMET, for his support in implementing the MoM for data generation.

References

1. R. Bancroft, Microstrip and Printed Antenna Design, Noble Publishing, Raleigh, NC, USA, 2-3 (2004).
2. J. R. James and P. S. Hall, Handbook of Microstrip Antennas, Peter Peregrinus, London, U.K., 1-2 (1989).

3. Y. J. Guo, A. Paez, R. A. Sadeghzadeh and S. K. Barton, *IEEE Trans. Antennas Propag.*, A Circular Patch Antenna for Radio LAN's, 45 (1997).

4. N. Kumprasert and W. Kiranon, *IEEE Trans. Antennas Propag.*, Simple and Accurate Formula for the Resonant Frequency of the Circular Microstrip Antennas, 43 (1995).

5. N. Kumprasert and W. Kiranon, *IEEE Trans. Antennas Propag.*, Simple and Accurate Formula for the Resonant Frequency of the Equilateral Triangular Microstrip Patch Antenna, 42 (1994).

6. R. K. Mishra, *Int. J. RF. and Microwave CAE*, An Overview of Neural Network Methods in Computational Electromagnetics, 12 (2002).

7. G. Angiulli, M. Versaci, *International Journal of Infrared and Millimeter Waves*, A Neuro-Fuzzy Network Model for the Design of Circular and Triangular Equilateral Microstrip Patch Antennas, 23 (2002).

8. F. Wang and Q. Zhang, *IEEE Trans. Microw. Theory Tech.*, Knowledge-Based Neural Models for Microwave Design, 45 (1997).

9. R. K. Mishra and A. Patnaik, *IEEE Trans. Antennas Propagat.*, Neural Network-Based CAD Model for the Design of Square-Patch Antennas, 46 (1998).

10. C. Cortes and V. Vapnik, *Machine Learning*, Support vector network, 20 (1997).

11. M. Deshpande, D. Shively and C. R. Cockrell, *NASA Technical paper*, Resonant frequencies of irregularly shaped microstrip antennas using Method of Moments, 3386 (1993).

12. V. N. Vapnik, The Nature of Statistical Learning Theory, Springer Verlag, New York, USA (1995).

13. A. J. Smola, Regression estimation with support vector learning machines, Master's thesis, Tech. Univ., Munchen, Germany (1996).

14. N. Cristianini and J. Shawe-Taylor, An Introduction to Support Vector Machines, Cambridge Univ. Press, Cambridge, U.K. (2000).

15. O. Chapelle and V. Vapnik, Model selection for support vector machines, In: S. A. Solla, T. K. Leen, and K.-R. Muller, Eds. *Advances in Neural Information Processing Systems*, MIT Press, Cambridge, USA, 12 (2000).

PARALLEL-HIERARCHICAL TRANSFORMATION AS THE SYSTEM MODEL OF EFFECTIVE ARTIFICIAL INTELLIGENCE TOOLS

L. I. TIMCHENKO, N. I. KOKRIATSKAIA

Department Telecommunication Technologies and Automation,

State University for Transport Economy and Technologies,

19 Lukashevich Street, Kyiv, 03049, Ukraine

E-mail: timchen@list.ru

www.detut.edu.ua

I. D. IVASYUK

Management of Education and Science of Winnitca Regional State Administration

33 Kozizkiy Street, Vinnytsa, Ukraine

E-mail: ihor_vin@ukr.net

G. L. KOSENKO, R. V. MAKARENKO

Department Telecommunication Technologies and Automation,

State University for Transport Economy and Technologies,

19 Lukashevich Street, Kyiv, 03049, Ukraine

E-mail: violet_g@bk.ru, mrv_detut@bigmir.net

Multistage integration of visual information in the brain allows people to respond quickly to most significant stimuli while preserving the ability to recognize small details in the image. Implementation of this principle in technical systems can lead to more efficient processing procedures. The multistage approach to image processing, described in this paper, comprises both main types of cortical multistage convergence. One of these types occurs within each visual pathway and the other between the pathways. This approach maps input images into a flexible hierarchy which reflects the complexity of the image data. The procedures of temporal image decomposition and hierarchy formation are described in mathematical terms. The multistage system highlights spatial regularities, which are passed through a number of transformational levels to generate a coded representation of the image which encapsulates, in a computer manner, structure on different hierarchical levels in the image. At each processing stage a single output result is computed to allow a very quick response from the system. The result is represented as an activity pattern, which can be compared with previously computed patterns on the basis of the closest match.

1. Introduction

The given article offers new approach to the creation of computing medium - of parallel -hierarchical (PH) networks, being investigated in the form of model of neurolike scheme of data processing [1]. The approach has a number of advantages as compared with other methods of formation of neurolike media (for example, already known methods of formation of artificial neural networks). The main advantage of the approach is the usage of dynamics of multilevel parallel interaction of information signals at different hierarchy levels of computer networks, that enables to use such known natural features of organization of computations in cortex as: topographic nature of mapping, simultaneity (parallelism) of signals operation, inlaid cortex, structure, rough hierarchy of the cortex, spatially correlated in time mechanism of perception and training. The formation of multi-stage PH networks assumes the process of sequential transformation of correlated and formation of decorrelated in time elements of neural networks at its transition from one stable state into another. The key feature of the offered approach is analysis of dynamics of spatially correlated mechanism of transformation of current and formation of resultant elements of neural networks. Such mechanism allows presenting in a new way the processing in neural networks as the process of parallel-sequential transformation of various components of image and account of time responses of transformation. Physical contents of input elements of neural networks, which participate in correlation - decorrelation, such as, for example, the amplitude or frequency, phase or energy of signals, cohesion or texture of images, is determined by the type of transformation being used, the selection of which depends on the class of problems being solved. In general view the multistage concept regarding image processing can be formulated in the following way. The image analysis presents sequential transformation of concurrent and detection of discrepant in time image components at transition of neural networks elements from current energy state with certain space coordinates into states with less energy with other space coordinates. Such process of image analysis occurs at many stages, each of which includes fulfillment of above-stated procedure. The condition for transition of image components at higher level is availability of dynamics of mutual coincidence of intermediate results of processing in time in parallel channels of lower layer. The outcome of image analysis is formed from insulated in time-space area image components.

The development of computing facilities starts with transition from conventional computing frames of- von Neumann to "expert systems" and 'smart' neuroengineering systems, imitating cerebral activity of the human being intellectually - computing means of the sixth generation. We can state, that the "ideal" converter unit of the optical information of parallel type is an eye - probably most unique sensory systems of the human being. Human brain is - natural processor, which remakes sensor information. There is a problem. Is there a possibility to simulate the process of eye functioning- processor perception of the sensory information on neuroshaped circuits intended for data processing? The analysis of recent studies on neurobiology and publications on modeling of neural mechanisms of sensor information perception has shown that still some problems remain obscure, namely, how the interaction of neurounits take place in the cortex, their interaction on the level of natural local neural networks; how temporal integration of spatially–separated activated D.Kheb neuroassemblies in horizontal and vertical routes takes place at the moment of coordinated action of numerous simultaneously acting irritants? That is why our dissertation investigates hypothetical model of special integration and structuralization of information in the cortex of human brain, concerning problems of perception, information storage and pattern recognition. Models considered in the article, to a great extent, metaphorical similarity with computers; nevertheless they are supposed to provide new, more elaborated approach to computer-based calculations. Proceeding from this approach new microprocessor-based systems and computers of new architecture could be created. Besides, the models will allow having a new approach to biological systems. The prototype of suggested approach can be considered the principles of collective computations in neuroshaped circuits intended for collective decision making, requiring corporate interaction of large quantity of simple solutions, as a result, complex solution is taken by means of data combining during any period of time. After analysis of neurobiological data regarding the theory of sensor information stratification in the human brain and peculiarities of computation system organization a number of discrepancies concerning natural mechanisms of object perception and external environment were revealed. These discrepancies didn't find corresponding reflection in modern neuroshaped computators considerably limiting their technical possibilities and they don't meet main requirements relating to intellectual means of information processing. In spite of attempts that have been made for over half of the century, the problem of creation of artificial intelligence system based on application of computers is still far from its solution, although some interesting theoretical results have been obtained. In this connection the report delivered by Professor Hogard, Cambridge University, in the White House must be mentioned. Professor Hogard considers the creation of artificial intelligence to be the main scientific problem of the next millennium.

The given article studies one of the main problems of artificial intelligence (AI), formulated by Professor Yu.V. Kapitonova and V.I. Skurikhin. This is the problem of formation of "objects and external environment situations" perception model. The given problem is considered regarding its application for the solution of various applied problems. The idea of hierarchial organisation of links between structures of human brain, suggested by Professor Z.L. Rabinovich was taken into consideration while formation of general methodology of PH transformation creation. The idea is that "transmission of excitation between structures, that is, their activation can be carried out not only by vertical (hierarchical direct and reversal) links, but also horizontally-within the limits of one and the same field".

Computational modeling in of Brain-like function has over the last 50 years gone through enormous upheaval. From the early work due to Rosenblatt ("Perceptron") to later research in learning methods and representational function ("Hopfield Networks, Back Propagation") there has been no formal setting for the analysis of collective structures, like sets of neurons. Rather there has been a dependent island of research that focuses on memory, visual perception, speech recognition, handwriting recognition etc., as applications or focused models of cortical function in biological systems— typically in small circuits (lobster's gastro-intestinal system, motion detection circuits in crickets etc.). Despite a few researchers such as Steve Grossberg, there are almost no claims to general principles to organize and produce systematic results for neural systems.

Using collections of neural computing units with homogeneous learning rules are hardly a means to understand general system level function. The brain's dynamics is in orders of 1000s to millions of interacting subsystems, clearly the neuron is at the wrong level of analysis but treating the brain as if it were independent insulated modules is patently false. This scientific work is unique in that it focuses directly on this kind of problem: formulation of methodology, theory of the system and circuit engineering of hierarchy structures with space-multilevel data presentation and time-network principles of their analysis. Fundamentally, this type of research is about collective decision-making and work is focused on the time-space dynamics of this phenomenon which is common to every type of decision make in human problem solving.

2. Parallel-hierarchical transformation as the system model of effective artificial intelligence tools

The network structure is suggested and studied (Figure 1), it permits to simulate principle of operation of distributed neural network [2-9].

Such a network consists of a set of sub networks (Figure 2) of formation of special-temporal medium (STM) state signs, the structure of them is homogeneous and consists of a number of interdependent hierarchical levels.

Operational algorithm of the network is universal and provides parallel-hierarchical formation of a set of common and various signs-signals of STM state. Generalization of all types of sensor information takes place at the last stage of transformation outside hierarchical processing of each type of sensor information. "Intellectual" level of distributed networks is determined by the degree of sensor information generalization in its branches. The greater degree of sensor information generalization, while it's passing along branches of the network, the higher its "intellectual" level. In each branch of PH network the algorithm of pyramidal processing is realized.

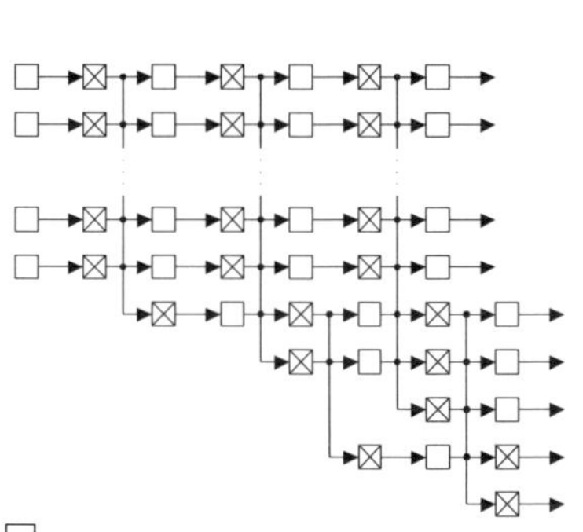

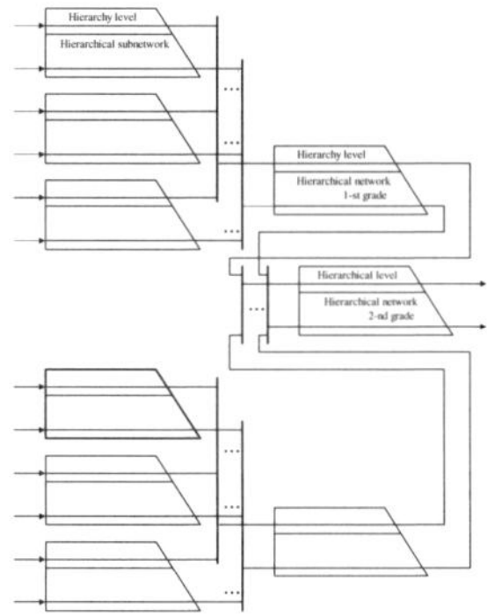

<table>
<tr><td>□</td><td>- set of different states of STM.</td></tr>
<tr><td>⊠</td><td>- common states of STM hierarchical.</td></tr>
</table>

Figure 2. Structure of multistage hierarchical network.

Figure 1. Structure of parallel-hierarchical network.

The essence of PH approach is in simultaneous usage of sequence of data arrays sets, which form sets of information fields at different levels of hierarchy. All this permits to realize the strategy of multilevel interaction from "total to partial". In general form the methodology of PH network formation can be presented in formalized form, proceeding from the following principles. Let the set of initial data be given. The following problem appears. How can parallel computing process be organized in real scale to obtain strictly distributed in time and hierarchy computing network? If sets of input data flows are processed at

670

different hierarchy levels, then each level represents a set of processing elements, functioning in strictly fixed time intervals (t_j). Let n_1 functions $f_1(t)$, $f_2(t),...,f_{n1}(t)$ be given. The given functions we shall describe at different hierarchical levels from the 1st to j-th $(j=2l, \ l=1,2...$ and $j=2l+3, \ l=0,1,2,...)$.

$$\sum_{j=1}^{n_1}\sum_{i=1}^{n_{j1}} f_{j1}\left(t-i\tau\right)=\sum_{j=1}^{n_2}\sum_{i=1}^{n_{j2}} f_{j2}\left(t-2ij\tau\right) = \sum_{i=1}^{n_{1(2l+3)}} f_{1(2l+3)}\left(t-\left(\ 2i \ + \ 6l \ + \ 3 \ \right)\tau\right) +$$

$$+ \sum_{i=2}^{n_{21(2l+3)}} f_{2(2l+3)}\left(t-\left(2i+6l+3\right)\tau\right)+... \ + \ \sum_{i=n-1}^{n_{(n-1)(2l+3)}} f_{(n-1)(2l+3)}\left(t-\left(2i+6l+3\right)\tau\right)+ \tag{1}$$

$$+ \sum_{i=n}^{n_{n(2l+3)}} f_{n(2l+3)}\left(t-\left(2i+6l+3\right)\tau\right) = \sum_{j=2}^{k} f_{i,j}\{t-(3j-4)\tau),$$

where τ – delay of the following function formation relatively previous, n_{kj} – number of functions of jth decomposition of kth functional level. The right part of the expression (1) forms tail functions, which are distributed in time on different hierarchical levels and are obtained as a result of this functional transformation. Analyzing networks transformation (1), we can make a conclusion that in the process of each level formation, the time shift (τ) is formed; its presence leads to tail functions obtaining.

The dissertation considers the networks method of PH transformation at models level.

Mathematical model of pyramidal decomposition of the set $\mu=\{a_i\}$, $i = \overline{1,n}$ has the form

$$\sum_{i=1}^{n} a_i \ = \ \sum_{j=1}^{R} \left(n - \sum_{k=0}^{j-1} n_k \right) \left(a^j \ - \ a^{j-1} \right), \tag{2}$$

where $a_i \neq 0, R$ -dimensionality of the given set, $S(S = 1,2,3...)$ - non-empty sets of elements, that preset the information. Let us form the subsets from the same elements, the elements of one set we denote by a^k, $k = \overline{1,R}$, n_k - number of elements in k^{th} subset (i.e. multiplicity of a_k), a^j - random element of the set $\{a^k\}$, chosen at j^{th} step, $j = \overline{1,R}$, $a^0 = 0$, $n_0 = 0$. Analyzing the expression (2) of pyramidal processing of numeric information we can make a conclusion, that while processing the quantity of numbers decreases at each step. If sets, obtained after each step, how to put in series one on another, in this case 3D contour, formed by them would have the form of the pyramid. Transformation of the set μ into the set μ^1 that is prescribed by the model (2) is the operator of transformation G.

$$G(\mu) = \mu^1 . \tag{3}$$

If for initial S arrays transformation operator G could be applied, that is prescribed by the formula (2), then for each array we will obtain corresponding decomposition:

$$\mu_1^1 = \bigcup_{i=1}^{R_1^1} a_{1i}^i , \quad \mu_2^1 = \bigcup_{i=1}^{R_2^1} a_{2i}^i , \quad \dots , \quad \mu_s^1 = \bigcup_{i=1}^{R_s^1} a_{si}^i , \tag{4}$$

where μ_s^1 - set under the number S on the first level, whereas for the kth level set the number 1 will be written as μ_1^k , correspondingly R_s^1 - number of elements in S set on the first level, R_1^k - number of elements in S set on k^{th} level. If we unite the obtained elements (5) into matrix M_1 , then the matrix of direct decomposition on the first level is being formed:

$$M_1 = \bigcup_{s=1}^{S} \left(\bigcup_{i=1}^{R_S^1} a_{si}^1 \right) . \tag{5}$$

If matrix M_1 is rewritten, having concentrated its elements not by lines, but by columns, then new matrix is formed:

$$M_1^T = \bigcup_{i=1}^{R_S^1} \left(\bigcup_{s=1}^{S} a_{si}^1 \right) , \tag{6}$$

that is matrix M_1 is transposed. Having designated by T the operator of matrix transposition, i.e. transition from (5) to (6), then $T(M_1) = M_1^T$.

New array μ_2 is formed at the second level ($k=2$) in case when operator G is applied to set μ_2 :

$$\mu_2 = \bigcup_{R^1=1}^{R^1} \mu_{R^1}^2 = \bigcup_{R^1=1}^{R^1} \left(\bigcup_{i=1}^{R_{R_1}^2} a_{R^1 i}^2 \right) .$$

Starting from the second level, formation of matrices M_2^T , M_3^T ,..., M_k^T is carried out not only by means of transposition, as in (7), but also along diagonals and obtained sets are diagonal. Matrix M_2^T can be obtained from M_2 in the same way as matrix M_1^T and M_1 , having excluded the first element a_{11}^2 - tail element of the network. Element a_{11}^2 - is the first result in S transformation of initial arrays. On each level, starting from the second, one element of a_{11}^k type is obtained, where k –number of level $(k = 2,3,...)$, as in the first columns of matrices $M_2 , M_3 ,\dots, M_k$ only one element can be found. Matrix M_2^T passes to the third level and servers as the bases for matrix M_3 construction etc., until only one element remains in matrix M_k (at a certain k^{th} level), that is

$T(S(M_k)) = M_k^T$ does not contain a single element. Serial application of three operators G, S, T forms functional Φ, that is $\Phi(M) = T[S(G(M))]$, where S - shift operator on the value that is less than the number of given line by one, and exclusion of the first column of matrix M_k as a result of decomposition. Network method of direct PH transformation comprises serial application to initial sets $\bigcup_{s=1} \mu_s$ transformation operator G and transposition operator T, and then $(k-1)$ times functional Φ.

$$\Phi_{t=2}^{k}\left[T\left(G\left(\bigcup_{s=1}^{S}\left(\bigcup_{i=1}^{n} a_i \right) \right) \right) \right] = \bigcup_{t=2}^{k} a_{11}^{t}, \tag{7}$$

where a_{11}^{k} - initial information (tail elements of the network) of direct PH transformation.

The following statements follow from expression (7).

Statement 1. The sum of input elements of PH network equals to the sum of its tail elements.

$$\sum_{j=1}^{S}\sum_{i=1}^{n_S} a_{ji} = \sum_{t=2}^{k} a_{11}^{t}.$$

Statement 2. The length of algorithm is determined in the following way:

$$L = R^1 + \sum_{t=1}^{k} P^{t+1} - (n^t - 1),$$

where $P^t = \max\left\{ R_1^t, R_2^t + 1; R_3^t + 2; \ldots; R_{n^{t-1}}^t + n^{t-1} - 1 \right\}$, and

n^{t-1} is the number of sets in matrix M'_{t-1}, which pass to t- level for further transformation. Using general idea of structural organization of artificial neural networks by the scheme: input ball $\to$ hidden ball $\to$ output ball, the teaching PH network can be synthesized, in which the first level of the network is used as an input ball, as the hidden ball levels $2 \div k$ could be used, and as output ball - traditionally used in artificial neural networks input layer. Using statement 2, which determines the length of network algorithm, the number of elements of hidden layer can be determined and procedure of its elements computation could be formalized.

The given article suggests comparative analysis of efficiency relatively other transformations by the number of operations for PH transformation that have been used. If there are k arrays, and by means of n_i we designate the number of elements in the array by number i $(n_i \geq 1)$, $i = \overline{1,k}$, $\Sigma n_i = N$ - total number of elements being processed; m_i - number of various elements in i^{th} array $(m_i \geq 1)$, p_i^j - probability of jth element appearance in i^{th} array, where $j = \overline{1, m_i}$, and $m = \max m_i$, then the number of operations will be:

$$N + \sum_{i=1}^{k} n_i p_i^1 + \sum_{i=1}^{k} n_i \left(1 - p_i^1\right) + \sum_{i=1}^{k} n_i \left(1 - p_i^1\right)p_i^2 + \sum_{i=1}^{k} n_i \left(1 - p_i^1\right)\left(1 - p_i^2\right) + \cdots + \sum_{i=1}^{k} \left[n_i \prod_{j=1}^{m-1} \left(1 - p_i^j\right)p_i^m \right] +$$

$$+ \sum_{i=1}^{k} \left[n_i \prod_{j=1}^{m-1} \left(1 - p_i^j\right) \right] = N + \sum_{i=1}^{k} n_i \left(p_i^1 + 1 - p_i^1 + \left(1 - p_i^1\right)p_i^2 + \left(1 - p_i^1\right)\left(1 - p_i^2\right) + \ldots + \right.$$

$$+ \prod_{j=1}^{m-1} \left(1 - p_i^j\right)p_i^m + \prod_{j=1}^{m-1} \left(1 - p_i^j\right)\bigg) = N + \sum_{i=1}^{k} [n_i \left(1 + \left(1 - p_i^1\right) + \left(1 - p_i^1\right)\left(1 - p_i^2\right) + \ldots + \right.$$

$$+ \prod_{j=1}^{m-1} \left(1 - p_i^j\right)] = N + \sum_{i=1}^{k} \left[n_i \left(1 + \sum_{z=1}^{m-1} \prod_{j=1}^{z} \left(1 - p_i^j\right)\right) \right].$$

If the appearance of elements in array will be equally probable event with the rate of probability p, then for N elements out of k n element sets is valid:

$$N + \sum_{i=1}^{k} \left[n_i \left(1 + \sum_{z=1}^{m-1} \prod_{j=1}^{z} \left(1 - p_i^j\right)\right) \right] = N + \sum_{i=1}^{k} \left[n_i \left(1 + \sum_{z=1}^{m-1} \left(1 - p\right)^z\right) \right] = N +$$

$$+ \left(1 + \sum_{z=1}^{m-1} \left(1 - p\right)^z\right) \sum_{i=1}^{k} n_i = N + N\left(1 + \sum_{z=1}^{m-1} \left(1 - p\right)^z\right) = N\left(2 + \sum_{z=1}^{m-1} \left(1 - p\right)^z\right) = N\left(2 + \frac{1-p}{p}\right) = \left(1 + \frac{1}{p}\right)N,$$

if $n = m$, then $p = \dfrac{1}{N}$.

Thus, the number of operations for PH transformation equals $N(N+1)$. For instance, for orthogonal transformations, widely used in practical spheres, the number of operations being used will be: for WPF - $4N^2 \log_2 N$, for Adamara - $2N^2 \log_2 N^2$ and for Haara - $4N(N+1)$.

3. Conclusions

In this paper, a novel three-dimensional architecture of multistage network is presented. Processing in this network is based on the principle of investigating partial spatio-temporal regularities between image components. Instead of using a fixed hierarchy of representations, the initial image is decomposed into structural components, which are then elaborated in order to investigate correlations between them at different hierarchical levels. Processing at higher levels involves decomposition, discovery of new regularities and interpretation of the extracted information. Any discovered correlations reduce redundancy of representation and indicate a certain underlying principle, which certainly deserves explanation. The central goal at all processing levels is to postulate new structural relationships and this task is performed by a uniform local transformation.

Performance of the multistage algorithm relies profoundly on the type of initial representation of the input data and on the type of local transformation. For the purpose of pattern analysis, the initial image is transformed so that each pixel is assigned the value of connectivity in order to represent local structure. For grey-scale images, a three-level structural representation is created so that not only the number of connected neighbours is specified, but also is the nature of the significant changes in brightness. The three connectivity levels are processed simultaneously by the same network algorithm.

Each level of the multistage network investigates spatial regularities between the simultaneously processed image components. The most spatially correlated components are promoted for further processing. The local transformation in each processing channel is realised in two stages, and it is applied to those components that have simultaneously arrived to a single point in the network. The first stage involves clustering of the most spatially correlated components. The value of a cluster is calculated according to the number of components in the cluster and to their structural information. The second stage is realised as the "winner takes all" competition in temporal decomposition for the future processing. Clustered components in the processing channel compete for the earliest possible promotion to the next processing level. This stage is realised as sorting. The structural image description created by the multistage hierarchical network can be represented as a pattern vector. This enables a different image representation, which is a compromise between a totally localised representation in the Kohonen network [10] and a totally distributed one in the Linsker network [11]. The components of the output pattern vector are computed one at a time, with the more correlated structural components appearing before the less correlated (noisy) ones. This makes possible preliminary analysis of the output.

The multistage clustering transformation can be assigned to the class of nonlinear techniques, which are powerful for description of local image regions. On the other hand, performance of such methods profoundly depends on the size of structuring element [12]. Although adaptive structuring elements have been considered in the literature [13, 14], the clustering procedure solves the problem of the size of processing window in a more elegant way.

We believe that the multistage structure can be associated with the theory of multistage integration of the visual information in the brain. Representation of the intermediate visual process in terms of conventional multilayer neural networks is improper. Certain complex structures must emerge in order to investigate inter-relations between consistently more complex components. The multistage network attempts to approach this problem from the functional point of view. It reflects the convergence of data flow in parallel channels. The data is processed according to the state in which it is found at the moment of processing.

The results of the multistage image analysis indicate the usefulness of this unified approach to image analysis. This approach can readily be applied to various visual pattern recognition problems with only minor changes in the algorithm. However, this is just a single example of the multistage strategy in signal processing. With some other local transformations used, the multistage network can be applied for different tasks. It is the task of researcher to find the proper information representation and suitable local transformation for each specific application.

References

1. Svechnicov S.V., Kozhemhako V.P., Timchenko L.I. "Quasipulse-potential optoelectronic elements and devices of logic-temporal type". – K.: Naukova Dumka, 1987.-256p.p.
2. Timchenko L.I. Multistage parallel-hirarchical networks as the model of neural-like computing scheme. /Cybernetics and system analysis. -2000. – N2-p.p. 114-134.
3. Grudin M.A., Harvey D.M., Timchenko L.I., Lisboa P.J.G. Face recognition method using a multistage hierarchical network / Proc of IEEE Int. Conf. Acoust., Speech and Signal Proc. (ICASSP97). – V.4. - Munich (Germany). - 1997. - P.2545 - 2548.
4. Grudin M.A., Timchenko L.I., Harvey D.M. and Gel V.P. A system-theoretical approach to multistage hierarchical image processing / Proceeding of EUROPTO Symposium Vision Systems Image Processing Techniques. - Vol. 2785. - Besancon (France). - 1996. - P. 225-234.
5. Timchenko L.I., Kutaev Y.F., Chepornyuk S.V., Grudin M.A., Harvey D.M., Gertsiy A.A., Brain A - Like approach to multistage hierarchial image / Lecture Notes in Computer Sciense. Image Analysis and Processing. Springer. - Vol.1311. -Florence (Italy) - 1997. - P.246 - 253.

6. Grudin M.A., Harvey D.M. and Timchenko L.I. Multistage hierarchy for fast image analysis / Proc. of the European Symposium on Satellite Remote Sensing III. - Vol.2955. - Taomina (Italy). - 1996. - P. 120 - 128.

7. Timchenco L., Chepornyuk S., Grudin M., Harvey D., Kutaev Y., Gertsiy A. Three-dimensional multistage network applying for facial image decomposition / Proc. Machine Vision Applications, Architectures, and Systems Integration IV. SPIE Symposium. - Pitsburg (USA). - 1997. - Vol. 3205.- P.90-95.

8. Timchenko L.I., Grudin M.A., Gel V.P. and Harvey D.M. A multistage hierarchical approach to image processing // IEE Colloquium on Mulitdimensional Systems. - London (UK). - 1996. - P. 2.1-2.6.

9. Kutaev Y., Timchenko L., Gertsiy A., Zagoruiko L. Compact representation of the facial images for identification in a parallel-hierarchical network / Proc. Machine Vision Systems for Inspection and Metrology VII. SPIE Symposium. - Boston (Massachusetts USA). - 1998. - Vol. 3521. - P. 157-167.

10. T. Kohonen, "The Self-Organizing Map," *Proc. of the IEEE*, Vol. 78, No. 9, pp. 1464-1479, Sept. 1990.

11. R. Linsker, "Self-Organization in a Perceptual Network," *IEEE Computer*, pp. 105-117, March 1988.

12. S. Zeki, *A Vision of the Brain.* Blackwell Scientific Publications, Oxford, 1993.

13. G. E. Hinton, "Mapping Part - Whole Hierarchies into Connectionist Networks," *Artificial Intelligence*, Vol. 46, No. 1-2, pp. 45-75, 1990.

14. Parallel-Hierarchical Transformation as the System Model of Optoelectronic Artificial Intelligence Tools. Monograph. / V.P.Kozhemyako, Yu.F. Kutaev, S.V. Svechnikov, L.I. Timchenko, A.A. Yaroviy – Vinnytsia: UNIVERSUM-Vinnytsia, 2003. – 324 p.

SPRING BRAKE ORTHOSIS FOR FES-ASSISTED WALKING WITH WHEEL WALKER

R. JAILANI[1,2], M.O. TOKHI[1] and S.C. GHAROONI[1]

[1]*Department of Automatic Control and System Engineering, University of Sheffield, UK*

[2]*Faculty of Electrical Engineering, Universiti Teknologi MARA, 40450 Shah Alam, MALAYSIA*
Email: r.jailani@sheffield.ac.uk

This paper presents a simulation of bipedal locomotion to generate stimulation pulses for activating muscles for paraplegic walking with wheel walker using functional electrical stimulation (FES) with spring brake orthosis (SBO). A new methodology for paraplegic gait, based on exploiting natural dynamics of human gait, is introduced. The work is a first effort towards restoring natural like swing phase in paraplegic gait through a new hybrid orthosis, referred to as spring brake orthosis (SBO). This mechanism simplifies the control task and results in smooth motion and more-natural like trajectory produced by the flexion reflex for gait in spinal cord injured subjects. The study is carried out with a model of humanoid with wheel walker using the Visual Nastran (Vn4D) dynamic simulation software. Stimulated muscle model of quadriceps is developed for knee extension. Fuzzy logic control (FLC) is developed in Matlab/Simulink to regulate the muscle stimulation pulse-width required to drive FES-assisted walking gait and the computed motion is visualised in graphic animation from Vn4D. The results show that SBO can reduce torque and stimulation pulses required for FES-assisted paraplegic walking with wheel walker.

1. Introduction

Paraplegic is impairment in motor and/or sensory function of the lower extremities. It is usually the result of spinal cord injury (SCI) which affects the neural elements of the spinal canal. Brown-Triolo et al. [1] in their study found that 51% of SCI subjects defined mobility in terms of life impact and autonomy, and gait was found to be perceived as the first choice in possible technology applications. Their subjects also indicated willingness to endure time intensive training and undergo surgery operation if mobility is guaranteed. Therefore, solutions to mobility loss were seen as an exciting prospect to these patients.

Restoring gait in SCI is a research challenge. Researchers have investigated various electrical, mechanical and combined techniques also called hybrid orthosis to restore functional movement in the lower limbs [2-4]. Among the gait phases, the swing phase is important in advancing the leg in order to contribute to movement of the body in the direction of gait progress. Hip flexion is an essential part of pick-up in the swing phase of reciprocal gait, whilst passive hip extension is important during the trunk glide in stance. Researchers have attempted to provide hip flexion to improve walking by a method called functional electrical stimulation (FES). Paraplegic walking with only FES has significant drawbacks in function restoration. Firstly, due to stimulated muscle contractions, muscle fatigue will quickly occur because of the reversed recruitment order of the artificial stimulated motoneurons. As a result, there are limitations in standing time and walking distance. Another disadvantage is erratic stepping trajectories because of poor control of joint torque [5].

Hybrid systems can overcome these limitations by combining FES with the use of a lower limb orthotic brace. Orthoses can guide the limb and reduce the number of degrees of freedom in order to simplify the control problem. The use of active muscle can also be reduced by locking orthosis joints. Furthermore, it rigidity improves walking efficiency and reduces overall energy cost [6].

In this paper, a hybrid FES gait system concept called Spring-Brake-Orthosis (SBO) which combines mechanical braces (with coordinated joint locking mechanism) with an energy storage element mounted on it and FES to generate the swing phase of paraplegic gait is presented [7]. This approach also substantially simplifies and reduces the problem of control tasks in a hybrid orthosis while offering more benefits on quality of a swinging leg. Previous work, Gharooni [7] has developed and validates SBO for leg swing phase while Huq [8] used SBO in body weight supported treadmill locomotion in simulation environment. In this paper, the application of SBO is widen where it is used for paraplegic walking with wheel walker. The new concept in hybrid orthotics provides solutions to the problems that affect current hybrid orthosis, including knee and hip flexion without relying on the withdrawal reflex or a powered actuator and foot-ground clearance without extra upper body effort.

2. Description of the model

2.1. *Humanoid model with wheel walker*

Humanoid model is built up using anthropometric data. Therefore, the quality and completeness of the anthropometric data are very important in this study. The anthropometric data considered in this study is based on Winter's work [9]. Human body is characterized by three main planes and directions with planes crossing in the centre of the body gravity. The length and mass of each body segment is expressed according to the overall weight and height of the humanoid model. The humanoid model developed in this work is based on a human body with height 1.73m and weight 80kg. The locations of the centre of mass together with segment density were also obtained from anthropometric data of Winter [9]. The density of each body segment was used to determine its volume which then determined their segment width.

The wheel walker model is developed using Vn4D software based on the design of a wheel walker sold by youreableshop^{TM}. The model developed incorporated all the basic parts of the real machine. For the wheel walker considered in this paper, the material, dimension and weight are duplicated from real wheel walker that is available in the market [10].

The final stage of the development of the humanoid with wheel walker model incorporated is the combination of both models. It is important to make sure that the humanoid model is attached to the wheel walker model at the right position and right joint.

2.2. *ANFIS muscle model*

In order to simulate FES, a physiological based muscle model is constructed with adaptive neuro-fuzzy inference system (ANFIS) based on previous work [11, 12]. A series of experiments using FES with different stimulation frequencies, pulse width and pulse duration to investigate the impact on muscle output torque are conducted. The collected data is used to develop the paraplegic muscle model. 500 training data and 300 testing data set are used in the development of muscle model. In this paper, the total joint moment generated by the muscle model to drive the walking gait depends on stimulated pulse width as the frequency is fixed to 33Hz. A fatigue model was incorporated in this muscle model which also takes into consideration that fatigue is increasing with rising stimulation frequencies. Additional explanation about muscle fatigue can also be obtained in earlier publication [13].

In the body-segmental dynamics, total joint moment is the sum of active and passive joint moments. Active joint moment is the addition of the joint moments produced by each muscle group and in this case, it will be represented by muscle model. Passive muscle properties have been separated from the active muscle properties, and are assigned to the joints in order to keep the number of muscle parameters low. In order to make sure the simulation accurately represents the real data, the knee passive properties used in this paper for moment of inertia, damping and stiffness are selected as 0.188 kgm^2, 0.0031055 Nms/deg and

0.024244 Nm/deg respectively. The optimisation and validation of these parameters can be found in earlier publications [14, 15]. Therefore, all the parameters used in this paper are extracted from one subject having T2/T3 incomplete lesion for 29 years and results obtained can be further validated by experimental work applied to the particular subject.

3. Walking gait

3.1. *Knee flexion leads to hip flexion*

There are two major forces that act during walking particularly the swing phase; gravity and segment interaction forces. Gravity acts on all masses comprising the body, and for the purpose of analysis, they can all be replaced with a single resultant force acting at the point of centre of mass (CoM). The projection of the centre of mass on the ground is called centre of gravity (CoG). In the SBO the spring acts as an external force on the knee joint and causes the knee to flex and potential energy is stored in the lower leg (by raising the CoM). Consequently, this causes firstly the shank to accelerate and secondly change in relative angle between the shank and thigh, with the lower extremity taking a new configuration. Both of these produce moments about the hip joint as will be illustrated in the following sections.

3.1.1. *Segment interaction*

In the movement of a multiple link mechanical structure such as the arm/forearm system, the torques at the joints arise not only from muscles acting on the joints but also from interactions due to movement of other links. These interaction torques are not present during movement at only a single joint and represent a significantly complicated function in the dynamic analysis of movement [16].

3.1.2. *Hip flexion kinetics*

During normal gait, flexion and extension of the hip and knee are linked by bi-articular muscles such as the rectus femoris and the hamstrings group, as well as kinematically and kinetically. Normal gait is initiated by hip flexion with little muscular action around the knee; the inertial properties of the shank cause the knee to flex in response to the accelerating thigh, producing ground clearance [17]. Additionally, as the hip flexes the shank remains in the lowest potential energy position and this leads to additional knee flexion.

These inter-segment linkages also apply when knee flexion occurs without muscular activity at the hip. If the knee is flexed the action of the accelerating shank will cause the hip to flex; additionally, the new orientation of the knee will cause the leg to adopt a new minimum energy configuration with a flexed hip as illustrated in Figure 1(a). The static relationship between the knee angle (α) and hip angle (θ) [7] based on anthropometric data used from [9] is given as:

$$tan\theta = sin\alpha/(2.426 + cos\alpha) \tag{1}$$

This relationship is plotted in Figure 1(b), which represents an ideal situation and assumes no spasticity or muscle contracture. Additional hip flexion is produced by the dynamic inter segment coupling and is dependent on the angular acceleration of the knee. Thus, it can be seen that if the knee can be made to flex by any means then this will also lead to hip flexion. The amount of hip flexion produced by the dynamic inter segment coupling is dependent on the angular acceleration of the knee.

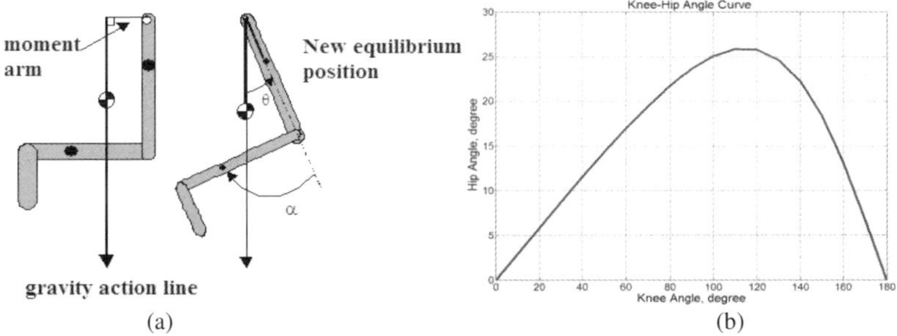

Figure 1: (a) Hip flexion resulting from flexed knee (b) Static relation between knee and hip flexion angle.

As indicated earlier, the swing phase is important in advancing the leg and hence movement of the body in the direction of gait progress. During pick-up, hip flexion, knee flexion, and ankle dorsiflexion all combine to clear the toe. In this study it is shown that hip flexion can be produced by the knee flexion.

In this paper, combination of spring and brake at the knee is introduced. The stimulated quadriceps muscles group can usually produce much more torque than is required to extend the leg, even with the thigh horizontal. A spring acts to resist knee extension, then the additional quadriceps torque can be used to 'charge' (store potential energy in) the spring when the leg is extended. A brake can then be used to maintain the knee in extension without further quadriceps contraction, preventing fatigue. When the brake is released the spring will contract, releasing its potential energy as kinetic energy and causing the knee to flex. The advantage of this approach over the use of a powered actuator is that a spring has a very high torque to weight and size ratio, efficient, robust and does not require any control signals or electrical power.

In order to prevent the dynamic hip flexion produced by the accelerating knee from being lost, a means of 'catching' the hip at its maximum flexion angle is required. This can be achieved by using a ratchet/brake at the hip. This leads to an orthosis combining a ratchet at the hip with a brake and spring at the knee and electrical stimulation of the quadriceps.

3.2. *Fuzzy control for knee extension*

There are 2 inputs selected as inputs for the controller. These are the error (difference between actual knee trajectory measured from Vn4D simulation output and reference knee trajectory) and change of error. The controller output is the stimulated pulse width. Five Gaussian (bell-shaped) type membership functions are used for each input and output. The inputs and output are normalised from 0 to 1 and the scaling factor used in left leg FLC are 0.1, 0.0025 and 70 while in the right leg FLC are 0.066, 0.0025 and 70 for error, change of error and output respectively. These values are obtained by trial and error process. Figure 2 shows a block diagram of the walking system. The stimulation pulse width from fuzzy controller will feed into the muscle model and produce muscle torque that drives the Vn4D model to follow the walking gait. Then the error and change of error are fed back to the fuzzy controller to adjust stimulation pulse-width to the optimum level.

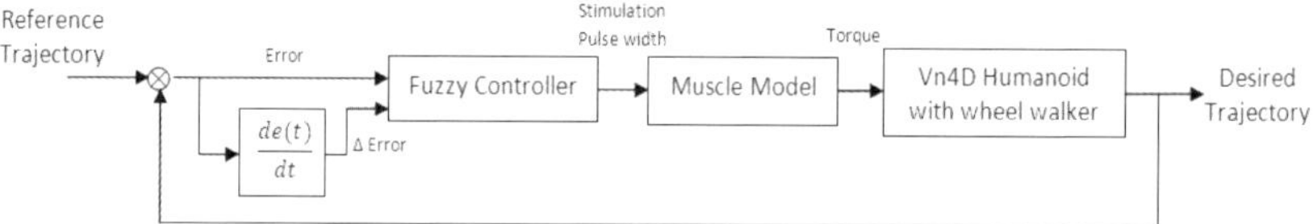

Figure 2: Block diagram of the control system.

4. Results

Simulations were carried out using Matlab/Simulink with incorporation of humanoid with wheel walker model in Vn4D to illustrate the effectiveness of SBO in FES-assisted walking with wheel walker. The control objective is to regulate the level of stimulated pulse width for muscle stimulation in knee extension by following the reference trajectory. The knee trajectories for walking gait from pre-defined trajectory and SBO are shown in Figure 3. Due to various perturbations and limited strength of the hip and knee flexor and extensor muscles, the shank and thigh may not perfectly track the reference trajectory.

The tasks of swing phase in view of its functional characteristics can be divided into two modes, namely passive and active. In passive mode, combination of functions of passive elements (brake and spring) initiates a swing phase by flexing the knee joint. A large range of knee flexion picks up the foot to make enough ground clearance. The inertia and pendular effects of the lower extremity advance the leg forward. In this study a spring constant of 200 N/m was used after a trial and error process. This spring constant value gives the best flexion trajectory referring to the predefined trajectory. In active mode, electrically stimulated knee extensor muscles groups provide the leg extension so that the heel reaches the ground. The timing block schedules and adjusts two passive and active modes by sending a strobe signal at appropriate times. It should be noted that the passive mode is double pendulum driven by only the spring torque in the knee joint and the active mode is a simple pendulum in which the joint trajectory is tracked by the electrically activated muscle torque. This is because the hip brake catches the hip at the maximum flexion angle, and does not allow the hip to move until the end of swing phase.

Figure 3 shows the stimulation pulse width, knee and hip trajectory for both legs. In the left knee, the stimulation starts at 0.48 second and at the time that knee is in full flexion. The same situation takes place with the right knee where the stimulation starts at 1.58 second. The results show that the controller designed work as expected. The results show that the left hip brake catches the maximum hip angle at 25° while the right hip brake catches the maximum hip angle at 27°. This is because the left leg is the beginning to provoke the start of periodic gait cycle and the right leg is where all body parts are in the movement condition where the centre of body is gravity and inertia driven in the direction of progression.

5. Conclusion

The objective of the SBO approach is to eliminate reliance on the withdrawal reflex and the associated problems of habituation and poor controllability. Instead, a simple switchable brake with a spring elastic element with well-defined properties provides the necessary function and trajectory. The technique seems promising in producing functional hip flexion. The results of the SBO typical behaviour with the model simulation confirm the effectiveness of the SBO for FES-assisted walking with wheel walker. It is also concluded that FLC can be successfully implemented to regulate the level of stimulation pulse-width used to stimulate the knee extensor muscle for FES-assisted walking with wheel walker. Based on the simulation developed, a stable walking gait with body weight transfer technique has been successfully achieved.

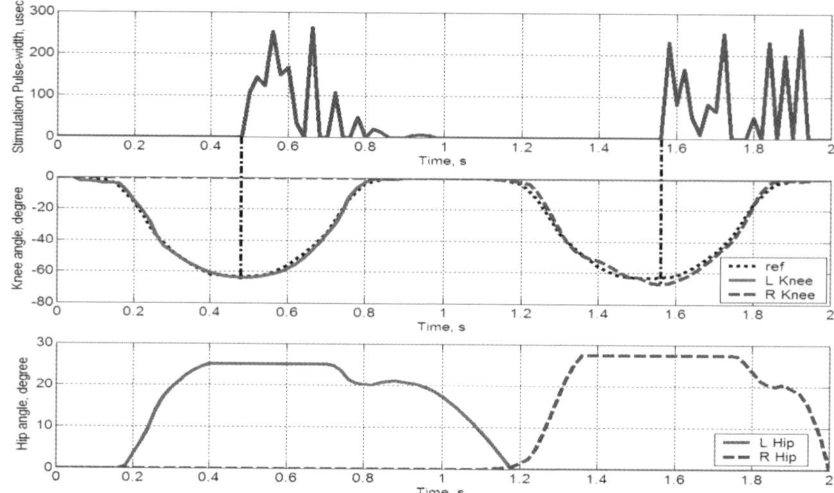

Figure 3: Stimulation pulse-width, knee and hip trajectory for complete walking gait.

References

1. D. Brown-Triolo, R. Triolo, and P. Peckham, "Mobility Issues and Priorities in Persons with SCI: A Qualitative Investigation," presented at Second Annual IFESS Conference, 1997.
2. K. Ferguson, G. Polando, R. Kobetic, R. Triolo, and E. Marsolais, "Walking with a hybrid orthosis system," *Spinal cord*, pp. 800-804, 1999.
3. D. Popovic, R. Tomovic, and L. Schwirtlich, "Hybrid assistive system-the motor neuroprosthesis," *Biomedical Engineering, IEEE Transactions on*, vol. 36, pp. 729-737, 1989.
4. M. Solomonow, E. Aguilar, E. Reisin, R. V. Baratta, R. Best, T. Coetzee, and R. D'Ambrosia, "Reciprocating gait orthosis powered with electrical muscle stimulation (RGO II). Part I: Performance evaluation of 70 paraplegic patients," *Orthopedics*, vol. 20, pp. 315-324, 1997.
5. J. Hausdorff and W. Durfee, "Open-loop position control of the knee joint using electrical stimulation of the quadriceps and hamstrings," *Medical and Biological Engineering and Computing*, vol. 29, pp. 269-280, 1991.
6. J. Stallard and R. E. Major, "The influence of orthosis stiffness on paraplegic ambulation and its implications for functional electrical stimulation (FES) walking systems," *Int. Prosthet. Orthot*, vol. 19, pp. 108-114, 1995.
7. S. Gharooni, B. Heller, and M. O. Tokhi, "A new hybrid spring brake orthosis for controlling hip and knee flexion in the swing phase," *Neural Systems and Rehabilitation Engineering, IEEE Transactions on*, vol. 9, pp. 106-107, 2001.

8. M. S. Huq, "Analysis and control of hybrid orthosis in therapeutic treadmill locomotion for paraplegia," in *Automatic Control and System Engineering*, vol. PhD: The University of Sheffield, 2009.

9. D. A. Winter, *Biomechanics and motor control of human movement*, 2nd ed. New York: Willey-Interscience, 1990.

10. "Where services and care matters, Mobility Smart," vol. 2008.

11. R. Jailani, M. O. Tokhi, S. C. Gharooni, and Z. Hussain, "A Novel Approach in Development of Dynamic Muscle Model for Paraplegic with Functional Electrical Stimulation," *Engineering and Applied Science*, vol. 4, pp. 272-276, 2009.

12. R. Jailani, M. O. Tokhi, S. C. Gharooni, and Z. Hussain, "Development of Dynamic Muscle Model with functional Electrical Stimulation," presented at International Conference on Complexity in Engineering (COMPENG 2010), Rome, Italy, 2010.

13. R. Jailani, M. O. Tokhi, S. C. Gharooni, and Z. Hussain, "The Investigation of The Stimulation Frequency and Intensity on Paraplegic Muscle Fatigue," presented at 14th Annual Conference of The International Functional Electrical Stimulation Society (IFESS 2009), Seoul, Korea, 2009.

14. R. Jailani, M. O. Tokhi, S. C. Gharooni, and Z. Hussain, "Estimation of Passive Stiffness and Viscosity in Paraplegic: A Dynamic Leg Model in Visual Nastran," presented at 14th International Conference on Methods and Models In Automation and Robotics, Miedzyzdroje, Poland, 2009.

15. R. Jailani, M. O. Tokhi, S. C. Gharooni, and Z. Hussain, "Passive Stiffness and Viscosity of Dynamic Leg Model: Comparison Between GA and PSO," presented at 12th International Conference on Climbing and Walking Robots and The Support Technologies for Mobile Machine (Clawar 2009), Istanbul, Turkey, 2009.

16. J. M. Hollerbach and T. Flash, "Dynamic interactions between limb segments during planar arm movement," *Biological Cybernetics*, vol. 44, pp. 67-77, 1982.

17. V. T. Inman, H. J. Ralston, F. Todd, and J. C. Lieberman, *Human walking* Williams & Wilkins Baltimore, 1981.

TOWARDS AN ADVANCED VIRTUAL TESTING ENVIRONMENT FOR CONCRETE MATERIALS

EDWIN DADO

*Faculty of Military Sciences, Netherlands Defence Academy, Hogeschoollaan 2, Breda,
The Netherlands*

EDDIE KOENDERS

*Faculty of Civil Engineering and Geosciences, Delft University of Technology,
Stevinweg 1, Delft, The Netherlands*

SJOERD MEVISSEN

*Faculty of Military Sciences, Netherlands Defence Academy, Hogeschoollaan 2, Breda,
The Netherlands*

Physical laboratory-based experiments and tests have become a fundamental learning, research and development tool in many areas of (civil) engineering education, science and practice. However, new areas of research in engineering analysis have come about as a result of the changing roles of computational models in respect to laboratory-based experiments. In this context, virtual testing is rapidly emerging as a key technology in civil engineering (CE). With the application of advanced existing or emerging information and communication technologies (ICT) - including grid computing, web services, product data technology, semantic web and soft computing - we are able to create so-called advanced 'virtual testing environments' (VTEs) that allow students, researchers and practioners to conduct virtual tests anytime and anyplace. In the first part of this paper the motivation and the current applications of virtual testing in CE is discussed. In the second part of this paper, the emphasis will be on the existing and emerging technologies for developing VTEs and the current efforts at Delft University of Technology to develop a VTE for concrete materials.

1. Introduction

Physical laboratory-based experiments and tests have become a fundamental learning, research and development tool in many areas of (civil) engineering education, science and practice. In the context of education, they have particularly enriched engineering education by helping students to understand fundamental principles by connecting theory and equations in their text books to real world applications with real equipment and data. In the context of science, physical experiments have been used to gain insight into a particular phenomenon in a real-life setting or to verify or validate scientific computational models for a long time. In both educational and research context, this type of physical experiments is generally governed by the available infrastructure and resources at the educational and research institutes, frequently limiting the exposure of valuable materials to a relatively small audience [1].

New areas of research in engineering analysis have come about as a result of the changing roles of computational models in respect to laboratory-based experiments. This new environment of engineering is forcing scientists to allocate experimental infrastructures and resources differently. Rather than trying to prove whether a calculation or computational simulation is correct, the focus is on learning how to use experimental data to 'improve' the accuracy of (existing) computational models. This process of improving the accuracy of calculations and computer models is using advanced statistical techniques of assessing the accuracy of computational predictions with respect to experimental measurements. In fact, it takes into account that both computer simulation and experimental data have uncertainties associated with them [2]. Thus providing a testing environment based on highly-validated computer models and associated experimental data that is able to make highly precise predictions of the outcome of laboratory-based tests without the need to perform them in a real laboratory.

With the application of advanced existing or emerging information and communication technologies (ICTs) - including, grid computing, web services, product data technology, semantic web and soft computing - we are able to create so-called 'virtual testing environments' (VTEs) that allow students, researchers and practioners to conduct virtual tests anytime and anyplace.

2. Brief overview of virtual testing in civil engineering

Virtual testing is rapidly emerging as a key technology in civil engineering (CE). Although some applications of virtual testing other than related to (composite) materials and components have been reported by a number of researchers, most effort has been put into the development of VTEs for composite materials (e.g. concrete materials) and components. [3] In this respect, virtual testing is mostly defined as a concept of making use of high performance computers in conjunction with high quality models to predict the properties and/or behavior of composite materials and components. Consequently, virtual testing is often seen as another new terminology for computer simulation, which is a wrong assumption. Although it is true that computer simulation is an important tool for virtual testing, it is only one of key components that constitute a VTE [3].

As discussed earlier, within a VTE computer models interact with experimental data in order to predict the properties and behavior of composite materials and components. In this context, one can discuss about the question whether a functional VTE actually increases the need for physical laboratory-based testing or not. Even the most convinced adepts of computer simulation consider that physical laboratory-based testing is essential to the success of correlative and predictive computer simulation work. Currently, we can only speak of complementary virtual testing, mainly for cost reduction and re-analysis purposes and it of prime importance not to confront this important topic to that of the experimental validation work which is at least of equal importance [4].

One of the most influential pioneers of virtual testing in CE is NIST[*] in the US. In January 2001, a NIST/industry consortium was formed to develop a 'virtual cement and concrete testing laboratory' (VCCTL). The main goal of the consortium was to develop a virtual testing system, using a suite of integrated computer models for designing and testing cement-based materials in a virtual environment, which can accurately predict durability and service life based on detailed knowledge of starting materials, curing conditions, and environmental factors. In 2001 an early prototype (version 1.0) of the VCCTL became public available and accessible through the Internet. The core of this prototype was formed by the NIST 3D Cement Hydration and Microstructure Development Model (CEMHYD3D). Using the web-based interface of the VCCTL, we can create an initial microstructure containing cement, mine mineral admixtures, and inert fillers following a specific particle size distribution, hydrate the microstructure under a variety of curing conditions and evaluate the properties of the simulated microstructures for direct comparison to experimental data. As the consortium proceeded, the prediction of rheological properties of the fresh materials and elastic properties of the hardened materials were incorporated into the VCCTL resulting in the release of version 1.1 of the VCCTL in 2003 [5].

3. Brief overview of existing and emerging ICT

In order to structure the discussion in this section, a conceptual scheme for a VTE is presented in Figure 1. As shown in Figure 1, a VTE consists of three main parts (or layers): (1) Virtual Testing Laboratory (system layer), (2) Computer Models (application layer) and (3) Data (data layer) embedded in (1) Hardware Environment and (2) Software Environment.

---

[*] National Institute of Standards and Technologies (NIST).

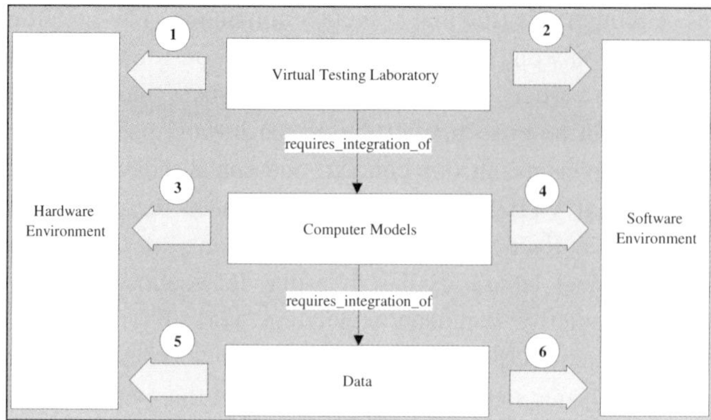

Figure 1: Conceptual scheme for a Virtual Testing Environment.

The Hardware Environment, as shown Figure 1, not only contains computer systems and infrastructure but also can contain (or interfaces with) traditional physical laboratory equipment. In the past, a number of approaches were based on this idea of a VTE as a virtual web-based interface providing 'virtual access' to physical laboratory equipment and accompanying materials [6]. As discussed in [3], VTEs are no longer regarded as isolated web-based computer environments, but as a set of integrated hardware and software components that, used together, form a distributed and collaborative space for virtual testing. Multiple, geographically dispersed (research) institutes use the virtual laboratories to establish their own VTE to perform experiments and tests as well as share their results. An emerging technology in this respect is grid computing technology. As an example, consider the prediction of properties of concrete-based structures. Concrete is a composite material which' aspects and corresponding properties need to be predicted on different levels of detail. A multi-scale modeling approach, where these different levels are integrated, leads to a more comprehensive basis for the description of the concrete material performance and increases the accuracy of the prediction of the properties of concrete [7]. However, research in the past has led to the development of specialized computer models that are developed by different research institutes. A shared access to and the use of these resources is an inevitable condition for multi-scale modeling. Grid computing technology addresses these needs (partly).

The Software Environment, as shown in Figure 1, is traditionally dominated by (programming) languages such as SQL for databases, Fortran and C(++) for implementing computer models, HTML for developing web-based interfaces for user interaction etc. An emerging technology in this area is platform technology[*]. Keywords in this respect are web services and interoperability. Web Services fundamentally concern about the interoperability, especially when the computer application programs concerned are developed using different languages tools and computer platforms. Web services standards and technologies offer a widely adopted mechanism for making computer programs work together.

Concerning the issue of interoperability we need to distinguish three layers of interoperability: (1) data interoperability, (2) application interoperability and (3) resource interoperability. As discussed in [8] the common agreement is that the solution of the data interoperability problem is at the information level. In the last two decades several research and development projects have shown that product data technology provides a good basis for the development of information models in the CE domain. Today, with the development of the Industry Foundation Classes (IFC), the product modeling paradigm has been implemented in many commercial and scientific computer applications[†]. An emerging technology in this area is semantic web technology. In the context of data interoperability, the semantic web derives its notion of meaning of content specialized vocabularies, referred to as 'ontologies'. Integrating ontologies with web services make them visible and accessible for other computer applications (i.e. application integration). Although Grid Computing can provide the technological backbone for resource integration, multi-scale modeling cannot be successful without incorporating ICTs related to data/application integration[‡].

Another emerging technology related to the data layer, as shown in Figure 1, is soft computing technology. As discussed earlier, one of the most important features of a VTE is assessing the accuracy of a computational prediction with respect to experimental measurements. In this respect, advanced statistical techniques for data analysis, such as multiple regression and correlation techniques, are often used. Soft computing technology is a container term which refers to complementary technologies such as neural computing, fuzzy logic, genetic algorithms, probabilistic reasoning etc. Soft computing and statistical techniques emphasize different aspects of data analysis. Soft computing focuses on obtaining working solutions quickly, accepting approximations and unconventional approaches. Its strength lies in its flexibility to create models that suit the needs arising in computer applications (e.g. model generation). Statistics - as branch of mathematics - is more rigorous and focuses on establishing

---

[*] E.g. Sun's J2EE and Microsoft's .NET platforms.
[†] More information: www.iai-international.org.
[‡] Examples of R&D projects can be found at: www.escience-grid.org.uk and www.semanticgrid.org.

objective conclusions based on experimental data by analyzing the possible situations and their likelihood (e.g. model validation) [9].

4. Progress towards a VTE for concrete materials

The section of Material and Environment of the Faculty Civil Engineering at Delft University of Technology has been involved in a number of trials in order to find out the basic principles of which a VTE should comply with and to find out the conditions at which this VTE would be attractive to establish. The first trials where focusing on the virtual testing of the concrete compressive strength. In physical-based concrete laboratories, the compressive strength is determined with an experimental device where a concrete cube is positioned in between two steel plates and compressed using a hydraulic force. The force imposed to the concrete cube is increased until failure occurs. When considering a VTE, this procedure has to be mimicked while using different complementary computer models. These computer models are used to simulate the failure behavior of the material during testing. The simulation of the development of the material properties is conducted with the hydration model Hymostruc and the failure behavior is simulated with the Lattice model [10,11].

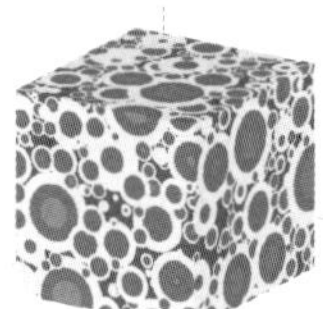 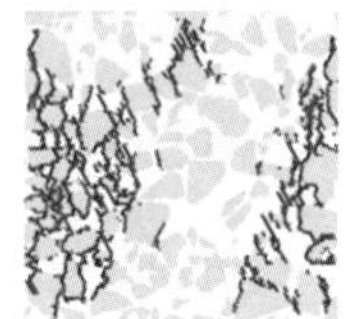 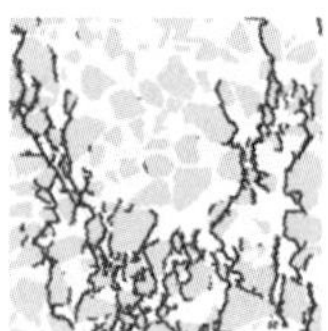

Figure 2: Left: Hymostruc virtual microstructure. Right: Lattice facture simulation.

After mixing of concrete, hardening takes place and the material properties start to develop. This process leads to a set of properties that is unique for every particular type of concrete. Determining the properties of an arbitrary type of concrete in general and the compressive strength in particular, is therefore a necessary need, every time a mix composition alters. Computer models can be used to predict the material properties. The Hymostruc model is used to predict the hardening process of cement-based materials as a function of the water-cement ratio, the reaction temperature, the chemical cement composition and the particle size distribution of the cement. The model calculates the inter-particle contacts by means of the 'interaction mechanism for the expanding particles' where hydrating particles are embedded in the outer shell of larger hydrating particles. This mechanism provides the basis of the formation of a microstructure which, on its turn, can be considered as the backbone of the hardening material.

Up till now, only the Hymostruc model has been partly amended and its functionality partly changed towards a future highly adaptive service kernel that is able to be integrated in a future VTE (Figure 3).

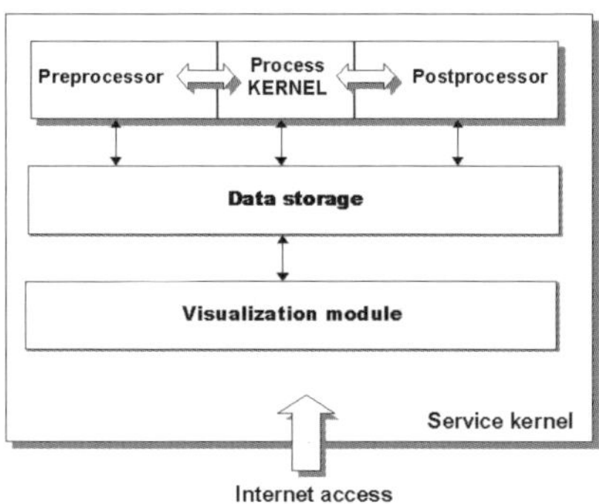

Figure 3: Schematic representation of the service kernel's structure.

Figure 3 gives the plain impression of the architectural model of the highly adaptive service kernel; build up from pre-processor-module, a process-kernel, and a post-processor-module. The pre-processor module comprises several functionalities about the generation of a virtual microstructure or particle structured materials. Initially, the microstructure's virtual basis can be generated by either a statistical or a random placement of the particles within the predefined material boarders. The process-kernel represents a module for calculation and calculates the formation of inter-particle contacts of microstructures by mechanisms based on chemical, physical and mechanical processes. The post-processing module addressed, calculates the materials properties from a generated microstructure. The visualization module provides for a real-time visualization of the calculated simulation process.

The next step in the development of the VTE is the embedment of the Lattice model for simulation of the ultimate capacity of concrete based on a fracture mechanics and necessary to predict the crack propagation of the material during loading. The model simulates fracture processes by means of mapping a framework of beams to the materials structure. For concrete materials in particular, the Lattice model reflects the high-level structure representing the paste and aggregates. The model should be able to detect failure paths through the material (weakest links) and to calculate the accompanying ultimate strength of the material. Once this failure path has been initiated, the inner structure of the material starts to disintegrate and affects the actual strength of the cube as well. Together, the Hymostruc model and the Lattice model have the potential to be the model core of the future VTE for compressive strength tests.

5. Conclusions

This paper depicts the development of 'advanced' VTEs in CE. In this respect, virtual testing is based on highly-validated computer models and associated experimental data that is able to make highly precise predictions of the outcome of laboratory-based tests without the need to perform them in a real laboratory. As discussed in this paper, with the promises of advanced existing and emerging ICTs a whole new realm of possibilities for developing VTEs has opened. In this paper we discussed one effort related to the development of VTE for concrete materials. Although the involved researchers denote the importance of advanced VTEs, the possibilities of existing and emerging ICT are largely ignored or very limited implemented in the current version of their VTE for concrete materials. It will take a huge investment in time and resources to come up with a VTE that meet the requirements of an advanced VTE as described in this paper.

References

1. F. Kuester, and T. Hutchinson, A virtualized laboratory for earthquake engineering education, Journal of Engineering Education, 15:13, 2007.
2. S. Doebling et al, Validation of Transient Structural Dynamics Simulations, Third Int. Conf. on Sensitivity Analysis of Model Output, 2001.
3. E. Dado, E. Koenders, and S. Özsariyildiz, Virtual Testing Environments for Composite Materials and Components in CE, CC2009 Conf., 2009.
4. K. Kayvantash, Virtual Testing & Modelling: State-of-the-Art Review, European Vehicle Safety Network 2, www.passivesafety.com/, 2004.
5. J. Bullard, The Virtual Cement and Concrete Testing Laboratory Consortium - Annual Report, NIST, 2002.
6. P. Bhargava et al, Web-based virtual torsion laboratory, Journal of Computer Applications in Engineering Eduction, 14:1, 2006.
7. E. Koenders et al, A Virtual Lab for Building Materials, AEC Conf. 2005.
8. E. Dado, ICT-Enabled Communication and Co-operation in Large-Scale On-Site Construction Projects, Delft University of Technology, 2002.
9. COST consortium, Combining Soft Computing Techniques and Statistical Methods to Improve Data Analysis Solutions, Fact Sheet, EU, 2008.
10. Hymostruc, www.microlab.tudelft.nl, 2009.
11. E. Schlangen, Experimental and Numerical Analysis of Fracture Processes in Concrete, Delft University of Technology, 1993.

MODELING, SIMULATION AND VHDL IMPLEMENTATION OF DISTRIBUTIONS BASED PWM CONTROLLER

EMIL POP, MONICA LEBA

System Control, Applied Informatics and Computer Engineering Department,
University of Petrosani, Str.Universitatii, 20
Petrosani, 332006, Romania

In this paper, the PWM controller is modeled and simulated based on distributions properties and then it is implemented using VHDL hardware description language. Using distributions it is possible to describe complex PWM equations in such a manner that it could be implemented in VHDL code. This solution allows a software-embedded controller implementation in a VLSI ASIC integrated circuit.

1. Introduction

The present PWM controller devices are mostly software oriented technologies based on microcontrollers for complex and non time critic applications.

Microcontroller programmable logic devices are a very good solution to implement the mathematical complex control algorithm with non critical time. But, when it is needed parallel processing then there must be chosen another solution available today using VHDL and ASIC programmed logic. This solution is a middle way between the hardware parallel processing and high speed capabilities and software control algorithm flexibility. This solution has big constraints regarding the mathematical formula implementation.

In some cases, a solution to avoid this barrier is to use the distributions and their remarkable properties. In this paper, we will use the following distributions definition: Distributions are real, linear and continuous functional f defined on fundamental functions space $\left\{ \varphi_i(x) \right\} = K^m$ having the properties [2], [4]:

$$\forall \varphi_1(x), \varphi_2(x) \in K^m, \ \alpha, \beta \in R^n : \alpha \cdot \varphi_1(x) + \beta \cdot \varphi_2(x) \in K^m \tag{1}$$

$$\forall \varphi_k(x) \in K^m : \lim_{k \to \infty} |\varphi_k(x)| = 0 \tag{2}$$

$$f : K^m \to R : \qquad f[\varphi(x)] \in R$$

Very important are the elementary distributions like pulse and step.

696

1.1. *Elementary distributions*

The pulse distribution or Dirac pulse is defined as follows [3], [5], [6]:

$$\delta : K^m \to R : \delta[\varphi(x)] = \varphi(0) = \begin{cases} 0; x \neq 0 \\ \infty; x = 0 \end{cases} ; \ \varphi(x) \in K^m ; \ \int_R \delta[\varphi(x)]dx = 1 \qquad (3)$$

The most important properties of Dirac distribution are:

$$\frac{d[f(x)]}{dx} = f(x)' + \sum_{i=1}^{p} s_i \cdot \delta(x - x_i); \ s_i = f(x_i + 0) - f(x_i - 0) \qquad (4)$$

$$\delta[f(x)] = \sum_{i=1}^{p} \frac{1}{\left|f'(x)\right|} \cdot \delta(x - x_i); \ x_i \text{ are real, simple solutions of } f(x) = 0 \qquad (5)$$

The step distribution or Heaviside distribution is defined bellow:

$$\theta : K^m \to R; \qquad \theta[\varphi(x)] = \begin{cases} 1; & x \geq 0 \\ 0; & x < 0 \end{cases} \qquad (6)$$

The important properties of the step distribution are the following:

$$f(x) \cdot [\theta(x - x_0) - \theta(x - x_1)] = \begin{cases} f(x), & x \in [x_0, x_1] \\ 0, & x \notin [x_0, x_1] \end{cases} \qquad (7)$$

$$\theta(-x) = 1 - \theta(x); \ \theta(x) - \theta(-x) = \text{sign}(x) ; \ \frac{d[\theta(x)]}{dx} = \delta(x) \qquad (8)$$

1.2. *Modeling and simulation*

In order to validate the theoretical results and then to find practical implementation solutions, there will be achieved the modeling and simulation both of the distributions and the PWM controller. In this section, the elementary distributions and their major properties will be tested. In figure 1 the model of $\delta(x - x_0)$, $\theta(x - x_0)$ and $\text{sign}(x)$ was designed and simulated. The same way there can be tested all the properties of each elementary distribution.

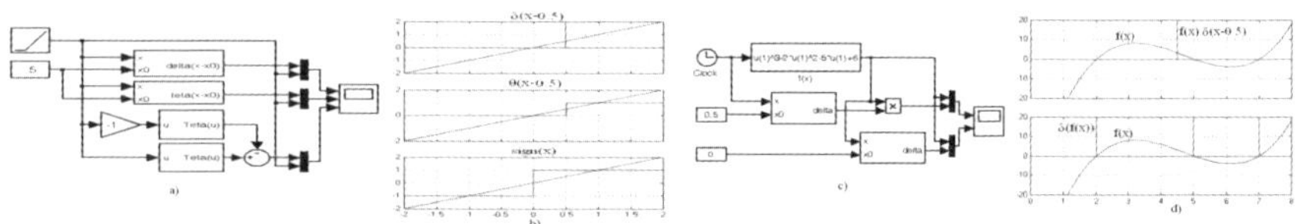

Figure 1. Distributions: a) Model; b) Delta, step and sign simulation results; c) Delta property model; d) Simulation results

Using the function $f(x) = x^3 - 2 \cdot x^2 - 5 \cdot x + 6$, that has the simple real solutions $x_1 = 2, x_2 = 5, x_3 = 7$ there is designed a model that implements (4) and (5) delta distribution properties, as shown in figure 1.c and d.

The property (7) of step distribution can be used as interval characteristic function. By this, it is possible to write as a closed formula any multi-intervals defined function. Let the following multi-intervals function:

$$f(x) = \begin{cases} x - 1, & x \in (-\infty, -1] \\ x, & x \in (-1, 1) \\ x - 1, & x \in [1, \infty) \end{cases} \tag{9}$$

The final closed formula is:

$$f(x) = x - 1 + \theta(x + 1) - \theta(x - 1) \tag{10}$$

Appling the derivation operator results:

$$\frac{df(x)}{dx} = 1 + \delta(x + 1) - \delta(x - 1) \tag{11}$$

The simulation model and results are presented in figure 2.

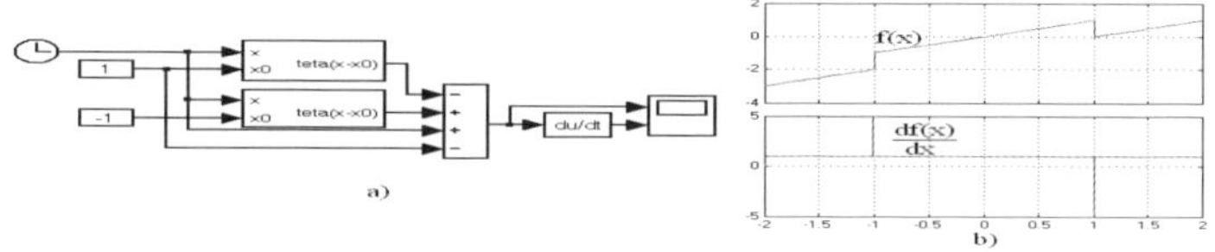

Figure 2. Multi-interval function simulation: a) Model; b) Function and its derivation

2. Three-Phased PWM Distributions Based Controller

2.1. *Principle*

The PWM controller must generate six appropriate PWM pulses that are 120 degrees unphased. This complicated process consists of sine wave modulation with a triangular carrier. In order to generate the triangular pulses train, like the one in figure 3, having variable parameters, like frequency (f) and modulation index (p) we have to apply the above theorem and distributions properties.

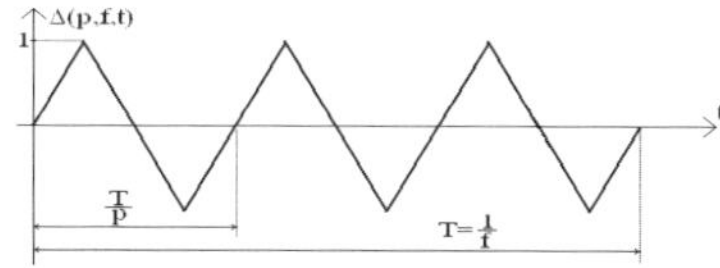

Figure 3. Triangular pulses train principle

698

The triangular wave formula in distributions is [9], [10]:

$$\Delta(p,f,t)=4p\cdot f\cdot\sum_{k=0}^{2\cdot p}(-1)^{k}\cdot\left(t-\frac{2k}{4p\cdot f}\right)\cdot\left[\theta\left(t-\frac{2k-1}{4p\cdot f}\right)-\theta\left(t-\frac{2k+1}{4p\cdot f}\right)\right] \quad (12)$$

The sine wave formula is:

$$\sigma(R,f,i,t)=R\cdot\sin\left(2\cdot\pi\cdot f\cdot t+\frac{2\cdot(i-1)\cdot\pi}{3}\right) \quad (13)$$

where R is the modulation ratio, i is the phase number (i=1,2,3) and k is the pulse number (k=1..2p).

The PWM pulses train is calculated from the intersection points between the two waves. Using the distributions properties, this problem can be solved very simple and precisely, applying the above theorem as follows:

$$PWM_{i}(t)=\theta[\sigma(R,f,i,t)-\Delta(p,f,t)] \quad (14)$$

The controller generates three pulses trains (PWM_{i}) and other three un-phased by 180° ($\overline{PWM_{i}}$) to these.

2.2. *PWM controller modeling and simulation*

Using the distributions equation (14), where σ and Δ are given by (12) and (13) equations, there is designed the model from figure 4.a. In figure 4.b is shown the detailed model of the distributions based triangular wave Δ.

In figure 4.c are presented the triangular carrier generated by distributions together with the three-phased modulation sine waves.

In figure 4.d are shown the six PWM pulses generated according to the (13) distributions equation.

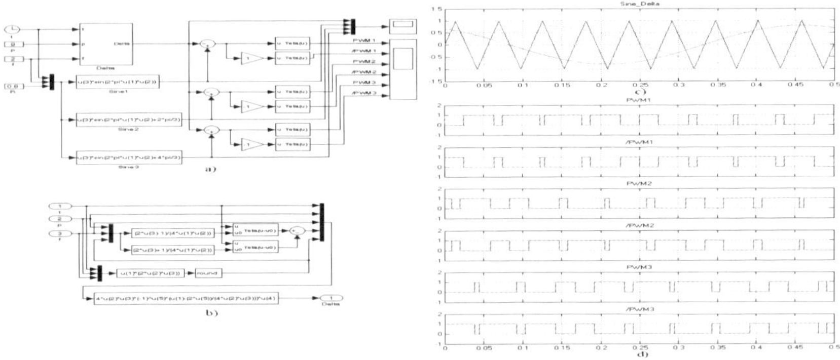

Figure 4. Three-phased PWM controller for p=9, f=2Hz and R=0.8: a) Model; b) Triangular wave generation; c) Modulation principle; d) PWM pulses

3. Distributions Based Three Phase PWM Controller VHDL Design

The controller is intended to be a standalone ASIC VHDL implementation. This solution has the major advantage of high speed operation, because it works in parallel hardware level processing. This speed is not achievable by microcomputers software implementation, like microcontroller or microprocessor. The block diagram of this new controller is proposed as shown in figure 5 [11], [12]. This solution has some hardware advantages like: low power consumption, ensures the necessary pins numbers and a minimum of RAM memory.

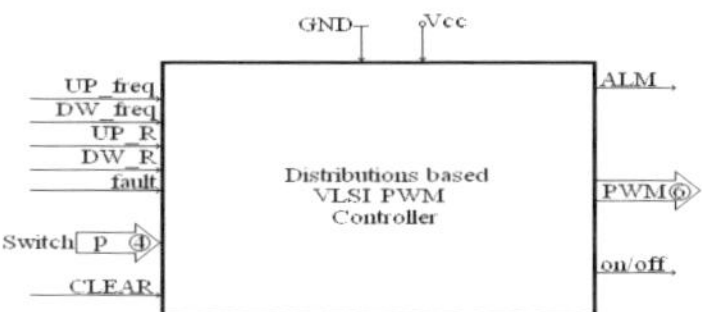

Figure 5. Distributions based VLSI PWM controller

The inputs are: two signals for frequency increment and decrement, two signals for R index increment and decrement, four signals from a switch for p (number of triangles per period) and other two signals for Clear that resets all the controller elements and Fault that get an error signal from the process. The outputs are: six PWM pulses, an Alarm (ALM) signal and an on/off signal from the power supply.

For this VLSI PWM controller was used the VHDL language. First there was detailed the structure of the project. In figure 6 is presented this detailed diagram. As can be seen most of the blocks are implemented based on the distributions properties. Among these, the followings sine and delta generators and Step block are implemented completely based on distributions theory. Also the clock generator uses several properties of distributions.

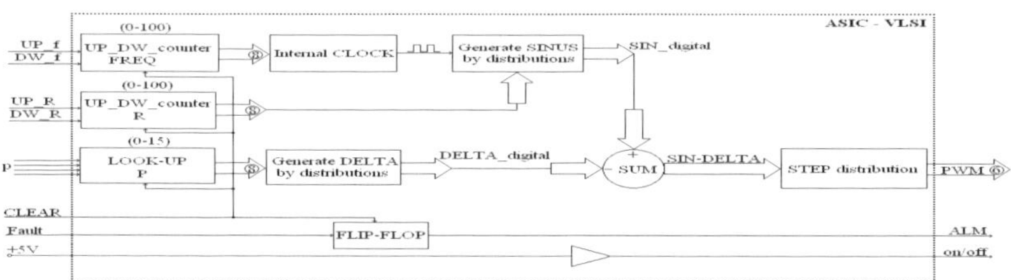

Figure 6. Detailed diagram of distributions VLSI PWM controller

700

There were used two up/down counters, one for frequency f control and one for index R control. The factor p is taken from a look-up table, where are memorized 16 possible values (odd multiple of 3). The frequency is used for an internal clock generator. This clock pilots the sine generator which is scaled with the index R. This clock together with the factor p generates the triangles. Sine and negated triangles are inputs for an adder. The resulted signal is input to the Step distribution block that generates directly the PWM pulses. This diagram was tested in MatLab-Simulink. In figure 7 is presented the simulation model. In figure 8 are presented the simulation results for f=20Hz, R=60% and p=15. In figure 8.a are the three phased PWM pulses and in figure 8.b are the line voltages. As can be seen from the results in figure 8.b the resulting line voltages are identical to the ones in the classical PWM controller.

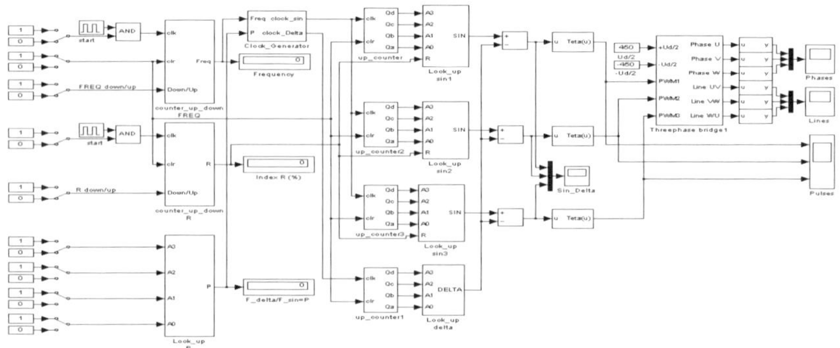

Figure 7. VLSI PWM controller simulation model

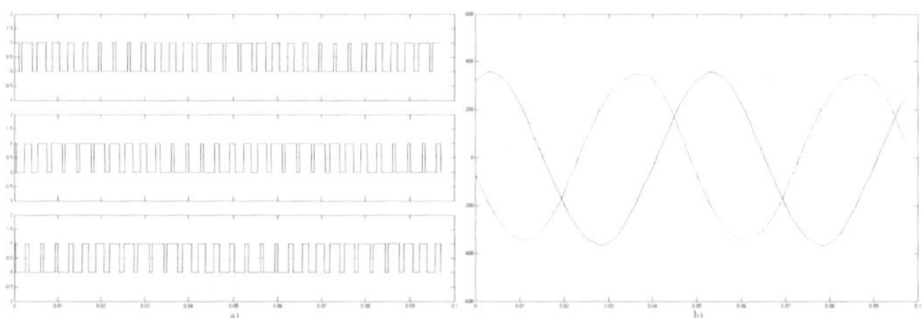

Figure 8. Simulation results

The VHDL code for the sine generator is presented in figure 9.

```
library IEEE;                                        "00100110",
use IEEE.STD_LOGIC_1164.ALL;                         "00000000",
use IEEE.STD_LOGIC_ARITH.ALL;                        "11011010",
use IEEE.STD_LOGIC_UNSIGNED.ALL;                     "10111001",
entity clk_sin_gen is                                "10100100",
Port ( clk,clr : in std_logic;                       "10011100",
sin_out: out std_logic_vector(7 downto 0));          "10100100",
end clk_sin_gen;                                     "10111001",
                                                     "11011010");
architecture Behavioral of clk_sin_gen is     begin
signal addr : std_logic_vector (0 to 3);      process(clk,clr)
type vector_array is array(0 to 15) of        begin
std_logic_vector(7 downto 0);                     if clr='0' then
constant memory: vector_array:=                     addr<="0000";
    ("00000000",                                  elsif (clk'event and clk='1')  then
        "00100110",                                 addr<= addr+ 1;
        "01000111",                                end if;
        "01011100",                             sin_out <= memory
        "01100100",                                 (conv_integer(addr));
        "01011100",                             end process;
        "01000111",                             end Behavioral;
```

Figure 9. VHDL code for sine generator

The simulation results for this sine generator are presented in figure 10.

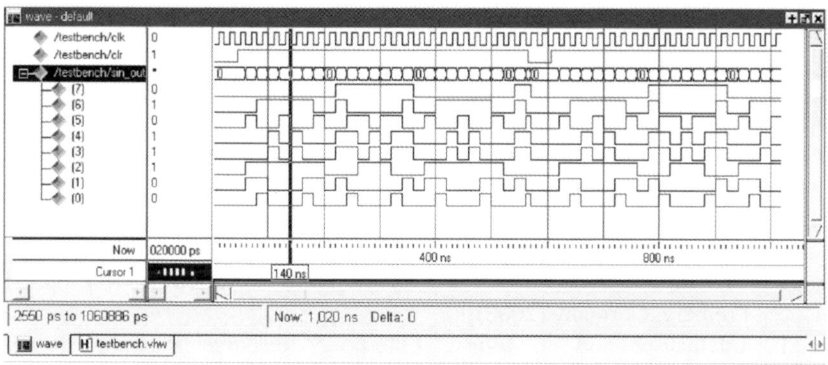

Figure 10. VHDL digital sine generator

4. Conclusions

Using the distributions theory properties the digital systems can be modeled and simulated analyzed and designed using the experience and tools of continuous systems. The properties of distributions can be useful in VLSI design in order to avoid the major problem of complex formula implementation. The designed distributions based VLSI controller is an alternative solution versus microcontroller or microprocessor, cheaper and more compact. It has the major advantage of high speed operation, because it implements parallel processing, has hardware level high speed and good reliability.

References

1. D. Perry, VHDL Programming by examples. *McGraw Hill* (2002).
2. L. Schwartz, Theorie des distributions, *Hermann*, Paris (1951).
3. M. Leba and E. Pop, New Distribution Properties and Applications in Digital Control, *Proceedings of the 7th WSEAS International Conference on ADVACED TOPICS on SIGNAL PROCESING, ROBOTICS and AUTOMATION (ISPRA'08)*, Cambridge, U.K., ISBN 978 960 6766 44 2, ISSN 1790 5117, pp. 43-48, **BHL87** (2008).
4. R.G. Buschman, Integral Transformation, Operational Calculus and Generalizated Functions, *Kluwer*, Netherlands (1996).
5. P. Dirac, The Physical Interpretation of Quantum Dynamics, *Proceedings of Royal Society*, Section A113, London, pp. 621-641 (1926-1927).
6. F. Farassat, Introduction to Generalized Functions with Applications in Aerodynamics and Aeronautics, *Langley Research Center*, Hampton (1994).
7. W. Kecs and P.P. Teodorescu, Introducere in teoria distributiilor cu aplicatii in tehnica, *Ed.Tehnica*, Bucuresti (1975).
8. F.G. Friedlander and M. Joshi, Introduction to the Theory of Distribution, *Cambridge University Press*, USA (1999).
9. R. Cristescu and G. Marinescu, Applications of Theory of Distributions, *John Wiley and Sons Inc*, USA (1973).
10. O. Heaviside, On Operators in Mathematical Physics, *Proceedings of Royal Society*, Section 52, London, pp. 504-529 (1893).
11. E. Edelhauser and A. Ionica, Software Solutions for the Romanian Underground Coal Mining, *Freiberger Forschungshefte Reihe C 526 - Geoingenieurwessen*, ISBN 978-3-86012-340-6, ISSN 0071-9404, pp. 31-38, Freiberg, Germany (2008).
12. E. Edelhauser and A. Ionica, Enterprise Resource Planning through Structural Founds in the Romanian Economy, *Proceedings of 6th International Conference Management Technological Changes*, Greece, **BMO93** (2009).

FUNDAMENTAL MATRIX APPROACH IN SOLVING PRACTICAL STABILITY FOR DISTRIBUTED PARAMETER SYSTEMS

DJORDJE N. DIHOVICNI

Department of Control Systems, Technical College, Bulevar Zorana Djindjica
Belgrade, Serbia 11070, Serbia

MIROSLAV MEDENICA

Department of Control Systems, Technical College, Bulevar Zorana Djindjica
Belgrade, Serbia 11070, Serbia

The practical stability for a class of distributed parameter system is presented. The system is described in state space and it is developed unique theory for such a problem, where is used fundamental matrix of system and matrix measure. From strictly engineering point of view it is extremely important to know on which interval is system stable, especially for very complex systems,such as distributed parameter systems, which state equation depends on time and space co-ordinate. In order to know successful theory results, numerical example and system motion are shown.

1. Introduction

During process of analysing and synthesis of control systems fundamental problem is stability. It is well-known fact, that we can share stability definitions to Ljapunov and non-Ljapunov concept that are arisen from various engineering needs. The most often case for consideration of control systems is Ljapunov approach, where the system behaving is considering on infinite interval, which in real cases has only academic importance. From strictly engineering point of view it is very important to know the boundaries where system trajectory comes during there's motion in state space. These practical technical needs are responsible for non-Ljapunov definitions, and among them is extremely important behaving on finite time interval- practical stability. Taking into account that system can be stable in classic way but also can posses not appropriate quality of dynamic behavior, and because that it is not applicable, it is important to take system in consideration in relation with sets of permitted states in phase space which are defined for such a problem. In theory of control systems, there are demands for stability on finite time interval that for strictly engineering view of point has tremendous importance. The basic difference between Ljapunov, and practical stability is set of initial states of system (S_α) and set of permitted disturbance (S_ε) in state space, for every opened set S_β permitted states and it is supplied that equilibrium point of that system will be totally stable, instead the principle of practical stability where are sets (S_α, S_ε) and set S_β which is closed, determined and known in advance.

Taking into account principle of practical stability, the following conditions must be satisfied:

- determine set S_β- find the borders for system motion;
- determine set S_ε- find maximum amplitudes of possible disturbance;
- determine set S_α of all initial state values.

In case that this conditions are regularly determined it is possible to analyse system stability from practical stability view of point.

2. Definitions and conditions of practical stability

Let us consider first order hyperbolic distributed parameter system, which is decribed by the following state- space equation:

$$\frac{\partial \underline{x}(t, z)}{\partial t} = A_0 \cdot \underline{x}(t, z) + A_1 \frac{\partial \underline{x}}{\partial z} \tag{1}$$

with appropriate function of initial state:

$$\underline{x}_0(t, z) = \underline{\psi}_x(t, z) \\ 0 \le t \le \tau, 0 \le z \le \zeta \tag{2}$$

where $\underline{x}(t, z)$ is n- component real vector of system state, A is matrix appropriate dimension, t is time and z is space coordinate.

Definition 1: Distributed parameter system described by equation (1) that satisfied initial condition (2) is stable on finite time interval in relation to [$\xi(t,z)$, β, T, Z] if and only if:

$$\underline{\psi}_x^T(t, z) \cdot \underline{\psi}_x(t, z) < \xi(t, z) \tag{3}$$

$$\forall t \in [0, \tau], \forall z \in [0, \varsigma]$$

then it follows

$$\underline{x}^T(t,z))\cdot\underline{x}(t,z)<\beta$$

$$\forall t\in[0,T]\forall z\in[0,Z] \tag{4}$$

where $\xi(t,z)$ is scalar function with feature $0<\xi(t,z)\le\alpha,\,0\le t\le\tau,\,0\le z\le\zeta$ where α is real number, $\beta\in R$ and $\beta>\alpha$.

Let calculate the fundamental matrix for this class of system:

$$\frac{d\Phi(s,\sigma)}{d\sigma}=A_1\cdot(sI-A)\cdot\Phi(s,\sigma) \tag{5}$$

where after double Laplace transformation, and necessary approximation finally it is obtained:

$$\Phi(t,z)=\exp(A\cdot t\cdot z) \tag{6}$$

where $A=\dfrac{I-A_0\cdot A_1}{A_1}$.

Theorem 1: Distributed parameter system described by equation (1) that satisfied internal condition (2) is stable on finite time interval in relation to $[\xi(t,z),\,\beta,\,T,\,Z]$ if it is satisfied following condition:

$$e^{2\mu(A)\cdot t\cdot z}<\frac{\beta}{\alpha}. \tag{7}$$

Proof: Solution of equation (1) with initial condition (2) is possible to describe as:

$$\underline{x}(t,z)=\Phi(t,z)\cdot\underline{\psi}(0,0) \tag{8}$$

By using upper equation it follows:

$$\underline{x}^T(t,z)\cdot\underline{x}^T(t,z)=\left[\underline{\psi}_x^{\,T}(0,0)\cdot\Phi(t,z)\right]\cdot\left[\underline{\psi}_x^{\,T}(0,0)\cdot\Phi(t,z)\right] \tag{9}$$

By using well-known inequality:

$$\left\|\Phi(t,z)\right\|=\left\|\exp[A\cdot t\cdot z]\right\|\le\exp\{\mu(A)\cdot t\cdot z\} \tag{10}$$

706

and taking into account that:

$$\underline{\psi}_x^T(0,0)\cdot \underline{\psi}_x(0,0)<\alpha$$

(11)

$$\left\|\underline{\psi}_x^T(0,0)\right\|=\left\|\underline{\psi}_x^T(0,0)\right\|<\alpha$$

then follows:

$$\underline{x}^T(t,z)\cdot \underline{x}(t,z)\le e^{2\mu(A\cdot t\cdot z)}\cdot \alpha.$$

(12)

Applying the basic condition of theorem 1 by using equation (7) to further inequality it is obtained:

$$\underline{x}^T(t,z)\cdot \underline{x}(t,z)<\left(\frac{\beta}{\alpha}\right)\cdot \alpha<\beta.$$

(13)

Theorem 2: Distributed parameter system described by equation (1) that satisfied initial condition (2) is stable on finite time interval in relation to [ξ(t,z), β, T, Z] if it is satisfied following condition:

$$e^{\mu(A)\cdot t\cdot z}<\frac{\sqrt{\beta/\alpha}}{1+\tau\cdot\zeta\|A\|},$$

$$\forall t\in[0,\tau]\forall z\in[0,\varsigma]$$

(14)

The proof of this theorem is given in (Dihovicni, 2007).

Definition 2: Distributed parameter system described by equation (1) that satisfied initial condition (2) is stable on finite time interval in relation to [ξ(t,z), β, T, Z] if and only if:

$$\left|\underline{\psi}_x(t,z)\right|_2<\xi(t,z)$$

(15)

then follows:

$$\left|\underline{x}(t)\right|_2<\beta$$

(16)

where ξ(t,z) is scalar function with feature $0<\xi(t,z)\le\alpha, 0\le t\le\tau, 0\le z\le\zeta)$ α is real number, β € R and β > α.

Theorem 3: Distributed parameter system described by equation (1) that satisfied initial condition (2) is stable on finite time interval in relation to [α, β, T, Z] if it is satisfied following condition:

$$e^{\mu_2(A)\cdot t\cdot z} < \frac{\sqrt{\beta/\alpha}}{1+\mu^{-1}{}_2(A)}. \tag{17}$$

$$\forall t \in [0,T] \forall z \in [0,Z]$$

Theorem 4: Distributed parameter system described by equation (1) that satisfied initial condition (2) is stable on finite time interval in relation to [α, β, T, Z], if it is satisfied following condition:

$$e^{\mu(A\cdot t\cdot z)} < \frac{\beta}{\alpha} \tag{18}$$

$$\forall t \in [0,T], \forall z \in [0,Z]$$

Proof: It follows from theorem 3 in case that $\mu(A) = 0$.

Theorem 5: Distributed parameter system described by equation (1) that satisfied initial condition (2) is stable on finite time interval in relation to [t_0, J, α, β, Z] if it is satisfied following condition:

$$\left[1 + (t - t_0)\cdot \sigma_{\max}\right]^2 \cdot e^{2(t-t_0)\cdot z\cdot \sigma_{\max}} < \frac{\beta}{\alpha}, \tag{19}$$

$$\forall t \in [0,J] \forall z \in [0,Z]$$

where $\sigma_{\max}$ represents maximum singular value of matrix. The proof of this theorem is given in (Dihovicni, 2007).

3. Example

Consider the distributed parameter system:

$$\frac{\partial \underline{x}(t,z)}{\partial t} = \begin{bmatrix} 2 & 1 \\ -2 & 4 \end{bmatrix} \frac{\partial \underline{x}}{\partial z} + \begin{bmatrix} 1 & 0 \\ 2 & -1 \end{bmatrix} \underline{x}(t,z)$$

where

$$A_0 = \begin{bmatrix} 1 & 0 \\ 2 & -1 \end{bmatrix}, A_1 = \begin{bmatrix} 2 & 1 \\ -2 & 4 \end{bmatrix} \tag{20}$$

and according with equation (6) it is obtained:

$$A = \begin{bmatrix} 0.548 & 0.904 \\ 0.1653 & 3.320 \end{bmatrix} \tag{21}$$

with initial condition

$$\underline{x}_0\left(t,z\right) = \underline{\psi}_x\left(t\right) = \begin{bmatrix} 0 & 1 \end{bmatrix}^T \tag{22}$$

Let us assume following values:

$$\alpha = 2.0; \ \beta = 60.22; \ \kappa_{est} = 0.7s \tag{23}$$

where $\kappa = t \cdot z$

and check initial condition

$$\left\| \underline{\psi}_x \right\|^2 = 1 < 2.01 \tag{24}$$

Let us calculate matrix measure μ and the norm:

$$\mu(A) = 3.37$$

$$\left\| A \right\| = 3.45 \tag{25}$$

Combining this values into equation (7), it is obtained

$$e^{2 \cdot t \cdot z} < 29.96$$
$$\forall t \in \left[0, T\right], \ z \in \left[0,1\right] \tag{26}$$

with solution

$$\kappa_{est} = 1.69s \tag{27}$$

Upon the theorem 2 it is obtained inequality

$$e^{t \cdot s} < 1.23$$
$$\forall t \in [0, T], \, z \in [0, 1] \tag{28}$$

with solution

$$\kappa_{est} = 0.207 s \tag{29}$$

By using theorem 3 it follows

$$e^{t \cdot s} < 23.31 \tag{30}$$

which solution is:

$$\kappa_{est} = 3.14 s \tag{31}$$

Upon the theorem 4 it is obtained inequality:

$$e^{t \cdot s} < 29.96 \tag{32}$$

and solution is:

$$\kappa_{est} = 3.39 s \tag{33}$$

If we use theorem 5 then it is obtained:

$$[1 + 3.45t]^2 \cdot e^{2 \cdot 3.45 \cdot t \cdot z} < 29.96 \tag{34}$$

with solution

$$\kappa_{est} = 0.06 s \tag{35}$$

By analising the values for estimation it is obvious that the best result is obtained by using the theorem 2.

Figure 1 represents system motion on time interval t € [0, 0.7], and space interval z € [0, 1].

710

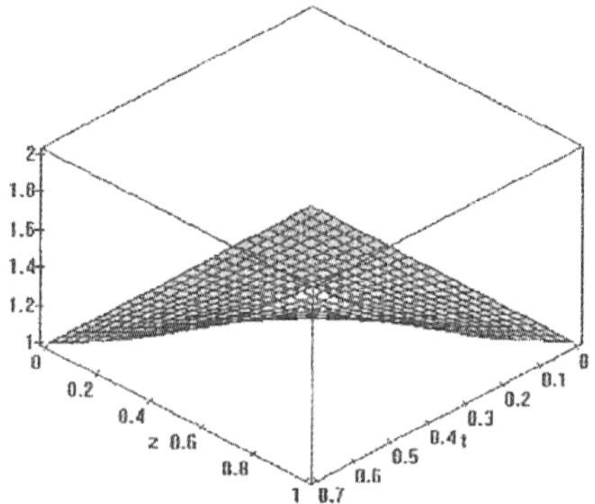

Figure 1. System motion on time interval and space interval z € [0, 1]

4. Conclusion

The main conclusion from the result is that estimated interval which is determined by using previous explained theorems, and which represents product of tz for this class of distributed parameter systems is very near to real value, so the theory is applicable and has wide-spread use in determination where is the system stable. Taking into account that the most natural processes and phenomena are distributed parameter systems, gives presented theory and results great importance.

References

1. L.R Tokashiki, T. Fujita. T Kagawa and W. Pan, *Dynamic Characteristics of Pneumatic Cylinders Including pipes*, 9th Bath International Fluid Power Workshop, September 1996, pp 1-14.
2. Dj. Dihovicni, N. Nedic, *Stability of Distributed Parameter Systems on Finite Space Interval*, 32-end Yupiter Conference, Zlatibor 2006, pp 306-312.
3. Edmond Richer, Yildirim Hurmuzlu, *A High Performance Pneumatic Force Actuator System*, ASME Journal of Dynamic Systems Measurement and Control, September 2000, pp 416-425.
4. B. Novakovic, "Metode vodjenja tehnickih sistema (Book style)," Skolska knjiga, Zagreb 1989.
5. Ernat- Dieter Gilles, "*A Systeme mit verteilten Parametern, (Book style),*" Wien 1973.
6. *Manual of Hydraulics and Pneumatics*, The Japan Hydraulics and Pneumatics Society, 1989.

7. Ikegami T. Fujita T. Kagawa T. *Pneumatic cylinder with meter-out velocity control*, 9th Symposium on Fluid Control Matsuayama, Japan 1994.

8. Brown FT. *The Transient Response of Fluid Lines. J. of Basic Engineering*, Trans of ASME, Series D, 84-4, 547/553, 1962.

9. Kagawa T Fujita T, Takeuchi M. *Dynamic Response and Simulation Model of Pneumatic Pipe Systems*, Proc 7th Bath International Fluid Power Workshop 1994.

10. N.N. ISO 6358, *Pneumatic Fluid Power Components using compressible fluids Determination of flow rate characteristics*, October 1989.

HYBRID MODELING OF CAPILLARY DISTRIBUTION SYSTEM IN THE FOOD CHAIN OF DIFFERENT LOCATIONS SOUTH OF BOGOTA

OSCAR JAVIER HERRERA OCHOA

Industrial Engineering Department,
Cooperative University of Colombia and District. Bogotá Colombia
Email: ojavierho@gmail.com

The following provides the results of simulation of the design of a hybrid model (combination of an optimization model based on mixed integer programming complemented by an approximation algorithm with further routes as discrete system simulation), the capillary distribution system (distribution logistics platforms from each of the distribution centers) in food chain in different locations in the south of Bogotá, which maximizes the food supply in these areas of the city.

1. Introduction and Justification

Given the problems that arise in the supply of food from suppliers to end users in a representative increase in food prices for several reasons, it poses a routing model that determines the optimal load to distribute and whose results are simulated discretely as a way to present a possible solution to the problem shown in some locations or areas in the south of the city of Bogotá, Colombia.

On the other side and from the perspective of the supply chain [1] where "should harmonize all activities associated with the flow and transformation of goods from the raw materials stage to the end user in both directions, from above and down into the supply chain "is that it presents difficulties for companies tasked with developing the handling of their products along the chain, bringing in a logistics management cost overruns, as specified by the lack of adequate planning routes and sources to optimal use to transport their goods to their customers.

Thus, it is challenged to plan and coordinate the distribution of goods handled, giving specific solution to the problem of routing the various processing centers or packet traffic to various consumer scepters or customers within the logistics operation developed by a firm or group of companies within the supply chain, and sets within this approach, the optimal quantities to be transported to thus minimize the costs associated with the operation of distribution, so that it scope in last, the two objectives pursued by all logistics activities, which are meeting the needs of customers (internal and external) to itself and the operational efficiency [2] and it is of great importance for regions and featuring sectors such as Bogotá, the use of technical tools and more, offered by the Operations Research contributing to the establishment of optimal values within the various problems identified in the management of logistics and operational activities especially those focused distribution and transportation of the products or goods to different customers of the respective companies.

These activities are part of the problems have been discussed in operations research as models for routing, which have yielded very outstanding and in many cases optimal values in response to the proposals set out in specific logistics systems, distribution with route planning.

Through load allocation models [3] complemented by the savings algorithm of Clarke-Wright [4], calculated the possible optimal routes for the supply of food, taking into account the capabilities of logistics platforms that serve as centers distribution and therefore vehicles (trucks) to be deployed. Possible routes should cover all the centers of consumption taking into account that part from the different logistics platforms. Decisions be made about the data produced by each of the above models as they are complementary but the results must comply with the conditions of viability compared to the real system capabilities and cost of hiring trucks bearing in mind that some truncations may arise between them.

In terms of geographical areas or localities of analysis, includes the installation of logistics platforms as stipulated by the District University study program in Bogotá Without Hunger, which store all food supply chains food already established in the basket and that are in demand in these areas. To meet this demand platforms were used as a means of supplying the most efficient way for the families of the respective localities, to thereby make a distribution to final customers for the chain through the existing market concentrations in these localities and the use of distribution centers set up by the zonal planning units in each locality. This distribution is done according to location, size and coverage that may have existing market concentrations in the respective localities. The following is the general outline that shows the process of procurement for their respective localities.

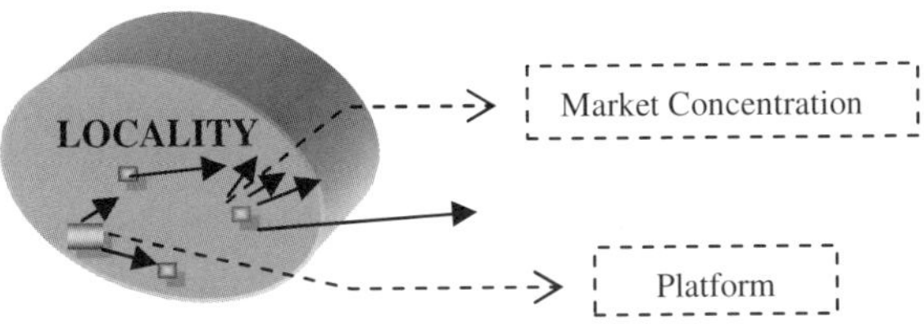

Figure 1. General scheme of distribution by location

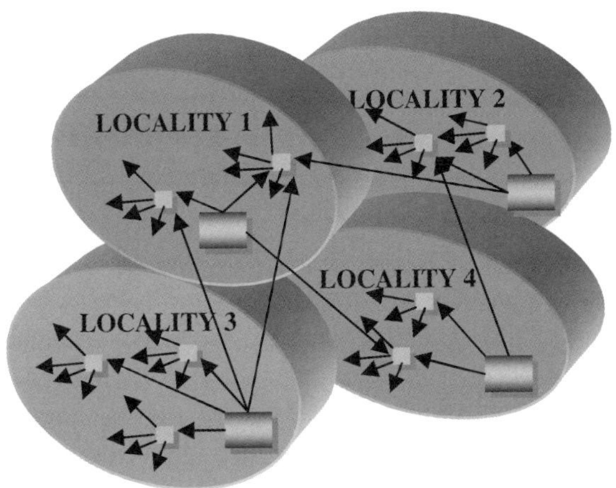

Figure 2. General scheme of distribution on all property subject of study

With the routing model with assignment of duties, we will see what are the optimal allocations for the capillary distribution of food from the respective logistic platforms. To develop the assessment model included variables such as access roads and the condition of roads for each market concentrations, and fixed cost items, wages of driver / vehicle, average speed / vehicle, fuel consumption / Km, Price of Fuel / gl. Fixed costs and other factors / km, including: duration of tires, washing and lubrication, oil and filters (air and diesel fuel) in the respective vehicles.

The initial step to the study of food distribution in the various localities to the south of Bogotá analysis was to identify the centers of consumption in each of the localities. Based on this information to the identification of market concentrations, assessing the demand for accessing public to buy their food in these areas, including coverage of these concentrations in the locality. The main objective of making optimal routing is to know exactly which segment of the town is supplied collection center or located in this platform and consumption centers which cater for other platforms are located in different locations.

2. Design Model

Although the problem of design and optimization of routes and frequencies has been less studied [5] lists the following difficulties:

1. Formulation of the problem: to define the decision variables (including the election by the line that transports) and the objective function.

2. Non-linearity and non-convexity of the problem.

3. Combinatorial nature of the problem with discrete variables.

4. Multiple objectives: a trade-off exists mainly among the objectives of the system users and operators, which means that there may be no single optimal solution, but several non-dominated solutions. One solution is not dominated when no other solution that improves on some objective function without worsening the other.

5. Spatial arrangement of the trades: a readiness formalization of them.

Applications of the TSP, and the problems deriving from it have many practical applications, especially in the field of product distribution and services. Hence the importance it has achieved in recent years the study of such problems. Because of this interest, there have been many methods and algorithms that have appeared in recent years in order to find optimal solutions of the TSP.

The TSP is a problem of type NP-Hard. When the number of grid points is high, it precludes the use of exact algorithms for solving such problems due to the large amount of time required for resolution. In these cases when other algorithms required to provide an approximate solution to the optimum, which required computing time is less, such as heuristic algorithms, and more specifically, the metaheuristics.

For the specific case of the TSP problem genetic algorithm was used for resolution. In order to analyze the results found by it, have developed local search heuristic algorithms used by other authors in solving the TSP problem [6]. These are algorithms: Savings and Integration.

To carry out this assignment and after reviewing the relevant literature addressing this topic model was established using the following mathematical model, which is framed within the mixed integer programming:

Load Allocation Model

Decision Variables:

X_{ij} = quantity of units to carry the same type, from the process plant i, the consumer or customer center j in the network node of the supply system.
Y_{ij} = binary variable that activates if you take the value 1, or off if you take the value 0, the use of the process plant i, the consumer or customer center j in the network node of the supply system.

Parameters:

ICJ = Unit cost of transporting the product, source or process plant i, the consumer or customer center j in the network node of the supply system.

CFij = Fixed cost of transport of the process plant i, the consumer or customer center j in the network node of the supply system.

Cmaxij = maximum allowable cost for transportation from the process plant i, the consumer or customer center j in the network node of the supply system.

ai = available capacity to supply the process plant i

bj = demand requirement by the consumer or customer center j

Mathematical Structure:

$$\text{Min Z:} \quad \sum_{i=1}^{m}\sum_{j=1}^{n} CijXij + \sum_{i=1}^{m}\sum_{j=1}^{n} CFijYij \qquad \text{Objective Function} \quad (1)$$

s.a.

$$\sum_{i=1}^{m} Yij = 1 \quad \forall \; j = 1,\dots,n \quad \text{Restricted Connectivity} \tag{2}$$

$$\sum_{j=1}^{n} CFijYij = C\max \quad \forall \; i = 1,\dots,m \quad \text{High cost constraint. allowed} \tag{3}$$

$$\sum_{j=1}^{n} Xij \leq ai \quad \forall \; i = 1,\dots,m \quad \text{Supply constraints or sleeps} \tag{4}$$

$$Xij - Yij * bi = 0 \quad \forall \; i = 1,\dots,m \; y \; j = 1,\dots n \quad \text{Restrict or Market Demand} \tag{5}$$

$$Xij \geq 0 \; \text{Nonnegativity constraints} \tag{6}$$

$$Yij = Binaria \tag{7}$$

Savings Method

The valuation method of Clarke-Wright savings [7] has been through the years by being flexible enough to handle a wide range of practical constraints, is relatively quick to calculate on a computer for problems with moderate number of stops and able to generate solutions that are near optimal. The method can handle many practical constraints, mainly because it is able to form routes and stops on the routes to order simultaneously.

The aim of the savings method is to minimize the total distance traveled by all vehicles and indirectly minimize the number of vehicles required to meet all the stops. The logic of the method is to start with a simulated vehicle that covers every stop and returns to the reservoir, as shown in Figure 3 (a). This gives the maximum distance to be experienced in the route design problem. Then combine two stops on the same route for a vehicle can be eliminated and the distance traveled is reduced. To determine the stops that are combined into a route, calculate the distance saved, before and after the merge. The distance saved by combining the two points (A and B) that are not otherwise in a route with any other stops, is algebraically subtracting the distance from the path shown in Figure 3 (b) of Figure 3 (a). The result is a saving value S = d0, A + dB, 0 - dA, B. This is calculated for all pairs of stops. The couple of stops with the largest savings value is selected for the combination. The revised route is illustrated in Figure 3 (b).

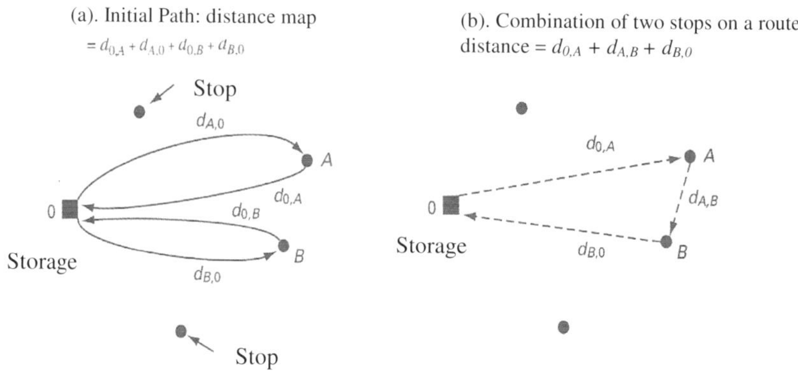

Figure 3. Travel distance reduced through consolidation of stops on a route

The strong nature of the assessments of savings to include many restrictions that seem so important in real applications. The strength of the method is due to the ability to assign simultaneously a stop to a route and place it in a place in the sequence of the route. Therefore, before accepting a stop on a route should provide the route with the new stop.

By using the load allocation model complemented by the savings algorithm, is to provide a possible solution to the food supply in the three study localities south of Bogotá.

Simulation Results

Load allocations obtained from each of the platforms located at each location and specific routes for distribution of food from each of these platforms to the respective centers of consumption and / or distribution by the criterion of greater savings in distance, was carried out the simulation taking into account the process of development [8] Promodel using for the four locations or areas of study. By way of facilitating the development of this whole procedure took 18 centers of consumption and / or division with four logistics platforms located in each geographical area or locality south of the city of Bogotá, so that this model could be developed hybrid several stages as a way of representing the development of this activity through the use of this model aimed at optimizing the distribution of food in these areas of the city and as a way of verifying the logistical operation of the system by using mathematical tools such. The following outlines some of the results of this simulation in which on average for each of the logistic platforms, we have the following average values for all the tours on different routes: 14.1, 6.9, 6.4 and 6.5 km. respectively for each platform, which makes it present in significant savings as compared to the currently developing and whose distances are 45, 25, 20, and 26 km respectively for each platform. Below is a map of the geographical areas of the four localities on which the simulation was conducted of the implementation of the hybrid model in question, where customers represent the different centers of consumption or distribution of food within the established system for mayor of the city of Bogotá, Colombia.

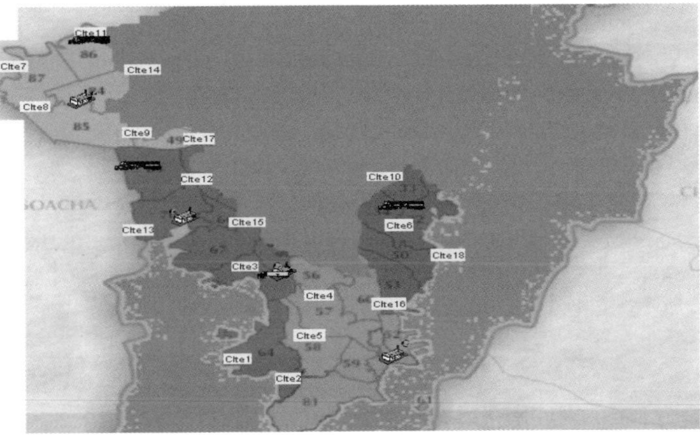

Graphic. No 1. Map locations for consumption centers

3. Conclusions

The development of this simulation model that began with the design of a routing model from multiple sources mixed integer programming with a classical model of transport, and apply the specific routing under the criterion of shortest distance to travel restrictions by the algorithm of Clark and Wright, allows for a fairly satisfactorily as the case where application for decision making in logistics which have various possibilities for the distribution and allocation later in a network routing node, plus have the possibility to carry out assignments logistics operators as the demands of the customers of that system while taking into account the capacity or availability to be taken from each of these operators or network distribution, resulting in Finally, near the optimal values with respect to costs associated with this operation. Importantly, this model includes fixed costs of transportation, which sets basic parameters as input information to facilitate and expedite the calculation of these costs over the distances between each of the customers and distribution centers in the network system, including for example drivers' wages, fuel consumption of vehicles, changes in the prices of these fuels and other items associated with the expense of machinery for the mobilization of goods, making it easier and provides greater accuracy in the calculation of these costs to be then used as input information to the mathematical development of this model. Moreover, also provides variable transport costs in handling the unit value that involves the mobilization of products from each processing center or source to the different consumption centers or destination, taking in this way, an integration of elements cost involved in developing the transport activity along the supply chain for a company dedicated to this work logistics.

Moreover, as a major contribution has to be this type of model had not been previously established, taking as a great help to those involved in establish routing logistics companies engaged in this activity, moreover, in those situations in which it has a wide variety of choices for placing the burden to carry, otherwise, and as already mentioned, this model takes into account the capabilities and availability of supply from different centers or storage process that takes in it, making it easier at any given time, making decisions in a fast and accurate address system requirements.

References

1. Robert B. Handfield, Ernest L. Nichols, Supply Chain Redesign: Transforming Supply Chains into Integrated Value Systems. Prentice Hall, **1P2** (2002).
2. State of Logistics report, Council Logistics Management, **1P3** Disponible en: http://cscmp.org/default.asp [citado el 22 de noviembre de 2007]
3. Modelo de Ruteo Mixto con varias fuentes con Asignación de Cargas. Oscar J. Herrera. Revista Fusión Industrial, Universidad Industrial de Santander UIS, Colombia. Septiembre **1P5** (2008).

4. PhD. Ing. J. Torres A. Compendio, Aspectos generales sobre Logística, Cátedra Gestión de Sistemas Logísticos. Maestría en Ingeniería Industrial, Universidad Distrital Francisco José de Caldas, Bogota Colombia. **1P5** 2008 I.

5. Baaj, M. H., and H. S. Mahmassani. An AI-based approach for transit route system planning and design. Journal of Advanced Transportation 25, 2: 187–210. **2P9** (1991).

6. Charkroborty, P., and T. Dwivedi. Optimal route network design for transit systems using genetic algorithms. Engineering Optimization 83-100 **2P13** (2002).

7. Ronald H. Ballou "Logística Administración de la cadena de suministro" Quinta edición Págs. 243–244. **2P21** (2004).

8. Ross Sheldon. Stochastic Processes. 4ta edición Ed. John Wiley and sons. New York, **2P25** (2007).

MODELLING AND SIMULATION AS INTEGRATED TOOL FOR RESEARCH AND DEVELOPMENT

FLORIN IONESCU[†]

Mechatronics Department, Konstanz University of Applied Sciences
Brauneggerstr. 5, D-78462 Konstanz, Germany

The paper presents some achievements in the field of Mechatronics, where large scale modelling and simulation (MS) have been involved and have shown, that they represent unavoidable tools for a high Quality/Price-Rate of research and development (R & D). It also produces a high positive gradient of evolution in education. Some information concerning the R & D process and the achieved results, applied on own products, like Industrial Robotics, the RoTeMiNa Micro-Nano-Robot and Precessional Drives as well as the own MS Platform, HYPAS, are devoted and apropiatelly commented. To this purpose MS using MATLAB/Simulink, SolidDynamics & MotionInventor Platforms, with some accent on industrial robots and precessional drives, are presented in the paper.

1. Introduction

The concept of mechatronics was born in Japan, Romania and Belgium 30 years ago, and is a complex concept in a continuous change. It had the meaning to use a synergetic combination of mechanics and electronics, being related to electro-mechanics, but differing in the criteria of design. Therefore, mechatronics bekame a significant interdisciplinary design trend, that involves the application of the latest techniques in precision mechanical engineering, control theory, computer science, and electronics to create and rapid implementate on the market more functional products optimally matched for higher performances. Some of the key elements of mechatronics, related to CAE, are presented in Figure 1. The new concepts have a strong influence not only on the product design towards/against an agresive competition on the market, but also on the gradient of the education in mechanical engineering, further training of research engineers or of engineering managers. Thus, the new products have specific characteristics, including the replacement of many mechanical functions with electronic ones. By applying new control approaches [16], one expect from the device to reach new performance.

[†] The research projects reported in the work have been partially supported by means of grants from: DFG (Deutsche Forschungsgemeinschaft), Bonn, AvH (Alexander-von-Humboldt-Foundation), Bonn, Otto-von-Guerické-Foundation, Essen, Steinbeis-Fundation, Stuttgart and HTWG (Konstanz University of Applied Research), all from Germany.

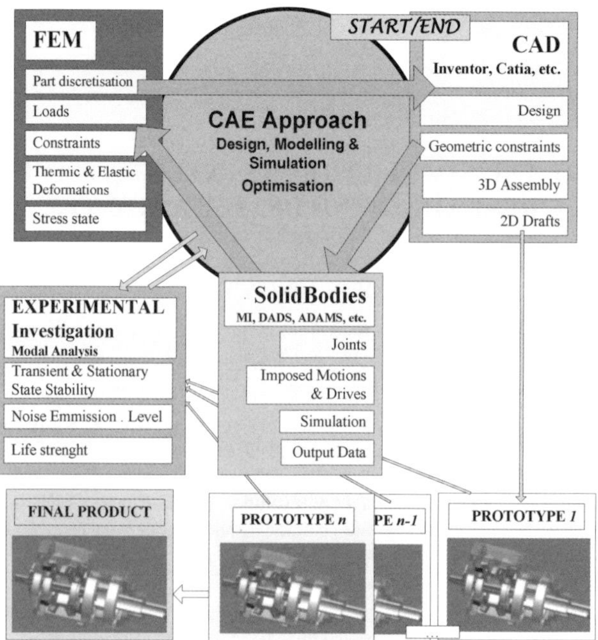

Figure 1. Fundamental Fields and Approaches in CAE (Source: Ionescu[©], 2007).

2. Optimised and Integrated Design in Mechatronics

Targeting permanently to achievement of a higher Quality-Price-Ratio and also performances, a product of relative high complexity has to satisfy the application of the simulation on physical models at real (or reduced) scale. This approach does not allow flexibility and is less appropriate. The optimization in experimental closed loop is not possible in those cases. Important stages of the presented cycle can be easily done by using a computer. Thus, one has to use high integrated methods of computer aided design ([8]). The use of Platforms in this domain are, due to their deep integration, specialized on 3D geometry generation, kinematic and dynamic simulation, static and dynamic behavior analysis, is very avantageous. In Figure 1 the diagram of the integration principle is shown. It starts with the pre-design and ends with de final product (Bostan [2], Ionescu [8, 12]). Figure 1 shows also the information model, with multiple loops, which allows the design and optimization at different levels. The information transfer is realized in multiple lops, the loops of optimization being of great importance. In the modern CAD three stages are used to optain an optimised product:

- **1st Stage**: CAD, which starts from the hand sketch and is delivering a first approach of the product;
- **2nd Stage**: SOLID BODIES modelling, which takes over the 3D-CAD design and, making use of an appropriate correlation movement - joint, delivers a simulation model; this will be completed with data which are helping to reconstruct the supposed/desired input-reality; at the end all kinetic information (static, transient, stationary -vibration and noise emission-) are delivered and will be used later for optimisation;
- **3rd Stage**: FEM optimization; preestablished performances concerning stress, deformation, heavines, own values and forms as well as price, etc., can be involved and obtained. The closed loop of the three stages can offer the perspective to virtually design a neu machine with a high degree of accuracvy, before any prototype will be achieved, some times solution impossible to be achieved because of economical reasons. The experimental investigation (to be performed in conjunction with prototypes), offers much supplimentary information for the optimisation and is (expansive but) a unovidable step of the CAE-process. Because of the extremly nonlinear structures (static and dynamic) of the layer properties of the modells, the dinamic analysis could be extremly sensitive to these behavoiur and also difficult to be achieved. Four types of analysis and implications of the modeling information at every level are identified: 1. Parameteric drawing; 2. Simple calculations on the real project; 3. Complex calculations on the idealized project; 4. Simulation.

3. Modelling and Simulation of Robots

3.1. *Robot for cell micro and nano manipulations*

The challenge of development of ultra-precise manipulating systems is to combine the unique features of piezo actuators with appropriate mechanics, sensors and control electronics. This challenge refers also to the scientists and design engineers working in that field as well. The experimental simulation produces, at its turn, multiple sets of data. More than one idealized drawing can be achieved for a single existing drawing. A robot system with 6,5 Dof utilizing the teleoperated control approach with impedance scaling was developed and called RoTeMiN-robot for cell micro and nano manipulations (Figures 2 and 3). It consists of 3 T-joints, with a stroke range of 55 (100) [mm], a repeatability of less than 0,2[μm], a linear sensor with resolution of 0,1[μm]. The local robot structure with 3 Dof has been developed in a way to guarantee the precise reference three-dimensional nano motion and control for sample manipulation or injection in sub-micrometer or nanometer range. Two of the joints are R-joints around x- and y-axes in a range of 30 [mrad] with an actuator's resolution of 1.6 10^{-3} [arcsec]. The last joint is a translational one, having a stroke of 65 [μm] and a resolution of 4 [nm]. The sensors used for the local robot structure are strain gauge sensors integrated in the piezo actuator bodies, with resolution of 35 [nm].

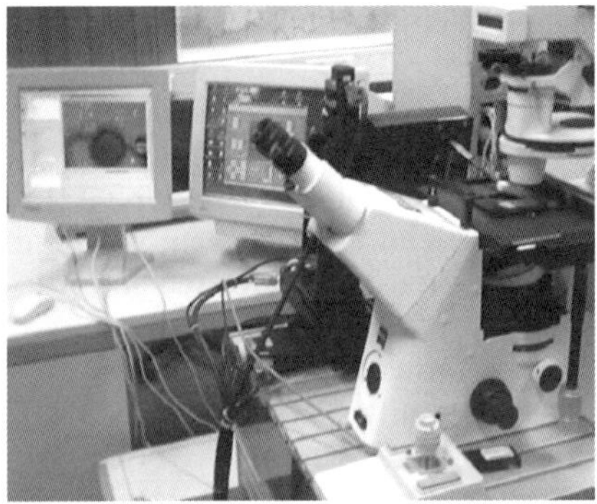

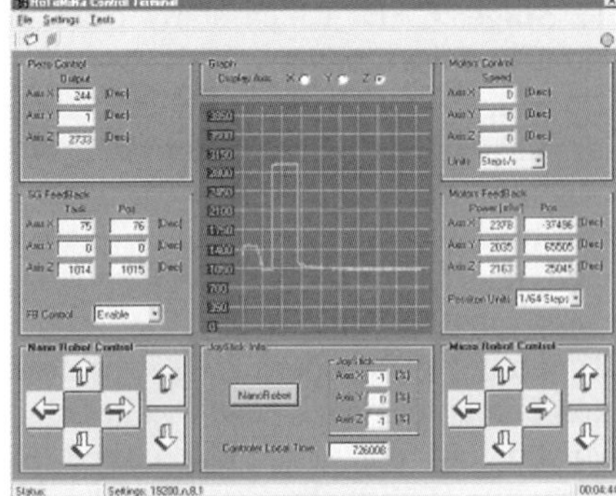

Figure 2. RoTeMiNa MicroNano-Robot with hybrid teleoperation for cell penetrations.

Figure 3. Interface of RoTeMiNa MicroNano-Robot (Source: Ionescu©, 2005).

Teleoperation hybrid approach transferring operator motion and manipulation developed based on the linear (velocity) or impedance scaling approach.

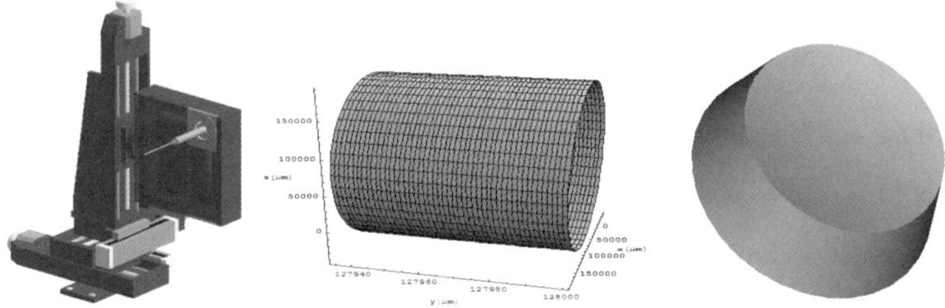

Figure 4. RoTeMiNa-Robot: Nano Stage, Macro and Nano Spaces (Source: Ionescu©, 2005).

The time for the operation to be performed is reducing using familiar for the operator dynamics which is the main request, especially for the cell manipulations. An approach of impedance scaling has been utilized here. The identification of the structure was made in MATLAB, using the obtained experimental results for the X-, Y- and Z-axes, for different identification methods and two different types of the input signal: sinus and triangle type.

The transfer functions of the three nano axes have been obtained for the control of the piezzo actuated stages. All the equations of motion of the Micro-Nano-Robot have been generated, basicly using an oriented edges graph method with multiple cycles. The concept of matroid, applied to independency of columns, was considered as a good approach for generating equations of motion.

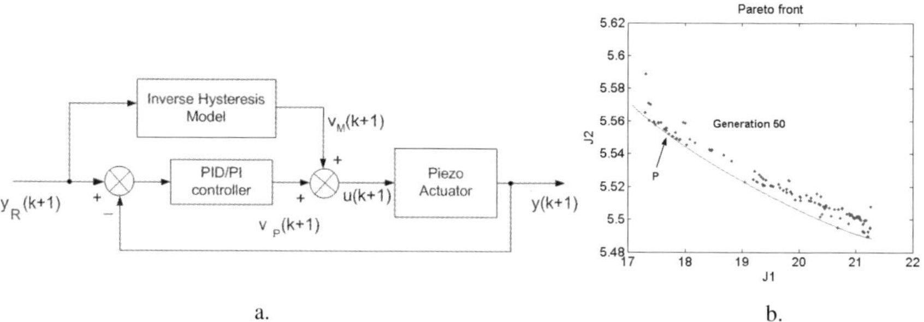

a.   b.

Figure 5a. Structure of a control system of RoTeMiNa Robot (Source$^©$: Ionescu, 2005).
Figure 5b. The PF after 50 generations. Point P indicates the selected individual for the PID tuning parameters (TP, TI, and TD) (Source$^©$: Ionescu, 2007).

A control schema was proposed in order to compensate the hysteresis of piezo actuators included in micro/nano robot (Fig. 5a). It uses a neuro-fuzzy inverse model with PID/PI error mapping compensator. We have adopted an originally mixed algorithm in order tune the PID/PID parameters using GEATbx toolbox. The results of simulation have shown the method as effective, with a very good linearization of the (electrical) hysteresis curve, even in the case of a very sharp upper a lower corner of hysteresis curve. The MSE was below 0.005 in all the tested cases. The control schema is based on inverse neuro-fuzzy model in a feed-forward connection. The piezzo-actuator is modelled by modified mathematical model in order to be simulated and tested in a mixed analogue-discrete schema. The mapping errors due to dynamic fuzzy model are compensated by PID/PI controllers. The PID/PI parameters are found using genetic algorithms applied to global optimization problem with two objectives. The Pareto front, that describes the optimal solutions, is found using a rank-based selection for local points that describe the Pareto front (Fig. 5b). The proposed method improves the linearization of the hysteresis and the performance of the piezzo-actuator.

3.2. *Modelling and simulation of industrial robots*

Two fashions of approaches for modelling and simulation are usual and were implemented for the theoretical- and 3D-approaches. It is generally accepted that a multi-body system is a set of rigid solids linked to each other by joints [1, 15]. A system can further consist of several independent subsystems. A rigid body is a physical body that suffers no deformation and stress. There is a permanent contact (joint) between two solids consisting of an articulation and a type of movement. The dynamic system is governed by two kinds of actions: the internal action, generated by actuators (engines, brakes, etc.) and the external actions due to environment (gravitation, impacts, perturbations, etc.). Own functions and driving structures can be as "code" created. During the simulation, the program provides information concerning positions, velocities, accelerations, point trajectories, the forces and moments applied to the articulations, the energies, as well as other data concerning the system, pre-defined by the software or defined by the user. SD simultaneously displays the evolution of the graphs and the 3D animation of the mechanical system (Fig. 6). Approaches can perfomed using a mathematical and/or a 3D-environment, The first one is folowed by an executions upon the M/S Platform and can be completted by own subprograms [15]. The second approach uses actually the same mathematical background, which not accessible to the user.

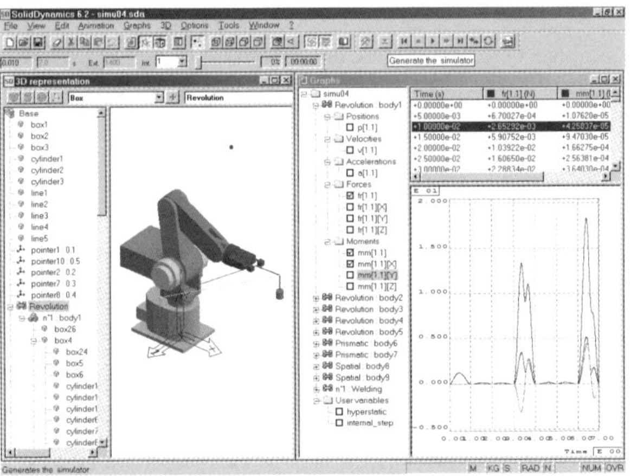

Figure 6. Revolute Robot with Indirect Dynamics (Source: Ionescu[©], 2005).

Mathematical approach. Mathematical approches, with their advantages for control and synthesis were developped in [1, 3, 4, 15] and are used for both types of dynamics: direct and inverse (Figures 7-11) as well as for the visio control [10].

The 3D-SD-Approch. The following example of modelling a simulation in SD deals with the off-line programming of robots and is equally a complex one. The programmer creates three dimensional graphic models of the robots and devices and applies inverse cinematic solutions to the models to control the device motion. The robots and devices are then placed in a graphic work cell environment to create an exact representation of a real world work cell. During the execution the models simulate the motion of the actual robot or device, allowing the programmer to check for robot work space, possible collisions, motion, and optimization. The ASCII file containing the joint coordinates is generated and used for the real robot control (Ionescu [12, 13]).

Different types of robot models are presented in Figures 7 through 11. (Source: Ionescu[©], 2005). All robots are driven, while forces and moments are the result of of the trajectory's computation.

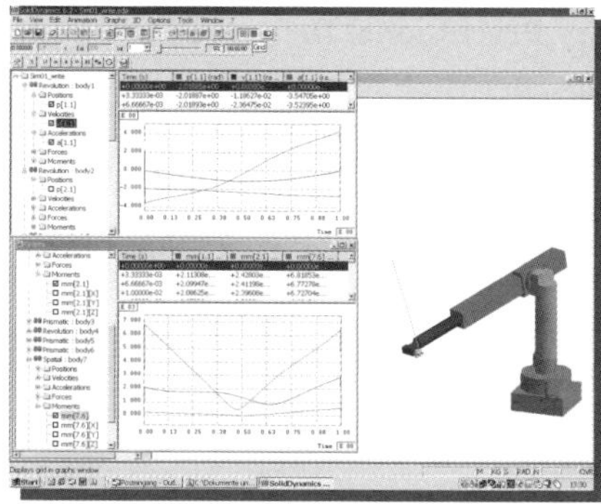

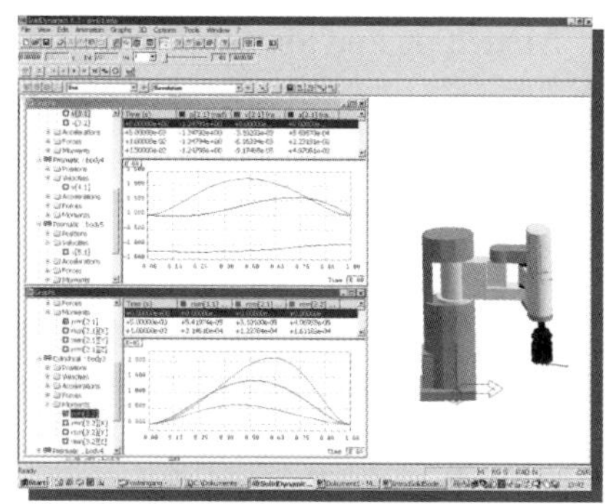

Figure 7. Model of a Spherical Robot.

Figure 8. Model of a SCARA-Robot.

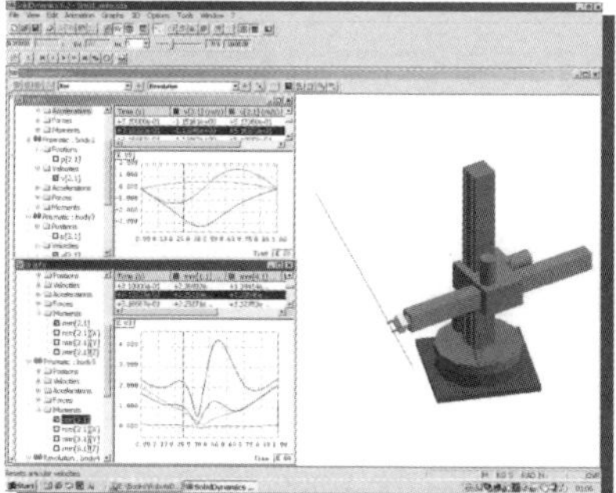

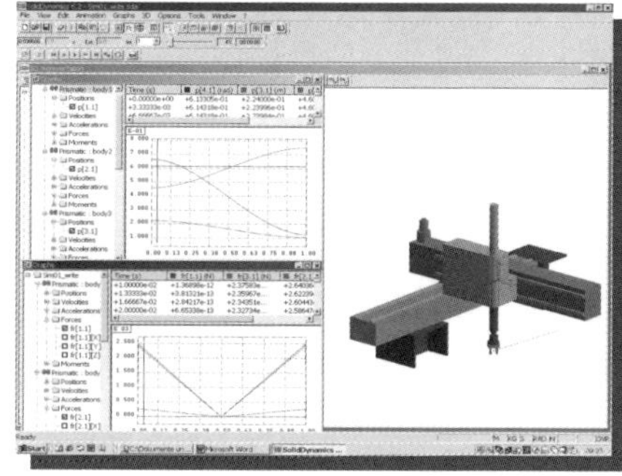

Figure 9. Model of a Cylindrical Robot.

Figure 10. Model of a Chartesian Robot.

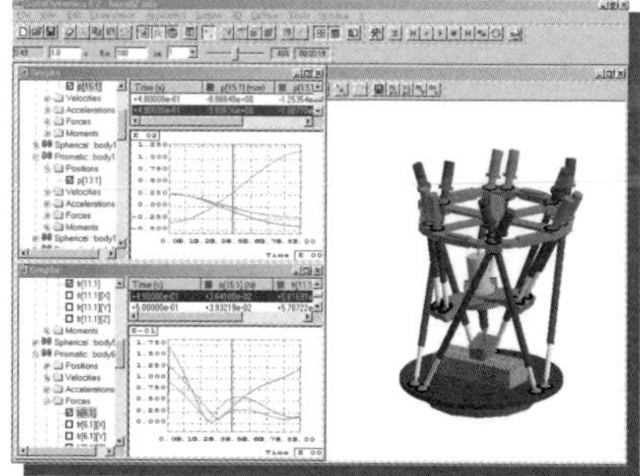

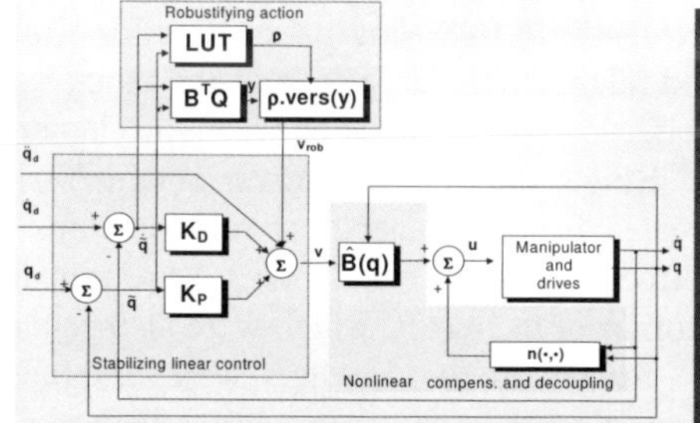

Figure 11. 3D-Modell and Direct Control of a Twelve Leggs Parallel Robot/Machine-Tool.

4. Modelling and Simulation of a Planetary Precessional Drive (PPD)

The next example of M & S presents an original concept, the appropriate design and the achieved results of simulations. It represents a planetary precessional drive mechanism (Source: Bostan[©] & Ionescu[©], 2006), with the following data: 1. The transfer ratios: $i = 78$ & 100 [-]; 2. The input speed: $n = 1480$ [rot/min]; 3. The output torques: $M = 1.480$ & 4.960 [Nm]. The calculation of the planetary precessional transmission and the simulation was carried out using the simplified 3D model created in program MI2004+, as shown in Figures 12-15.

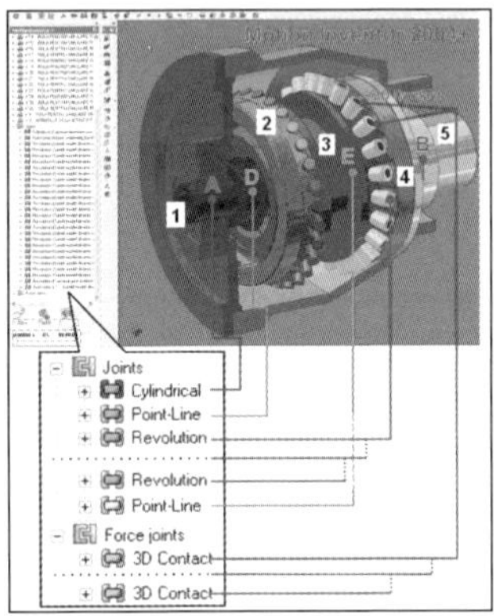

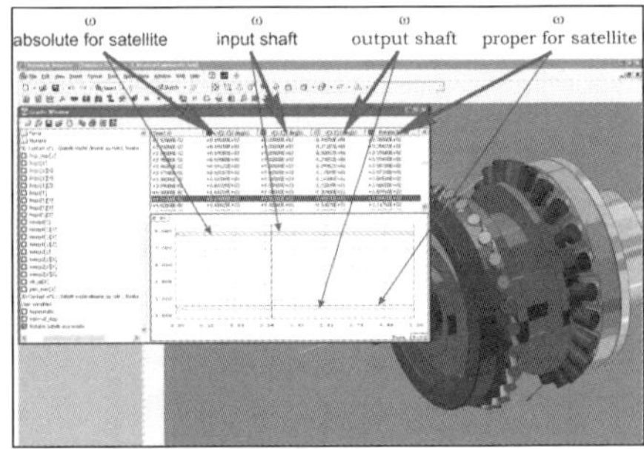

Figure 12. 3D-Model of the PPD Joints Tree.   Figure 13. Kinematic Simulation of PPD.

The contact between the rollers of the block-satellite and the fixed (2) and mobile (3) wheels are modelled through 3D-Herz-properties of material pairs (steel on steel). The model, accompanied by the "joints tree", is shown in Figure 12. The model study was achieved in several stages, as follows:

1st Stage: a primary design was "manually" computed and in a draft-CAD transposed. The computing of most kinematic data was carried out, which included the following parameters for simulation: the transfer ratio; the absolute and relative angular speeds of the block satellite; the angular speed on the output shaft; the transfer ratios between the elements of the drive;

2nd Stage: the first design was obtained without the profiles of teehts; these were created from the analytical relationsships and separatelly transposed, via excell software, in ACSII files. They were transformed afterwards by MI into cicloidal profiles of the teeths, which were also generated;

3rd Stage: all the bearings were designed, with both geometrical and contact properties; the contact properties between the teeht – steel on steel – of the two wheels (2 and 4) and the rollers were created and tested;

4th Stage: an own module for **noise generation** from the generated vibrations was created and implemented. Thus information concerning both, vibrations and noise were obtained and all sources with their personalised contributions were analysed. Some of the obtained results are shown on Fig. 14 & 15.

5th Stage: performs the dynamic simulation. It allows determining the loadings in bearings, (contact) forces in the drive, such as: the total force on a satellite roller (Fig. 14*a*), contact force on the tooth profile (Fig. 14*b*), contact forces roller-tooth including visualization (Fig. 15). A periode of one week/modell was used to virtually (re)design, simulate and optimize the first approach.

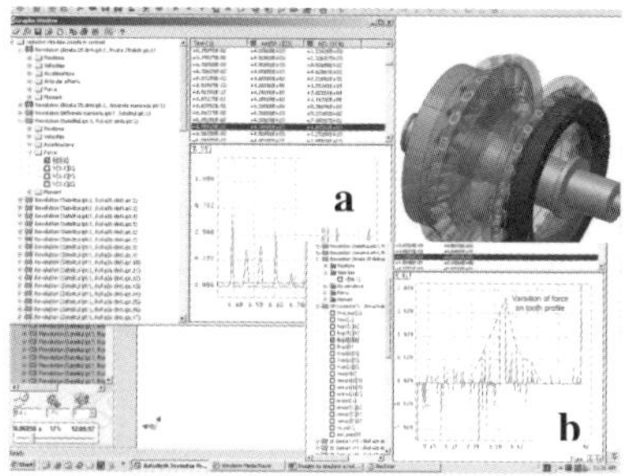

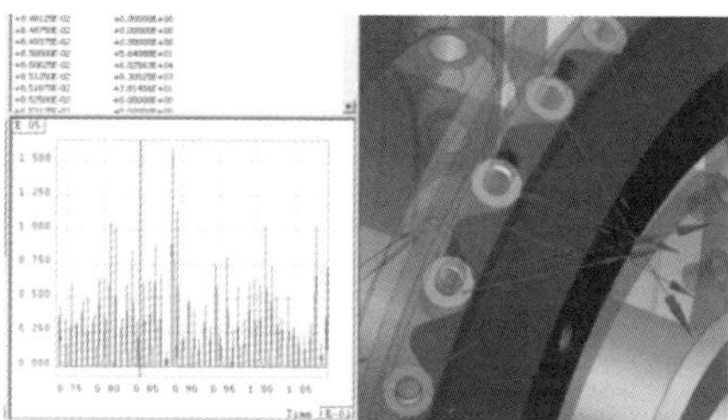

Figure 14. Dynamic simulation:
a. Variation of the total force on a roller axis;
b. Variation of the contact force on the tooth.

Figure 15. Forces between teeth and rollers.

5. Modell Generation and Simulation of Hybrid Systems with HYPAS

Hydraulic and pneumatic installations have a high rate of manufacturig's accuracy, are characterised be very personalised Mathematical Models and thus is definingg their particular approach. Some of them are listed below: 1. Their MM are have multiple static and dynamic nonlinearities; 2. They are involved in installations together with mechanic and electric components and are interfaced with elements making connection to the control process; 3. They variable with the plants are working are of different physical nature; 4. The administration and thus the evaluation of the obtained data is difficult, without any secure approach, because an entire spectrum of variables is available: from the very small ones, like flows Q [m³/s], to the very big values, like the pressures p [N/m²]) .

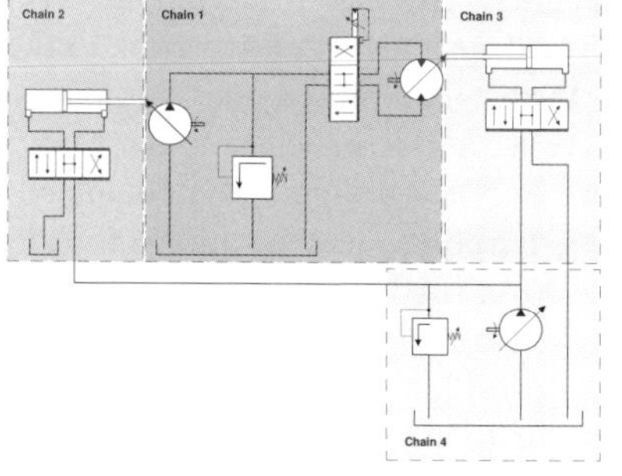

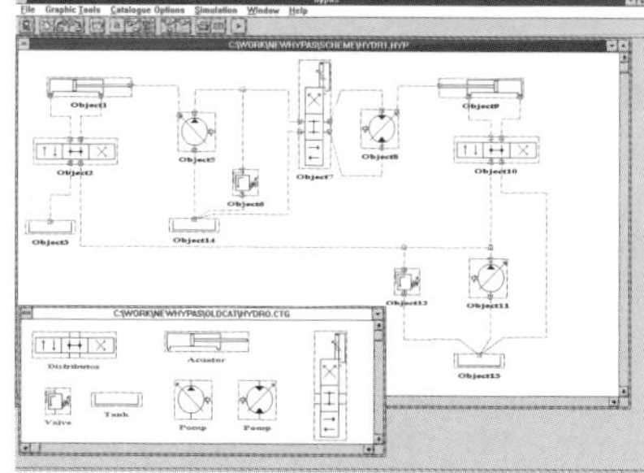

Figure 16. Block diagram of a system and its HYPAS α-approach (Source: Ionescu$^{©}$, 2005).

5. The elements are working as multiport subsystems, which variables are changing theis orientation, both as in- as as output variables. These are enough to conclude, that the Mathematical Modelling (MM) of a H & P - Installation necessitates high level knowledge and abilities. This is mostly reserved to the scientists. To overcome this situation and to let the engineers an open access to the MM, several technologies were developped and are available, like AMESIM and DSh+. As presented (Ionescu [5, 6, 7, 12, 13, 16]), an alternative platform to the above mentioned, called HYPAS, was developped. It allows to automatically modell (dynamic/steady state, linear/nonlinear, partial/ full, for H-, P-, E- and process control) modules and/or installations and to simulate them in: steady-state, stationary and in the transient domains.

One simulation result of the position control plant, from Figure 17a, is presented in Figure 17b. Different libraries of modules were implemented. They can be observed on the partial open windows. Also sepcial modules for the investigation of frequency behaviour and for identification are implemented in HYPAS-β.

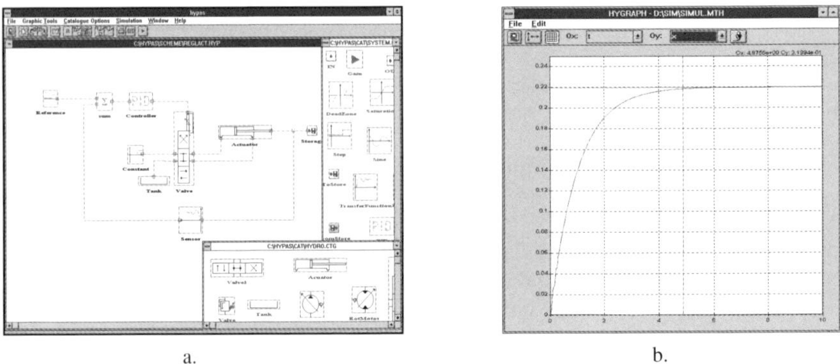

a.   b.

Figures 17. BSB of a positioning servo drive and result of simulations with α-HYPAS.

6. Conclusions

The presented features are based on the author's experience in modelling and simulation with technologies as MATLAB/Simulink, SD and MI programs, as well as with the own simulation software for hybrid systems, HYPAS. New PPD mechanisms were easy and with less R- &D-costs optimised and in many applications implemented. All these projects have led to the conclusion that M & S represents powerful and very useful tools, not only for design and a complety technological information, but also for training purposes, leading indirectly to improuvemet of development's gradient. Whyle MATLAB/Simulink dosn't offer bata bases with simulation modules of hybrid systems, Ionescu have carried out during the last decade to developp the HYPAS–Platform, offering a large spectrum of MMs. The presented examples were first modelled & simulated were presented just to underline their necessity for the R & D process (the educational domain being included). One may make a last remarc: (hybrid) systems can be fully modelled and simulated, with a high degree of decription accuracy.

Acknowledgments

This paper is dedicated to Professor Dr. Georges Mesnard, grounder of AMSE, to whom many scientists are thankfull for having offered them a platform for communication. It is also dedicated to Prof.Dr.Dr.h.c.mult. Johann LÖHN, President of Steinbeis-Foundation for Economical Promotion and of Steinbeis-University, Stuttgart, who organised the modern Technology Transfer and thus offered a high appreciated and wellcome support for Smal and Medium Sized Entreprises.

References

1. Th. Borangiu and Fl. Ionescu, Acad Press ISBN 973-27-0927-8, AGIR Press, ISBN 973-8130-64-6, (2003).
2. I. Bostan, Fl. Ionescu, V. Dulgheru, G. Constantin and A. Sochireanu. Academic Press, Bucharest, ISSN 1842-3183, pp. 21-28, (2006).
3. Fl. Ionescu, G. Constantin and V. Platagea. WCNA, Pergamon Press, PII: S0362-546X(97)00204-6, Vol 30, Part 4, pp.1969-1976, (1996).
4. Fl. Ionescu. WCNA, Pergamon Press, PII: S0362-546X(97)00204-6, Vol 30, Part 3, pp. 1447-1461, (1997).
5. Fl. Ionescu. HYPAS. ISCFP`99, 6th Scand Intern Fluid Power Confer, Tampere, Finland, pp. 947-961, (1999).
6. Fl. Ionescu and D. Stefanoiu. HYPAS, Acta Press, ISBN 0-88986-35-X & ISSN 1482-7913, (2002).
7. Fl. Ionescu. Forum, ISSN 1619-9812, pp. 77-86, (2005).
8. Fl. Ionescu, F. Choynovski and G. Constantin. ARA-Journal, Alma-Mater Press, ISBN 3-00-011583-8, Vol 2000-2002, Nr. 25-27, pp. 150-157, (2003).
9. Fl. Ionescu and D. Stefanoiu (Eds). Steinbeis-Edition, ISBN 3-938062-13-4 & Acad Press, Bulgaria, ISBN 954-322-107-3, (2005).
10. Th. Borangiu and Fl. Ionescu. (Eds.: Fl. Ionescu & D. Stefanoiu), Steinbeis-Edition, ISBN 3-938062-13-4 & Acad Press, ISBN 954-322-107-3, (2004).
11. Fl. Ionescu, I. Talapasanu, D. Arotaritei, R. Hradynarski and K. Kostadinov, IAFA 2007, Academic Press, ISBN 978-973-718-741-3 pp. 20-27, (2007).
12. Fl. Ionescu. IFAC-MCPL, Romania, ISBN 978-973-739-481-1, (2007).
13. Fl. Ionescu. IAFA2007, Printech Edition, ISBN 978-973-718-741-3, (2007).
14. Fl. Ionescu. NanoTech Conf, Oakland Univ, MI, USA, (2008).
15. Fl. Ionescu, I. Talpasanu, K. Kostadinov, D. Arotaritei and G. Constantin. ISBN 978-1-59693-254-8, Artech House, SA, pp. 215-252, (2008).
16. D. Stefanoiu, Th. Borangiu and Fl. Ionescu, Academic Press, ISBN 973-27-1082-9 & AGIR Press, ISBN 973-8466-74-1, (2004).
17. Fl. Stratulat and Fl. Ionescu (Ed.), Steinbeis-Edition, ISBN 978-3-938062-72-2, (2009).

PART 7:
APPLICATIONS IN OTHER FIELDS

APPROACH OF EVALUATION OF ENVIRONMENTAL IMPACTS USING BACKPROPAGATION NEURAL NETWORK

JELENA JOVANOVIĆ, ZDRAVKO KRIVOKAPIC

*University of Montenegro, Faculty of Mechanical Engineering Podgorica,
Dzordza Vasingtona bb, 81000 Podgorica, Montenegro*

SABRIJA RAMOVIĆ, MSC

AD Barska plovidba, Bar, 85000 Bar, Montenegro

ALEKSANDAR VUJOVIĆ, PhD

*University of Montenegro, Faculty of Mechanical Eengineering Podgorica,
Dzordza Vasingtona bb, 81000 Podgorica, Montenegro*

The paper is dealing with the problems of the reliable and objective of evaluation environmental impacts. In order to realize our objectives, we collected a great number of data from the organizations with the ISO 14001 certificate. The data related to identified and evaluated (according organization's methodology) as a significant environmental impacts. In the paper were created two models for evaluation of the environmental impacts based on artificial neural network applied in the pilot organization. The results were compared with the results obtain by the application of the AHP (Analytic hierarchy process) MCDM method what defined the access for evaluation of the environmental impacts supplying the necessary level of reliability and objectivity.

1. Introduction

The base of EMS (Environmental management system) lies in a good identification and evaluation of environmental aspects and impacts. The great part of the key ISO 14001 [2] standards requirements is based on knowledge about the significant environmental aspects and impacts, while the other ISO 14001 standards requirements are in certain correlation with them even though they are not completely dependent on them [13],[14],[15]. Having in mind the great importance of the requirement 4.3.1 (ISO 14001) "Environmental aspects", nonexistence of reliable and objective approach for evaluation environmental aspects and impacts presented the stimulant for the research in this direction.

In fact, the standard ISO 14004 [3], requirement 4.3.1.5 ***"the importance is relative concept and cannot be defined in absolute terms"*** leaves to the organizations fully freedom regarding evaluation environmental aspects and impacts. In order to find the possibility to establish a unique approach to the evaluation of environmental impacts, applicable in all organizations independent of their activity and which will at the same time supply all necessary objectivities and reliability, we collected a large number of marks of significance environmental aspects according to criteria of methodology ISO 14001 certified organizations. Because of great number of data heterogeneity (marks of environmental impacts related 4 important criteria using their evaluation methodology) we argue that use of artificial neural network [11],[12] could offer the desired results, what established the following hypothesis:

H1: Two models based on neural networks provide objective and reliable evaluation of environmental aspects when used them together

This hypothesis represents another view of problem which we analized in paper [17]. Neural networks are useful if you have great number of inputs for the short period of time and when the rules of connection data aren't known [4].

2. The approach of evaluation environmental impacts

In order to prove the possibility to manipulate with register of the significant environmental aspects and impacts (because ISO 14001 certified organizations created their own method for evaluation environmental impacts), we perform the comparative analysis of the evaluation methodologies and results of the evaluation in the 3 ISO 14001 certified organization [16],[17]. Comparing parallel the evaluation methodologies and results of evaluation by JAVA computer's program, it has been proved that depending on the applied evaluation method of environmental impacts, the register of significant environmental impacts could change the level up to 20%. Because of necessity of creating the models based on neural networks we collected the data related to identificated and evaluated as significant environmental impacts from 6 organizations with ISO 14001 certificate which will be further noted with letters (A,B,C,D,E,F) in order to respect data set confidentiality secret. The objectivity and reliability of these models will be perform using the AHP(Analytic Hierarchy process) method in the pilot organization noted as X. AHP [8],[9],[10] represents frequently used MCDM method for problems that could be transformed into hierarchical structure. In order to establish the objective and reliable final register of significant environmental impacts for 4 environmental media's (air, people, water and ground), the evaluation of environmental impacts identified in organization X will be realized in three ways:

1. AHP model
2. Model of classical neural network
3. Model of neural network of reduced matrix approach

Having in mind that for the appliance of all models requests the initial evaluation of identified environmental impacts in X organization, according chosen criteria, we will first apply the AHP model. Output values of all models are obtained according to the same input values. In order to establish the most convenient way for objective and reliable evaluation of environmental impacts it is necessary to make comparative analysis between all three methods.

3. Using AHP model for evaluation of environmental impacts in pilot organization

AHP is reliable and easy to use MCDM (Multi Criteria Decision Making) method for decision-making jobs especially for problems that could be transforming into hierarchical structure. For this evaluation, AHP model has on the lowest level alternatives (environmental impacts) on the middle level the criteria for evaluation of the impacts and on the highest level goal. Evaluation using the AHP model coordinates the EMS (Environmental management system) manager from organization X. Three criteria in the hierarchy AHP model (for the evaluation of environmental impacts marked) are also signed as the most significant in ISO 14004 standards. These criteria are:

- Volume of impacts
- Power of impacts (The seriousness of the consequences of the impact)
- Probability of the appearance of impacts

Therefore, with this approach it has been created the AHP model for evaluation of environmental impacts for all environmental media's (air, people, water, and ground) as it is prescribed on Figure 1.

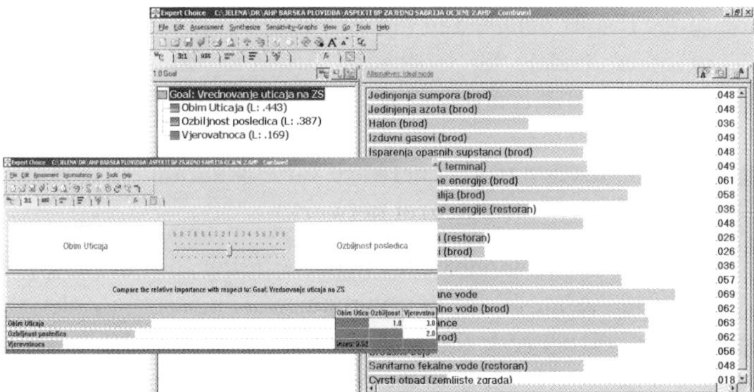

Figure 1. AHP model for evaluation of environmental impacts in organization

Valued by applying the AHP method, represent certain improvement compared to methodology of ISO 14001 certified organizations, because that is the wide spread mathematical model for the decision bring on facts whose verification is realized worldwide, not only on the local level. The valuing of the criteria compared to goal was performed by mutual comparison, while the valuing of impacts compared to the criteria was done by direct input of values from the scale from 1 to 4. After the evaluation of all the hierarchical levels, the model performed the synthesis of the results what gave us the list of importance of the identified environmental impacts (Figure 2).

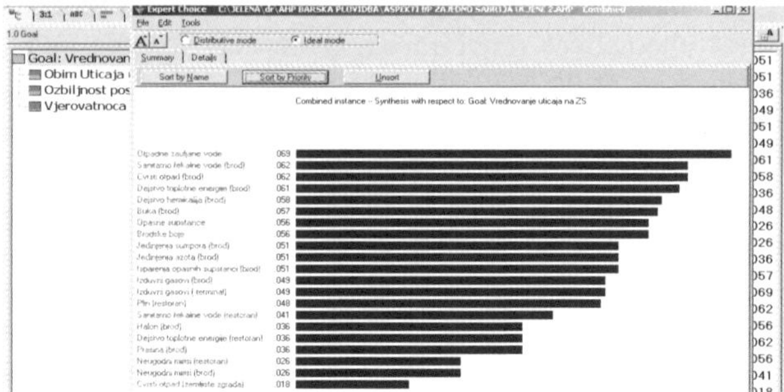

Figure 2. Rang list of environmental impacts significance

The limit of significance environmental impacts is defined by detailed analysis with EMS manager from organization X. The limit is 0.048 what indicates that there is 13 significant impacts from total 21 identified. The discussion of the results obtained in this way is possible to realize only after the appliance of other models for evaluation, when it will also be possible to perform their comparative analysis.

4. Using backpropagation neural network for evaluation environmental impacts (Model of classical neural network)

For evaluation of environmental impacts using neural networks it is necessary to do the arrangement of environmental impacts in order to get the special instruction of network for each media separately. The arrangement of environmental impacts according to the considered environmental media for the entire training sample (from organization A,B,C,D,E,F) is shown on Figure 3.

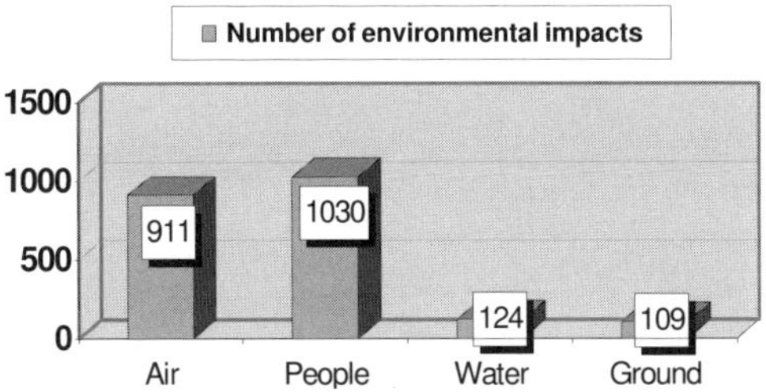

Figure 3. Distribution of impacts according the environmental media for 6 organizations from the training sample

Data in the users' graphic interface of the software package MATLAB for the work with neural network must be normalized. As the marks for all the organization are obtained on the base of different methodologies, it is necessary to normalize the input data according to the organization with the biggest range of marks. After the normalization of data we come to the training of neural network separately for each environmental media and the checking of results i.e. the stimulation of model is performed on the data of organization X according to the input marks from AHP model. This model is called classical neural network. Performances of neural network for media air are presented on figure 4.

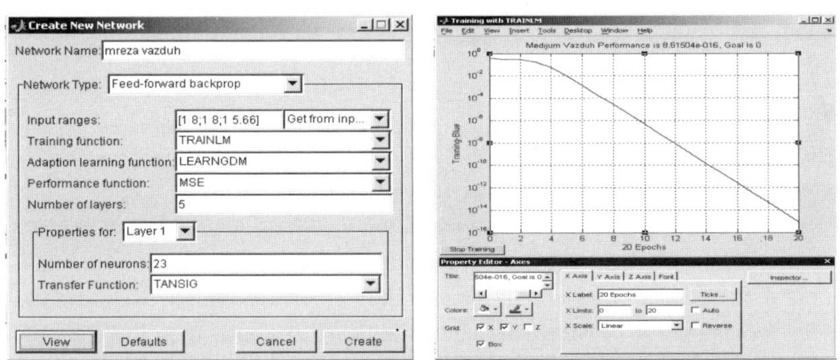

Figure 4. Performances of neural network with diagram of convergence (media air)

After testing network on the simulative sample for media air in the organization X, we obtained the outputs as it is showed in Figure 5.

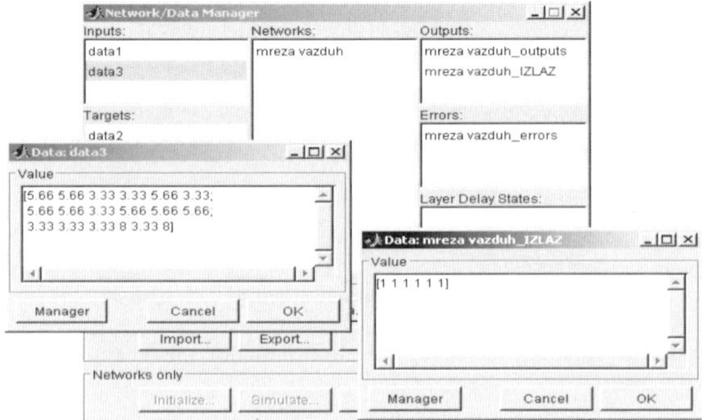

Figure 5. Simulation of neural network (media air)

By simulation of classical neural network with the data of organization X we obtained the marks which refer to 6 identified impacts on the media air. The mark close to the value +1 categorizes the impact as "significant" while the mark close to lower limit value -1 categorizes the impact as "insignificant". Analyzing the results obtained in this way we noticed that all identified impacts on media air as significant what doesn't match for only one impact obtained by the AHP model. This procedure was applied also for the other environmental media's and we obtained very good match of results. Concerning the media people and ground, the result is identical, while for the media water we notify the deviation for 2 of 6 impacts.

5. The appliance of neural network of reduced matrix model

We collected data from certified organizations (A, B, C, D, E and F) in order to analyze their own methodologies for evaluation environmental impacts. According that, we created a model which represents the attempt to eliminate the visible defects analyzed methodologies. The model was called "Reduced matrix model for evaluation of environmental impacts" because it is inspired by the theory of "Risk Management" ... [5]. "Reduced matrix model..." is composed by 2 matrixes. Each matrix is consisted of 2 criterions for evaluation. Mandatory criterion of every matrix is called: "Power of impacts". Other criterions in matrix are same as in model of classical neural network ("Volume of impacts" and "Probability of the appearance of impacts").

This model seem simple but for many environmental impacts can be quite rough because it demands to fulfill a large number of matrix for their final evaluation. In order to accelerate and automatic the process of evaluation we used also backpropagation neural network based on data received from organization A,B,C,D,E and F which are previously evaluated according Reduced matrix model. Before creating and training Backpropagation neural network based on reduced matrix model it is necessary to transform marks of evaluated environmental impacts from 6 observed organizations into marks in reduced matrix model.

Comparing the detailed description of the individual marks for all organization from the training sample we determined correlation in evaluation. For such defined input marks of environmental impacts in organization A,B,C,D,E and F according to mathematic established correlation inside the matrix and using the program made in JAVA programming language [6],[7] we obtained the outputs for all input values. When we obtained training sample in this way we could start with training backrpopagation neural network. In this paper, in order to shorten the procedure of evaluation of environmental impacts, we created one Feed forward backpropagation neural network based on Reduced matrix model with the training sample collected from all environmental media's of the organizations A,B,C,D,E and F. Neural network for such a big sample converge relatively fast as it shown in Figure 6.

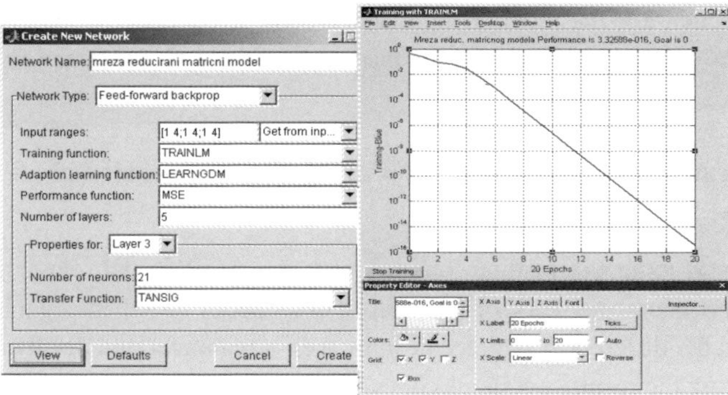

Figure 6. Performance of Backpropagation neural network based on reduced matrix model with diagram of convergence

Simulation of such created and trained neural network is possible for all identified environmental impacts at the same time. Due to more simplified comparative analysis of the results obtained between the applications of all three models. We performed the simulation of neural network reduced matrix model for each environmental media separately. The results of the simulation for the media air of the organization X are shown in Figure 7.

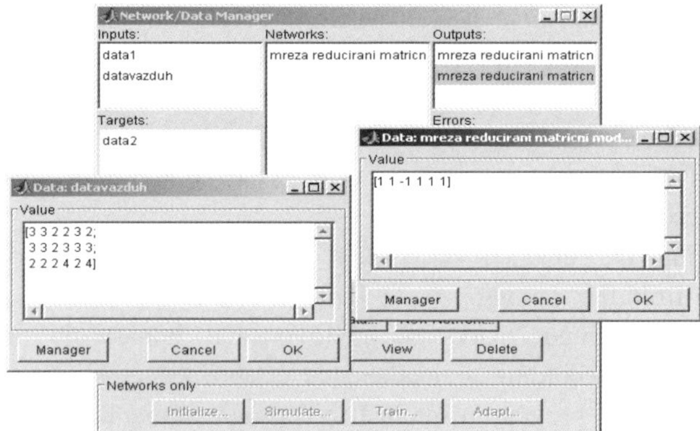

Figure 7. Simulation of neural network of reduced matrix model (media air)

With the simulation for media air we obtained the result that completely match with the results obtained in the AHP model, while with the model of classical neural network there is some deviation in the result. This procedure is also applied for other environmental media's, and we obtained very good match of the results with AHP model and the identical results with classical neural network model. For the media people and ground we obtained completely same results as in AHP model while for the media water there was a deviation in 2 of 6 impacts.

6. Comparative analysis of models for evaluation environmental impacts

Having in mind the results obtained with the AHP model, classical neural network and neural network of reduced matrix model tested in organization X we notified the differences which can show their advantages and disadvantages.

Analyzing the results we should have in mind that for models based on neural networks the normalization of input and output value has been performed. The input for the classic neural network were normalized according to the data of the organization with biggest mark of importance and that also has the largest number of identified impacts (organization A) and the output according to the limits enabled by the model of neural network and according to the own methodologies of evaluation of organization A, B, C, D, E and F. Meanwhile in the MATLAB in the range of output values was limited on interval (-1, 1). Therefore all the impacts considered so significant were marked with 1 while all insignificant marked with -1. Relating to outputs of neural networks with reduced matrix model situation is similar. Normalization of the inputs for this model is performed according to the rules defined with reduced matrix model and correlation of the marks of this model with own methodology of the organizations (A,B,C,D,E, F). Further in the text for comparative analysis of the models we will use signs(Model 1- AHP model of organization X, Model 2 - Classical neural network, Model 3 -Neural network of reduced matrix model). Figure 8 shows the analysis of the relation of the numbers of compatible results obtained on the test sample of the pilot organization X by applying the Models 2 and 3 compared with Model 1.

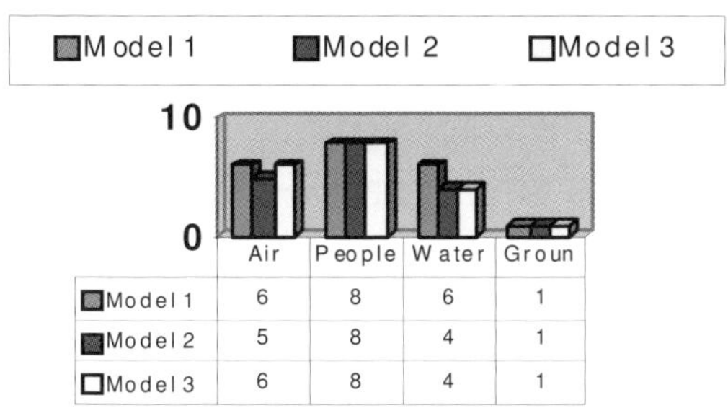

	Air	People	Water	Groun
Model 1	6	8	6	1
Model 2	5	8	4	1
Model 3	6	8	4	1

Figure 8. Comparative analysis of the results compatibility obtained by applying Models 2 and 3 in relation with model 1

We can see that for the media people where the training sample was the biggest Models 2 and 3 gave the same results as the Model 1. Analyzing the input marks for all impacts of test sample for each criteria separately we can conclude that such defined significance of impacts on media people is completely expected. Training sample for the media air is smaller then for media people. It is widely known that size of training sample is the most important factor for the validity of the model of neural network. Accordingly we can say that the compatibility in 5 of 6 impacts for media air is quite satisfactory. Anyway, analyzing the controversial impact which according to the model of classical neural network was marked as significant, we notify that probability of its appearance evaluated with very small mark was crucial for defining its significance. This indicates that the model of classical neural network for the media air has some greater sensibility for evaluation significance of impacts.

When we talk about media water we can say that we had not enough big training samples when we compare it with training samples for media people and air. But since we obtained completely identical results of evaluation of environmental impacts on media water by Models 2 and 3, it needs some more detailed analysis. The two controversial impacts have completely identical marks for all three criteria of evaluation, so we can talk about one type of impact. Anyway, regarding the probability of appearance of this impacts which are valued with the lowest possible mark (mark 1) result based on neural networks (Models 2 and 3) which means insignificant of this impacts was expected. The fact is that for all environmental media's, Models 2 and 3 threats the impact with especially low probability of appearance always us insignificant what makes them to be the potential danger which should be treated separately with the special procedures according standard ISO 14001. On the other hand to the criteria "probability of appearance of impacts" in the Model 1 was given the lowest importance referring to the other two criteria what quite lowered his part in the synthesis of the results by applying the AHP model. This approach resulted to categorize these impacts as significant. Relatively small training sample for the media water, from one side, doesn't permit completely acceptance of the results obtained on Model 2. But on the other side it points to the compatibility of the results in 4 of 6 impacts and to enlarge the training sample in order to provide completely objective evaluation of impacts for the media water. For the media ground we obtained the results which are completely compatible for all models but because of quite small training sample and test sample it couldn't be withdrawn the general conclusion about the validity of Model 2 for this media.

7. Conclusion

Methodology for evaluation of environmental impacts isn't explicitly defined in standard ISO 14001 or standard ISO 14004, but analyzing the different accesses of the ISO 14001 certified organization whose data in course of preparing of this paper were accessible, we came to the conclusion that in this area have a lot of possibilities for manipulation with data. Therefore in this paper are presented the accesses of the evaluation of environmental impacts by applying of the models based on neural networks and model based on AHP method of multicriteria decision.

Even if completely compatible the results of evaluation of all three models for media people, in the case of the media air there is some deviation in the mark of one impact obtained with the Model 2 compared the marks of same by applying the Models 1 and 3. Having in mind that two models of which one is based on the evaluation of AHP method gave the same results for the contradictory impact and which after later inspection of input marks was confirmed as valid, for the media air we can set the final results offered by the Models 1 and 3. On the other hand even if not enough big training sample for the media water among them parallel results of the Model 2 and 3 offered the deviation in 2 of 6 impacts in relation to Model 1. Analyzing the input marks of the contradictory impacts we concluded that the probability of their appearance is so little that they could be treated as controlled significant impacts and we recommend that they should be treated using procedure for prevention of possibility dangers. When we talk about the media ground even if all the models have among them parallel results it is not recommended to use only the Model 2. Each evaluation is subjective as well as the evaluation by using the neural network of the reduced matrix model, so that as the most reliable solution we recommend the double evaluation of environmental impacts:

1. Evaluation by applying neural network of reduced matrix model
2. Reviewing of the results by applying classical neural network

In the judgment of significance of environmental impacts the advantage is, anyway, given to the neural network of the reduced matrix model having in mind that we still don't have big enough training sample for all environmental media and because this model (Model 3) gave us the best results. By comparative analysis of the Models (2 and 3) in relation to Model 1 and having in mind the limitation regarding the size of training sample we can point to quite big reliability and objectivity of the models based on the neural networks in the evaluation of environmental impacts. With this way we confirm the hypothesis from beginning of this paper which refers to the fact that the models based on neural networks could provide objective and reliable evaluation of environmental impacts.

References

1. Jovanović J., Primjena ICT na modeliranje kvantifikovanja aspekata životne sredine, *Magistarski rad*, Podgorica, (2006)
2. ISO 14001:2004., Sistemi upravljanja zaštitom životne sredine - Zahtjevi sa uputstvom za primjenu, *ISO 2004*, (2004)
3. ISO 14004:2004, Sistemi upravljanja zaštitom životne sredine - Opšte smjernice za principe, sisteme i postupke, *ISO 2004*, (2004)
4. Arsovski Z., Informacioni sistemi, *Univerzitet u Kragujevcu*, (2008)
5. AS/NZS 4360:2004, Risk management, *Standards Australia*, Sydney, (2004)
6. Lemay L., Cadenhead R., JAVA 1.2, *Kompjuter biblioteka*, Čačak, (2001)
7. Charatan Q., Kans A., JAVA in two semesters, *McGraw Hill*, UK, (2002)
8. Moreno-Jimenez, J.M., Aguaron, J., Escobar, M.T, Decisional tools for consensus building in AHP-group decision making, *12^a mini Euro Conference Brussels* (Belgium)
9. Saaty, T.L. Group decision-making and the AHP

10. Ramanathan, R., Ganesh, L.S., Group preference aggregation methods employed in AHP: An evaluation and intrinsic process for deriving members weightages, *European journal of operational research 79, (*1994)
11. Subašić P. Fazi logika i neuronske mreže, *Tehnička knjiga*, Beograd, (1997)
12. Milenković S., Veštačke neuronske mreže, *Zadužbina Andrejević*, Beograd, (1997)
13. Sayre D., Inside ISO 14000: The competitive advantage of environmental management. *Delray Beach*, FL: St Lucie Press, (1996)
14. Rondinelli D., Panacea V.G., Common sense, or just a label? The value of ISO 14001 environmental management systems, *European Management*, 18(5):499e510, (2000)
15. Andrews, R. N., Charm J., Habicht H., Knowlton T., Sale M. and Tschinkel V., Third-Party Auditing of Environmental Management Systems: U.S. Registration Practices for ISO 14001.
http://www.ndol.org/documents/emsreport.pdf. (2001)
16. Melnyk, Sroufe, and Calantone, Assessing the Impact of Environmental Management Systems on Corporate and Environmental Performance, *Journal of Operations Management 21*: 329–351, (2003)
17. J. Jovanović, Z. Krivokapić, S Ramović, M. Perović, Evaluation Of The Environmental Impacts By Applying The Neural Networks, *ICQME 2009 conferenc*e, Paris, (2009)

PROJECTING DEMOGRAPHIC SCENARIOS FOR A SOUTHERN ELEPHANT SEAL POPULATION

MARIANO A. FERRARI[*]

Facultad de Ingeniería, UNPSJB, Blvd. Brown 3700
Puerto Madryn, 9120, Argentina

Centro Nacional Patagónico, CONICET, Blvd. Brown 2915
Puerto Madryn, 9120, Argentina

CLAUDIO CAMPAGNA

Wildlife Conservation Society (Argentina), Amenabar 1595 - Piso 2 - Oficina 19
Ciudad Autonoma de Buenos Aires, C1426AKC, Argentina

MIRTHA N. LEWIS

Centro Nacional Patagónico, CONICET, Blvd. Brown 2915
Puerto Madryn, 9120, Argentina

A standard age-structured model was used to model and project population growth, for the expanding southern elephant seal, *Mirounga leonina*, population at Península Valdés (PV, Argentina), considering alternative environmental scenarios.

1. Introduction

Southern elephant seals, *Mirounga leonina*, are distributed mostly in subantarctic environments [8]. One colony, Península Valdés (PV), in coastal Patagonia (Argentina), is exceptional. The number of seals on the Patagonian coast has been increasing for decades. This unique trend in the species is supported by detailed censuses of the PV colony conducted annually during the last 25 years [9].

Despite the positive trend in PV seals, the precedent of several populations of southern elephant seals declining for decades [6, 12] suggests that timely conservation action may benefit from long-term time series in demographic data.

---

[*] Email: ferrari@cenpat.edu.ar

Indeed, the main purpose of achieving long-term data on population numbers, particularly pup production, at PV was to detect eventual declines.

We applied theoretical demographic and environmental parameters to analyze trend scenarios for PV and discuss quantitative results relative to adopting simple precautionary decisions in the absence of data. The unique characteristic of PV as the only growing colony for a widely distributed species allows comparisons with shrinking populations that may help determine which life history stages are most relevant in explaining present trends.

2. Methods

2.1. *Demographic model*

We used a standard age-structured model (Table 1). Juvenile females were seals up to age 4 and adults were older than 4. We assume an equal fertility parameter (α) for all reproductive females (juvenile females at age 3 and adult females). The mean vital rates were gathered from different sources (see Table 1). First year survival (c) was taken from a life table of South Georgia elephant seals [10]. The sex ratio at birth (ρ) and adult survival (p) were taken from previous mark-recapture estimates for this population [1, 12]. Juvenile survival (s) and fertility (α) were estimated by a standard maximum likelihood approach [5] using census counts of pups and females from 1995 to 2006.

2.2. *Environmental stochasticity*

We assumed the environment, thus the vital rates, varying randomly over time [3] and this environmental variation was assumed to affect juvenile and adult survival (s, p). Year-to-year variations of s and p are likely to be correlated, and this correlation can have significant impact on population growth [13]. To include correlation effects in our projections, we considered two environmental factors, A and B which were related to s and p. This follows [4] in that the correlations between vital rates are related to a shared dependence of each demographic rate on an environmental factor. An attempt was made to associate environmental factors with foraging success. Female foraging trips were categorized as: (a) to the Patagonian Basin and the edge of the continental shelf (Basin) and (b) to the continental shelf (Shelf), according to the time spent foraging on each region of the SW Atlantic, e.g. [2] and unpublished data. A was assumed as an environmental factor that determines the mortality of Basin seals and B as an environmental factor, independent of A, which determines the mortality of Shelf seals. All adult females and a proportion δ of juvenile females follow a Basin-strategy whereas the rest of juvenile females follow a Shelf-strategy. Thus adult survival p was determined directly by A and juvenile survival s was determined by $\delta A'+(1-\delta)B$, where A' is an environmental factor completely correlated with A. We used an estimation of $\delta = 0.5$ according to our records of juvenile foraging trips to project scenarios. On the other hand, we varied δ as a free parameter in a second analysis, this allowed considering several alternatives of correlation between s and p (in a simple way) to project population numbers.

Table 1. Matrix population model and alternative projected scenarios. Environmental factor A determines the mortality (survival) of Basin seals (see Methods) whereas the independent environmental factor B determines the mortality (survival) of Shelf seals.

Current demographic parameter estimates

Parameter	Mean value	Source
First year survival (c)	0.6	South Georgia (McCann 1985)
Proportion of females at birth (ρ)	0.5	Península Valdés (Unpublished)
Adult survival, 4 years old and older (p)	0.842	P.V. (Pistorius et al. 2004)
Juvenile survival, 1 to 3 years old (s)	0.804	P.V., Maximum likelihood
Fertility (α)	0.94	P.V., Maximum likelihood

Population projection matrix

$$\begin{pmatrix} 0 & 0 & 0 & \alpha & \alpha \\ \rho.c & 0 & 0 & 0 & 0 \\ 0 & s & 0 & 0 & 0 \\ 0 & 0 & s & 0 & 0 \\ 0 & 0 & 0 & s & p \end{pmatrix}$$

Projected scenarios

Scenario	Mean value of factor A ($\bar{a}$)	Mean value of factor B ($\bar{b}$)	Environmental variance (*var*)	Juveniles affected by A (δ)
1. Current conditions	0.842	0.804	0.0003	0.5
2. Moderate decrease of A	0.830	0.804	0.0003	0.5
3. Strong decrease of A	0.818	0.804	0.0003	0.5

To determine the environmental variance (*var*) we consider the adult survival mark-recapture estimates [12]. The observed variance of these estimates includes variance due to demographic stochasticity and measurement error [7].

These components must be removed to estimate environmental variance, otherwise, the environmental variability may be considerably overestimated. We do not have an estimate of measurement error and demographic stochasticity for the current survival mark-recapture estimates. Thus, to get an acceptable value of environmental variance, we rejected three extreme values and calculated observed variance.

2.3. *Projected scenarios*

When we ran a simulation in a specific scenario, we first selected a value for each environmental factor A and B from a beta distribution with mean $\bar{a}$ and $\bar{b}$ respectively, and variance *var*, according to Table 1. We assumed that the mean value of A' and B coincides under current conditions. Then we directly calculated $A' = c_1 A + c_2$, with $c_1 = \sqrt{2}$ and $c_2 = \bar{b} - c_1(0.842)$, and the population projection parameters: $p = A$, $s = \delta A' + (1 - \delta) B$. In this way, when we varied δ in the following analysis, p and s have a correlation of $\delta / \sqrt{\delta^2 + (1-\delta)^2}$, and the variance of s is greater than *var*, regardless of the δ value.

Assuming an initial population corresponding to the number of pups estimates (directly from census data) prior to 2006, the population was projected for 50 years, and we performed 1000 replicate runs for each scenario. We assumed that environmental states (annual values of A and B) were independent and identically distributed. We excluded density dependence and demographic stochasticity from our model since it was a first approximation to modeling this southern elephant seals population.

2.4. *Stochastic population dynamics*

Two metrics are commonly used to summarize the stochastic population dynamics: the growth rate of mean population size (r), and the stochastic growth rate (r_s). The former corresponds to the deterministic growth rate of mean population parameters and it is not influenced by environmental variability. The latter correspond to the average of growth rates of many replicate simulations. It is particularly important because it depends of environmental variability [3]. We used the Tuljapurkar's approximation of the stochastic growth rate [13, 14] to calculate r_s as an explicit function of three parameters: adult mortality, proportion of juveniles affected by factor A (δ, which determines the correlation between adult and juvenile mortality) and the environmental variance (*var*). Then, for different values of δ and *var*, we calculated how much should increase adult mortality so that $r_s = 0$, which allow us to distinguish between an increasing and a decreasing population in a variable environment.

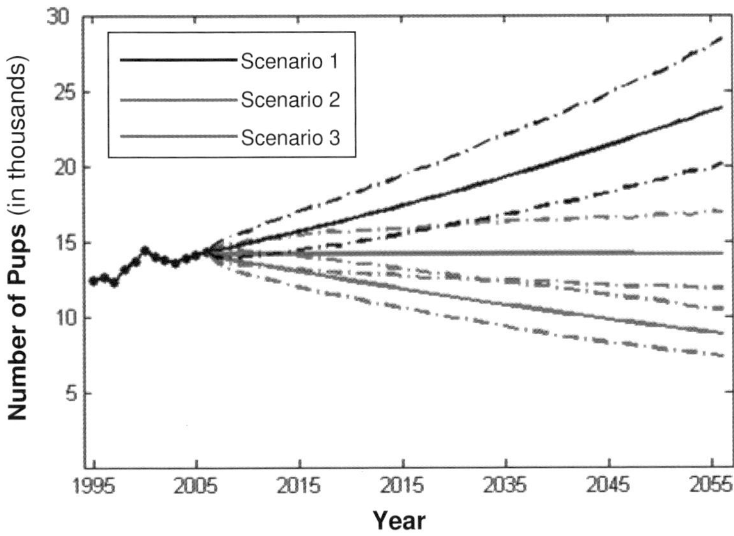

Figure 1. Projections of the number of pups for the three scenarios described in Table 1. Solid lines are mean population projections. Dotted lines are 90% confidence limits from 1000 simulations.

3. Results

Projecting population trends for the period 2006-2056 yielded three theoretical scenarios (Figure 1), none of them conducting to extinction in 50 years. Scenario 1 reflected the continuity of present conditions for an annual mean population growth of 1.04% (Tuljapurkar approximation of the stochastic growth rate was $r_s = 0.0101$ and the growth rate of mean population $r = 0.0103$). The 90% confidence interval after 1,000 simulations projected a range in the number of pups born for 2056 of $20,110 - 28,360$ individuals.

Scenario 2 simulated a worsening of environmental conditions that caused 1.4% decrease of the mean value of factor A, corresponding to an increase of 8% in adult female mortality and of 4.5% in mean mortality of juvenile females. The stochastic growth rate estimate was $r_s = -0.0002$, and the growth rate of mean population $r = -0.0001$ (stable population). The projected range of pups born in 50 years from 2006 ranged $11,830 - 16,870$ animals.

Scenario 3 illustrated an important environmental deterioration with a decrease of 2.9% in the mean value of factor A, with a 15% increase in adult female mortality and an 8.6% increase in juvenile female mortality. The stochastic growth rate estimate was $r_s = -0.0096$, and the growth rate of mean population $r = -0.0094$, corresponding to a 1% annual decrease in mean population size. The 90% confidence interval for the number of pups born ranged 7,290 – 10,466 seals.

Table 2. Percent of increase in adult female mortality that will explain a decrease in number of pups born ($r_s < 0$) as a function of the effect of environmental factor A on juveniles. Four cases are tested with different environmental variance: $var = 0$ represents the mean population behavior, $var = 0.0003$ is the value assumed as current environmental variance, $var = 0.006$ is the observed variance of adult survival mark-recapture estimates [12] and $var = 0.01$ is a speculative increase in environmental variance proposed as a worse case.

Environmental variance (var)	Proportion of juveniles affected by environmental factor A (δ)				
	0	0.25	0.5	0.75	1
0	11.9 %	9.45 %	7.83 %	6.69 %	5.84 %
0.0003	11.8 %	9.36 %	7.74 %	6.59 %	5.74 %
0.006	9.79 %	7.65 %	6.07 %	4.81 %	3.74 %
0.01	8.35 %	6.45 %	4.91 %	3.56 %	2.35 %

On the other hand, a potentially decreasing population (in a stochastic environment) will result from small changes in the mean of environmental factor A, by considering a combined increase of environmental variance and the proportion of juveniles affected by A (Table 2).

4. Discussion

4.1. *General conclusions*

Expectations are that a PV elephant seal colony will continue to exist in the next 50 years with a number of pups born that range from over 7,000 (the colony size in the late 1960s) to close to 30,000 individuals, depending on the scenario.

A deterioration of environmental factor A would be the equivalent of a worsening of the environmental conditions that today support the population. Two kinds of environmental modifications: a decrease in the A mean and an increase in the environmental variance were analyzed in the present work. However, the impact of A was restricted to adult and juvenile females, which is a strong simplification. Moreover, projections could certainly be improved by a better understanding of environmental variance.

4.2. *The practical conservation value of estimating future scenarios*

One motivation to conduct detailed counts during decades is the early detection of population changes to advice management accordingly and to contribute to species conservation. However, in an eventual decrease in pup production we would not be able to determine with certainty if the trend represents a shift from scenario 1 to scenarios 2 or 3. Moreover, the causes of a shift in scenarios may also be difficult, if not impossible, to tackle. A decrease in numbers may reflect either a large scale environmental change or a negative interaction with humans.

Therefore, chances are that a decrease in numbers will only serve for the record. Elephant seals suggest that our best chance to protect them is the precautionary alleviation of actual and potential threats. We know that seals forage on the Argentine continental Basin. Therefore, the developing of deep sea fishery in the Basin is likely to be a potential source of interaction. If the interaction occurs and causes population impacts, we will most likely be unable to document the direct cause, although we will be accurately documenting the demise.

The constrains that our data may have for conservation beyond the Precautionary Principle find a counterpart in their potential for comparing growing and shrinking populations and determine which life history stages are most relevant to explain present trends. The demographic model presented here (Table 1) implies that adult female survival is the vital variable with greatest impact on population growth, followed by juvenile survival, first year survival and fertility. This can be made explicit by performing a standard elasticity analysis [3], the respective elasticity values for p, s, c and α are: 0.46, 0.32, 0.11 and 0.11. This elasticity distribution is different from populations that were decreasing, such as Macquarie Island or Marion Island, where juvenile survival seems to be the vital rate of greatest impact on population growth [11].

References

1. C. Campagna and M.N. Lewis, *Marine Mammal Science* **8**, 387 (1992).
2. C. Campagna, B.J. Le Boeuf, S. Blackwell, D.E. Crocker and F. Quintana, *Journal of Zoology* **236**, 55 (1995).
3. H. Caswell, *Matrix population models, 2nd edn.* Sinauer Associates, Inc., Sunderland, MA, USA (2001).
4. D. Doak, P. Kareiva and B. Klepetka, *Ecological Applications* **4(3)**, 446 (1994).
5. R. Hilborn and M. Mangel, *The Ecological Detective: confronting models with data.* Princeton Uninersity Press, New Jersey (1997).
6. M.A. Hindell and H.R. Burton, *Journal of Zoology* **213**, 365 (1987).
7. B.E. Kendall, *Ecological Applications* **8(1)**, 184 (1998).
8. B.J. Le Bouef and R.M. Laws, *Elephant seals.* University of California Press (1994).
9. M.N. Lewis, C. Campagna, F. Quintana and V. Falabella, *Mastozoología Neotropical* **5**, 29 (1998).

10. T.S. McCann, pages 1-17 in J.K. Ling and M.M. Bryden, eds. *Studies of sea mammals in South Latitudes*. Northfield, South Australian Museum (1985).

11. C.R. McMahon, M.A. Hindell, H.R. Burton and M.N. Bester, *Marine Ecology Progress Series* **288**, 273 (2005).

12. P.A. Pistorius, M.N. Bester, M.N. Lewis, F.E. Taylor and C. Campagna, *Journal of Zoology* **263**, 107 (2004).

13. S. Tuljapurkar, *Population dynamics in variable environments*. Springer-Verlag, New York, USA (1990).

14. S. Tuljapurkar, pages 59-87 in S. Tuljapurkar and H. Caswell, eds. *Structured-population models in marine, terrstrial and freshwater systems*. Chapman and Hall, New York, USA. (1997).

EFFECT OF HEAT INPUT AND ENVIRONMENTAL TEMPERATURE ON THE WELDING RESIDUAL STRESSES USING ANSYS APDL PROGRAM COMPARISON WITH EXPERIMENTAL RESULTS

NAZHAD A. HUSSEIN

Mechanical Dept, Univ. of Salahaddin, Erbil, Iraq

The aim of this paper is to investigate the effect of increase in the value of heat input due to change in the welding speed and its influence on residual stress distribution in steel weldments at different environmental temperature. The residual stresses were determined by FE simulation using ANSYS APDL program and hole-drilling strain gage method of ASTM standard E837-01 during experimental works. The experimentally determined axial and transverse residual stresses on the surface compared with simulation results. The numerically calculated stresses were in good qualitative agreement with experimental results and successfully describe stress profile. The result showed that increasing in heat input decreasing the residual stresses in x-deflection by 10%, 15%, and 17% and z-stress by 13%, 16%, and 20% at environmental temperature of 10°c, 25°c and 40°c respectively.

1. Introduction

You Residual stress distribution and distortion in a welded plate are strongly affected by many parameters and by their interaction. In particular, there are structural, material and welding factors. The structural parameters include geometry of the plates, thickness and width and joint type. Among the material parameters mechanical and physical properties and type of filler-metal were considered. Welding process parameters include type of process employed, welding procedure: current, voltage, arc travel speed, and arc efficiency. As a consequence of the non-uniform temperature distribution, parts of materials close to the weld are subject to different rates of expansion and contraction developing a three-dimensional complex residual stress state. This usually because brittle fracture, cracking, diminishes buckling load, affecting therefore the load-bearing capacity of welded structure. To understand the formation of residual stress, node temperature history during the welding process must be calculated. Physical and mechanical material properties are a function of temperature. The temperature history of the welded components has a significant influence on the residual stresses, distortion and hence the fatigue behavior of the welded structures. Classical solutions for the transient temperature field such as Rosenthal's solutions [1] dealt with the semi-infinite body subjected to an instant point heat source, line heat source or surface heat source. These solutions can be used to predict the temperature field at a distance far from the heat source but fail to predict the temperature in the vicinity of the heat source. Eagar and Tsai [2] modified Rosenthal's theory to include a two dimensional (2-D) surface Gaussian distributed heat source with a constant distribution parameter (which can be considered as an effective arc radius) and found an analytical solution for the temperature of a semi-infinite body subjected to this moving heat source. Their solution is a significant step for the improvement of temperature prediction in the near heat source regions. Jeong and Cho [3] introduced an analytical solution for the transient temperature field of a fillet-welded joint based on the similar 2-D Gaussian heat source but with different distribution parameters (in two directions x and y). Using the conformal mapping technique, they have successfully transformed the solution of the temperature field in the plate of a finite thickness to the fillet welded joint. Even though the available solutions using the Gaussian heat sources could predict the temperature at regions closed to the heat source, they are still limited by the shortcoming of the 2-D heat source itself with no effect of penetration. This shortcoming can only be overcome if more general heat sources are implemented.

Goldak, et al. [4], first introduced the three-dimensional (3-D) double ellipsoidal moving heat source. Finite element modeling (FEM) was used to calculate the temperature field of a bead-on-plate and showed that this 3-D heat source could overcome the shortcoming of the previous 2-D Gaussian model to predict the temperature of the welded joints with much deeper penetration. However, up to now, an analytical solution for this kind of 3-D heat source was not yet available [5], and hence, researchers must rely on FEM for transient temperature calculation or other simulation purposes, which requires the thermal history of the components.

Therefore, if any analytical solution for a temperature field from a 3-D heat source is available, a lot of CPU time could be saved and the thermal-stress.

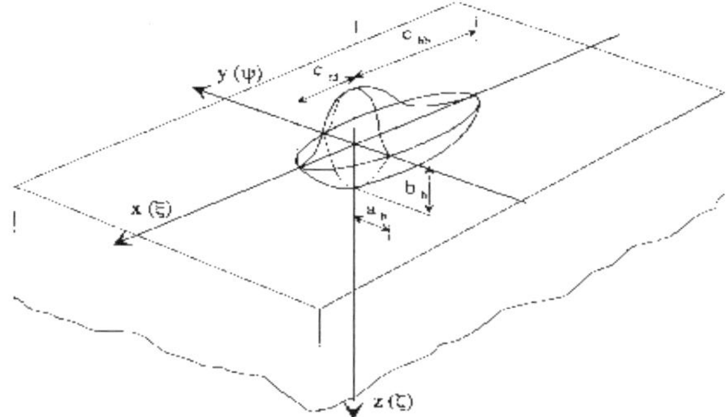

Figure 1. Double ellipsoidal density distributed heat source.

Double ellipsoidal density distributed heat source analysis or related simulations could be carried out much more rapidly and conveniently. The heat source model developed by Goldak is used in this research, which distributes the heat throughout the volume of the molten zone.

2. Experimental Procedure

These experiments were conducted as per the design matrix using semiautomatic thyrister-controlled GMAW equipment. A servomotor-driven manipulator was used to maintain uniform welding speed. Copper-coated steel wire AWS ER70S-6 (BW-2), 1.2 mm diameter, in the form of coil was used, with CO_2 as the shielding gas. Structural steel plate (ISO 2062) specimens $300 \times 150 \times 12$ mm were welded together.

Before the start of actual welding, the plates were tack welded at the ends. The tack welded plates were supported like the boundary conditions selected in FE simulation. The residual stresses were determined by using hole-drilling strain gage method of ASTM standard E837-01 during experimental works.

3. Finite Element Model

Eight- node brick elements with linear shape function are mostly listed in the model. Linear elements are preferred because, in general, favors more lower-order elements than fewer high-order elements in non-linear problems. The basic FE model is shown in figure-2. This model consist of nodes associated 34800 elements.

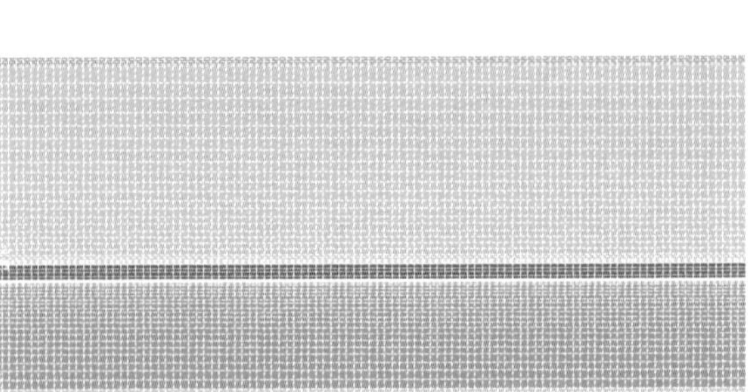

Figure 2. Basic Finite Element Model.

In order to facilitate data mapping between thermal and structural analysis, the same FE model is used with respective element types. For structural analysis the element type is solid 45 with three translational degree of freedom at each node. Due to anticipated high temperature and stress gradients near the weld, a relatively fine mesh is used in distance of 10 mm on both sides of the weld centerline. The boundary conditions during the structural analysis applied as shown in figure-3.

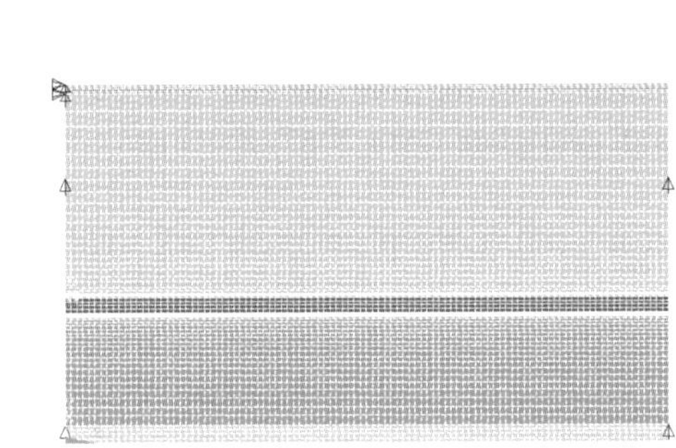

Figure 3. Boundary conditions during the structural analysis.

4. Results and Discussions

The experimentally determined residual stresses were in good qualitative agreement with the numerically calculated residual stresses and successfully describe stress profile. The deviation of experimental data from the calculated stresses may be because of several reasons including approximation in mechanical properties of material involved, possible eccentricity in the hole, probability of hole depth measurement error etc. Figure 4&5 show the comparison between FE and experimental results at 40°C.

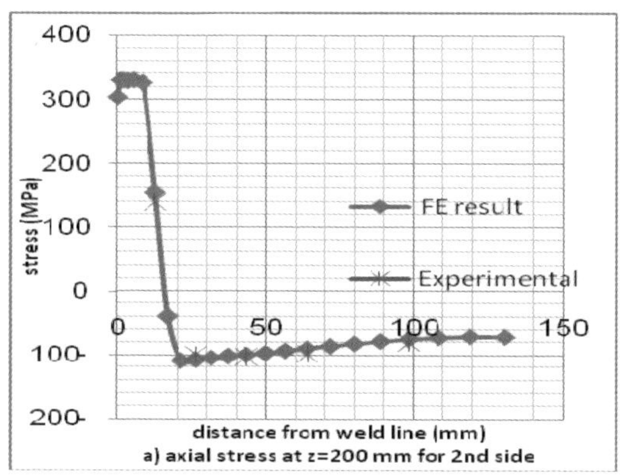

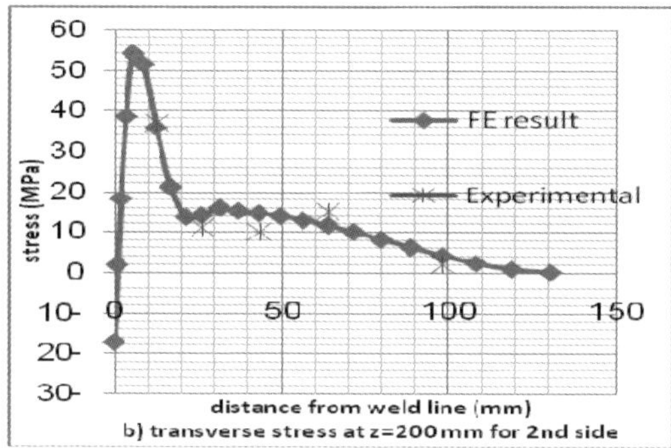

Figure 4. Comparison between Residual Stresses of Flange at z=200 mm from Experimental and FE Results for Welding at 10 °C.

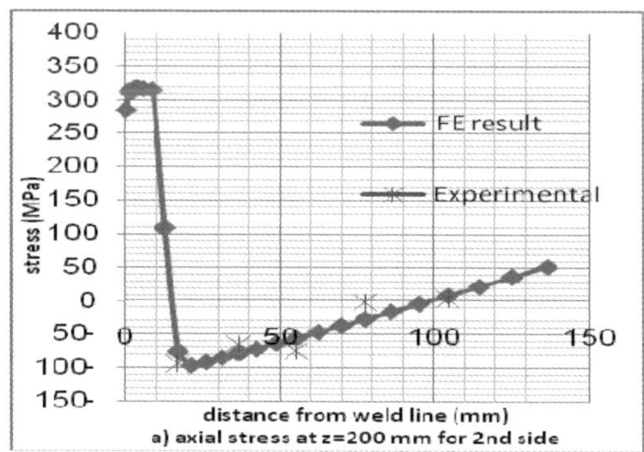

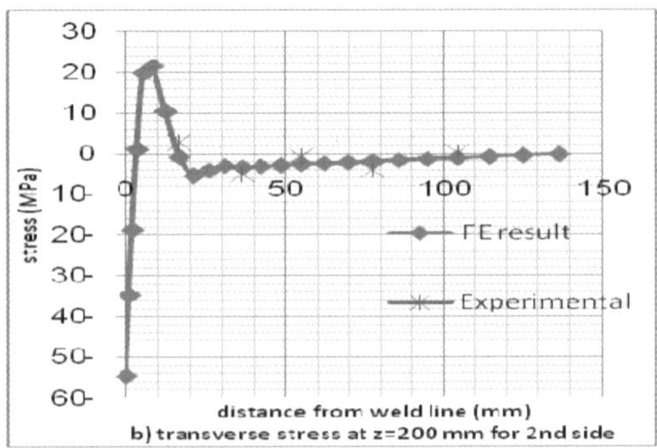

Figure 5. Comparison between Residual Stresses of Web from Experimental and FE Results for Second Side Welding at 10 °C.

4.1. *Effect of environmental temperature*

Another factor that received attention is the initial temperature of the work pieces. Welding done at three different environmental temperatures, therefore welding modeled for the selected temperatures and axial stresses extracted as shown in figure (4). Increasing the environmental temperature from 10°c to 40°c resulted in decreasing the residual stresses. The decreasing of residual stresses attributed to reduce the cooling rate in a weld by lowering the temperature gradient between the weld zone and the unheated metal. Because the temperature gradient is very steep between the melt and cold base metal, the metal starts to very rapidly during the first second after the heat source is extinguished and cooling rate increased. The temperatures between the points are, of course, subject to either positive or negative gradient depending on distance from the weld and the amount of time that elapsed after start of welding. [6]

In welded joints, the higher the peak temperature reached at a point during welding, the faster the cooling rate will be after cooling has began. Temperature rise is most rapid in the heat-affected zone at the start of welding, when the flame or arc dwells against cold metal. As a consequence of this rapid temperature rise, many develop a microstructure in the HAZ that is prone to become semi-hardened. The microstructural condition in steel develops when a constituent containing cementite undergoes only partial dissolution during heating. As a consequence, localized areas in the microstructure surrounding particles of un dissolved cementite becomes abnormally rich in carbon content, and these high-carbon areas easily may from marten site in a matrix of un hardened microstructure on cooling; hence the expression semi-hardened. This microstructural condition can cause in higher residual stresses. [7]

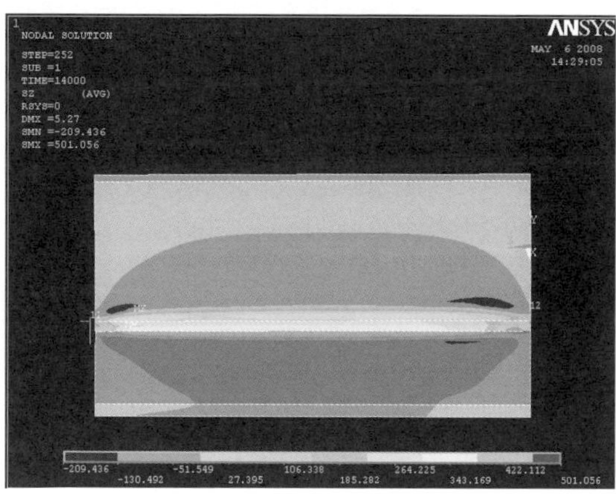

Figure 6.a. Distribution of Residual Stresses on the Model at Environmental Temperature of 10°C. (Smax=501 MPa)

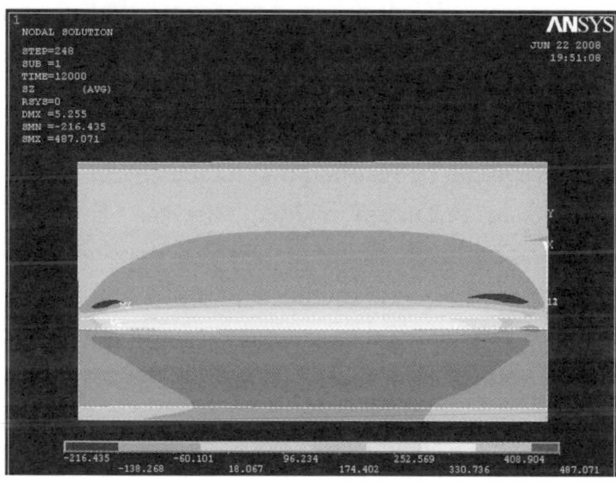

Figure 6.b. Distribution of Residual Stresses on the Model at Environmental Temperature of 25°C. (Smax=487 MPa)

764

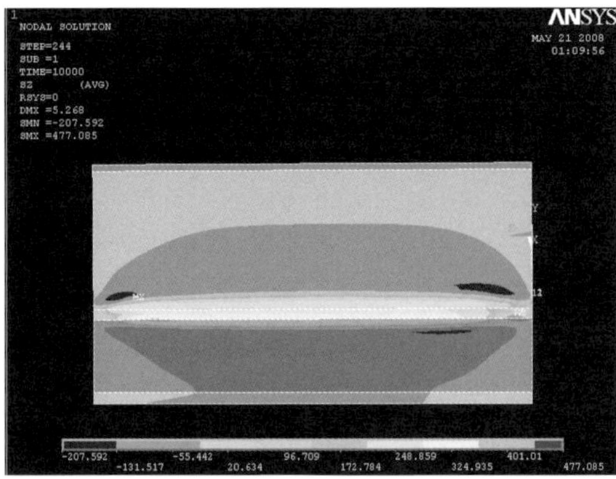

Figure 6.c. Distribution of Residual Stresses on the Model at Environmental Temperature of 40°C. (Smax=477 MPa)

4.2. *Effect of heat input at different environmental temperature*

In this section the effect of heat input at different environmental temperature discussed in order to reach better results for the welded part with less residual stresses. The table (1) showed the change in residual stresses and deflection due to increasing heat input by 13% at selected environmental temperature i.e. 10°c, 25°c and 40°c. It was obvious from Table (1) that increasing in heat input decreasing the residual stresses in x-axis by 10%, 15%, and 17% and z-axis by 13%, 16%, and 20% at environmental temperature of 10°c, 25°c and 40°c respectively. Therefore it can be resulted that increasing in heat input with higher environmental caused in minimum residual stresses. Higher input at higher environmental temperature used to regulate HAZ cooling rate and thus favor deflection and residual stresses. The higher environmental temperature caused in less cooling rate and the effect of increasing heat input add for lowering cooling rate more and caused tougher microstructure with lower residual stresses. [8]

Table 1. Change in Residual Stresses due to Increasing Heat Input by 13% at Selected Environmental Temperature

Temperature	Sx(%)	Sy(%)	Sz(%)
10°C	10	---	13
25°C	15	---	16
40°C	17	---	20

5. Conclusions

1- A good qualitative agreement obtained between the finite element and experimental results.

2- Increasing the environmental temperature in which specimens were welded caused significant decreasing in residual stresses.

3- Increasing the heat input by 13% accompany with increasing of environmental temperature from 10°c to 40°c showed the maximum decreasing of residual stresses by 17% for x-direction and 20% for z-direction and no change in y-residual stresses.

References

1. Rosenthal, D., Mathematical theory of heat distribution during welding and cutting. Welding Journal 20(5): 220-s to 234-s, (1941).
2. Eager, T. W., and Tsai, N. S., Temperature fields produced by traveling distributed heat sources. Welding Journal 62(12): 346-s to 355-s, (1983).
3. Jeong, S. K., and Cho, H. S., An analytical solution to predict the transient temperature distribution in fillet arc welds. Welding Journal 76(6): 223-s to 232-s, (1997).
4. Goldak, J., Chakravarti, A., and Bibby, M., A Double Ellipsoid Finite Element Model for Welding Heat Sources, IIW Doc. No. 212-603-85, (1985).
5. Painter, M. J., Davies, M. H., Battersby, S., Jarvis, L., and Wahab, M. A., A literature review on numerical modelling the gas metal arc welding process. Australian Welding Research, CRC. No. 15, Welding Technology Institute of Australia, (1996).
6. J. Choi, J. Mazumder, Numerical and Experimental Analysis for Solidification and Residual Stress in the GMAW Process for AISI 304 Stainless Steel, J. of Material Science, Vol. 37, PP. 2143-2158, (2002).
7. G. H. Jung, C. L. Tsai, Fundamental studies on the Effect of Distortion Control Plans on Angular Distortions in Fillet Welded T-Joints, Welding Journal, PP. 213s-223s, (2004).
8. D. Dang, W. Liang, H. Murakawa, Determination of Welding Deformation in Fillet-Welded Joint by means of Numerical Simulation and Comparison with Experimental Measurements, J. of Material Processing Technology, Vol. 183, PP. 219-225, 2007.

SPHALERITE DISSOLUTION ACTIVITY IN THE PRESENCE OF SULPHURIC ACID BY USING THE PITZER'S MODEL

BEGAR ABDELHAKIM[1]

[1] *Department of Mechanical Engineering, University of Biskra, BP145 Biskra, Algeria*
begarabdelhakim@yahoo.fr

M.A. DJEGHLAL[2], A. BEGAR[3], A. DOUAIR[4]

[2] *LSGM Laboratory, Department of Metallurgy, ENP, B.P182, El-Harrach, Algeria*

[3] *Department of Mechanical Engineering, University of Biskra, BP145 Biskr Algeria*

[4] *E.M.G.M. Barika 05400 Batna Algeria*

The study presented here relates to the process of dissolution of the synthetic sphalerite in aqueous solution of sulphuric acid which makes it possible to obtain from zinc sulphate, the constant of balance of the reaction of dissolution is given by using the model of Pitzer for calculating coefficient of activity. The experiments of leaching of this study covering the active temperature range of temperature 25°C until 200°C, it is necessary to determine the expressions thus giving the coefficients of activities of zinc sulphate the coefficients of activities of sulphuric acid to 25°C, by introducing the dependence compared to the temperatures.

1. Introduction

During the last decades, attention has been given to the leaching of zinc sulphide ores/concentrates by aqueous sulfuric acid (Demopoulos and Baldwin, 1999; Peng 2005; T.Pecina and al, 2007) [6,7,11].

Electrolytes play an important role in many applications which occur typically in the fields of ores leaching, in the fields of corrosion, the effects of water pollution abatement, the transformation of foodstuffs, and in the treatment of the oil reservoir. Many attempts were made to develop models to represent the thermodynamic properties of the solutions of electrolyte. Pitzer and al. [3,9,10] developed a model of calculation of the properties of the electrolytes starting from an improved analysis of the model of Debye Huckel and semi numerical models. This model connects the intermolecular forces and the distribution of the ions to the osmotic pressure and takes into account the influence of forces with short distance in the binary interactions. The obtained equations are analogous to those of Guggenheim. The expressions of the coefficient of activity and the osmotic coefficient are deduced from the equation of the excess free energy of Gibbs (Gex).

2. Thermodynamic model

2.1. *Sulphuric acid is alone in solution*

In water, Sulphuric acid is separated according balances

$$H_2SO_4 \Leftrightarrow H^+ + HSO_4^- \qquad K_1$$
$$HSO_4^- \Leftrightarrow H^+ + SO_4^{-2} \qquad K_2$$

The constant equilibrium is linked to the standard free energy of the reaction by the relation Vanthoof. He just: $k_1=80,72$ and $k_2=0,0125$.

The high values of the equilibrium constant K_1, Translated into strong shift in the balance towards the formation of HSO_4^- and H^+. We admit that in the future the first dissociation sulphuric acid is total. Only the second equilibrium dissociation will be taken into account $HSO_4^- \Leftrightarrow H^+ + SO_4^{-2}$.

Pitzer and al. [9] gave value perceptibly different K_2. They adopted the value 0.0105, which corresponds to a compromise.

An application of Pitzer's expression for estimating the coefficient of activity for a mixture of electrolytes to the couple of ions H^+ and SO_4^{-2} in the presence of ions HSO_4^- gives:

$$\ln(\gamma_H^2 \gamma_{SO_4}) = 6f^{\gamma} + 4m_1 B_{H_1} + (4m_2 + 2m_H)B_{H_2}^{(0)} \\ + (8m_2 + 2m_H).m_H C_{H_2} + 6m_1 m_H B'_{H_1} \tag{1}$$

Now let us apply the expression of the coefficient of activity for a mixture of electrolytes to the couple of ions H^+, HSO_4^- in the presence of ions SO_4^{-2}.

$$\ln\gamma_H \ln\gamma_{HSO_4} = 2f^{\gamma} + 2(m_1 + m_H)B_{H_1} + 2m_2 B_{H_2}^{(0)} + 4m_2 m_H C_{h_2} + 2m_1 m_H B'_{H_1} \tag{2}$$

The former relationships must be compatible with the balance of dissolution. Hence the expression of the product of the coefficients of activity is as follows:

$$\frac{\gamma_{H^+} \gamma_{SO_4^-}}{\gamma_{HSO_4^-}} = \exp(4f^{\gamma} + 2(m_1 - m_H)B_{H_1} + 2(m_2 + m_H)B_{H_2}^{(0)} \\ + 2(2m_2 + m_H)B_{H_2}^{(0)} + 2(2m_2 + m_H)m_H C_{H_2} + 4m_1 m_H B'_H) \tag{3}$$

At weak concentrations, the molality is close to the concentration on the basis of the second balance of the dissolution of the sulphuric acid $HSO_4^- \Leftrightarrow H^+ + SO_4^{-2}$ the concentration of the sulphate ions in the solution makes it possible to write the following relationship:

$$m_H = \frac{\dfrac{K_2 m_1}{m_2}}{(\dfrac{\gamma_H \gamma_2}{\gamma_1})} \tag{4}$$

An averaged coefficient of activity $\gamma^\pm$ can be defined by assuming that the sulphuric acid is completely dissociated. The following relationship:

$$4\gamma_\pm^3 m^3 = \gamma_H^2 \gamma_{SO_4} m_H^2 m_2 \tag{5}$$

allows the calculation of the average coefficient of activity $\gamma_\pm$. Indeed the molality of ions H^+ was determined and one calculates $(\gamma_H^2 \gamma_{SO_4})$ as follows:

$$\ln(\gamma_H^2 \gamma_{SO_4}) = 6F^\gamma + 4m_1 B_{H_1} + (4m_2 + 2m_H)B_{H_2}^{(0)} \\ + (8m_2 + 2m_H)m_H C_{H_2} + 6m_1 m_H B'_{H_1} \tag{6}$$

With
$$C_{H_2} = \frac{C_{H_2}^\gamma}{2^{\frac{3}{2}}} \tag{7}$$

$$f^\gamma = A^\gamma (\frac{I^{\frac{1}{2}}}{1+1.2 I^{\frac{1}{2}}} + \frac{2}{1.2} \ln(1+1.2 I^{\frac{1}{2}})) \tag{8}$$

$$A^\gamma = 0{,}0000043\, T^2 + 0{,}002709\, T + 0{,}583022 \tag{9}$$

$$B_{H1} = B_{H1}^{(0)} + \frac{B_{H1}^{(1)}}{2I}(1 - (1 + 2I^{\frac{1}{2}})e^{(-2I^{\frac{1}{2}})}) \tag{10}$$

$$B'_{H1} = \frac{B_{H1}^{(1)}}{2I^2}(1 - (1 + 2I^{\frac{1}{2}} + 2I)e^{(-2I^{\frac{1}{2}})}) \tag{11}$$

For an aqueous sulphuric solution, the ionic species involved are: H^+, HSO_4^- and SO_4^{-2}. Therefore $I = \frac{1}{2}m_H + \frac{1}{2}m_1 + \frac{1}{2}m_2 2^2$

Pitzer [8] provides the following equations, depending on the temperature:

$$k_2 = e^{-14{,}0321 + \frac{2825{,}2}{T}} \tag{12}$$

$$B_{H1}^{(0)} = 0{,}05584 + \frac{46{,}040}{T} \tag{13}$$

770

$$B_{H_1}^{(1)} = -0,65758 + \frac{336,514}{T} \tag{14}$$

$$B_{H_2}^{(0)} = -0,32806 + \frac{98,607}{T} \tag{15}$$

$$C_{H_2} = 0,25333 - \frac{63,124}{T} \tag{16}$$

2.2. Sulphuric acid and sphalerite in solution

The principal ionic species in solution are here H^+, HSO_4^-, SO_4^- and Zn^{+2}.
An application of Pitzer's expression for estimating the coefficient of activity for a mixture of electrolytes to the couple of ions H^+ and SO_4^{-2} in the presence of ions HSO_4^- and Zn^{+2} in neglects the coefficients of B'_{Zn_1} et C_{Zn_1} in front of the interactions of the species Zn^{+2} and SO_4^{-2} gives:

$$
\begin{aligned}
\ln(\gamma_H^2 \gamma_{SO_4}) = {} & 6f^\gamma + 4m_2(B_{H_2}^{(0)} + (m_H + 2m_{Zn})C_{H_2}) + 4m_1(B_{H_1}) \\
& + 2m_{Zn}(B_{Zn_2} + (m_H + 2m_{Zn})C_{Zn_2}) + 2m_H(B_{H_2}^{(0)} \\
& + (m_H + 2m_{Zn})C_{H_2}) + 6m_1 m_H B'_{H_1} + 4m_2 m_H C_{H_2} \\
& + 6m_2 m_{Zn} B'_{Zn_2} + 4m_2 m_{Zn} C_{Zn_2}
\end{aligned} \tag{17}
$$

Now let us apply the expression of the coefficient of activity for a mixture of electrolytes to the couple of ions H^+, HSO_4^- in the presence of ions SO_4^{-2} and Zn^{+2}.

$$
\begin{aligned}
\ln(\gamma_H \gamma_{HSO_4}) = {} & 2f^\gamma + 2m_1 B_{H_1} + 2m_2(B_{H_2} + (m_H + 2m_{Zn})C_{H_2}) + 2m_H B_{H_1} \\
& + 2m_1 m_H B'_{H_1} + 2m_2 m_H C_{H_2} + 2m_2 m_{Zn}(B'_{Zn_2} + C_{Zn_2})
\end{aligned} \tag{18}
$$

By making the difference, one obtains the term $\ln(\gamma_H^2 \gamma_{SO_4}/\gamma_{HSO_4})$ who is used for calculates molarity in ions H^+.

$$
\begin{aligned}
\ln(\frac{\gamma_H^2 \gamma_{SO_4}}{\gamma_{HSO_4}}) = {} & 4f^\gamma + 2m_2(B_{H_2}^{(0)} + (m_H + 2m_{Zn})C_{H_2}) + 2m_1(B_{H_1}) + 2m_{Zn}(B_{Zn_2} \\
& + (m_H + 2m_{Zn})C_{Zn_2}) + 2m_H(B_{H_2}^{(0)} - B_{H_2}^{(1)} + (m_H + 2m_{Zn})C_{H_2}) \\
& + 4m_1 m_H B'_{H_1} + 2m_2 m_H C_{H_2} + 4m_2 m_{Zn} B'_{Zn_2} + 2m_2 m_{Zn} C_{Zn_2}
\end{aligned} \tag{19}
$$

B_{Zn_2} is a function expressed the binary interaction between the ions Zn^{+2} and ions sulphated SO_4^{-2}, its expression is:

$$B_{Zn_2} = B_{Zn_2}^{(0)} + \frac{2B_{Zn_2}^{(1)}}{\alpha_1^2 I}(1 - (1 + \alpha_1 I^{\frac{1}{2}})\exp(-\alpha_1 I^{\frac{1}{2}})) + \frac{2B_{Zn_2}^{(2)}}{\alpha_2^2 I}(1 - (1 + \alpha_2 I^{\frac{1}{2}})\exp(-\alpha_2 I^{\frac{1}{2}})) \tag{20}$$

B'_{Zn_2} it is derived from B_{Zn_2} compared to the ionic force.

$$B'_{Zn_2} = \frac{2B^{(1)}_{Zn_2}}{\alpha_1^2 I^2}(-1+(1+\alpha_1 I^{\frac{1}{2}}+\frac{1}{2}\alpha_1^2 I)\exp(-\alpha_1 I^{\frac{1}{2}}))$$

$$+\frac{2B^{(2)}_{Zn_2}}{\alpha_2^2 I^2}(-1+(1+\alpha_2 I^{\frac{1}{2}}+\frac{1}{2}\alpha_2^2 I)\exp(-\alpha_2 I^{\frac{1}{2}}))$$

(21)

It is necessary for the electrolyte 2-2 which is $ZnSO_4$ to introduce an additional coefficient $B^{(2)}$ compared to the similar expression valid for the electrolytes 1-1 and 1-2, $B^{(0)}_{Zn_2}$, $B^{(1)}_{Zn_2}$, $B^{(2)}_{Zn_2}$ are parameter depends on the temperature.

Pitzer and Mayorga[10] gave the values of this parameter to 25°C:

$$B^{(0)}_{Zn_2} = 0{,}1949; \ B^{(1)}_{Zn_2} = 2{,}883; \ B^{(2)}_{Zn_2} = 32{,}81$$

$$\frac{\partial B^{(0)}_{Zn_2}}{\partial T} = -3{,}68.10^{-3}; \ \frac{\partial B^{(1)}_{Zn_2}}{\partial T} = 2{,}33.10^{-2}; \ \frac{\partial B^{(2)}_{Zn_2}}{\partial T} = -3{,}33.10^{-1}$$

The experiments of leaching of this study covering the active temperature range of the ambient temperature until 200°C, it is necessary to supplement the expressions giving the coefficients of activities of zinc sulphate to 25°C, by introducing the dependence compared to the temperatures.

The average coefficient of activity of zinc sulphate will thus be expressed in the form by developing the terms f^{γ}, B^{γ} et C^{γ} :

$$\ln\gamma_{ZnSO_4} = -4A^{\varphi}(\frac{I^{\frac{1}{2}}}{I+bI^{\frac{1}{2}}}+\frac{2}{b}\ln(I+bI^{\frac{1}{2}}))+\frac{3}{2}m^2 C^{\varphi}_{ZnSO}$$

$$+m\left\{\begin{array}{l} B^{(0)}_{ZnSO_4}+2\dfrac{B^{(1)}_{ZnSO_4}}{\alpha_1^2 I}[1-(1+\alpha_1 I^{\frac{1}{2}})\exp(-\alpha_1 I^{\frac{1}{2}})] \\[2mm] +2\dfrac{B^{(2)}_{ZnSO_4}}{\alpha_2^2 I}[(1+\alpha_2 I^{\frac{1}{2}})\exp(-\alpha_2 I^{\frac{1}{2}})] \end{array}\right\}$$

(22)

In this expression coefficients $B^{(0)}_{ZnSO_4}, B^{(1)}_{ZnSO_4}, B^{(2)}_{ZnSO_4}$ like $C^{\varphi}_{ZnSO_4}$ and A^{φ} depend on the temperature. The derivative partial of the coefficient of activity of zinc sulphate compared to the temperature is equal to:

$$\frac{\partial \ln\gamma_{ZnSO_4}}{\partial T} = -4(\frac{\partial A^{\varphi}}{\partial T})_p(\frac{I^{\frac{1}{2}}}{(1+bI^{\frac{1}{2}})} + \frac{2}{b}\ln(1+bI^{\frac{1}{2}})) + m\{2(\frac{\partial B_{ZnSO_4}^{(0)}}{\partial T})$$
$$+ (\frac{2}{\alpha_1^2 I})(\frac{\partial B_{ZnSO_4}^{(1)}}{\partial T})[1-(1+\alpha_1 I^{\frac{1}{2}})\exp(-\alpha_1 I^{\frac{1}{2}})]$$
$$+ (\frac{2}{\alpha_2^2 I})(\frac{\partial B_{ZnSO_4}^{(2)}}{\partial T})[1-(1+\alpha_2 I^{\frac{1}{2}})\exp(-\alpha_2 I^{\frac{1}{2}})]\} + \frac{3}{2}m^2(\frac{\partial C_{ZnSO_4}^{\varphi}}{\partial T}) \qquad (23)$$

The resolution of this equation requires the knowledge off the derivatives partial of $A^{\varphi}, B_{ZnSO_4}^{(0)}, B_{ZnSO_4}^{(1)}, B_{ZnSO_4}^{(2)}$ and C^{φ} compared to the temperature.

The molar enthalpy connects A_H is related to the osmotic variation of coefficient according to the temperature by the relation: $A_H = 4RT^2 \frac{\partial A^{\varphi}}{\partial T}$ $\qquad$ (24)

Pitzer and Bradley [3] provided the values of the molar enthalpy connect reduced A_H / RT for temperatures going of 0 to 350°C.

For the convenience of numerical calculation, the apparent molar enthalpy is expressed according to the temperature Kelvin and for a pressure equal to the saturating steam pressure, in the form;

$$\frac{A_H}{RT} = 11,0679053 - 0,145798089T + 6,95581035T^2 \qquad (25)$$
$$- 1,41494867.10^{-6}T^3 + 1012268758.10^{-9}T^4$$

3. Optimization of the parameters of the model

The model of Pitzer was applied to calculate the average coefficients of activity thus the molality in ion H^+ of solution aqueous. We worked out for this purpose that a computer code in language of Fortran which allows us calculating the molality in ion H^+ of solution aqueous and the coefficients of activities.

4. Results and comments

Fig.1 shows a linear dependence between the molarity of H_2SO_4 and the molality of H + whatever the temperature. It can be noted that the temperature does not have any influence on the calculated molality in ion H^+ as a function of the molality in sulphuric acid at 25°C.

Let m be the stœchiometric concentration in sulphuric acid, and m_H the concentration in ion H^+ in equilibrium. The expression giving the balance of the sulphate ions can be written as:

$$m_H^3 + k_1 m_H^2 + (k_1 k_2 - mk_1)m_H - 2k_1 k_2 = 0 \qquad (26)$$

The solving of this cubic equation in m_H gives a concentration in ion H^+ at equilibrium for 25°C approximately with a concentration of ions H^+ equals to

0,135M. The stœchiometric concentration m being equal to 0,125M. The comparison with the value extracted from fig.1 for the same stœchiometric concentration gives a value of the concentration in ion H^+ equal to 0,1566519M i.e a difference of 16,038% compared to the value of the same concentration obtained without taking into account the activities.

Fig.2 show that whatever the molality, the coefficient of activity $\gamma_\pm$ for the sulphuric acid decreases when the temperature increases.

The curves give the coefficients of activity of the sulphuric acid for molalities ranging between 0,01 and 5 mol.kg^{-1} to 25°C, and of the molality of 0,01, 0,05, 0,1 Zinc sulphate mol.Kg^{-1}, allows to say that the presence of zinc sulphate influences the coefficient of activity average $\gamma_{H_2SO_4}$ by undervaluing it, especially with the weak stœchiometric molality in acid sulphuric.

The curves which correspond to the temperatures of 50°C until 200°C, show that the presence of zinc sulphate decreases the coefficients of means activity of the sulphuric acid, whatever the temperature.This influence becomes neglected with the weak zinc sulphate molalities for important molalities in sulphuric acid.

The variation of coefficient of activity of the sulphuric acid according to the temperature for molalities given out of zinc sulphate and sulphuric acid is comparable with those obtained in the absence of zinc sulphate.

One can note that contrary has what is observed with 25°C the coefficient $\gamma^\pm_{H_2SO_4}$ of a solution without Zinc sulphate is higher to 190°C, than the coefficient $\gamma^\pm_{H_2SO_4}$ solution containing of Zinc sulphate.

The values of the coefficient of activity of Zinc sulphate at the ambient temperature are slightly higher enters 10^{-3} and 10^{-2} mol/kg to the values with 50°C. To a given temperature, the average coefficient of activity of zinc sulphate passes by a minimum which is at a zinc sulphate molality lain between 1mol/kg with 25°C and 0,01 mol/kg to 200°C.

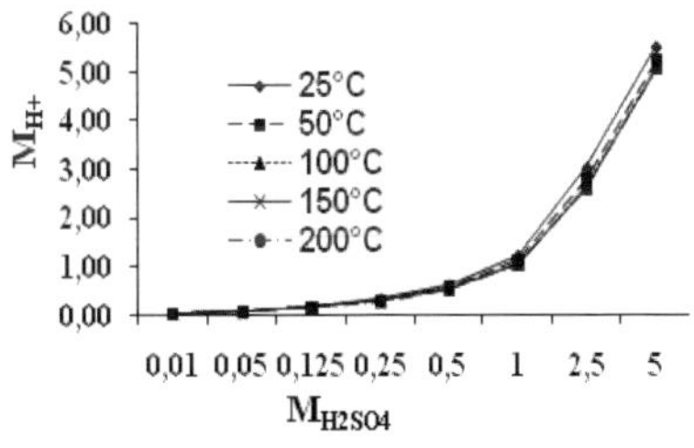

Fig. 1. Molality in H^+ according to the molality in sulphuric acid at various temperature

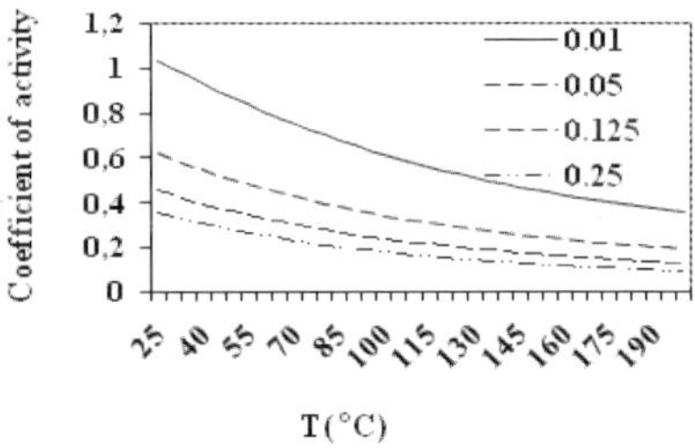

Fig. 2. Coefficient of stoechiometric activity of the sulphuric acid according to the temperature for solutions sulphuric

774

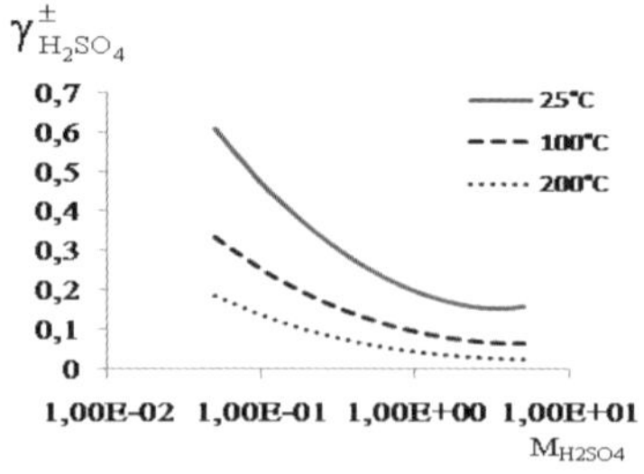

Fig. 3. Coefficient of sulphuric activity of acid in the presence of zinc sulphate according to the molality in sulphuric acid

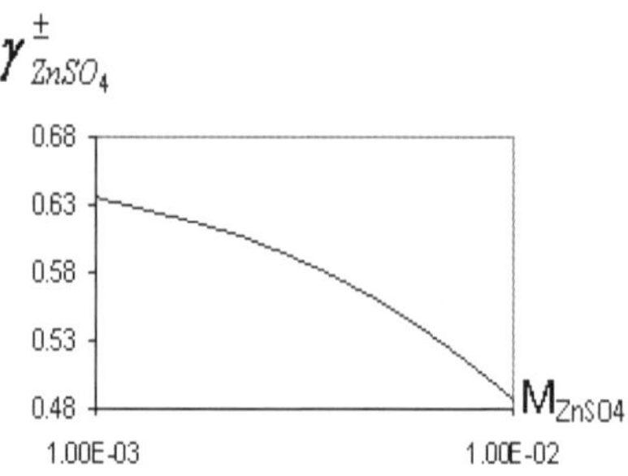

Fig. 4. Stoechiometric coefficient of activity of sulphuric zinc sulphate in the presence of sulphuric acid according to the zinc sulphate molality with 25°C

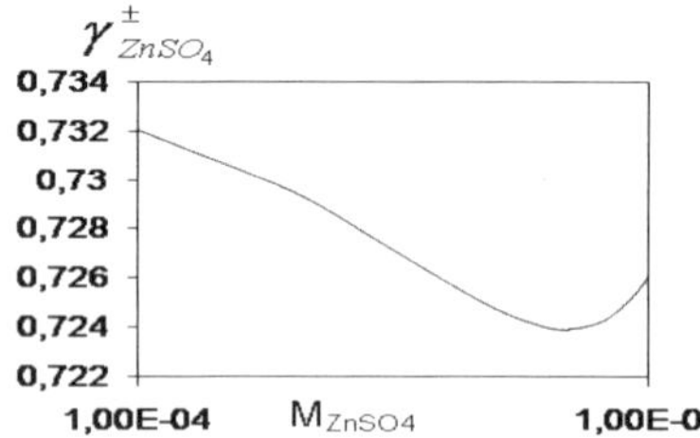

Fig. 5. Stoechiometric coefficient of activity of zinc sulphate in the presence of sulphuric acid according to the zinc sulphate molality with 100°C

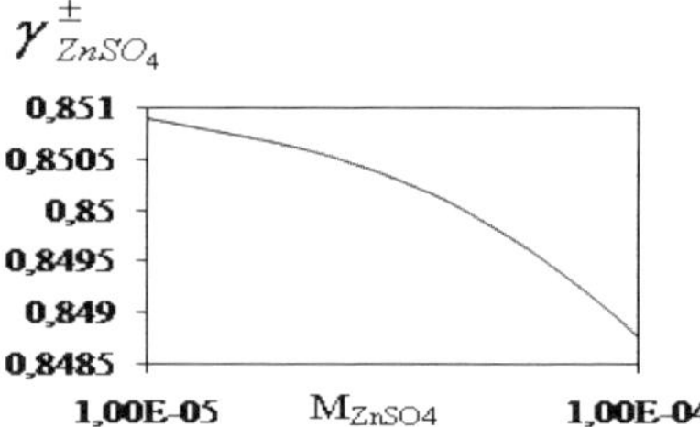

Fig. 6. Stoechiometric coefficient of activity of zinc sulphate in the presence of sulphuric acid according to the zinc sulphate molality with 200°C

5. Conclusion

In the temperature range considered: 25 to 200°C this study allows the determination of concentration in ion H^+ and the coefficients of activity of different kinds of the sulfuric acid is alone in solution. In an aqueous solution of sulphuric acid, the species reacting are H^+, HSO_4^- and SO^{4-2}. We can consider that the sulphuric acid with the two kinds of anions HSO_4^-, SO_4^{-2} and the cations H^+, make up a mixed electrolyte for the equation of Pitzer.

The values indicated of coefficient of activity of zinc sulphate in the presence of sulphuric acid, show that to a given temperature the presence of sulphuric acid lowers the coefficient of activity of zinc sulphate.

It decreases when the zinc sulphate molality believes; doubting quickly that the molality in sulfuric acid is weak. The field of study is broken up into three distinct parts: between 25 and 100°C, 110 and 150°C and 160 and 200°C. These various fields seem related to the structure of sulphur, the melting point of crystalline sulphur ranging between 110 and 120°C while the temperature of 160°C corresponds to the transition $S_{\lambda \to} S_p$.

References

1. JR. Bailar et al. *Press NewYork* (1973).
2. L.f. Silvester, Ks. Pitzer. *J.sol.chem* 7(5), 327-37 (1978).
3. D.j. Bradley, Ks. Pitzer. *J.Phys.chem* 83(12), 1599-603 (1979).
4. LT. ROMANKIW and PL BRUYN *Wadsworth and Devis Eds.* 45-66 (1984).
5. JP. BAUR et al. *The Metall. Soc. Of AIME pamphlet* 72B, 96, 62 (1972).
6. Demopoulos, G.P., Baldwin, S.A. *In: Mishra, B. (Ed.), TMS Annual Meeting, San Diego*, 567-583 (1999).
7. Peng, P., Xie, H., Lu, L. *Cl4. Hydrometallurgy* 80, 265-271 (2005).
8. M.E. Wadsworth, *Plenum Press pp133-197 NewYork* (1979).
9. Pitzer k.s. ROY R.N. *silvester L.F j am chem. Soc* 99(15), 4930-6 (1977).
10. PITZER K.S. Mayorga G. *J.sol.chem.* 3(7), 539-46 (1974).
11. T. Pecina, T. Franco, P. Castillo, E.Orrantia, *Minerals Engineering* 23-30 (2008).

FAST FOURIER TRANSFORM ENSEMBLE KALMAN FILTER WITH APPLICATION TO A COUPLED ATMOSPHERE-WILDLAND FIRE MODEL

JAN MANDEL, JONATHAN D. BEEZLEY,
VOLODYMYR Y. KONDRATENKO

*Department of Mathematical and Statistical Sciences
University of Colorado Denver, Denver, CO 80217-3364, USA*

We propose a new type of the Ensemble Kalman Filter (EnKF), which uses the Fast Fourier Transform (FFT) for covariance estimation from a very small ensemble with automatic tapering, and for a fast computation of the analysis ensemble by convolution, avoiding the need to solve a sparse system with the tapered matrix. The method is combined with the morphing EnKF to enable the correction of position errors, in addition to amplitude errors, and demonstrated on WRF-Fire, the Weather Research Forecasting (WRF) model coupled with a fire spread model implemented by the level set method.

1. Introduction

Data assimilation is a statistical technique to modify the state of a running model in response to data, based on sequential Bayesian estimation.[1] The EnKF[2] accesses the model only as a black box. It is suitable for a wide range of problems and relatively easy to combine with existing modeling software. However, the ensemble size needed can be large, and the amount of computation required in EnKF can be significant when the EnKF is modified to suppress spurious long-range correlations. We propose a new variant of EnKF that can overcome these difficulties by the use of FFT. The new method is applied to the morphing EnKF,[3] which is needed for the fire application, but the FFT EnKF can be used with or without morphing.

2. Data Assimilation

We first briefly describe the EnKF for reference. The EnKF advances in time an ensemble of simulations $u_1,...,u_N$, which approximates the probability distribution of the model state u. The simulations are then advanced in time until the *analysis time*, when new data d arrives. It is assumed that the data error is known, $d - Hu \sim N(0, R)$ given u, where H is the *observation operator* and R is the *data error covariance matrix*. The ensemble, now called the *forecast ensemble*, is combined with the data to give the *analysis ensemble* by the EnKF formulas[4]

$$u_k^a = u_k + C_N H^T (H C_N H^T + R)^{-1}(d + e_k - H u_k^f), \tag{1}$$

where C_N is an estimate of the covariance of the model state, and e_k is random perturbation $e_k \sim N(0, R)$. The analysis ensemble $u_1^a, ..., u_N^a$ is then used as the initial condition for a new simulation, advanced to a new analysis time, and the *analysis cycle* repeats.

In the standard EnKF,[4] C_N is the sample covariance computed from the ensemble. Under suitable assumptions, it can be proved that the ensemble converges for large N to a sample from the Kalman filtering distribution and C_N converges to the true covariance.[5]

2.1 *FFT EnKF and Covariance Estimation by FFT*

The EnKF formulation (1) relies on linear algebra only and it is oblivious to any structure of the model state. Large ensembles (30-100 and more) are often needed[2]. We are interested in obtaining a reasonable approximation of the covariance matrix from a very small sample. For this, we take advantage of the fact that the simulation state u is a block vector, where the blocks are values of the modelled physical fields on grids of points in a spatial domain Ω, which are (discrete versions of) smooth random functions, i.e., realizations of random fields. The covariance of a random field drops off quickly with distance, and it is often the case in geostatistics that random fields are stationary, that is, the covariance between two points depends on their distance vector only.[6] But for a small sample, the ensemble covariance is a matrix of low rank with large off-diagonal elements even at a great distance. Therefore, localization techniques are used, such as tapering, which consists of multiplication of the terms of the sample covariance by a fixed function to force the drop-off of the covariance away from the diagonal, resulting in a more accurate approximation of covariance for small samples.[7] However, solving a system with the resulting approximate covariance matrix is expensive, because efficient dense linear algebra, which relies on the representation of the sample covariance matrix as the product of two rectangular matrices,[8] can no longer be used.

For simplicity, we explain the FFT EnKF in the 1D case. Higher-dimensional cases work exactly the same. Also, we consider first the case when the model state consists of one block only.

The basic operation in the EnKF (1) is the multiplication $v = C_N u$ of a vector u by an approximate covariance matrix C_N. Denote by $u(x_i)$ the entry of vector u, corresponding to node x_i and suppose for the moment that the random field is stationary, that is, its covariance matrix satisfies $C(x_i, x_j) = c(x_i - x_j)$ for some covariance function c. Then v is the convolution

$$v(x_i) = \sum_j C(x_i, x_j) u(x_j) = \sum_j u(x_j) c(x_i - x_j).$$

The discrete Fourier transform changes convolution to multiplication entry by entry. Hence, if the random field is stationary, multiplication by its covariance matrix becomes multiplication by a diagonal matrix in the frequency domain.

The proposed method of covariance estimation consists of computing the sample covariance of the ensemble in the frequency domain, and neglecting all of its off-diagonal terms. This is justified by the assumption that the covariance depends mainly on the distance.

(1) Given ensemble $[u_k]$, apply a FFT operator F to each member to obtain the member $\hat{u}_i = F u_k$ k in the frequency domain.

(2) Compute the approximate forecast covariance matrix $\hat{C}_N$ in the frequency domain as the diagonal matrix with the diagonal entries c_i equal to the diagonal entries of the sample covariance of the ensemble $[u_k]$

$$c_i = \frac{1}{N-1} \sum_{k=1}^{N} \left| \hat{u}_{ik} - \overline{\hat{u}_i} \right|^2, \quad \overline{\hat{u}_i} = \frac{1}{N} \sum_{k=1}^{N} \hat{u}_{ik}. \tag{2}$$

Multiplication by the approximate covariance matrix C_N then becomes in the frequency domain

$$u = C_N v \iff \hat{u} = Fu, \ \hat{v} = \hat{c} \bullet \hat{u}, \ v = F^{-1} \hat{v},$$

where $\bullet$ is entry-by-entry multiplication, $(\hat{c} \bullet \hat{u})_i = \hat{c}_i \hat{u}_i$. In the important case when $H = I$ and $R = rI$ (the whole state is observed and the data errors are uncorrelated and the same at every point), considered here, the EnKF (1) in the frequency domain reduces to entry-by-entry operations,

$$\hat{u}_k^a = \hat{u}_k + \hat{c} \bullet \left(\hat{c} + r \right)^{-1} \bullet \left(\hat{d} + \hat{e}_k - \hat{u}_k^f \right). \tag{3}$$

In an application, the state has multiple variables. The state vector, its covariance, and the observation matrix then have the block form

$$u = \begin{bmatrix} u^{(1)} \\ ... \\ u^{(n)} \end{bmatrix}, \quad C = \begin{bmatrix} C^{11} & ... & C^{1M} \\ ... & ... & ... \\ C^{M1} & ... & C^{MM} \end{bmatrix}, \quad H = \begin{bmatrix} H^1 & ... & H^M \end{bmatrix} \quad (4)$$

Assume that the first variable is observed, then $H^{(1)} = I, H^{(2)} = 0, ..., H^{(M)} = 0$. The EnKF (1) then simplifies to

$$u_k^{(j),a} = u_k^{(j)} + C_N^{(j1)}(C_N^{(11)} + R)^{-1}(d + e_k - u_k^{(1)}), j = 1, ..., M, \quad (5)$$

which becomes in the frequency domain

$$\hat{u}_k^{(j),a} = \hat{u}_k^{(j)} + \hat{c}^{j1} \bullet \left(\hat{c}^{(11)} + r \right)^{-1} \bullet (\hat{d} + \hat{e}_k - \hat{u}_k), \quad (6)$$

where the spectral cross-covariance between field j and field 1 is approximated from

$$\hat{c}_i^{(j1)} = \frac{1}{N-1} \sum_{k-1}^{N} \left(\hat{u}_{ik}^{(j)} - \overline{\hat{u}}_i^{(j)} \right)^* \left(\hat{u}_{ik}^{(1)} - \overline{\hat{u}}_i^{(1)} \right), \quad \overline{\hat{u}}_i^{(j)} = \frac{1}{N} \sum_{k=1}^{N} \hat{u}_{ik}^{(j)}. \quad (7)$$

2.2 Morphing EnKF

To treat position errors in addition to amplitude errors, FFT EnKF is combined with the morphing EnKF.[3,8] The method uses an additional ensemble member u_{N+1} called the *reference member*. Given an initial state u, the initial ensemble is given by $u_{N+1} = u$ and

$$u_k^{(i)} = (u_{N+1}^{(i)} + r_k^{(i)}) \circ (I + T_k), k = 1, ..., N, \quad (8)$$

where $r_k^{(i)}$ are random smooth functions on Ω, T_k are random smooth mappings $T_k : \Omega \to \Omega$, and $\circ$ denotes composition. Thus, the initial ensemble has both amplitude and position variability, and the position change is the same for all blocks. Random smooth functions and mappings are generated by FFT as a Fourier series with random coefficients that decay quickly with frequency.

The data d is an observation of $u^{(1)}$, and it is expected that it differs from the model in amplitude as well as in the position of significant features, such as firelines. The first blocks of $u_1, ..., u_N$ and d are then registered against the first block of the reference member u_{N+1}. We find *registration mappings* $T_k : \Omega \to \Omega$ $k = 0, ..., N$ such that

$$u_k^{(1)} \approx u_{N+1}^{(1)} \circ (I + T_k), \ T_k \approx 0, \nabla T_k \approx 0, \ k = 0, ..., N,$$

where $d = u_0^{(1)}$. Define the registration residuals $r_k^{(j)} = u_k^{(j)} \circ (I + T_k)^{-1} - u_{N+1}^{(j)}$, $k = 0,...,N$. The *morphing transform* maps each ensemble member u_k into the extended state vector

$$u_k \mapsto \tilde{u}_k = M_{u_{N+1}}(u_k) = (T_k, r_k^{(1)}, ..., r_k^{(M)}). \tag{9}$$

Similarly, the data becomes the extended data vector $d \mapsto \tilde{d} = \left(T_0, r_0^{(1)}\right)$. The FFT EnKF method (6) is applied to the transformed ensemble $\tilde{u}_1, ..., \tilde{u}_N$ with the observation operator given by $(T, r^{(1)}, ..., r^{(M)}) \mapsto (T, r^{(1)})$. The cross-covariances between x and y components of T and $r^{(1)}$ are neglected, so the covariance $C^{(11)}$ in (5) consists of three-diagonal matrices, and (6) applies. The new transformed reference member is obtained as

$$\tilde{u}_{N+1}^a = \frac{1}{N} \sum_{k=1}^{N} \tilde{u}_k^a$$

and the analysis ensemble $u_1, ..., u_{N+1}$ by the *inverse morphing transform*

$$u_k^{a,(i)} = M_{u_{N+1}}^{-1}(\tilde{u}_k^a) = \left(u_{N+1}^{(i)} + r_k^{a,(i)}\right) \circ (I + T_k^a), \quad k = 1,...,N+1. \tag{10}$$

3. The Wildland Fire Model

We only summarize the model very briefly. See Ref. 8 for further details, references, and acknowledgements.

The fire model runs on a 2D rectangular grid on the Earth surface, called the fire grid. The model postulates fire line propagation speed as a function of wind and terrain slope, and an exponential decay of fuel by combustion after the ignition. The fire area is represented by a level set function as the set of points where the level set function is negative. The level set function satisfies a partial differential equation, which is solved numerically on the fire grid by explicit time stepping. Ignition is achieved by setting the value of the level set function so that it is negative in the ignition region. The state of the fire model consists of the level set function and the ignition time at the fire grid nodes. Other derived quantities included in the state vector are the fuel fraction burned and the heat flux from the combustion.

The fire model is coupled with the Weather Research Forecasting (WRF) atmospheric model,[9] which runs on a much coarser 3D grid. In every time step, the fire model inputs the horizontal wind velocity, and the heat and vapor fluxes output from the fire model are inserted into the atmospheric model. The fire model is distributed as WRF-Fire with WRF, and the latest development version is also available from the authors.

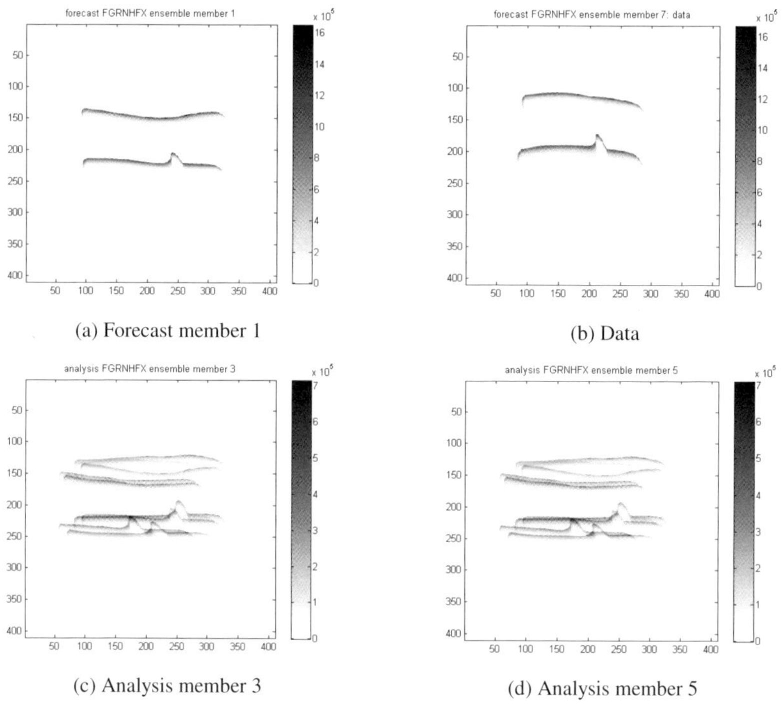

(a) Forecast member 1

(b) Data

(c) Analysis member 3

(d) Analysis member 5

Figure 1. The morphing EnKF with 5 ensemble members, applied to the ground heat flux from the WRF-Fire model. The ensemble size is not sufficient, the correct analysis is not even approximately in the span of the forecast, and the EnKF cannot reach it.

4. Computational Results

We have used the optimization method from Ref. 3 for registration. We have used the real sine FFT, which forces zero change on the boundary. We have used a standard ideal problem distributed with WRF-Fire. The model has a 420×420 fire mesh and a 42×42×41 atmospheric mesh. The fuel was the same on the whole domain. The model was initialized with the wind blowing diagonally across the grid, and two line ignitions and one circle ignition occur within the first 4 seconds of simulation time. After one minute of simulation time, when the fire was established and one of the line fires has merged with the circular fire, the simulation was stopped and an initial ensemble was generated by random smooth perturbation both in position and in amplitude. Artificial data was created by a similar perturbation. The forecast was taken the same as the initial ensemble. The described data assimilation algorithm was then applied with 5 members, with the results shown in Figure 1 for the morphing EnKF and

Figure 2 for the morphing FFT EnKF. We see that the EnKF was not able to approach that data at all with such a small ensemble, while the FFT EnKF delivered an ensemble around the correct data shape.

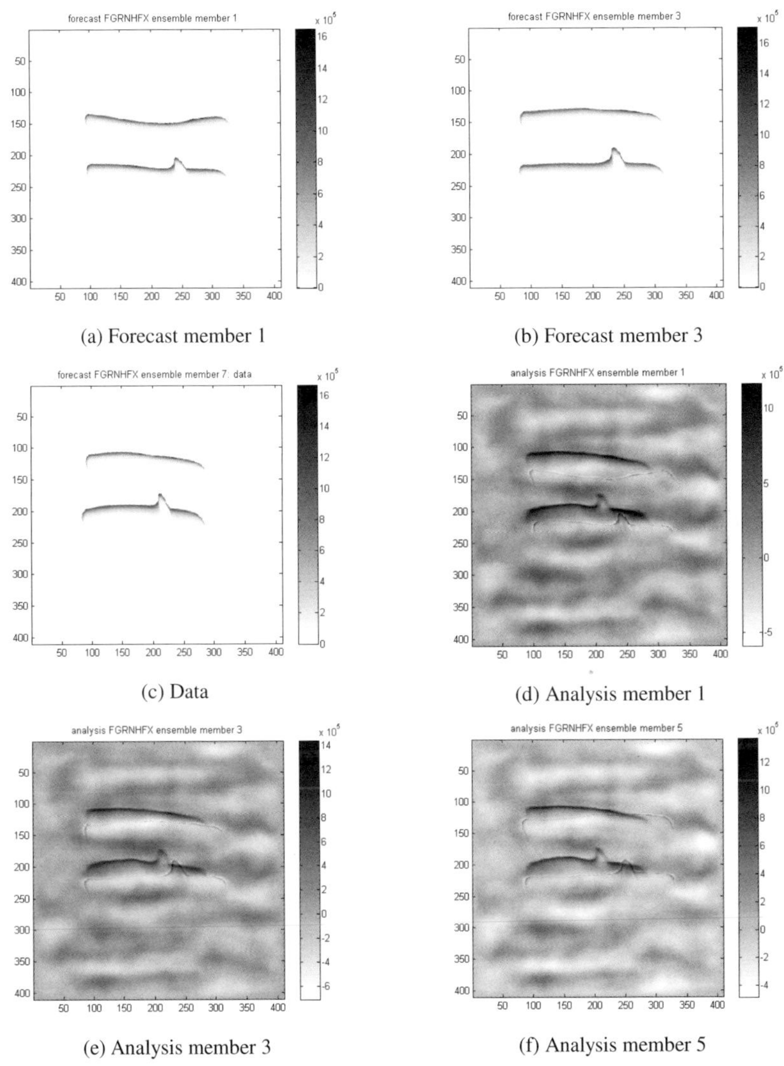

Figure 2. The morphing FFT EnKF with 5 ensemble members, applied to the ground heat flux from the WRF-Fire model. The analysis ensemble moved towards the data.

5. Conclusion

We have shown that the morphing FFT EnKF is capable of data assimilation in a wildfire simulation, which exhibits sharp boundaries and coherent features. We have shown that the FFT EnKF can deliver acceptable results with a very small ensemble (5 members), unlike the standard EnKF, which is known to work with morphing for this application, but only with a much larger ensemble.[3] Further development, involving multiple variables and multiple analysis cycles, will be presented elsewhere.

Acknowledgements

This work was supported by NSF grants CNS-0719641 and ATM-0835579.

References

1. E. Kalnay, *Atmospheric Modeling, Data Assimilation and Predictability* (Cambridge University Press, 2003).
2. G. Evensen, *Data assimilation: The ensemble Kalman Fiter*, 2nd edn. (Springer Verlag, 2009).
3. J. D. Beezley and J. Mandel, *Tellus* **60A**, 131 (2008).
4. G. Burgers, P. J. van Leeuwen and G. Evensen, *Monthly Weather Review* **126**, 1719 (1998).
5. J. Mandel, L. Cobb and J. D. Beezley, *On the convergence of the ensemble Kalman Filter*, Applications of Mathematics, to appear. arXiv:0901.2951 (January, 2009).
6. N. A. C. Cressie, *Statistics for spatial data* (John Wiley & Sons Inc., New York, 1993).
7. R. Furrer and T. Bengtsson, *J. Multivariate Anal.* **98**, 227 (2007).
8. J. Mandel, J. D. Beezley, J. L. Coen and M. Kim, *IEEE Control Systems Magazine* **29**, 47 (June 2009).
9. WRF Working Group, Weather Research Forecasting (WRF) Model, http://wrf-model.org, (2010).

MAGNETIC FIELD EFFECT ON THE NEAR AND FAR CYLINDER WAKES

M. AISSA

Unit of Applied Research in Renewable Energies Ghardaia, Algeria

A. BOUABDALLAH

LTSE, Physics Faculty, University of Sciences and Technology Houari Boumedienne B.P. 32 El Alia Bab Ezzouar 1611, Algiers. Algeria

H. OUALLI

[3]MDF, EMP, Bordj El Bahri, Algeriers, Algeria

The present numerical simulation focuses on the elecro-conductor fluid flow over a circular cylinder. Our principal goal is to control the upstream and downstream flows by external applied magnetic aligned field. A different values of magnetic interaction number N (Stuart number) have been selected for this control method, and the Reynolds number flow control to be maintained invariant Re= 550.

The results show that the downstream flow deceleration is associated to the disappearance of shedding eddies mechanism, On the other hand, on upstream side stagnation point, the boundary layer thickness increase with Stuart number increasing. We note also the appearance of new eddies at near side shear layers that degenerate in the transversal direction with high Stuart number. These last eddies influenced considerably the boundary layer separation point's position over cylinder.

1. Introduction

Bluff body flows are of great importance in various engineering fields. This is certainly due to the large scale vortices induced by such shear flows. Protas and Wesfreid [1] reported that the presence of big concentrated eddies , the so called Bénard-von Kármán vortices intrinsically related to forces acting on the obstacle makes the bluff body wakes playing a very important role in technical applications. In spite of the continuously devoted efforts to their understanding, they remain poorly understood. Consequently many phenomena are waiting to be enlightened as several investigations are initiated.

We present herein a numerical results find by fluent software, that resolve a problem of external magnetic field effect in the flow fluid over circular cylinder.

Where, the study of magneto-hydrodynamic flows (MHD) is of great importance in view of various scientific and industrial applications that can associate such as geophysics and astrophysics or metallurgical engineering and future fusion reactors. These flows are modeled by coupling Maxwell's and Navier Stokes equations. As in fluid dynamics, in general, the computational and numerical simulations are essential and which allow for predictions of results. This is very useful to the complexity experiments realization. There are two major problems: the technology for achieving this magnetized medium and physics involved to study the flow parameters influence which causes in such medium. Physically, the most interesting of these parameters is the boundary layer separation phenomenon on a body wall immersed in flow fluid. This boundary layer separation control around profile find many and varied applications in aircraft configurations various. This is because its ability to delay or eliminate the separation phenomenon, and thus leads to enhanced lift forces levels, to reduce drag forces and noise generated on the aircraft engines. These represent major challenge economic and technological obvious. Many studies have so far been conducted on the experimental design to test the effectiveness of different actuators can control the separation and different methods of action are extremely diverse. For example, regarding the methods called "active" which introduce energy into the external fluid, it distinguishes the use of movable walls [2], methods based on suction or blowing [3.4], acoustic [5], thermal [6] or electromagnetic [7] and micro jets to blow continuously methods [8]. This list is not exhaustive and many of these works provide excellent results and great promise. A method, based on the electromagnetic forces injection in the Navier Stokes equations, provided an approach to flow control. The magneto-hydrodynamic flow control studies have been realized investigations in the framework on the magneto-hydrodynamic propulsion boat. (Mengs, 1994) [9].

2. Problem description

In this study, we examine the effect of an external magnetic field applied in the motion fluid (air), with uniform velocity U_∞, kinematic viscosity v and mass density ρ. A cylinder of diameter $D = 1m$ is subjected to aerodynamic forces generated by the movement of air affected by an external applied magnetic field. According to these physical conditions, the Reynolds number that characterizes this flow is fixed at $Re = 550$. Other control parameters, namely, the magnetic interaction number N (Stuart number) and the magnetic Reynolds number R_m vary with the applied external magnetic field intensity.

In the flow control objective air interacting with the cylinder, we study the effect of magnetic field in the near wake and far wake formed a downstream of the cylinder, thus its influence on boundary layer and the separation point position. We simulate the flow through a computer code fluent after submitting its geometric configuration by the Gambit software that creates the geometry and the associated mesh. While Fluent solves the Navier Stokes equations system combined with Maxwell equations.

We have characterized the flow field shown in Figure 1 by the following dimensions:

The length flow field after the cylinder L = 40D = 40m.

The length flow field before the cylinder l = 5D = 5m.

The width flow field d = 10D = 10m.

A constant magnetic field B0 is applied along direction of the flow.

The meshing is made in 65,940 triangular cells and well refined near the cylinder and expands more we recede into the infinite flow away from the cylinder.

The differential equations governing the problem of fluid mechanics "continuity, Navier-Stokes, energy .... "Are discretized into algebraic expressions and built on each mesh. Solving the system obtained after linearization of the discretized equations can have the new values of the various unknowns: velocity, pressure, temperature, etc.

3. Governing equations and boundary conditions

Figure 1 shows a computational domain and the polar coordinate system used in this present study. By FLUENT computational software we resolve the continuity and motion equations defined as:

Mass conservation equation:

$$\nabla.V = 0 \ \ or \ \ \frac{\partial}{\partial x}(ru_r) + \frac{\partial u_\theta}{\partial \theta}$$

Where

$$\nabla = \frac{\partial}{\partial r}\vec{e}_r + \frac{1}{r}\frac{\partial}{\partial \theta}\vec{e}_\theta$$

Navier-Stockes equation:

$$\frac{\partial V}{\partial t} + (V.\nabla)V = -\frac{1}{\rho}\nabla p + v\nabla^2 V + g + \frac{1}{\rho}j*B$$

Where

$$\nabla^2 = \Delta = \frac{\partial^2}{\partial r^2} + \frac{1}{r}\frac{\partial}{\partial r} + \frac{1}{r^2}\frac{\partial^2}{\partial \theta^2}$$

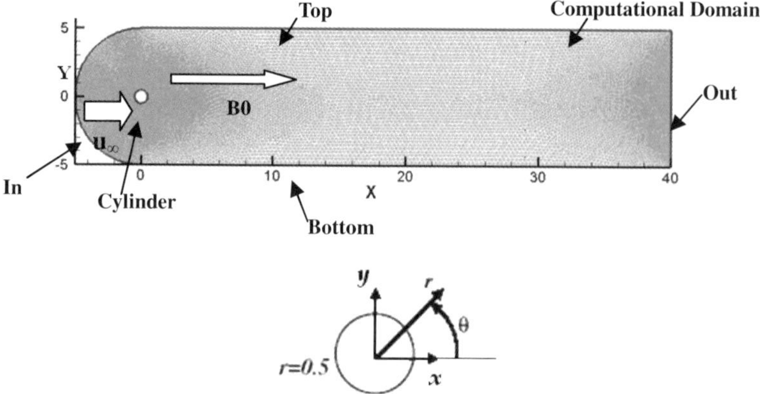

Fig. 1. Computational domain and polar coordinates system

We project the Navier Stockes equation in radial (r) and angular (θ) directions we obtain successively:

$$\frac{\partial u_r}{\partial t}+\frac{\partial u_r^2}{\partial r}+\frac{1}{r}\frac{\partial(u_r u_\theta)}{\partial\theta}+\frac{u_r^2-u_\theta^2}{r}=-\frac{\partial p}{\partial r}+\frac{1}{R_e}\left[\nabla^2 u_r-\frac{u_r}{r^2}-\frac{2}{r^2}\frac{\partial u_\theta}{\partial\theta}\right]+f_r$$

and

$$\frac{\partial u_\theta}{\partial t}+\frac{\partial(u_r u_\theta)}{\partial r}+\frac{1}{r}\frac{\partial u_\theta^2}{\partial\theta}+\frac{2u_r u_\theta}{r}=-\frac{1}{r}\frac{\partial p}{\partial r}+\frac{1}{R_e}\left[\nabla^2 u_\theta-\frac{u_\theta}{r^2}+\frac{2}{r^2}\frac{\partial u_r}{\partial\theta}\right]+f_\theta$$

The magnetic field applied in the X direction with constant value B_0 can be created the Lorentz forces acting on the fluid defined as:

$$f_r = N[u_r(\sin\theta)^2+u_\theta\sin\theta\cos\theta]$$

$$f_\theta = N[u_\theta(\cos\theta)^2+u_r\sin\theta\cos\theta]$$

The Amper low:

$$j=\mu^{-1}\nabla*B$$

The Faradai low

$$\frac{\partial B}{\partial t}=-\nabla\times E$$

The ohm low

$$j=\sigma(E+V\times B)$$

Dimensionless control parameters:

1) Reynolds number:

$$R_e=\frac{inertial\ \ forces}{viscous\ \ forces}=\frac{U_\infty D}{v}$$

2) Magnetic Reynolds number:

$$R_{em} = \frac{convection\ of\ B}{diffusion\ of\ B} = \frac{U_\infty D}{v_m} = \mu \sigma U_\infty D$$

3) Stuart number (magnetic interaction number)

$$N = St = \frac{magnetic\ forces}{inertial\ forces} = \frac{H_a}{R_e} = \frac{\sigma B_0^2 D}{\rho U_\infty}$$

4) Hartmann number:

$$H_a = \left(\frac{electromagnetic\ forces}{viscous\ forces} \right)^{1/2} = B_0 D \sqrt{\frac{\sigma}{v\rho}}$$

5) Alfaven Number:

$$Al = \frac{magnetic\ field\ energy}{cenit\ energy} = \frac{N}{R_{em}} = \frac{B_0^2}{\mu \rho U_\infty^2}$$

6) Batchlor number (magnetic Prandtl number):

$$Bt = Pr_m = \frac{Re_m}{Re} = \mu \sigma v = \frac{v}{v_m}$$

Boundary Conditions

In this study we have taken a count the no slip condition on the cylinder surface which given by: $u(R, \theta) = v(R, \theta) = 0$

We have imposed the Nwman type boundary condition in the beginning flow domain, which it has been carried on the velocity flow parameter (velocity inlet)

The boundary condition Direclet type associated for both sides of computational domain (Top and Bottom), it has been carried on the velocity flow parameter (velocity inlet).

In out side computational domain we considered the boundary condition Diriclet type on the pressure magnitude (pressure outlet), which is equal to the atmospheric pressure.

4. Results and discussion

4.1. *The cylinder wake evolution with Stuart number N*

Figure 2 shows on instantaneous iso-values vorticity distribution with different Stuart numbers (interaction magnetic number) N = 0, and N = (0.05, 0.1, 0.2, 0.4, 0.8, 3, 10) with fixed Reynolds number Re = 550. When N = 0, which correspond to the case without applied magnetic field, the flow remains unsteady, where there is the regular vortices shedding in the cylinder wake. We note the dislocation and degradation of the Von Karman streets vortices farther when the flow fluid to be submitted to the low intense magnetic field. Furthermore, that last vortices have been well trained in the magnetic field absence case. This result may be explained by the predominance of the magnetic forces relative to the inertial forces. HS Yoon et al [10] used the spectral method to study a flow fluid with Reynolds number Re = 100 and Stuart numbers N = 0, 0.1, 0.2, they found that the vortex shedding phenomena to be disappears at N = 0.2 for obtaining a stationary wake. Lahjomri et al [11] realized an experimental study and shows that an aligned magnetic field leading to the suppression shedding vortex. In figure 2 we observe the pair of vortex appearance in the vicinity of the two recirculation zones that shrink the size of the wake close between the two shear layers generated by boundary layers separation on the surface of the cylinder, and thus boundary layers thickness increases on upstream before separation point, this is result with the Stuart numbers N = (0.8, 1.6, 3. 10). These events begin in a manner not remarkable with low Stuart number, to become more important when increasing this number. This can be interpreted by magnetic forces applied perpendicularly negative direction to the high side shear layer, and in the positive direction of the from dawn side shear layer. These forces lead to decrease in the flow velocity around the cylinder, as these forces become more important when we increase the Stuart number. We note the degeneration pairs vortices in the transverse direction of the flow that occurs during the disappearance of the Von Karman's vortex. This degeneration increases with the Stuart number increasing in beyond N = 0.8. At N = 3 we observe the starting formation of second pair vortex, where as N = 10 the complete formation of the third pair vortex.

4.2. *Pressure variation around cylinder versus Stuart number N*

In Figure 3 we represented the pressure coefficients curves around the cylinder, associated with different Stuart numbers considered, according to Y-coordinates (blue curve). This give evidence of the pressure difference between the upstream and downstream cylinder (Cp (x <0)-Cp (x> 0)), which can give us a forecast on the drag force be created when increases the applied external magnetic field intensity. And the second appearance (green curve) represents the pressure coefficient evolution versus X-coordinates, which highlights the difference in pressure between the upper and lower cylinder surfaces (Cp (y <0)-Cp (y> 0)), it can give us prediction lift forces applied on the cylinder. It is noted in the natural case (N = 0) that this pressure difference is significant negative in absolute value, reflecting the lift forces absence in the natural case. This absolute value to reduce in the case of N = 0.05. The pressure difference in the case of N = 0.1 is significant positive, reflecting the presence of important lift forces around the cylinder. The positive difference pressure persists in all three cases of N = 0.2, N = 0.4, N = 0.8 with very low absolute value. However, when we increase the value of more Stuart number N = 3 and N = 10 the pressure difference becomes negative with small absolute values which tend to zero.

In figure 2 we observe thus the maximum pressure at upstream stagnation point of the cylinder, so that it decreases in the direction flow until it reaches a minimum value of pressure at neighboring X =- 0.05 in the natural case (N = 0), when the Stuart number has increased, N = 0.05, N = 0.1 and N = 0.2, we find the same form of pressure variation, however, that the point of minimum pressure moves back slightly to X =- 0.1, beyond this Stuart number values we get the position corresponding to the minimum pressure change direction in the x positive way for to reach x = 0 with N = 0.8. When the Stuart number more increases to N = 3 and N = 10 we note that the shear layer contracted by the vortices generated in transversal side of the wake. So that the separated boundary layer delayed and the minimum pressure mark their positions near x = + 0.1.

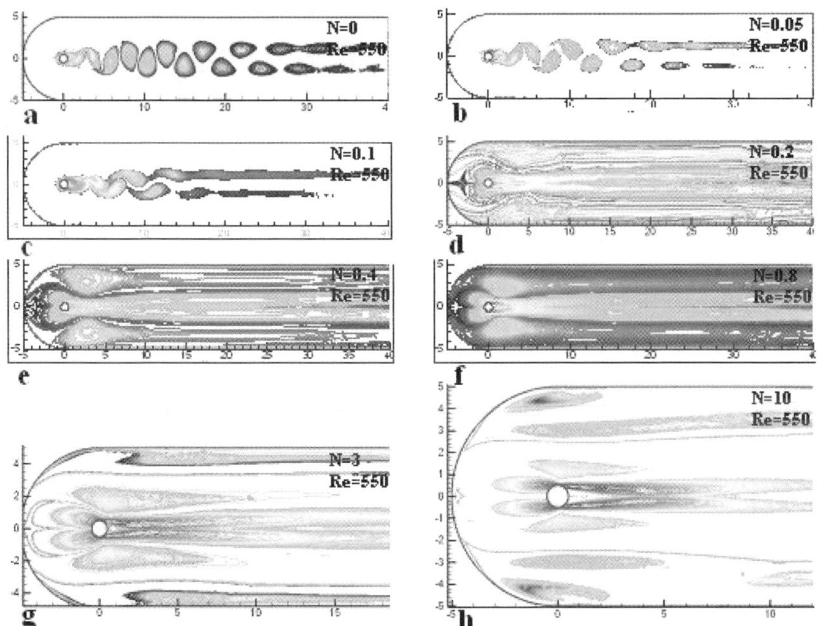

Fig. 2. The vorticity field distribution with various Stuart number (**a :N=0, b :N=0.05, c :N=0.1, d :N=0.2, e :N=0.4, f :N=0.8, g :N=3, h :N=10**)

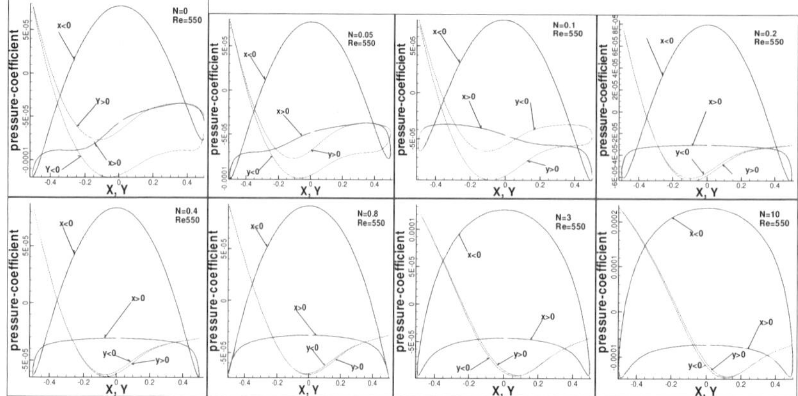

Fig. 3. The pressure differences (intrados-extrados) (upstream-donstream) over the cylinder whith various Stuart number N

5. Conclusion

This study has been realized by a computational software Fluent after drawing the geometrical configuration provided with a suitable mesh and boundary conditions chosen. We found that a magnetic field can significantly affect the near and far wakes and the boundary layer formed around a cylinder. We noticed that the length of the weak vortices decreases with magnetic fields intense. In order that these vortices disappear completely with moderate magnetic fields corresponding to interaction magnetic number $N \geq 0{,}2$. Where they are replaced by two recirculation areas with other eddies that are born in the transverse direction. These phenomena are caused by forces opposed to the flow those how created by the applied magnetic field aligned to the flow, it significantly affects the near wake, and consequently on the boundary layer thickness, detachment points, pressure profile and aerodynamic forces.

References

1. Protas and Wesfreid, On the relation between the global modes and the spectra of drag and lift in periodic wake flow C. R. Mecanique 331 (2003) 49-54.
2. V.J.Modi, FMoktarian, T.Yokozimo, Moving surface boundary layer control as applied to 2D airfoils, AIAA paper, 1998, pp.89-0296.
3. I.Wyganski, Boundary layer flow control by periodic addition of momentum, in: 4th AIAA schear flow control conference, Silvertree Hotel Snomass village, CO, June 29-July 2, 1997.
4. D.C.Me Cormick, boundary layer separation control with directed synthetic jets, AIAA paper, 2000, 0519, Janaury 2000.

5. F.G.Collins, boundary layer control on wings using sound and leading edge serrations, 1979, pp.1875-1979.
6. P.K.Chang, control of flow separation, hemisphere, Washington, DC, 1976.
7. M.Gad-el-hak, flow control, Passive, Active and Reactive Management, Cambridge Univ. Press, Cambridge, UK, 2000.
8. J.Favier, A.Kourta, Etude du contrôle du décollement sur un profil d'aile par mesures PIV et analyse POD, C.R.Mécanique, Toulouse, France, 2006.
9. Meng, J.C.S., 1994. Seawater electromagnetics. A new frontier. Magnétohydrodynamics 30, 401-418.
10. H.S.Yoon, H.H.Chun, M.Y.Ha, H.G.Lee. A numerical study on the fluid flow and heat transfer around a circular cylinder in an aligned magnetic field, International Journal of Heat and Mass Transfer 47(2004) 4075-4087.
11. J.Lahjomri, P.Caperan, A.Alymany, The cylinder wake in a magnetic field aligned with the velocity, J. Fluid Mech 253(1993) 421-448.

STABILITY THEORY METHODS IN MODELLING PROBLEMS

LYUDMILA K. KUZMINA

*Kazan Aviation Institute, KSTU of A.N.Tupolev name – NRU,
Adamuck, 4-6, Kazan, 420015, Russia*

Main aim of research is methods of modelling in Complex systems dynamics. In this way generalized approach, based on Lyapunov's stability theory and Chetayev's idea, is developed. Besides the investigated objects are treated for unified view point on formed basic postulates (stability and singularity) as singularly perturbed ones.

It offers ample scope to obtain the reduction principle analogue, valid for general qualitative analysis and synthesis problems; to establish the effective technique. The concepts and methods of classical stability theory are developed for modelling problems of considered systems, with extending the statements of N.G.Chetayev, V.V.Rumyantsev and P.A.Kuzmin. The original system is decomposed on a few subsystems, that are describing the behavior of different-frequency variables, in accordance with multiple time scales.

The problems of mechanical-mathematical modelling are solved from unified positions [1,2,3]. Besides the hierarchy of state variables is established by natural way automatically; the sequences of nonlinear comparison systems are built in accordance with hierarchic structure of variables; the compatibility between original model and shortened one is revealed. With reference to Mechanics the rigorous theoretic justification is obtained for considered approximate models and theories, both traditional and new ones.

1. Introduction

The first rigorous results in this direction were obtained by H.Poincare and by A.M.Lyapunov. In classical works of A.M.Lyapunov the comparison method (general method of qualitative analysis) was developed with the strong justification for the solving of stability problems. This method led to the reduction principle, well-known one in stability theory (A.M.Lyapunov, K.P.Persidskiy,...), and to the comparison principle (R.Bellman-V.Matrosov).

There is the direct methodological connection between stability theory and singular perturbations theory (I.S.Gradstein, N.G.Chetayev); between modelling problems and parametric stability theory (N.G.Chetayev, P.A.Kuzmin). With reference to Mechanics problems, formulated here, it leads to the singularly perturbed problems, with various singularities types, with specific critical cases.

This research is formed on accepted here basic proposition about global, in-depth fundamental, connection between the singularly perturbed problems (and modelling problems in Mechanics) and the stability methods of Lyapunov's theory. Such tenet is ascending to well-known stability postulate (N.G.Chetayev), and singularity postulate (L.K.Kuzmina), with the extending statement about stability with parametric perturbations on singular case. All original objects may be treated from unified view point of systems of singularly perturbed class. The object state may be described by the equations with small (or big) parameters. The original mathematical model (as example, in Lagrange's form) may be represented in standard form, as singular model, with small parameters in different powers. For this it is necessary to construct the corresponding non-linear, non-singular, evenly-regular transformation of variables. It is postulated (L.K.Kuzmina), that such suitable transformation exists always, and it may be constructed by special, non-formal manners. Besides the original dynamic problems are solved as singular ones; shortened (approximate) systems are introduced as subsystems of s-level (s-systems); reduced models are obtained as asymptotic s-models. Here these s-systems are also singularly perturbed ones. It is non-traditional approach, combining the methods of stability theory and perturbations theory that allows to come near to the solving fundamental problem of modelling in Mechanics via understanding it as problem of singularly perturbed class.

Following to ideas of N.G.Chetayev's, in accordance with Lyapunov's methods, the singular problems may be solved (stability, proximity, optimality, quickness,...) both for non-critical and for critical cases; with simple and multiple roots;... Also for singular systems with the peculiarities (critical spectrums) the reduction conditions may be determined. In these cases the direct use of known results of singular perturbations theory (A.N.Tikhonov, A.Naifeh,...) is non-suitable: eigen-values of corresponding matrices are zero- and imaginary ones. Mechanical systems are "quasi-Tikhonov's systems" (N.N.Moiseev). Therefore special, novel, manners are necessary. Methods, based on Lyapunov's methodology, Chetayev's ideas, elaborated here, give powerful tool; bring new interesting results, perspective both for perturbations theory (singular problems in specific, critical cases are solvable) and for applications to Mechanics, for general modelling theory.

2. Initial principles

It is well known [3-15], many applied investigations lead to the mathematical problems, having important general features: the reduction of the order of the differential equations, the loss of continuity, boundary condition. We shall call the singular systems such ones, when the transition to the reduced system is accompanied by the lowering of the model order, the structural change. For these systems the initial mathematical model may be presented in standard form of system with the singular perturbations. It enables to consider the original objects on typical scheme, to construct by regular manners the idealized mechanical-mathematical models, that are interesting for applications, to get strict conditions of their acceptability in dynamics.

For singularly perturbed objects a motion consists of components of various classes, from fast to slow, and their differential equations (mathematical models) can be led to the form of equations with small parameters before higher derivatives. Therefore in practice for analysis of such systems the reduced models of lower order are being used as working models. Let the differential equations of the perturbed motion of considered system can be led to a form (let consider the systems with the steady states set)

$$M(\mu)\frac{dy}{dt} = Y(t,\mu,y) \tag{1}$$

where $y = \|z, x\|^T$, z, x are m-, n-dimensional vectors; $\mu > 0$ is a small dimensionless parameter; $Y(t,\mu,y) = \|Z(t,\mu,y); P(\mu)x + X(t,\mu,y)\|^T$; $M(\mu) = \|M_{i,j}(\mu)\|$; $P(\mu) = \|P_{i,j}(\mu)\|$; $M_{i,j}$, $P_{i,j}$ are submatrices of the appropriate sizes; $Z(t, \mu, y)$, $X(t, \mu, y)$ are non-linear vector-functions, holomorphic (in appropriate domain) on the totality of variables z, x, in which coefficients are continuous, limited functions of t, μ; $Z(t, \mu, z, 0)$, $X(t, \mu, z, 0)$; $M_{i,j}(\mu) = \mu^{\alpha_i} I$, $0 \le \alpha_i \le r$; I are identity matrices. We shall be able to consider the critical cases of system (1), where z are critical variables [1]. Taking into consideration in (1) only members containing μ in power not more than s, $s < r$, we shall receive the shortened approximate system of type

$$M_s(\mu)\frac{dy}{dt} = Y_s(t,\mu,y) \tag{2}$$

We shall call (2) the shortened system of s-level, s-system (s-approximation on μ). For singularly perturbed systems that are considered here, the order of system (2) is lower than order of full system (1). In applications to mechanics this shortened system leads to the reduced model as the asymptotic model of s-level. From the point of view of mechanics a transition to the reduced model is accompanied by a decrease of freedom degrees number.

We shall be able to obtain the sequence of asymptotic models (as designing-basic models) in mechanics, corresponding the sequence of shortened s-systems $(s=0,1,2,\ldots r\text{-}1)$. The following problem is important both for the theory and applications: in which cases and under what conditions it is possible to reduce system (1) to shortened s-system? The similar problem for equations with small parameter under higher derivatives was considered by many authors [2-8]. We shall show the solving of some concrete problems of mechanics, that lead to particular cases of the system (1) of special class, that are not embraced by already known results.

3. Mechanical system with nonrigid elements

As an example of such mechanical system we shall consider the systems of gyrostabilization, modelling ones as mechanical (electromechanical) systems with controlling gyroscopic elements. Here there is a critical case of zero roots. We shall solve a stability problem of the steady motion for such system, supposing that the elements of the system are not absolutely rigid (we neglect the mass of elastic elements). Differential equations of perturbed motion we shall accept in a form of Lagrange's equations (as in [5, 15])

$$\frac{d}{dt} a\dot{q}_M + (b + g)\dot{q}_M + cq_M = Q''_M, \qquad \frac{dq_M}{dt} = \dot{q}_M \qquad (3)$$

Here $q_M = \left\| q_1, q_2, q_3, q_4 \right\|^T$ is n - dimensional vector of mechanical generalized coordinates, where q_1 is l-dimensional vector of the gyroscopes precessions angles; q_2 is $(m\text{-}l)$-dimensional vector of angles deviations of own rotations of gyroscopes from their values in steady motion; q_3 is $(s\text{-}m)$-dimensional vector of stabilization angles, $s=m+1$; q_4 is $(n\text{-}s)$-dimensional vector of elastic elements deformations; a, b, g are square $n{\times}n$ -matrices of forms of the system kinetic energy, dissipative function of friction forces, gyroscopic coefficients accordingly; $c = \left\| c_{i,j} \right\|$, $b = \left\| b_{i,j} \right\|$ $(i,\ j=1,\ldots,4)$, c_{ij} and b_{ij} are submatrices of an appropriate sizes; b_{44} is square $(n\text{-}s){\times}(n\text{-}s)$ -matrix of dissipative function of internal friction forces in material of elastic bodies; c_{44} is square $(n\text{-}s){\times}(n\text{-}s)$ -matrix, corresponding to potential energy of elasticity forces.

We assume that all functions in (3) are holomorphic (on the totality of their variables) in certain area.

For solving of this problem (and choosing of a reduced model) we shall lead equations (3) to a form (1) with singular perturbations. For this, first, we must introduce in equations (3) a small parameter, using physical considerations. We suppose, that the elements of the considered systems are of a sufficiently high rigidity and according to that $c_{44} = c_{44}^* / \mu^2$, $b_{44} = b_{44}^* / \mu$, where $\mu > 0$ is a small parameter. Now, using the constructed transformation of variables:

$$z = \|a_1, a_2\|^T \dot{q}_M + \|b_1^0 + g_1^0, b_2^0 + g_2^0\|^T q_M, \quad \kappa_1 = \|a_1, a_2, a_3\|^T \dot{q}_M, \quad \kappa_2 = a_4 \dot{q}_M,$$

$q_j = q_j$, $(j = 1, 4)$ where a_i, b_i, g_i $(i = 1, \ldots, 4)$ are submatrices of matrices a, b, g correspondingly, we shall lead equations (3) to the singularly perturbed form. This transformation is the non-linear, non-singular under condition that $\left| b_{i,j}^0 + g_{i,j}^0 \right|_{i=1,2}^{j=2,3} \neq 0$, evenly regular [6], not changing the statement of the stability problem. System (3) in new variables has a form (1)

$$\frac{dz}{dt} = Z(t, \mu, z, x), \quad M(\mu)\frac{dx}{dt} = P(\mu) + X(t, \mu, z, x) \tag{4}$$

where $x = \|x_1, x_2, x_3\|^T$, $x_1 = \|\kappa_1, q_1\|^T$, $x_2 = \kappa_2$, $x_3 = q_4$; $\alpha_1 = 0$, $\alpha_2 = 2$, $\alpha_3 = 0$; $P_{2i}(\mu) = \mu P_{2i}'(\mu)$ $(i = 1, 2)$.

The characteristic equation has m zero-roots. Other roots can be found from the equation $d(\lambda, \mu) = 0$. We assume the shortened system of 0-level (degenerated system) as an approximate one for a system (4), marking it (4′) without writing. In old variables it is the system

$$\frac{d}{dt} a^* \dot{q} + (b^* + g^*)\dot{q} + c^* q = Q^*, \quad \frac{dq}{dt} = \dot{q} \tag{5}$$

where $q = \|q_1, q_2, q_3\|^T$ is s-dimensional vector of generalized coordinates, describing the state of an absolutely rigid system; a^*, b^*, c^*, g^* are $s \times s$-matrices of absolutely rigid system.

The equation (5) describes a motion of an idealized model of mechanical system. This model corresponds to an approximate system (4′) of 0-level. We shall call it a "limit model". A problem: in what conditions a transition from the initial model (3) to its idealized model (to absolutely rigid system) is possible? Using methods of stability theory [1, 2], combined with the singular perturbations methods [7,8] and introducing the differential equations for deviations that respond to non-critical (basic) variables x, we can find out the acceptability conditions for transition validity from system (4) to the system (4′) in concrete dynamical problems. After returning to old variables, taking into account the properties of the considered mechanical system, we receive the corresponding statements.

3.1. *Stability problem*

When the stability property for reduced model (5) will be ensuring same property for original (full) model (3)?

Theorem 1. If $\left| b_{i,j}^0 + g_{i,j}^0 \right|_{i=1,2}^{j=2,3} \neq 0,$ $\left| c_{31}^0 \right| \neq 0$ and all roots (except m zero roots) of characteristic equation of reduced system (5) have negative real parts, then with sufficiently small values of μ (sufficiently high rigidity of the system elements) the zero solution stability of the full system will be succeeding from the zero solution stability of reduced system (5). And reduced system (5) has integral

$$\left\| \begin{matrix} a_1^* \\ a_2^* \end{matrix} \right\| \dot{q} + \left\| \begin{matrix} b_1^{*0} + g_1^{*0} \\ b_2^{*0} + g_2^{*0} \end{matrix} \right\| q + \varphi(q,\dot{q}) = B$$

and full system (3) has integral of Lyapunov:

$$\left\| \begin{matrix} a_1 \\ a_2 \end{matrix} \right\| \dot{q}_M + \left\| \begin{matrix} b_1^0 + g_1^0 \\ b_2^0 + g_2^0 \end{matrix} \right\| q_M + F(q_M, \dot{q}_M) = A.$$

3.2. *Estimations of approximate solutions*

Let $q_i = q_i(t,\mu)$, $\dot{q}_i = \dot{q}_i(t,\mu)$, $(i=1...4)$ be the solution of system (3) with the initial conditions $q_{i0} = q_i(t_0,\mu)$, $\dot{q}_{i0} = \dot{q}_i(t_0,\mu)$; we shall designate $q_i^* = q_i^*(t)$, $\dot{q}_i^* = \dot{q}_i^*(t)$, $(i=1,...4)$ as the solution of approximate system (5), defined by the initial conditions $q_{j0}^* = q_j^*(t_0)$, $\dot{q}_{j0}^* = \dot{q}_j^*(t_0)$ $(j=1, 2, 3)$, where $q_4^* \equiv 0$, $\dot{q}_4^* \equiv 0$.

Making use of stability theory methods we can prove the following statement:

Theorem 2. If the characteristic equation for system (5) has all roots in the left half-plane (except m zero roots) for $d(0, 0) \neq 0$, then under sufficiently big stiffness of the system elements (i.e. μ is sufficiently small) there exists such a μ_*-value for $\xi > 0$, $\eta > 0$, $\gamma > 0$ given in advance (no matter how small ξ and γ are), that in a perturbed motion:

$$\left\| q_i - q_i^* \right\| < \xi, \qquad \left\| \dot{q}_i - \dot{q}_i^* \right\| < \xi \qquad (i=1,...,4) \quad \text{when } 0 < \mu < \mu_* \text{ for } t \geq t_0 + \gamma, \text{ if}$$

$$q_{j0} = q_{j0}^*, \qquad \dot{q}_{j0} = \dot{q}_{j0}^*, \, (j=1,2,3) \, \left\| q_{40} \right\| < \eta, \quad \left\| \dot{q}_{40} \right\| < \eta.$$

It should be pointed out that while demonstrating and using variables z, x we introduce deviations $a = z - z^*$, $b = x - x^*$ and consider a differential equation for b.

The analysis of these equations as well as the integral structure enable to derive the statement of Theorem.

These results, complementing already known [9], justify for the systems, considered here, admissibility of approximate limit model (as asymptotic model of 0-level) and determine the conditions, under which the considered transition is correct (in a meaning, adopted here).

Remark. According to this we can introduce other approximate model (as designing-basic model) for (3). This is asymptotic model of 1-level (μ-approximation), that has $(s+(n-s)/2)$ of freedom degrees (if in (4) take into consideration members containing μ in power not more than 1). This model is new one (it is very interesting result).

System (4) belongs to the special critical case, when all eigenvalues of matrix P_{22}, corresponding to the fast x_2, are zero.

4. Systems with fast rotors

Using the same asymptotic approach, we can solve a problem of the transition strict substantiation to a reduced (approximate) model for the mechanical systems with the fast rotors (gyroscopes) [13]. No-giving the formulas and computations here, we note only the some results. In this case original mathematical model is accepted in a form of Lagrange's equations [5]; big parameter is introduced through gyroscopic forces [5, 13]; the necessary transformation of state variables is constructed; the initial equations are reduced to standard form (1). The reduced models are got on our scheme. According to elaborated method, by strict mathematical manner we obtained the known (precessional) model and new («limit») model (as shortened model of 1-st level and 0-level, correspondingly). The conditions of acceptability of these models are determined.

5. Systems with small delay time

Here the electromechanical systems (EMS), modelling the gyrostabilization systems, are investigated. Original model is presented in general form of Lagrange-Maxwell (Gaponov) equations [14]. The problems: the constructing of reduced model; and their acceptability (in corresponding sense) for these systems. For case of fast-acting systems, interpreting ones as singularly perturbed system, according to our method, we solve these problems. The required transformation is constructed; the reduced models (two types) are obtained; the domains of acceptability are determined.

6. Conclusion

We notice that by analogy with these systems, using the same methods, other singularly perturbed problems and systems of mechanics may be considered.

The subject-matter of investigations is general problem of modelling in mechanics. The development of mathematical modelling questions of mechanics is closely concerned with actual tasks of mechanical systems dynamics, of differential equations theory with big and small parameters, of stability theory. In one's turn it is generating new trends in mathematics, interesting mathematical-mechanical problems.

The received results are generalizing and supplementing ones, known in theory of perturbations; these results are developing interesting applications in engineering. With reference to Mechanics the rigorous theoretic justification is obtained for considered approximate models and theories, both traditional (K.Magnus, A.Andronov, D.Merkin,…) and new ones; the separation of state variables on different-frequency groups is developed from first stages of designing; the acceptability of approximate theories, models is discussed, including "exotic" Aristotle's model in Dynamics.

Deep philosophical aspect of idealization problem in Mechanics is highlighted.

Acknowledgments

The author is grateful to Russian Foundation of Fundamental Investigation for support in this research.

References

1. A.M.Lyapunov, *The general problem of motion stability*. Moscow, USSR AS Coll. of papers, vol.2, 7-264 (1956).

2. N.G.Chetayev, *Appl. Math. and Mech.* Vol.21, No.3, 419-421 (1957).

3. L.K.Kuzmina, Proceedings of 9-th National All-Russian Congress on Theor. and Appl. Mech. Nizh. Novgorod, vol.1, 76 (2006).

4. N.N.Moiseev, Mathematical Problems of Systems Analysis. Moscow, Nauka (1981).

5. L.K.Kuzmina, *Appl. Math. and Mech.* Vol.46, No.3, 382-388 (1982).

6. S.Lefshetz, Differential Equations: geometric theory. New York, 1957.

7. I.M.Gradstein, *Math. Rev.* Vol.32, No.3, 533-544 (1953).

8. A.N.Tikhonov, *Math. Rev.* Vol.31, No.3, 575-586 (1953).

9. F.L.Chernousko, A.S.Shamaev, *Proc. USSR AS, Mech. of Solid Body*. No.3, 33-42 (1983).

10. Y.Z.Tsypkin, P.V.Bromberg, *Izv.AS USSR, OTS*. No.2, 1163-1167 (1945).

11. A.A.Feldbaum, *Avtomatika and telemech*. No.4, 253-279 (1948).

12. A.A.Voronov, Introduction in dynamics of complex controlled systems. Moscow, Nauka (1985).

13. D.R.Merkin, Gyroscopic systems. Moscow, 1956.

14. L.K.Kuzmina, *Appl. Math. and Mech*. Vol.55, No.4, 594-601 (1991).

15. L.K.Kuzmina, *Applied Mechanics in the Americas* Vol.12, AAM, USA, 178-181 (2008).

AUTHOR INDEX